Bibliographies and Indexes in Science and Technology

Publishing Opportunities for Energy Research: A Descriptive Guide to Selective Serials in the Social and Technical Sciences
Roberta A. Scull, compiler

Toxic and Hazardous Materials: A Sourcebook and Guide to Information Sources
James K. Webster, editor

Three Mile Island: A Selectively Annotated Bibliography
M. Sandra Wood and Suzanne M. Shultz, compilers

Food and Nutrition in the Middle East, 1970-1986: An Annotated Bibliography
Gail G. Harrison, Osman M. Galal, and Mary E. Mohs, compilers

Hypertext/Hypermedia: An Annotated Bibliography
Michael Knee and Steven D. Atkinson, compilers

**A Bibliographic Guide to the
History of Computing, Computers, and
the Information Processing Industry**

A Bibliographic Guide to the History of Computing, Computers, and the Information Processing Industry

Compiled by
James W. Cortada

Bibliographies and Indexes in Science and Technology, Number 6

Greenwood Press

NEW YORK
WESTPORT, CONNECTICUT
LONDON

Library of Congress Cataloging-in-Publication Data

Cortada, James W.
    A bibliographic guide to the history of computing, computers, and
the information processing industry / compiled by James W. Cortada.
        p. cm.—(Bibliographies and indexes in science and
technology, ISSN 0888-7551 ; no. 6)
    Expanded version of: An annotated bibliography on the history of
data processing.
    ISBN 0-313-26810-X (lib. bdg. : alk. paper)
    1. Computers—History—Bibliography. 2. Electronic data
processing—History—Bibliography. I. Cortada, James W.   Annotated
bibliography on the history of data processing. II. Title.
III. Series.
Z5640.C67   1990
[QA76.17]
016.004'09—dc20   90-3093

British Library Cataloguing in Publication Data is available.

Library of Congress Catalog Card Number: 90-3093
ISBN: 0-313-26810-X
ISSN: 0888-7551

First published in 1990

Greenwood Press, 88 Post Road West, Westport, CT 06881
An imprint of Greenwood Publishing Group, Inc.

Printed in the United States of America

The paper used in this book complies with the
Permanent Paper Standard issued by the National
Information Standards Organization (Z39.48-1984).

10 9 8 7 6 5 4 3 2 1

Contents

Preface

The history of data processing is now an established
field for study, joining with a contemporary fascination for
events taking place in the area of computing and the information processing industry. Just in the past ten years the
number of publications on the subject has exploded. Publications are coming from vendors and users of information
processing products; from journalists writing biographies,
company exposés, or surveys of the industry; and from participants in the industry and professionally trained historians.
Increasingly, those viewing the industry are taking its past
into consideration. That development should be of no surprise.
The portion of the data processing industry that has relied on
computers dates back some forty years, and its predecessor—
the office appliance industry—came into existence a century
ago. In addition, computers are being put into the hands of
millions of users who did not have access to this technology
a decade ago, thanks to the introduction of micro-computers.
That exposure to computing has encouraged growing interest in
the general subject.

The purpose of this bibliographic guide is to serve as a
general introduction to the literature of the industry. Cast
in historical terms, it provides an annotated list of published materials describing the history of the industry as well as
items of importance to those interested in the general topic.
It includes listings of current publications of relevance to
those focusing on today's events, such as computer magazines.
There are also citations of a strictly historical nature.
The bibliography includes many historically important contemporary publications, such as those describing hardware and
software of past decades, seminal technical papers (some dating back more than a half century), application briefs, and
industry surveys. I included contemporary material on punch
card technology and its use, since tabulating equipment was a
source of technology inspiring the emergence of the computer
and later, an incentive for early users of the new machines.
The volume also includes developments of the 1970s and 1980s,
such as the expanding role of Japan and other countries in the
industry and the emergence of microcomputers.

In 1983 I published a short Bibliography on the history
of computers (An Annotated Bibliography on the History of Data
Processing, released by Greenwood Press). That volume was an

initial survey of materials focused on history and included
only minimal references to technical or contemporary materials.
This second publication is quite different in a number of ways.
It is much broader in scope, reflecting the changing needs of
those looking at the subject. Although this second project
encompasses all the titles listed in the original book with
corrections, those titles represent a minority of the entries.
Historical surveys missed the first time are included here as
well as those that have appeared since the first volume. The
number of chapters has increased from four to nine and the
number of subheadings from 63 to nearly 100. The number of
titles has more than tripled. The material has been reorganiz-
ed and new subheadings added to reflect emerging topics and the
growth of literature on particular aspects of the industry.
Thus, for example, as devices or organizations appeared in the
literature, these were grouped in new sections. Each chapter
is introduced with a short review of historically important
issues, comments on the literature and on the challenges
awaiting those interested in understanding the industry and
its technology. As an attempt to keep the bibliography's
usefulness current, the reader is guided to ongoing publications for new references that might appear after the publication of this book. Finally, the index has been greatly expanded to include subject references as well as author citations.
As in the earlier work, all bibliographic citations are
annotated with a brief description of either the work's contents or on its historical importance.

The nature of the literature has been changing, as
reflected in this book. With an increased appreciation of
data processing's history, which dates back many decades
before the arrival of the computer, historians have been
uncovering thousands of publications relevant to the topic.
To a large extent this bibliography reflects a growing broad-
ness of definition, which was not obvious as recently as the
mid-1980s. The need to acknowledge the extensive impact of
punch card, adding and calculating machinery, and their applications as precursors of modern computing is recent. That
implies a recognition of the office appliance industry and a
broad range of technologies, which laid the foundation for
modern data processing, stretching back to at least the
1860s. The listings in this book, while reflective of this
view, are nonetheless limited to what could fit into a single
volume. The actual number of descriptions, for instance, of
how machines were used in any decade would fill many volumes.
What becomes obvious from the titles included is the growing
importance of the role played by office equipment and that
industry in the economic activities of large organizations in
the twentieth century. As historians move away from a narrow
technological view of computing dating back to the 1930s and
toward a complex perspective on economic and technical activities internationally and over the past century, bibliographic
needs change. That evolution alone makes most bibliographic
collections too narrow, requiring the kind of tool offered
with this volume.

This publication continues Greenwood Press's commitment
to publishing essential reference tools dealing with the
history of information processing and with American industries
at large. These are critical aids for historians and those
working in American industry. Cynthia Harris at Greenwood
encouraged me to work on the project and advised me on how

best to pull together such a work of reference. I also want
to acknowledge my appreciation to my two daughters, Beth and
Julia, who helped with the indices. I hope that this book
provides the kind of tool the reader is looking for; errors
that might be found are a reflection of my own limitations
for which I apologize in advance.

A Bibliographic Guide to the
History of Computing, Computers, and
the Information Processing Industry

1

Reference and
Introductory Materials

Chapter One contains reference materials, such as
bibliographies, surveys of archives, and dictionaries, along
with general surveys, major periodicals, and other titles
related to the general theme of information processing.
While there has been a substantial increase in the number of
basic reference materials on the subject over the past five
years, much remains to be done, particularly guides to the
collections of archives, bibliographies of major libraries,
and biographical or institutional histories.

Several developments currently underway are augmenting
the sources available to researchers. The Charles Babbage
Institute (CBI), housed at the University of Minnesota in
Minneapolis, publishes a newsletter that lists new publications and reviews developments in archives related to
information processing. This publication is a useful
barameter of events and stays current. The Annals of the
History of Computing also reviews new publications in addition
to publishing articles of historical interest. CBI publishes,
on a periodic basis, detailed bibliographies and other
reference materials. These publications are essential tools
for students of the history of computing and information
processing. Finally a number of American publishers are
beginning to introduce books on the subject. Two recent
leaders include Greenwood Press with works of reference and
The MIT Press with monographs, memoirs, and reprinted
classics. Increasingly during the 1980s, commercial and
university presses have released books on the subject as well.

In the United States major collections are being
developed at various archives. The U.S. National Archives,
the National Museum, and the Library of Congress have active
programs to expand their holdings and are continually
cataloging their existing and large collections. Major
corporations in the data processing industry also maintain
archives and are increasingly allowing historians to use
them. Examples of the better organized ones include those
at IBM and Unisys. NCR's archive contains massive amounts
of material, but it is not organized and at this time is
understaffed. Others exist but are not available to the
public at all. Important collections are growing at Harvard,
MIT, Stanford, the University of Illinois, University of
Pennsylvania, and Dartmouth College. Smaller collections are

now expanding at smaller state universities and at all the
U.S. national laboratories. MIT and Dartmouth have published
guides to their technical collections; one can expect other
guides to appear in the next several years. Clearly, there
is a move afoot to build collections and publicize their
contents within the United States. To a lesser extent, the
same is true in Great Britain and sporadically across
Western Europe. Surveys of collections are now routinely
published along with descriptions of the archives themselves.
For example, the IEEE Center For the History of Electrical
Engineering includes such surveys in its Newsletter.

Museums provide another source of currently expanding
reference materials. The National Museum in Washington,
D.C. (part of the Smithsonian) maintains a permanent exhibit
on mechanical computing and periodically creates others on
the same theme. The Computer Museum in Boston is a monument
to computing and focuses primarily on computers and software
since the 1940s. It is rapidly becoming the attic for the
industry as more old devices are contributed to its collection.
Each major vendor also stores, restores, and occasionally
exhibits its old products. Recent examples of this kind of
activity involved IBM, NCR and AT&T.

Minimal work has been done on the historiography of
computing and its industry. Some attempts have been made,
however, to link issues in information processing to themes
commonly looked at in the field of technological history.
Linkages and issues are periodically reviewed in such
publications as the Annals of the History of Computing. Much
of the historically useful publications have been memoirs or
histories of specific machines. Better work has been done
on the history of printing and publishing, telephony, and
mathematics than in the field of computing and its related
industry. What little general survey work has appeared is
included in this chapter. Publications that review in general
terms narrower subjects or limited periods are listed in
subsequent chapters.

Archives

1   AFIPS. Preserving Computer Related Source Material.
        Arlington, Va.: AFIPS, n.d.

    This publication describes the kinds of materials
    which should be preserved for historians and how to
    do it. It is available free by writing to AFIPS,
    N. Lynn St., Arlington, Va. 22209.

2   "AFIPS/Smithsonian Project on Computer History,"
        Communications ACM 14, No. 7 (1971): 494.

    This project involved collecting oral histories of
    pioneers in the development of the computer and
    related technologies.

3   AFIPS History of Computing Committee. What Is the Best
        Memory Protection Device? Reston, Va.: AFIPS, 1985.

    The brochure describes what to save and why and is
    very similar to the first entry above.

4   Aspray, William. "Literature and Institutions in the
         History of Computing," ISIS 75, No. 1 (1984): 162-
         170.

         This article is on the status of historical research
         in computing activities and defines the mission of
         CBI.

5   Aspray, William and Bruemmer, Bruce (eds). Guide to the
         Oral History Collection of the Charles Babbage
         Institute. Minneapolis, Mn.: Charles Babbage
         Institute, 1986.

         This describes CBI's collection of over 150
         transcripts of oral history abstracts and includes
         an index.

6   Aspray, William and Bruemmer, Bruce. "Oral Histories of
         Information Processing," Oral History Association
         Newsletter 18, No. 4 (1984): 2.

         This work describes the major holdings in the U.S.
         at such places as the Computer Museum (Boston),
         Smithsonian Institution (Washington, D.C.), MIT
         Archives (Boston) and at CBI (Minneapolis) with a
         total of nearly 500 interviews.

7   Bruemmer, Bruce H. Resources for the History of Computing:
         A Guide to U.S. and Canadian Records. Minneapolis,
         Mn.: Charles Babbage Institute, 1987.

         This guide provides brief descriptions of U.S. and
         Canadian archival collections related to the history
         of computing primarily since 1935. It does not
         survey holdings retained by government archives and
         agencies.

8   Bruemmer, Bruce H. and Hochheiser, Sheldon. The High-
         Technology Company: A Historical Research and
         Archival Guide. Minneapolis, Mn.: Charles Babbage
         Institute, 1989.

         They describe typical industrial actions in high-
         technology companies and then illustrate a method
         for collecting relevant documentary materials on
         such activities. Their intent is to identify the
         kinds of records that should be preserved and used.

9   Cortada, James W. (ed). Archives of Data Processing
         History: A Guide to Major U.S. Collections.
         Westport, Conn.: Greenwood Press, 1990.

         The chapters in this guide, written by archivists,
         survey major holdings dealing with computing, data
         processing, and its industry back to the nineteenth
         century.

10   Dollar, Charles M. "Computers, the National Archives,
         and Researchers," Prologue (Spring 1976): 29-34.

This describes current actions taken to preserve
the history of computer-related materials and the
problems associated with that mission.

11   Goldstein, Marcy G. "Bell Laboratories Archives:
      Collector and Collections," IEEE Center For the
      History of Electrical Engineering Newsletter 4
      (Fall 1983): 6.

      This guide describes the collection, including
      photographs, manuscripts, and artifacts.

12   Gullard, Pamela. "The Charles Babbage Institute for the
      History of Information Processing," Annals of the
      History of Computing 2, No. 1 (January 1980): 71-74.

      This article is a survey of CBI's activities between
      1977 and 1980, of its objectives and role as
      computing's archive and historical research center.

13   Hagley Museum and Library. Computers, Automation, and
      Cybernetics at the Hagley Museum and Library.
      Wilmington, Del.: Hagley Museum and Library, 1989.

      This survey of the collection includes the papers of
      Elmer Sperry, Sperry Gyroscope Company, Sperry-
      UNIVAC, on the IBM antitrust and technical lawsuits
      of the 1960s and 1970s.

14   Kidwell, Peggy A. and Morris, Juanita A. (eds). A
      Combined Index to Oral Histories Open to Readers.
      Washington, D.C.: Smithsonian Institution, 1986.

      This survey is part of the Smithsonian Computer
      History Project and an early description of its work.

15   Lewis, Robert G. "The AT&T Corporate Archives," IEEE
      Center For the History of Electrical Engineering
      Newsletter 13 (Fall 1986): 6-7.

      This is an illustrated history of the archive which
      dates back to 1913.

16   "Museums and Archives," Annals of the History of
      Computing 10, No. 4 (1989): 305-329.

      This surveys current activities of the Computer
      Museum, Smithsonian Institution, National Museum of
      American History, Science Museum, Deutsches Museum,
      CBI, IEEE Center For the History of Electrical
      Engineering, National Archives, British National
      Archives for the History of Computing, AFIPS History
      of Computing Committee, and activities in France.

17   Rider, Robin E. and Lowood, Henry E. Guide to Sources
      in Northern California for History of Science and
      Technology. Berkeley, Cal.: Office for History of
      Science and Technology, University of California,
      1985.

This includes material on Silicon Valley, Stanford, and other institutions on the west coast of the United States.

18 Samuels, Helen W. Selective Guide to the Collections. Cambridge, Mass.: Institute Archives and Special Collections, The Libraries, Massachusetts Institute of Technology, 1988.

The guide to MIT's archival collections includes over a dozen entries dealing with computing, research projects and individuals, primarily for the period between the 1930s and the 1960s.

19 Simon, Sally and Merz, Nancy M. "Texas Instruments Archives: A Corporate Resource," IEEE Center For the History of Electrical Engineering 10 (Fall 1985): 6-7.

This describes TI's archives, which includes files on Jack S. Kilby's integrated circuits of the late 1950s.

20 Tropp, Henry S. "The Smithsonian Computer History Project and Some Personal Recollections," in N. Metropolis et al. (eds). A History of Computing in the Twentieth Century: A Collection of Essays (New York: Academic Press, 1980): 115-122.

Tropp was very active in supporting historical examination of data processing's past and in the preservation of its records in the 1970s.

21 Tropp, Henry S. et al. Preserving the History of Computers. Montvale, N.J.: AFIPS, 1972.

This pamphlet describes the initial purpose and goals of the Computer History Project supported by AFIPS for the preservation of historical materials.

22 White, W.C. "Evolution of Electronics," Electronics 25, No. 9 (1952): 98-99.

He provides a family tree with roots leading from basic research to branches, such as types of vacuum tubes.

23 Zemanek, Heinz. "The New Department 'Informatics Automatics' at the Deutsches Museum in Munich," Annals of the History of Computing 10, No. 4 (1989): 329-335.

He describes the creation of this department and its activities of the late 1980s.

Bibliographies

24 ABI/SELECTS. The Annotated Bibliography of Computer Periodicals. Louisville, Ky.: Data Courier Inc.,1983.

This 576-page bibliography is the single most
useful publication on the subject available.

25   ACM Guide to Computing Literature (1964--annual).

This is an index of publications dealing with all
aspects of data processing literature. The first
volume (1964) covers publications which appeared in
1963. Many of the issues are massive with thousands
of titles.

26   Aspray, William. "An Annotated Bibliography of Secondary
Sources on the History of Software," Annals of the
History of Computing 9, Nos 3-4 (1988): 291-343.

This contains hundreds of citations organized
alphabetically by author.

27   Aspray, William. Charles Babbage Institute Selective
Bibliography on the History of Computing and
Information Processing. Minneapolis, Mn.: Charles
Babbage Institute, 1981.

This is a four-page annotated list of 32 titles
that serve as an introduction to the subject.

28   Bain, R.E. A Bibliography for Management Support
Systems. Menlo Park, Ca.: Stanford Research
Institute, 1971.

This bibliography was prepared for the U.S. Office
of Naval Research (ONR) as a guide to DP publications
on applications, management issues, and technology.
It is a good introduction to the growing body of
literature which appeared during the 1960s on data
processing, particularly in the United States.

29   Barnes, Colin I. Computer Applications; A Select
Bibliography. Hatfield, Herts, England: Hatfield
College of Technology, 1967.

This 66-page bibliographies was one of the first to
focus on the literature of computer uses, listing a
wide assortment of publications, mostly published
during the early to mid-1960s.

30   Barnes, O.D. and Schbrieber, D.B. Computer-Assisted
Instruction: A Selected Bibliography. Washington,
D.C.: Association for Educational Communications and
Technology, 1972.

This was an early specialized bibliography on
computer applications. It is the major list of
publications on the use of data processing in
education during the 1960s.

31   Beach, Ann F. et al. Bibliography on the Use of IBM
Machines in Science, Statistics, and Education. New
York: International Business Machines Corporation,

1954; 2nd edition, 1956.

This publication, and the revised and expanded
second edition of 81 pages, offer a variety of IBM
and trade publications describing specific uses of
this company's products. This was the first of many
such publications issued by IBM.

32   Bessent, J.R. et al. The Impact of Microelectronics: A
      Review of the Literature. London: Frances Pinter,
      1981.

      This lists 400 non-technical publications on
      microelectronics.

33   Besterfield, D.H.   A Bibliography of Selected RAND
      Publications: Computing Technology.   Santa Monica,
      Ca.: RAND Corporation, 1971.

      RAND was a major consultant to U.S. Government and
      defense industry organizations on computing and
      related technologies during the 1960s. and thus its
      publications can aid in understanding how computers
      were used, especially by the government.

34   "Bibliography on Automatic Digital Calculating Machines"
      in Report of a Conference on High Speed Automatic
      Calculating Machines, 22-25 June 1949 (Cambridge:
      Mathematical Laboratory, January 1950): 134-141.

      This bibliography surveys scientific literature for
      the period 1946-1949, offering over one hundred
      titles.

35   Bibliography on Electronic Computing Machines.
      Teddington, Middlesex: Mathematics Division, National
      Physical Laboratory, June 1948.

      This three page document lists 52 articles and books
      from the period 1940-1947. They are technical
      publications especially useful on the work of British
      and American scientists working on computers.

36   Bramer, Max A.   The Fifth Generation: An Annotated
      Bibliography. Wokingham, England and Reading, Mass.:
      Addison-Wesley, 1985.

      This is the first bibliography to appear on the
      Japanese computing projects of the 1980s known as
      "Fifth Generation" hardware and software.

37   Chroust, G.   Bibliography for the History of World Data
      Processing. Vienna: IBM Laboratory, 1974.

      This is a bibliography of artifacts, photographs,
      articles and books in an exhibit entitled "The
      History of Data Processing" at the Museum of Industry
      and Technology at Vienna, Austria.

38   Cortada, James W. <u>An Annotated Bibliography on the</u>
      <u>History of Data Processing</u>. Westport, Conn.:
      Greenwood Press, 1983.

      This bibliography covers all aspects of the subject
      and is an earlier edition of the current publication.
      All of its entries are included in this volume.

39   Dartmouth College Library. <u>An Inventory of the Papers</u>
      <u>of George Robert Stibitz Concerning the Invention</u>
      <u>and Development of the Digital Computer</u>. Hanover,
      N.H.: Dartmouth College Library, 1973.

      George Stibitz developed a series of computers at
      Bell Laboratories, beginning in the late 1930s and
      through the 1940s. This inventory catalogs his
      papers housed at Dartmouth and includes a short
      biography of him.

40   Deighton, Suzan et al. (eds). <u>Computers and Information</u>
      <u>Processing World Index</u>. Phoenix, Arizona: Oryx
      Press, 1984.

      This 616 page book includes material on societies,
      directories, catalogs, and publishers.

41   Dick, Elie M. <u>Current Information Sources in Mathematics</u>.
      Littleton, Col.: Libraries Unlimited, Inc., 1973.

      This is an annotated bibliography of over 1,500
      titles, and although primarily on mathematics, it
      has sections dealing with the science of computing
      and about information processing in general.

42   Dotterweich, Dolores and Gebhardt, Friedrich.
      <u>Sammlungen zur Geschichte der Datenverarbeitung</u>.
      (Collections Concerning the History of Data
      Processing). Gesellschaft für Mathematik und
      Datenverarbeitung, No. 11. Bonn, West Ger.: January
      1983.

      This is a 26-page list of German collections on data
      processing and includes documents, pictures, machines
      and parts, and descriptions of 22 locations with
      addresses and telephone numbers. One is in Vienna,
      the others in West Germany.

43   Gotterer, Malcolm H. <u>Kwic Index; A Bibliography of</u>
      <u>Computer Management</u>. New York: Brandon/Systems
      Press, 1968 (?).

      This is a general binliography covering all aspects
      of data processing technology, applications, and
      management.

44   Gros, Eugene. <u>Russian Books on Automation and Computers</u>.
      London: Scientific Information Consultants, 1967.

      This is the first bibliography to appear in English

on the subject of Soviet computing publications.
The focus is on materials of the mid-1960s.

45   Hahn, Roger. A Bibliography of Quantitative Studies on
     Science and Its History. Berkeley Papers in History
     of Science 3. Berkeley: University of California,
     1980.

     This 33-page paper has some material concerning data
     processing. The primary concern is with quantitative
     applications and sociological issues.

46   Harvard University. Subject Catalog of The Baker
     Library. Graduate School of Business Administration,
     Harvard University. 10 vols & 1 supplemental vol.
     (1974). Boston: G.K. Hall & Co., 1971.

     This is a bibliography of the Harvard Business
     School's library, covering all aspects of business
     and includes data processing both by topic and
     alphabetically. It has hundreds of titles on data
     processing through the early 1970s along with
     standard library call numbers and references.

47   Hildebrandt, Darlene Myers. Computing Information
     Directory. Federal Way, Wa.: Pedaro, 1985.

     This directory includes bibliographic references,
     lists of organizations within the information
     processing industry and other data on the subject.

48   IBM. Atlas of Applications. 3 vols. White Plains, NY:
     IBM Corporation, 1973-1976.

     This is a list of publications from a wide variety
     of periodicals (some 7,000 titles) covers computer-
     based applications in business, science, engineering
     and other fields, published during the 1960s and
     early 1970s. It is the largest bibliography on the
     subject of applications.

49   Lowenstein, L.K. An Annotated Bibliography on Urban
     Games. Monticello, Ill.: Council of Planning
     Libraries, 1971.

     Lowenstein focuses primarily on the literature of
     modelling, covering both basic elements involved and
     the use of computers to execute such games.

50   Malassis, L. et al. "Bibliographie Relative à l'Arith-
     métique, au Calcul Simplifié et aux Instruments à
     Calculer," Bulletin de la Societe d'Encouragement
     pour l'Industrie Nationale 132 (September-October
     1920): 739-757.

     This reviews over 300 entries dealing with calcula-
     ting machinery, slide rules, etc., of the late 1800s
     and early 1900s. There are materials on applications
     and machine descriptions.

51   May, Kenneth O. <u>Bibliography and Research Manual of the</u>
        <u>History of Mathematics</u>. Toronto: University of
        Toronto Press, 1973.

        This bibliography does for mathematics what this
        bibliography does for data processing by providing
        a broad brush review of the literature by topic. It
        includes some material on the relationship of
        mathematics to computers.

52   McCormick, Edward M. <u>Bibliography on Mechanized Library</u>
        <u>Processes</u>. Washington, D.C.: Office of Science
        Information Service, National Science Foundation,
        1963.

        While largely a bibliography of application material,
        it includes considerable data on punched-card
        systems and on the use of computers.

53   Miller, Edward F. <u>Bibliography and Kwic Index on</u>
        <u>Computer Performance Measurement</u>. Santa Barbara,
        Ca.: General Research Corporation, 1973.

        This provides an evaluation of computers that were
        available during the late 1960s and 1970s with
        considerable reference to other publications.

54   Morrill, Chester. <u>Computers and Data Processing:</u>
        <u>Information Sources; An Annotated Guide to the</u>
        <u>Literature, Associations, and Institutions</u> Concerned
        <u>With Input, Throughput, and Output of Data</u>.
        Detroit: Gale Research Company, 1969.

        This is a highly specialized, 275-page listing of
        material on manufacturers, consultants, companies,
        and publications.

55   National Computing Center. <u>International Computer</u>
        <u>Bibliography</u>. Manchester, England: National
        Computing Center, 1968.

        This is a monumental two volume collection of over
        6,000 titles on all aspects of the subject.

56   Neeland, Frances. <u>Bibliography on Information Science</u>
        <u>and Technology</u>. 4 vols. Detroit: American
        Documentation Institute, 1967-1969.

        This presents a large collection of publications on
        data processing, library science, and other related
        fields of information handling. Primary focus is
        on publications which appeared during the 1950s and
        early 1960s. Technical material is presented along
        with items dealing with applications in a wide
        variety of fields.

57   Nossbaum, H.A. <u>Bibliography on Time Sharing</u>. Amsterdam:
        Netherlands Automatic Information Processing

        Research Centre, 1969.

This 49-page publication is dedicated to literature
on time sharing applications existing in the mid-
1960s, a period when this form of computer usage
spread widely both in the United States and in Europe.

58   Operations Research Group, Case Institute of Technology.
      <u>A Comprehensive Bibliography on Operations Research</u>.
      New York: John Wiley & Sons, Inc., 1958.

      Forty subject groups of publications appearing in
      print prior to 1958 are presented with cross-
      references listed by author with categories. It is
      an important list of the first decade of operations
      research, involving the use of computers.

59   Pitkin, Gary M. <u>Serials Automation in the United States:</u>
      <u>A Bibliographic History</u>. Metuchen, N.J.: Scarecrow
      Press, 1976.

      This covers publications which appeared between 1951
      and 1974, offering some 100 titles, a subject area
      which early-on caught the attention of librarians
      attempting to use computers effectively.

60   Pritchard, Alan. <u>A Guide to Computer Literature</u>.
      Hamden, Conn.: Archon Books, 1969.

      This bibliography covers all types of information in
      a narrative form and is an excellent introduction to
      the literature of computer science.

61   Randell, B. "An Annotated Bibliography on the Origins
      of Computers," <u>Annals of the History of Computing</u>
      1, No. 2 (October 1979): 101-207.

      This was the first complete bibliography on the
      subject of computing's history to be published. It
      is annotated and includes some unpublished material
      not included in the Cortada bibliography. All other
      citations are, however, included.

62   Randell, B. "The Origins of Digital Computers: Supple-
      mentary Bibliography," in N. Metropolis <u>et al</u>. (eds).
      <u>A History of Computing in the Twentieth Century</u> (New
      York: Academic Press, 1980): 629-653.

      The primary focus is from Charles Babbage (1800s)
      through the 1950s, with the majority of titles
      concerning computing from the 1930s to the late 1950s.

63   <u>Reader's Guide to Periodical Literature</u>. (Begin with
      1945).

      This is an excellent source for articles on all
      aspects of data processing. It is an essential
      source for the study of contemporary developments
      as reflected in widely-read magazines in the United
      States. The material is grouped by topics and
      indexed.

64   Rezus, A. <u>A Bibliography of Lamda-Calculi, Combinatory</u>
      <u>Logics and Related Topics</u>. Amsterdam: Mathematisch
      Centrum, 1982.

      One thousand titles are presented that deal with
      technical issues, logics and mathematics. Von
      Neumann's papers are listed, beginning with his
      earliest publications to the 1950s.

65   Solomon, Martin B. and Lovan, Nora G. <u>Annotated Biblio-</u>
      <u>graphy of Films in Automation, Data Processing and</u>
      <u>Computer Science</u>. Lexington: University of Kentucky
      Press, 1967.

      This bibliography surveys material which appeared
      during the 1950s and 1960s, offering valuable source
      material on public attitudes toward data processing,
      descriptions of computer technology, and about its
      uses and impact.

66   Stolurow, Lawrence M. and Peterson, Theodore I. <u>Computers</u>
      <u>in Educational Technology—Selected Bibliography,</u>
      <u>1969-1972</u>. White Plains, N.Y.: IBM Corporation, 1972.

      More than 600 titles are presented. It suggests
      that the interest in computers in education was far
      more than is usually noted by historians.

67   Subramanyam, K. <u>Directory of Primary Journals in</u>
      <u>Computer Science</u>. Monticello, Ill.: Council of
      Planning Libraries, 1976.

      This is a 34-page list of key journals of the 1970s
      making this an essential reference work on a growing
      list of data processing applications.

68   Thayne, Rulon <u>et al</u>. <u>Computers and Data Processing</u>
      <u>Systems</u>. Arlington, Va.: Armed Services Technical
      Information Agency, August 1962.

      This is a massive, annotated bibliography of papers
      prepared by or for the U.S. Department of Defense
      between 1953 and 1963.

69   United States, Bureau of Domestic Commerce. <u>Data</u>
      <u>Communications: Market Information Sources</u>.
      Washington, D.C.: Government Printing Office, 1972.

      This is a 53-page bibliography on all aspects of the
      data processing industry and is not limited just to
      a review of computers.

70   United States, Department of Labor. <u>Automatic Technology</u>
      <u>and Its Implications: A Selected Annotated Biblio-</u>
      <u>graphy</u>. Bulletin No. 1198, Bureau of Labor Statistics.
      Washington, D.C.: Government Printing Office, August
      1956.

      This is one of the earliest bibliographies to appear

on the subject of data processing technology and its applications.

71   Wood, D.   "A Bibliography of Formal Language Theory," in John Cocke and J.T. Schwartz (eds), Programming Languages and Their Compilers (New York: Courant Institute of Mathematical Science, New York University, 1970): 693-728.

This bibliography concentrates on publications of the 1960s, a period of considerable activity in the field of computer languages.

72   A World List of Computer Periodicals. Manchester: National Computer Centre, 1970.

This is a newer edition of bibliographic entry No. 55.

73   Youden, W.W.   Computer Literature Bibliography, 1946-1963. Washington, D.C.: National Bureau of Standards, 1965.

This is an excellent bibliography covering articles, conference reports, and books on all aspects of data processing: the industry, technology, economics, and uses. Other volumes were published, most notably No. 2 (1967) covering 1964-1967.

Courses on Data Processing History

74   Cutliffe, Stephen H.   The Machine in the University: Sample Course Syllabi for the History of Technology and Technology Studies. Bethlehem, Pa.: Science, Technology, and Society, 1983.

Associated with Lehigh University, the author offers an early attempt to provide instruction on the subject.

75   Rosenberg, Robert. "The Origins of EE Education: A Matter of Degree," IEEE Spectrum 21, No. 7 (July 1984): 60-68.

This surveys how electrical engineering, as a subject of study, evolved between 1880 and 1900. The topic was a root of modern computer science. For additional comments on the theme see Annals of the History of Computing 74, No. 1 (January 1985): 72-73.

76   Smillie, K.W. "A Service Course in Computing Science Presented From a Historical Point of View," SIGCSE Bulletin 13, No. 2 (June 1981): 27-33.

This article describes a course for computing students taught at the University of Alberta. It covers the subject from the ancient Egyptians to the present.

77   Stern, Nancy. "The History of Computing: Its Place in

the Curriculum," Interface (Fall 1980): 33-36.

She argues for the teaching of data processing's history in college curriculums.

78   Williams, Michael R. "A Course in the History of Computation," Annals of the History of Computing 7, No. 3 (July 1985): 241-244.

He describes a course taught on the subject at the University of Calgary. The focus of the class is on the evolution of calculations down to the present.

Electricity and Electronics

79   Antebi, Elizabeth. The Electronic Epoch. New York: Van Nostrand—Reinhold, 1982.

This is a history of the evolution of European electronics from 1930 to the 1980s and is well illustrated.

80   Davis, Henry B.O. Electrical and Electronic Technologies: A Chronology of Events and Inventors from 1940 to 1980. Metuchen, N.J.: Scarecrow Press, 1985.

This is a detailed (over 300-pages) chronology covering all aspects of the subject and includes material on computer science.

81   Electronics editors. An Age of Innovation: The World of Electronics, 1930-2,000. New York: McGraw-Hill, 1981.

Chapter One discusses the technical and social environment of the 1930s while the second reviews major technical events prior to 1930. Computer history is discussed throughout the book. Chapters Seven and Eight are dedicated to computers. The book is well illustrated.

82   Greenwood, Ernest. Aladdin USA. New York: Harper, 1928.

This is a general history of electricity in the United States. Although not a good study, it does, however, set the background and illustrates the motivation for electrification of calculating devices during the early years of the 1900s.

83   Grob, Bernard. Basic Electronics. New York: McGraw-Hill, 1984.

Although it has no history in it, the volume helps to set the technological stage for what computers are all about and thus serves as good technical background material.

84   Handel, S. The Electronic Revolution. London: Penguin, 1967.

This history of electronics goes from the 1700s to the transistor in an easy-to-read style for the non-technical reader. It is useful for placing into context the role transistors played in the broader field of electronics.

85   Morton, Jack A. Organizing for Innovation. New York: McGraw-Hill, 1971.

The author invented the term "tyranny of numbers," which he describes in this book on electronics. It is a phrase that has influenced historical perspectives on the role of electronics in the post-1950 period.

Encyclopedias and Dictionaries

86   American National Standards Committee X3, Information Processing Systems. American National Dictionary for Information Processing Systems. Homewood, Ill.: Dow Jones-Irwin, 1984.

To many in the data processing industry, ANSI standards on technology and, in this case definitions, are the norm. This dictionary is complete accumulation of many technical terms.

87   American National Standards Institute (ANSI). American National Standard Vocabulary for Information Processing. New York: ANSI, 1970.

This is an excellent, detailed source for terms used in the 1950s and 1960s. The book reflects a continuing project by ANSI to define the vocabulary of computer technology down to the present.

88   Association for Computing Machinery. ACM Guide to Computing Literature. New York: ACM, 1977.

While essentially a bibliography, it introduces definitions of terms. It appeared continuously in various editions throughout the 1970s.

89   Belzer, J. et al. (eds). Encyclopedia of Computer Science and Technology. New York: Dekker, Inc., 1977.

This contains a variety of articles relative to early computers and their developers. It runs to multiple volumes in several editions.

90   Berkeley, E.C. and Lovett, L.A. Glossary of Terms in Computers and Data Processing. Newtonville, Mass.: Berkeley Enterprises, Inc., 1960.

This is a useful publication on the terms in use

during the 1950s and contains some words no longer
in use. Edmund Berkeley was a major consultant in
the field of data processing in the 1950s and 1960s.

91   Buchholz, W. "Origin of the Word Byte," Annals of the
      History of Computing 10, No. 4 (1989): 340.

      He dates its origin to the 1950s and explains how
      it came into existance.

92   Edmunds, Robert A. The Prentice-Hall Standard Glossary
      of Computer Terminology. Englewood Cliffs, N.J.:
      Prentice-Hall, Inc., 1985.

      This is a typical, but good, example of many such
      dictionaries available in the 1980s on data
      processing terms.

93   Goodman, Edith H. (ed.). Data Processing Systems
      Encyclopedia: A Guide to Electronic and Electrome-
      chanical Equipment, Software, Applications and
      Related Services. Detroit: American Data Processing,
      1967.

      This loose-leaf publication appeared in various
      editions and additions in the late 1960s and is a
      comprehensive collection of information on all
      aspects of the data processing industry of the 1960s.

94   Horn, Jack. Computer and Data Processing Dictionary
      and Guide. Englewood Cliffs, N.J.: Prentice-Hall,
      Inc., 1966.

      More than a dictionary of terms common in the 1960s,
      Horn's book is also a guide to managerial issues of
      the period and to its technology.

95   Illingworth, Valerie et al. Dictionary of Computing.
      Oxford: Oxford University Press, 1983.

      3750 terms are presented covering all aspects of
      computer science as of the early 1980s.

96   IBM. Vocabulary for Data Processing, Telecommunications,
      and Office Systems. Poughkeepsie, N.Y.: International
      Business Machines Corporation, 1981.

      This massive dictionary has appeared in various
      editions throughout the 1970s and 1980s. This
      particular edition reflects the convergence of
      computer science, telecommunications and application
      terms through its content. Its definitions rely on
      industry standard interpretations, such as those
      from ANSI.

97   Meek, Chester L. Glossary of Computing Terminology.
      New York: CCM Information Corporation, 1972.

      This dictionary provides definitions commonly

in use during the 1970s. The phrases presented
also reflect terms used in the 1960s.

98   Ralston, A. and Meek, C.L. <u>Encyclopedia of Computer
      Science</u>. New York: Petrocelli/Charter, 1976.

      This is a massive and fundamental reference work on
      data processing. It covers all aspects, including
      the history of machines, software and biographies.

99 Ralston, A. and Reilly, Jr., E.D. (eds). <u>Encyclopedia
    of Computer Science and Engineering</u>. New York: Van
    Nostrand Reinhold, 1983.

      Essentially a second, expanded edition of the 1976
      work, it contains 550 articles written by 301
      contributors. It also contains more entries of an
      historical nature than in the first edition. A
      third edition is in preparation.

100   Sippl, Charles J. <u>Computer Dictionary</u>. Indianapolis:
      H.W. Sams, 1974.

      This second edition is 488 pages in length, making
      it one of the more complete and larger dictionaries
      of the period.

101   Sippl, Charles J. <u>Computer Dictionary and Handbook</u>.
      Indianapolis: Howard W. Sams & Co., Inc., 1966.

      This is the first edition of No. 100 above. It
      contains some 300 pages on the DP industry,
      contemporary products, services and software.

102   Spencer, Donald D. <u>The Computer Programmer's
      Dictionary and Handbook</u>. Waltham, Mass.: Blaisdell,
      1968.

      One of many such dictionaries to appear in the
      1960s on the subject. It does contain, however,
      material on programming, circa 1960s.

103   Tropp, Henry S. "Origin of the Term Bit," <u>Annals of
      the History of Computing</u> 10, No. 4 (1989): 336-340.

      He traces the term back to its origins in the 1940s
      and provides its most complete history available.

104   United States, Executive Office of the President,
      Bureau of the Budget. <u>Automatic Data Processing
      Glossary</u>. Washington, D.C.: Government Printing
      Office, 1962.

      This is the first known dictionary to appear on the
      subject published by the U.S. Government and reflects
      growing need for such tools within government
      agencies.

105   "What Those Words Mean," Science Digest 57 (April
       1965): 78-79.

       The focus is on data processing language.

                    General Histories of Calculators

106   Baxandall, D. "Calculating Machines, " Encyclopaedia
       Britannica (14th edition) (1929): 545-553.

       This particular issue reviews briefly the work of
       Napier, Pascal, Leibniz, Thomas, Odhner, Felt,
       Bollée, Hollerith, Babbage and Scheutz, and thus
       serves as an introduction to the history of
       calculators prior to the advent of electronic
       digital computers.

107   Brauner, L. "Wichtige Abschnitte der Rechenmaschinen-
       Entwicklung," Beitr. Gesch. Techn. Ind. 16 (1926):
       248-260.

       This is a lengthy chronology on the invention of
       calculating machines. It is illustrated with
       pictures of inventors and their devices.

108   Chapuis, A. and Droz, E. Automata: A Historical and
       Technological Study. London: V.T. Batsford, Ltd.,
       1958. French edition: Les Automates, Figures
       Artificielles d'Hommes et d'Animaux: Histoire et
       technique. Neuchatel: Griffon, 1949.

       These authors provide a major study of mechanical
       devices, most specifically of automons, mostly
       driven by pegged cylinders, from the 1600s down to
       chess playing machines developed by Torres y
       Quevedo.

109   Cooke, C.W. Automata Old and New. London: Chiswick
       Press, 1893.

       This is a short history of automata, well illustrated.

110   Cousins, F.W. "The Calculating Machine; Its History and
       Basic Principles," Newnes Practical Mechanics (July-
       September 1946): 342-344, 389-391, 427-428.

       This is a general history of calculating machines,
       beginning with the abacus down to Napier's bones,
       and includes the work of Leibniz, Odhner and others.

111   d'Ocagne, M. "Histoire des Machines à Calculer,"
       Bulletin de la Societe d'Encouragement pour
       l'Industrie Nationale 132 (September-October 1920):
       554-569.

       This is a speech focusing on the work of Pascal,
       Leibniz, Thomas, and Torres y Quevedo.

112   d'Ocagne, M. "Vue d'Ensemble sur les Machines à

Calculer," Bulletin des Sciences Mathematique, 2e
Série 46 (1922): 102-144.

This is a solid review of how calculating machines
developed. He discusses Pascal, Tchebichef, Felt,
Leibniz, Thomas, Maurel, Odhner, Burroughs, Bollée,
Scheutz, Babbage, and Torres y Quevedo.

113   Galle, A. Mathematische Instrumente. Leipzig: B.G.
Teubner, 1912.

Pages 23 through 48 review devices made by Pascal,
Leibniz, Thomas, Mercedes-Euklid Machine, Odhner,
the "Gauss" circular device built by Hamann,
Steiger's "Millionaire" Machine and other difference
machines.

114   Horsburgh, E.M. "Calculating Machines," Glasgow
Institution of Engineers and Shipbuilders in
Scotland 63 (1920): 117-162.

This is a detailed history of calculating devices.
It includes the abacus, Napier's rods, Pascal,
Leibniz, Thomas, difference engines, arithmometers,
Odhner wheel machines, key driven adding machines,
and the "Millionaire."

115   Horsburgh, E.M. "Calculating Machines," Glazebrook's
Dictionary of Applied Physics 3 (1923): 193-201.

This reviews briefly devices from the abacus to the
then current devices, and how they were designed
and used.

116   Horsburgh, E.M. (ed). Napier Tercentenary Celebration:
Handbook of the Exhibition. Edinburgh: Royal Society
of Edinburgh, 1914. Published also as Modern
Instruments and Methods of Calculation: A Handbook
of the Napier Tercentenary Celebration Exhibition.
Reprinted by Tomash Publishers (Los Angeles, 1983)
and distributed by The MIT Press.

This publication provides details on commonly
available devices of the early 1900s: their history,
description, and use, along with illustrations.

117   Jackson, Hugo T. "Who's Who in Hardware: A Short
History of Early Computer Pioneers," Computek 1,
No. 1 (September-October 1984): 28-36.

This covers briefly people from Schickard to the
inventors of the transistor.

118   Lilley, S. "Machinery in Mathematics: An Historical
Survey of Calculating Machines," Discovery 6, Nos
5 and 6 (1945): 150-156, 182-185.

This covers both digital and analogue devices in
addition to the more standard topics of Pascal,

Babbage, Thomas and others, particularly of the 1800s.

119   Lilley, S. "Mathematical Machines," Nature 149 (1942): 462-465.

Essentially this is an earlier version of his article cited in No. 118.

120   Locke, L.L. "Synchronism and Anarchronism," Scripta Mathematica 1 (1932): 147-152.

This discusses a variety of calculating machines and their inventors such as Leibniz, Grant, Baldwin and Rechnitzer.

121   Martin, E. Die Rechenmaschinen und ihre Entwicklungs-geschichte. Pappenheim: n.p., 1925.

Part 1 of this book is an historical survey of calculators. Subsequently some 250 pages are taken up with listing over 200 calculators, beginning with Pascal's of 1642 down to the 1920s. The book is well illustrated.

122   Reinecke, H. "Neuere entwicklungen mechanischen rechenmaschien," in 350 Jahre Rechenmaschen, ed. by M. Graef (Munich: Carl Hanser, 1973): 43-50.

This surveys developments in mechanical calculating machinery of the 19th and 20th centuries.

123   Stanley, W.F. Mathematical Drawing and Measurement Instruments. London: W.F. Stanley, Co., 1888.

This is a good reflection of a large number of slide rules, adding machines, surveying equipment, many of which are reviewed here, available in the 1880s.

124   Taton, R. and Flad, J.P. Le Calcul Mécanique. 2nd ed. Paris: Presses Universitaires de France, 1963; 1st ed., 1949.

This is a history of devices for calculating with primary attention going to those beginning with the abacus and ending with mechanical desk calculators. There is only a passing discussion of digital computers.

125   Trinks, F. Geshichtliche Daten aus der Entwicklung der Rechenmaschinen von Pascal bis zur "Nova-Brunsviga". Braunschweig: Grimme, Natalis and Co., A.G., 1926.

This illustrated 48-page booklet tells the history of European calculators and of the Brunsviga devices.

126   Verry, A. "History and Development of Calculating Machines and Instruments," Coventry England Society Journal 21 (1940): 143-186.

This summarizes applications of many devices, including those of Morland, Stanhope, Hamann, Burroughs, and Scheutz.

127   Williams, J.M. "Antique Mechanical Computers," Byte 3 (July 1978): 48, 50, 52-58; (August 1978): 96-98, 100, 102, 104-107; (September 1978): 82, 84, 86, 88, 90, 92.

This reviews early devices by such inventors as Vaucanson, von Knaus, Maillardet, and Torres y Quevedo. Many were automata devices.

128   Williams, Michael R. "The Difference Engines," Computer Journal 19, No. 1 (1976): 82-89.

This starts with Müller's 1786 proposal and ends with the use made by Comrie and others of commercially available desk calculators and accounting machines as difference engines. There are thoughts of Deacon, Grant, Ludgate, Bollée, Hamann, Thompson, Scheutz, Babbage and others. It ends chronologically in the period just before World War II.

129   Worlton, W.J. "Pre-Electronic Aids to Digital Computation,' in S. Fernbach and A.H. Taub (eds), Computers and Their Role in the Physical Sciences (New York: Gordon and Breach, 1970): 11-50.

He covers the period from early calculating methods to electromechanical calculators of the 1940s.

130   Zemanek, H. "Central European Prehistory of Computing," in N. Metropolis et al. (eds), A History of Computing in the Twentieth Century (New York: Academic Press, 1980): 587-609.

Written by an important computer scientist, eight stories are told: Broesel's programmed weaving device of the 1740s, Maelzel's programmable music machine of the early 1800s, Petzel's calculator of the 1840s and 1850s, Schaeffler's work in the 1870s, on Torres y Quevedo's work of the early 1900s and especially with chess machines, and ends with Tauschek's bookkeeping systems of the 1930s. There is also material on post World War II computing including on the Vienna Definition Language which evolved between 1958 and 1960.

General Histories of Computers and Data Processing

131   Antebi, Elizabeth. The Electronic Epoch. New York: Van Nostrand Reinhold, 1983.

This is a beautifully illustrated history with many photographs of old computers and their developers.

132   Apokin, I.A. and Maistrov, L.E. Rasvitie Vyichislite-lynich Mashin. Moscow: Nauka, 1974.

This is a general history of computing, covering all
aspects from the ancient abacus to the electronic
digital computer. The bibliography included suggests
a thorough job of research covering developments
worldwide.

133   Association for Computing Machinery. A Quarter Century
       View. New York: Association for Computing Machinery,
       1971.

       This publication focuses primarily on the evolution
       of computers in the USA during the 1950s and 1960s
       and is well illustrated.

134   Augarten, Stan. Bit by Bit. An Illustrated History of
       Computers. New York: Ticknor & Fields, 1984.

       This is a beautifully illustrated, very reliable
       account of the machines, including the micro
       computer—a technical history for the layman. It
       includes a chronology.

135   Bernstein, Jeremy. The Analytical Engine. Computers—
       Past, Present and Future. New York: William Morrow,
       1981; 1st ed., Random House, 1963.

       This is a popular history of computers, covering all
       the obvious people and their work from Babbage to
       Aiken, Stibitz, Eckert, Mauchly, von Neumann and
       others. It is a short but competent introduction
       to the history of computers.

136   Blohm, Hans et al. Pebbles to Computers. The Thread.
       Toronto: Oxford University Press, 1986.

       This is a general overview of computing devices
       from ancient times to the present. The main thrust
       of the work is to provide an illustrated survey;
       the photographs make this an important source work
       on illustrations.

137   Bowden, B.V. (ed). Faster Than Thought. London: Sir
       Isaac Pitman and Sons, 1953.

       This is an important publication—a minor classic in
       the historiography of computing—on the history of
       calculating and computing equipment. It contains a
       great deal of useful information on Babbage and on
       projects of the 1940s.

138   Buyer, Raymond. La Cybernetique et l'Origine de
       l'Information. Paris: Universitaris de France, 1954.

       This is as much a history of information processing
       by mankind as a history of computing equipment.

139   Campbell-Kelly, Martin. The Computer Age. East Sussex:
       Wayland Publishers, 1978.

This is a photo essay by an historian of computing.
He takes the story from the Stone Age to the present
with particular emphasis on the impact of computers
on people's lives.

140   Chase, George C. "History of Mechanical Computing
        Machinery," Proceedings of the ACM Pittsburgh 2-3
        May 1952: 1-28; reprinted with an introduction in
        Annals of the History of Computing 2, No. 3 (July
        1980): 198-226.

        This is a slide show with text on calculating
        devices beginning with the abacus down through the
        Harvard Mark I. It offers considerable information
        on American scientists such as Baldwin, Monroe,
        Avery, Friden, Hopkins, Grant, Burroughs, Dalton,
        Sundstrans, Ellis and Felt. Also covered are the
        projects by Hollerith, Aiken, Scheutz and Babbage.

141   The Computer. Madison, WI: Hawkhill Associates, Inc.,
        1988.

        This is a 33.5 minute-long VHS video cassette that
        reviews the general history of computers and then
        how computers work. It is suitable for basic
        class room use.

142   Computers and Computing. Herbert Ellsworth Slaught
        Memorial Papers, No. 10, American Mathematical
        Monthly 72, No. 2 (February 1965). Menasha, WI:
        Mathematical Association of America, 1965.

        This was published as a supplement to the journal.
        It has some material on computers written by pioneers
        in their development. They include: Dick Hamming,
        Nick Metropolis, Kelly Gotlieb, Allen Newell, and
        Tony Oettinger.

143   Cortada, James W. Historical Dictionary of Data
        Processing: Technology. Westport, Conn.: Greenwood
        Press, 1987.

        This has entries on all major computers, peripheral
        equipment, software, technical concepts, on calcula-
        tors and other mechanical devices ranginf rom ancient
        times down through the early 1980s. Each entry also
        includes bibliography.

144   Couffignal, L. Les Machines à Penser. Paris: Les
        Editions de Minuit, 1952.

        He reviews a number of then currently available
        calculators, punched card devices, and computers
        such as the Mark I, ENIAC, that of the Institut
        Blaise Pascal, and Babbage's Analitcal Engine.

145   de Beauclair, W. "Geschichte Entwicklung," in K.
        Steinbuch (ed), Taschenluch der Nachrichten Verar-

beitung. 2. Uberarbeite. (Berlin: Springer Verlag,
1967): 1-39.

The history of digital computers is presented in a
brief fashion, taking the story down to the 1960s
and with a detailed bibliography.

146   de Beauclair, W. Rechen mit Maschinen: Eine Bildgesch-
       ichte der Rechentechnik. Braunschweig: Friedr.
       Vieweg und Sohn, 1968.

       This is a well illustrated account of the origins
       of digital computers up through the early 1960s. It
       is an extremely informative survey of all the key
       technologies involved.

147   de Beauclair, W. and Schmid, D. "Geschichtliche
       Entwicklung," in K. Steinbuch and W. Weber (eds),
       Taschenbuch der Informatik 1 (Berlin: Springer
       Verlag, 1974): 1-45.

       This reviews how the digital computer came about in
       general terms; complete with a bibliography that is
       extensive.

148   Erskine, G.A. "The History of the Computer," Proceed-
       ings, 1976 School of Computing, CERN 76-24 (1976):
       26-279.

       The author provides considerable data on machines
       from Schickard's calculator to the early stored
       program computer.

149   Evans, Christopher. The Making of the Micro: A History
       of the Computer. New York: Van Nostrand Reinhold,
       1981.

       This takes the story of the micro computer down to
       the 1970s, beginning with the abacus and ending with
       the transistor and integrated circuits. Evans is a
       participant in the computer industry and wrote a
       useful, short introduction to the subject. This
       book is an illustrated version of his earlier volume,
       The Micro Millenium (New York: Viking Press, 1979).

150   Fernbach, Sidney. "Supercomputers—Past, Present,
       Prospectus," FGCS (Future Generation Computer
       Systems) 1, No. 1 (July 1984): 23-30.

       He defines super computers, describes various early
       attempts to build such machines in the period from
       the 1950s. He describes the role of IBM, governments
       and other organizations. The author is an active
       participant in the super computer sector of the data
       processing industry.

151   Fleck, G. (ed). A Computer Perspective. (By the Office
       of Charles and Ray Eames). Cambridge, Mass.: Harvard
       University Press, 1973.

This is a profusely illustrated history based on an
IBM exhibit. It is organized by decade and contains
considerable amounts of little-known pieces of data
and photographs on the history of computing.

152   Franksen, Ole I. "The Nature of Data—From Measurements
       to Systems," <u>Bit</u> 25, No. 1 (1985): 24-50.

This publication traces the history of measurements
and data in physics since the days of Newton.

153   Freiherr, Gregory. <u>History of Computing: Abacus to
       ENIAC and Beyond</u>. Reprinted from <u>The Seeds of Arti-
       ficial Intelligence</u> (Rockville, Md.: NIH Publications,
       1979): 9-19.

This is a brief illustrated history and has some
errors in facts.

154   Ganzhorn, K. and Walter, W. <u>Die Geschichtliche
       Entwicklung der Datenverarbeitung</u>. Stuttgart: IBM
       Deutschland GmbH, 1975.

This is a beautifully illustrated introduction to
early counting systems and mechanical devices,
automata, and to the work of Charles Babbage,
Herman Hollerith, Zuse, and to such machines as the
Mark I, SSEC, and early IBM electronic multipliers.

155   Giarratano, Joseph C. <u>Foundations of Computer Techno-
       logy</u>. Nc.: Howard W. Sams, 1982.

This is a short history of computers.

156   Goldscheider, P. and Zemanek, H. <u>Computer: Werkzeug der
       information</u>. Berlin: Springer Verlag, 1971.

This reviews computers and old mechanical devices
of the pre-computer era by two scientists active
in computer science.

157   Goldstine, Herman H. "A Brief History of the Computer,"
       <u>Proceedings of the American Philosophical Society</u>
       121, No. 5 (October 1977): 339-345.

Written by a close associate of von Neumann, this
brief account takes the story from Schickard (1592-
1635) down to his own work on the computer at the
Institute for Advanced Studies at Princeton, NJ in
the 1940s.

158   Gonick, L. <u>The Cartoon Guide to Computer Science</u>. New
       York: Barnes and Noble Books, 1983.

This covers all aspects of computer science with
cartoons. It contains an enormous amount of detail
hard to find on history, systems, logics, etc.
while offering some humor.

159   Graef, Martin (ed). <u>350 Jahre Rechenmachinen</u>.
      Munich: Carl Hanser Verlag, 1973.

      This reviews 350 years of computing machines in a
      series of lectures given at the University of
      Tuebingen.

160   Harmon, M. <u>Stretching Man's Mind: A History of Data
      Processing</u>. New York: Mason/Charter, 1975.

      This is a popular history that focuses on machines
      and their inventors and less on the modern industry
      that bears its name.

161   Hartree, D.R. <u>Calculating Instruments and Machines</u>.
      Urbana: University of Illinois Press, 1949; reptin-
      ted by MIT Press, 1984.

      Douglas Hartree was an early computer scientist and
      this book, considered a minor classic in the field,
      describes differential analyzers, the technology of
      the digital computer of the 1940s, and then the work
      of Babbage, Aiken, the IBM SSEC and other projects
      and technical issues of the day.

162   Hartree, D.R. "A Historical Survey of Digital
      Computing Machines," <u>Proceedings of the Royal
      Society. London A</u> 195 (1948): 265-271.

      This is a brief overview of Charles Babbage's
      Analytical Engine, the Harvard Mark I, and the ENIAC.

163   Hoffman, W. "Entwicklungsbericht und Literaturzusamm-
      enstellung über Ziffern-Rechenautomaten," in his
      <u>Digitale Informationswandler</u> (Braunschweig: Vieweg,
      1962) and also in <u>Digital Information Processors</u>
      (New York: Wiley, 1962): 650-717.

      This is a useful, well-documented overview of
      computers within an historical context.

164   Hollingdale, S.H. and Tootill, G.C. <u>Electronic Compu-
      ters</u>. Middlesex: Penguin Books, 1965.

      They survey the history of computers from the
      abacus to the early 1960s with most of the atten-
      tion paid to post-World War II developments.

165   Huskey, H.D. "The Development of Automatic Computing,"
      in Demme Van Tassel (ed), <u>The Compleat Computer</u>
      (Chicago: SRA, Inc., 1976): 12-18.

      This computer scientist provides a general,
      illustrated history of computers from Babbage to
      the 1970s.

166   Huskey, H.D. and Huskey, V.R. "Chronology of Computing
      Devices," <u>IEEE Transactions on Computers</u> C-25, No.
      12 (December 1976): 1190-1199.

This has a large variety of short entries from counting tables to modern machines; includes a bibliography.

167   Last, J. "Digital Calculating Machines," The Charted Mechanical Engineer (December 1962): 572-579.

This is a brief survey with its focus on very early digital devices.

168   Margerison, Tom A. "Computers," in Trevor I. Williams (ed), A History of Technology, 7: The Twentieth Century, pt 2 (Oxford: Oxford University Press, 1978): 1150-1203.

This general history is one of the better short surveys and takes the story down to about 1950. The Oxford publication of these multi-volumes (16 in total) was a major event in the historiography of technology as a whole.

169   McCarthy, J. "Information," Scientific American 215, No. 3 (1966): 65-72.

This is a short history of computers.

170   Moreau, René. The Computer Comes of Age: The People, The Hardware, and the Software. Cambridge, Mass.: MIT Press, 1984.

This French IBM technical manager/executive provides a history of computers and of his industry, with primary focus on the period from the 1930s to the 1980s.

171   Mowshowitz, Abbe (ed). Inside Information: Computers in Fiction. Reading, Mass.: Addison-Wesley, 1977.

This reviews the role computers have played in fiction, especially in that of H.G. Wells, A. Bierce, E.L. Rice and others. The author also has a section on the role of post-World War II literature and the social impact of computers.

172   Penzias, Arno. Ideas and Information: Managing in a World of Computers. New York: W.W. Norton, 1989.

The author is the head of the research division at Bell Labs. He describes basic computer architecture with a short history of its evolution. His focus is on information handling from cave wall drawings to computers.

173   Pollack, Seymour V. "The Development of Computer Science," in S.V. Pollack (ed), Studies in Computer Science (Washington, D.C.: Mathematical Association of America, 1982): 1-51.

This focuses very much on hardware developments.

174   Randell, B. "The History of Digital Computers,"
       Bulletin of the I.M.A. 12, Nos 11-12 (November-
       December 1976): 335-346.

       This is a very brief history of digital computers
       from Babbage to the first stored program devices.

175   Randell, B. (ed). The Origins of Digital Computers.
       New York: Springer-Verlag, 1973; rev. 3rd ed., 1982.

       This is an important publication on the history of
       computer technology. It contains over 30 papers on
       the subject; a critical source on scientific
       developments.

176   Rochester, Jack B. and Gantz, John. The Naked Computer.
       New York: William Morrow and Co., 1983.

       This is a collection of brief stories, old tales,
       some oral history, and trivia written more for
       entertainment than scholarship.

177   Rosenberg, Jerry. The Computer Prophets. Lodon:
       Macmillan, 1969.

       This reviews the early history of computer technology
       through histories of inventors and machines, most of
       the period since the 1930s.

178   Serrel, R. et al. "The Evolution of Computing Machines
       and Systems," Proceedings of the IRE 50 (May 1962):
       1039-1058.

       This is an early, illustrated history of computers
       in the USA with considerable material on the evolu-
       tion of data processing technology in the 1940s and
       1950s.

179   Smith, Thomas M. "Origins of the Computer," in Paul J.
       Grogan and Donald F. Kaiser (eds), Technology in
       Western Civilization (New York: Oxford University
       Press, 1967), 2, pp. 309-323.

       Computer history is presented as a general overview
       from its earliest days down to the mid-1960s with
       illustrations.

180   Smith, Thomas M. "Some Perspectives on the Early
       History of Computers," in Z.W. Pyhyshyn (ed),
       Perspectives on the Computer Revolution (Englewood
       Cliffs, N.J.: Prentice-Hall, Inc., 1970): 7-15.

       A variety of inventors are surveyed. The author
       argues that many concurrent activities led to the
       development of the computer.

181   Stine, G. Harry. The Untold Story of the Computer
       Revolution: Bits, Bytes, Bauds and Brains. New York:
       Arbor House, 1985.

This is a general survey of people and machines
intended for a non-technical audience. The author
also speculates about the future of computers; well
written.

182   Tee, Garry J. "Computers and Mathematicians," The New
      Zealand Mathematics Magazine 24, No. 3 (September
      1987): 3-12.

      Although a general overview of the relationship of
      computers to mathematics, there are included examples
      from Babbage, Turing, crystallography and tomogra-
      phy.

183   Thomas, S. Computers: Their History, Present Applica-
      tions and Future. New York: Holt, Rinehart and
      Winston, 1964.

      This has a great deal of information on data
      processing activities in the United States up to
      the early 1960s with primary focus on the 1950s.

184   3M Company. The Birth of the Computer. London: 3M
      Company, 1971.

      This is a collection of six illustrated brochures
      surveying the history of calculators and companies
      and computers from Napier through the first genera-
      tion of processors.

185   Time-Life Books. Computer Basics, 1, Understanding
      Computers. Alexandria, Va.: Time-Life Books, 1985.

      This beautifully illustrated volume has a short
      chapter on the history of various computers.

186   Weiss, Eric A. "Biographies; Oh, Pioneers!," Annals
      of the History of Computing 10, No. 4 (1989): 348-
      360.

      This is an illustrated history with brief comments,
      on the significance of individuals important to the
      history of computing. It includes a list of some
      260 important individuals.

187   Willers, F.A. Mathematische Maschinen und Instrumente.
      Berlin: Akademie-Verlag, 1951.

      Pages 5 through 91 deal with calculators and
      computers in an historical context down to 1950.
      It discusses how they work and offers considerable
      bibliographic references.

General Histories of Technologies

188   Byrn, Edward. The Progress of Invention in the Nine-
      teenth Century. New York: Munn, 1900.

      While it glories in the accomplishments of the past

century, it nonetheless talks about what happened
in some detail, thereby providing useful background
material.

189   Crowther, J.G. <u>Discoveries and Inventions of the
      Twentieth Century</u>. New York: Dutton, 1966.

      This is a general introduction by a leading histo-
      rian of technology in this century.

190   Devaux, Pierre. <u>Automates et automatisme</u>. Paris:
      Presses Universitaires de France, 1944.

      More than simply a history of automatas, particularly
      of the eighteenth century, this is also a technical
      explanation of how they worked.

191   Dijksterhuis, E.J. <u>The Mechanization of the World
      Picture</u>. Translated by C. Dikshoorn. London: Oxford
      University Press, 1969.

      Originally published in Dutch in 1950, this scholarly
      book is a survey of the mechanical philosophy of
      science down to Leibnitz.

192   Giedion, Siegfried. <u>Mechanism Takes Command</u>. New York:
      Oxford University Press, 1948.

      This book is dedicated to the broad theme of plant
      and assembly-line automation, mechanized transporta-
      tion and the general acceptance of machines to do
      the jobs of society. It identifies many of the
      social and economic impacts which were to be repeated
      with the wide use of computers and its variants of
      automation.

193   Gilfallan, S.C. <u>The Sociology of Invention</u>. Cambridge,
      Mass.: MIT Press, 1935.

      This was one of the first serious studies made on
      the dynamics of change in science. Many of the
      issues raised in this book have subsequently become
      standard topics for historians of data processing.
      It is a useful introduction to the understanding of
      how a variety of technical innovations could build
      on each other, allowing for the digital computer,
      for example, to develop.

194   Gruenberger, F. "Editor's Readout—.06 Ideas/Kiloman
      Year," <u>Datamation</u> 8 (1962): 23.

      He lists 30 ideas that had the greatest influence
      on the development of computer science and data
      processing.

195   Hall, Courtney. <u>History of American Industrial Science</u>.
      New York: Library Publishers, 1954.

      This discusses the evolution of industry and, in the

United States, industrial arts with its associated
technologies.

196   Hindle, Brooke. _Emulation and Invention_. New York:
      Basic Books, 1981.

      This surveys the history of the Morse telegraph.
      That technology had a profound influence on future
      engineers who worked on radios and later, on digital
      and analog computers.

197   Kaempffert, Waldemar (ed). _A Popular History of
      American Inventions_. New York: Burt, 1924.

      Included in this book is a discussion of a variety
      of business machines, precursors to the modern
      calculators and computers.

198   Kuhn, Thomas S. _The Structure of Scientific Revolutions_.
      Chicago: University of Chicago, 1962.

      This is a very influential book that suggests how
      technology and science evolve. It was the most
      important book on the subject for nearly a quarter
      of a century and significantly influnced the think-
      ing of many historians of science during the 1960s,
      1970s and 1980s.

199   Mason, W.P. "Electrical and Mechanical Analogies,"
      Bell Systems Technical Journal 20 (October 1941):
      405-414.

      Mason offers an historical survey of electrical and
      mechanical filters from the 1800s, when electricity
      was in its infacy as an area of scientific activity
      down to the 1940s.

200   Morison, Elting E. _From Know-How to Nowhere: The
      Development of American Technology_. New York: Basic
      Books, 1974.

      This is a fundamental book for understanding the
      environment in the United States which made research
      and development of high technology possible.

201   Morison, Elting E. _Men, Machines, and Modern Times_.
      Cambridge, Mass.: MIT Press, 1966.

      The author focuses on the theme of technological
      innovations and how they came about. These were
      ideas expanded further in his 1974 book (entry No.
      200).

202   Noble, David. _Forces of Production: A Social History
      of Industrial Production_. New York: Oxford Univer-
      sity Press, 1986.

      This is a widely read study on the subject, highly
      influential on historians of technology.

203   Pyke, Magnus. The Science Century. New York: Walker,
       1967.

       Attention is drawn to developments of the nineteenth
       century and their influence on American economic
       affairs.

204   Roller, Duane H. Perspectives in the History of Science
       and Technology. Norman, Okla.: University of
       Oklahoma Press, 1981.

       This offers background on the growth of technology
       in general over the past several hundred years.

205   Singer, Charles et al. A History of Technology. 16 vols.
       Oxford: Clarendon Press, 1954-1978.

       This is a treasure of articles by specialists on all
       aspects of technology from ancient times to the
       present. Comments on the rise of computers can be
       found in the volumes after No. 4.

206   Stimson, Dorothy. Sarton on the History of Science.
       Cambridge, Mass.: Harvard University Press, 1962.

       This provides background information on scientific
       developments in genral and on their characteristics,
       many of which are repeated with the evolution of
       computer-based technology.

207   Stokes, John W. 70 Years of Radio Tubes and Valves.
       Vestal, N.Y.: Vestal Press, 1982.

       This contains a great deal of information on the
       history of radio tubes for home radios but also
       vacuum tubes which were early components of the
       digital computer of the 1940s and 1950s.

208   Swartzlander, Earl E. (ed). Computer Design Development
       Principal Papers. Rochelle Park, N.J.: Hayden Book
       Co., 1976.

       These are scientific papers published on logic
       design, arithmetic algorithms and computer architec-
       ture which appeared for the first time from 1919
       through the 1950s that would be of interest to
       historians of such technology. They are all period
       pieces.

209   Tyne, Gerald F. Saga of the Vacuum Tube. Indianapolis:
       Howard W. Sams and Co., 1977.

       Its focus is on the role these tubes played in the
       development and use of radio. These components were
       also used in early digital computers.

210   White, Lynn T. Medieval Technology and Social Change.
       Oxford: Clarendon Press, 1962.

This very interesting book has a discussion of mechanical-dynamic technology in the era before the creation of early mechanical calculators and adding machines.

211   Williams, Trevor I. A Short History of Twentieth Century Technology. New York: Oxford University Press, 1982.

This is a basic text on all aspects of the subject and has a section on computer developments set within the context of social, economic and political issues. It is of great value to historians wishing to pursue the history of data processing outside the confines of technical details.

Historiography

212   Burke, J.G. "Comment: The Complex Nature of Explanation in the Historiography of Technology," Technology and Culture 11 (1970): 22-26.

He argues that technology in general is not a society's product as a whole but comes from parts of it which in turn then can create social change.

213   Ceruzzi, Paul. "An Unforseen Revolution: Computers and Expectations, 1935-1985," in Joseph J. Corn (ed), Imagining Tomorrow: History, Technology, and the American Future. Cambridge, Mass.: MIT Press, 1986.

Ceruzzi is a leading historian of the early digital computer. His article focuses on the development of the computer as unplanned and underappreciated in its potential.

214   Daniels, G. "The Big Questions in the History of American Technology," Technology and Culture 11 (1970): 1-21.

One of his arguments was that technological innovation simply encouraged Americans to do what they seem to do well. His comments applied to all forms of technology, not just to computer science.

215   Gaines, Brian R. and Shaw, Mildred L. "A Learning Model for Forecasting the Future of Information Technology," Future Computer Systems 1, 1 (1986): 31-69.

Although not an historical piece, it nonetheless offers a model of possible use to historians by which to measure past events.

216   Hamming, R.W. "We Would Know What They Thought When They Did It," in N. Metropolis et al (eds), A History of Computing in the Twentieth Century: A Collection of Essays (New York: Academic Press, 1980): 3-10.

        This is a very short philosophic essay introducing
        the subject of computing history.

217   Mahoney, Michael S. "The History of Computing in the
        History of Technology," Annals of the History of
        Computing 10, No. 2 (1988): 113-125.

        He surveys literature on the history of computing
        and, more importantly, the issues raised as they
        apply to general themes in the history of technology.

218   May, Kenneth O. "Historiography: A Perspective for
        Computer Scientists," in N. Metropolis et al. (eds),
        A History of Computing in the Twentieth Century: A
        Collection of Essays (New York: Academic Press,
        1980): 11-18.

        This is on the historiography of computing with
        emphasis on the attitude of people that should be
        taken toward the subject.

219   Norberg, Arthur L. "Another Impact of the Computer—
        The History of Computing," IEEE Transactions on
        Education, E-27, No. 4 (1984): 197-203.

        Norberg, the director of the Charles Babbage
        Institute, evalues the status of research on the
        history of data processing as of the mid-1980s.

220   Pugh, Emerson W. "A Report on the IBM Technical
        History Project," Charles Babbage Institute News-
        letter 9, No. 4 (Summer 1987): 4.

        This IBM engineer/executive describes the effort to
        produce IBM's Early Computers (Cambridge, Mass.:
        MIT Press, 1986) and the work on its sequel dealing
        with the IBM S/370 line of computers.

221   Zemanek, Heinz. "Wird der Computer die Technik
        vermenschlichen?—Ein Beitrag zum 100. Geburtstag
        des OVE," Elektrotechnik und Maschinenbrau 100
        (1983): 448-458.

        This distinguished IBM scientist shares his thoughts
        on what computer science is about and what it teaches
        us.

                          Mathematics

222   Arbib, Michael A. Theories of Abstract Automata.
        Englewood Cliffs, N.J.: Prentice-Hall, 1979.

        This book discusses the mathematical basis of
        automata. This essential aspect of the evolution
        of computer technology is covered in detail. It
        also has a section on Turing machines.

223   Asimov, Isaac. Asimov on Numbers. New York: Doubleday,
        1977.

He discusses, in part, binary numbers, their systems and significance to science and computers.

224   Ball, W.W. <u>A History of the Study of Mathematics at Cambridge</u>. Cambridge: University of Cambridge, 1889.

Of particular interest is the material on Charles Babbage's writings (pp. 125-126) for their impact on other mathematicians.

225   Bell, Eric. <u>Mathematics, Queen and Servant of Science</u>. New York: McGraw-Hill, 1951.

This is a fun, clever book on all aspects of mathematics, including Boolean and binary systems.

226   Bledsoe, W.W. and Loveland, D.W. (eds). <u>Automated Theorem Proving: After 25 Years</u>. Providence: American Mathematical Society, 1984.

This is volume 29 of the AMS Contemporary Mathematics Series. It discusses mathematics since 1950s as applied to proving theorems.

227   Bliss, Gilbert A. <u>Lectures on the Calculus of Variations</u>. Chicago: University of Chicago Press, 1945.

This was his major work on the calculus of variation, a subject critical to the mathematics of ballistics and hence motivation for the development of calculation devices of great capacity, such as computers.

228   Boyer, C.B. <u>A History of Mathematics</u>. New York: John Wiley, 1968.

This massive work covers all aspects of the subject and thus is good background material. It takes the history of mathematics well into the age of computer technology.

229   Cajori, Florian. <u>A History of Mathematics</u>. New York: The Macmillan Co., 1919.

This is the second edition and has passing references to Charles Babbage and to a variety of calculating devices popular in the late 1800s/early 1900s.

230   Cohen, Patricia Cline. <u>A Calculating People: The Spread of Numeracy in Early America</u>. Chicago: University of Chicago Press, 1982.

This book does not contain any discussion of mechanical aids to calculation. However, it does provide a good survey of the role of numbers in American society of the 1600s and 1700s.

231   Dauben, Joseph W. <u>The History of Mathematics from Antiquity to the Present: A Selective Bibliography</u>.

New York: Garland Publishers, 1985.

This selective bibliography offers some 2,000 titles which are annotated covering all aspects of the subject.

232   Davis, Phillip J. and Hersh, R. The Mathematical Experience. Boston: Birkhäuser, 1981.

This is a good one volume introduction to the history of mathematics. It also discusses computational devices and why they were needed, offering a partial explanation for the incentives leading to the development of the computer.

233   Folkerts, M. and Lindgren, U. (eds). Mathemata: Festschrift für Helmuth Gericke. Stuttgart: Franz Steiner, 1985.

This collection of essays contains a paper by E.M. Bruins on "Numerical Solutions of Equations Before and After al-Kashi."

234   Genaille, H. "Piano Arithmétique pour la Vérification des Grandes Nombres Premiers," Association Française pour le Avance de Science 20, No. 1 (1891): 159.

This is a one paragraph review of the piano arithmétique designed to determine if certain types of numbers were prime.

235   Glaser, Anton. History of Binary and Other Nondecimal Numeration. Los Angeles: Tomash Publishers, 1981.

This is a well-written history covering the years 1500-1965. It ends with the ENIAC computer project.

236   Graham, R.L. and Hell, Pavol. "On the History of the Minimum Spanning Tree Problem," Annals of the History of Computing 7, No. 1 (January 1985): 43-57.

This is a history of algorithmic solutions to this problem. It is a highly technical paper.

237   Hamming, R.W. Introduction to Applied Numerical Analysis. New York: McGraw-Hill, 1971.

This textbook was written by a leading computer mathematician on a subject basic to much computer science and technology of the 1960s and 1970s.

238   Hurd, Cuthbert C. "A Note on Early Monte Carlo Computations and Scientific Meetings," Annals of the History of Computing 7, No. 1 (January 1985): 141-155.

This is an illustrated article and contains material on IBM as well. It is a very technical paper.

239   Kaufmann, H.   Die Ahnen des Computers: Von der phönizi-
        schen schrift zur datenverarbeitung.   Dusseldorf:
        Econ-Verlag, 1974.

        A great deal of information is provided on the
        evolution of arithmetic and calculators down to the
        early days of computer technology.

240   Kepler, J.   Harmonices Mundi.   Lince, Austria: n.p.,
        1619.

        This is a primary source of his ideas on mathematics.

241   Kepler, J.   Tabulae Rudolphinae.   Ulm: n.p., 1627.
        This is a primary source of his ideas on mathematics.

242   Murray, F.J.   The Theory of Mathematical Machines.
        New York: King's Crown Press, 1948.

        He offers theory on how mechanical aids work and
        has good material relevant to the precursors of the
        computer of the late 1940s and early 1950s.

243   Newan, James R.   The World of Mathematics.   4 vols.   New
        York: Simon & Schuster, 1956.

        All 4 volumes serve as excellent introductions to
        the subject and hence as background to computer
        science.   Volume 3 has a discussion of Boolean
        logic.

244   Phillips, Esther R. (ed).   Studies in the History of
        Mathematics.   M.A.A. Studies in Mathematics, 26
        (1987).

        Its focus is primarily on contemporary mathematics
        but also has some material on the history of
        computing: logic and computers (pp. 137-165) and on
        von Neumann and the IAS (pp. 166-194).

245   Rosser, J. Barkley.   "Highlights of the History of the
        Lambda-Calculus," Annals of the History of Computing
        6, No. 4 (October 1984): 337-349.

        Lambda-calculus, combinatory calculus, is key to
        computational theory.   This technical paper explains
        its features and recent history.

246   Smith, D.E.   History of Mathematics.   2 vols. New York:
        Dover Publications, 1923-1925.

        This older general history is still useful since it
        reviews the work of some nineteenth century mathema-
        ticians, such as Charles Babbage.

247   Tarwater, Dalton (ed).   The Bicentennial Tribute to
        American Mathematics, 1776-1976.   New York: Mathema-
        tical Association of America, 1977.

It has three chapters with material concerning
computers.

248   Taton, R. <u>Histoire du Calcul</u>. Paris: Presses Universitaires de France, 1969. (5th ed.).

Emphasis is placed on the evolution of mathematics
from earliest times to the introduction of mechanical
aids to calculations.

249   Thompson, Thomas M. <u>From Error-Correcting Codes Through</u>
<u>Sphere Packings to Simple Groups</u>. Washington, D.C.:
Mathematical Association of America, 1984.

This is a history of work done at Bell Labs by
Richard Hamming on error-correcting codes in
mathematics and includes the work of others on
information theory. It is a clearly, thorough
study.

250   Zemanek, Heinz. <u>Al-Khorezmi: His Background, His</u>
<u>Personality, His Work and His Influence</u>. Urgench,
Uzbek, USSR: Privately printed, 1979.

This is a biography and analysis of the work of a
mathematician who lived in the 800's A.D. It is
illustrated and well done.

Museums and Exhibits

251   "A Walk Through the Computer Museum with Gordon Bell,"
<u>Computerworld</u>, October 14, 1985, pp. ID/10-11, 13-
14, 16-17, 19-22.

This is an illustrated history and description of
the Boston-based Computer Museum and about his
views as its director. He is also famous for having
developed the DEC PDP-11 mini-computer.

252   Bell, Gwen and Bell, C. Gordon. "Digging for Computer
'Gold' (in Computer Archaeology)," <u>IEEE Spectrum</u> 22,
No. 12 (December 1985): 56-62.

They describe the work being done at the Computer
Museum by its directors. The Computer Museum is a
major repository of computer hardware and software.

253   Chroust, G. and Zemanek, H.   "80 und mehr jahr
computer—ein austellungswand," <u>Electronische Rech-</u>
<u>enanlagen</u> 25, No. 6 (1983): 58-65.

This is an illustrated description of the 12 panels
in the exhibit on the history of data processing
from Pascal to the chip at the Museum of Technology
in Vienna developed by Zemanek.

254   Cohen, I. Bernard. "Home of the New Dinosaurs,"
<u>American Heritage of Invention & Technology</u> 1, No.
3 (Spring 1986): 64.

He describes the Computer Museum in Boston.

255   Lubar, Steven. "The Computer Museum, Boston, Massachu-
       setts," Technology and Culture 27, No. 1 (January
       1986): 96-105.

       This is a detailed, positive account of the museum
       which opened in late 1984. It is a description of
       its exhibits and objectives.

256   Mayr, Otto. Feedback Mechanisms in the Historical
       Collections of the National Museum of History and
       Technology. Washington, D.C.: Smithsonian Institu-
       tion Press, 1971.

       This illustrated account has a chapter entitled,
       "Electronic Computers: PHILBIC electronic analog
       computer" and also describes the Ramo-Woolridge
       RW-300 used for process control at Texaco's
       refinery at Port Arthur, Texas beginning on March
       13, 1959.

257   Raines, Jane M. "History of Computing at the Science
       Museum, London," Annals of the History of Computing
       2, No. 1 (January 1980): 76-77.

       This is a description of the large exhibit at the
       Museum by a staff member covering items from early
       slide rules to Babbage machinery and finally, to
       electronic digital computers.

258   Weiss, Eric A. "The Computer Museum," Annals of the
       History of Computing 7, No. 3 (July 1985): 258-266.

       This is an illustrated, detailed description of
       what was on exhibit as of 1985. At that time it
       had over 1,000 items from 250 companies in its
       collection.

Periodicals

259   Abacus (1982-1988).

       This contained numerous articles on the history of
       computing.

260   Association for Computing Machinery. Bibliography of
       Current Computing Literature (New York: ACM, 1969-
       1975).

       These seven volumes contain thousands of titles on
       computers, applications, programming, data processing
       and other related topics.

261   Association for Computing Machinery. Comprehensive
       Bibliography of Computing Literature, 1966-1967.
       New York, ACM, 1967-1968.

       This two volumes represent a variant of numerous

bibliographies published by ACM of current technical
publications on data processing.

262   Association for Computing Machinery. <u>Computing Reviews</u>.
        New York: ACM, 1977.

        These two volumes are similar in scope to No. 261.

263   Association for Computing Machinery. <u>Computing Reviews</u>.
        <u>Permuted (kwic) Index to Computing Reviews, 1960-</u>
        <u>1963</u>. (New York: ACM, 1964).

        A second volume covering 1964-1965 was published in
        late 1965.

264   <u>Association for Computing Machinery Journal</u> (1954--
        Present).

        This is the main publication of the ACM and often
        where the first formal explanation of a new technology
        or programming language appeared.

265   Association for Computing Machinery. <u>ACM Transactions</u>
        <u>on Mathematical Software</u> (1975--Present).

        This is a technical journal, reflecting the signifi-
        cant amount of activity present in the area of
        software development.

266   <u>Burroughs Clearinghouse</u> (1916--Present).

        This is a monthly, internal organ on all aspects of
        the company's activities.

267   <u>Burroughs System Service Bulletin</u> (1912-1914).

        The focus was on the company's products.

268   <u>Charles Babbage Institute Newsletter</u> (1979--Present).

        This quarterly is a major source of information on
        historical activities. For details it is the best
        quick reference. Charles Babbage Institute, 103
        Walter Library, University of Minnesota, Minneapolis,
        Minnesota 55455 (USA).

269   <u>Computer Journal</u> (1958--Present).

        This British journal is the organ of the British
        Computer Society and is a technical publication.

270   <u>Computer Talk</u> (1967--Present).

        This quarterly offers information on current
        industry trends and news.

271   <u>Computer Yearbook and Directory</u>. Detroit: American Data
        Processing, 1966-1972. Then as <u>Computer Yearbook</u>
        (1972--Present).

As the data processing industry acquired definition, such publications appeared. This one is the most complete and widely-used publication of this type.

272   Computers and Automation (1951--Present).

This monthly is one of the oldest publications in the industry and is a technical journal.

273   Computerworld (2967--Present).

This is the data processing industry's weekly newspaper. It began publication in June, 1967. Issues run to over 100 pages and cover all aspects of the industry's activities.

274   Datamation (1957--Present).

This is the single most widely-read magazine in the data processing industry until the advent of PC-oriented publications by the late 1980s. This monthly carries articles on vendors, analysis of the industry, product and application news, managerial issues, and periodically on the history of the industry.

275   Digital Computer Newsletter (1948--Present).

This quarterly focuses primarily on technical issues.

276   Honeywell Computer Journal (1967--Present).

This has articles on applications, products, technologies, and on rare occasions, on historical issues.

277   IBM Journal of Research and Development (1957--Present).

This is a technical journal covering major developments in computer science. On occasion it will publish articles on the history of IBM technology.

278   IEEE Center For the History of Electrical Engineering. Newsletter (1982--Present).

This contains news about IEEE activities, news about research on the history of electricity, computing, and other related fields. It publishes a bibliography and articles on key archival collections.

279   Journal of Data Management (1963--Present).

This monthly is useful for understanding technical developments in computer science, especially for the period of the 1960s and 1970s.

280   Mathematical Tables and Other Aids to Computation (1943-1960).

This was the most important source of articles
dealing with computer science in the 1940s and very
early 1950s. It served as the primary publication
outlet for many technical articles of the period.
In total 14 volumes of issues were published.

281   McGrath, Bob. IBM Alumni Directory (1971--Present).

Published semi-annually (at least in the 1970s),
this has listed over 3,000 names by 1985, providing
an individual's name, title, company, address,
when and where with IBM.

282   Simulation (1963--Present).

This journal is devoted to contemporary work with
analog computers and hybrid systems.

283   Springer International and American Federation of
Information Processing Societies. Annals of the
History of Computing (1979--Present).

This is the single most important source of material
on the history of information processing, particularly on its technology. It also contains book
reviews, bibliography, obituaries and other useful
information. For details write to Springer-Verlag,
44 Hartz Way, Secaucus, N.J. 07094 (USA).

284   Think (1935--Present).

This is IBM's employee magazine. It contains
articles on the company's major activities, operations in various countries, and biographies of key
executives. It is published monthly.

285   Williams, M.R. "History of Computation," CIPS Review
(1980--Present).

This is a two-page column appearing since 1980 on
all aspects of the industry's history.

Printing

286   Eisenstein, Elizabeth. The Printing Press As An Agent
for Change: Communications and Cultural Transforma-
tions in Early-Modern Europe. 2 vols. Cambridge:
Cambridge University Press, 1979.

This is the best account of the subject with its
focus on the consequences of this communicating
technology. It teaches us a great deal about the
issues facing historians of data processing's
technology.

287   Febvre, Lucien and Martin, Henri-Jean. The Coming of
the Book: The Impact of Printing, 1450-1800. Trans.
by David Gerard. London: NLB, 1976; original edition,
L'Apparition du Livre. Paris: Edicions Albin Michel,
1958.

This is a well-organized and detailed history that
views the coming of this technology in terms useful
to historians of computer technology. Many of the
issues faced hundreds of years ago were replicated
in the 1950s and 1960s with computers.

288   Hirsch, Rudolf. Printing, Selling, and Reading, 1450-
       1550. Wiesbaden: n.p., 1967; revised ed., 1974.

       He focuses on the first century following the develop-
       ment of Gutenberg's printing methods for social and
       intellectual historians. Many of the issues faced
       by printers are instructive for the 20th century
       data processing industry.

289   McLuhan, Marshall. The Gutenberg Galaxy: The Making
       of Typographic Man. Toronto: University of Toronto
       Press, 1972.

       The high priest of the "media is the message" in
       this book discusses the impact printing had on
       information handling and culture. It is a semenal
       work on the subject.

                        Telephony

290   Chapuis, Robert J. 100 Years of Telephone Switching,
       1878-1978: Part I: Manual and Electromechanical
       Switching, 1878-1960s. Amsterdam, N.Y.: Elsevier
       North-Holland, 1982.

       This comprehensive book focuses on all types of
       technology, including early computer-like devices.

291   Paine, Albert B. Theodore N. Vail: A Biography. New
       York: Harper, 1921.

       This is a biography of an early, influential
       president of AT&T. At the turn of the century Vail
       took a small high-tech company and made it a major
       industrial force.

292   Pool, Ithiel de Sola (ed). The Social Impact of the
       Telephone. Cambridge, Mass.: MIT Press, 1977.

       In this brilliant study, Pool examines the telephone's
       sociological role and historic impact on society. It
       is a classic study illustrating how to examine the
       impact of one form of communications on society.

293   Smith, George David. The Anatomy of A Business
       Strategy: Bell, Western Electric, and the Origins
       of the American Telephone Industry. Baltimore:
       The Johns Hopkins University Press, 1985.

       This describes the acquisition of Western Electric
       by the American Bell Telephone Company and is thus
       an early example of how technological and strategic
       business problems were solved.

294   Wasserman, Neil. From Invention to Innovation: The
         Case of Long-Distance Telephone Transmission At the
         Turn of the Century. Baltimore: The Johns Hopkins
         University Press, 1985.

      The author surveys the invention and implementation
      of long-distance telephonic technology. Besides
      contributing to our knowledge of a company active in
      the data processing world, it offers insight on the
      tactics required of a firm to implement and expand
      the use of a communications technology.

2

Pre-History of
Information Processing

This chapter focuses on the development of the earliest
aids to computing, with particular emphasis on seventeenth-
century European events and others of the Far East. This is
an especially fertile period in the history of computing and
it has been well studied by historians, although historians
have usually had the intent of either writing biographies or
of studying the development of early European mechanical
adding/calculating machines rather than the intention of
studying computing. Such studies were asides to broader
concerns regarding scientific explorations. Many of the
inventors of early mechanical aids to computing were also
major figures in the history of mathematics and physics.
John Napier (1550-1617) developed logorithms, while Gottfried
Wilhelm von Leibniz (1646-1716) and Blaise Pascal (1623-1666)
were both important mathematicians. In a later period,
Joseph-Marie Jacquard (1752-1834), the last of this group,
invented the programmable loom. Their work with computing
devices was generally described as an integral part of the
development of modern science and it was described more
effectively than the work of others during later periods.
The bulk of all histories of computing machines—particularly
for the nineteenth and twentieth centuries—have not
integrated such events as completely into the mainstream of
the history of technology.
     In fact, the literature on computing during the
eighteenth and nineteenth centuries remains too limited,
suggesting opportunities for historians. Many of the monographs listed below were the by-products of research conducted
in archival collections in Europe for the period prior to the
early 1800s. Those holdings, often housed at national or
royal academies of science or mathematics, remain sources yet
to be studied in light of the development of the modern
computer. The one major subject of the 1800s that did see
attention, and thus is an exception to the otherwise weak
historiography, is Charles Babbage about whom there are many
fine studies.
     Titles listed below contain the most important materials
focusing attention on mechanical computing activities. They
are not complete on the lives of such individuals as Pascal
or Leibniz since a complete list of all references would have
been book-length. Items have been selected for inclusion on

the basis of their contribution to the general theme of the
bibliography. Many of the themes covered below are also the
subject of many titles listed in the previous chapter as well.

Abacus and Soroban

295   Araki, Isao et al. (eds). Encyclopedia of Soroban (In
        Japanese). Tokyo: Akatsuki Publishing Co., 1956;
        2nd Ed., 1969.

        Seventy-three contributors wrote over 1600 pages on
        the Soroban and its use. This book has a history
        covering over one hundred pages. It is a definitive
        work on a device which still is made and used.
        Currently some four million are manufactured each
        year.

296   Knott, C.G. "The Calculating Machine of the East: The
        Abacus," in E.M. Horsburgh (ed), Napier Tercentenary
        Celebration: Handbook of the Exhibition (Edinburg:
        Royal Society of Edinburg, 1914): 136-154.

        This is a short history of the abacus that explains
        how it is used to do multiplication, division, square
        roots and cube roots.

297   Li, Shu-T'ien. "Origin and Development of the Chinese
        Abacus," Journal of A.C.M. 6, No. 1 (1959): 102-
        110.

        The history is taken back to 1100 B.C.

298   Porter, G.N. From Abacus to Addo. London: Addo Ltd.,
        1965.

        This pamphlet is an illustrated history of calcula-
        tors with special emphasis on the Addo series of
        devices first introduced by H. Agrell in 1917. It
        also describes the abacus.

299   Pullan, J.M. The History of the Abacus. London:
        Hutchinson, 1968.

        This is a 127-page history covering its origins as
        a calculating device. It describes variations,
        including jetons.

300   Smith, D.E. "Computing Jetons," Numismatic Notes and
        Monographs, No. 9. New York: American Numismatic
        Society, 1921.

        This surveys the abacus, along with an explanation
        of how it works.

301   Yamazaki, Yoeman et al. The Soroban in Japan (In
        Japanese). Tokyo: Akatsuki Publishing Co., 1968.

        This is a history of the Soroban—Japanese abacus
        of Chinese origin. It is well illustrated.

302   Zemanek, Heinz. "Abacus: The Word and the Device,"
      Abacus 1, No. 3 (1984): 22-27.

      This history of the abacus also traces the etymology
      of the word. It is a useful, enthusiastic introduc-
      tion to the subject by a computer scientists.

                    Ancient Devices and Methods

303   al-Razzaz al-Jazzari, Ibn. The Book of Knowledge of
      Ingenious Mechanical Devices. Translated and edited
      by D.R. Hill. Dordrecht: D. Reidel, 1974.

      This is an annotated and illustrated translation of
      a 13th century Arab document describing mechanical
      automata, many using pegged cylinder sequencing
      mechanisms. Most were driven by water wheels to
      control the movements of model figures.

304   Ascher, Marcia. "The Logical-Numerical System of Inca
      Quipus," Annals of the History of Computing 5, No.
      3 (July 1983): 268-278.

      This illustrated history and description of an Inca
      mathematics system is the only known publication
      devoted to the subject; it covers the period 1400-
      1560 A.D.

305   Gardner, M. "Logic Machines," Scientific American 183
      (March 1952): 68-73.

      Reviews the evolution of such machines including the
      designs of Ramon Lull (13th century Catalan),
      Stanhope, Jevons, Kalin, Burkhart and others.

306   Hero of Alexandria. Di Herone Alessandrino De gli
      automati . . . tradotte dal greco da Bernardino
      Baldi. Venice: Appresso Girolamo Porro, 1589.

      This describes a robotic automata device.

307   Kennedy, E.S. "A Fifteenth-Century Planetary Computer:
      al-Kāshī's Tabaq al-Manāteq," Parts 1 and 2, Isis
      41 (1950): 180-183; 43 (1952): 41-50.

      This reviews a Moslem mathematician's work with
      calculating equipment.

308   Kennedy, E.S. "Al-Kāshī's 'Plate of Conjunctions',"
      Isis 38 (1947): 56-59.

      This describes a special purpose machine used in
      calculating decimal fractions.

309   Kennedy, E.S. The Planetary Equatorium of Jamshid
      Ghiath al-Din al-Kāshī. Princeton, N.J.: Princeton
      University Press, 1960.

      This suveys the life and work of a fifteenth-century

Moslem mathematician who studied astronomy and
designed devices to help in such work.

310   Knuth, D.E. "Ancient Babylonian Algorithms," Communi-
       cations of the ACM 15 (1972): 671-677; 19 (1976): 108.

This is on the early history of mathematics, important as evidence of early needs for aids to calculations.

311   Morris, L. Robert. "Derek de Solla Price and the
       Antikythera Mechanism: An Approciation," IEEE Micro
       4, No. 1 (February 1984): 15-21.

This includes a biography of Derek (a computer
scientist) and then some information on an old
Greek device; includes bibliography.

312   Needham, Joseph. Science and Civilization in China.
       Cambridge: Cambridge University Press, 1959. Vol. 3.

This third volume contains material on mathematics
and aids to computing in China.

313   Price, Derek de Solla. "An Ancient Greek Computer,"
       Scientific American 200, No. 6 (1959): 60-67.

He describes the Antikythera device which he believes
could have been used to determine longitude and
solve equations of the sun.

314   Rogers, J.L. "The Sumador Chino.Comm." Communications
       of the ACM 3, No. 11 (1960): 621-622.

Rogers offers an illustrated description of an
instrument used for addition similar to Napier's
rods which he discovered in Mexico.

315   Walther, W. "Die Gespeicherten Programme des Heron von
       Alexandria: Heron's of Alexandria Stored Program,"
       Elektronische Rechenanlagen 15, No. 3 (1973): 113-
       118.

This is an illustrated article on using pegged
cylinders and ropes to control a sequence of programs
in ancient times.

Counting Systems and Aids

316   Bernard, F.P. The Casting Counter and the Counting
       Board. Oxford: Clarendon Press, 1916.

This is an excellent history of the subject. These
aids to computation were in wide use up through the
early modern period in Europe.

317   Cheng, D.C. "The Use of Computing Rods in China,"
       American Mathematical Monthly 32 (1925): 492-499.

The author describes an aid to counting in ancient
China, probably dating from before the birth of
Christ.

318   De La Couperie, T. "The Old Numerals, the Counting
       Rods, and the Swan Pan in China," Numismatic
       Chronicle 3 (1883): 297.

       This briefly surveys aids to counting in ancient
       China.

319   Gandz, S. "The Knot in Hebrew Literature," Isis 14
       (1930): 189-214.

       The knotted cord is an ancient aid to counting. The
       early Hebrews used it to aid memory, even in the
       days of Moses.

320   Hadas, Moses. Ancilla to Classical Reading. New York:
       Columbia University Press, 1954.

       This is a good survey of ancient writing and oral
       reading methods.

321   Karpinski, L. "Augrim Stones," Modern Language Notes
       27, No. 7 (undated, circa 1920s-1930s): 206-209.

       This describes an early system for counting using
       stones, in Europe.

322   Pady, Donald S. and Kline, Laura S. "Finger Counting
       and the Identification of James VI's Secret Agents,"
       Cryptologia 4, No. 3 (July 1980): 140-149.

       This describes a medieval calculating device and its
       cryptological use in the 1600s in England. They
       argue that research and development on such a device
       had been done earlier by Venerable Bede (673-735)
       and by Robert Recorde (1510-1558); illustrated.

323   Penniman, C. "Philadelphia's 179 Year Old Android,"
       Byte (August 1978): 90-92, 94.

       This is an illustrated review of a mechanical writing
       machine that also drew, made by Maillardet in about
       1805. It is now at the Franklin Institute.

                    Joseph-Marie Jacquard

324   Barlow, A. History and Principles of Weaving by Hand
       and Power. London: S. Low, Marsten, Searle and
       Rivington, 1878.

       The works of Bouchon, Falcon, Vaucanson, Jacquard,
       Bonelli, Bolmida, Vicenzia and others are reviewed.
       Vincenzia's efforts in the 1850s with electro-magne-
       tic methods for reading patterns and controlling
       looms receives considerable attention in this book.

325   Brown, John Howard (ed). Textile Industries of the
        United States. Boston: James Lamb, 1911.

        He discusses early programming methods for looms
        using cards to set weaving patterns in the 1700s.

326   Eymard, P. "Historique du Métier Jacquard," Annales
        des Sciences Physiques et Naturelles (Société d'
        Agriculture, d'Histoire Naturalles, et des Arts
        Utile de Lyon) 3rd Series, 7 (1863): 34-56.

        This details the work of Bouchon, Falcon, Vaucanson,
        Jacquard and others in the development of looms.

327   Forbes, R.J. Studies in Ancient Technology. 9 vols.
        Leiden: E.J. Brill, 1964.

        This is an extremely detailed study. Some material
        on textiles and looms may be found in volume four.

328   Poncelet, M. "Machines et Outils Appliqués aux Arts
        Textiles," Travaux de la Commission Française.
        Exposition Universelle de 1851, 3, Part 1, Section
        2 (1857): 346-373.

        This details the work of Bouchon, Falcon, Vaucanson,
        Breton, and Jacquard on the draw loom.

329   (Porter?). A Treatise on the Origin, Progressive
        Improvement and Present State of the Silk Manufacture
        Lardner's Cabinet Cyclopaedia, vol. 48. London:
        Longman, 1831.

        This contains details on the Jacquard loom.

330   Posselt, E.A. The Jacquard Machine Analyzed and
        Explained: With an Appendix on the Preparation of
        Jacquard Cards, and Practical Hints to Learners of
        Jacquard Designing. Philadelphia: Pennsylvania
        Museum and School of Industrial Art, 1887.

        This is a detailed account on the workings of the
        loom and is heavily illustrated. It is particularly
        useful for understanding how the cards were used,
        often considered an early form of machine programm-
        ing.

331   Usher, Abbott. A History of Mechanical Inventions.
        Cambridge, Mass.: Harvard University Press, 1962;
        3rd Edition.

        This contains a discussion of Bouchon, Falcon,
        Vaucanson, and Jacquard among others.

                    Gottfried Wilhelm von Leibniz

332   Hoffman, J.E. Leibniz in Paris, 1672-1676. London:
        Cambridge University Press, 1974.

This volume has a great deal of information on his
mathematical ideas and about his calculators. It
does not provide an adequate amount of technical
details on the device. Otherwise, this is a useful,
scholarly book.

333   Jones, C.V. "Gottfried Wilhelm von Leibniz," in A.
      Ralston and Meek, C.L. (eds), Encyclopedia of
      Computer Science (New York: Petrocelli/Charter,
      1976): 775-776.

      This short, illustrated biography also defines his
      significance for the history of data processing. It
      focuses also on the development of Leibniz's device.

334   Kormes, M. "Leibniz on His Calculating Machine," in
      D.E. Smith (ed), A Source Book in Mathematics (New
      York: McGraw-Hill, 1929): 173-181.

      This is a translation of a 1685 document describing
      the four basic arithmetic operations.

335   Kreiling, F.C. "Leibniz," Scientific American 218,
      No. 5 (May 1968): 94-100.

      This illustrated biographical note contains a review
      of his calculator.

336   Leibniz, Gottfried Wilhelm von. "De Progressione
      Dyadica-Pars I," dated 15 March 1679, reprinted in
      Herron von Leibniz' Rechnung mit Null und Einz
      (Berlin: Siemens Aktiengessellschaft, 1966): 42-47.

      This describes binary representations and the design
      of a binary calculator with the use of moving balls
      to represent digits.

337   Leibniz, Gottfried Wilhelm von. The Philosophical
      Writings of Leibniz. Selected and Translated by Mary
      Morris. London: Everyman's Library, 1934.

      This is a basic reference on Leibniz, covering all
      aspects of his scientific work and ideas, not just
      about calculators.

338   Locke, L.L. "The Contributions of Leibniz to the Art
      of Mechanical Calculation," Scripta Mathematica 1
      (1933): 315-321.

      This is a useful source for basic information on his
      calculators. He built the first one and designed a
      second.

339   Wilkins, John. An Essay Towards a Real Character and
      a Philosophical Language. London: n.p., 1668.
      Reprint, edited by R.C. Alston. English Linguistics
      1500-1800, No. 119. Menston, U.K.: Scolar Press,
      1968.

> This collection of calligraphic symbols suggested
> ideas in favor of a logical language of thought
> similar to Leibniz's.

340   Williams, Mike. "History of Computation: Leibniz Takes
      The Calculating Machine One Step Closer to Perfec-
      tion," CIPS Review 6 (May-June 1982): 10-13.

      This is a short review of Leibniz's device.

341   Wittke, H. Die Rechenmaschine und ihre Rechentechnik.
      Berlin: Grunewald, 1943.

      He briefly reviews Leibniz's wheel, Odhner's device
      and then the Mercedes-Euclid and Millionaire calcu-
      lators.

Samuel Morland

342   Dickinson, H.W. Sir Samuel Morland, Diplomat and
      Inventor, 1625-1695. The Newcomen Society for the
      Study of the History of Engineering and Technology:
      Extra Publication No. 6. Cambridge: Heffer and Sons,
      1970.

      The author has prepared a well-researched monograph
      which includes discussion of pumps, steam engines,
      cryptography, and calculators; includes illustra-
      tions.

343   Gleiser, Molly. "Samuel Morland: From Seals to
      Wheels," Computer Decisions (April 1976): 54-57.

      She surveys the life of Morland (1625-1695) and the
      development of his calculating machines, including
      two hand held devices (1673), using gear wheels
      driven by a stylus.

344   Morland, Sir Samuel. A New and Most Useful Instrument
      for Addition and Subtraction of Pounds, Shillings,
      Pence and Farthings. London: n.p., 1672.

      He describes his own machine, making this both an
      early "product" publication and one of the first
      "application briefs" to be published.

345   Morland, Sir Samuel. The Description and Use of Two
      Arithmetick Instruments. London: n.p., 1673.

      This 164-page book focuses on the mathematics of
      the devices and less on their mechanisms. Sir
      Samuel did not hesitate to publicize the virtues of
      his inventions, and this publication was part of
      the effort to make known his own creations.

346   Turner, G. L'E. "Samuel Morland," Dictionary of Scien-
      tific Biography 9, pp. 529-530.

      This has a biography complete with detailed notes

on bibliography covering this inventor of the 1600s.

347   Whitelocke, B. _Journal of the Swedish Embassy (New Edition)_. London: n.p., 1855.

It contains some material on Morland in Sweden.

John Napier

348   Baron, M.E. "Napier, John," in _Dictionary of Scientific Biography_ (New York: Charles Scribner's Sons, 1970) 9, pp. 609-613.

This is a short biography with details on logarithms.

349   D'Ocagne, P.M. "Some Remarks on Logarithms Apropos to Their Tercentenary," in _Annual Report of the Smithsonian Institution_ (Washington, D.C.: The Smithsonian Institution, 1914): 175-181.

An early twentieth century expert on calculating machines discussed the importance of logarithms in an historical context.

350   Erskine, D.S. and Minto, W. _An Account of the Life, Writings and Inventions of John Napier of Merchiston_. Perth: n.p., 1778.

Napier's rods received detailed attention early-on. These authors described his "multiplicationis promptuarium" for multiplication.

351   Ginsburg, J. "Napier on the Napier Rods," in _A Source Book in Mathematics_ (New York: McGraw-Hill, 1929): 182-185.

The author reproduces a translation of a paper by Napier, dated 1617, explaining the use of rods to help process multiplications.

352   Gridgeman, N.T. "John Napier and the History of Logarithms," _Scripta Mathematica_ 29, Nos 1-2 (1969): 49-65.

This is one of the better accounts of the subject.

353   Hawkins, William F. "The Mathematical Work of John Napier," _Bulletin of the Australian Mathematical Society_ 26, No. 3 (December 1982): 455-468.

This is an abstract of the author's Ph.D. dissertation in which he reviews the origins of logarithms, _Rabdologia_ and other topics. The dissertation itself is 1,044 pages in length.

354   Jones P.S. "Tangible Arithmetic I: Napier's and Genaille's Rods," _Mathematics Teacher_ 47 (1954): 482-487.

Jones focuses on the origins of the rods developed
by these two mathematicians and discusses the relationship of their work to each other.

355   Leybourn, William. <u>Arithmetik, Vulgar, Decimal und
      Instrumental</u>. 7th Edition. London: Churchill, 1700.

      Pages 259-295 reviews Napier's rods and their use in
      determining square and cube roots of a number. The
      rest of the book is a good reflection of mathematical
      thinking of the late 1600s.

356   Leybourn, William. <u>The Art of Numbering By Speaking
      Rods: Vulgorly Termed Nepeir's Bones</u>. London: n.p.,
      1667.

      This is a very early account of Napier's logarithms,
      clear evidence of their immediate impact on mathema-
      ticians.

357   Napier, John. <u>A Plaine Discovery of the Whole Revelation
      of Saint John</u>. Edinburgh: n.p., 1593.

      Written by the inventor of logarithms, this book is
      not about mathematics but instead on society and
      mankind in general.

358   Napier, John. <u>Rabdologia</u>. Edinburgh: n.p., 1617.

      It is in this book that he describes for the first
      time in detail his "bones"--logarithms.

359   Napier, Mark. <u>Memoirs of John Napier of Merchiston,
      His Lineage, Life and Times, With a History of the
      Invention of Logarithms</u>. Edinburgh: William Blackwood
      and in London: Thomas Cadell, 1834.

      This is a biography and description of his invention.

360   Schott, Gaspard. <u>Organum Mathematicum.</u> Nuremberg: n.p.,
      1668.

      Besides reviewing his own ideas on mathematics, he
      discusses the use of Napier's bones.

361   Vanhee, Louis. "Napier's Rods in China," <u>American
      Mathematical Monthly</u> 23 (1926): 326-328.

      The article is proof of Napier's logarithms being
      accepted in many parts of the world quickly after
      their development.

Blaise Pascal

362   Archibald, R.C. "Seventeenth Century Calculating
      Machines," <u>Mathematical Tables and Other Aids to
      Calculation</u> 1 (1943): 27-28.

      He discusses Pascal's work with early calculators.

363   Bishop, M. Pascal: The Life of Genius. London: Bell
       & Sons, 1937.

       This is a full biography of the mathematician and
       about his work. Although Pascal died at the early
       age of 39, he accomplished a great deal, including
       the development of a calculator described in this
       book. The majority of the volume, however, is
       devoted to his work in mathematics.

364   Chapman, S. "Blaise Pascal (1623-1662): Tercentenary
       of the Calculating Machine," Nature 150 (31 October
       1942): 508-509.

       This brief biography focuses on his work with the
       calculator.

365   Diderot, D. "Arithmétique," Encyclopédie, ou Dictionn-
       aire Raisonné des Sciences, des Arts e des Métiers
       (Paris: n.p., 1751): 1, pp. 664-684.

       In this, the most famous encyclopedia ever published,
       a leading French light wrote the first full account
       of how Pascal's machine worked.

366   Fonsny, J. "Pascal et la Machine Arithmétique," Les
       Études Classiques, Namur 20 (1952): 181-191.

       He surveys Pascal's role and views regarding
       calculating machines.

367   Jones, C.V. "Blaise Pascal," in A. Ralston and C.L.
       Meek (eds), Encyclopedia of Computer Science (New
       York: Petrocelli/Charter, 1976): 1048.

       This short, illustrated biography also places
       Pascal's contribution into perspective as it affects
       computer science. The article also describes clearly
       Pascal's calculator.

368   Locke, L.L. "Pascal on His Calculating Machine," in D.
       E. Smith (ed), A Source Book in Mathematics (New
       York: McGraw-Hill, 1929): 165-172.

       This is a translation of an advertisement prepared
       by Pascal in 1649 for his calculator.

369   Payen, J. "Les Exemplaires Conservés de la Machine de
       Pascal," Revue d'Histoire des Sciences et de leurs
       Applications 16, No. 2 (April-June 1963): 161-178.

       The author describes eight copies of Pascal's calcu-
       lators.

370   Von Mackensen, L. "Von Pascal zu Hahn: Die Entwicklung
       von Rechenmaschinen im 17 und 18 Jahrshundert," in
       M. Graef (ed), 350 Jahre Rechenmaschinen (Munich:
       Carl Hanser, 1973): 21-33.

He covers a variety of inventors such as Pascal,
Schickard, Leupold, Braun, Hahn and others.

Wilhelm Schickard

371   Flad, J.P.   "L'Horloge à Calcul de l'Astronome W.
      Schickard semble avoir été la Premières Machines à
      Calcul à Engrenages Propre aux 4 Opérations,"
      Chiffres 1 (1958): 143-148.

      The author describes how this man's work was intro-
      duced and how the machine functioned. Although a
      brief article, it is well done.

372   Hammer, F.   "Nicht Pascal sondern der Tübinger Professor
      Wilhelm Schickard erfund die Rechenmachine!,"
      Buromarkt 20 (1958): 1023-1025.

      The author tells how he found letters by Schickard
      addressed to Kepler about his calculating device and
      on its use.

373   "Tercentenary of Wilhelm Schickard (1592-1635)," Nature
      136 (19 October 1935): 636.

      Focus is on the astronomer's work in a very short
      biography.

374   Von Freytag Löringhoff, B.   "Die Erste Rechenmaschine:
      Tübingen 1623," Humanismus und Technik 9, No. 2 (20
      April 1964): 45-55.

      This describes Schickard's machine.

375   Von Freytag Löringhoff, B.   "Eine Tübingen Rechenma-
      schinen aus dem Jahre 1623," Heimatkundliche Blätter
      für den Kreis Tübingen 11, No. 3 (July 1957): 25-28.

      This is a brief overview of the device based largely
      on Schickard's letters to Kepler on the subject.

376   Von Freytag Löringhoff, B.   "Prof. Schickards Tübinger
      Rechenmaschine von 1623 im Tübinger Rathaus," Kleine
      Tübinger Schriften 4 (1973).

      He continues the same theme as the previous two
      entries but this time with illustrations.

377   Von Freytag Löringhoff, B.   "Über die erste Rechenmas-
      chine," Physikal Blätter 14, No. 8 (1958): 361-365.

      He focuses on recently discovered descriptions of
      Schickard's machine.

378   Von Freytag Löringhoff, B.   "Wiederenentdeckung und
      Rekonstruktion der Allesten Neuzeitlichen Rechenma-
      schine," V.D.I.—Nachrichten 14, No. 39 (21 December
      1960): 4.

This is a brief, illustrated description of Schickard's device.

379   Von Freytag Loringhoff, B.   "Wilhelm Schickard und seine Rechenmaschine von 1623," in M. Graef (ed), 350 Jahre Rechenmaschinen (Munich: Carl Hanswer, 1973): 11-20.

This is a survey of the life and work of Schickard by the most knowledgable expert on the man.

380   Von Mackensen, L.   "Zur Vorgeschichte und Entstrehung der ersten digitalen 4-spezies-Rechenmaschine von Gottried Wilhelm Leibniz," Akten des Leibniz-Kongr., Hannover, 1966 2 (Weisbaden: Franz Steiner, 1969): 34-68.

Although this contains a great deal of material on Leibniz, and to early aids to enumeration and calculation, it is also a good source on Pascal and on Schickard.

381   Williams, M.R.   "From Napier to Lucas: The Use of Napier's Bones in Calculating Instruments," Annals of the History of Computing 5, No. 3 (July 1983): 279-296.

This illustrated history of calculating machines reviews devices made or designed by Schickard, Morland, Schott, Kircher, Lucas and Genaille.

Jacques Vaucanson

382   Doyon, A. and Liaigre, L.   Jacques Vaucanson, Mécanicien de Génie.   Paris: Presses Universitaires de France, 1966.

This is a lengthy biography with considerable attention paid to his mechanical automata and his draw loom.

383   Droz, E.   "From Jointed Doll to Talking Robot," New Scientist 14 (1962): 37-40.

This illustrated account discusses how mechanical automata emerged, with particular focus on Vaucanson, von Knaus and other inventors of the eighteenth century.

384   Foucaud, E.   The Book of Illustrious Mechanisms of Europe and America. Translated by J. Frost. Aberdeen: George Clark and Sons, 1848.

This has several chapters on automata and about the work of Vaucanson and Maelzel.

385   Vaucanson, Jacques.   An Account of the Mechanisms of An Automaton or Image Playing on the German-Flute. London: Parker, 1742.

This is a translation of his 1738 publication along
with another piece on other automata: a duck and a
flute and drum playing figure.

386   Vaucanson, Jacques. Le Mécanisme du Fluteur Automate.
      Paris: Guerin, 1738.

      This describes a device automating a flute, with its
      blowing and fingering using pegged cylinders for
      sequence action control. Unfortunately, the 15-page
      pamphlet was not illustrated.

Machines and People (1500-1800)

387   Adam, A. Von Himmlischen Uhrwerk zur Statischen Fabrik.
      Vienna: Verlag O. Munk, 1973.

      This reviews from primitive astronomical devices
      through Hollerith machines in Vienna. It provides
      details on Schickard's calculating device, draw-looms
      and "Broselmachine" (1680-1690), and modifications
      to Hollerith machines by Schäffler.

388   Archibald, R.C. Mathematical Table Makers. New York:
      Yeshiva University, 1948.

      This is a collection of biographies of and bibliogra-
      phies about 53 compilers including Babbage, Burgi,
      Comrie, Napier and Wiberg.

389   Arrington, Joseph Earl. "John Maelzel, Master Showman
      of Automata and Panoramas," Pennsylvania Magazine
      of History and Biography 84, No. 1 (January 1960):
      56-92.

      Maelzel was an early nineteenth century German
      builder of musical automata.

390   Asimov, Isaac. Asimov's Biographical Encyclopedia of
      Science and Technology. Garden City, N.Y.: Double-
      day, 1982. 1st Edition, 1964.

      The second edition contains 1,510 entries with all
      the major figures of computing represented.

391   Ballot, C. L'Introduction du Machinisme dans l'Indus-
      tria Française. Lille: O. Marquandt, 1923.

      This has a great number of historical details on the
      work of Bouchon, Falcon, Vaucanson and Jacquard.

392   Beck, T. Beiträge zur Geschichte des Maschinenbaues.
      Berlin: Springer, 1900.

      This is an illustrated history of machinery begin-
      ning with Heron of Alexandria down through James Watt.
      Included are devices by Vitruvius' (Hodometer) and
      another by Leonardo da Vinci, both of which recorded

travelled distance by the controlled release of
counting balls into a container. In reality, da
Vinci developed a design for geared counting wheels.

393   Beckmann, John. "Odometer," in A History of Inventions
      and Discoveries (London: J. Bell, 1790): 9-19.

      This suggests that the odometer existed in the fif-
      teenth century and definitively by the late 1500s.

394   Bedini, S.A. "The Role of Automata in the History of
      Technology," Technology and Culture 5, No. 1
      (1964): 24-42.

      This is a good survey covering hydraulic and pneuma-
      tic equipment, mechanical clockworks, pegged cylin-
      ders, and presents the highlights of Vaucanson's
      work. This article is illustrated and contains
      bibliographic references.

395   Buchner, A. Mechanical Musical Instruments. London:
      Batchworth Press, 1950.

      As with weaving devices, various methods were
      developed to command musical machines to perform
      specific functions. A variety of automatophonic
      instruments are described and illustrated, including
      barrel organs, music boxes and pianolas.

396   Chevalier, J. L'Invention du Calcul Mécanique. Confé-
      rence donnée au Conservatorire des Arts et Métiers
      le 19 Mai 1942. Paris: Outhier, 1942.

      This 48-page illustrated review covers Gerbert,
      Pascal, such devices as jetons, Campos bookkeeping
      units and logarithms. It has an illustration of a
      Campos machine.

397   De Solla, Derek. "A History of Calculating Machines,"
      IEEE Micro 4, No. 1 (February 1984): 23-52.

      The focus is on pre-electric calculators; illustra-
      ted.

398   Diderot, D. Memoires sur Différens Sujets Mathématiques.
      Paris: Durand, 1748.

      This philosophe of the eighteenth century dedicated
      a chapter of this work to automatic pipe organs,
      described how they worked, and offered details on
      their construction, finally comparing their pros and
      cons to manual systems.

399   d'Ocagne, M. "Thomas de Colmar, Inventeur de l'Arithmo-
      metre," Revue Scientifique 73 (1935): 783-785.

      He discusses Colmar's work and device on the occasion
      of the inveiling of a statue to Colmar.

400   Drake, S. "Galileo and the First Mechanical Computing
       Device," Scientific American 234, No. 4 (1976): 104-
       113.

       This discusses the gunner's compas, a tool used to
       help set the elevation of the barrel.

401   Drake, S. Galileo Galilei: Operations of the Geometric
       and Military Compass. Washington, D.C.: Smithsonian
       Institution Press, 1978.

       The author provides a description of the compass,
       which is a sector, made in the first decade of the
       1600s or in the very late 1500s.

402   Dumas, M. Scientific Instruments of the 17th and 18th
       Centuries and Their Makers. London: B.T. Batsford
       & Co., 1972.

       This is a good overview of calculators used to do
       simple mathematical functions. It also surveys
       astronomical instruments.

403   Feldhaus, F.M. Über die Entwicklung und das Wesen des
       Maschinenrechens. Thun: Zella-Mehlis, 1928-1930.
       14 pamphlets.

       These short 14 pamphlets survey manual and machine
       calculation. Topics include Pascal, Morland, Schott,
       Leibniz, Perrault, Poleni, and Leupold.

404   "Find Ancient Computer; Greek Computer," Science News
       Letter 75 (January 17, 1959): 36.

       This was a press report on the discovery of the
       Antikythera Device which scientists later concluded
       was a very early drive mechanism used to help in
       performing astronomical calculations.

405   Flad, J.P. Les Trois Premières Machine à Calculer:
       Schickard (1623), Pascal (1642), Leibniz (1675).
       Paris: Palais de la Decouverte, Université de Paris,
       1963.

       This is an illustrated description of each device.

406   Gersten, C.L. "The Description and Use of An Arithme-
       tical Machine Invented by Christian-Ludovicus
       Gersten, F.R.S., Professor of Mathematics in the
       University of Giessen," Philosophical Transactions
       39 (July-September 1735): 79-97.

       This briefly covers Morland, Leibniz, Poleni, Leupold
       and Pascal before offering considerable details about
       his own machine: what it is, how it works, and when
       it should be applied.

407   Gleisser, M. "Men and Machines Before Babbage," Datama-
       tion 24, No. 10 (October 1978): 124-128, 130.

This is a superficial account of Pascal, Morland, and Leibniz.

408   Grillet, René. <u>Curiositez Mathematiques</u>. Paris: n.p.,
       1673.

       He describes his own calculator, one of several built
       by European mathematicians in the 1600s.

409   Grillet, René. "Nouvelle Machine d'Arithmétique de
       l'invention du Sieur Grillet Horlogeur à Paris,"
       <u>Journal de Scavans</u> (1678): 164-166.

       He describes a machine designed by him based on the
       use of Napier's rods; illustrated.

410   Heath, F.G. "Pioneers of Binary Coding," <u>Journal of
       the Institute of Electrical Engineering</u> (London) 7,
       No. 81 (1961): 539-541.

       This is on Sir Francis Bacon, Gray and Baudot,
       surveying their work in mathematics.

411   Johnston, Mark D. <u>The Spiritual Logic of Ramon Llull</u>.
       Oxford: Clarendon, 1987.

       He describes this 13th century monk's ideas for a
       mechanically produced set of syllogisms, making it
       an early logic system.

412   Kangro, H. "Kircher, Athanasius," in <u>Dictionary of
       Scientific Biography</u> (New York: Charles Scribner's
       Sons, 1970): 7, pp. 374-378.

       This is a biography of the mathematician of the
       1600s.

413   Keller, A.G. "Schott, Gaspard," in <u>Dictionary of
       Scientific Biography</u> (New York: Charles Scribner's
       Sons, 1970): 12, pp. 210-211.

       This is a biography and contains a description of
       his calculator.

414   Kennedy, E.S. "A Fifteenth Century Lunar Eclipse
       Computer," <u>Scripta Mathematica</u> 17 (1951): 91-97.

       This reviews a Moslem mathematician's work on
       calculating equipment.

415   Kreindl, F. "Jacquards Prinzip bereits 200 Jahr alt?,"
       <u>Sonderdruck Melliand Textilber</u> (Heidelberg) 2
       (1935): 1-2.

       This describes a draw loom with sequence control
       mechanisms made up of wooden pegs on a canvas. It
       was invented in Austria in about 1740 independently
       of Bouchon's and Falcon's machines.

416   Price, D.J. De Solla. "Ancient Greek Computer,"
      Scientific American 200 (June 1959): 60-67,200;
      Reply by D.R. Schwartz, Ibid., 201 (August 1959):10.

      This surveys the Antikythera Device and its possible
      use in ancient Greece.

417   Price, D.J. De Solla. "Automata and the Origins of
      Mechanisms and Mechanistic Philosophy," Technology
      and Culture 5, No. 1 (1964): 9-23.

      He argues there was a parallel development from
      Greek times of astronomical and anthropomorphic
      devices.

418   Racknitz, J.F. Uber den schachspieler des herrn von
      Kempelen und dessen nachbildung. Dresden: n.p.,
      1798.

      This is an early account of Wolfgang von Kempelen
      (1734-1804) and of his fraudulant chess-playing
      machine, the Turk, which toured Europe in the late
      1700s.

419   Scriba, C.J. "Review of Maistrov, I.E. and Cenakal, V.
      L.: A Very Old Calculating Machine," Math. Review
      40, No. 3 (1970): 456-457.

      This discusses a calculating machine made by a
      Hebrew clockmaker named Jewna Jacobson at Neiswiez,
      Lithuania, no later than about 1770. It could add,
      subtract, multiply, and divide up to nine digits,
      although it was used for up to five.

420   Taton, R. "Sur l'Invention de la Machine Arithmétique,"
      Revue d'Histoire des Sciences et de leurs Applica-
      tions 16 (1963): 139-160.

      He reviews Pascal's calculator and those of early
      developers in Europe.

421   Vartanian, Aram. La Mettrie's L'Homme-Machine: A Study
      in the Origins of An Idea. Princeton: Princeton
      University Press, 1960.

      This tracks the idea from Descartes' machine to
      La Mettrie. The latter stated that man was simply
      a machine.

422   Waters, David W. The Art of Navigation in England in
      Elizabethan and Early Stuart Times. London: Hollis
      and Carter, 1958.

      The needs of navigation led to such aids to calcula-
      tion as the astrolobe which are described here.

423   Weiss, Eric A. "Jonathan Swift's Computing Invention,"
      Annals of the History of Computing 7, No. 2 (April
      1985): 164-165.

This is an illustrated account of a fictional device
in Gulliver's Travels that could write.

424   Willers, F.A. "Aus der Frühzeit der Rechenmaschinen,"
       Wiss. z. Techn. Hochschule Dresden 2, No. 2 (1952-
       1953): 151-158.

       This is on the evolution of calculators. Some which
       are mentioned include those by Pascal, Gersten,
       Leibniz, Poleni, Leopold, Hahn and Müller.

425   Wolf, A. "Calculating Machines," in A History of
       Science, Technology, and Philosophy in the Eighteenth
       Century (London: George Allen and Unwin, 1938): 654-
       660.

       The author reviews some calculators built by Pereire,
       Leupold, and Stanhope in the 1700s.

3

Origins of Modern Computing

During the period from roughly 1800 to the end of World War I, both Europe and the United States shifted from an overwhelmingly agricultural economy to one dosed heavily with industrialization. Mechanical devices for all manner of human labor came into their own, and that included aids to computing. Modern adding and calculating machines, typewriters, slide rules of all sizes and shapes, the cash register, and punch card technology were introduced on both sides of the Atlantic. Elegant and complex "engines" were conceived by Charles Babbage (1791-1871), while others worked out the theoretical backgrounds in mathematics and logic used in the twentieth century in the creation of the computer. Thus, for example, the work of George Boole (1815-1864) proved important to computing in general.

This chapter contains recent monographic works and contemporary publications detailing the large number of developments in the era of the Industrial Revolution. These two types of materials reflect the available sources, since the period as a whole has not been effectively covered by historical surveys. Literature on Babbage himself represents an exception, almost a growth industry, while materials on other inventors are only now beginning to appear. The section on adding machines and calculators contains references to the major vendors of the age, as do those on Felt and Hollerith. Someone interested in early punch card activities would consult the sections on both that subject and Hollerith. The general subject was broken out into two because of the large amount of material of a biographical nature and on the nature and use of his technology.

The most useful studies todate for the period are biographical surveys of Hollerith and Babbage. Much is yet to be done on other inventors of the period. Full-length biographies, based on significant research, are lacking for such major figures as William S. Burroughs (1855-1898) and Leonardo Torres y Quevedo (1852-1936). Institutional histories of adding and calculating machine vendors, such as Burroughs and Felt & Tarrant, and of cash register companies, such as NCR, have yet to be written. There are useful studies of the role technology has played in national census-taking for both the nineteenth and the twentieth centuries, primarily in the United States.

Material in this chapter has been organized largely by biographical categories, since many of the developers worked independently of any institution and were not a part of some recognizable industry-wide movement. When sub-sets of equipment existed, such as punch card devices and adding machines, separate sections on these were created. This work does not attempt to provide a detailed catalog of fiction dealing with computing; one exception has been made—The Wizard of Oz, since that body of publications became extensive and proved very visible at the time. Monographs dealing with mechanistic motifs, such as Frankenstein, can be found most easily through the general index to this bibliography. However, as a general comment, the amount of monographic material on computer/robot fiction is very limited.

Adding Machines and Calculators

426   "Adding Machine," Scientific American 53, No. 9 (Augst 29, 1885): 132.

This is a short review of ten important adding machines developed by W.J. MacNider.

427   An Illustrated Chronicle of "A Machine to Count On". Goteborg, Sweden: Aktielbolaget Original Odhner, 1951.

This is a history of W.T. Odhner's calculator which dominated European and Russian calculating machine technology from the 1870s to the 1920s. It is a company history but also contains biographical data on the inventor himself.

428   Barnard, F.A.P. Report on the Machinery and Processes on the Industrial Arts and Apparatus of the Exact Sciences. Paris Universal Exposition 1867. New York: van Nostrand, 1869.

This is nearly 700 pages in length, and reviews in part mechanical calculators at the Paris show. Two which are described were made by Musina—a pocket calculator for adding—and the other a Thomas Arithmometer. The book also has a survey of the history of calculators in general; see especially pages 629-648.

429   Baxandall, David. Calculating Machines and Instruments. London: Science Museum, 1926; Revised Edition, 1975.

This is a catalog of the Museum's collection of early calculating devices, and including pieces of machine's built by Babbage and Scheutz. The publication describes these in some detail.

430   Boys, C.V. "Calculating Machines," Journal of the Society of Arts 34 (March 5, 1886): 376-389.

This author lectured on then current technology, surveying efforts by Babbage, Morland, Stanhope,

Thomas de Colmar. He paid particular attention to
a device made by Tate called an improved Thomas
Arithmometer and another called the Edmondson "circular machine".

431   "The Burroughs Adding and Listing-Machine," Engineering
       83 (May 3, 1907): 580-581.

       This is an illustrated description of the device.
       Burroughs was, by 1907, one of the largest suppliers
       of calculating equipment in the world.

432   Burroughs Adding Machine Company. Burroughs, A Complete
       Line of Desk Figuring, Listing and Bookkeeping
       Machines. Detroit: Burroughs Adding Machine Company,
       1943.

       This is a ten-page catalog of technology that had
       not changed fundamentally since the turn of the
       century.

433   Burroughs Adding Machine Company. Handbook of Instruc-
       tions for Operators of Burroughs Adding and Listing
       Machines. Detroit: Burroughs Adding Machine Company,
       1911.

       This 98-page publication describes the complex use
       of many products offered by Burroughs by 1911 and
       illustrates typical applications of the age.

434   Chatfield, Michael. A History of Accounting Thought.
       Melbourne, Fla.: Krieger, 1977 (Revised Edition);
       Originally published 1925.

       This author traced the rise and evolution of the
       accounting profession, particularly during the 19th
       century with some mention of the role of technology
       in the performance of an accountant's job.

435   Clark, R. "Barbara Froena Domi Promittunt Foedera
       Mala," in Somerset Anthology (York: Sessions, 1975):
       96-102.

       Originally written in 1951, this is on a device that
       composes Latin hexameter verse and on the inventor,
       John Clark (1785-1852). The title is a verse created
       by the device. This machine was exhibited in London
       in 1845. The article includes a photograph of the
       machine.

436   "Combined Adding, Listing and Computing Machine," Indus-
       trial Management 53, Supplement-2 (May 1917).

       By 1917 complex adding/calculating devices were
       available for accounting applications, particularly
       from Burroughs.

437   Crew, E.W. "Calculating Machines," The Engineer 172
       (December 1941): 438-441.

This offers a good explanation of Napier's rods, and a brief review of machines circa 1940.

438   Davies, Margery W. Woman's Place Is At the Typewriter: Office Work and Office Workers, 1870-1930. Philadelphia: Temple University Press, 1983.

This is based on a large number of business histories and corporate records to present an extremely crucial story. It was in this environment that all manner of office machines were used.

439   Description and Instructions for the Use of Edmondson's Circular Calculating Machine. Halifax: Jos. Edmundson, Heath Ave., 1885.

This 24-page, illustrated pamphlet is an operational guide to an arithmometer with a description of its design.

440   Dicksee, Lawrence R. Machinery As An Aid to Accountancy. London: Gee & Co., 1916.

This is a pamphlet written by a professor of accounting at the University of London. He describes existing machines, their recent history, and how they are beneficial.

441   Dietzschold, C. Die Rechenmaschine. Leipzig: n.p., 1886.

The author built a variable motion drive mechanism to do arithmetic in the 1880s.

442   d'Ocagne, M. Le Calcul Simplifié. 2nd Ed. Paris: Gauthier-Villars, 1905.

This is an important publication that reviews calculators, slide rules, nomograms, difference engines, and devices by Babbage, Pascal, Burroughs, Felt, Leibniz, Müller, Thomas, Maurel, Tchbebichef, Odhner, Selling, Scheuz, and the work of Bollée. A third edition (published in 1928) was completely rewritten to account for technology introduced since 1905. The third edition includes material on Torres y Quevedo.

443   Dyck, W. Katalog Mathematische unsw. Instrumente. Munich: Wolf und Sohn, 1892.

It lists calculating devices with short descriptions. This is particularly useful for a quick appreciation of what was available in Europe in the 1890s.

444   Edmondson, J. "Summary of Lecture on Calculating Machines, Delivered Before the Physical Society of London, March 28, 1885," Philosophical Magazine 5th Series, 20 (July-December 1885): 15-18.

This discusses difference engines, and machines made

by Morland, Stanhope, Thomas, and Grant.

445   Gardner, M. Logic Machines and Diagrams. New York:
      McGraw-Hill, 1958.

      This covers the development of devices to help
      reasoning and problem solving in formal logic. It
      argues that Marquand was the first to design an
      electric logic device in 1885 and that Burack was
      the first to make one in 1936.

446   Genaille, H. "Sur une Nouvelle Machine à Calculer par
      Genaille," Association Française Avanc. de Science
      (1878): 181-182.

      This is a lecture he gave on a system of rods similar
      to Napier's.

447   Goldberg, H.E. "Arithmetical Machines: Their History,
      Theory and Methods of Construction," Scientific
      American Supplement 79 (January 23, 1915): 59, 60,
      79 (January 30, 1915): 75-76.

      This is primarily about calculating devices drawn
      from U.S. patent records and describes the work of
      Castle (1850) 10 key adding machine, Riggs (1854)
      similar device, Teasdale's multiplication machine
      (1871), and then a variety of equipment from Felt,
      Burroughs, Dalton, Moon-Hopkins, Grant, the Million-
      aire and others.

448   Grant, G.B. "A New Calculating Machine," American
      Journal of Science 3rd Series, 4, No. 8 (1874): 277-
      284.

      This is a good review of the author's device for
      calculating and about its technology.

449   Grant, G.B. "Calculating Machine," American Journal
      of Science 108 (1881): 277.

      This reviews his work with calculating machines as
      of about 1880.

450   Grant, G.B. "On a New Difference Engine," American
      Journal of Science, 3rd Series, 2, No. 8 (1871): 113-
      117.

      The author was the founder of the U.S. gear-cutting
      industry. In this article he describes a device he
      built in the 1860s which weighed over a ton and had
      15,000 parts.

451   Haga, E.J. Understanding Automation. Elmhurst, Ill.:
      The Business Press, 1965.

      Chapter One gives an historical overview on the
      origins of computer and about the effort to make a
      commercially viable calculator in the 1800s.

452   Hart, Walter. Arithmetic Without Figuring. Book of
        Instructions for the Equationer, Or Universal Calcu-
        lator. New York: The Equationer Co., 1892.

        This 24-page pamphlet describes the use of an early
        mechanical calculator.

453   Henneman, A. Die Technische Entwicklung der Rechen-
            maschine. Aachen: Verlag Peter Basten, 1953.

        This is an illustrated and detailed survey of the
        evolution of calculating and bookkeeping devices
        such as punch cards, relay and electrical computers,
        and such older devices as were made by Leibniz,
        Poleni, Roth, Odhner, Baldwin, Müller, Thomas,
        Burkhardt, Hamann, Bollée, Steiger and Burroughs.

454   Jacob, L. Le Calcul Mecanique. Paris: Doin, 1911.

        The author was a French military officer interested
        in mathematics and ballistics. He describes various
        uses for mechanical aids to calculations.

455   Krebs, E. "Die Rechenstable und Rechenmaschinen einst
            und jetzt," Beitr. Gesch. Techn. Ind. 3 (1911): 147-
            162.

        This has a description of calculating devices made
        by Hahn, Burkhardt, Unitas, Archimedes, Brunsviga,
        Monopol, Mercedes-Gauss, and Millionaire, all from
        the very early 1900s.

456   Lenz, R. "Die Rechenmaschinen," Verein zur Berförderung
            des Gewerbfleisses in Preussen 85 (1906): 111-138.

        This is an illustrated review of calculating machines
        made by Goldman, von Mayer, Felt & Tarrant, Burroughs
        and by Brunsviga, Thomas, Selling and Baldwin all of
        the late 1800s/early 1900s.

457   Locke, L.L. "The First Direct-Multiplication Machine,"
            Typewriter Topics (November 1926): 16-20.

        This details a machine made by Ramon Verea in 1878
        which employed a mechanical multiplication table
        equaling ten faced prisms each of which had nine pairs
        of holes.

458   Locke, L.L. "The History of Modern Calculating Machines:
        An American Contribution," American Mathematics
        Monthly 31 (1924): 422-429.

        He surveys develops from the 1870s to the 1920s, a
        period in which enormous strides were made in the
        United States in the development of many calculating
        machines.

459   Mays, W. "First Circuit for an Electric Logic Machine,"
            Science 118 (September 4, 1953): 281-282.

This offers a description of a circuit diagram made
up in about 1885 by Alan Marquand for an electrical
relay device executing logical inferences.

460   Mehmke, R. and d'Ocagne, M.   "Calcul Numériques,"
       Encyclopedie des Sciences Mathématiques Pures et
       Applicquées. Edition Française. Tome 1 (vol. 4).
       Fascicule 2 (1908): 196-320.

       Pages 236-267 offers a useful historical review of
       calculators from Pascal to Felt and includes those
       of Leibniz, Thomas, Maurel, Bollée and Steiger. It
       also discusses difference engines and contains
       bibliographic references.

461   "Mind Races With Machines," Literary Digest 82 (August
       30, 1924): 20.

       A contest was held in France between a man and a
       calculator; the machine proved faster.

462   "New Multiplication Machine," Scientific American 125A
       (November 1921): 62.

       This is a description of a French device for doing
       fast multiplications and is illustrated.

463   "Naval Devices for the Office," World's Work 12
       (August 1906): 7910-7911.

       This describes the use of calculators to do such
       work as design ships.

464   Patterson, G.W.   "The First Electric Computer, A
       Magnetological Analysis," Journal of the Franklin
       Institute 270 (1960): 130-137.

       This focuses on Marquand's electrical binary logic
       machine of the 1880s.

465   Randell, Brian.   "From Analytical Engine to Electronic
       Digital Computer: The Contributions of Ludgate,
       Torres, and Bush," Annals of the History of Comput-
       ing 4, No. 4 (October 1982): 327-341.

       He describes the work of Percy E. Ludgate (1883-
       1922), Leonardo Torres y Quevedo (1852-1936), and
       Vannevar Bush (1890-1974). It is detailed, well
       documented, clear and illustrated.

466   Schellen, H.   Der Elektromagnetische Telegraph.
       Braunschweig: Vieweg, 1870.

       He has a section devoted to "read-only" memory in
       Morse code.

467   Scheyer, E.   "Control of Machines by Perforated Records
       Based on the Jacquard Mechanism," American Machinist
       55, No 10 (1921): 743-747.

The author describes Jacquard and player piano technology and the role of perforated paper tape in controlling instruction of machines.

468   Schulze, J. William. The American Office: Its Organi-
      zation, Management and Records. New York: Ronald
      Press, 1914.

      As a part of a new type of business literature on
      how best to manage offices, this book reviews data
      processing technologies of its day as part of that
      discussion. It comments on tabulators, adding and
      calculating machines, and typewriters.

469   Scott, L. "New Methods of Office Work," World's Work
      9 (March 1905): 5973-5976.

      This refers to the increased use of computing
      equipment in American offices at the turn of the
      century.

470   Sebert, H. "Rapport fait par M. Sebert, au Nom du
      Comité des Arts Économiques, sur la Machine à Cal-
      culer, dit Arithmomètre, inventée par M. Thomas (de
      Colmar) et perfectionée par M. Thomas de Bojano, 44
      rue de Chateudur, à Paris," Bulletin de la Societé
      d'Encouragement pour l'Industrie Nationale (August
      1879): 393-425; reprinted in Ibid. 132 (1920): 694-
      720.

      This is an illustrated description of an arithmome-
      ter and on the work of Thomas de Colmar, and his
      son Thomas de Bojano, inventors of the device. It
      is a useful and detailed article.

471   Thompson, Erwin W. Book-keeping by Machinery; A Treatise
      on Office Economics. New York: The Author, 1906.

      Like a new wave of office management books to appear
      in the early 1900s, this one acknowledges the useful
      features of using office equipment. It describes
      also how to cost-justify their acquisition.

472   United States, Department of Commerce, Bureau of Foreign
      and Domestic Commerce. Foreign Import Duties on
      Office Appliances: Typewriters, Typewriter Ribbons,
      Carbon Paper, Manifolding Apparatus, Adding Machines,
      and Cash Registers. Tariff Series No. 29. Washington,
      D.C.: Government Printing Office, 1914.

      This has some analysis on the world-wide industry but
      is most useful for its detailed tariff schedules. It
      is surprising how many countries at that time already
      had focused on office equipment.

473   Von Bohl, W. Instruments and Machines for Mechanical
      Calculation (in Russian). Moscow: n.p., 1906.

      There was considerable interest in office equipment

in Russia, similar to what was going on in Western Europe. The most popular devices were Odhner-based technology for calculators. These are described in this publication.

474   Von Dyck, W. <u>Katalog Mathematischer und Mathematisch-physikalisher Modelle Apparate und Instrumente</u>. Munich: n.p., 1892, 1893.

This is an early European source on mechanical aids to calculation available in the late nineteenth century.

475   Walford, C. "Calculating Machines," <u>The Insurance Cyclopaedia</u> 1 (1871): 411-425.

This is an historical review along with an account of the mechanization of calculations of actuarial tables. It is a very early publication on nineteenth century calculators and indicative of which industry was one of the earliest to adopt such technology.

Charles Babbage

476   "Addition to the Memoir of M. Menabrea On the Analitical Engine," <u>Philosophical Magazine</u> 23 (September 1843): 235-239.

This reviews Babbage's relations with the British government and his work on the design of an analytical engine.

477   Adler, R.R. "Mr. Babbage's Calculating Engine," <u>Machine Design</u> 30, No. 3 (November 13, 1958): 125-129.

This is a short review of both the Difference and Analytical Engines.

478   Archibald, R.C. "Bibliographia de Mathematicis X: Charles Babbage (1792-1871)," <u>Scripta Mathematica</u> 3 (1935): 266-267.

This is a short bibliiography on the life and work of Charles Babbage.

479   Babbage, B.H. <u>Babbage's Calculating Machine; or Difference Engine</u>. London: Science and Art Department, South Kensington Museum, 1872.

This describes the Difference Engine made in 1833 and an exhibit on it at the Museum.

480   Babbage. Charles. "A Note Respecting the Application of Machinery to the Calculation of Astronomical Tables," <u>Memoirs of the Astronomical Society</u> 1 (June 1822): 309.

This was his first publication on the Difference Engine.

481   Babbage, Charles. "The Calculating Machine of M.
      Scheutz," Mechanics Magazine 64, No. 1705 (1856):
      343-346.

      He reports on Scheutz's engine in a positive light.
      This machine had been under development throughout
      the 1830s and 1840s and was completed in the 1850s.

482   Babbage, Charles. "Correspondence. (Une lettre à M.
      Quetelet de M. Ch. Babbage relativement à la machine
      à Calculer)," Académie royale des sciences, des
      lettres et des beaux-arts de Bruxelles 2 (1835): 123-
      126.

      This is the first article in which Babbage discussed
      the design of the Analytical Engine and what made it
      unique from the Difference Engine.

483   Babbage, Charles. The Exposition of 1851; or, Views
      of the Industry, the Science and the Government of
      England. London: John Murray, 1851.

      He has a chapter on "Calculating Engines" and another
      on "Intrigues of Science" which reviews the relations
      of the government regarding calculating machines.
      Here we see some of his views about the impact of the
      government on his own work and on the anlytical
      engine while providing much social commentary.

484   Babbage, Charles. How to Invent Machinery. Edited and
      supplemented by W.H. Atherton. Manchester: Vulcan,
      1899.

      This 16-page pamphlet reproduces a paper written by
      Babbage in 1829.

485   Babbage, Charles. "Letter to M. Quetelet," Bulletins
      de l'Académie Royale des Sciences et Belles-Lettres
      de Bruxelles 2, No. 5 (May 1835): 124-125.

      This suggests that Babbage spent the past six months
      working on a new machine that could execute sequences
      of mathematical operations.

486   Babbage, Charles. The Ninth Bridgewater Treatise: A
      Fragment. London: John Murray, 1837.

      He discusses his views on various projects and
      machines, and offers a history of his efforts at
      making difference and analytical devices.

487   Babbage, Charles. "Note sur la Machine Suédoise de MM.
      Scheutz pour Calculer les Tables Mathématiques par
      la Méthode des Differences et en Imprimer les Résul-
      tats sur les Planches Stéréotypes," Comptes Rendus
      Académie des Sciences (Paris) 41 (October 8, 1855):
      557-560, Ibid., 42 (April 28, 1856): 798-800.

      The first part describes his son's drawings using

"mechanical notation" of Scheutz's engine. Part two
is correspondence regarding his engine.

488   Babbage, Charles. "Observations on the Application of
      Machinery to the Computation of Mathematical Tables,"
      Memoirs of the Astronomical Society 1, No. 2 (1825):
      311-314.

      This is a paper he read on December 13, 1822 on the
      value of removing restrictions of the Difference
      Engine to functions with some order of difference
      being constant.

489   Babbage, Charles. "On a Method of Expressing by Signs
      the Action of Machinery," Philosophical Transactions
      116, Part 3 (1826): 250-265.

      This is a significant paper because for the first
      time he describes mechanical notation, a fundamental
      concept behind his engines.

490   Babbage, Charles. "On the Mathematical Powers of the
      Calculculating Engine," Unpublished mss (December 1,
      1837), reprinted in B. Randell (ed), The Origins of
      Digital Computers (Berlin: Springer Verlag, 1973):
      19-54.

      This is his most complete description of the Analy-
      tical Engine.

491   Babbage, Charles. "On the Theoretical Principles of
      the Machinery for Calculating Tables," Edinburgh
      Philosophical Journal 8 (1823): 122-128.

      This is an early discourse on mathematical machinery
      and how it relates to his own work with engines.

492   Babbage, Charles. Passages From the Life of a Philoso-
      pher. London: Longman, Gree, Longman, Roberts and
      Green 1864; reprinted New York: Augustus M. Kelley,
      1969.

      Several chapters deal with the difference engine and
      the subsequent analytical engine.

493   Babbage, Charles. "Sur la machine suédoise de MM.
      Schuetz pour calculer les tables mathématiques,"
      Comptes rendus hebdomadaires des séances 4 (1855):
      557-560.

      He describes the machine made in Sweden which won a
      gold medal in Paris in 1855. Babbage admired the
      machine.

494   Babbage, Henry P. "Babbage's Analytical Engine,"
      Monthly Notices of the Royal Astronomical Society 70
      (1910): 517-526, 645.

      This describes the work oh H.P. Babbage following

the death of his father, Charles Babbage, and involves the construction of the mill and printing device for the analytical engine.

495   Babbage, Henry P. (ed). Babbage's Calculating Engines: Being a Collection of Papers Relating to Them, Their History, and Construction. London: E. and F.N. Spoon, 1889; reprinted, Los Angeles: Tomash, 1983.

This reprints many papers; the volume is edited by his son.

496   Babbage, Henry P. Memoirs and Correspondence of Major-General H.P. Babbage. London: Privately Printed, 1910.

Although primarily devoted to his career in India, he does describe childhood memories of his father and the analytical engine, later of similar activities involved in invention in 1854-55 and of his own inventive activities following his retirement from active service in 1874.

497   Babbage, Henry P. "On the Mechanical Arrangement of the Analytical Engine of the Late Charles Babbage F.R.S.," Report of the British Association for the Advancement of Science (1888): 616-617.

This is a paper by H.P. Babbage arguing that his father anticipated advances in carriage, counting apparatus, and mechanical notation in calculating equipment design.

498   Babbage, Henry P. "On Mechanical Notation, As Exemplified in the Swedish Calculating Machine of Messrs. Scheutz, "Report of the British Association for the Advancement of Science (1885): 203-205.

He offers a brief description of mechanical notation.

499   Babbage, R.H. "The Work of Charles Babbage," Proceedings of a Symposium on Large Scale Digital Calculating Machinery, 7-10 Jan. 1947. Annals of the Computation Laboratory of Harvard University, 16 (Cambridge, Mass.: Harvard University Press, 1948): 13-22.

500   Baily, F. "On Mr. Babbage's New Machine for Calculating and Printing Mathematical and Astronomical Tables," Philosophical Magazine 63 (May 1824): 355-367.

This surveys various mathematical tables for which the difference engine would be useful.

501   Baum, Joan. The Calculating Passion of Ada Byron. Hamden, Conn.: Archon Books, 1986.

This is a very readable account of Ada Byron that is

weak on facts but useful for discerning her perso-
nality. It also describes her relationship with
Charles Babbage to some degree.

502   Baxandall, D. "Calculating Machines and Instruments,"
       Catalogue of the Collections in the Science Museum.
       London: H.M.S.O., 1926.

       This is a useful catalog of the Museum's collection
       of early calculating devices, including Babbage's
       difference engine, and another made by Scheutz.
       Parts of Babbage's analytical engine are also here
       and described in this publication.

503   Bell, Walter Lyle. "Charles Babbage, Philosopher,
       Reformer, Inventor: A History of His Contributions
       to Science" (Unpublished Ph.D. dissertation, Oregon
       State University, 1975).

       This is a serious biography of Babbage.

504   Booth, A.D. Review of "Charles Babbage and His Calcula-
       ting Engines," edited by P. and E. Morrison, Journal
       of the Royal Statistical Society, Series A, 125, No.
       3 (1962): 491-492.

       Booth comments that early pioneers in computers did
       not know of Babbage's work or that he had already
       developed the logic of a digital computer—a contro-
       versy that continued throughout the historical
       literature into the 1980s.

505   Bowden, B.V. "Charles Babbage, Father of the Mechani-
       cal Brain," Science Digest 49 (1961): 82-88.

       This is a shorter version of his 1960 article on
       the same subject (see entry number 506).

506   Bowden, B.V. "He Invented the Computer—Before Its
       Time," Think (July 1960): 28-32.

       He reviews in general terms the work of Charles
       Babbage and Lady Lovelace.

507   Bowden, B.V. "Science Milestone: Charles Babbage,"
       Science Digest 49 (January 1961): 82-88.

       He delivers the same message and material as in the
       previous two publications.

508   Brainerd, J.G. Review of "Charles Babbage (1792-1871),"
       Computer Reviews 6, No. 5 (1965): 284.

       The author headed up the ENIAC project in the 1940s
       and states that that work was done without anyone
       being aware of Babbage's accomplishments with regard
       to digital devices, especially concerning the Analy-
       tical Engine.

509   Brewster, David. "History of Mechanical Inventions and
      Processes in the Useful Arts," Edinburgh Journal of
      Science 1, No. 1 (1824): 141-151.

      He describes Babbage's Difference Engine.

510   Brewster, David. "Mr. Babbage's Calculating Engine,"
      Letters on Natural Magic, Addressed to Sir Walter
      Scott, Bart. New Edition. London: William Tegg,
      1868, pp. 340-345.

      This contains a short account of Babbage's Difference
      Engine, first published in 1832, along with an
      account of Babbage's demonstration of the device.

511   Brewster, David. "Mr. Babbage's Calculating Machine,"
      New Scientist 88, No. 1232/1233 (December 18/25,
      1880): 831-832.

      This is the same as item number 510 reprinted.

512   Briguglio, L. and Bulferetti, L. (eds). Luigi Federico
      Menabrea. Memorie. Florence: Giunti, 1971.

      These are the memoirs of Menabrea, in French, which
      in part (pages 36-38) reviews his meeting with
      Babbage and also about the relations of both men
      with Lady Lovelace.

513   Bromley, Allan G. "Charles Babbage's Analytical
      Engine, 1838," Annals of the History of Computing
      4, No. 3 (July 1982): 196-217.

      This is a useful, technical review of his engine
      and of its design.

514   Bromley, Allan G. "The Evolution of Babbage's Calcula-
      ting Engines," Annals of the History of Computing
      9, No. 2 (1987): 113-136.

      This is a detailed, technical review of Babbage's
      architecture and design for both the Difference and
      Analytical Engines; excellent.

515   Bulferetti, L. "I Corrispondenti Italiani di Charles
      Babbage," Le Machine: Bollettino dell'Instituto
      Italiano per la Storia della Tecnica 1, nos 2-3
      (1967-1968): 119-126.

      Babbage's correspondence with various Italian scien-
      tists regarding his work is presented here, a great
      deal is from the 1840s. These papers are today at
      the British Library.

516   Bulferetti, L. "Un Amico di Charles Babbage: Fortunato
      Prandi," Memorie dell'Instituto Lombardo (Academia
      di Scienze e Letterie. Classe di Lettere, scienze
      morali e storiche 30, No. 2 (1968): 83-116.

This is a competent biography of Prandi, friend of
Babbage, while in London. The paper is based on
primary sources.

517   Buxton, H.W. *Memoir of the Life and Labours of the
       Late Charles Babbage Esq. F.R.S.* Edited with intro-
       duction by Anthony Hyman. Cambridge, Mass.: MIT
       Press, 1988.

       Buxton, with the cooperation, wrote this biography
       which he completed after Babbage's death in the late
       1800s but which is published now for the first time.
       It is edited by a leading biography of Charles
       Babbage.

518   Buxton, L.H.D. "Charles Babbage and His Difference
       Engine," *Transactions of the Newcomen Society* 14
       (1934): 43-65; Plate 4.

       This is a detailed review of the engine, with some
       discussion of his other devices and those of other
       people of the period.

519   C., P.S. "Mr. Babbage and His Rivals," *Mechanics
       Magazine* 23, No. 614 (May 16, 1835): 119.

       This is a defense of Babbage's efforts; rivals is
       used here to define his critics.

520   "Calculating by Machinery," *Manufacturer and Builder*
       2, No. 8 (August 1870): 225-227.

       This focuses on difference engines, including those
       of Babbage and Scheutz.

521   Campbell-Kelly, Martin. "Charles Babbage's Table of
       Logarithms (1827)," *Annals of the History of Com-
       puting* 10 No. 3 (1988): 159-169.

       The article reviews how he produced what was con-
       sidered the most accurate logarithmic table of its
       day.

522   "Charles Babbage," *Nature* 5, No. 106 (November 9, 1871):
       28-29.

       This is a brief overview of Babbage's work; an
       obituary notice.

523   Colebrook, Henry T. "Address of Henry Thomas Colebook,
       President of the Astronomical Society of London . . .
       On Presenting the Honorary Gold Model to Charles
       Babbage, Esq. F.R.S.," *Mem. Astronomical Society* 1,
       No. 2 (1825): 509-512.

       The material includes the quote "It substitutes
       mechanical performance for an intellectual process"
       to describe the functioning of his Difference Engine.

524   Collier, Bruce. "The Little Engines That Could've; The
       Calculating Machines of Charles Babbage" (Unpublished
       Ph.D. dissertaion, Harvard University, 1971).

       This is a well-researched technical review of Babb-
       age's work.

525   Crosse, A. "A Twilight Gossip With Past," Temple Bar
       96 (October 1892): 179-201.

       These are recollections of a visit to Charles Babb-
       age's home and discussion of the Difference Engine.

526   Crosse, A. "John Kenyon and His Friends," Temple Bar
       88 (April 1890): 477-496.

       He includes material on a conversation with Babbage
       and Lady Lovelace.

527   Crosse, A. "Science and Society in the Fifties,"
       Temple Bar 93 (September 1891): 33-51.

       He reviews a conversation with Babbage during the
       1850s concerning analog devices and Lady Lovelace.

528   de Fonblanque, E.B. The Life and Labours of Albany
       Fonblanque. London: Bentley, 1871.

       He includes a one-page obituary of Lady Lovelace
       which appeared originally in the Examiner.

529   de Morgan, S.E. Memoir of Augustus de Morgan, With
       Selections From His Letters. London: Longmans,
       Green and Co., 1881.

       He has passing comments on Babbage and of a visit to
       him.

530   "Disputes in the Royal Astronomical Society," Mechan-
       ics Magazine 61, No. 1649 (1855): 242-246, 267-271.

       It comments in part on Charles Babbage.

531   Dodge, N.S. "Charles Babbage," Annual Report, Smith-
       sonian Institution (Washington, D.C.: Smithsonian
       Institution, 1873): 162-197.

       Published nearly two years after his death, this is
       a report on Charles Babbage's life and work. It does
       include quotes from his writings and an obituary
       notice.

532   Dubbey, J.M. "Charles Babbage and His Computers,"
       Bulletin of the Institute of Mathematics and Its
       Applications 9, No. 3 (March 1973): 662-669.

       He presents an essay on his (Babbage's) thinking
       as it applied to his "computers" or engines. The
       term computer is used prematurely in this article.

533   Dubbey, J.M.   "The Mathematical Work of Charles
      Babbage" (Unpublished Ph.D. dissertation, University
      of London, 1968).

      This is a scholarly review of the subject and of his
      machines based on the Babbage Papers.

534   Dubbey, J.M.   The Mathematical Work of Charles Babbage.
      Cambridge: Cambridge University Press, 1978.

      This is the revised, improved, and published version
      of his 1968 dissertation.

535   Felt, D.E.   "Mechanical Arithmetic," Scientific Ameri-
      can 69 (November 11, 1893): 310-311.

      The author had invented and brought to market a very
      widely used desk-top calculator by the time he wrote
      this article. In this piece he describes the diff-
      erence machines built by Babbage and Scheutz and
      compares their design and function to his own Comp-
      tometer.

536   Fitzgerald, W.C. "The Romance of Our Museums," The
      Strang Magazine 9 (1895): 709-715.

      Babbage's work is reviewed based on an interview
      with H.P. Babbage.

537   Forbes, E.G.   "The Crawfor Collection of the Royal
      Observatory," Science Research Council Publications
      9, No. 1 (1973): 7-13.

      It lists some 2,600 items from Babbage's personal
      library with discussion.

538   Franksen, Ole Immanuel.   "Mr. Babbage, the Difference
      Engine, and the Problem of Notation: An Account of
      the Origin of Recursiveness and Conditionals in
      Computer Programming," International Journal of
      Engineering Science 19, No. 12 (1981): 1657-1694.

      This surveys Babbage's work, offering an abstract
      simulation of the Difference Engine, written in APL.
      For a useful analysis of this article see Annals of
      of the History of Computing 5, No. 4 (October 1983):
      411-415.

539   Franksen, Ole Immanuel. Mr. Babbage's Secret. The Tale
      of a Cypher and APL. Birkerbød, Denmark: Strand-
      bergs Forlag, 1984.

      Reviews Babbage's work on deciphering and his mathe-
      matics. For a detailed analysis and summary of this
      work see Annals of the History of Computing 7, No. 2
      (April 1985): 185-187.

540   Fyvie, J.   "The Calculating Philosopher," Some Literary
      Eccentrics (London: Constable, 1906): 179-209.

This a biography for the general reader and which is critical of his engines.

541   Garwig, P.L. "Charles Babbage (1792-1871)," <u>American</u> Documentation 20, No. 4 (October 1969): 320-324.

This is a short biography of Babbage.

542   Goddard, D. <u>Eminent Engineers: Brief Biographies of</u> <u>Thirty-Two of the Inventors and Engineers Who Did</u> <u>Most to Further Mechanical Progress</u>. New York: Deray-Collard, 1906.

Pages 240-254 reviews Babbage's life and work, paying attention to his two important machines.

543   Gunther, R.W.T. <u>Early Science at Cambridge</u>. Cambridge: Cambridge University Press, 1937.

This important book has some material on the role Babbage played in the field of nineteenth century British mathematics.

544   Halacy, D. <u>Charles Babbage, Father of the Computer</u>. New York: Crowell-Collier, 1970.

This is a popular, functional biography of Charles Babbage, based on secondary sources in large part.

545   Hammersley, J.M. "The Technology of Thought," in J. Neyman (ed), <u>The Heritage of Copernicus</u> (Cambridge, Mass.: MIT Press, 1974): 394-415.

The author includes some thoughts on Babbage, on his relations with Lady Lovelace, and on their contribution to computation.

546   Hollingdale, S.H. "Charles Babbage and Lady Lovelace— Two 19th Century Mathematicians," <u>Bulletin of the</u> <u>Institute of Mathematics and Its Applications</u> 2, No. 1 (1966): 2-15.

This is especially useful for the phases Babbage went through to arrive at his views on general programming of sequence control and about Lovelace's calculations of Bernoulli numbers.

547   Howlett, J. "Charles Babbage and His Computer," in M. Graef (ed), <u>350 Jahre Rechenmaschinen</u> (Munich: Carl Hanser, 1973): 34-42.

This is simply a summary view of Babbage and his work on calculating engines.

548   Huskey, Velma R. and Huskey, Harry D. "Ada, Countess of Lovelace, and Her Contribution to Computing," <u>Abacus</u> 1, No. 2 (1984): 22-29.

This is an introduction to Babbage's friend.

549   Huskey, Velma R. and Huskey, Harry D. "Lady Lovelace
      and Charles Babbage," Annals of the History of
      Computing 2, No. 4 (October 1980): 299-329.

      This is an illustrated account of the correspondence
      between Lovelace and Babbage and on their work.

550   Hyman, Anthony. Charles Babbage: Pioneer of the Compu-
      ter. Princeton: Princeton University Press, 1982.

      This is the best biography on Babbage. The research
      is thorough, is based on primary materials, and
      covers his life and work in a balanced, full manner.

551   Hyman, Anthony. Computing: A Dictionary of Terms,
      Concepts and Ideas. London: Arrow Books, 1976.

      More than a dictionary, it contains material on
      Babbage.

552   Hyman, Anthony. "Letter to the Editor," Computer
      Weekly, December 11, 1975, p. 8.

      He details the place and birth of Charles Babbage.

553   IBM Corporation. Charles Babbage Computer Pioneer,
      1791-1891. London: IBM United Kigdom, 1972.

      Although the birth year is off, this wall chart has
      accurate information on Babbage's engines, especially
      the Analytical Engines of 1834 and 1856.

554   Judex Juris (pseud. for Joseph Jarvis). On the Calcu-
      lation and Printing of Mathematical Tables by
      Machinery: The Inventor and His Treatment. London:
      C. Whiting, circa 1861.

      This 53-page pamphlet defends Babbage and is critical
      of the British government and the Royal Society for
      not supporting his work with engines.

555   Kean, D.W. "The Computer and the Countess," Datamation
      19, No. 5 (1973): 60-63.

      This details the life of Lady Lovelace and her work
      with Babbage on analytical engines and a gambling
      scheme.

556   Lardner, D. "Babbage's Calculating Engines," Edinburgh
      Review 120 (July 1834)and reprinted by P. Morrison
      and E. Morison (eds), Charles Babbage and His Calcu-
      lating Engines: Selected Writings by Charles Babbage
      and Others (New York: Dover, 1961).

      This is a survey of mathematical tables and of the
      Difference Engine.

557   "The Late Mr. Babbage," Illustrated London News, Novem-
      ber 4, 1871, p. 423.

This is an obituary notice for Charles Babbage with portrait. He was recognized as a major mathematician in his own day, resulting in numerous obituary articles.

558   "The Late Mr. Babbage," The Times, October 23 and 30, 1871, p. 5.

This obituary notice is particularly detailed on his early years.

559   Lewis, T.C. Heroes of Science: Mechanicians. London: Society for Promoting Christian Knowledge, 1884.

Pages 302-340 contain a biography of Babbage drawn from his own writings. There is nothing on the Analytical Engine.

560   Losano, M.G. Babbage: La Macchina Analitica, Un Secolo di Calcolo Automatico. Milan: ETAS Kompass Libri, 1973.

This has many papers previously unpublished by Babbage housed at the library of the Academy of Sciences of Turin. It includes police records on Babbage's activities and those of his friend Fortunato Prandi.

561   Losano, M.G. "Charles Babbage e la Programmazione delle Machina da Calcolo," Atti dell'Academia delle Scienze di Torino 106 (1971/72): 25-37.

He surveys Babbage's ideas regarding program control of machinery.

562   Losano, M.G. (ed). Machines Arithmétiques: Invenzioni francesi del Settecento. Turin: Bottega D'Erasmo, 1976.

These are reproductions of eighteenth century French articles on calculating machines such as the adding device of Perrault and calculators of Lepine, Pascal, Hillerin de Boistissandeau by an expert on Charles Babbage.

563   Lovelace, Augustus Ada, Countess of. "Sketch of the Analytical Engine Invented by Charles Babbage, by L.F. Menabrea of Turin, Officer of the Military Engineers, With Notes Upon the Memoir by the Translator," Taylor's Scientific Memoirs 3 (1843): Article 29: 666-731.

This has a significant paper on Babbage's Analytical Engine, reflecting a clear view of the device.

564   MacFarlane, A. Lectures on Ten British Physicists of the Nineteenth Century. New York: Wiley, 1919.

Pages 71-83 contains a chapter on Babbage's life and

includes a good description of his deas for an
analytical engine.

565   Marshall, W.P.   "Babbage's Calculating Machine," <u>Proceed-
      ings of the Birmigham Philosophical Society</u> 1 (1879):
      33-48.

      This describes how the Difference Engine was intended
      to function.

566   Mayne, E.C.   <u>The Life and Letters of Anne Isabella, Lady
      Noel Byron</u>.   New York: Scribner's Sons, 1929.

      The epilogue was written by May, Countess of Lovelace
      and contains a short biography of her husband's
      mother, Ada Augusta, also the Countess of Lovelace.

567   McLaughlin, T.   "Ada Byron—The Romantic Computer Pro-
      grammer," <u>Spectrum</u> 147 (1977): 6-7.

      This is general, short account.

568   Menabrea, L.F.   "Notions sur la Machine Analytique de
      M. Charles Babbage," <u>Bibliothèque Universelle de
      Genève</u> 82 (October 1842): 352-376.

      This was written by a friend of Babbage and may
      perhaps be the first account published of the analy-
      tical engine's concept on the European continent. It
      is well illustrated.

569   Menabrea, L.F.   "Sur la Machine Analytique de Charles
      Babbage," <u>Comptes Rendus. Academie des Sciences</u>
      (Paris) (July 28, 1884): 179-182.

      This includes a letter to the author from Babbage on
      the subject of the Analytical Engine.

570   Merrifield, C.W.   "Report of the Committee, Consisting
      of Professor Cayley, Dr. Farr, Mr. J.W.L. Glaisher,
      Dr. Pole, Professor Fuller, Professor A.B.W. Kennedy,
      Professor Clifford and Mr. C.W. Merrifield, Appointed
      to Consider the Advisability and to Estimate the
      Expense of Constructing Mr. Babbage's Analytical
      Machine, and of Printing Tables by Its Means," <u>Report
      of the British Association for the Advancement of
      Science, Dublin, August 1878</u>. (London: John Murray,
      1879): 92-102.

      This reviews Babbage and his ideas. It concluded that
      his machine was not sufficiently designed yet to be
      built at that time.

571   Microforms International Marketing Corporation.   <u>The
      History of Computing: A Memoir of the Life of Charles
      Babbage</u>. Elmsford, N.Y.: Microforms International,
      1985.

      This is a collection of 13 microfiche cards with the

papers of Charles Babbage for use by researchers on his life and work.

572   Moore, Doris Langley. <u>Ada, Countess of Lovelace: Byron's Legitimate Daughter</u>. New York: Harper & Row, 1977.

      This is an excellent biography which has material on her work with mathematics and her relations with Charles Babbage.

573   Morrison, Philip and Morrison, Emily (eds). <u>Charles Babbage and His Calculating Engines: Selected Writings by Charles Babbage and Others</u>. New York: Dover, 1961.

      This contains 400 pages of material on his engines. It is a convenient collection of primary source materials.

574   Morrison, Philip and Morrison, Emily. "Strange Life of Charles Babbage," <u>Scientific American</u> 180 (April 1952): 66-73.

      This is a biography with some description of his engines.

575   Mosley, Mabeth. <u>Irascible Genius: A Life of Charles Babbage, Inventor</u>. London: Hutchinson, 1964.

      For many years this was the standard biography on Babbage.

576   Moulton, Lord. "The Invention of Logarithms, Its Genesis and Growth," in C.G. Knott, <u>Napier Tercentenary Memorial Volume</u> (London: Longman, Green and Company, 1915): 1-24.

      Pages 19-20 recount a visit to Charles Babbage by the author and has some sad comments about the unfinished analytical engine.

577   "Mr. Babbage and His Calculating Engines," <u>Mechanics Magazine</u> 21, No. 578 (September 6, 1834): 391-392.

      This was a report on the current status of the Difference Engine and of its problems. The article suggests that the British government investigate what is going on so that the work could be completed.

578   "Mr. Babbage's Calculating Machine," <u>Mechanics Magazine</u> 10, No. 263 (August 23, 1828): 64.

      Like the previous article, it reviews the status of the project.

579   "Mr. Babbage's Calculating Machinery," <u>Mechanics Magazine</u> 18, No. 488 (1832): 173-175.

      This reviews calculators made before Babbage's and

then surveys the status of work on the Difference
Engine.

580   "Mr. Charles Babbage," The Illustrated Times, October
        28, 1871, p. 267.

        This is an obituary notice that contains some details
        on how he built the Difference Engine (or parts of
        it).

581   Nievergelt, J. "Computers and Computing—Past, Present,
        and Future," IEEE Spectrum 5, No. 1 (1968): 57-61.

        He argues that modern designers did not know of
        Babbage or of his work when they developed the digi-
        tal computer.

582   Nudds, D. "Charles Babbage (1871-1871)," in J. North
        (ed), Mid-Nineteenth Century Scientists (Oxford:
        Pergamon Press, 1969): 1-34.

        This biography has a good overview of Babbage's work.

583   "Our Obituary Record," The Graphic, November 18, 1871,
        p. 495.

        This is an obituary notice on Charles Babbage.

584   Pengelly, H. (ed). A Memoir of William Pengelly of
        Torquay, F.R.S., Geologist. London: Murray, 1897.

        This was written by a friend of Babbage and has
        material on the inventor.

585   P.S.C. "Mr. Babbage and His Rivals," Mechanics Magazine
        23 (1835): 119.

        This article is somewhat critical of Babbage's
        efforts in regard to the Difference Engine.

586   Publicola (pseud.). "Mr. Babbage's Calculating Machine,"
        Mechanics Magazine 171, No. 466 (1832): 256.

        This is a letter to the editor regarding Babbage's
        book, On the Economy of Machinery and Manufacturing,
        published in 1832, asking why the inventor has not
        finished building his calculating machine instead.

587   Quetelet, A. "Notice sur Charles Babbage, Associé de
        l'Académie," Annual de l'Académie Royale sur les
        Sciences, Lettres e Beaux-Arts De Belgique (1872):
        149-165.

        The author describes memoirs of meetings and letters
        with Babbage, a close friend of the author.

588   Richardson, C.J. A Popular Treatise on the Warming and
        Ventilation of Buildings. 3rd ed. London: John
        Neale, 1856.

Pages 90-102 discuss a self-regulating heating system installed at Babbage's home in 1837. Plate 16
has a layout of the house while Plate 17 the machine
to control water flow in four circulation loops. The
machine was devised by Babbage.

589   Rosse, Lord. "Presidential Address," Proceedings of
      the Royal Society 7 (1854-1855): 248-258.

      He reviews the Society's relations with Babbage and
      the inventor's attempts to bid for government con-
      tracts in the early 1850s.

590   R.T. Mathematical and Scientific Library of the Late
      Charles Babbage of No. 1, Dorset Street, Manchester
      Square. London: Hodgson and Son, 1872.

      This was the 191-page sale catalog with sections on
      pure mathematics, astronomy, mechanics, optics,
      electricity, pneumatics, mathematical tables for a
      total of over 2,000 items.

591   S., A. "Obituary: Charles Babbage," Monthly Notices.
      Royal Astronomical Society 32, No. 4 (February 9,
      1872): 101-109.

      Babbage was closely associated with this organization.

592   Sarton, G. The Study of the History of Mathematics.
      New York: Dover, 1936.

      There are some references to Babbage and his calcu-
      lating machines.

593   Shuster, A. and Shipley, A.E. Britain's Heritage of
      Science. London: Constable & CO., 1917.

      This book has passing comments on Babbage and his
      role relative to other scientists of his time in
      industrial England. Such books are important to
      appreciate the relative impact of people who later
      were seen as giants of as yet an unborn industry,
      such as data processing.

594   Sinderen, Alfred Van. "Babbage and the Scheutz Machine
      at Dudley Observatory," Annals of the History of
      Computing 10, No. 2 (1988): 136-139.

      He describes the role played by Babbage in acquiring
      a calculator for the Albany, NY observatory in the
      nineteenth century.

595   Sinderen, Alfred Van. "The Printed Papers of Charles
      Babbage," Annals of the History of Computing 2, No.
      2 (April 1980): 169-185.

      This lists the papers and discusses them in detail.
      The article is very thorough and complete.

596   Smiles, S. Industrial Biography: Iron Workers and Tool
            Makers. London: John Muray, 1908.

            First published in 1863, this has a chapter on Joseph
            Clement who did some work for Charles Babbage. An
            appendix written by Babbage explains their relation-
            ship.

597   Smith, D.E. "Among My Autographs," American Mathema-
            tics Monthly 29 (1922): 114-115.

            This is based on a letter written by Babbage on his
            own work in 1840.

598   Stein, Dorothy. Ada: A Life and a Legacy. Cambridge,
            Mass.: MIT Press, 1985.

            This is a full biography of Ada Lovelace, Charles
            Babbage's companion. The author focuses a great
            deal of attention on how he worked with her to pro-
            mote his various projects.

599   S.Y. "Calculating Machinery," Mechanics Magazine 23,
            624 (July 25, 1835): 317-318.

            This publishes a letter defending Babbage's plans
            for calculating and printing mathematical tables
            automatically.

600   Tee, Garry J. "Charles Babbage (1791-1871) and His
            New Zealand Connections," in M.E. Hoare et al.,
            In Search of New Zealand's Scientific Heritage
            (Wellington: Royal Society of New Zealand, 1986):
            81-90.

            While minor, a connection existed with interest in
            his engines covering many years in duration. Work on
            early digital computers also took place in New
            Zealand.

601   Timbs, J. Stories of Inventors and Discoverers. 2nd
            Ed. London: Lockwood, 1863.

            Pages 134-135 discuss Babbage's work mentioning that,
            in addition to his engines and automatic speaking
            machines by others, there is a review of work by
            Morland and Jacquard.

602   Traconi, F.G. "Un Precursore delle Moderne Macchine
            Calcolotrici: Charles Babbage (1792-1871)," Atti
            dell'Academia delle Scienze di Torino 106 (1971/72):
            17-24.

            This is a short biography and review of Babbage's
            work, and about his visit to Turin in 1840, based
            on manuscripts in the collection of the Academy of
            Sciences in Turin.

603   Tucker, R. Mathematical and Scientific Library of the

Late Charles Babbage. London: C.F. Hodgson and Son, 1872.

As part of the effort to liquidate Babbage's estate, this catalog of some 2,000 items on science in general was published.

604   Tumbleson, R.C. "Calculating Machines," Electrical Engineering 67, No. 10 (1948): 6-12.

This is a light account of Babbage's Analytical Engine and has some comments on American computers, including on the method of programming the ENIAC.

605   Turner, H.D. "Charles Babbage F.R.S. (1792-1871)," Research Application Ind. 149, No. 9 (1961): 342-352.

This is a short account of Babbage's machines with a quote from him in a letter dated December, 1839 to an associate on the use of the Jacquard card technique.

606   Van Sinderen, Alfred W. "Babbage's Letter to Quetelet, May 1835," Annals of the History of Computing 5, No. 3 (July 1983): 263-267.

This reprints the letter with analysis, on the concept of the Analytical Engine.

607   Verrijn, Stuart A.A. Lezen en Schrijven. Inaugural Lecture, University of Leiden, March 5, 1971. Gronigen: Walters-Noordhoff NV, 1971.

He discusses Babbage and the implications of his work.

608   Weld, C.R. The Eleventh Chapter of the History of the Royal Society. London: Richard Clay, 1849.

This booklet has two articles concerning Babbage's arguments with the British government over his difference engine. The argument is critical of the government's lack of support. The pamphlet may have been edited by Babbage himself.

609   Weld, C.R. History of the Royal Society with Memoirs of the Presidents. 2 vols. London: J.W. Parker, 1848.

Chapter nine reviews Babbage's relations with the Royal Society and the government regarding his engines. He uses primary materials housed at the Society's library.

610   Wilkes, Maurice V. "Automatic Calculating Machines," Journal of the Royal Society of Arts C, No. 4862 (1951): 56-90.

This is a detailed view of Babbage's Analytical Engine by a leading computer scientist.

611   Wilkes, Maurice V. "Babbage As a Computer Pioneer,"
      Report of Proceedings, Babbage Memorial Meeting,
      London, 18 October 1971. London: British Computer
      Society, 1971.

      He relies extensively on Babbage's notebooks for
      material with which to write this article on his
      Analytical Engine.

612   Wilkes, Maurice V. "Charles Babbage," in A. Ralston
      and C.L. Meek (eds), Encyclopedia of Computer
      Science (New York: Petrocelli/Charter, 1976): 157-
      159.

      This is a short biography that also explains his
      significance to the general field of computing's
      history; illustrated.

613   Wilkes, Maurice V. "The Design of a Control Unit—
      Reflections on Reading Babbage's Notebooks,"
      Annals of the History of Computing 3, No. 2 (April
      1981): 116-120.

      Wilkes focuses on why Babbage wrote little about a
      control system for the Analytical Engine. He offers
      details as well from the notebooks.

614   Williams, Michael R. "Babbage and Bowditch: A Trans-
      atlantic Connection," Annals of the History of
      Computing 9, Nos 3-4 (1988): 283-290.

      Babbage wrote a letter on August 2, 1835, which is
      reprinted here, describing his thoughts concerning
      the Analytical Engine.

615   Williams, Michael R. "History of Computation: Charles
      Babbage (1791-1871)—Grandfather of the Computer
      Age," Canadian Information Processing Society Review
      6 (September-October 1982): 20-23.

      This is a short biography.

616   Williams, Michael R. "The Scientific Library of
      Charles Babbage," Annals of the History of Comput-
      ing 3, No. 3 (July 1981): 235-240.

      The author describes the contents of Babbage's
      library of some 2,000 items, suggesting possible
      intellectual influences on him.

617   Wittenberg, G. Charles Babbage: Biographical Notes and
      Notes on Exhibits Compiled for the Babbage Display at
      the Computer Exhibition, Llandudno, July, 1970.
      Llandudno: Computer Consultants, Ltd., 1970.

      This contains a bibliography, photographs and notes.

618   Y., S. "Calculating Machinery," Mechanics Magazine
      23, No 264 (July 25, 1835): 317-318.

This is a letter supporting Babbage's plans for an
analytical engine to prepare mathematical tables.

Leon Bollée

619   Bollée, Leon. "Sur une Nouvelle Machine à Calculer,"
       Comptes Rendus Academie de Sciences (Paris) 109
       (1889): 737-739.

       This is a short description of his machine with a
       good explanation of how it works to do direct multi-
       plication.

620   d'Ocagne, M. "On the Origin of Machines of Direct
       Multiplication," in C.G. Knott (ed), Napier Tercen-
       tenary Memorial Volume (London: Longman, Green and
       Company, 1915): 283-285.

       He describes Bollée's direct multiplier first built
       in 1887. Some biographical data is also included.

621   Sebert, H. "Rapport fait par M. Le Général Sebert, au
       nom du Comité des Arts Economiques, sur les Machines
       à Calculer de M. Leon Bollée, du Mans," Bulletin de
       la Societe d'Encouragement pour l'Industrie (1885):
       977-996; reprinted in Ibid. 132 (1920): 723-738.

       This surveys Bollée's machines and provides a very
       useful of his life and work.

George Boole

622   Bell, Eric. Men of Mathematics. New York: Simon &
       Schuster, 1937.

       This is insightful, well-written, and offers a good
       review of the life and work of George Boole.

623   Boole, George. The Laws of Thought. New York: Dover
       Press, 1953.

       This is a reprint of his famous book, An Investiga-
       tion of the Laws of Thought, on Which Are Founded
       the Mathematical Theories of Logic and Probabilities,
       first published in 1854. This is the book in which
       he presents what came to be the basis for Boolean
       mathematics.

624   Boole, Mary Everest. A Boolean Anthology. N.c.: Asso-
       ciation of Teachers of Mathematics, 1972.

       This contains a good survey of his thinking in origi-
       nal source material.

625   Broadbent, T.A.A. "George Boole," in Dictionary of
       Scientific Biography (New York: Scribners, 1970), 2
       pp. 293-298.

       This is a good introduction to the nineteenth century

mathematician who applied arithmetic (mathematical) principles to logical thought, hence the term Boolean logic. His work was essential to the mathematics underpinning the development of computer technology in the following century.

626   Minker, Jack and Minker, Rita G. "Optimization of Boolean Expression—Historical Developments," Annals of the History of Computing 2, No. 3 (July 1980): 227-238.

This is an illustrated, technical discourse on the evolution of Boolean logic and how it applies to compilers.

627   Tropp, H. "George Boole," in A. Ralston and C.L. Meek (eds), Encyclopedia of Computer Science (New York: Petrocelli/Charter, 1976): 177-178.

This is a useful biography that also explains his significance to computer scientists.

Dorr E. Felt

628   "An Improved Calculating Machine," Scientific American 59 (1888): 265.

This provides a description of the machine he invented and that became the basis of Felt & Tarrant Manufacturing Company of Chicago; illustrated.

629   Boys, C.V. "The Comptometer," Nature 64 (1901): 265-268.

This is on one of the more popular calculators of the turn-of-the-century. It is a description of its use in performing basic arithmetic functions and offers a comparison to the functions of slide rules and arithmometers.

630   Felt, Dorr E. "Mechanical Arithmetic or the History of the Counting Machine," Lectures on Business. Chicago: Washington Institute, 1916.

He describes his comptometer and comments on developments by other vendors. It offers useful information on the history of Felt & Tarrant Manufacturing Company.

631   Felt & Tarrant Manufacturing Company. Applied Mechanical Arithmetic as Practised on the Comptometer. Chicago: Felt & Tarrant Manufacturing Company, 1914; Revised edition, 1920.

This is a very important publication not only on Felt & Tarrant's products and history of the company, but on calculators in general: their technology and use. The 1920 edition is over 600 pages in length and has many illustrations.

Herman Hollerith

632   Austrian, Geoffrey D. Herman Hollerith: The Forgotten
       Giant of Information Processing. New York: Columbia
       University Press, 1982.

       This is the definitive biography of Hollerith, cover-
       ing his life and work, while providing considerable
       information on punch card technology and the industry
       it fostered from the 1880s to World War I.

633   Austrian, Geoffrey D. "Hollerith," Think (May/June
       1982): 3-37.

       This consists of excerpts from his book cited above.

634   Austrian, Geoffrey D. "Winning the Merchants," Datama-
       tion 28, No. 2 (Fall 1982): 156-172.

       This deals with Hollerith's efforts to sell his devi-
       ces to commercial users from 1900 to 1910.

635   Blodgett, John H. "Herman Hollerith: Data Processing
       Pioneer" (Unpublished M.A. thesis, Drexell Institute
       of Technology, 1968).

       This is a short biography.

636   Blodgett, John H. and Schultz, C.K. "Herman Hollerith:
       Data Processing Pioneer," American Documentation 20,
       No. 3 (July 1969): 221-226.

       This is a short version of the M.A. thesis and, like
       it, relies on research done in the Hollerith family
       papers.

637   de Beauclair, W. "Herman Hollerith," V.D.I.-Nachrichten
       (February 17, 1960): 6.

       This is a short biography.

638   Engelbourg, S. "From Invention to Innovation: The Half-
       way House of Herman Hollerith," Technikgeschichte
       42 (1975): 26-34.

       This is a good analysis of his business career and
       on his personality. Emphasis is on the years after
       1890, ending in 1911 when his firm became part of
       C-T-R.

639   Feindler, R. Das Hollerith-Lochkarten-Verfahren für
       Maschinelle Buchhaltung und Statistik. Berlin: Ver-
       lag von Reimar Hobbing, 1929.

       This is a textbook on how to use contemporary gear
       developed by Hollerith. It is over 400 pages in
       length and well illustrated, suggesting what Holler-
       ith accomplished.

640   Fisher, A.M. The Hollerith Devices. New York: n.p.,
          1913.

          While primarily a survey of Hollerith's equipment,
          it is a useful, if short, introduction to his work.

641   "Herman Hollerith," American Society of Mechanical
          Engineers Record and Index 3 (1929): 320-321.

          This is an obituary.

642   "Herman Hollerith," Systems and Procedures Journal 14,
          6 (November-December 1963): 18-24.

          This illustrated article reviews his first tabulating
          system and use in the census of 1890. There are
          passing comments on the origins of IBM.

643   Hollerith, Herman. "An Electric Tabulating System,"
          The Quarterly (Columbia School of Mines) 10, No. 3
          (April 1889): 238-255.

          This is Hollerith's own description of his punch
          card equipment and how it could be used for the
          census.

644   Hollerith, V. "Biographical Sketch of Herman Hollerith,"
          Isis 62, No. 1 (1971): 69-78.

          The article was written by his daughter. She focuses
          on how he developed his tabulating system and about
          his trips to Europe to find users.

645   Koon, S.G. "Hollerith Tabulating Machinery in the
          Business Office," Machinery 20 (1913): 25-26.

          While primarily an application brief on the use of
          his devices, along with photographs of these as
          installed at Southern Pacific Railroad, Carnegie
          Steel, Cleveland Electric Illuminating Co., it is
          suggestive of what he sold and to whom.

646   Luebbert, W.F. "Herman Hollerith," in A. Ralston and
          C.L. Meek (eds), Encyclopedia of Computer Science
          (New York: Petrocelli/Charter, 1976): 610-611.

          This biography also defines his historical signifi-
          cance to the data processing industry.

647   Moore, James P. A Life of Francis Amasa Walker. New
          York: Holt, 1923.

          There are passing references to Walker's relations
          to Hollerith.

648   Murphy, L.J. "Herman Hollerith and His Electric Data
          Tabulating System" (Unpublished M.A. thesis, Case
          Institute of Technology, June, 1968).

This is a well documented biography and of his work up to about 1914.

649   Rex, F.J.   "Herman Hollerith, The First 'Statistical Engineer'," Computers and Automation 10, No. 8 (August 1961): 10-13.

This is a brief review of his life and work, complete with a useful bibliography.

650   Takahashi, Y.   "The Invention of the Electrical Census Machines" (In Japanese) Statistical Bulletin of Japan 129-130 (1892): 165-168, 206-211.

This is a translation of an article in English and good evidence of the publicity Hollerith was receiving in many parts of the world.

651   Willcox, W.F.   "Herman Hollerith," Mathematical Tables and Other Aids to Calculation 3 (1948): 6263; reprinted from Dictionary of American Biography 21 (New York, 1944): 415-416.

It pays particular attention to the evolution of his punch card devices.

652   Willcox, W.F.   "John Shaw Billings and Federal Vital Statistics," Journal of the American Statistical Association 21 (1926): 257-266.

This has a short passage on Billing's relations with Hollerith.

Percy E. Ludgate

653   Ludgate, Percy E.   "Automatic Calculating Engines," in E.M. Horsburgh (ed), Napier Tercentenary Celebration: Handbook of the Exhibition (Edinburgh: Royal Society of Edinburgh, 1914): 124-127.

While the focus of this piece is on Babbage and his work, it offers a rare glimpse into Ludgate's own thoughts.

654   Ludgate, Percy E.   "On A Proposed Analytical Machine," Scientific Proceedings of the Royal Dublin Society 12, No. 9 (1909): 77-91.

Written by a lesser-known pioneer of computing of the first decade of the 1900s, this article describes a tape drive calculator.

655   Randell, Brian.   "Ludgate's Analytical Machine of 1909," Computer Journal 14, No. 3 (1971): 317-326.

This is the only serious article to appear on Ludgate's career and work on an analytical machine.

656   Riches, D. An Analysis of Ludgate's Machine Leading to

a Design of a Digital Logarithmic Multiplier.
Swansea: Department of Electrical and Electronic
Engineering, University College, June, 1973.

This 94-page monograph analyzes Ludgate's ideas and
has designs and other illustrations included.

Otto Schaffler

657   Zemanek, H.   "Datenveranbeitung von 100 Jahren: Otto
       Schäffler (1838-1928) ein zu Unrecht vergessener
       österreichischer Pionier der Nachrichten- und Lochk-
       artentechrick," Elektrotech. Maschinenbau 90, 11
       (1973): 543-550.

       This is an illustrated review of Schaffler's life
       and work by a computer scientist.

658   Zemanek, H.   "Otto Schäffler (1838-1928)—Ein vergessen-
       er Österreicher," Jahrb. Österreich Gewerbevereins
       (1974): 71-92.

       This illustrated and well-documented biography
       illustrates how early machines could be programmed
       using a telephone-like switchboard.

659   Zemanek, H.   "Otto Schäffler, Wiener Pionier der Lochk-
       artentechnik," Elektronische Rechenanglagen 12, No.
       3 (1970): 133-134.

       This is on the life and work of Schaffler who paten-
       ted a plugboard in 1895 for controlling punch card
       equipment.

Georg and Edvard Scheutz

660   Anderson, T.   "Första Svenska Räknemaskinen," Daedalus
       (1932): 106-109.

       This reviews the work of Georg Scheutz and of his
       interest in Babbage's machine between 1833 and 1853.
       It covers work done the workshop of J.W.Bergström
       in Stockholm during those years on improved versions
       of Babbage's designs.

661   Archibald, R.C.   "P.G. Scheutz, Publicist, Author, Sci-
       entific Mechanician, and Edvard Scheutz, Engineer—
       Biography and Bibliography," Mathematical Tables
       and Other Aids to Computation 2 (1947): 238-245.

       This is a short biography of the father and son team.
       It is well done and fully annotated with bibliogra-
       phy.

662   Bülow, Ralf.   "The Windmill Computer—An Eyewitness
       Report of the Scheutz Difference Engine," Annals of
       the History of Computing 11, No. 1 (1989): 44.

       Austrian astronomer Edmund Weiss (1837-1917) saw the

Scheutz machine at the Dudley Observatory in 1872 at Albany, New York. His observations are published in English.

663 Haga, E.J. "More About Difference Engines," <u>Journal of Business Education</u> 39, No. 3 (December 1963): 120-121.

This focuses on two Scheutz machines and in their use to calculate and print English life tables. This article has bibliographic references on difference engines in general.

664 Jacob, L. "Le Calcul Mécanique," <u>Encyclopédie Scientifique: Bibliothèque des Mathématiques Appliquees</u>. Paris: Octave Doin et Fils, 1911.

It has a great deal on difference engines, on Scheutz and about Wiberg and Torres y Quevedo.

665 Lindgren, Michael. <u>Glory and Failure: The Difference Engines of Johann Muller, Charles Babbage and Georg and Edvard Scheutz</u>. Linkoping Studies in Arts and Science, 9. Kristianstads Boktryckeri, AB, 1987.

These three machine builders of the 19th century are well reviewed both in terms of the social context in which they worked and their actual technical achievements. It is a major source of material that uses new primary sources for a very well documented study.

666 Lindgren, Michael and Lindquist, S. "Scheutz's First Difference Engine Rediscovered," <u>Technology and Culture</u> 23 (1982): 207-213.

This is a serious study that is well documented.

667 Losano, M.G. "Le radici Europee dell'elaboratore elettronico," <u>Le Scienze</u> 89 (1976): 57-72.

This is an illustrated account of four European contributors to computers involving the work of Leibniz, Pascal, Scheutz and Zuse, with passing commentary on Babbage. The most useful portion covers Scheutz.

668 Losano, M.G. <u>Scheutz: La Macchina alle Differenze</u>. Milan: Etas Libri, 1974.

This series of articles on Scheutz includes translations of original documents on his difference engine. Included is an extensive bibliography by C.F. Bergstedt.

669 Manby, C. <u>Scheutz' Difference Engine and Babbage's Mechanical Notation</u>. London: William Clowes, 1856.

This contains excerpts of meetings held at the

Institution of Civil Engineers during 1855-1856 at
which Babbage talked about his own device and that
of Scheutz.

670   Merzbach, Uta C. George Scheutz and the First Printing
      Calculator. Smithsonian Studies in History and Tech-
      nology, No. 36. Washington, D.C.: Smithsonian Insti-
      tution Press, 1977.

      This is a thorough and competent study of the 19th
      century project complete with illustrations and bib-
      liography.

671   Scheutz, Georg and Scheutz, Edvard. Specimens of Tables
      Calculated, Stereomoulded and Printed by Machinery.
      London: Privately printed, 1857.

      This was one of the first "application briefs" ever
      published describing the use of a difference engine.
      It details the use of their machine of the 1850s.

672   "The Swedish Tabulating Machine of G. and E. Scheutz,"
      Annals of the Dudley Observatory 1 (1866): 116-126.

      This observatory, located in Albany, NY, used a
      Scheutz difference engine for the bulk of the second
      half of the 19th century which is described here.

673   Wiberg, Martin. Tables de Logarithmes Calculées et
      Imprimées au moyen de la Machine à Calculer. Stock-
      holm: n.p., 1876.

      He describes a Scheutz difference engine and its
      printing of logarithms completed in 1874.

674   Williams, F.J. "The Swedish Calculating Machine at the
      General Register Office, Somerset House," British
      Almanac and Companion (London: Knight and Co., 1866):
      5-16.

                    Leonardo Torres y Quevedo

675   d'Ocagne, M. "Torres-Quevedo," Larousse Mensuel 364
      (June 1937): 727-728.

      This obituary notice reviews his work on all manner
      of scientific research, including on computation
      devices and automata. It is substantive, written by
      a technically competent writer.

676   d'Ocagne, M. "Torres-Quevedo et son Oeuvre Mécanique,"
      Revue des Questions Scientifiques (July 20, 1938):
      5-14.

      Although an obituary, this is a detailed review of
      his work, including on analog and digital devices.

677   Homenaje a D. Leonardo Torres Quevedo (1852-1936).

Madrid: Centro de la Informática Técnica y Material
Administrativas, 1977.

This has a 1951 article on Torres by G. Torres
Quevedo Polanca and a 1953 catalog of an exhibition
of the inventor's machines; illustrated.

678   Leonardo Torres Quevedo. Madrid: Colegio de Ingenieros
      de Caminos, Canales y Pertos, 1978.

      This is a short, illustrated account growing out of
      an exhibition of Torres' work. It includes a biogra-
      phy and a bibliography.

679   Rodríguez Alcalde, L. Biografía de D. Leonardo Torres
      Quevedo. Santander: C.S.I.C., 1974.

      This is a biography containing a great deal of infor-
      mation, including illustrations and photographs of
      the inventor and his machines.

680   Rodríguez Alcalde, L. Torres Quevedo y la Cibernética.
      Madrid: Ediciones Cid, 1966.

      This is a fuller treatment of Torres and his work
      than the 1974 publication.

681   Santesmases, José García. Obra é Inventos de Torres
      Quevedo. Madrid: Instituto de España, 1980.

      This is the most detailed, best biography of Torres
      y Quevedo and of his work. For a review in English,
      see Annals of the History of Computing 3, No. 4
      (October 1981): 416-417.

682   "Torres and His Remarkable Automatic Devices," Scienti-
      fic American Supplement 80 (November 6, 1915): 296-
      298.

      This is an illustrated account of his scientific work
      and especially about his chess machine.

683   Torres-Quevedo, G. "Présentation des Appareils de
      Leonardo Torres y Quevedo," Les Machines à Calculer
      et la Pensée Humaine. Coloques Internationales du
      CNRS. Paris, 8-13 Jan. 1951. (Paris: Editions du
      CNRS, 1953): 383-406.

      He describes the machine invented by his father for
      playing chess and for remote control of a boat.

684   Torres-Quevedo, G. Les Travaux de l'Ecole Espagnole sur
      l'Automatisme," Ibid., 361-381.

      This is on the life and work of Torres y Quevedo prior
      to World War I, and particularly regarding an electro-
      mechanical analytical engine.

685   Torres y Quevedo, L. "Arithmomètre Électromécanique,"

Bulletin de la Societe d'Encourangement pur l'Industrie Nationale 119 (September-October 1920): 588-599.

He describes his electromechanical arithmometer. It was an important development of the time for arithmetic calculations, controlled by a typewriter.

686   Torres y Quevedo, Leonardo. "Easais sur l'Automatique. Sa definition. Étendue theorique de ses applications." Revue de l'Academie des Sciences de Madrid (1914); also in Revue Générale des Sciences Pures et Appliquées (November 15, 1915): 601-611.

He discusses digital methods for automatic process control and then describes how a program controlled calculator might work, years ahead of many other designs.

687   Torres y Quevedo, Leonardo. "Ensayos sobre Automatica. Su definición. Extensión teórica de sus aplicaciones," Real Academia de Ciencias Exactas Naturales, Revista 12 (1913): 391-418.

This is the original version of the material presented in citation No. 686.

688   Vigneron, H. "L'Arithmomètre de M. Torres y Quevedo," La Nature (August 7, 1920): 89-93.

This is an illustrated article describing the inventor's typewriter-controlled arithmometer.

689   Vigneron, H. "Les Automates," La Nature (June 13, 1914): 56-61.

This is a short survey done, especially concerning a chess-playing machine.

690   Zamanek, H. "Spanische automaten: Leonardo Torres y Quevedo (1852-1936)," Electron. Rech., 8 No. 6 (1966): 217-218.

This is a short, illustrated article on the inventor and about his electro-mechanical devices and, in particular, about the chess machine and arithmometer.

Martin Wiberg

691   Anderson, T. "Wibergs Räknemaskin," Daedalus (1933): 98-99.

This is a short biography of Martin Wiberg (1826-1905) which also describes his difference machine. The article is based on primary source material.

692   Archibald, R.C. "Martin Wiberg, His Tables and His Difference Engine," Mathematical Tables and Other Aids to Computing 2 (1947): 371-373.

While a biography, and a survey of his work, its focus is primarily on his contributions within the field of mathematics. It does review his efforts to make calculating devices.

693   Delaunay, C.E.   "Rapport sur la Machine à Calculer présentée par M. Wiberg," Comptes Rendus. Academie des Sciences (Paris) 56 (1863): 330-339.

This details the method of finite differences and of Wiberg's device. There are comparisons to those of Babbage and Scheutz.

Census

694   Alterman, Hyman.   Counting People: The Census in History. New York: Harcourt, Brace & World, 1969.

This mentions the introduction of data processing technology to help counting in Europe and in the United States. This is a standard history of census taking.

695   Bertillon, J.   "La Statistique à la Machine," La Nature (September 1, 1894): 218-222.

This is an illustrated description of Hollerith devices used in the 1890 U.S. census. It also has a review of its use in Canada, Austria, Italy, France and Germany.

696   Billings, John S.   "Mechanical Methods Used in Compiling Data of the Eleventh U.S. Census, with Exhibition of A Machine," Proceedings of the American Association for the Advancement of Science, 40th Meeting, Washington 1891 (Salem: American Association for the Advancement of Science, 1891): 407-409.

The author argues that he first suggested the use of punch card technology for the 1880 census and that Hollerith took up the idea and implemented it for the subsequent U.S. census.

697   Cheysson, E.   "La Machine Electrique à Recensement," Journal de la Societe de Statistique de Paris (March 1892): 87-96.

He reviews Hollerith type devices constructed by Schaffler, used in the census taken by Austria. Over 24 million cards were processed in this census alone.

698   Cragg, W.B.   "How Census Data Is Tabulated," Credit Monthly 32 (August 1930): 48-49.

This reviews U.S. census practises with tabulating equipment as employed for the 1920 count and in use for that of 1930.

699   d'Auria, L. et al. "The Hollerith Electric Tabulating

System," <u>Journal of the Franklin Institute</u> 129, No.
4 (April 1890): 300-306.

This is an explanation of Hollerith's equipment,
particularly the tabulator and sorter, and how they
were used in the U.S. census of 1890.

700   Durand, E.D. "Counting Our Population by Machine,"
       <u>Scientific American</u> 69 (February 12, 1910): 108-110.

       This is a review of the use of tabulating machines
       in the U.S. census of 1910.

701   Durand, E.D. "Tabulation by Mechanical Means—Their
       Advantages and Limitations," <u>Transactions of the
       Fifteenth International Congress on Hygiene and
       Demography, Washington, September 23-28, 1912</u>, 6:
       <u>Proceedings of Section 9, Demography</u> (Washington,
       D.C.: U.S. Government Printing Office, 1913): 83-90.

       A great number of facts about card punch technology
       at the U.S. Bureau of the Census is presented, espe-
       cially concerning performance rates, configurations,
       and features of the hardware.

702   Eckler, A. Ross. <u>The Bureau of the Census</u>. New York:
       Praeger, 1972.

       The book recounts the introduction of Hollerith's
       punch card system for use in the census of 1890 as
       part of an overall history of the Bureau.

703   Garrison, Fielding H. <u>John Shaw Billings: A Memoir</u>.
       New York: Putnam, 1915.

       This was written by a U.S. official at the Census
       Bureau. It is an important contemporary publication
       on the role Hollerith's technology played in the
       census of 1890.

704   "Handling of the Census Returns for the Whole United
       States," <u>American Machinist</u> (May 5, 1910): 809-812.

       This is an illustrated account of James Powers' card
       punch and tabulators made at the U.S. Bureau of the
       Census as an effort to improve Hollerith's equipment.

705   Hansen, Morris H. and McPherson, James L. "Potentiali-
       ties and Problems of Electronic Data Processing," in
       Lowell H. Hattery and George P. Bush (eds), <u>Electro-
       nics in Management</u> (Washington, D.C.: The University
       Press of Washington, D.C., 1956): 53-66.

       The authors survey the use of computers at the U.S.
       Bureau of the Census of the 1950s, providing a
       balanced, detailed view of their experience with this
       new technology.

706   Hollerith, Herman. "The Electrical Tabulating Machine,"

Journal of the Royal Statistical Society 57, No. 4
(1894): 678-682.

This is one of the earliest statements by Hollerith
in print on how to use his equipment to conduct an
analysis of a census.

707   Lydenberg, Harry Miller. *John Shaw Billings*. Chicago:
      American Library Association, 1924.

      A biography of a key official in the U.S. Bureau of
      the Census, it is useful for appreciating the early
      use of punch card technology at the agency.

708   Martin, T.C. "Counting a Nation by Electricity,"
      Electrical Engineer 12, No. 184 (November 11, 1891):
      521-530.

      The author describes how Hollerith's equipment was
      used to tabulate the U.S. census of 1890; illustra-
      ted.

709   "Mechanical Tabulation," *Engineering* 74 (August 8,
      1902): 165.

      This is a short review of Hollerith's devices and
      use in the U.S. census of 1890, and later in the
      U.S. agricultural census taken in 1900. His equip-
      ment is compared to those employed in looms and in
      railroad signal interlocking mechanisms.

710   Merriam, W.R. "The Evolution of Modern Census Taking,"
      Century Magazine (April 1903): 831-842.

      An illustrated article, this describes various add-
      ing devices used in the U.S. census of 1880 and of
      the equipment employed in 1900.

711   Munroe, James Phinney. *A Life of Francis Amasa Walker*.
      New York: Holt, 1923.

      This is a biography of the superintendent of the U.S.
      Bureau of the Census in 1880 and contains some
      details on his introduction of technology into the
      Bureau.

712   Newcomb, H.L. "The Development of Mechanical Methods
      of Tabulation in the United States," *Transactions,
      Fifteenth International Congress on Hygiene and
      Demography, Washington, September 23-28, 1912*, 6:
      Proceedings of Section 9, Demography (Washington,
      D.C.: U.S. Government Printing Office, 1913): 73-83.

      This is an excellent and very early complete history
      of Hollerith devices and their role in the U.S.
      census, 1890-1910.

713   Newton, Bernard. *The Economics of Francis Amasa Walker:
      American Economics in Transition*. New York: A.M. Kel-
      ley, 1968.

Walker was the superintendent of the U.S. Bureau of the Census responsible for the 1880 count.

714   "Our Machine-Made Census," Literary Digest 64 (February 28, 1920): 26.

The article describes the use of tabulating equipment for the U.S. census of 1920.

715   Porter, R.P.   "The Eleventh Census," Journal of the American Statistical Society 2, No. 15 (1891): 321-379.

He details the devices and programs of the 1890 census in the U.S.   This is an informative report of the mechanics of collecting and analyzing data from an official of the Census Bureau.

716   Rauchberg, H.   "Die Elektrische Zählmaschine und ibre Anwendung insbesondere bei der Osterreichischen Volkszählung," Allgemeines Statisches Archiv 11 (1892): 78-126.

This is a detailed review of Schaffler's tabulators and their role in the Austrian census of the time.

717   Stewart, J.A.   "Electricity and the Census," Scientific American 122 (January 31, 1920): 109.

Stewart describes the use of tabulating equipment for the U.S. census of 1920.

718   Takahashi, Y. and Shoji, S.   "On the Electrical Tabulating Machines" (In Japanese), Researches of the Electrotechnical Laboratory 146 (1924): 1-13.

This is a translation of Cheysson's article of 1892 (No. 697 above).

719   Truesdell, Leon E.   The Development of Punched Card Tabulation in the Bureau of the Census, 1890-1940. Washington, D.C.: U.S. Government Printing Office, 1965.

This is the most complete study of the subject and the major source on the use of Hollerith and Powers equipment in this U.S. agency, by an employee.

720   Walker, Francis A.   Report to the Secretary of the Interior on the "Temporary Nature of Census Operations" (November 15, 1879). Washington, D.C.: U.S. Government Printing Office, 1879.

The Superintendent of the U.S. Bureau of the Census and also a well-known economist, reports that he would gather data on 215 items (as opposed to 5 in 1870) and that to carry out this task encourages the use of card tabulating equipment for the first time in the taking of a U.S. census.

721   Wright, Carroll. The History and Growth of the United
       States Census. Washington, D.C.: U.S. Government
       Printing Office, 1900.

       There is a great deal of contemporary information on
       Hollerith's technology as used in U.S. census-taking.

               Punch Card Applications (1880s-1930s)

722   Applied Mechanical Arithmetic: As Practised on the
       Controlled Key Comptometer Adding and Calculating
       Machine. Chicago: Felt & Tarrant Manufacturing
       Company, 1920.

       This is a user guide over over 600-pages for the
       application of Duplex-Key-Controlled Comptometers in
       business. It also has illustrations and makes this
       volume a good source on both applications in general
       and on Felt's equipment for the early years of the
       1900s.

723   Berkeley, Edmund C. "Boolean Algebra (The Technique
       for Manipulating "And," "or," "Not," and Conditions)
       and Applications to Insurance," Record of the Ameri-
       can Institute of Actuaries 26 (October 1937): 373-
       414.

       He describes an early use of such algebra with a
       logic-truth calculator approach, suggestive of how
       far the use of punch card technology had come by the
       mid-1930s.

724   Billings, John S. "On Some Forms of Tables of Vital
       Statistics. With Special Reference to the Need of
       the Health Department of a City," Public Health
       Papers and Reports, American Public Health Associa-
       tion 13 (1887): 203-221.

       He discusses punch card layout conventions using
       Hollerith's equipment. It is one of the first arti-
       cles to appear on the use of such technology. The
       author was a highly regarded statistician.

725   Campos, F.P. Applications Mécano-Comptables des Machines
       à Totalisateurs Multiples. Paris: Etienne Chiron,
       1944.

       This describes 18 ways of using the Logabox bookkeep-
       ing machine, drawn primarily from accounting and
       banking applications. Some simultaneous linear equa-
       tions are also illustrated along with harmonic analysis
       applications.

726   Comrie, Leslie J. "Computing by Calculating Machines,"
       Accountants Journal 45 (1927): 42-51.

       He reviews various calculating methods, such as
       "short-cutting," that used machine available in the
       British office appliance market.

727   Comrie, Leslie J. "Scientific Applications of the
       National Accounting Machine," Supplement to the
       Journal of the Royal Statistical Society 3, No. 2
       (1936).

       The author managed the British agency that used the
       National Accounting Machine to do mechanical forms
       of scientific calculations, most importantly, in
       doing calculations associated with the movements of
       the moon.

728   Eastwood, Robert Parker. Sales Control by Quantitative
       Methods. New York: Columbia University Press, 1940.

       In the early decades of the 20th century, quantita-
       tive methods were applied to all manner of business
       activity. In part, punch card machines and calcula-
       tors made that possible.

729   Eckert, Wallace J. Punched Card Methods in Scientific
       Computation. New York: T.J. Watson Astronomical
       Computing Bureau, Columbia University, 1940; Reprint-
       ed by MIT Press, 1984.

       This is a major application brief for punch card
       applications in science, written by an expert who
       was supported by IBM. He describes the technology
       and then gives special emphasis to astronomical uses.

730   Eckert, Wallace J. "The Role of the Punched Card in
       Scientific Computation," Proceedings of the Indus-
       trial Computation Seminar, September 1950 (New York:
       IBM Corporation, 1951): 13-17.

       This is a short account using examples of uses of
       punch card technology from IBM at Columbia University
       in the period 1928-1950.

731   Edwards, W.E. "The Story of the Locking Frame," The
       Railway Magazine (March 1911): 199-213.

       This illustrated article surveys the development and
       use of an interlocking mechanism to control sequences
       of railroad signal settings.

732   "The Electrical Tabulating Machine Applied to Cost
       Accounting," American Machinist 25 (August 16,
       1902): 1073-1075.

       Using Hollerith's key punch and tabulator, this is an
       early example of cost accounting done by mechanical
       means at a time when cost accounting was becoming a
       normal accounting process in American industry.

733   Elliott-Fisher Company. Bookkeeping by Machinery; A
       Text Book for the Guidance of the Novice or Expert.
       Harrisburg, Pa.: Elliott-Fisher Co., 1916; Revised
       ed., 1918.

While this volume surveys the use of bookkeeping
machinery and not punch card equipment, the applications it describes were also being implemented on
Hollerith and Powers products. This volume is
massive in detail, over 1,100 pages in length.

734   Gaines, M.W.   "Tabulating-Machine Cost-Accounting for
      Factories of Diversified Product," Engineering
      Magazine 3 (December 1905): 364-373.

      In the first two decades of the 20th century, this
      became an important application of punch card devices
      and, by the end of the 1930s, standard in most large
      corporations.

735   Goddard, A.   "Putting the Payroll On An Automatic Bases,"
      Scientific American 123 (September 18, 1920): 275.

      The author describes the use of tabulating equipment
      to do payroll and gives a very early explanation of
      the justification for such automation.

736   "J. Rayden Pierce IBM Engineer Dies Suddenly," Business
      Machines 15, No. 2 (January 12, 1933): 1.

      This is an obituary of an IBM engineer of the 1920s
      and 1930s who had developed a series of inventions
      for mechanical accounting.

737   Jordan, George.   "A Survey of Punched Card Development"
      (Unpublished M.A. Thesis, MIT, School of Industrial
      Management, 1956).

      This is a history of punch card equipment from 1880
      to 1950 with particular emphasis on the period 1930-
      1940. It is a major source on applications and
      bibliography.

738   Maul, M.   "Die Elektrischen Lochkarten-Maschinen,"
      Elektrolechnische Zeitschrift 48 (1927): 1789-1794.

      It reviews, in part, the development of punch card
      devices since 1890 down to the 1920s.

739   McCormack, H.S.   "Keeping Books by Machine: The Punched
      Card As A Saver of Brain Energy," Scientific Ameri-
      can 108 (March 1, 1913): 194-195.

      This is a short, early brief on accounting applica-
      tions in the United States and their justification.

740   "The Mechanical Accountant," Engineering 74 (December
      26, 1902): 840-841.

      This early publication describes tabulating machines
      and their use in calculating and managing statistics.

741   Nagler, J.W.   "In Memoriam Gustav Tauschek," Blätter
      für Technikgeschichte 26 (1966): 1-14.

    Tauschek was an engineer who built punch card equip-
ment for both European and American firms in the
1920s and 1930s, including for IBM.

742   The Pierce Automatic Accounting Machines. Woonsocket,
    R.I.: Pierce Accounting Machine Co., 1910 (?).

    This is a sales brochure describing card perfora-
tors, cash registers, and other office appliances
capable of priting and punching simultaneously.

743   Scheyer, E. "When Perforated Paper Goes to Work: How
    Strips of Paper Can Endow Inanimate Machines with
    Brains of Their Own," Scientific American 127 (Dec-
    ember 1922): 394-395, 445.

    He argues that Jacquard mechanisms can help automate
manufacturing applications, e.g., in cutting out
cloth. The use of such technology was a rival to
punch cards and even in the late 1980s was still the
basis of much machine instructed activities.

744   Seward, H. "Mechanical Aids in Factory-Office Economy,"
    Engineering Magazine 27 (July 1904): 605-625.

    This was typical of many such publications that began
to appear at the turn of the century on the use of
office equipment to do accounting or manufacturing
(shop floor) applications.

745   Shaw, Arch Wilkinson. An Approach to Business Problems.
    Cambridge, Mass.: Harvard University Press, 1916,
    1926.

    Accounting practises were undergoing many signifi-
cant changes in the first two decades of the 20th
century. This book surveys some of those and how
managers were responding to these.

746   Snedecor, C.W. "Uses of Punched Card Equipment in
    Mathematics," American Mathematics Monthly 35 (1928):
    161-169.

    This is a short review of sorters and calculators in
use for statistical work.

747   "Tabulating Statistics and Accounts By Machinery,"
    Electrical Railway Journal 41 (May 10, 1913): 853-
    854.

    This short article describes how Hollerith equipment
was used by the Portland Railway, Light and Power
Company to do accounting and statistical work. This
represented one of the earliest commercial users of
Hollerith's equipment.

748   Tauschek, G. Die Lochkarten-Buchhaltung-maschinen mein-
    es Systems. Vienna: n.p., 1930.

This describes a bookkeeping system employing punch-
es, sorters, collators and tabulators during the
1920s.

749   Thompson, H.A.   Joint Man/Machine Decisions: The Phase
      Beyond Data Processing and Operations Research.
      Cleveland: Systems and Procedures Association, 1965.

      Pages 103-105 discuss a railway signal machine called
      the Saxby and Farmer Machine, first made in the
      1850s.   The author refers to it as "non-numeric,
      symbolic logic simulator" device employing Boolean
      logic.

750   U.S. War Department.   The Medical Department of the
      United States Army in the World War, 15: Statistics,
      Part 1, Army Anthropology.   Washington, D.C.: U.S.
      War Department, 1921.

      This surveys activities during World War I, including
      the use of Hollerith devices to establish the sizes
      of men for sewing uniforms, along with other appli-
      cations.

751   "Wanted: An Electric Nerve-Saver," Literary Digest 48
      (June 20, 1914): 1484-1485.

      This describes developments and uses of card punch
      equipment.

752   Williams, N.   "Les Machines à Calculer et à Classer
      Hollerith et leur Emploi dans la Comptabilité des
      Chemins de Fer," Génie Civil 61 (May 18, 1912): 57.

      The author describes the use of Hollerith equipment
      by American railroads.

753   Woodruff, L.F.   "A System of Electric Remote-Control
      Accounting," Transactions of the IEEE 57 (February
      1938): 78-87.

      This provides a description of a system in a depart-
      ment store using terminals, telephone lines, and
      tabulators in the 1930s.   Perhaps this was the first
      use of on-line applications.

Research and Development

754   Boys, C.V.   "A New Analytical Machine," Nature 81
      (July 1, 1909): 14, 15.

      This surveys Ludgate's proposal for a tape driven
      calculator.

755   Church, R.   Review of L.E. Sadovskii, "Topics From The
      History of the Development of Mechanical Mathematics
      in Russia," Mathematical Reviews 12, No. 2 (1951): 69.

      This concentrates on the efforts of Tchebichef on a

device having automatic multiplication and division
developed in 1881. It also reviews an Odhner wheel
of about 1878. Other machines are mentioned intended
for analogue work developed during the same period.

756   Clark, R. et al. Somerset Anthology. Ed. by P. Lovell
      (York: Sessions, 1975): 96-102.

      This is the discussion of a device that composes
      Latin hexameter verses made by John Clark (1785-1852)
      and shown in London in 1845 called "The Eureka."
      Babbage said of the man: "He was as great a curiosity
      as his machine." It has a photograph of the device.

757   Eccles, W.H. and Jordan, F.W. "A Trigger Relay Utili-
      zing Three-Electrode Thermionic Vacuum Tubes," The
      Radio Review 1 (1919): 143-146.

      This is one of the earliest papers to discuss a relay
      system driven by electrical impulses causing "great
      changes . . . in its electrical equilibrium, and
      then remains in the new condition until re-set." That
      became the basis of the use of electrical impulses
      in computers decades later.

758   Hudson, T.C. "Nautical Almanac Office Anti-Differencing
      Machine," in E.M. Horsburgh (ed), Napier Tercentenary
      Celebration: Handbook of the Exhibition (Edinburgh:
      Royal Society of Edinburgh, 1914): 127-131.

      This illustrated article is on a difference engine
      based on a Burroughs adding machine prototype.

759   Jevons, W.S. "On the Mechanical Performance of Logical
      Inference," Philosophical Transactions of the Royal
      Society (London) 16, No. 2 (1870): 497-518.

      This offers details on a mechanical device to evalu-
      ate Boolean logic up to four forms.

760   Ketner, Kenneth L. "The Early History of Computer
      Design: Charles Sanders Peirce and Marquand's Logical
      Machines," Princeton University Library Chronicle 45,
      No. 3 (1984): 186-211.

      While the case is overstated on computer design, the
      article does provide useful material on two important
      scientists working on logic machines.

761   Marquand, Allan. "A New Logical Machine," Proceedings
      of the American Academy of Arts and Sciences 21
      (1886): 303-307; Reprinted in Princeton University
      Library Chronicle 45, No. 3 (1984): 213-217.

      Marquand was an important 19th century designer of
      logic machines; this was one of his more important
      articles on the subject.

762   Pastore, Annibale. Logica Formale: dedotta della
       considerazione di modelli meccanici. Turin: Bocca,
       1906.

       This book describes a logic machine the author
       invented in 1903 which could represent 256 syllogisms
       expressed on the machine.

763   Peirce, Charles Sanders. "Logic Machines," American
       Journal of Psychology 1 (1887): 165-170; Reprinted
       in Princeton University Library Chronicle 45, No. 3
       (1984): 219-224.

       This was an important article by a designer of logic
       machines in 19th century America.

764   Suplee, H.H. "The Principle of Reversal: A Suggestion
       for Inventors," Scientific American 109 (November
       1, 1913): 344.

       He focuses on music boxes, pianolas, looms, etc.,
       involving a way of recording actions that need to be
       recreated. He suggests how this can be done using
       one master record.

765   Tee, Garry J. "The Early History of Computing," Search
       18 (September-October-November-December 1987): 234-
       236, 292-295.

       This surveys the research of Babbage, Hollerith,
       Comrie, about analog devices, Zuse, cryptology,
       Turing, Colossus, ENIAC, and EDVAC.

766   Thomson, Sir William (Lord Kevin). "On an Integrating
       Machine Having a New Kinematic Principle," Proceed-
       ings of the Royal Society 24 (February 1876): 262-
       275.

       This technical description is of a device to solve
       differential equations; it was designed, not built.

Slide Rule

767   Cajori, F. A History of the Logarithmic Slide Rule.
       London: Constable, 1909.

       This is a reliable history of the conventional slide
       rule with details on many of its late 19th century
       variants.

768   Cajori, F. "Notes on the History of the Slide Rule,"
       American Mathematical Monthly 25 (1908): 1-5.

       This carrier on the same theme explored in his book.

769   Cajori, F. William Oughtred—A Great 17th Century
       Teacher of Mathematics. Chicago: Open Court Publi-
       shing Co., 1916.

       This biography is of a proponent of the slide rule.

770   Fuller, G.   A New Calculating Slide Rule Equivalent to
      a Straight Slide Ule 83 Feet 4 Inches Long.   London:
      n.p., 1879.

      The period of the 1870s and 1880s saw many new slide
      rules introduced.   This documents one of hundreds that
      were built.

771   Garvan, A.N.B.   "The Slide Rule and the Sector," Proceed-
      ings of the 10th International Congress of the History
      of Science (1962): 397-399.

      This is a very brief history of the subject; almost
      useless.

772   Thompson, J.E.   The Standard Manual of the Slide Rule.
      New York: Van Nostrand Co., 1952.

      This is a user's guide for the slide rule, one of the
      most popular aids to computations in the U.S. and
      Europe from the 1880s to the 1970s.

                          Typewriter

773   Adler, M.H.   The Writing Machine—A History of the
      Typewriter.   London: George Allen and Unwid, Ltd.,
      1973.

      This is a general, useful history of the typewriter.
      It came into use during the 1870s and was a common
      feature of major offices by World War I.

774   Beattie, H.S. and Rahenkamp, R.A.   "IBM Typewriter
      Innovation." IBM Journal of Research and Development
      25, No. 5 (September 1981): 729-739.

      This article begins with pre-IBM typewriters then
      focuses on post-1933 developments down to 1980.   A
      clear discussion of the technology that went into
      the IBM Selectric is presented with illustrations.
      This machine was frequently used as a console by
      various computer manufacturers in the 1960s, inclu-
      ding IBM and Honeywell.

775   Beeching, W.A.   Century of the Typewriter.   New York:
      St. Martin's Press, 1974.

      Like Adler's book, this is a good introductory history
      of the typewriter.

776   Blanchard, Carroll H., Jr.   The Early Word Processors.
      Research Report 3.   Lake George, N.Y.: State Univer-
      sity at Farmingdale Educators Project IV, 1981.

      This is a very detailed, highly illustrated compen-
      dium of early typewriters and their technology,
      from the 1860s down to 1925.   It reproduces many
      advertisements and marketing brochure-text of the
      period.

777   Bliven, Bruce, Jr. The Wonderful Writing Machine. New
        York: Random House, 1954.

        This has some material on pre-electronic typewriters
        not found in Adler or Beeching.

778   "Carbon Paper After 150 Years," The Office Magazine 76
        (1972): 124-125.

        This is a short history that also includes some
        material on other typewriter supplies in passing.

779   Engler, George Nichols. "The Typewriter Industry: The
        Impact of a Significant Technological Innovation"
        (Unpublished Ph.D. dissertation, University of Cali-
        fornia at Los Angeles, 1969).

        This is the only full study of the subject. Essen-
        tially an economic analysis covering the period from
        the 1870s to the 1960s in the U.S., it surveys the
        major suppliers and analyzes market conditions.

780   History of the Typewriter. Detroit: Metropolitan Type-
        writer Co., 1923.

        This is a brief overview of the types of machines
        made from the late 1870s to the early 1920s.

781   Tolley, William P. Smith-Corona Typewriters and H.W.
        Smith. New York: Newcomen Society in North America,
        1951.

        This is a history of the company from the 1920s to
        1950 and contains comments on early typewriters.

782   U.S. Department of Labor, Bureau of Labor Statistics.
        Industrial Survey in Selected Industries in the
        United States, 1919. Washington, D.C.: U.S. Govern-
        ment Printing Office, May, 1920.

        Pages 487-509 reproduce tables of salaries for manu-
        facturing jobs across the U.S. in typewriter compa-
        nies, for adding machines and cash registers, for
        male and female workers.

783   Wittwer, B.W. "A History of the Development of the IBM
        SELECTRIC," Paper No. 63-MD-11-a. New York: American
        Society of Mechanical Engineers, 1963.

        This covers the period 1933-1963 and IBM's most popu-
        lar typewriter.

784   Zellers, John A. The Typewriter: A Short History, On
        Its 75th Anniversary, 1873-1948. New York: Newcomen
        Society of England, 1948.

        This offers considerable coverage of the role played
        by Remington Rand; the author was a vice president
        of that company.

Wizard of Oz

785   Baum, L. Frank. The Wizard of OZ. Ed. by Michael
       Patrick Hearn. New York: Schocken Books, 1983.

       This is a reproduction of the original 1900 book
       with a biography of the author and historical essays
       on his work.

786   Baum, Frank Joslyn and MacFall, Russell P. To Please
       A Child. Chicago: Reilly & Lee, 1961.

       This is a biography of L. Frank Baum; one of the
       co-authors was his eldest son.

787   Eyles, Allen. The World of OZ. Tucson, Ariz.: HP
       Books, 1985.

       This is a beautifully illustrated history of OZ:
       plays, stories, and movies.

788   Gardner, Martin and Nye, Russel B. The Wizard of OZ
       and Who He Was. East Lansing: Michigan State Univer-
       sity Press, 1957.

       This is a serious study of the literature and movies
       of OZ.

789   Greene, David L. and Martin, Dick. The OZ Scrapbook.
       Random House, 1977.

       This details the iconography of OZ and Ozian arti-
       facts; well illustrated.

790   Greene, Douglas G. and Hearn, Michael Patrick. W.W.
       Denslow. Mt. Pleasant, Mich.: Central Michigan
       University, 1976.

       Denslow was the original illustrator of the OZ books.

791   Hanff, Peter E. and Greene, Douglas G. Bibliographia
       Oziana. Kinderhook, Ill.: The International Wizard
       of OZ Club, 1976.

       This is the only extensive bibliography on the
       subject and includes material on Baum's successors.

792   Hearn, Michael Patrick. The Annotated Wizard of OZ.
       New York: Clarkson N. Potter, 1973.

       This reproduces early drawings by W.W. Denslow and
       includes a biography of L. Frank Baum with biblio-
       graphy.

793   Snow, Jack. Who's Who in OZ. Chicago: Reilly & Lee,
       1954.

       Reviews more than 630 Ozian characters in 39 books;
       includes biographies of OZ authors and illustrators.

4

Between Two World Wars

The period between the two world wars was marked by two
fundamental events in the history of computing and data processing. First, there was wide acceptance and use of punch
cards and other office equipment by government agencies and
commercial enterprises on both sides of the Atlantic. That
development, in turn, led to continued expansion of the office
appliance industry. Second, differential analyzers and other
analog devices were constructed, which encouraged additional
work on mechanical computing. Concurrently, mathematicians
and engineers worked out the theoretical underpinnings of
information theory to a point where projects could be started
leading to the construction of the first digital computers
during World War II.

This chapter organizes materials around those themes.
Headings include key scientists, punch card applications,
types of equipment and technologies, and institutional histories. As in the previous chapter, both contemporaneous and
monographic materials are listed when they contribute to an
understanding of the history of both the technology and its
nascent industries. For the first time, a particular technology was widely used enough to make it necessary to have sections on its applications. Punch cards, in effect, gave
thousands of users their first exposure to the kind of information processing that later evolved into computer systems.
Thus considerable attention has been paid to including contemporary articles and books dealing with what those devices were
used for on both sides of the Atlantic. Although this chapter
focuses on the interwar period, materials on punch cards
during the late 1940s and early 1950s were also included to
round out the subject.

Serious historical attention has focused more on particular scientists and their machines, such as on Vannevar Bush
(1890-1974) and Douglas R. Hartree (1897-1958), than on a
particular class of machines. Yet to be examined fully are
the uses of punch card equipment, network analyzers, calculating and adding machines (particularly in business), and
company histories. Exceptions include John V. Atanasoff
(1903-   ), Bush, and cryptoanalysis. If we know little of
American developments during the interwar period, that is
even truer for Europe, Japan, and Latin America.

Analog Calculators

794   Booth, Andrew D.   "Two Calculating Machines for X-Ray
       Crystal Structure Analyses," Journal of Applied
       Physics 18 (July 1947): 664-666.

       This describes the use of an analog type device
       first perfected during World War II based on a plan-
       imeter mechanism. The second machine he describes
       had a digital counter.

795   Dietzold, Robert L.   "The Isograph—A Mechanical Root-
       Finder," Bell Laboratories Record 16, No. 4 (Decem-
       ber 1937): 130-134.

       The author describes an analog calculating machine
       used to do algebraic calculations at Bell Laborator-
       ies in the 1930s.

796   Duncan, W.J.   "Some Devices for the Solution of Large
       Sets of Simultaneous Linear Equations," London,
       Edinburgh, and Dublin Philosophical Magazine and
       Journal of Science 35, Series 7 (1944): 660-670.

       Duncan surveys an analog computing machine used in
       Europe and in the U.S. to do algebraic calculations
       in the 1930s.

797   Frame, J. Sutherland.   "Machines for Solving Algebraic
       Equations," Mathematical Tables and Other Aids to
       Computation 1, No. 9 (January 1945): 337-353.

       Frame reviews analog devices built in the early
       1940s and growing out of projects from the 1930s.

798   Hart, H.C. and Travis, Irven.   "Mechanical Solution of
       Algebraic Equations," Journal of the Franklin Insti-
       tute 225 (January 1938): 63-72.

       This technical paper reviews how an analog calculator
       could be used in the 1930s to do algebra just before
       the dawn of the digital computer.

799   Herr, D.L. and Graham, R.S.   "An Electrical Algebraic
       Equation Solver," Review of Scientific Instruments
       9 (October 1938): 310-315.

       The decade of the 1930s saw considerable work done
       with analog computers, particularly in their appli-
       cation to higher mathematics. This article reflects
       that activity.

800   Mallock, R.R.M.   "An Electrical Calculating Machine,"
       Proceedings of the Royal Society, Series A, No. 140
       (1933): 457-483.

       Mallock's detailed technical description of an ana-
       log calculator showed how his machine could solve 10
       linear simultaneous equations in 10 unknowns.

801   Mercner, R.O. "The Mechanism of the Isograph," Bell
       Laboratories Record 16, No. 4 (December 1937): 135-
       140.

       This device, an analog calculator, was used for
       research at Bell Labs. The article is a useful
       description of an isograph, a device used to do
       algebra mechanically.

802   Stibitz, George R. "Electric Rost-Finder," Mathematical
       Tables and Other Aids to Computation 3, No. 24 (Octo-
       ber 1948): 328-329.

       This giant of early computing at Bell Labs discusses
       his use of an analog computer (really a calculator)
       in the 1940s to do algebraic functions.

803   Tomayko, James E. "Helmut Hoelzer's Fully Electronic
       Analog Computer," Annals of the History of Computing
       7, No. 3 (July 1985): 227-240.

       This is a history of a German machine built in 1941,
       based on Hoelzer's earlier work, and was used with
       the A-4 rocket; illustrated.

804   Weiss, Eric A. "The Number 2-B Regrettor: A 1937
       Engineering Parody That Foreshadowed Thinking Machin-
       es," Annals of the History of Computing 7, No. 2
       (April 1985): 167-176.

       This is an illustrated spoof on computing in the
       late 1930s.

805   Wilbur, J.B. "The Mechanical Solution of Simultaneous
       Equations," Journal of the Franklin Institute 222
       (December 1936): 715-724.

       He shows how to use an analog calculator to solve up
       to 9 simultaneous equations in the 1930s.

                        John V. Atanasoff

806   Atanasoff, John Vincent. "Advent of Electronic Digital
       Computing," Annals of the History of Computing 6,
       No. 3 (July 1984): 229-282.

       This is his most detailed account of his own work
       during the 1930s especially; illustrated.

807   Atanasoff, John Vincent. "Atanasoff Recalls Early Days
       of Computers," SIAM News (May 1984): 7-8.

       This has the same theme as the previous citation; it
       defends his claim to being the earliest developer of
       the digital computer.

808   Atanasoff, John Vincent. "Computing Machine for the
       Solution of Large Systems of Linear Algebraic
       Equations," (unpublished memorandum, Iowa State

College, Ames, Iowa (August 1940); Reprinted in B. Randell, _The Origins of Digital Computers: Selected Papers_ (Berlin: Springer-Verlag, 1982): 315-335.

This is an illustrated description of his machine and about the research that went into it. It accounts for the use of binary registers, add/subtract mechanism, and the decimal/binary converter.

809   Atanasoff, John Vincent. _From One Dr. John Vincent Atanasoff_. New York: Phoenix/BFA, 1984.

This is a 28-minute film; his anecdotes and views about the role he played in the development of the digital computer.

810   Berry, Clifford E. "Design of Electrical Data Recording and Reading Mechanism" (Unpublished M.S. thesis, Iowa State College, 1941).

Berry was Atanasoff's graduate student when he was working on the ABC machine in the late 1930s and early 1940s. The thesis was a byproduct of some of that work.

811   Burks, Alice R. and Burks, Arthur W. _The First Electronic Computer: The Atanasoff Story_. Ann Arbor: University of Michigan Press, 1988.

This is a major review of Atanasoff that argues in favor of his significant contribution to the development of the digital computer.

812   David, H.A. and David, H.T. (eds). _Statistics: An Appraisal. Proceedings of a Conference Marking the 50th Anniversary of the Statistical Laboratory, Iowa State University, June 13-15, 1983_. Ames: Iowa State University Press, 1984.

This contains several papers which discuss the use of data processing technologies there from the 1930s to the present.

813   Gardner, W. David. "The Independent Inventor," _Datamation_ 28, No. 10 (September 1982): 12-22.

This is an interview with Atanasoff which focuses on his role in the development of the digital computer.

814   Gross, George L. "Approximate Solution of Linear Differential Equations" (Unpublished M.S. thesis, Iowa State College, 1937).

This was written by a student of Atanasoff at the exact time he was working on the design of the ABC machine. This paper influenced the logic design of the device.

815   Kern, J.L.   _The Development of Computer Science at Iowa_

State University. Report ERI-342, Engineering
Research Institute. Ames: Iowa State University,
1968.

This contains data on the early use of punch card
technology, then on the beginnings of computer
research by Atanasoff and others as far back as the
1920s, then carries the story into the period of the
electronic computer.

816   Mackintosh, Allan R.   "Dr. Atanasoff's Computer,"   Scien-
      tific American 259, No. 2 (August 1988): 90-96.

      This is a brief, but competent survey of the subject.

817   Mackintosh, Allan R.   "The First Electronic Computer,"
      Physics Today 40, No. 3 (March 1987): 25-32.

      He argues that Atanasoff was the first, not the ENIAC
      team.

818   Mollenhoff, Clark R.   Atanasoff: Forgotten Father of the
      Computer. Ames: Iowa State University Press, 1988.

      The author (journalist/lawyer) argues that Atanasoff
      developed the initial ideas for the digital computer.
      This is a well-rounded biography, not just a history
      of a computer.

819   Mollenhoff, Georgia.   "John Vincent Atanasoff," in A.
      Ralston and C.L. Meek (eds), Encyclopedia of Computer
      Science (New York: Petrocelli/Charter, 1976): 136-137.

      This is an illustrated biography of the computer
      scientists that also defines the historical signifi-
      cance of his work.

820   Mollenhoff, Georgia.   "John V. Atanasoff, DP Pioneer,"
      ComputerWorld 8 (March 13, 1974), pp. 1, 13; (March
      20, 1974), pp. 15-16; (March 27, 1974), pp. 9-10.

      This is an account of his life and work based on
      interviews with the computer scientist.

821   Silag, William.   "The Invention of the Electronic Digi-
      tal Computer at Iowa State College, 1930-1942," The
      Palimpsest 65 (September-October 1984): 150-164, 173.

      This was published by the Iowa State Historical
      and unhesitatingly takes Atanasoff's side in the
      debate over who developed the digital computer.

822   Stewart, Robert M.   "The End of the ABC," Annals of the
      History of Computing 6, No. 3 (July 1984): 317.

      Says it was junked in 1948 by the author who, at that
      time, did not realize its historical significance.

823   Stern, Nancy.   "Who Invented the First Electronic

Digital Computers," <u>Abacus</u> 1, No. 1 (Fall 1983): 7-15.

She argues that Atanasoff did not and that the team that put together the ENIAC did.

824   Turner, Judith Axler. "Almost Half a Century Later, the Father of the Computer Gets a Celebration," <u>Chronicle of Higher Education</u> 27, No. 8 (October 18, 1983): 17.

This includes an interview. The DP industry also noted the celebration; see Robert M. Stewart, "John Vincent Atanasoff Celebration." <u>Annals of the History of Computing</u> 6, No. 3 (1984): 313-315.

825   Zemanek, H. "John Vincent Atanasoff: Ein Amerikanischer Computer-Pionier Bulgarischer Abstammung," <u>Elektron. Rech.</u> 16, No. 3 (1974): 91-92.

This brief article is one of the first to recognize that Atanasoff had played an important role in the development of the computer.

Vannevar Bush

826   "All the Answers at Your Fingertips; In the Laboratory of M.I.T.," <u>Popular Mechanics</u> 85 (March 1946): 164-167.

This has a description of the second differential analyzer built at MIT by Bush.

827   Bush, Vannevar. "The Differential Analyzer: A New Machine for Solving Equations," <u>Journal of the Franklin Institute</u> 212 (October 1931): 447-488.

This is a major statement by Bush on his work at MIT in the late 1920s to develop an analog device to solve problems in electrical engineering.

828   Bush, Vannevar. "Instrumental Analysis," <u>Bulletin of the American Mathematical Society</u> 142 (1936): 649-669.

He surveys available calculating devices, some digital and others analogue. He suggests a control unit attached to a conventional punch card device to address some of the function proposed by Babbage.

829   Bush, Vannevar. <u>Pieces of the Action</u>. New York: William Morrow, 1970.

These are his memoirs, the man who built sigificant differential analyzers in the 1930s and served as an important advisor to the U.S. Government in subsequent decades.

830   Bush, Vannevar and Caldwell, S.H. "A New Type of

Differential Analyzer," <u>Journal of the Franklin Institute</u> 240 (1945): 255-326.

This is about a faster machine for programming a differential analyzer available at MIT in 1942 than was previously in operation there.

831   Bush, Vannevar and Caldwell, S.H. "Thomas-Fermi Equation Solution by the Differential Analyzer," <u>Physical Review</u> 38, No. 10 (1931): 1898-1902.

This is one of the earliest papers by Bush on research done at MIT on the Difference Analyzer, an early analogue calculator.

832   Bush, Vannevar and Hazen, H.L. "Integraph Solution of Differential Equations," <u>Journal of the Franklin Institute</u> 204 (1927): 575-615.

They describe a device that could solve second order differential analyzers they were building.

833   Bush, Vannevar <u>et al</u>. "A Continuous Integraph," <u>Journal of the Franklin Institute</u> 203 (1927): 63-84.

He describes work on a device at MIT that could solve integral equation problems. It was, like all his other machines, an analogue creation.

834   Caldwell, Samuel H. "Educated Machinery," <u>Technology Review</u> 48, No. 1 (1945): 31-34.

This describes the second differential analyzer at MIT that he and Bush worked on together.

835   Genet, N. "100-Ton Brain at M.I.T.," <u>Scholastic</u> 48 (February 4, 1946): 36.

The article describes the second differential analyzer then at MIT and which grew out of Bush's work of the 1930s.

836   Gleiser, Molly. "Analog Inventor," <u>Datamation</u> 26, No. 10 (October 1980): 141-143.

This is a light biography of Bush and review of his work; includes four photographs.

837   "The Great Electro-Mechanical Brain; M.I.T.'s Differential Analyzer," <u>Life</u> 20 (January 14, 1946): 73-74.

The public was exposed to a number of "computers" in 1945-1946 of which this was one of the more famous. This is a non-technical description of Bush's machine.

838   Hartree, Douglas R. "The Bush Differential Analyzer and Its Applications," <u>Nature</u> 146 (1940): 319-323.

He reviews the machine and possible uses in mathematics.

839   Hartree, Douglas R. "A Great Calculating Machine: The
       Bush Differential Analyser and Its Applications in
       Science and Industry," Proceedings of the Royal
       Institution of Great Britain 31 (1940): 151-170.

       This important computer scientist wrote one of the
       first application briefs for an analog device, in
       this case, for MIT's differential analyzer of the
       1930s.

840   "Mathematical Machine; New Electronic Analyzer," Science
       News Letter 48 (November 10, 1945): 291.

       This is a brief description of the second differen-
       tial analyzer at MIT.

841   "M.I.T.'s 100-Ton Mathematical Brain is Now to Tackle
       Problems of Peace," Popular Science 148 (January
       1946): 81.

       This is a brief description of MIT's second differen-
       tial analyzer. Like many other computer/calculator
       projects not publicized during the Second World War,
       this one received considerable attention.

842   Owens, Larry. "Vannevar Bush and the Differential
       Analyzer: The Text and Context of An Early Computer,"
       Technology and Culture 27, No. 1 (January 1986): 63-
       95.

       The author presents a well-researched account of early
       analog computing, in particular Bush's, covering the
       period of the 1920s-1930s.

843   Radford, W.H. Report on Investigation of the Practica-
       bility of Developing A Rapid Computing Machine.
       Cambridge, Mass.: MIT, 1939.

       This reports on one year's work funded by NCR to work
       on a machine proposed by Bush. This 98-page report
       offers a highly detailed and illustrated account of
       the work done by him.

844   "Robot Einstein: Differential Analyzer at M.I.T.,"
       Newsweek 26 (November 12, 1945): 93.

       This offers a non-technical description of MIT's
       analog machine, as designed and built by Bush.

845   Shannon, C. "Mathematical Theory of the Differential
       Analyzer," Journal of Mathematics and Physics 20
       (1941): 337-354.

       This is a good survey of Bush's work during the
       1930s and the results of it.

                            Calculators

846   Apraxine, N. "Machine à Calculer mue Électriquement,"

Comptes Rendus de Academie des Sciences (Paris) 195
(November 1932): 857-858.

This briefly reviews of an accumulator with multiple
decimal digits, using electromechanical relays.

847   Benge, Eugene Jackson. Cutting Clerical Costs. New
        York: McGraw Hill Book Co., 1931.

        This is a useful survey of office applications for
        "office appliances" as of the late 1920s with empha-
        sis on their benefits.

848   Brieux, A. Malassis-Chauvin Collection. (Typescript
        catalog). Paris: Alain Brieux, rue Jacob, n.d.

        This 97-page catalog of sales items includes descrip-
        tions of abaci, adding machines, typewriters, sub-
        tracting devices, etc. of all types. These were on
        exhibit at the Société d'Encourangement pour l'Indus-
        trie Nationale show in 1920 which was then purchased
        from Malassis and expanded by Chauvin to a total
        size of 442 items. The devices date from 1914 to
        1939. Forty-one illustrations and 15 photographs
        support the detailed descriptions of these items.

849   Brunsviga-Maschinenwerke Grimme, Natalis. 60 Jahre
        Brunsviga. Braunschweig: Brunsviga-Maschinenwerke-
        Grimme, Natalis and Co., 1931.

        This offers a history of desk calculators and current
        models of this company's products. It also describes
        the Trinks-Brunsviga Museum.

850   Brunsviga-Sonderhelft 1936. Braunschweig: Brunsviga-
        Maschinenwerke, Grimme, Natalais and Co., A.G., 1936.

        This describes, with illustration,s, the collection
        of the Trinks-Brunsviga Museum. That contains devices
        from the 19th and early 2-th centuries; includes a
        bibliography.

851   Buelow, Ralf. "Ein Unbekannter Computerpionier,"
        Kulter und Technik 3 (1987): 161-166.

        A German lawyer, Emil Schilling, patented a machine
        in Germany in 1926 which was program-controlled as a
        calculator. It used punch tape and pneumatics. This
        is also a biography of Schilling.

852   "Call for Business Machines," Business Week (January
        12, 1935): 16.

        The article reviews sales for various firms in 1933
        and 1934, forecasting a strong 1935. It is well
        informed.

853   Comrie, Leslie J. "Calculating Machines, Appendix III,"
        in L.R. Connor (ed), Statistics in Theory and Prac-
        tice (London: Pitman, 1938): 349-371.

This surveys widely available machines of the 1930s, their features and functions, operational character- istics, and their uses.

854   Comrie, Leslie J. "Mechanical Computing," Plane and Geodetic Surveying (ed. by D. Clark) (London: Con- stable, 1934): 11, pp. 284-294.

This is a short discussion of the Odhner wheel type of calculator and some uses it can be applied to in science.

855   Comrie, Leslie J. Modern Babbage Machines. Bulletin. London: Office Machinery Users Association, Ltd., 1932.

This 29-page booklet deals with difference engines and methods. While he surveys machines by Babbage, Scheutz, Wiberg, Grant and Hamann, he also spends considerable effort and space on more contemporary devices such as the Brunsviga-Dupla, the Nova-Bruns- viga Iva, Burroughs bookkeeping machines, and on NCR's.

856   Couffignal, L. Les Machines à Calculer, leurs Principes, leur Évolution. Paris: Gauthier Villars, 1933.

The discussion centers around card punch devices of the 1930s and of their possible linkage together to solve problems raised by Babbage relating to program control.

857   d'Ocagne, Maurice. Le Calcul Simplifié: Graphical and Mechanical Methods for Simplifying Calculation. Trans by J. Howlett and M.R. Williams. Cambridge, Mass.: MIT Press, 1986.

This book was first published in the 1890s; the translation is of the 1928 edition and has an intro- duction. It is a good source for the subject cover- ing the period from the late 1800s down through the 1920s.

858   Fasnacht, Harold D. How to Use Business Machines; A Brief Introductory Course. New York: Gregg Publish- ing Co., 1947.

This is a useful introduction to existing calculating machines of the 1940s and their possible uses.

859   "The First Alphabetical Printing Unit," Powers-Samas Gazette (March-April 1956): 8-9.

This is a description of a 1916 device built by Charles Foster using punch card tabulating equipment.

860   "Freeing the Operator," Illustrated World 27 (July 1917): 704.

This discusses the use of calculators in business.

861   French, W.F.   "Don't Tell Me It Can't Be Done," Illus-
      trated World 36 (February 1922): 836-838.

      This describes what calculators could be useful for
      as of the early 1920s, a period of enormous expansion
      in the use of such devices by all offices.

862   Garner, S. Paul.   Evolution of Cost Accounting to 1925.
      University: University of Alabama Press, 1954, 1976.

      He argues that with the availability of data cap-
      turing on the plant floor possible by the early 1900s,
      cost accounting was now a practical thing to do.
      Especially useful is Chapter Five.

863   Hamann, Charles.   Uber Elektrische Rechenmaschinen.
      Neu-Babelsberg: Privately Printed, 1932 (?).

      This 32-page booklet describes various devices, such
      as multipliers, sorters, calculators and other tabu-
      lating equipment.

864   Hartree, Douglas R.   Calculating Instruments and Machin-
      es.   Urbana: University of Illinois Press, 1949;
      Reprinted with introduction by Maurice V. Wilkes.
      Cambridge, Mass.: MIT Press, 1984.

      He surveys differential analyzers, their use in
      mathematics, digital equipment, Babbage's engine,
      and the general question of program control; excell-
      ent technical bibliography.

865   Hoyau, L.A.D.   "Description d'une Machine a Calculer
      nommée Arithmomètre de l'invention de M. Le chevalier
      Thomas de Colmar," Bulletin de la Societe d'Encourage-
      ment pour l'Industrie Nationale (November 1822): 355-
      365; Reprinted in Ibid. 132 (1920): 662-670.

      Although the original publication was of a then
      state-of-the-art device, the Thomas machine was still
      in use a century later, mainly at under-budgeted
      university laboratories.

866   Hull, C.L.   "An Automatic Correlation Calculating
      Machine," Journal of the American Statistical Assoc-
      iation 20, No. 15 (1925): 522-531.

      He describes an electric calculator using numbers
      read from paper tape. It was a special purpose cal-
      culator.

867   Instruments et Machines à Calculer.   Paris: Conservatoire
      National des Arts et Métiers, Cat. du Musee, Section
      A, 1942.

      This is a catalog of calculators and other related
      equipment in the collection; illustrated.

868   Last, J.   "Digital Calculating Machines," Chartered

Mechanical Engineering 9, No. 11 (1962): 572-579.

Last describes many of the pre-1900 calculators, along with early card mechanisms (such as Hollerith and Powers). It is useful and well organized.

869   Lind, W. "Getreibe der Addiermaschinen," Z. Ver. Deutsch. Ing. 75 (1931): 201-205.

This surveys current adding machines and their principles of operation; illustrated.

870   Lind, W. "Getreibe der Multipliziermaschinen," Z. Ver. Deutsch. Ing. 75 (1931): 985-990.

He describes currently available calculators capable of performing multiplication; illustrated.

871   Littauer, Sebastian B. "The Development of Statistical Quality Control in the United States," American Statistician 4, No. 5 (1950): 14-20.

The process of quality control of production depended on the collection and anlysis of a great deal of shop floor data made possible only by the introduction of data processing technologies of the late 1800s.

872   "Making the Mechanical Mathematician," Popular Mechanics 41 (April 1924): 568.

This is useful for explaining the state of the technology commonly available in the 1920s in calculators.

873   McCarthy, J.H. The American Digest of Business Machines: A Compendium of Makes and Models With Specifications and Principles of Operation Described, and Including Used Machine Valuations. Chicago: American Exchange Service, 1924.

This volume of 640 pages is detailed and very complete for devices from the last quarter of the 1800s to the early 1920s of all types. This is the best source available for used market conditions as well.

874   "Mechanical Calculations Moves On," Scientific American 156 (February 1937): 114.

This is a technical description of a device to do repetitive applications such as payroll, cost accounting among others.

875   Meyer Zur Capellen, W. Mathematische Instrumente. Leipzig: Akademische Verlagsgesellschaft, 1949.

Pages 53-122 describe how contemporary calculators and adding machines work. A quick review of computer developments may be found in an appendix.

876   Modernes Rechnen. Zurich: Heinrich Daemen, 1930.

       This is a sales catalog for contemporary adding
       machines and calculators; illustrated.

877   Office Equipment Catalogue, Inc. Office Equipment
       Catalogue. Chicago: Office Equipment Catalogue,
       Inc., 1925.

       This the second annual edition. It lists devices
       by vendors by the hundreds, and provides some infor-
       mation on the suppliers themselves. It is an
       excellent source for information on the office
       appliance world of the early to mid-1920s.

878   The Office Machine Manual: A Loose-Leaf Reference Book
       on Office Machines and Appliances. 4 vols. London:
       Gee, 1938 et. seq.

       This contains massive quantities of information on
       current adding and calculating devices, tabulators,
       bookkeeping machines, etc., how they work, design,
       applications; illustrated. Historical backgrounds
       of some machines is also presented. It is an
       exceptional review of British and American devices
       of the 1930s.

879   "Parade of the Business Machines; 32nd Annual National
       Business Show," Business Week (October 19, 1935):
       10-11.

       This is one of the first articles to argue that
       some machines designed in the 1930s were made to
       handle data handling requirements of New Deal
       programs.

880   Pugh, J. Calculating Machines and Instruments. London:
       Science Museum, 1975.

       This is not to be confused with Baxandall's 1926
       publication issued by the same museum. The newer
       catalog is twice the length of the first one and
       contains devices from after 1926 but with the same
       useful information about them.

881   Purinton, E.E. "Machines Instead of Men," Independent
       and Weekly Review 97 (January 18, 1919): 92-93.

       This was published just on the verge of a massive
       injection of office appliances into American and
       European offices in the 1920s. It argues in favor
       of their use.

882   Radford, George S. The Control of Quality in Manufac-
       turing. New York: Ronald, 1922.

       He was the first to write and lecture extensively
       on what would become known decades later as quality
       control and quality circles. It was possible to

focus on the issue because of the now existing
capability of capturing necessary data in efficient
and cost-effective ways that involved a continual
process of data gathering, feedback, and response
to events in a factory.

883   Shewhart, Walter A. Economic Control of Quality of
       Manufactured Product. New York: Van Nostrand, 1931.

       This is another example of a growing body of liter-
       ature, beginning in the 1920s, on the use of contin-
       uous data gathering in process and manufacturing
       operations to control quality of production and
       hence lowering of unit costs. The data gathering
       effort involved the use of hardware from the office
       appliance industry.

884   Tee, Garry J. "Two New Zealand Mathematicians," in
       John N. Crossley (ed), Proceedings of the First
       Australian Conference on the History of Mathematics
       (Clayton, Victoria, Australia: Monash Univer, 1981).

       This surveys the life and work of Leslie John Comrie
       (1893-1950) and Alexander Craig Aitken (1895-1967).
       Comrie encouraged the use of calculating equipment
       in the 1920s and 1930s, particularly by mathemati-
       cians while Aitken did the same for numerical ana-
       lysis.

885   "The Thirsk Totalisator," The Electrical Review 106
       (February 7, 1930): 268-269.

       This was a mobile totalisator at the Thirsk race
       course in 1930.

886   Toulon, P. "Les Machines à Calculer et leurs Applica-
       tions dans l'Organisation de l'Industrie et du
       Commerce," Bulletin de la Société d'Encouragement
       pour l'Industrie Nationale 132 (September-October
       1920): 570-584.

       Toulon describes a variety of devices in the posse-
       ssion of this society which includes a Thomas
       arithmometer, Millionaire, Comptometer and such
       other equipment as adding machines from Burroughs
       to devices by Torres y Quevedo. All were 19th
       century and early 20th century vintage.

887   Turck, J.A.V. Origin of Modern Calculating Machines;
       A Chronicle of the Evolution of the Principles that
       Form the Generic Make-Up of the Modern Calculating
       Machine. Chicago: The Western Society of Engineers,
       1921.

       This nearly 200-page monograph is a detailed review,
       primarily of early 20th century technology.

888   U.S. Bureau of the Census. Census of Manufactures,
       1933: Cash Registers and Adding, Calculating, and

Card-Tabulating Machines. Washington, D.C.: U.S.
Government Printing Office, 1935.

This 8-page census was published for various years
in the entire 20th century. These are especially
useful for sizing American volumes of manufacture
of such devices. This one reflects the impact of
the Great Depression on the industry.

889   Wright, F.E. "Trigonometric Computer," Scientific
       American Monthly 1 (March 1920): 228.

Wright describes the use of a calculator in higher
mathematics. All during the 1920s mathematicians
would stress the limits of existing calculator
technologies which would force additional enhance-
ments to adding and calculating machines, to bookkeeping and punch card devices too.

Company Events

890   "Business Machines," Business Week (December 7, 1935):
       36.

The article reports on some of the early legal
battles between the U.S. Government and both IBM
and Remington Rand concerning dominance of the
tabulating machine market.

891   "Rand Reshuffle," Time 27 (June 22, 1936): 70, 74.

This describes a strike at Remington Rand, one of
the office appliance industry's largest vendors.

892   "Tabulating Machines Target of Trust Suit," Business
       Week 129 (April 6, 1932): 16.

Both Remington Rand and IBM were involved in liti-
gation over the issue with the U.S. Justice Department during the 1930s.

893   Victor Adding Machine Company. Victor Sales Training
       Manual. Chicago: Victor Adding Machine Co., 1948.

In addition to some sales training, it offers
insight into the company of the 1930s and 1940s.

Leslie J. Comrie

894   Comrie, Leslie J. "Inverse Interpolation and Scienti-
       fic Application of the National Accounting Machine,"
       Supplement to the Journal of the Royal Statistical
       Society 3, No. 2 (1936): 87-114.

He reviews the history of special purpose difference
machines and then this particular one and its application.

895   Comrie, Leslie J. "On the Application of the Brunsvig

Dupla Calculating Machine to Double Summation with
Finite Differences," Monthly Notices, Royal Astronomical Society 88, No. 5 (March 1928): 447-459.

Offers a quick survey of difference machines, then
the features of this device and its use in differen-
cing applications.

896   Comrie, Leslie J. (Untitled article). The Observatory
      51 (April 1928): 105-108.

      This is a summation of the paper referred to in
      entry No. 895.

897   Lehmer, D.H. "Leslie John Comrie (1893-1950),"
      Mathematical Tables and Other Aids to Calculation
      5 (1951): 108-109.

      This is an obituary. For a biography see entry No.
      884.

898   Scientific Computing Service Limited. Scientific
      Computing Service Limited: A Description of Its
      Activities, Equipment and Staff. London: Scientific
      Computing Service, Ltd., 1946.

      In addition to describing its services, this has a
      review of Comrie's career and a bibliography of his
      publications.

                        Cryptology

899   Davies, Donald W. "The Early Models of the Siemens
      and Halske T52 Cipher Machines," Cryptologia 7,
      No. 3 (July 1983): 235-253.

      This description of a German cipher machine of
      the World War II period covers a class of devices
      called Sturgeon, Tunny and Thrasher (British)
      machines. The descriptions are accurate and are
      illustrated.

900   Davies, Donald W. "Sidney Hole's Cryptographic Device,"
      Cryptologia 8, No. 2 (April 1984): 115-125.

      This is an illustrated account of a machine built
      in 1926 which is described as "two modified type-
      writers connected by a pneumatic rotor mechanism"
      with 5 moving cylinders. It was judged to be ine-
      ffective.

901   Deavours, Cipher A. and Kruh, L. Machine Cryptography
      and Modern Cryptoanalysis. Dedham, Mass.: Artech
      House, 1985.

      This offers a review of devices used between 1920
      and 1945 which they author call machines from "the
      golden age of machine cryptography." The book is
      an important source on the subject.

902   Ewing, Alfred. "Some Special War Work—Part I,"
       Cryptologia 4, No. 4 (October 1980): 193-203, "Part
       II," *Ibid*. 5, No. 1 (January 1981): 33-39.

       This is a lecture delivered by the author on December
       13, 1927 dealing with work done during World War I
       in breaking German codes for the Allies. He worked
       on the Zimmerman Telegram for the British.

903   Ferris, J. "The British 'Enigma': Britain, Signals
       Security and Cipher Machines, 1906-1946," *Defense
       Analysis* 3 (Oxford: Brassey's Defence Publishers,
       1987): 153-163.

       This is a useful survey of British activities, with
       details on the Typex Enigma and the Rockex machine.

904   Gouaze, Linda Y. "Needles and Haystacks: The Search
       for Ultra in the 1930s (An Excerpt)," *Cryptologia*
       11 (April 1987): 85-92.

       This is an excerpt from her 1983 thesis done at the
       Naval Postgraduate School, in which she argues that
       little data exists on activities prior to 1940 but
       then explains in detail the French role.

905   Kahn, David. "A New Source for Historians: Yardley's
       Seized Manuscript," *Cryptologia* 6, No. 2 (April
       1982): 115-119.

       This describes a search for a World War I paper by
       Herbert O. Yardly, then head of MI-8, the U.S.
       Army's cryptologic agency.

906   Kahn, David. "Churchill Pleads for Intercepts,"
       Cryptologia 6, No. 1 (January 1982): 47-49.

       He reproduces two letters, dated 1924, by Churchill.

907   Kahn, David. "In Memoriam: Georges-Jean Painvin,"
       Cryptologia 6, No. 2 (April 1982): 120-127.

       This is an obituary notice for a World War I
       cryptoanalyst. It provides details of his role.

908   Kahn, David. *Kahn on Codes: Secrets of the New Crypt-
       ology*. New York: Macmillan, 1984.

       Among the topics is a discussion of how he came to
       write *The Codebreakers* (1967), he also discusses
       Enigma, Polish cryptoanalysis and World War II. It
       is a collection of many articles published elsewhere.

909   Kruh, Louis. "The Day the Friedmans Had a Typo in Their
       Photo," *Cryptologia* 3, No. 4 (October 1979): 236-
       241.

       It contains a discussion on two flaws in a cipher
       hidden in a group photograph of a World War I

cryptographic class (1918) in Geneva, Illinois.

910   Kruh, Louis. "Devices and Machines: The Hagelin Cryp-
       tographer, Type-C-52," Cryptologia 3, No. 2 (April
       1979): 78-82.

       He describes a mechanical unit of the 1950s; it is
       a technical discussion.

911   Kruh, Louis. "The Genesis of the Jefferson/Bazeries
       Cipher Device," Cryptologia 5, No. 4 (October
       1981): 193-208.

       He describes the M-94, a U.S. Army device of 1922.
       A similar machine had been invented by Thomas Jeffer-
       son between 1790 and 1793 and also by Babbage in
       1854. In 1891 Etienne Bazeries also conceived one
       which stimulated later the development of the M-94,
       M-138, M-138A. This is illustrated and contains an
       extensive bibliography.

912   Kruh, Louis. "Memoirs of Friedman" and "Reminiscences
       of a Master Cryptologist," Cryptologia 4, No. 1
       (January 1980): 23-26, 45-50.

       The first piece is on World War I, the second assess-
       es various World War II efforts of the British and
       Americans and concludes that American efforts yielded
       the greatest results.

913   Meyer, Carl and Matyas, Stephen M. Cryptography: A New
       Dimension in Computer Data Security. New York:
       Wiley-Interscience, 1982.

       This very large book reflects thinking of the 1970s
       and early 1980s, including lines of development
       within IBM to provide protection to messages sent
       across telecommunication lines.

914   Snyder, Samuel S. "Computer Advances Pioneered by
       Cryptologic Organizations," Annals of the History
       of Computing 2, No. 1 (January 1980): 60-70.

       He reviews the role, in the 1940s and 1950s, of
       various agencies, such as NSA (1948-1962). He has
       a technical discussion with chronology and some
       memoir material of his own role.

915   Snyder, Samuel S. Influence of U.S. Cryptologic
       Organizations on the Digital Computer Industry.
       Fort Meade, Md.: National Security Agency, 1977.

       Some of the computers discussed include the Atlas,
       ERA 1101, UNIVAC 1103, and other machines from the
       1930s through the 1950s.

916   Sorkin, Arthur. "Lucifer, A Cryptographic Algorith,"
       Cryptologia 8, No. 1 (January 1984): 22-42.

The device described was designed by Horst Feistel
in the early 1970s to provide a secure cipher that
had both diffusion and confusion features to confuse
any statistical analysis.

917   Stuerzinger, Oskar. "The A-22 Cryptograph," Cryptologia 5, No. 3 (July 1981): 175-183.

The A-22 was the first device used in a commercial
telegraph system. It was a hand-held unit for
mechanical cryptography. The article is illustrated
and offers a good description of how the A-22 worked.

918   Stuerzinger, Oskar. "The B-21 Cryptograph," Cryptologia 7, No. 4 (October 1983): 333-346.

This is an illustrated description of the B class
electromechanical cipher machine, first developed
in 1925 and used against Enigma during World War II.

919   Tilt, Borge. "On Kullback's x-Tests for Matching and
Non-Matching Multinomial Distributions," Cryptologia 8, No. 2 (April 1984): 132-141.

Solomon Kullback was one of 3 mathematicians hired
in 1930 for the Signal Intelligence Service in the
U.S. Army. This article describes a 1935 test he
devised.

920   Weller, Robert. "Rear Admiral Joseph N. Wenger USN
(Ret.) and the Naval Cryptologic Museum," Cryptologia 8, No. 3 (July 1984): 208-234.

This describes the museum's holdings and is located
in Washington, D.C. The collection ranges from 1900
to the 1950s. This also has material on the role
Wenger played from 1924 to 1958.

921   Yardley, Herbert O. "The Achievements of the Cipher
Bureau (MI-8) During the First World War," Cryptologia 8, No. 1 (January 1984): 62-74.

This is the fullest, contemporary account in print
of the role played by U.S. Army cryptologists in
World War I. It was written by a participant of
the period who also continued his activities into
the 1920s.

Differential Analyzers

922   Beard, R.E. "The Construction of a Small Scale Differential Analyser and Its Application to the Calculation of Actuarial Functions," Journal of the
Institute of Actuaries 71 (1942): 193-227.

This is a description of a small British differential
analyzer of the early 1940s.

923   Berry, T.M. "Polarized-Light Servo System,"

Transactions of the American Institute of Electrical Engineers 63 (April 1944): 195-197.

This describes a differential analyzer built at GE, a device that followed motion by using polarized light.

924   Boelter, L.M.K. et al. _The Differential Analyzer of the University of California_. Los Angeles: University of California, 1947.

This 25-page document is on a differential analyzer built at U.C.L.A. in the 1940s.

925   Bratt, J.B., Lennard-Jones, J.E. and Wilkes, Maurice V. "The Design of a Small Differential Analyzer," _Proceedings of the Cambridge Philosophical Society_ 35 (1939): 485-493.

This was one of the earliest computing projects that Wilkes was involved with.

926   Comrie, Leslie J. "Modern Babbage Machines," _Bulletin, Office Machinery Users Association, Ltd._ London: Office Machinery Users Association, Ltd., 1932.

Comrie reviews difference devices and their applications and history. It is useful for devices of the 1920s and 1930s.

927   Kuehni, H.P. and Peterson, H.A. "A New Differential Analyzer," _Transactions of the American Institute of Electrical Engineers_ 63 (May 1944): 221-227.

This is a description of GE's differential analyzer. See also entry No. 923.

928   Maginnis, F.J. "Differential Analyzer Applications," _General Electric Review_ 48, No. 5 (May 1945): 54-59.

The article discusses briefly GE's differential analyzer.

929   Massey, H.S.W. et al. "A Small Scale Differential Analyzer: Its Construction and Operation," _Proceedings of the Royal Irish Academy_ 45 (1938): 1-21.

This was one of nearly a half dozen such machines constructed in Great Britain during the 1930s.

930   Porter, Arthur. "The Construction of a Model Mechanical Device for the Solution of Differential Equations with Applications to the Determination of Atomic Wave Functions" (Unpublished M.S. thesis, Victoria University of Manchester, 1934).

This reflected research done by a graduate student of Douglas R. Hartree. Porter helped him build the

first differential analyzer in Great Britain. It
was modeled after Bush's machine at MIT. The thesis
is an early description of the analyzer.

931   Saver, R. and Poesch, H. "Integrated Machine for Solv-
       ing Ordinary Differential Equations," Engineers
       Digest (American Edition) 1 (May 1944): 326-328.

       This is a description of a German differential
       analyzer.

932   Trvis, Irven. "Differential Analyzer Eliminates Brain
       Fag," Machine Design (July 1935): 15-18.

       Trvis describes an analog differential analyzer built
       at the Moore School of Electrical Engineering, nearly
       a decade before the same institution constructed the
       ENIAC, the first fully operational electronic digital
       computer.

                Harmonic Analyzers and Synthesizers

933   Archer, R.M. "Projecting Apparatus for Compounding
       Harmonic Vibrations," Journal of Scientific Instru-
       ments 14 (1937): 408-410.

       Archer details work done with harmonic analyzers
       which were early analog computational equipment.

934   Brown, S.L. "A Mechanical Harmonic Synthesizer-Analy-
       zer," Journal of the Franklin Institute 228 (1939):
       675-694.

       Brown provides one of the first descriptions of this
       kind of analog device which he used to study wave
       motions and various other physical or mathematical
       functions.

935   Brown, S.L. and Wheeler, L.L. "A Mechanical Method
       for Graphical Solution of Polynomials," Journal of
       the Franklin Institute 231 (1941): 223-243.

       These two scientists discussed how they used a
       harmonic analyzer.

936   Brown, S.L. and Wheeler, L.L. "Use of the Mechanical
       Multiharmonograph for Graphing Types of Functions
       and for Solution of Pairs of Non-Linear Simultaneous
       Equations," Review of Scientific Instruments 13
       (November 1942): 493-495.

       This article reflected a growing interest within
       the U.S. scientific community of the 1920s-1940s in
       using ever increasingly complex devices to do the
       work of research in mathematics.

937   Fürth, R. and Pringle, R.W. "A New Photo-Electric
       Method for Fourier Synthesis and Analysis," London,
       Edinburgh and Dublin Philosophical Magazine and

Journal of Science 35, Series 7 (1944): 643-656.

This is an example of British research done using a harmonic analyzer in the 1930s and 1940s.

938   International Hydrographic Bureau. _Tide Predicting Machines_. N.c.: International Hyrographic Bureau, Special Publication 13, July 1926.

The use of analog devices to do tide predicting had been underway since the 19th century and served as an important motivator for harmonic analyzers and synthesizers in the early decades of the 20th century.

939   Kranz, Frederick W. "A Mechanical Synthesizer and Analyzer," _Journal of the Franklin Institute_ 204 (1927): 245-262.

This is an early description of an analog computer-like device of the 1920s.

940   Marble, F.G. "An Automatic Vibration Analyzer," _Bell Laboratories Record_ 22 (April 1944): 376-380.

Marble describes work done at Bell Labs on analog devices, suggestive that there was more computer-like activity there at the time than simply Stibitz's.

941   Maxwell, L.R. "An Electrical Method for Compounding Sine Functions," _Review of Scientific Instruments_ 11 (February 1940): 47-54.

The method described is one that relied on the use of a harmonic analyzer.

942   Michelson, A.A. and Stratton, S.W. "A New Harmonic Analyzer," _American Journal of Science_ 4th Series, 5 (1898): 1-13.

This discusses, in part, problems of current calculations using mechanical calculators and what was needed. The authors were two great physicists.

943   Miller, Dayton. "A 32-Element Harmonic Synthesizer," _Journal of the Franklin Institute_ 181 (1916): 51-81.

Miller's work took place at the high point of early 20th century development of harmonic analyzers.

944   Miller, Dayton C. "The Henrici Harmonic Analyzer and Devices for Extending and Facilitating Its Use," _Journal of the Franklin Institute_ 182 (1916): 285-322.

Miller worked at the dawn of electrical computational devices and at the same time as Ludgate and Torres y Quevedo.

945   Milne, J.R. "A 'Duplex' Form of Harmonic Synthesiser
      and Its Mathematical Theory," Proceedings of the
      Royal Society of Edingburgh 39 (1918-1919): 234-242.

      This British harmonic analyzer was one of the first
      described in print built in Europe.

946   Montgomery, H.C. "Optical Harmonic Analyzer," Bell
      System Technical Journal 17, No. 3 (July 1938):
      406-415.

      A great deal of work was done at Bell Labs in the
      1920s and 1930s with a variety of analog computa-
      tional machines. This was one of the projects of
      the 1930s.

947   Raymond, W.J. "An Harmonic Synthesizer Having Compo-
      nents of Incommensurable Period and Any Desired
      Decrement," Physical Review 11, Series 2 (1918):
      479-481.

      This is a technical description. Raymond was one
      of the first scientists to design harmonic analyzers.

948   Robertson, J.M. "A Simple Harmonic Continuous Calcula-
      ting Machine," London, Edinburgh and Dublin
      Philosophical Magazine and Journal of Science 13
      (1932): 413-419.

      This is a technical piece on a British harmonic
      analyzer, one of many built in the 1920s and 1930s.

949   Somerville, J.M. "Harmonic Synthesizer for Demonstra-
      ting and Studying Complex Wave Forms," Journal of
      Scientific Instruments 21 (October 1944): 174-177.

      This is a study of tidal waves, providing additional
      motivation for the construction of harmonic analy-
      zers during the first half of the 20th century.

950   Straiton, A.W. and Terhune, G.K. "Harmonic Analysis
      by Photographic Method," Journal of Applied Physics
      14 (1943): 535-536.

      Although a technical piece, it describes some of
      the most advanced work being done on harmonic
      analyzers in the late 1930s and early 1940s.

951   Wegel, R.L. and Moore, C.R. "An Electrical Frequency
      Analyzer," Bell System Technical Journal 3 (1924):
      299-323.

      Bell Labs was one of the premier centers for U.S.
      computational research in the 1920s. These two
      authors were part of a staff of hundreds doing
      research at Bell.

Douglas R. Hartree

952   Hartree, Douglas R. "The Differential Analyzer,"
      Nature 135 (June 8, 1935): 940.

      He describes an early British differential analyzer
      built in the 1930s at Manchester University.

953   Hartree, Douglas R. "The Wave Mechanics of an Atom
      With a Non-Coulomb Field," Proceedings of the
      Cambridge Philosophical Society 24 (1928): 89-110;
      Part II: 111-132; Part III: 426-437.

      This was one of his earliest papers on the Hartree-
      Fock method of using a differential analyzer.

954   Hartree, Douglas R. and Porter, A. "The Construction
      of a Model Differential Analyzer," Memoirs and
      Proceedings of the Manchester Literary and Philoso-
      phical Society 79 (July 1935): 51-72.

      He describes an early differential analyzer built
      at the Manchester University with comments on the
      experience of construction. Most accounts of such
      devices only reviewed how they were used.

955   Hartree, Douglas R. and Womersley, J.R. "A Method for
      the Numerical or Mechanical Solution of Certain
      Types of Partial Differential Equations," Proceed-
      ings of the Royal Society of London, Series A, 161
      (1937): 353-366.

      They discuss mathematical applications of a differ-
      ential analyzer.

956   Medwick, Paul A. "Douglas Hartree and Early Computa-
      tions in Quantum Mechanics," Annals of the History
      of Computing 10, No. 2 (1988): 105-112.

      The article reviews Hartree's work during the 1920s
      and 1930s on mathematical solutions for problems in
      quantum mechanics. This led him to realize the need
      for analog and digital computational aids to help do
      the necessary calculations.

Network Analyzers

957   Enns, W.E. "A New Simple Calculator of Load Flow in
      A.C. Networks," Transactions of the American Insti-
      tute of Electrical Engineers 62 (1943): 786-790.

      This analog device was used to model the flow of
      electricity—a major application area since World
      War I.

958   Hazen, Harold L. et al. The M.I.T. Network Analyzer.
      Cambridge, Mass.: MIT Department of Electrical
      Engineering, Serial No. 69, April 1931.

Hazen and his associates describe one of the most famous of the early analog computational devices.

959   Kron, Gabriel. "Electric Circuit Models for the Vibration Spectrum of Polyatomic Molecules," Journal of Chemical Physics 14, No. 1 (January 1946): 19-31.

Network analyzers provided much information on how such analog devices could be used. One use is described here.

960   Kron, Gabriel. "Equivalent Circuits of the Elastic Field," Journal of Applied Mechanics A11 (September 1944): 146-161.

This describes how Kron used a network analyzer for a non-traditional application.

961   Kron, Gabriel. "Numerical Solution of Ordinary and Partial Differential Equations by Means of Equivalent Circuits," Journal of Applied Physics 16 (1945): 172-186.

Kron, a leading figure in the use of network analyzers, explains his study of electrical circuits.

962   Kron, Gabriel. "Tensorial Analysis and Equivalent Circuits of Elastic Structures," Journal of the Franklin Institute 238 (December 1944): 399-442.

This was one of the author's most detailed publications involving the use of network analyzers to study electrical circuits.

963   Kron, Gabriel and Carter, G.K. "A.C. Network Analyzer Study of the Schrodinger Equation," Physical Review 67 (1945): 44-49.

This continues the discussion begun in earlier articles and late in the history of network analyzers of the 1930s.

964   Kron, Gabriel and Carter, G.K. "Network Analyzer Tests of Equivalent Circuits of Vibrating Polyatomic Molecules," Journal of Chemical Physics 14, No. 1 (January 1946): 32-34.

This was one of the last of Kron's papers in a series begun in the early 1940s involving the use of a network analyzer.

965   Kuehni, H.P. and Lorraine, R.G. "A New A.C. Network Analyzer," Transactions of the American Institute of Electrical Engineers 57 (1938): 67-73.

This is a technical description of an electric network modeling exercise, which came in a period of extensive work with such analog devices.

966   Parker, W.W. "A.C. Network Calculator," Electrical
        Engineering (May 1945): 182-183.

        This describes the GE network analyzer used to model
        electrical circuits in upstate New York in the mid-
        1940s. The effort, however, had been going on for
        nearly two decades with various types of analog
        devices.

967   Parker, W.W. "The Modern A.C. Network Calculator,"
        Transactions of the American Institute of Electrical
        Engineers 60 (November 1941): 977-982.

        This description illustrates how network analyzers
        were built in the late 1930s to help electrical
        companies manage their large networks of electrical
        circuits by modelling their behavior.

968   Peterson, H.A. "An Electric Circuit Transient Analyzer,"
        General Electric Review (September 1939): 394-400.

        The article describes GE's network analyzer installed
        in Schenectady, NY, called the A.C. Network Analyzer.

969   Peterson, H.A. and Concordia, C. "Analyzers for Use in
        Engineering and Scientific Problems," General Elec-
        tric 48, No. 9 (September 1945): 29-37.

        The two scientists prepared a useful overview of
        how network analyzers were being used in the 1940s.

970   Varney, R.N. "An All-Electric Integrator for Solving
        Differential Equations," Review of Scientific
        Instruments 13 (January 1942): 10-16.

        Varney describes a network analyzer to solve problems
        in electrical networking.

        Punch Card Applications: Commercial, 1920s-1930s

971   "A.B. & A. Introduces Tabulating Machine Checks," Rail-
        way Age 75 (July 14, 1923): 76-77.

        U.S. railroad companies were some of the first,
        extensive users of such technology, along with the
        U.S. Government.

972   "Accurate Statistics," Systems and Management Methods
        62 (July 1933): 305-306.

        The Polish National Alliance of the United States
        of North America, an insurance company, saved on
        clerical expenses by using punch card methods and
        machines.

973   Angstadt, L.H. "Mechanical Accounting for Store
        Inventories," Management Engineering 4 (August
        1923): 267-268.

During the 1920s one of the fastest growing areas for the use of punch card equipment was inventory control. The logic for such an application is explained.

974   Atkins, P.M. "Industrial Cost Accounting for Executives," _American Machinist_ 59 (October 18, 1923): 591-594.

The notion of cost accounting was a relatively new one at the end of World War I. It is explained here along how it can be implemented with punch cards.

975   "Austin Works Systems," _Automobile Engineering_ 17 (October 1927): 380-384.

Automobile factories were some of the largest in the U.S. and they quickly became major users of office appliances in manufacturing.

976   Baehne, G.W. (ed). _Practical Applications of the Punched Card Method in Colleges and Universities_. New York: Columbia University Press, 1935.

This was a major work, at the time, on the use of cards, primarily in scientific applications but also in administration.

977   Benge, Eugene J. _Cutting Clerical Costs_. New York: New York: McGraw-Hill Book Co., 1931.

Pages 157-179 has an illustrated description of office equipment of the late 1920s, with comments on their use, cost justification and impact.

978   "Billing Procedures of the Brooklyn Union Gas Company," _American Gas Journal_ No. 151 (December 1939): 15-17.

The installed Powers equipment managed 550,000 accounts. This was probably Powers' first account outside of the U.S. Bureau of the Census, dating back to 1911.

979   Bosworth, A.W. "Advances in Trust Accounting and Control," _Trust Companies_ 62 (January 1936): 25-32.

Old Colony Trust Company and the First National Bank of Boston employed punch card equipment to cut nearly in half all duplicated existing data in the 1930s in the area of trust accounting.

980   Bower, E.C. "On Subdividing Tables," _Lick Observatory Bulletin_ 16, No. 455 (November 1933): 143-144.

Although on mathematics for scientists, the article concerns issues relevant to the business community involving the use of punch cards.

981   Briggs, G.B. "Economies in Trust Accounting,"

Trust Companies 64 (May 1937): 551-553.

This illustrates benefits experienced in the 1930s
as banks moved rapidly to tabulating equipment to
cut operating costs and improve efficiencies.

982   Butz, R.H. "Punched Cards Speed Stock Control," Food
       Industries 8 (December 1936): 631.

       Punch card equipment at the Luden Corporation did
       perpetual inventory, stock control and production
       accounting.

983   "Cards for Customers: Making and Printing Tabulating
       Machine Cards," American Machinist 81 (June 16,
       1937): 556-558.

       Tabulating machine applications frequently required
       either pre-printed or pre-punched cards. This
       article is a rare account of this topic.

984   "Cards Tell Facts," Systems and Management Methods 62
       (August 1933): 357.

       Production control at the Model Laundry Company in
       the early 1930s is described.

985   "Census Tabulating Machine," Engineer 131 (May 20, 1927):
       523-533.

       The hardware is described along with its most famous
       and first use.

986   "Compiling Operating Statistics by Punched Cards,"
       Railway Review 79 (October 30, 1926): 647-648.

       During the 1920s railroad companies continued to
       find more uses for tabulating equipment and its
       trade press continuously published articles on the
       subject.

987   Connover, J.L. "Report of Committee on Office Labor
       Saving Devices," American Gas Association, Account-
       ing Section 1 (May 1927): 15-34.

       It not only reportedly favorably on tabulating
       equipment but describes as well a series of appli-
       cations already in place within the industry.

988   Cradit, R.Y. "Punched Cards Method in Accounting,"
       Journal of Accountancy 57 (April 1934): 272-285.

       This is a text on how to use punched cards in
       accounting and why as of the 1930s. The journal
       was a highly regarded publication.

989   Curtis, C.R. "Mechanization in Gas Offices," Gas Jour-
       nal No. 202 (June 14, 1933): 807-809.

Utilities early became users of punched cards for
billing and accounting management. The article is
a survey of common uses as of the 1920s and early
1930s.

990   Davidson, W.V. "Punched Card Systems of Inventory
      Control," N.A.C.A. Bulletin 4 (1923): 23.

      This is a relatively early article on the logic of
      using tabulating equipment for this application.

991   Davidson, W.V. "How A Wholesaler Became Efficient,"
      Food Industries 9 (March 1937): 120-123.

      The focus is on inventory control with punch cards
      but it also discusses stock control, billing, and
      sales analysis in 10 warehouses.

992   Dean, C.W. "Gates Rubber Company's New Budgetary
      Control System," American Business 7 (May 1937):
      34-35ff.

      This company's tabulating equipment was used to
      compare expenses to budget by doing detailed sales
      analysis.

993   Denton, Elwood V. "Sales and Statistical Analysis for
      A Metal Manufacturer," N.A.C.A. Bulletin 21 (Decem-
      ber 15, 1939): 491-499.

      The application was at the American Rolling Mill
      Company.

994   Eisertola, F. "Mechanical Devices in Accounting
      Department of San Antonio and Arkansas Railway,"
      Railway Review 68 (January 8, 1921): 44-48; Ibid.
      (January 15, 1921): 80-85.

      This represents an early description of the use of
      tabulating equipment for accounting at a railway
      company.

995   Ford, C.M. "Alphabetical and Mneomonic Symbols on
      Tabulating Machine Cards," Industrial Management
      61 (May 1, 1921): 347-350.

      By the end of World War I engineering applications
      were becoming more common, using punch card equip-
      ment.

996   "Fuel Accounting with Punched Cards," Railway Review
      79 (November 31, 1926): 719-721.

      This was a variant of inventory control accounting
      applied to railroads and fuel management.

997   Gardner, G.A. "Improving Operation of Tabulating
      Machine Installations," N.A.C.A. Bulletin 21
      (December 15, 1939): 481-490.

This tells of how the Schenley Distillery Corporation used punch card equipment to manage the large volume of orders it received after the repeal of prohibition.

998   "Gas Accounts and Records by Punched Cards," <u>Gas Journal</u> No. 227 (April 16, 1939): 395-396.

This describes accounts receivable and billing applications.

999   Glacy, G.F. "Improved Car Accounting and Statistics at Lower Costs," <u>Railway Age</u> 94 (April 15, 1933): 548-552.

This is a study of the Boston and Maine Railroad's approach to information management systems begun in the 1920s. It led to the installation of a Powers system in 1932 for a variety of statistical applications.

1000   Graham, Willard J. <u>Cost Accounting and Office Equipment</u>. Chicago: American Technical Society, 1929.

This is a detailed description of office applications and in particular about cost accounting, using both punch card and bookkeeping methods.

1001   Graham, Willard J. "Distribution Methods by Hand and Machine," <u>Journal of Accountancy</u> 53 (March 1932): 171-185.

Manual versus semi-automated methods are compared with specific examples; a very useful piece for the late 1920s/early 1930s.

1002   Howell, M.J. "Punch Cards for Bills Receivable," <u>Railway Age</u> 79 (August 15, 1925): 321-322.

This was one of the earliest uses railroads put punch cards to in the United States.

1003   Ingram, F.C. "Mechanical Bookkeeping of Consumers' Accounts," <u>American Gas Journal</u> (October 15, 1921): 349-351.

This reviews billing and gas consumption data capture and management using punch card equipment.

1004   International Business Machines Corporation. <u>The Electric Tabulating and Accounting Machine Method</u>. Endicott, N.Y.: International Business Machines Corporation, 1925.

This describes IBM's tabulating products of 1925, what applications they were useful for, and gives details on use and justification.

1005   International Business Machine Corporation. <u>A</u>

Hollerith Handbook. Rio de Janeiro: International
Business Machines Corporation, 1934.

This contains descriptions of IBM punch card products of the 1930s, how to use them, and offers a
series of descriptions of applications. It ends
with hints on better methods of using such equipment.

1006 International Business Machines Corporation. Machine
Methods of Accounting. Endicott, N.Y.: International Business Machines Corporation, 1936.

This is very much a collection of application
briefs using punch card technology.

1007 International Business Machines Corporation. Managerial Accounting by Machine Method. Endicott, N.Y.:
International Business Machines Corporation, 1939.

As with most of IBM's punch card publications, this
one focuses on applications of such technology:
what, how, and why.

1008 Jacobson, C.A. "Universal Calculating Machine for
Chemical Calculations," Chemical Age 30 (February
1922): 51-52.

Chemical applications called for calculations and
were a major set of uses for such equipment in
industry.

1009 Kimball, J.H. and Sedgwick, R.M. "Tabulating Machines
in Customer Accounting," Journal of the American
Water Works Association 23 (November 1931): 1891-
1894.

The authors describe the use of tabulating equipment at the East Bay Municipal Utility District of
California (1916-1931).

1010 Leffingwell, William Henry. Office Management: Principles and Practice. Chicago: A.W. Shaw Co., 1925.

This is a valuable source for early 1900s office
management issues, including the use of office
appliances in the United States.

1011 Linton, D.H. "How We Make a Market Survey," American
Gas Journal No. 146 (March 1937): 18-20.

This is on the use of punched cards at the New
England Gas and Electric Association. Data taken
from meter readers was analyzed by an IBM tabulating service bureau during the 1930s.

1012 Little, H.C. "Time Saving Sales and Quota Record,"
American Business 8 (January 1938): 32ff.

The Excelsior Insurance Company used punch card
equipment to manage data on premiums and quotas.

1013   "Machine-Made Records," Factory and Industrial Manage-
        ment 82 (October 1931): 492-493.

        The article describes the use of punch card equip-
        ment at Kaufmann's Department Store to do inventory
        management in the 1930s.

1014   "Mechanical Aids in Preparing the Railroad Payroll,"
        Railway Review 66 (March 13, 1920): 423-424.

        Large employers saw the benefits of managing payroll
        through a punch card system; this is an early appli-
        cation brief on the topic.

1015   "Mechanical Aids to Merchandise Control in Department
        Stores," Harvard Business Review 6 (April 1928):
        330-342.

        The article explains the logic for using a punch card
        system for inventory control and the issues involved
        in the implementation and management of such a system.
        This was published at a time when large department
        stores were implementing new systems for this
        application.

1016   "Mechanical Method Provides Accurate Control of Ware-
        house Stocks,"System 62 (December 1933): 560-561.

        The Frank H. Fleer Corporation used punch cards to
        control stocks in 28 warehouses during the 1930s.

1017   Mills, Gail A. Accounting Manual for Colleges. Prince-
        ton: Princeton University Press, 1937.

        Appendix A (pages 157-163) surveys business machines
        available as of the mid-1930s, suitable for use by
        accountants.

1018   Morse, Perley. Business Machines; Their Practical
        Application and Education Requirements. London:
        N.p., 1932.

        This lengthy book is a wealth of material on what
        uses people could put business machines to, includ-
        ing punch card systems. It has application descrip-
        tions along with a survey of existing hardware and
        some bibliography.

1019   "New Methods to Order and Inventory Control in Rubber
        Footwear," Rubber Age 25 (September 25, 1929): 671-
        672.

        This is a postive story on inventory control and of
        its methods, using punch card equipment.

1020   Paetzold, F.L. "Use of Mechanical Devices in Treasury
        Department," Railway Age 73 (November 4, 1922): 839.

This accounting brief discuses of punch cards in
financial applications as they apply to a railroad.

1021   Parker, R.H.   "Punched Card Method in Circulation
        Work; Duplicate Key Punch and Horizontal Sorter,"
        Library Journal 61 (December 1, 1936): 903-905.

        The author describes how to use punch card equipment
        to help manage the library book circulation process.

1022   "Payroll Machine," Management and Administration 8
        (September 1924): 312-313.

        This describes the use of punch cards for payroll
        management at a time when this application was
        spreading widely among large organizations.

1023   Perry, R.P. "General Accounting With Bookkeeping
        Machines," Electric Railway Journal 61 (March 10,
        1923): 413-414.

        The industry's trade publications continued to pub-
        licize installations of tabulating equipment even
        though by the 1920s the use of such technology had
        been evident in the railroad business for over 30
        years.

1024   Porteous, Kenneth. "Factory Orders and Inventory
        Records: Case History of Their Mechanical Prepara-
        tion," Factory Management and Maintenance 95
        (September 1937): 70-80.

        The Union Switch and Signal Company installed IBM
        punch card equipment in the 1930s to manage infor-
        mation on routing, tooling and materials.

1025   Price, C.O. "Calculating Machine in Railroad Account-
        ing," Railway Review 64 (June 28, 1919): 972-976,
        Ibid. 65 (October 25, 1919): 600-601.

        Articles on railroad accounting applications, pub-
        lished before the 1920s, are few. This one describes
        work begun several years earlier on the use of
        tabulating equipment.

1026   "Railroad Accounting by Use of Perforated Cards,"
        Railway Review 76 (May 30, 1925): 980-985.

        Like the previous entry, this is a positive account
        of the use of punch card applications.

1027   "Railway Accounting With Punched Cards," Railway Rev-
        iew 79 (September 4, 1926): 353-354.

        This continues a type of publication popular in the
        1920s within this industry.

1028   "Rock Island Goes Modern in Material Accounting,"
        Railway Age 106 (June 10, 1939): 976-984.

The application described here is accounting with
statistical analysis. Card punch equipment was first
used in January, 1939, in material handling. It was
a huge application of such equipment, employing 66
IBM machines.

1029   Rowland, F.H. "Textile Accounting and Punched Cards,"
        Textile World 69 (May 1, 1926): 3025-3026.

        This is the earliest, or one of the first, articles
        published on the use of punch cards in this industry.

1030   Scheyer, C. "Control of Machines by Perforated
        Records," American Machinist 55 (November 10, 1921):
        743-747.

        Shop floor automation became increasingly important
        during the 1920s. This article describes how punch
        cards can play a role in such automation.

1031   Scheyer, C. "When Perforated Paper Goes to Work,"
        Scientific American 127 (December 1922): 394-395.

        This continues the theme first developed in the
        previous bibliographic entry.

1032   Schnackel, H.G. and Lang, Henry C. Accounting by
        Machine Methods: The Design and Operation of Modern
        Systems. New York: Ronald Press Co., 1929.

        This is a 563-page "how to" book on equipment and
        applications of the 1920s; an important source for
        the period.

1033   "Sorting and Tabulating Machines in Disbursement Work,"
        Railway Review 67 (July 10, 1920): 51-52.

        Railroads were, along with insurance companies, the
        leading commercial users of punch card equipment by
        1920. In this article disbursement accounting is
        described.

1034   Sperling, I.I. "Reducing Routine to Minutes," Banking
        30 (May 1938): 66-68.

        The Cleveland Trust Company installed punch card
        equipment to handle large volumes of data and to
        produce reports on trust accounts, lists of securi-
        ties, income and analysis sheets.

1035   "Station Accounting by Punched Card Systems," Railway
        Review 79 (October 16, 1926): 575-578.

        The topic is obvious; it relied on punch card equip-
        ment doing a new application.

1036   "Statistical Bureau of Freight Auditor's Office,"
        Railway Review 77 (July 11, 1925): 41-47.

This was one of the first departments within a railroad to use punch card equipment (1890s), the article one of the last to appear on the subject.

1037   Twohy, Frank. "Application of Tabulating Equipment
       in Accounting Procedures," Journal of the American
       Water Works Association 28 (November 1936): 1704-
       1711.

       The Bureau of Water Works and Supply at Los Angeles
       used punch card equipment first to do customer bill-
       ing, bookkeeping, and accounting before finding
       other uses for such hardware.

1038   Van Bibber, A.E. "Using Punched Cards for Controlling
       Materials," American Machinist 51 (August 14, 1919):
       295-300.

       Materials control, particularly in manufacturing
       facilities, early became a logical inventory manage-
       ment application suitable for automation with punch
       card equipment. A case is described of the benefits
       of such an implementation.

1039   Van Drooge, H. "Orders, Inventory, Billings Under
       Automatic Control," Factory Management 97 (June
       1939): 56-59.

       At McKesson and Robbins, Inc., the central tabula-
       ting center offered a wide variety of services much
       like computer data centers did more than 20 years
       later. The services are described.

1040   Vannais, L.E. "Punched Card Accounting From the Audit
       Viewpoint," Journal of Accountancy 70 (September
       1940): 200-217; Ibid. 70 (October 1940): 339-356.

       This is a major review of the subject in which the
       author explains how best to create audit trails in
       punch card systems and then how to audit these in
       comparison to manual accounting applications. The
       principles developed by accountants in the punch card
       era were applied almost directly for over two decades
       in the post mid-1950s era of computer-based applica-
       tions.

1041   Waite, Frederick A. "The Electrographic System of
       Trust Accounting," Trust Companies 63 (August 1936):
       187-194, 439-443.

       Merchants National Bank of Boston used punch card
       equipment for trust accounting in the 1930s, using
       IBM products. The article describes this applica-
       tion and includes the cost justification for it.

1042   Weig, W.J. "Punched Card Accounting for Mortgages,"
       Banking 29 (January 1937): 28.

       The Guaranty Trust Compant of New York installed

this application. The firm used IBM products from
the earliest days of the punch card company's marketing to banks.

1043   Woodruff, L.F. "Systems of Electric Remote Control
       Accounting," Electrical Engineering 57: Transact-
       ions (February 1938): 78-87.

       Kaufmann's Department Store used punch card equip-
       ment for inventory control at the store level, which
       is described here.

1044   Workman, E.W. "Cost Accounting by Machinery, The
       Hollerith System," Engineering and Industrial
       Management 6 (September 1921): 314-318.

       This is an early description of how to do cost
       accounting with punch card equipment. It was to be
       during the 1920s that cost accounting became a
       widespread accounting application, in part because
       of the convenience of punch card equipment.

       Punch Card Applications: Commercial, 1940s

1045   Adamson, J.R. "Punched Card System Speeds Accounting
       at Trion Division, Riegel Textile Corporation,"
       Textile World 99 (June 1949): 114-115ff.

       This is a self-congratulatory account of the system.

1046   Albach, O.H. "Economy in Interline Accounting,"
       Railway Age 128 (January 28, 1950): 224-227.

       This is on tracking charges and inventory for goods
       and rolling stock used by multiple railroad compa-
       nies.

1047   "Automatic Calculator: Remington Rand," Business Week
       657 (April 4, 1942): 69.

       This describes the use of a new Remington Rand
       machine that had a 10 key calculator introduced in
       1939 doing automatic multiplication of constants.

1048   Baird, D.G. "Buick Speeds Orders with Punched Cards,"
       American Business 20 (September 1950): 50.

       This describes order processing for the sale of
       Buick automobiles.

1049   Baird, D.G. "Speed Order Handling With New Speed at
       Chrysler Corporation," American Business 19 (April
       1949): 10-11.

       This is like the previous article, except this is
       about Chrysler automobiles.

1050   Baird, D.G. "Hudson Parts Control Method," American
       Business 17 (October 1947): 12-13.

This surveys parts control and inventory management
using punch cards within the automotive industry.

1051 Benjamin, K. "Problems of Multiple Punching with
      Hollerith Machines," Journal of the American Sta-
      tistical Association 42 (March 1947): 46-71.

      The use of punch cards in statistical work is des-
      cribed. It is interesting to note the use of the
      word Hollerith so many years after the term had lost
      currency and had been replaced with e.g., IBM.

1052 Beswick, G.J. and Littlewort, H.G. "Use of the Multi-
      plying Punch," American Gas Association Monthly 29
      (September 1947): 401-404.

      By the 1940s some punch card machines were becoming
      calculator-like, even computer-like in function,
      leading to more complex uses. This is a good reflec-
      tion of that process at work.

1053 Block, B.J. and Olds, E.B. "Punched Card Method for
      Presenting, Analyzing and Comparing Many Series of
      Statistics for Areas," Journal of the American
      Statistical Association 41 (September 1946): 347-355.

      As punch card products became more sophisticated,
      with enhanced calculating capability, such applica-
      tions became more possible. This describes such a
      use.

1054 Bolger, L.T. "California Fruit Growers Exchange
      Cooperates on Low Cost Methods," American Business
      19 (July 1949): 32ff.

      One way they cooperated was through punch card based
      accounting systems that included inventory control.

1055 Bond, G.D. "Continuous Meter Reading," Electrician
      125 (December 27, 1940): 336-336.

      Although implemented initially in the 1930s, this
      use of punch cards became increasingly widespread in
      the late 1940s with the post-World War II housing
      boom.

1056 Bruce, H.W. "Keeping Meter Records With Business
      Machines," Electrical West 94 (December 1946): 58-
      59.

      As with the previous bibliographic citation, this
      one is concerned with how to manage customer account
      information and billing through the use of punch
      card equipment.

1057 Bryan, R.N. "Mechanical Brain Aids Canadian Census
      Takers," Compressed Air Magazine 47 (July 1942):
      6793-6794.

Census taking, by the 1940s, had been done with punch cards for half a century in North America. Each time it took place, however, articles such as these would marvel at the extensive use of punch cards and explain why.

1058   Brown, J.K. "Punched Card Payroll Accounting," American Gas Association Proceedings (1947): 273-275.

This is a typical description of the benefits of payroll management using punch cards.

1059   Cady, G.H. and Boley, C.C. "Methods of Recording Coal Data," Economic Geology 35 (November 1940): 876-882.

This is almost like an inventory control application in which punch cards are used in a mining business.

1060   "Canadian Pacific Speeds Car Tracing," Railway Age 128 (December 1949): 311-312.

This is an inventory application for managing the location and allocation of rolling stock. This use of punch cards was not new in the 1940s but had been applied since the turn of the century.

1061   "Census Machine Does Work of 500 People," American Business 19 (December 1949): 24.

Each time a census was taken, articles such as these appeared, explaining the benefits of accounting equipment. The term "census machine", although very old fashioned in the 1940s, was the original name of Hollerith's equipment in the 1880s/1890s within U.S. Government circles.

1062   Chapin, T.A., Jr. "Some Problems of Installing a Punched Card System," N.A.C.A. Bulletin 27 (October 1945): 99-116.

The author published some widely-distributed books in the 1950s on the management of data processing. This early article recounts experiences with both installation and initial use of punch card systems with recommendations on how best to do that.

1063   Clemence, G.M. and Herget, Paul. "Optimum-Interval Punched-Card Tables," Mathematical Tables and Other Aids to Computation 1, No. 6 (April 1944): 173-176.

While the application described is a technical one, the use of tables was increasingly an issue in punch card tabulation in the 1940s within businesses.

1064   Cochran, J.W. "Recent Progress in Patent Classification," Industrial and Engineering Chemistry 40 (April 1948): 721-723.

The use of punch cards here is not a technical or

scientific application but rather a records keeping
function.

1065   Collins, L.S.   "Mechanical Labor Distribution for Job
        Cost Accounting," Ceramic Industry 36 (March 1941):
        45ff.

        Although not a new application for punch cards, it
        continued to experience new users all through the
        1940s.

1066   Conley, R.   "Check Handling Made Easier," American
        Business 16 (January 1946): 14-15.

        Banking applications of punch card technology were
        often on the leading edge of new uses. Check handl-
        ing was continuously automated and standardized all
        during the 1940s and 1950s as the volume of checks
        increased. This is an early explanation of one case
        of the process at work.

1067   "Conventional and Mechanical Search Methods," Indus-
        trial and Engineering Chemistry 42 (August 1950):
        1456-1457.

        This describes the use of punch card technology in
        a primative "data base" application.

1068   Crandall, G. and Brown, B.   "Information Service Using
        Both Hand and Machine Sorted Cards," Journal of
        Chemical Education 25 (April 1948): 195-196.

        This reviews the use of machine and hand punched
        card record keeping to list references at Socony -
        Vaccum Laboratories. The benefits of each approach
        are explained and the conclusion is drawn that a
        combination of the two is most efficient.

1069   Critchlow, E.F.   "Measurement and Prediction of Air-
        craft Vibration by Punched Card Systems," S.A.E.
        Journal 52 (August 1944): 368-379.

        The aircraft industry has always been a major user
        of mechanical aids to computing, particularly in
        design engineering. This punch card-based applica-
        tion is an early example of that kind of use.

1070   "Customer Inquiries Are Handled by Machine," American
        Business 19 (May 1949): 30.

        Punch cards are used to log customer information.

1071   "Daily Production Material Control Cuts Inventory and
        Speeds Planning," American Machinist 88 (August 3,
        1944): 94-96.

        Inventory control for raw materials and work-in-
        process (WIP) became a major application area for
        manufacturing companies, as illustrated here.

1072   "Data Detector: IBM System for Correlation of Large
        Numbers of Chemicals," Chemical Industries 67
        (August 1950): 183.

        This does not describe a purely scientific research
        and development application but rather a more common
        industrial one.

1073   Deemer, W.L. "Use of Mark Sensing in Large Scale
        Testing," Journal of the American Statistical
        Association 43 (March 1948): 40-52.

        Mark sensing experiments had been going on since
        the 1920s as a method of data collection by the use
        of electronics. This describes such a use but based
        on a punch card system.

1074   Delong, F.G. "Punched Card Method of Trust Accounting,"
        Trusts and Estates 72 (April 1941): 407-410; (June
        1941): 79-82.

        This is simply another application brief on a well-
        established use of punch cards in banking.

1075   Demming, W.E. "Errors in Card Punching," Journal of
        the American Statistical Association 37 (December
        1942): 525-536.

        This may be the most detailed study of punch errors
        published. In the case of card verification, its
        samples showed that errors varied from 0.5 to 5.0
        percent. This is important information since so
        much was spent on data verification.

1076   "Depreciation of Machine Accounting for Insurance
        General Agency," Pathfinder Service Bulletin 186
        (April 1949), unpaginated.

        This bulletin describes one application that requires
        calculating worth of insured items for purposes of
        establishing loss values.

1077   Donaldson, R.W. "Control of Accounts Payable by
        Punched Card Methods," N.A.C.A. Bulletin 30 (Novem-
        ber 1, 1948): 257-263.

        This is an application brief on accounts payable
        using punch card files and technology.

1078   Dunstan, L.A. "Machine Computation of Power Network
        Performance," Electrical Engineering 66 (September
        1947): 901-906.

        This outlines a system employed in computing power
        network performance, listing advantages and disadvan-
        tages of the described methods.

1079   Egan, D.J. "It's All in the Cards," Business Trans-
        portation 23 (November 1944): 48-51.

This is a short description of a scheduling application.

1080   Elliot, J.D.   "Customer Billing in a Electric Utility,"
       Edison Electric Institute Bulletin 13 (December
       1945): 354-356.

       Beginning in the 1930s, utilities automated billing
       and this case study of a New York utility, was
       simply the latest in process.

1081   Epstein, A.P.   "Practical Uses of Trade Union Records,"
       Monthly Labor Review 68 (March 1949): 300-301.

       This is a description of data manipulated and studied
       by using punch card equipment within the U.S. Govern-
       ment to analyze the American workforce.

1082   Fairbanks, E.E.   "Punched Card Identification of Ore
       Minerals," Economic Geology 41 (November 1946):
       761-768.

       The use of punch cards in mining had been limited to
       normal administrative processing. This describes a
       unique use of punch cards.

1083   "Figures That Help Top Management Decide," American
       Business 19 (July 1949): 18-19.

       By the 1950s decision-making reports and "what if"
       analysis generated by computational devices became
       very normal. This is an early description of such
       an application, based on the use of punch card files
       and equipment.

1084   Forest, J.H.   "Liberty Mutual Develops Machine Writing
       of Automobile Policies by Punched Cards," National
       Underwriters 52 (October 28, 1948): 2ff.

       Printing policies with the injection of appropriate
       data specific to a policy was tried using punch card
       systems.

1085   French, R.G.   "Quick Figures Cut Shipping Delays at
       Chrysler Plant," American Business 11 (June 1941):
       30-31.

       Chrysler invested $100,000 in Remington Rand products
       which are described and their use explained.

1086   French, R.G.   "This Record Reveals Extra Skills of
       Workers," American Business 15 (December 1945): 12-
       13.

       This describes a personnel record system in an auto-
       motive plant.

1087   "From Hand to Electrical Accounting Methods of Sorting
       and Billing Operations," American Business 18 (July
       1948): 12-13.

Accounts receivable applications were a logic use
of punch cards. This article describes a case of
its application.

1088   Gallagher, A.M. "Week's Work Done in 8 Hours," American Business 18 (November 1948): 22ff.

While productivity gains were usually experienced
when manual operations were put on punch card systems,
few articles were specific on quantification of time
saved, speed gained. This article offers evidence
of productivity.

1089   Gallagher, A.M. "Wholesale Figures for the Millions,"
American Business 19 (January 1949): 18-19.

Gallagher describes a punch card system in which
efficiency and productivity justified the investment.

1090   "Government Moves to Stabilize Office Salaries,"
American Business 13 (July 1943): 17-18.

One June 8, 1943 the Wage Labor Board was established by the U.S. Government to stabilize salaries. The
article describes salary levels and ways of measuring
data relevant to these.

1091   "Handling Partial Payments on Cash Splits With Mark
Sensing Tabulating Cards," American Gas Association
Monthly 26 (October 1944): 418-419.

Punch cards were used in this case to document cash
splits at Consolidated Edison of New York, employing
IBM mark sensing equipment.

1092   Harper, W.F. and McGinnity, W.J. "Completely Mechanical Material Control System," N.A.C.A. Bulletin 31
(July 1950): 1371-1377.

This describes material inventory control in a
factory environment using punch cards.

1093   Hartkemeier, H.P. and Miller, H.E. "Obtaining Differences From Punched Cards," Journal of the American
Statistical Association 37 (June 1942): 285-287.

This is a sophisticated article on mathematics but
for applications relevant to business.

1094   Hayward, R.J. "Street Lighting Record Control Modern-
ized," Electrical World 123 (January 6, 1945): 104ff.

This application became increasingly evident in the
1940s although some U.S. cities had begun working
with it in the 1920s.

1095   Hood, T.A. "Punched Cards for Field of Metal Finish-
ing," Metal Progress 56 (July 1949): 75-78.

Complex manufacturing processes adopted punch card systems for record keeping and job performance analysis in the 1930s and 1940s; one is described here.

1096   "How Lightolier's Punched Card Installation Produces Statements in 6 Instead of 20 Days," _Journal of Accounting_ 90 (August 1950): 136-140.

This manufacturer of lights uses punch card technology in the 1950s to produce its bills and to manage accounts receivable.

1097   "How to Set Up Property Records on Punched Cards to Facilitate Depreciation Accounting," _Journal of Accounting_ 90 (October 1950): 341-342.

The use of tabulating equipment that had computer-like processing capabilities after World War II made such applications easier to develop.

1098   "Insurance Accounting Urged to Use Card Systems," _National Underwriters (Life Edition)_ 50 (May 17, 1946): 7.

The rise in amount of information, caused by expanded business and increased government requirements, made it imperative that insurance companies manage data more efficiently and use to greater effect. Punch card technology was a way of helping that process.

1099   International Business Machines Corporation. _War Accounting Service_. Endicott, N.Y.: International Business Machines Corporation, 1943.

This is an application brief that describes how to perform the various war-related accounting functions required by the U.S. government using punch card equipment.

1100   "Inventory Records Kept 99% Accurate," _American Business_ 20 (June 1950): 10-11.

By the late 1940s this application of punch card technology was a well-established one with a proven track record of success. This article is simply a very late description of such a use.

1101   Israel, W.C. "Sensing Marks on Tabulating Cards," _American Gas Association Proceedings 1941_ (1941): 198-205.

More than a description of hardware, the article also surveys new uses for such technology as of the late 1930a/early 1940s.

1102   "It's All in the Cards," _Bus Transportation_ 27 (April 1948): 66-68.

This describes the use of punch cards in such typical applications in transportation as scheduling.

1103   Jacobs, N.B. "Coordinating Operating System Records
        With Accounting Records," Journal of the American
        Water Works Association 32 (February 1940): 225-241.

        While reflecting experiences with 1930s' vintage
        technology, it is a useful description of how to
        manage such equipment and not merely an application
        brief.

1104   Johnson, R.I. "Post Sales Record for Manufacturing
        Equipment," N.A.C.A. Bulletin 29 (April 1, 1948):
        955-960.

        This describes an application that had not received
        much publicity prior to the 1960s using information
        handling equipment.

1105   Kassenhohen, W. "Preventing Press Work Problems,"
        American Machinist 84 (March 1940): 162-163.

        During the 1930s and 1940s many shop floor applica-
        tions for punch card equipment came into existence.
        This article reflects that process by describing one
        case.

1106   Machine Sorts Information Fast," Business Week No. 1055
        (November 19, 1949): 41-42.

        While a description of hardware, the article descri-
        bes sorting. Sorting was a fundamental feature of
        all punch card applications: shuffling data into
        different piles that made sense to a user.

1107   "Management Reports Reveal Trends," American Business
        18 (September 1948): 18-19.

        By the 1940s punch card equipment was being used to
        produce summary reports for management based on
        substantial amounts of information in punch card
        form. It is the most important justification for
        the use of such technology.

1108   "Mark Sensing Aids in Taking Inventory," Railway Age
        129 (July 29, 1950): 16-17.

        This describes a well-known application using punch
        card equipment of the late 1940s.

1109   McGann, H. "Combination Billing Service," American
        Gas Association Monthly 31 (July 1949): 25-26; Ibid.
        (August 1949): 50.

        Billing applications in this industry was a basic
        function made complicated by this industry's early
        efforts to tie many of its activities to billing,
        managing the process with punch card equipment.

1110   McNeill, J.C. "Machine Methods Promote Efficiency in
        Mine Accounting," Coal Age 50 (November 1945): 109-
        114.

        This is a general overview of a series of applica-
        tions in the coal mining business employing punch
        card equipment.

1111   McNeill, J.C. "Payroll Work Speeded Up By Modern
        Machine Equipment," Coal Age 51 (August 1946): 109-
        114.

        This is a description of a common use of punch card
        equipment within a coal mining company, however,

1112   McPherson, J.C. "Mathematical Operations With Punched
        Cards," Journal of the American Statistical Associa-
        tion 37 (June 1942): 275-281.

        This is a well written description of available
        machines and uses, circa 1940/41, with statements
        about their capabilities.

1113   "Mechanized Accounting," Mass Transportation 37
        (October 1941): 141ff.

        This is more of a description of accounting with
        punch cards by a city than a general review of the
        subject.

1114   "Milwaukee's Street Inventory Record Will Facilitate
        Prediction of Future Pavement Requirements,"
        Engineering News 136 (January 10, 1946): 63-67.

        This was a common application of punch cards, in
        effect, to do inventory management and job schedu-
        ling.

1115   "Modern Machines for Trust Operating Economy," Trusts
        and Estates 89 (July 1950): 470-472.

        This describes the application in one bank. The
        benefits of such a system are also touted.

1116   Moore, E.L. "Paperwork for Smooth Flow and Close
        Control," Factory Management 103 (October 1945):
        134-138.

        IBM products are described being used for parts and
        material control, payroll and other accounting
        applications. It also lists the equipment used and
        their capacities; circa early 1940s.

1117   "Moraine Products Improves Payroll with New Check,"
        American Business 16 (September 1946): 36ff.

        The check is a punch card technology output docu-
        ment.

1118   Muncy, W.G.   "Accounting Control with Punched Card
        Procedures," Bus Transportation 28 (April 1949):
        62-64.

        This is a case study of the use of punch cards at
        one bus company with explations of why and how.

1119   "New Billing System Cuts Time and Errors for Common-
        wealth Edison," American Business 18 (June 1948):
        12-13.

        Edison had long been a user of punch card equipment
        for billing. This describes an enhanced version of
        that application, with new function and using hard-
        ware of the late 1940s.

1120   "New Electronic Statistical Machine to be Used in
        Census," Electrical Engineering 69 (February 1950):
        147ff.

        This describes hardware but also offers a review of
        the plans for the 1950 US census for the implementa-
        tion of data processing equipment.

1121   "New Payroll Procedures in Canadian National," Railway
        Age 129 (July 29, 1950): 18-20.

        This describes the use of punch cards in a payroll
        application, reflecting common trends in usage
        evident in other North American railroad lines.

1122   "New Pre-Billing System Ups Office Output for Service
        Parts," American Business 18 (May 1948): 14-15.

        This describes a combination inventory control and
        accounts receivables application of punch card
        equipment.

1123   Nilson, C.J.   "Putting the Factory Ledger on Punched
        Cards," N.A.C.A. Bulletin 31 (September 1949): 67-
        76.

        This describes one factory's experience and includes
        details on specific applications unique to a manu-
        facturing environment.

1124   "No More Cut-Ups, New Haven Has Mechanized Entire Car
        Service Procedures," Railway Age 128 (February 18,
        1950): 356-357.

        This comuter railroad's experience with continued
        automation of maintenance, scheduling, inventory and
        other controls is described.

1125   Noah, S., Jr.   "Payroll Accounting by Punched Card
        Methods," N.A.C.A. Bulletin 28 (August 15, 1947):
        1512-1531.

        This is a description of the application with bene-
        fits.

1126   Norris, W. "Better Methods Shatter Glass Company's
        Costs," _American Business_ 19 (March 1949): 8-9.

        The better methods involved manufacturing accounting
        using punch card methods.

1127   Notaro, M.R. "Punched Card Service Equally Applicable
        to Small Agency," _National Underwriter_ 53 (June 16,
        1949): 6ff.

        The article offers the argument that not only large
        insurance companies can benefit from punch card
        applications.

1128   "Novel System Mechanizes All Car Reports," _Railway_
        Age 120 (February 23, 1946): 394-398.

        The system is a punch card based one and involved
        rolling stock inventory and scheduling control.

1129   Otcasek, C.D. "Tabulating Cards Control of Meters,"
        American Gas Association Monthly 28 (April 1946):
        173-176.

        Utilities increasingly went to punch card accounting
        systems during the 1930s and 1940s. This is yet
        another, of a series of reports, of such companies
        migrating to more automated methods of controlling
        operations.

1130   "Paramount Studio Saves $36,000 Per Year: Uses Punched
        Card Accounting," _American Business_ 20 (March 1950):
        10-11.

        This is one of the earliest articles to address the
        issue of data processing in the movie making busi-
        ness. The applications described are routine
        accounting ones.

1131   Patton, W.G. "Pontiac Using Punched Card System for
        Distributing Available Cars," _Iron Age_ 159 (March
        27, 1947): 74ff.

        This is an inventory control application description.

1132   "Payroll System Saves $10,000 Per Year," _American_
        Business 20 (February 1950): 12-13.

        Punch card payroll systems were still being reported
        on since many businesses had not yet installed them.
        It was still new news in the 1940s and 1950s in mid-
        sized companies.

1133   Peakes, G.L. "Report Indexing by Punched Card,"
        Journal of Chemical Education 26 (March 1949): 139-
        146.

        This is more of an academic or library data manage-
        ment application found in American industry.

1134   "Pencil Entries Now Recorded Automatically on Punched
        Cards," Journal of Accountancy 81 (April 1946):
        332ff.

        This is one of a series of articles published by the
        journal in the 1940s on the value and use of punch
        card technology in accountancy.

1135   Pennington, P.R. "Sales and Production Outran Office
        Methods," American Business 17 (November 1947): 10-
        17.

        After describing the problem of loss of control, the
        author discusses the response made to it by using
        punch card equipment to handle more data, faster,
        and less expensively than before.

1136   Perry, J.W. "A.C.S. Punch Card Committee: Interim
        Report," Chemistry and Engineering News 27 (March
        14, 1949): 754-756.

        This report argues that existing punch card techno-
        logy restricted use of cards to only a small number
        of possible permutations of combinations in chemical
        research and applications but that changes in the
        technology should change that, offering greater
        flexibility.

1137   Perry, J.W. et al. "Round Table Discussion: Indexing
        and Classifying Results of Chemical Research in
        Relation to Punched Card Investigations," Journal
        of Chemical Education 24 (February 1947): 71-74.

        This offers various opinions concerning the value
        of punched cards in chemical research and applica-
        tions. The general concensus was that it is a
        time and cost saving tool.

1138   "Price Tag Accounting Automatically," Business Week
        No. 1034 (June 25, 1949): 84.

        This discusses price tags for products in retail
        business being managed by punch card methods.

1139   "Punched Card Accounting System at Sun Shipyard,"
        Marine Engineering 54 (March 1949): 71-72.

        This essentially describes production control and
        manufacturing applications.

1140   "Punched Card Installations Must be Planned," N.A.C.A.
        Bulletin 32 (September 1950): 27-38.

        This details the experience of one company install-
        ing punch card equipment.

1141   "Punched Card Machines and Studies of Flutter and
        Vibration in Planes," Journal of the Civil Aeronau-
        tics Administration 7 (January 15, 1946): 2ff.

This describes modelling with punch cards in the design of aircraft.

1142   "Punched Card Method Offers Agencies Real Cost Control," National Underwriters 53 (June 2, 1949): 6ff.

This describes punch card applications in the insurance industry with specific reference to underwriting.

1143   "Punched Card System for Information Data," Petroleum Processing 3 (June 1948): 527-528.

This is an early publication on the use of punch cards in the petroleum industry.

1144   Raywind, J. "Punched Card System for My Agency?," Spectator (Prperty Edition) 14 (June 1949): 16.

The answer was yes with an explanation of why.

1145   "Restoring Lost Babbage," Bus Transportation 23 (October 1944): 28-30.

This describes a novel inventory control system using tabulating equipment and punch card files.

1146   Riddle, L.P. "Analytical and Accounting Control of Sales and Gross Profit by Punched Cards," N.A.C.A. Bulletin 29 (November 15, 1947): 323-334.

This is an excellent description of the application and of the costs and benefits of the same.

1147   Root, W.J. "Block Rate Computations," American Gas Association Monthly 25 (February 1943): 75-77.

Root describes analysis of product costs and accounting using punch cards, for a single utility.

1148   Rostler, K.S. "Applications of Punched Cards to Indexing Rubber Compounds," India Rubber World No. 120 (September 1949): 698-701.

This is essentially a description of a process control/manufacturing data base management system using punch card files.

1149   "Scales Management Survey of Buying Power: Data Available on IBM Punched Cards," Sales Management 62 (May 1, 1949): 66.

This is a short piece on the acquisition of cards and data rather than on a specific application.

1150   Sargent, A.M. "Accurate Personnel Selection by Punched Card Systems," Factory Management 62 (May 1, 1949): 66.

One of a very few articles on the use of punch card
technology to manage personnel. It became an important application, however, during the computer age.

1151   Selgoie, T.A.   "Case Study of Accounting for Fixed
       Assets," N.A.C.A. Bulletin 23 (October 15, 1941):
       221-232.

       This is probably the first article published in the
       U.S. dedicated to this application for punch card
       equipment. It is a detailed, useful description.

1152   Sherman, C.W.   "Personnel Accounting," Electrical
       World No. 132 (October 8, 1949): 112-113.

       This is similar in subject to No. 1150 above.

1153   Sidak, J.G.   "Property Records and Depreciation Account-
       ing on Punched Cards," N.A.C.A. Bulletin 28 (July 1,
       1947): 1352-1358.

       This is a case study of one organization's experience
       and rationale for such a system.

1154   "Slash Order Handling Errors and Costs," American
       Business 19 (February 1949): 26ff.

       The application and its benefits are described.
       This was an important application by the mid-1950s
       in the United States.

1155   "Some Precautionary Notes on Audit of Sales and Receiv-
       ables When Accounts Are Kept on Punched Cards,"
       Journal of Accounting 89 (June 1950): 522-523.

       Errors and audability are important issues. Advice
       on these are offered here.

1156   Sparks, C.C.   "Fitting the Audit Program to Punched
       Card Accounting Systems," Journal of Accounting 86
       (September 1948): 196-200.

       This was a major issue with accountants throughout
       the era of punched cards. Some advice on dealing
       with it is offered in this article.

1157   Spowart, D.J.   "Car Records on Tabulating Equipment,"
       Railway Age 126 (May 14, 1949): 946-948.

       This is one of many such articles to describe
       inventory control in the railway industry.

1158   "Stock Control System Uses Punched Cards," American
       Business 20 (May 1950): 12-13.

       This was a widely used application, particularly in
       the retail business. This is more a brief announce-
       ment of its use in one organization rather than a
       description.

1159   "Taking a Big Bite Out of Costs," American Business
        16 (September 1946): 18-19.

        This is a typical testimonial of the period to the
        benefits of punch card technology's use in managing
        organizations.

1160   Tanner, Cyrus. "Talent Tabulator," Personnel Journal
        23 (April 1945): 375-377.

        He describes how the National Roster of Scientific
        and Specialized Personnel performed important work
        in the U.S. during World War II in locating people
        with specific skills, using punch card equipment.

1161   Tassie, J.M. "Three Way Control for Low Cost Opera-
        tion," Factory Management 104 (December 1946): 110-
        112.

        This is a short description of punch card applica-
        tions in manufacturing.

1162   "Taxpayers Refunds Are Speeded by Machine," American
        Business 19 (March 1949): 18-19.

        This is a description of a U.S. tax application, one
        that would be described later in many articles when
        it was computerized.

1163   "Teletyped Bills Save A Million A Year," American
        Business 19 (August 1949): 18-19.

        By the late 1940s major organizations had automated
        billing applications using punch cards. This is a
        description of one such case.

1164   Thomas, J.D. "Mechanized Accountancy and Statistical
        Work As Applied to Middlesex Gas Company," Gas
        Journal 250 (May 14, 1947): 336-338.

        The work describes is an example of management
        information systems in the utility industry. This
        uses punch card equipment to do the work.

1165   Turner, J. "Four Major Departments Profit From
        Mechanized Sales and Accounting Reports," American
        Business 18 (January 1948): 10-11.

        Punch cards are part of the technological base used
        in the case study described here.

1166   Turner, J. "Payroll, Costs, and Personnel Figures
        From One Machine," American Business 16 (December
        1946): 16-17.
        The equipment was a tabulator system.

1167   Turner, J. "Stock Control Plans to Increase Profits,"
        American Business 17 (January 1947): 12-13.

This represents a brief, but useful, description of punch cards in inventory management.

1168   Turner, J. "Top Management Gets the Figures," American Business 16 (November 1946): 8-9.

He describes summary accounting reporting using punch card equipment.

1169   "Two Clerks Do the Bookkeeping for 26,000 Consumer Loans," Bankers Monthly 66 (November 1949): 5-7.

The case is specific and deals with consumer loans, an application area hardly touched on by other articles on banking applications of the 1930s and 1940s.

1170   Unton, R.W. "Mechanization Cuts Time for Rewriting Meter Sheets," Electrical World 133 (March 27, 1950): 108ff.

This is a public utility application.

1171   Vannais, L.E. "The Accountant's Responsibility for Making Punched Card Installations Successful," Journal of Accountancy 88 (October 1949): 282-298.

Most punch card installations were controlled by accounting or financial departments. This article addresses the responsibilities and tasks involved.

1172   "Volume Up 50%, Few Workers Added," American Business 19 (October 1949): 12-13.

Productivity continues as a theme of this, the latest of a series of articles published in this journal on the use of punch cards in the late 1940s.

1173   "Walkie-Talkie Inventory Cuts Shut Down Time," Modern Industry 15 (March 1948): 83-84.

This is specifically a warehouse management and inventory control application.

1174   Wall, S.G. "Detail Posted General Ledger Through Use of Tabulatory Equipment," N.A.C.A. Bulletin 31 (September 1949): 59-66.

This is a useful article on the "how" of this application.

1175   Weibenson, H.C. "Expense Accounting Simplified by Electrical Accounting Machine," Bankers Monthly 59 (December 1942): 552-553.

Most banking articles deal with their products and services; this concerns overhead.

1176   Wornick, J.G.   "Machine Prorates Freight Revenues,"
        Railway Age 126 (May 14, 1949): 950-952.

        Railroads often shared goods being transported which
        called for a sharing as well of fees for that ser-
        vice.   The general application is described with a
        specific case study.

Punch Card Applications: Scientific, 1930s-1940s

1177   Alt, Franz L.   "Multiplication of Matrices,"   Mathema-
        tical Tables and Other Aids to Computation 2, No. 13

        He describes the use of card punch calculators in
        mathematics.

1178   Atanasoff, John V. and Brandt, A.E.   "Application of
        Punched Card Equipment to the Analysis of Complex
        Spectra,"   Journal of the Optical Society of America
        26, No. 2 (February 1936): 83-88.

        They detail the use of a tabulator with a "cross-
        connecting board" to store numerical values.

1179   Bailey, C.F. et al. "Punch Cards for Indexing Scienti-
        fic Data,"   Science 104 (August 23, 1946): 181.

        Punch cards were used in scientific research in the
        1940s both in physics and mathematics. This is a
        description of such a use.

1180   Comrie, Leslie J., "The Application of Commercial
        Calculating Machines to Scientific Computating,"
        Mathematical Tables and Other Aids to Computation 2
        (1946): 149-159.

        He reviews desk calculators, adding machines and
        punch card devices for applications in science.

1181   Comrie, Leslie J.   "The Application of the Hollerith
        Tabulating Machine to Brown's Tables of the Moon,"
        Monthly Notices, Royal Astronomical Society 92, No.
        7 (1932): 694-707.

        This describes a famous piece of work done with
        punch card equipment in 1929 at the Nautical Almanac
        Office by the author.

1182   Comrie, Leslie J. et al. "The Application of Hollerith
        Equipment to an Agricultural Investigation," Supple-
        ment to the Journal of the Royal Statistical Society
        4, No. 2 (1937): 210-224.

        This is a detailed review of how punch card equipment
        from IBM was used in one application, involving the
        entire range of gear: tabulators, sorters, and multi-
        plying punches. This was a complex use of such tech-
        nology.

1183   Cox, G.J.   "Punched Cards for a Chemical Bibliography,"
        Chemical and Engineering News 23 (September 25,
        1945): 1623-1626.

        This is an early description of a mechanized biblio-
        graphy in the sciences. By the 1960s, all scientific
        literature in English, for example, was being abstrac-
        ted by some mechanical means.

1184   Culley, Frank L.   "Use of Accounting Machines for Mass
        Transformation From Geographic to Military-Grid
        Coordinates," in American Geographical Union Trans-
        actions of 1942 (Washington, D.C.: National Research
        Council, 1942), Part 2, pp. 190-197.

        This describes how the work was done using punch card
        equipment.

1185   Deming, W. Edwards and Hansen, Morris H.   "On Some
        Census Aids to Dampling," Journal of the American
        Statistical Association 38, No. 225 (September 1943):
        353-357.

        This is a description of the use of punch cards in
        solving sampling problems in the late 1930s and early
        1940s in a precursor to an operations research pro-
        ject.

1186   Dunlap, Jack W.   "The Computation of Means, Standard
        Deviations, and Correlations by the Tabulator When
        the Numbers Are Both Positive and Negative," Proceed-
        ings of the Educational Research Forum (New York:
        IBM Corp., August 1940): 16-19.

        This reflected work encouraged by IBM in mathematics
        using its products.

1187   Dwyer, Paul S.   "Summary of Problems in the Computation
        of Statistical Constants with Tabulating and Sorting
        Machines," Proceedings of the Educational Research
        Forum (New York: IBM Corp., August 1940): 20-28.

        This was written by an expert in the use of punch
        card equipment for statistical analysis. Here he
        reviews work done by himself in the late 1930s.

1188   Dwyer, Paul S.   "The Use of Tables in the Form of
        Prepunched Cards," Proceedings of the Educational
        Research Forum (New York: IBM Corp., August 1940):
        125-127.

        In the 1930s pre-punched cards with mathematical
        data on them could be bought from IBM for use by
        customers in accounting and scientific applications.
        These are described.

1189   Dwyer, Paul S. and Meacham, Alan D.   "The Preparation
        of Correlation Tables on a Tabulator Equipped with
        Digit Selection," Journal of the American Statisti-
        cal Association 32 (1937): 654-662.

Two authorities on the subject of how to use punch
cards in scientific and statistical computing in
the 1930s comment on the use of such technology in
statistical analysis.

1190   Dyer, H.S. "Making Test Score Data Effective in the
        Admission and Course Placement of Harvard Freshmen,"
        Proceedings of the Research Forum (New York: IBM
        Corp., 1946): 55-62.

        The work was done using IBM punch card calculating
        equipment.

1191   Eckert, Wallace J. "Facilities of the Watson Scienti-
        fic Computing Laboratory," in Proceedings of the
        Research Forum (New York: IBM Corp., 1946): 75-80.

        This laboratory at Columbia University was funded
        by IBM and supplied with punch card equipment by
        the same firm. Its purpose was to expand the use of
        such technology in scientific research. Eckert
        describes the equipment there, its mission, and
        recent work.

1192   Eckert, Wallace J. Punched Card Methods in Scientific
        Computation. New York: Thomas J. Watson Astronomical
        Computing Bureau, Columbia University, 1940. Reprin-
        ted with introduction by J.C. McPherson by MIT Press,
        1984.

        This was a very important publication on the subject.
        It also contains descriptions of tabulators, sorters,
        and multiplying punches.

1193   Eckert, Wallace J. "Punched Card Techniques and Their
        Applications to Scientific Problems," Journal of
        Chemical Education 24 (February 1947): 54-57.

        He describes applications such as quality control,
        structural vibration, stress, and other forms of
        analysis using punch card equipment from IBM.

1194   Eckert, Wallace J. and Haupt, Ralph F. "The Printing
        of Mathematical Tables," Mathematical Tables and
        Other Aids to Computation 2, No. 17 (January 1947):
        196-202.

        Eckert taught at Columbia University where he found
        many ways to use card equipment in scientific appli-
        cations. This describes one of his projects.

1195   Feinstein, Lillian and Schwarzchild, Martin. "Automa-
        tic Integration of Linear Second-Order Differential
        Equations by Means of Punched-Card Machines," Review
        of Scientific Instruments 12, No. 8 (August 1941):
        405-408.

        This is a very technical period piece in mathematics.

1196   Florence, H. "New Era for Business Machines," Review
        of Reviews 89 (January 1934): 30-33.

        This is an illustrated history of the office equip-
        ment industry with details on the influence of the
        New Deal on it and new application areas, including
        scientific.

1197   Hotelling, Harold. "New Methods in Matrix Calcula-
        tion," The Annals of Mathematical Statistics 14,
        No. 1 (March 1943): 1-34.

        These new methods involve the use of punch card
        calculating machines.

1198   International Business Machines Corporation (ed).
        Proceedings of the Educational Research Program.
        Endicott, N.Y.: IBM Corp., 1941.

        This is a collection of papers dealing with the use
        of punch card applications, primarily in education
        but also in science.

1199   International Business Machine Corporation (ed).
        Proceedings of the IBM Research Forum. Endicott,
        N.Y.: IBM Corp., 1946.

        This collection of papers focused on applications
        using punch card equipment, primarily in science
        and mathematics.

1200   Johns, V. "On the Mechanical Handling of Statistics,"
        American Mathematical Monthly 33 (1926): 494-502.

        This was one of the first papers published on the
        general subject of mathematical-statistical problems
        and punch card equipment. There is a commentary on
        the evolution of mechanical key punches, electrical
        key punches and of other devices.

1201   King, Gilbert W. "Punched-Card Tables of the Exponen-
        tial Function," Review of Scientific Instruments
        15, No. 12 (December 1944): 349-350.

        Kind did considerable work employing punch card
        equipment in mathematics, some of which is described
        here.

1202   King, Gilbert W. "Some Applications of Punched Card
        Methods in Research Problems in Chemistry and Physi-
        cs," Journal of Chemical Education 24 (February
        1947): 61-64.

        King states that current technology is limited to
        addition, subtraction, and multiplication but that
        the machines which can divide would soon appear. He
        ends the article with a list of applications possible
        with punch card technology in science.

1203   Kormes, Mark. "Numerical Solution of the Boundary
        Value Problem for the Potential Equation by Means
        of Punched Cards," Review of Scientific Instruments
        14, No. 8 (August 1943): 248-250.

        Beginning in the 1920s, and considerably by the
        1930s, scientists and mathematicians were using
        punch card equipment to do their work. This exams
        one such application.

1204   Kuder, G. Frederic. "Use of the IBM Scoring Machine
        for Rapid Computation of Tables of Intercorrela-
        tions," Journal of Applied Psychology 22, No. 6
        (December 1938): 587-596.

        This is an early article on the scientific uses of
        punch card equipment from IBM; it uses a specializ-
        ed piece of equipment developed in the 1930s.

1205   Maxfield, D.K. "Library Punched Card Procedures,"
        Library Journal 71, No. 12 (June 15, 1946): 902-
        905.

        Although focused on library applications, the
        problem of scientific publications had to be solved
        as part of the solution of getting materials into
        the hands of researchers fast.

1206   McPherson, John C. "Mechanical Tabulation of Poly-
        nomials," Annals of Mathematical Statistics 12
        (September 1941): 317-327.

        This describes the use of punch card equipment in
        complex mathematics problems at the hight of experi-
        mentation with punch card equipment for such appli-
        cations.

1207   Milliman, Wendell A. "Mechanical Multiplication By
        the Use of Tabulating Machines," Transactions of
        the Actuarial Society of America, 35 Pt. 2 (October
        1934): 253-264.

        This is an early piece on the use of punch card
        equipment in complex mathematics.

1208   Snedecor, C.W. "Uses of Punched Card Equipment in
        Mathematics," American Mathematical Monthly 35
        (1928): 161-169.

        This is a convenient survey of the subject as of the
        late 1920s.

1209   Watson Scientific Computing Laboratory. Bibliography
        on Use of IBM Machines in Science, Statistics, and
        Education. New York: Columbia University Press,
        1954.

        This is an extremely useful publication and contains
        material on IBM's calculators at the dawn of the age
        of computers.

1210   Watson Scientific Computing Laboratory. Bibliography:
       The Use of IBM Machines in Scientific Research,
       Statistics, and Education. New York: IBM Corp., 1947.

       This is the first bibliography to appear on the
       subject. This 25-page publication was essentially
       an earlier edition of the previous citation (No.
       1209).

                     Punch Card Equipment

1211   Alden, William et al. The Automatic Office. Westboro,
       Mass.: William Alden Co., 1953.

       While this has material on the Alden product line,
       it contains material on applications and equipment
       in general for offices, including data processing
       products.

1212   American Office Machines Research Service. New York:
       Office Machine Research, Inc., 1937.

       This is one of many such guides to existing hardware
       available during the 1930s.

1213   Arkin, H. "Development and Principles of the Punched
       Card Method," in G.W. Baehne (ed), Practical Appli-
       cations of the Punched Card Method in Colleges and
       Universities (New York: Columbia University Press,
       1935): 1-20.

       This is a short review of the development of punch
       card technology with an illustrated account of IBM
       equipment of the 1930s.

1214   Baehne, G. Walter et al.(eds). Practical Applications
       of the Punched Card Method in Colleges and Univer-
       sities. New York: Columbia University Press, 1935.

       The volume of articles is filled with comments on
       punch card equipment of the 1930s.

1215   Beitlich, E. Buromaschinenkunde: Maschinenrechnen,
       Maschinenbuchhaltung, Vervielfältigungsgeräte.
       Hanover: Verlag von Carl Meyer, 1938.

       This is a 112-page, illustrated description of
       features and uses of various accounting and book-
       keeping equipment of the 1930s.

1216   Berger, R. "Die Lochkartenmaschine," Z.V.D.I. 72
       (1928): 1799-1807.

       This is a review of the evolution of punch card
       technology, discussing both Hollerith and Powers
       equipment, with illustrations. There are comments
       about attaching such technology to typewriters and
       calculating machines.

1217   Casey, Robert and Perry, James W. (eds). Punched
        Cards. New York: Reinhold Publishing Corporation,
        1953.

        This is a general overview of punch card equipment
        and applications, late in the era of the technology.
        It is useful for late punch card hardware.

1218   Comrie, Leslie J. The Hollerith and Powers Tabulating
        Machines. London: Privately printed, 1933.

        This is a 48-page review of how to operate such
        devices, their features, and applications; illus-
        trated.

1219   Curtis, C.R. Mechanised Accountancy: Veing A Review
        of the Latest Methods of Mechanical Book-keeping,
        Together Wtih a Survey of the Machines Used.
        London: Charles Griffin, 1932.

        This 143-page book is a guide to contemporary hard-
        ware and applications. It includes comments on
        products from Brunsviga, National, Underwood, Reming-
        ton, Hollerith, Campos and others.

1220   Deveaux, P. "Present Status of Calculating Machines,"
        Revue Industrielle 56 (1926): 113-117, 166-171.

        This is on contemporary calculating devices, their
        features and functions, with material on both
        Hollerith and Powers equipment; illustrated.

1221   Doss, Milburn, P. Information Processing Equipment.
        New York: Reinhold Publishing Corporation, 1955.

        This is similar to citation No. 1217.

1222   Ford, C.M. "Alphabetical and Mnemonic Symbols on
        Tabulating Machine Cards," Industrial Management
        61 (May 1, 1921): 347-350.

        The author, a plant manager, describes the use of
        tabulating equipment in factory applications.

1223   Franklin Institute. Report on the Hollerith Electric
        Tabulating System. Philadelphia: Franklin Institute,
        1890.

        This is the first publication from this organization
        on mechanical/tabulating computing. It would be
        followed by dozens in the decades to come.

1224   Freeman, W.E. (ed). Automatic, Mechanical Punching,
        Counting, Sorting, Tabulating, and Printing Machin-
        es. New York: National Electric Light Association,
        1915.

        This is a compendium of early uses of tabulating
        equipment in the U.S., complete with descriptions.

1225   Fry, Macon. Designing Computing Mechanisms. Cleve-
        land, Ohio: Penton Publishing Co., 1946.

        This pamphlet concerns the use of computing devices
        to do thinking and data manipulation.

1226   Geier, George J. and Mantner, Oscar. Systems Installa-
        tion in Accounting. New York: Burrel-Snow, Inc.,
        1932.

        This is an early "how to" users guide to mechanical
        aids to calculation. Emphasis is on systems, not
        single machines but groups of machines working in
        concert.

1227   Gillespie, Cecil. Accounting Systems: Procedures and
        Methods. New York: Prentice-Hall, Inc., 1951.

        While focusing more on accounting practises than on
        hardware, there is considerable material on the use
        of tabulating machines in accounting applications.

1228   Hartkemeier, Harry Pelle. Principles of Punch-Card
        Machine Operation: How to Operate Punch-Card Tabu-
        lating and Alphabetic Accounting Machines. New
        York: Thomas Y. Crowell Co., 1942.

        The author taught statistical analysis employing
        IBM tabulating equipment. There is no discussion
        of collators or multiplying punch equipment, only
        other tabulating gear.

1229   Heckert, J.B. Accounting Systems: Design and Insta-
        llation. New York: Ronald Press, 1936.

        This is a "how to" for configuring, installing and
        managing hardware systems of the early 1930s.

1230   Hedley, K.J. The Development of the Punched Card
        Method. N.c.: Acturial Society of Australasia,
        1946.

        This is a 20-page survey and general reference work.

1231   International Business Machines Corporation. The
        Control of Material. Endicott, N.Y.: International
        Business Machines Corp., 1924.

        While an application brief, it contains descriptive
        material on IBM products.

1232   International Business Machines Corporation. Interna-
        tional Business Machines. A-4036-6-45. New York:
        International Business Machines Corp., 1945.

        This is an illustrated description of nearly 20
        punch card machines, vintage 1945.

1233   International Business Machines Corporation. Machine

Methods of Accounting. Endicott, N.Y.: International Business Machines Corp., 1936-1941.

This is a group of 28 pamphlets providing details
on how to use IBM's punch card machinery, complete
with descriptions of the hardware. The intended
audiences were IBMers and users of the products.

1234   International Business Machines Corporation. Manual
        of Business Instruction: Equipment and Supplies
        Furnished. New York: International Business Machines
        Corp., 1933.

        This was issued by the Tabulating Machine Division
        (the old Hollerith company), and it was a salesman's
        Bible, their sales manual. It lists all products,
        prices, features, terms and conditions, and contracts
        under which customers could acquire the machines and
        supplies. Other than for product updates, this was
        the salesman's manual for the years of the Great
        Depression.

1235   International Business Machines Corporation. Modern-
        izing with International Business Machines. New
        York: International Business Machines, 1938.

        This is an illustrated, 80-page description of IBM's
        products intended as a sales document, circa 1938.
        The majority of the devices presented are tabulating
        and accounting machines and peripherals.

1236   International Business Machines Corporation. Pre-Punch-
        ed Cards. Endicott, N.Y.: International Business
        Machines Corp., 1934.

        This brochure describes IBM's products in both stock
        and pre-punched cards.

1237   International Business Machines Corporation. Princi-
        ples of Operation. Endicott, N.Y.: International
        Business Machines Corp., 1941-1948.

        This is a series of booklets describing IBM's
        punch card equipment of the 1940s, and how to use
        them. By the 1930s all IBM products were accompan-
        ied with a principles of operation publication, a
        publishing program that continues down to the 1990s.

1238   Lasser, J.K. Handbook of Accounting Methods. New
        York: D. Van Nostrand Co., 1943.

        This is limited acknowledgement of the role of
        played by hardware in accounting. It does, however,
        provide background on accounting as of the late
        1930s.

1239   Leffingwell, William Henry. The Office Appliance
        Manual. New York: National Association of Office
        Appliance Manufacturers, 1926.

This is a massive compendium of hardware as of the
early 1920s. It is an outstanding publication on
devices, companies, marketing, and industry information.

1240   Lilley, S. "Mathematical Machines," Nature 149 (April
       25, 1942): 462-465.

       This is a brief survey of computing devices, such as
       those of Babbage, Hollerith and calculators down to
       the 1940s.

1241   "Machines That Do All But Say Thank You; National
       Business Show," Literary Digest 120 (October 26,
       1935): 36.

       This particular show had many new devices on exhibit
       which are briefly described here.

1242   "Many New Machines at Business Show," Business Week
       (October 28, 1931): 22-23.

       This is the same show, different year, just cited
       above and which exhibited many products designed
       during the 1920s.

1243   McPherson, J.C. "Mathematical Operations With Punched
       Cards," Journal of the American Statistical Associa-
       tion 37 (June 1942): 275-281; Reprinted in Annals of
       the History of Computing 7, No. 4 (October 1985):
       368-371.

       This reflects the wide use of punch card technology
       in scientific and engineering applications with some
       discussion of the equipment used.

1244   Neuner, J.W. and Neuner, V.J. Accounting Systems:
       Installations and Procedures. Scranton, Pa.: Inter-
       national Text Book Co., 1949.

       The volume covers both hardware installations and
       the design of information flows in accounting.

1245   Parsons, Carl C. Machinery of the Office. Chicago:
       La Salle Extension University Press, 1921.

       The focus is on a broad range of equipment, not just
       tabulators or calculators.

1246   Remington Rand, Inc. "Know-How" Makes Them Great.
       New York: Remington Rand, Inc., 1941.

       This is a good exposure to the company's products.

1247   Remington Rand, Inc. Powers Reference Manual. Buffalo,
       N.Y.: Remington Rand, Inc.; Powers Accounting Machine
       Division, 1935.

       This is an illustrated survey of its products.

1248   Schnackel, H.G. and Lang, H.C. Accounting By Machine
       Methods. New York: Ronald Press, Co., 1939.

       This is a 53-page description of how to use punch
       card equipment of the 1930s in commercial applica-
       tions.

1249   "Speaking of Pictures: New Mechanical Monsters Ease
       Life's Growing Pains," Life (September 15, 1947):
       15-16.

       This is a popularized description of card punch
       equipment of the 1940s and then as they were being
       used at Life magazine.

1250   Tabulating Machine Company. Salesmen's Catalogue.
       New York: The Tabulating Machine Co., n.d. (circa
       early 1920s).

       This is a sales manual issued to marketing repre-
       sentatives of Hollerith's company. It describes
       all the punch card products, features, services,
       and prices as of the 1920s or late teens.

1251   "Tabulating Machines," Encyclopedia Britanica 21
       (1954 edition): 733.

       This offers a short history and description of
       tabulating equipment at that technology's pinnicle
       of development.

1252   Thompson, William R. Accounting Systems. Chicago:
       La Salle Extension University Press, 1921.

       This is a text accounting book but with some
       acknowledgment of mechanization.

1253   Traweek, Stella. Case Studies of Texas Business.
       Austin: Bureau of Business Research, Texas Univer-
       sity, 1953.

       This includes the use and explanation of, punch
       card equipment.

1254   Wolf, Arthur W. and Berkeley, Edmund C. Advanced
       Course in Punched Card Operations. Newark, N.J.:
       Prudential Insurance Company of America, 1942.

       This described IBM's punch card calculating devices
       and how to use them.

                    Research and Development

1255   Beevers, C.A. "A Machine for the Rapid Summation of
       Fourier Serier Series," Proceedings of the Physical
       Society (London) 51, No. 4 (1939): 660-663.

       This is about a small, special-purpose calculator
       containing 16 electromechanical counters.

1256   Berry, C.E. "Design of Electrical Data Recording and
        Reading Mechanism" (M.S. theis, Iowa State College,
        1941).

        This describes card reading and punching devices
        worked on for Dr. Atanasoff.

1257   Caley, D.H.N. "Electicity and the 'Tote'," The
        Electrician 103, Nos 3-4 (July 19 and 26, 1929):
        71-73, 108-109.

        Various automatic totalisator systems being develop-
        ed for race courses in Great Britain are described.
        Essentially three systems are involved in which the
        total bets on each course are recorded and calcula-
        ted.

1258   Ceruzzi, Paul. "An Unforseen Revolution: Computers
        and Expectations, 1935-1985," in Joseph J. Corn
        (ed), Imagining Tomorrow: History, Technology, and
        the American Future (Cambridge, Mass.: MIT Press,
        1986): 188-201.

        This is a good overview of R&D activities and give
        insight into the thinking of scientists and engineers
        over this considerable period of time, by an histor-
        ian.

1259   Couffignal, L. "Calcul Mécanique: Sur l'emploi de la
        numeration binaire dans les machines à calculer et
        les instruments nomomecaniques," Comptes. Rendus
        Academie de Science (Paris) 202 (1936): 1970-1972.

        He argues the case in favor of presenting numbers
        in binary form for computers and reviews the design
        of electrical calculators of the day.

1260   Couffignal, L. "Sur l'Analyse Mécanique. Application
        aux machines à calculer et aux calculs de la mécani-
        que celeste," Thèses présentées a la Faculté des
        Sciences de Paris, Series A (Paris: Gauthier-Villars,
        1938).

        This thesis is on how an electrco-mechanical program
        controlled binary calculator might work.

1261   Couffignal, L. "Sur un Problème d'Analyse Mécanique
        Abstraite," Comptes. Rendus Academie de Science
        (Paris) 206 (1938): 1336-1338.

        He discusses the electrical evaluation of logical
        expressions and is part of a series of articles he
        wrote growing out of his thesis on programmable
        calculators.

1262   Couffignal, L. "Sur une Nouvelle Machine à Calculer,"
        Comptes. Rendus Academie de Science (Paris) 191
        (1930): 924-926.

        This is on a machine that could perform four

function and chain the events in sequence. This article is an outgrowth of his graduate work.

1263   Crawford, P.O., Jr. "Instrumental Analysis in Matrix Algebra, Part V," (Unpublished B.Sc. thesis, MIT 1939).

Pages 60-65 has a design for "an automatically controlled calculating machine" to do matrix calculations. It has a means for scanning digital data represented on punched tape for the four mathematical functions, and for storing and printing or punching out data.

1264   Davis, Martin. "Mathematical Logic and the Origins of Modern Computers," MAA Studies in Mathematics 26 (1987): 137-165.

Davis reviews Turing's work and influence on the development of computers.

1265   Fry, T.C. "Industrial Mathematics," Bell System Technical Journal 20 (July 1941): 255-292.

Fry headed Bell Lab's mathematical consulting program in the interwar period. This article was an important review of the subject as of the 1930s. His thoughts and work influenced the developers of computers in the late 1930s.

1266   Gandy, R.O. "The Simple Theory of Types," in Logic Colloquium 76, edited by R.O. Gandy and J.M.E. Hyland (Amsterdam: North-Holland, 1977).

It has a section on Turing's work during World War II.

1267   Gray, T.S. "A Photo-Electric Integraph," Journal of the Franklin Institute 212 (1931): 77-102.

This is a description of an early analog computational machine developed in the 1920s.

1269   Hazen, H.L. and Brown, G.S. "The Cinema Integraph, A Machine for Evaluating a Parametric Product Integral, With an Appendix by W.R. Hdeman, Jr.," Journal of the Franklin Institute 230 (1940): 19-44, 183-205.

This surveys work done in the 1930s at MIT on evaluating integrals by analog means.

1270   Hazen, H.L. et al. "The MIT Network Analyzer, Design and Application to Power System Problems," Quarterly Transactions of the American Institute of Electrical Engineers 49 (1930): 1102-1114.

This is on work involving Bush's ideas as applied to electrical power networks.

1271   Herken, Rolf (ed). The Universal Turing Machine: A
        Half Century Survey. Oxford: Oxford University Press,
        1988.

        This collection of 28 papers, on the occasion of the
        50th anniversary of the publication of Alan Turing's
        famous 1937 paper, deal with Turing, 23 with contem-
        porary events in logic and theoretical computer
        science.

1272   Holst, Per A. "George A. Philbrick and Polyphemus—
        The First Electronic Training Simulator," Annals of
        the History of Computing 4, No. 2 (April 1982): 143-
        156.

        This surveys a device called the Automatic Control
        Analyzer for analog process control. It is an illus-
        trated, technical presentation.

1273   Kleene, Stephen C. "Origins of Recursive Function
        Theory," Annals of the History of Computing 3, No.
        1 (January 1981): 52-67.

        This surveys mathematics in the 1930s and focuses
        on Turing computability; a highly technical paper.

1274   Klir, J. "An Invention That Might Have Accelerated
        the Development of Mathematical Machines," Technical
        Digest 5, No. 5 (1963): 39-41.

        A patent of Bernard Weiner, 1923, for electrical
        computer and typewriter, is discussed in which relays
        are used with fixed built-in programs. It also in-
        cludes a short biography of Weiner. Work on this
        project came to an end when the Germans occupied the
        Vitkovice Iron Works where he had his ship. Weiner
        died in 1942.

1275   Kranz, F.W. "A Mechanical Synthesizer and Analyzer,"
        Journal of the Franklin Institute 204 (1927): 245-
        262.

        This is on early work done with analog computing at
        the Riverbank Laboratories, Geneva, Illinois, during
        the 1920s.

1276   Lehmer, D.H. "A History of the Sieve Process," in N.
        Metropolis et al.(eds), A History of Computing in
        the Twentieth Century (New York: Academic Press,
        1980): 445-456.

        This is an illustrated account by a participant in
        the development of machines to solve specific sieve
        mathematical problems during the 1930s and 1940s.

1277   Lehmer, D.H. "A Photo-Electric Number Sieve," American
        Mathematical Monthly 40, No. 7 (1933): 401-406.

        This reviews technical developments during the 1930s.

1278   "Letter-Printing Cathode-Ray Tube," Electronics 22
        No. 6 (June 1949): 160-162.

        Work with CRTs (terminals) had begun in the 1930s
        and intensified after World War II. Here is an
        expose on their use with digital electronic computers.

1279   Lewis, W.B. "A 'Scale of Two' High-Speed Counter Using
        Had Vacuum Triodes," Proceedings of the Cambridge
        Philosophical Society 33 (1937): 549-558.

        This surveys technical developments in Great Britain
        in the 1930s.

1280   Lewis, W.B. Electrical Counting: With Special Referen-
        ce to Alpha and Beta Particles. London: Cambridge
        University Press, 1942.

        Covers the same material as his previous publication
        except in more detail.

1281   Lifschutz, H. and Lawson, J.L. "A Triode Vacuum Tube
        Scale-of-Two Circuit," Review of Scientific Instru-
        ments 9 (March 1938): 83-89.

        The authors discuss a binary counter they developed
        during the 1930s.

1282   Massey, H.S.W. et al. "A Small Scale Differential
        Analyser—Its Construction and Operation," Proceed-
        ings of the Royal Irish Academy 45 (1938): 1-21.

        This describes a device developed to solve problems
        in physics.

1283   Montgomery D. "Oswald Veblen," Bulletin of the Mathe-
        matical Society 69 (1963): 26-36.

        This is an obituary on Veblen (1880-1960), an
        American mathematician who did research on ballistics
        during World War I and later built up the mathematics
        department at Princeton University and at the Insti-
        tute of Advanced Studies.

1284   Moulton, F.R. New Methods in Exterior Ballistics.
        Chicago: University of Chicago Press, 1926.

        This is on his research on ballistics and mathematics.

1285   Myers, D.M. "An Integraph for the Solution of Differ-
        ential Equations of the Second Order," Journal of
        Scientific Instruments 16 (1939): 209-222.

        Myers describes an analog device, perhaps could
        even be called an analog calculator, which he worked
        on during the 1930s.

1286   Nicoladze, C. "Arithmomètre à Multiplication Directe
        Purement Electrique," Comptes Rendus de la Academie

de Science de Paris 186 (1928): 123-124.

This is a short review of a device based on Genaille's
numbering rods and compares it to the work done by
Torres y Quevedo.

1287   Perkeris, C.L. and White, W.T.   "Differentiation With
       the Cinema Integraph," _Journal of the Franklin
       Institute_ 234 (July 1942): 17-29.

The describes their work with an analog device in
the 1930s and early 1940s.

1288   Phillips, E.W.   "Babbage, Electronic Computers and
       Scales of Notation," _The Post Insurance Magazine
       and Insurance Monitor_ 123, No. 49 (December 1962):
       1735-1737; Reprinted in _Computer Bulletin_ 6, No. 4
       (1963): 128-130.

The author acknowledges that he was aware of Babbage's
work while doing his own on computing in 1936.

1289   Phillips, E.W.   "Binary Calculation," _Journal of the
       Institute of Actuaries_ 67 (1936): 187-221.

He suggests actuarial data files be kept in octal
and doing calculations in binary notation. He then
argued how this might be done by mechanical means.

1290   Phillips, E.W.   "Birth of the Computer (Letter to the
       Editor)," _Sunday Times_ (September 5, 1965): 10.

He says he was always interested in Babbage. Further,
it first occurred to him that a binary computer
should be developed in 1934.

1291   Post, Emil L.   "Finite Combinatory Processes—Formula-
       tion, I," _Journal of Symbolic Logic_ 1, No. 3 (1936):
       103-105.

Post describes problem solving that mirrored programming from logic to machine-like "primitive acts" thus
joining with Turing and Shannon in the 1930s in describing programming a computer as one of logics not
of mathematics. This was a semenal paper.

1292   Shannon, Claude E.   "A Symbolic Analysis of Relay and
       and Switching Circuits," in Earl E. Swartzlander,
       Jr. (ed), _Computer Design Development: Principal
       Papers_ (Rochelle Park, N.J.: Hayden, 1976): 3-24.

Originally published in 1938, this was his masters
thesis project at MIT in which Shannon applied pro-
positional calculus to the design of electrical
circuits. This paper made possible scientific methods
of circuit design, helping to make information subject
to manipulation by electronic digital machines.

1293   Shannon, Claude E.   "A Symbolic Analysis of Relay and

Switching Circuits," Transactions of the AIEE 57
(1938): 712-713.

This is an illustrated account of how symbolic logic
can be applied to the design of circuits as, for
example, in adding two binary numbers.

1294   Silverman, J. Herbert. "A Process of Reduction,"
        Sky (October 1986): 40-46, 49.

        This is an illustrated history of microfische from
        1839 to 1986.

1295   Stokes, John W. 70 Years of Radio Tubes and Valves
        . . . A Guide for Electronic Engineers, Historians
        and Collectors. Vestal, N.Y.: Vestal Press, 1982.

        The emphasis is on components from the years between
        1927 and 1937, a period during which rapid develop-
        ments came in tube technology.

1296   Tucker, R.L. "A Matrix Multiplier," Psychometrika 5
        (1940): 289-294.

        This describes a machine which was a takeoff of an
        IBM test scoring device, used to help in the multi-
        plication of matrices.

1297   Turing, Alan M. "Intelligent Machinery" (September
        1947), reprinted in B. Meltzer and D. Michie (eds),
        Machine Intelligence 5 (Edinburgh: Edinburgh Univer-
        sity Press, 1969): 3-23.

        This paper discusses work done on Colossus and is a
        contribution to the early development of computer
        science in Great Britain.

1298   Turing, Alan M. "On Computable Numbers, With An
        Application to the Entscheidungsproblem," Proceedings
        London Mathematical Society Series 2, 42 (1937): 230-
        267; Correction, Ibid. 43: 544-546.

        This is one of the most famous, influential papers
        ever written on computer science. In it Turing
        describes the theoretical design of a computer and
        how such a device might solve complex problems.

1299   Valtat, R.L.A. "Calcul Mécanique: Machine à calculer
        fondée sur l'emploi de la numération binaire,"
        Comptes Rendus Academie des Sciences (Paris) 202
        (1936): 1745-1748.

        The author proposes a calculator that transforms
        input into binary and then performs calculation. He
        argued the case for representing binary digits by
        mechanical and electrical means.

1300   Wainwright, Lawrence L. "A Ballistic Engine," (Unpub-
        lished M.A. thesis, University of Chicago, 1923).

This short description of a device foreshadowed the differential analyzer common in the 1930s.

1301   Weygandt, A.   "Die elektromechanische Determinanten-maschine," _Z. Instrumentenkde_ 53 (1933): 114-121.

The paper is a description for evaluating 3 x 3 determinants using electromagnetic relays.

1302   Wilbur, John V.   "Mechanical Solution of Simultaneous Equations," _Journal of the Franklin Institute_ 222 (December 1936): 715-724.

This technical piece describes a machine by the same name built by this MIT professor in the late 1920s and early 1930s. It represented one of the earliest calculators constructed at MIT.

1303   Wilkinson, James H.   "The Birth of a Computer" _Byte_ 10, No. 2 (February 1985): 177-194.

This interview discusses the Turing Machine.

1304   Willers, F.A.   "Rechenmaschinen," _Archiv für Technisches Messen_ J01 Nos 1-5 (January, March, May, June, October 1940).

He presents five articles on various mathematical devices with illustrations and bibliography.

1305   Wynn-Williams, C.E.   "Electrical Methods of Counting," _Reports, Progr. Physics_ 3 (1937): 239-261.

This was written by an important British computing scientist. He reviews his work of the 1930s on the design of electronic counting circuits, electronic counters, printing, and decimal-to-binary conversion.

1306   Wynn-Williams, C.E.   "The Scale of Two Counter," _Year Book Physics Society_ (1957): 56-60.

He reviews his work at the Cavendish Laboratory, and later, at the Imperial College on Thyraton-based counters. He made his first counter in 1930s. The article carries the story down to World War II.

1307   Wynn-Williams, C.E.   "A Thyraton 'Scale of Two' Automatic Counter," _Proceedings of the Royal Society_ (London) Series A, No. 136 (1932): 312-324.

This summarizes his work with counters at the start of the 1930s.

1308   Wynn-Williams, C.E.   "The Use of Thyratons for High Speed Automatic Counting of Physical Phenomena," _Proceedings Royal Society_ (London) Series A No. 132 (1931): 295-310.

He discusses various methods using thyratrons as

recorders and suggests how an electronic counting
device might be made.

Tide Predictors

1309   Claudy, C.H. "A Great Brass Brain," Scientific American 110 (March 7, 1914): 197-198.

He describes a machine made by E.G. Fischer and R.A.
Harris, of the U.S. Coast and Geodetic Survey, to
predict waves, using gears and pulleys. The machine
became operational in 1914 after 15 years of development.

1310   Harris, R.A. "The Coast and Geodetic Survey Tide
Predicting Machine," Scientific American 110 (June
13, 1914): 485.

The co-inventor of the machine describes how it could
take 37 different tides to calculate tide forecast
and produce a plot which worked. The device was used
during World War I to help Allied ships avoid German
U-boats.

1311   Rauschelbach, H. "Die Deutsche Gezeitenrechenmaschine," Zeitschrift fur Instrumentenkunde 44 (July
1924): 285-303.

He describes a machine used to predict tides built
in Germany in 1916 at the Imperial Observatory. It
was a German version of the U.S.'s Great Brass Brain.

5

Hardware, 1939–1960s

The quantity of material in this chapter, which exceeds that in any earlier one, reflects the period when the digital computer and its associated data processing industry came into their own. In the decades between the start of World War II and the mid-1960s, computers were built, used, and distributed widely. The major concepts behind the von Neumann machine were worked out and significant progress made in its associated technologies. These ranged from the initial use of vacuum tubes to the creation of the transistor, and finally to multiple generations of semiconductor components. Almost all the major computing projects that historians have studied so far come from this period, as do the bulk of the memoirs associated with computing. The majority of the subheadings are by machine type with some notable exceptions when the volume of literature warranted separate headings for individuals such as Grace Hopper, John von Neumann, and Konrad Zuse. The body of literature on activities during World War II alone is rapidly rivaling that on Babbage. Since robots first emerged during this period, a section on robots is included here, although it covers their role through the 1980s.

Much of the material in this chapter is contemporary. Careful attention has been paid to collecting descriptive publications, contemporary coverage of events to provide a perspective on expectations, technical literature on base technologies, memoirs of scientists and engineers, and available historical monographs. Early computers from the period 1940–1965 have received the most focus from historians, archivists, and museum curators, and they continue, as of this writing, to draw the greatest amount of attention. Yet almost nothing has been devoted to the customers' uses of these technologies or to the vendors who worked with them. What little available literature exists is listed in the final chapter on the information-processing industry as a whole. Because of the considerable success of IBM's processors during the 1950s, especially its 650 system, this chapter includes a number of contemporary materials on them. Left out were nearly two hundred one- or two-page descriptions from American newspapers, newsletters, and periodicals, since these did not contribute substantially to one's understanding of the subject.

The body of available materials on European developments
is better for the 1940s and 1950s than for any earlier period,
with the possible exception of the seventeenth century. It is
particularly good for British computing projects. French,
Italian, German, Russian, and East European developments are
not well represented. Existing publications on the industry
in these nations are included in the final chapter.

ACE and Alan M. Turing

1312   "ACE—The Automatic Computing Machine," Electronic
        Engineering 18 (December 1946): 372-373.

        This is a brief description of the computer at the
        National Physical Laboratory, home of much computer
        development during the 1940s.

1313   "Automatic Computation at the N.P.L.," Engineering
        171 (1951): 608.

        This reviews British computers of the period 1945-
        1951 and in particular, Turing's work on ACE at the
        National Physical Laboratory.

1314   "Calculations and Electronics: Automatic Computer /sic7
        Designed By the National Physical Laboratory,"
        Electrician 137 (1946): 1279-1280.

        This is a quick survey of recent work done at the
        NPL, including on ACE.

1315   Campbell-Kelly, Martin. "The Development of Computer
        Programming in Britain (1945-1955)," Annals of the
        History of Computing 4, No. 2 (April 1982): 121-
        139.

        This historian of British computing provides an
        illustrated and well documented technical review of
        a variety of computers, including the EDSAC at
        Cambridge University, Manchester's Mark I, NPL's
        Pilot ACE, and discusses the impact of these devices
        on stored-program computing.

1316   Campbell-Kelly, Martin. "Foundations of Computer
        Programming in Britain (1945-1955)" (Unpublished
        Ph.D. dissertation, Sunderland Polytechnic, 1980).

        This is a more detailed survey of the same theme
        published in the previous entry (No. 1315).

1317   Campbell-Kelly, Martin. "Programming the Pilot ACE:
        Early Programming Activity at the National Physical
        Laboratory," Annals of the History of Computing 3,
        No. 2 (April 1981): 133-162.

        He provides an illustrated history of the design of
        the British ACE between 1945 and 1952. It is a
        technical history of the computer and on its programm-
        ing. It is well documented and clear.

1318   Carpenter, B.E. and Doran, R.W. (eds).   A.M. Turing's
       ACE Report of 1946 and Other Papers.   Cambridge,
       Mass.: MIT Press, 1986.

       This is a collection of his papers from the 1940s
       and 1950s, and includes a short, illustrated biogra-
       phy of this important British scientist.

1319   Carpenter, B.E. and Doran, R.W.   The Other Turing
       Machine. Report 23, Massey University. Computer
       Unit, Palmerston North, New Zealand (August 1975).
       Reprinted in Computer Journal 20, No. 3 (August
       1977): 269-279.

       They review the design and features of Turing's ACE
       in the mid-1940s and compare this to the work being
       done by von Neumann. The article concludes that
       Turing's perspectives on the characteristics of a
       computer were more complete than von Neumann's. It
       is a highly technical discussion.

1320   Carpenter, B.E. and Doran, R.W.   "The Other Turing
       Machine," Computer Journal 20 No. 3 (August 1977):
       269-279.

       See previous citation.

1321   Gleiser, M. "The Curious Life of Alan Turing,"
       Computer Decisions (August 1976): 30-31, 34, 36.

       The author reviews Turing's work on computers and
       cryptoanalysis in the 1940s. This should be used
       with caution, it has errors of facts.

1322   Hodges, Andrew. Alan Turing: The Enigma. New York:
       Simon & Schuster, 1983.

       This is an excellent, full biography of Turing. For
       a detailed review of the book see Annals of the
       History of Computing 6, No. 2 (April 1984): 176-178.

1323   Huskey, Harry D. "Early Stored Program Computing in
       England," Proceedings of the Third Jerusalem Confer-
       ence on Information Technology (August 1978).

       His focus is on Bletchley Park and World War II,
       Turing and the ACE, work done at Cambridge Univer-
       sity with an EDSAC, and research at both Manchester
       University and at the University of London in the
       1940s.

1324   Huskey, Harry D. "From ACE to G-15," Annals of the
       History of Computing 6, No. 4 (October 1984): 350-
       371.

       He discusses Turing's ideas and the author's role
       in early computing, including memoirs of the Bendix
       G-15; illustrated.

1325   Kahn, David. "Cryptology and the Origins of Spread
        Spectrum," IEEE Spectrum (September 1984): 70-80.

        He talks of Turing's visit to Bell Labs during
        World War II to look at a telegraph scrambler to
        secure telephone calls; illustrated.

1326   Malik, R. "In the Beginning—Early Days with ACE,"
        Data Systems (1969): 56-59, 82.

        This assesses British computing projects of 1945-47
        and has a discussion of people, projects, places
        and, in particular, about the ACE. Turing receives
        considerable attention and the ACE's progress is
        presented down to the late 1950s.

1327   Menzler, F.A.A. "William Phillips," Journal of the
        Institute of Actuaries 94, No. 2 (1968): 269-271.

        This obituary notice includes material on his work
        with ACE at the NPL in 1943.

1328   Morris, F.L. and Jones, C.B. "An Early Program Proof
        by Alan Turing," Annals of the History of Computing
        6, No. 2 (April 1984): 139-143.

        The time was 1949, the event is documented with a
        description of the mathematics involved, and the
        original paper by Turing reprinted.

1329   Newman, M.H.A. "Alan Mathison Turing, 1912-1954,"
        Biographical Memoirs of Fellows of the Royal Society
        4 (1955): 253-263.

        This is an obituary/biography of a British computer
        pioneer and mathematician with material on his work
        with computer science.

1330   Phillips, E.W. "Irascible Genius (Letter to the Editor)
        Computer Journal 8 (1965): 56.

        He discusses work done toward the design of ACE in
        January 1943 and then about Turing's involvement in
        the project in the autumn of 1945.

1331   Randell, Brian. "On Alan Turing and the Origins of
        Digital Computers," in B. Meltzer and D. Michie (eds),
        Machine Intelligence 7 (Edinburgh: Edinburgh Univer-
        sity Press, 1972): 3-20.

        This is a good analysis of his contributions to the
        field of computer science from the mid-1930s to the
        early 1950s. It is also useful for information on
        Colossus.

1332   Turing, Alan M. "Computing Machinery and Intelligence,"
        Mind 59 (1950): 433-460.

        He argues that Babbage's work was known to him and

to other developers of computers of the 1940s, thus
adding fuel to the fire of controversy about how
much influence he had on computer scientists of the
1930s and 1940s.

1333   Turing, Alan M. Proposal for the Development of An
        Electronic Computer. National Physical Laboratory
        Report, Computer Science 57. London: NPL, 1972;
        Reprinted from original with foreward by D.W. Davies.

        This is a good source of material on Turing's work
        of the 1940s.

1334   Turing, Alan M. Proposals for Development in the
        Mathematics Division of An Automatic Computing
        Engine (A.C.E). Report E.882. Executive Committee,
        National Physical Laboratory. Teddington, Middle-
        sex: National Physical Laboratory, 1945.

        In his own words Turing offers the design of the
        ACE and an analysis of the work being done on it
        during the 1940s.

1335   Turing, Alan M. et al. The Automatic Computing Engine.
        Shrivenham: Military College of Science, 1947.

        His 62-page booklet contains lectures he gave with
        others on the ACE and he shares his views on the
        general design of computers.

1336   Turing, Alan M. and Woodger, Michael. A.M. Turing's
        ACE Report of 1946 and Other Papers. Cambridge,
        Mass.: MIT Press, 1985.

        This 125-page book reprints key papers published
        between 1945 and 1958 on the British ACE computer.

1337   Turing, S. Alan M. Turing. Cambridge: Heffer, 1959.

        This is a biography written by his mother. It is
        not limited to his personal life but also includes
        discussion of his work on computers.

1338   Wilkinson, J.H. "Alan M. Turing," in Anthony Ralston
        and Edwin D. Reilly, Jr. (eds), Encyclopedia of
        Computer Science and Engineering (New York: Van Nos-
        trand Reinhold, 1983): 1538-1539.

        This is a short, useful biography that defines his
        historical significance; it offers a good bibliogra-
        phy and is illustrated.

1339   Wilkinson, J.H. "The Automatic Computing Engine at
        the National Physical Laboratory," Proceedings of
        the Royal Society Series A, No. 195 (1948): 285-286.

        He focuses on the nature of optimum code as a means
        of reducing delays from delay-line storage.

1340   Wilkinson, J.H.   "Coding On Automatic Digital Comput-
       ing Machines," Report of a Conference on High Speed
       Automatic Calculating Machines, 22-25 June 1949
       (Cambridge: University Mathematical Laboratory,
       January 1950): 28-35.

       He compares order codes of both the Manchester and
       NPL ACE computers.

1341   Wilkinson, J.H.   "The Pilot ACE at the National Physi-
       cal Laboratory," The Radio and Electronic Engineer
       45, No. 7 (1975): 336-340.

       This reviews the development of an important early
       British digital computer in the 1940s, and with
       the role of Alan Turing explained.

1342   Wilkinson, J.H.   Progress Report on the Automatic
       Computing Engine. Teddington, Middlesex: National
       Physical Laboratory, April 1948.

       It contains a good survey of the work done on both
       hardware and software from 1946 to 1948; highly
       technical.

1343   Wilkinson, J.H.   "Some Comments From a Numerical
       Analyst," Journal of the ACM 18, No. 2 (1970): 137-
       147.

       This was the A.M. Turing Lecture for 1970 in which
       the author commented on the life and work of the
       British mathematician who developed the Turing
       Machine and worked on the ACE Computer.

1344   Wilkinson, J.H.   "Turine's Work at the National Physi-
       cal Laboratory and the Construction of Pilot ACE,
       DEUCE, and ACE," in N. Metropolis et al. (eds),
       A History of Computing in the Twentieth Century: A
       Collection of Essays (New York: Academic Press,
       1980): 101-114.

       This is Wilkinson's most complete report on the ACE
       project and the important role played by Turing in
       its development during the 1940s.

1345   Womersley, J.R.   ACE Machine Project. Executive Commi-
       ttee. Teddington, Middlesex: National Physical
       Laboratory, February 13, 1946.

       This is a progress report on the ACE computer at
       the NPL.

1346   Woodger, M.   "Automatic Computing Engine of the National
       Physical Laboratory," Nature 167 (February 17, 1951):
       270.

1347   Woodger, M.   "The History and Present Use of Digital
       Computers at the National Physical Laboratory,"

Process Control and Automation (November 1958): 437-443.

This reviews the construction of the final ACE at the NPL between 1953 and 1957. It also mentions the DEUCE.

American Computers

1348   Adams, Charles W.   "Automatic Data-Processing: A Survey," in Special Report No. 3 (New York: American Management Association, 1955): 125-139.

This was one of the first published reports for users of computers in business surveying existing computers and peripherals as of 1955 in the U.S.

1349   Alexander, Samuel N.   "Input and Output Devices for Electronic Digital Calculating Machinery," in Proceedings of a Symposium on Large-Scale Digital Calculating Machinery (Cambridge, Mass.: Harvard University Press, 1948): 248-253.

This brief article is an excellent survey of the period 1947/1948 of U.S. equipment, their features and functions.

1350   "Almost Human," Home Office News. Newark, N.J.: Prudential Insurance Company of America, February 1947.

This is an 8-page description of digital computational devices.

1351   Alt, Franz L.   "New High-Speed Computing Devices," The American Statistician 1, No. 1 (August 1947): 14-15.

This is a light statement that digital computers existed and how they worked. Alt worked at Bell Labs where much research had been done on computers since the 1920s.

1352   Association for Computing Machinery.   "Preprints: ACM SIGPLAN History of Programming Languages Conference," Los Angeles, June 103, 1978, ACM SIGPLAN Notices 13, No. 8.

This collection of papers (310 pages) on the history of programming eventually became an excellent and detailed history of the subject edited by R.L. Wexelblat, History of Programming Languages (New York: Academic Press, 1981).

1353   Auerbach, A.   "The Elecon 100 General Purpose Computer," Report on ACM Meeting (May 1952): 47-51; Reprinted in U.S. Department of Commerce, Publication No. 111043 (May 1952): 24-30.

He describes the Elecon 100, an early digital device.

1354   Berkeley, Edmund C. Giant Brains or Machines That
        Think. New York: John Wiley, 1949.

        This was one of the more widely distributed books
        on computers in the U.S. available in the early 1950s.
        It discusses how computers are designed and offers
        descriptions of Harvard's Mark I and the ENIAC. The
        book also contains a wide ranging collection of
        bibliographic references.

1355   Birkhoff, Garrett. "Computer Developments 1935-1955,
        As Seen From Cambridge, U.S.A.," in N. Metropolis
        et al. (eds), A History of Computing in the Twentieth
        Century: A Collection of Essays (New York: Academic
        Press, 1980): 21-30.

        He discusses Vannevar Bush and work done at MIT, in
        particular when he was there, all on computers.

1356   Brown, Gordon S. and Wiener, Norbert. "Automation,
        1955. A Retrospective," Annals of the History of
        Computing 6, No. 4 (October 1984): 363-372.

        This is on a talk Wiener gave in 1955, his views and
        activities at MIT. It was addressed to MIT alumni.

1357   Bush, Vannevar. "As We May Think," Atlantic Monthly
        (July 1945): 101-108.

        Bush was a professor at MIT who built analog devices
        and in this article, now comments on digital compu-
        ters.

1358   Carroll, John M. "Electronic Computers for the
        Businessman," Electronics (June 1955): 122-131.

        He surveys 38 commercial computers from 24 manufac-
        turers available in the U.S. in 1954-1955.

1359   Chase, S. "Machines That Think," Readers Digest 64
        (January 1954): 143-146.

        This is a period piece, reflecting what the U.S.
        public was told about computers just as they were
        becoming commercially viable.

1360   Comrie, Leslie J. "Babbage's Dream Comes True," Nature
        158 (1946): 567-568.

        He reviews a publication called A Manual of Operation
        for the Automatic Sequence Controlled Calculator.

1361   Crossman, L.P. "The Remington Rand Type 409-2 Elec-
        tronic Computer," Proceedings of the IRE 41 (October
        1953): 1332-1340.

        This describes a very early computer from Remington
        Rand.

1362   Curtiss, J.H.   The National Applied Mathematics Labo-
        ratories of the National Bureau of Standards: A
        Progress Report Covering the First Five Years of Its
        Existence. Washington, D.C.: National Bureau of
        Standards, Department of Commerce, 1953.

        This reviews work done between 1946 and 1953 on
        early American computers.

1363   Davis, Harry M.   "Mathematical Machines," Scientific
        American 180, No. 4 (April 1949): 29-39.

        This is on digital computers, very early in their
        development in the United States.

1364   Erickson, R.S.   "The Logistics Computer," Proceedings
        of the IRE 41 (October 1953): 1325-1332.

        This describes an early U.S. government computer.

1365   Felker, J.H.   "Performance of TRADIC Transistor Digi-
        tal Computer," Proceedings of the Eastern Joint
        Computer Conference, Philadelphia, December 1954, 46-48.

        This describes a computer built by Bell Labs for the
        U.S. Air Force, and was one of the earliest, if not
        first, to be built with transistors.

1366   Forrester, Jay W. et al. Lectures by Project Whirlwind
        Staff on Electronic Digital Computation. Cambridge,
        Mass.: MIT, Servomechanisms Laboratory, March and
        April, 1947.

        These are technical papers, including some by Warren
        S. Loud, Robert R. Everett and David R. Brown, cover-
        ing a broad range of topics by people knowledgable
        about computers of the 1940s.

1367   "Friendly Machine; DYSEAC," Scientific American 191
        (September 1954): 74ff.

        Besides being a formal description of the features
        of this early digital computer, there are comments
        about American computers in general.

1368   Fuller, Harrison W.   "The Numberoscope," in Proceedings
        of a Symposium on Large-Scale Digital Calculating
        Machinery (Cambridge, Mass.: Harvard University Press,
        1948): 238-247.

        This is the only known formal description of this
        device.

1369   Gluck, S.E.   "The Electronic Discrete Variable Compu-
        ter," Electrical Engineering 72 (1953): 159-162.

        This is a short survey of the device, primarily of
        number formating. The machine was installed in the
        fall, 1949, at the U.S. Ordnance Deapartment, and
        became operational in March 1952.

1370   Greig, J. "The Circle Computer," U.S. Department of
        Commerce, Publication No. 111043 (May 1952): 18-24;
        Reprinted in Mathematical Tables and Other Aids to
        Computation 7 (October 1953): 249-255.

        This is a description of an early U.S. digital
        computer project.

1371   Gridley, D.H. and Sarahan, B.L. "Design of the Naval
        Research Laboratory Computer," Electrical Engineer-
        ing 70 (February 1951): 111.

        This is a technical description of the NAREC, an
        early digital computer for the U.S. Navy.

1372   Gruenberger, F.J. "A Short History of Digital Comput-
        ing in Southern California," Computer News (1958):
        145.23-145.31.

        The subject is computing in Los Angeles between 1942
        and 1957. It is a light account with the names of
        many participants and specific dates of events relat-
        ed.

1373   Hartmanis, Juris. "Observations About the Development
        of Theoretical Computer Science," Annals of the
        History of Computing 3, No. 1 (January 1981): 42-51.

        This is the author recollections about activities
        in the general subject area of automata theory during
        the 1950s and 1960s.

1374   Hoberg, G.G. "The Burroughs Laboratory Computer,"
        Report on AIEE-IRE Computer Conference (February
        1952): 22-29.

        Hoberg describes Burroughs' first digital computer.

1375   Householder, A.S. "Reminiscences of Oak Ridge," in N.
        Metropolis et al (eds), A History of Computing in the
        Twentieth Century (New York: Academic Press, 1980):
        385-388.

        These are his recollections of early computer work
        dating from 1947 to 1954. It contains very few
        details.

1376   Huskey, Harry D. "Characteristics of the Institute
        for Numerical Analysis Computer," Mathematical
        Tables and Other Aids to Computation 4, No. 30
        (1950): 103-108.

        He describes the technical features and functions of
        an early computer housed at the University of Cali-
        fornia at Los Angeles for the National Bureau of
        Standards (1948-1949).

1377   Huskey, Harry D. The Development of Automatic Comput-
        ing. Proceedings of the First U.S.A.-Japan Computer

Conference, 3-5 October 1972, Tokyo. Montvale,
N.J.: A.F.I.P.S. Inc., 1972.

The papers focus on computer projects of the 1940s
and 1950s, such as about the ENIAC and EDVAC.

1378   Huskey, Harry D. "Electronic Digital Computing in the
       United States," in Report of a Conference on High
       Speed Automatic Calculating Machines, 22-25 June
       1949 (Cambridge, Mass.: University Mathematics Labo-
       ratory, January 1950): 109-111.

       He surveys quickly major projects such as IBM's
       electronic calculator, ENIAC, BINAC, Harvard Mark
       III, and the EDVAC.

1379   Jacobs, D.H. "The JAINCOMP-B1 Computer," U.S. Depart-
       ment of Commerce, Publication No. 111043 (May 1952):
       1-6.

       This is a brief, technical description of an early
       digital computer in the U.S. called the JAINCOMP-B1.

1380   Kempf, K. Electronic Computers Within the Ordnance
       Corps. Aberdeen, Md.: U.S. Army Ordnance, Aberdeen
       Proving Ground, November 1961.

       This is a detailed account of some early U.S. digi-
       tal computers, including the ENIAC, EDVAC, ORDVAC,
       BRLESC, and about the role played by the Corps in
       their development.

1381   Klass, P. "Fast Computer Handles Fluctuating Data;
       DYSEAC," Aviation Week 61 (October 4, 1954): 52ff.

       While a news article, it is an early, non-technical
       description of the DYSEAC computer, a member of the
       SEAC series built by the U.S. Government in the
       1950s.

1382   Leiner, A.L. "System Specifications for the DYSEAC,"
       Journal of the Association for Computing Machinery
       1 (1954): 57-81.

       The DYSEAC was an early "portable" computer, built
       under the auspices of the National Bureau of Stand-
       ards, following the design of the SEAC, and was
       installed at the U.S. Army Signal Corps in 1954.

1383   Leiner, A.L. et al. "DYSEAC," National Bureau of
       Standards, Circular 551 (1955): 39-71.

       This was NBS's third computer project, built between
       1952 and 1954, and described by its builders and is
       a formal technical description of its features and
       functions.

1384   Maynard, M.M. "Livermore Automatic Research Computer
       (LARC)," in A. Ralston and C.L. Meek (eds),

Encyclopedia of Computer Science (New York: Petro-
celli/Charter, 1976): 802-803.

This is a short, illustrated history of one of the
earliest electronic digital computers, developed by
Sperry UNIVAC (1959-1960).

1385   Meagher, R.E. and Nash, J.P.   "The ORDVAC," Report on
AIEE-IRE Computer Conference (February 1952): 37-43.

This is a technical description of the features and
functions of the ORDVAC, an early U.S. Government
electronic digital computer.

1386   Mitchell, J.L. and Olsen, K.H.   "TX-0: A Transistor
Computer," AFIPS Conference Proceedings EJCC 10
(1956): 93-101.

This describes one of a series of computers built
at MIT (TX-0, TX-1, TX-2, etc.), which were very
advanced in the 1950s and grew out of work done on
Whirlwind.

1387   Morton, P.L.   "The California Digital Computer,"
Mathematical Tables and Other Aids to Computation
5 (April 1951): 57-61.

Morton describes the CALDIC as a user but also gives
details on its design and function.

1388   Mullaney, F.C.   "Design Features of the ERA 1101
Computer," Report on AIEE-IRE Computer Conference
(February 1952): 43-49; Reprinted in Electrical
Engineering 71 (November 1952): 1015-1018.

This is a technical description of an important
digital computer, the ERA 1101.

1389   Newman, James R.   "Custom-Built Genius," New Republic
(June 23, 1947): 14-18.

The article reflects the infatuation with digital
computers evident on the part of the U.S. press
which began in the late 1940s and remained firm down
to the present. He also describes various projects
then underway.

1390   Office of Naval Research. A Survey of Large Scale
Digital Computers and Computer Projects. Washington,
D.C.: Department of the Navy, 1950.

This 28-page survey of government projects is relatively complete as a catalog of government computers
of the late 1940s.

1391   Perry, D.P.   "Minimum Access Programming," Mathematical Tables and Other Aids to Computation 6 (July
1952): 172-182.

In addition to its focus on programming, the article addresses hardware issues since programming in the early 1950s involved close interaction with machines.

1392   Quinby, E.J. "The MONROBOT Electronic Calculators,"
       U.S. Department of Commerce, Publication No. 111043
       (May 1952): 7-12.

       This may be the only published description of the
       MONROBOT computer.

1393   Ridenour, Louis N. "Mechanical Brains," Fortune 39,
       No. 5 (May 1949): 108-118.

       This is a positive outlook on the future of computing
       and offers a good look back on recent developments,
       including on the work of Eckert and Mauchly on the
       ENIAC and subsequent machines.

1394   Rigby, Fred D. "Tailored Electronic Data Processing
       Equipment," in Lowell H. Hattery and George P.
       Bush (eds), Electronics in Management (Washington,
       D.C.: The University Press of Washington, D.C.,
       1956): 31-37.

       Rigby was, in the mid-1950s, head of the Logistic
       Branch, Mathematical Science Division, Office of
       Naval Research. He reviews computing projects at
       ONR, its technology and their applications.

1395   Robinson, L.P. "Model 30-201 Electronic Digital
       Computer," U.S. Department of Commerce, Publication
       No. 111043 (May 1952): 31-36.

       This is a technical description of the CEC Model
       30-201 digital computer of the early 1950s.

1396   Rolph, William J. "The Last ALWAC," Datamation (Sep-
       tember 1962): 86-91.

       The ALWAC digital computer arrived at Southwestern
       Computing Services in July, 1956. This describes
       the system and is illustrated.

1397   Robertson, James E. "The ORDVAC and the ILLIAC," in
       N. Metropolis et al. (eds), A History of Computing
       in the Twentieth Century (New York: Academic Press,
       1980): 347-364.

       This is written by a participant in the use of these
       early U.S. digital computers, covering the period
       1949-1952. This is an illustrated, technical survey
       of these two systems.

1398   Sharpless, T.K. "Mercury Delay Lines As a Memory Unit,"
       Proceedings of a Symposium on Large Scale Digital
       Calculating Machinery, 7-10 January 1947, Annals of
       the Computation Laboratory of Harvard University 16

(Cambridge, Mass.: Harvard University Press, 1948):
103-109.

He argues that the Moore School intended to apply this
technology to its next computer. It was at the Moore
School that the ENIAC was built during World War II.

1399   Slotnick, D.L.   "The Conception and Development of
        Parallel Processors—A Personal Memoir," Annals of
        the History of Computing 4, No. 1 (January 1982):
        20-30.

        This is an illustrated account of his work (1953-75)
        and about a Westinghouse computer system called
        SOLOMON. It also comments on the University of Illi-
        nois ILLIAC IV.

1400   Smith, Richard E.   "A Historical Overview of Computer
        Architecture," Annals of the History of Computing
        10, No. 4 (1989): 277-303.

        This is a review of the logical aspects of a computer
        at the design level, surveying architectural changes
        over the past four decades.

1401   Sprague, R.E.   "The CADAC," U.S. Department of Commerce,
        Publication No. 111043 (May 1952): 13-17.

        The CADAC was a very early digital computer which
        Sprague describes in this article.

1402   Stibitz, George R.   "A New Class of Computing Aids,"
        Mathematical Tables and Other Aids to Computation 3,
        No. 23 (July 1948): 217-221.

        This Bell Labs scientist reviews the current develop-
        ments in the design of digital computers in the
        United States.

1403   Stibitz, George R.   Relay Computers. Applied Mathema-
        tics Panel Report 171.1R. Washington, D.C.: National
        Defense Research Council, February 1945.

        This is an excellent overview of the kind of computers
        being built at Bell Labs in the mid-1940s and has
        comments on the general development of computers in
        the United States.

1404   Sumner, F.H. et al. "The Central Control Unit at the
        'Atlas' Computer," Proceedings of the IFIP Congress
        (1962): 657-662.

        The Atlas was a 1950's digital computer project
        supported by the U.S. Government and which is par-
        tially described here.

1405   U.S. Navy Department, Office of Naval Research. A
        Survey of Automatic Digital Computers. Washington,
        D.C.: U.S. Government Printing Office, November, 1954.

This 109-page publication is an early, detailed
analysis of existing computer systems and about how
they were being used, covering U.S. processors.

1406   Welsh, H.F. and Porter, V.J.   "A Large Drum-File
       Memory System," Proceedings of the Eastern Joint
       Computer Conference: New Developments in Computers
       (New York: American Institute of Electrical Engineer-
       ing, 1957): 136-139.

       This describes storage for the Univac-Larc (also
       called the LARC in some publications) computing
       system. It was a system characterized by relatively
       inexpensive but slow memory.

1407   Wolff, J.J.   "The Office of Naval Research Relay
       Computer," Mathematical Tables and Other Aids to
       Computation 6, No. 40 (1952): 207-212.

       Wolff described a computer under construction through
       funding from ONR in the late 1940s and early 1950s.
       It was one of several being sponsored by the ONR at
       the time.

                     Analog Computers

1408   Allison, William.   "A Broad Look at Analog Computers,"
       Control Engineering 2 (February 1955): 53-57.

       This is a brief survey of existing analog computers
       and their advantages, circa mid-1950s.

1409   Black, H.W.   "Stabilized Feedback Amplifiers," Bell
       System Technical Journal 13 (January 1934): 1-18.

       Black described his 1937 invention of a feedback
       amplifier which made the potential for accurate
       analog computers possible.

1410   Bode, H.W.   Network Analysis and Feedback Amplifier
       Design. New York: D. Van Nostrand Co., 1945.

       This Bell Labs scientist developed amplifiers of
       tollerances needed for analog computers of the
       1930s. This book, although a technical treatise,
       summarizes his work.

1411   Currie, A.A.   "The General Purpose Analog Computer,"
       Bell Laboratories Record 29 (March 1951): 101-108.

       GPAC, also called Gypsy, was an early post World War
       II analog computer built at Bell Labs for complex
       mathematical applications. Currie describes the
       system in this article.

1412   Grandi, L.L. and Lebell, D.   "Analog Computers Solve
       Complex Problems," Radio and TV News 46 (November
       1951): 70-71FF.

This is an early publication on the use of analog computers in post-World War II USA.

1413   Holst, P.A. "A Note of History," Simulation 17, No. 3 (September 1971): 131-135.

This briefly describes analog computers.

1414   Jenkin, C.F. The Astrolabe—Its Construction and Use. Oxford: Oxford University Press, 1925.

This is a detailed study of the device which was used for centuries to predict movement of the stars and planets in Europe as an aid to navigation. The concepts of analog computing and feedback are described in this book as part of the effort to explain the astrolabe.

1415   Johnson, Clarence L. Analog Computer Techniques. New York: McGraw-Hill Book Co., 1956.

This is a technical treatise with some history. It is best used to understand early electronic analog computers of the late 1940s and early 1950s.

1416   Korn, Granino A. and Korn, Theresa M. Electronic Analog and Hybrid Computers. New York: McGraw-Hill, 1964.

This is a good technical snapshot of existing technologies in analog computing as of the early 1960s and late 1950s.

1417   Korn, Granino A. and Korn, Theresa M. Electronic Analog Computers: CD-c Analog Computers. New York: McGraw-Hill Book Co., 1956.

This second edition (first published in 1952) was a standard technical survey of the subject in the 1950s. The first chapter (pp. 1-29) has a useful summary of 1950s' analog machines. It also has an extensive bibliography (1950-1955) on analog devices and their uses.

1418   North, J.D. "The Astrolabe," Scientific American (January 1974): 96-106.

This is a very recent publication on the analog device used to help predict the movement of stars and planets since ancient times down to at least the 1600s in the West.

1419   Paynter, H.M. (ed). A Palimpsest on the Electronic Analog Art. Boston: George A. Philbrick Researches, Inc., 195(?).

This 270-page book is a collection of reprinted papers and articles on the features and applications of analog computers, mainly during the 1950s.

1420   Price, D. De Sola. <u>The Equatorie of the Planets</u>.
        Cambridge: Cambridge University Press, 1955.

        He reviews many analog devices used for navigation
        and the prediction of the movements of stars in
        general.

1421   Price, D. De Sola. <u>Gears From the Greeks</u>. New York:
        Science History Publications, 1975.

        He describes the Greek Antikythera device which was
        a mechanized astolabe found in a sunken ship. He
        discovered it at the Greek National Archaeological
        Museum and sees it as a very early analog computer.

1422   Ragazzini, J. <u>et al</u>. "Analysis of Problems in Dynamics
        by Electronic Circuits," <u>Proceedings, IRE</u> 19, No.2
        (May 1947): 444-452.

        The authors describe an analog construct of theirs
        which served as an early general purpose electronic
        computer.

1423   "Rocket Reckoner; Analogue Computer for Aiming Rockets,"
        <u>Newsweek</u> 39 (June 16, 1952): 61.

        Analog computers enjoyed a limited but useful period
        of popularity in the 1950s, particularly for milita-
        ry uses. This is a brief, and rare, look at such an
        early post-World War II use.

1424   Roedel, Jerry. <u>An Introduction to Analog Computers</u>.
        Papers Presented at 8th National Instrumentation
        Conference, Chicago, September 1953. Boston: George
        A. Philbrick Researchers, Inc., 1953.

        This is an early, useful introduction to the subject.
        It also contains material on the history of analog
        devices.

1425   Sheretz, P.C. "Electronic Circuits of the NAREC,"
        <u>Proceedings, IRE</u> (October 1953): 1313-1320.

        The author reviews the computer at the U.S. Naval
        Research Laboratory, an early military computer.

1426   Sienkiewicz, J.M. "Introduction to Analog Computers,"
        <u>Popular Electronics</u> 15 (December 1961): 65-68ff.

        By 1961 there were many functioning analog computers
        some of which are described in this article. It is
        also a useful introduction to their technology.

1427   Soroka, Walter W. <u>Analog Methods in Computation and
        Simulation</u>. New York: McGraw-Hill Book Co., 1954.

        This is an excellent, detailed, and technical descrip-
        tion published when analog computers were enjoying a
        great deal of popularity and just before the digital
        came to dominate.

1428   Travis, I. "The History of Computing Devices," in C.
        C. Chambers, <u>Theory and Techniques for the Design of</u>
        <u>Electronic Digital Computers. Lectures Delivered 8</u>
        <u>July-31 August 1946</u> (Philadelphia: Moore School of
        Electrical Engineering, University of Pennsylvania,
        1947): 2.1-2.3.

        Travis reviews briefly calculating methods that are
        both analog and digital.

                                BINAC

1429   Auerbach, A.A. <u>et al</u>. "The BINAC," <u>Proceedings of the</u>
        <u>Institute of Radio Engineering</u> 40 (1952): 12-29.

        The authors describe the BINAC and include circuit
        diagrams. They called this computer the "first CPU
        of its type to be completed successfully in the
        United States." They include a sample program run
        on the processor.

1430   "BINAC Demonstrated, New Electronic Brain," <u>Journal</u>
        <u>of the Franklin Institute</u> 248, No. 4 (October 1949):
        360-361.

        This is a review of a demonstration of the BINAC
        held at the Eckert-Mauchly Computer Corporation. It
        includes some technical details on the machine.

1431   "Faster, Smaller Computer; BINAC," <u>Science News Letter</u>
        55 (April 2, 1949): 222.

        This is a brief, but competent, overview of the
        military "portable" computer called the BINAC.

1432   "Northrop Acquires Electronic 'Brain'," <u>Aviation</u>
        <u>Week</u> 29 (September 19, 1949): 29.

        This details the purchase and plns for the BINAC.
        It was one of the first commercial transactions for
        a digital computer in the United States.

1433   Shaw, R.F. "Arithmetic Operations in a Binary Compu-
        ter," <u>Review Sci. Instr</u>. 21 (August 1950): 687-693.

        Shaw offers a description of how to perform addition,
        subtraction, multiplication and division on the
        BINAC in the most formative period in the develop-
        ment of what would later be called programming.

1434   Stern, Nancy. "The BINAC: A Case Study in the History
        of Technology," <u>Annals of the History of Computing</u>
        1, No. 1 (July 1979): 9-20.

        This is a well-researched and written history of the
        machine built by Eckert and Mauchly between 1947 and
        1949.

1435   Booth, Andrew D. "Computers in the University of
        London, 1945-1962," Radio and Electrical Engineer-
        ing 45, No. 7 (1975): 341-345; reprinted in N.
        Metropolis et al. (eds), A History of Computing in
        the Twentieth Century (New York: Academic Press,
        1980): 551-561.

        This is an illustrated survey of machines Booth
        worked on, starting in the early 1940s, from mecha-
        nical counters to analog machines, and relay calcula-
        tors. Some of the machines were the APEX, ARC, MAC
        and M3. A few were developed for the British Tabu-
        lating Macine Company.

1436   Cameron, K.E. "The Design of the M3 Computer,"
        (Unpublished M.S. thesis, University of Saskatche-
        wan, 1964).

        This was a computer developed, in part, at the Uni-
        versity of London with Andrew Booth's early involve-
        ment.

1437   Carter, R.H.A. "The TRE High-Speed Digital Computer,"
        Automatic Digital Computation (Proceedings of a
        Symposium Held at NPL, March 1953) (London: HMSO,
        1954): 56-64.

        This describes the TREAC, an early British computer
        which was very advanced in design for its day.

1438   Clarke, S.L.H. "The Elliott 400 Series and Before,"
        Radio and Electronic Engineer 45, No. 8 (August
        1975): 415-421.

        Clarke discusses the development of British commer-
        cial electronic digital computers of the 1950s.

1439   Comrie, Leslie J. "Recent Progress in Scientific
        Computing," Journal of Scientific Instruments 21
        (August 1944): 129-135.

        He reviews calculating devices and their applica-
        bility for scientific work. He discusses difference
        analyzers, the National Accounting Machine, various
        electrical and desk calculators, and commonly used
        punch card devices.

1440   Cooke-Yarborough, E.H. et al. "A Transistor Digital
        Computer," Proceedings of the IEE 103B, Supp. 1-3
        (1956): 364-370.

        The authors describe work they did on an early
        transistor computer at the United Kingdom Atomic
        Energy Research Establishment, Harwell, called the
        CADET computer.

1441   Coombs, A.W.M. "An Electronic Digital Computer, Parts
        1-4," Post Office EEJ 48 (July and October 1955,
        January 1956): 114, 137, 212; 49 (April and July
        (1956): 18, 126.

He describes MOSAIC, a British processor built
between 1947 and 1954, a machine for military radar
users.

1442   Coombs, A.W.M. "MOSAIC—The Ministry of Supply Auto-
        matic Computer," Automatic Digital Computation
        (Proceedings of a Symposium Held at NPL, March 1953)
        (London: HMSO, 1954): 38-42.

        The computer is described and was used for aircraft
        tracking experiments in the mid-1950s.

1443   Coombs, A.W.M. and Chandler, W.W. Automatic Computing:
        An Analysis of Arithmetical Operations. Post Office
        Research Station Report. Dollis Hill: Post Office,
        August 1946.

        They review adding, multiplication and other functions
        on machines in detail. It is, however, very much a
        theoretical discourse, circa mid-1940s.

1444   Davis, G.M. "The English Electric KDF9 Computer
        System," Computer Bulletin (December 1960): 119-120.

        This was a high-speed transistor, British computer.

1445   Huskey, Harry D. "Electronic Digital Computers in
        England," Mathematical Tables and Other Aids to
        Computation 3 (1948): 213-216.

        This is a status report on various computer projects
        in Great Britain as of 1947-1948.

1446   Kitz, N. "A Discussion of Automatic Digital High-Speed
        Calculating Machines, With Special Reference to S.E.C.
        —A Simple Electronic Computer" (M.Sc. thesis, Uni-
        versity of London, 1951).

        He offers a quick review of modern devices (nearly
        25) and then surveys work done at Birkbeck College.
        About half of the 152-page report is historical in
        content.

1447   Shire, E.S. and Runcorn, S.K. An Apparatus for the
        Computation of Serial Correlations and Its Use in
        Frequency Analysis, Report No. 7, Selected Government
        Report, 5: Servomechanisms (London: HMSO, 1951): 98-
        121.

        The report is based on an RRDE research survey of
        January 1945, on a machine using 2 paper tape readers
        and 1 multiplier built out of relays and uniselectors.

1448   Williams, M.R. and Campbell-Kelly, Martin (eds). The
        Early British Conferences. Cambridge, Mass.: MIT
        Press, 1989.

        This is a reprint, with introduction, of technical
        papers on computers from conferences held at

Cambridge University (June 22-25, 1949), Manchester
University (July 9-12, 1951), and at the National
Physical Laboratory (March 1953).

Colossus

1449   Chandler, W.W. "The Installation and Maintenance of
       Colossus," Annals of the History of Computing 5,
       No. 3 (July 1983): 260-262.

       Chandler worked at Bletchley Park during World War
       II and with this secret computer. These are his
       recollections of the period and about the machine.

1450   Coombs, Allen W.M. "Colossus and the History of Comput-
       ing: Dollis Hill's Important Contribution," Post
       Office Electrical Engineers' Journal 70, No. 2 (July
       1977): 108-110.

       Coombs reviews conference discussions on Colossus
       held at the Los Alamos Conference on the History of
       Computing, June, 1976.

1451   Coombs, Allen W.M. "The Making of Colossus," Annals
       of the History of Computing 5, No. 3 (July 1983):
       253-259.

       The author participated in the creation of computers
       at Bletchley Park during World War II and had a good
       knowledge of the Colossus system which he describes
       here.

1452   Flowers, T.H. "The Design of Colossus," Annals of the
       History of Computing 5, No. 3 (July 1983): 239-252.

       This is an illustrated account by an engineer at
       Bletchley Park during World War II.

1453   Flowers, Thomas H. et al."The Code Breaking Computers
       of 1944," in H. Hinsley, Colossus and the German
       High-Grade Cyphers, Lectures and Discussion, 26 March
       1987 (Hitchin Hertfordshire: IEEE Publications, 1987).

       These are four 90-minute videocassettes with develop-
       ers of Colossus. Speakers included Flowers, A.C.
       Lynch, A.W.M. Coombs, and H.H. Hinsley.

1454   Peltu, M. "How Secrecy Lost Britain a Lead," Computer
       Weekly (July 28, 1977): 4.

       This is about a lecture made by T.H. Flowers on
       Colossus. Flowers argues that the British lost the
       lead in the race to develop computers because of the
       need to keep quiet about the Colossus rather than
       share knowledge of the machine with other scientists.

1455   Randell, Brian. "The COLOSSUS," in N. Metropolis et
       al. (eds), A History of Computing in the Twentieth
       Century:A Collection of Essays (New York: Academic

Press, 1980): 47-92.

This is a detailed review of the British processor
of World War II vintage. It is a technical piece,
illustrated and by an author with hands-on experience
with the machine.

1456   Randell, Brian. "Colossus: Godfather of the Computer,"
        New Scientist 73 (February 10, 1977): 346-348.

        This is a short history of the early British compu-
        ter.

1457   Seale, P. and McConville, M. Philby: The Long Road to
        Moscow. London: Hamish Hamilton, 1973.

        This is discussion of various British computers and
        scientists, including the COLOSSUS and about Turing.

        Computer Design Automation Technology

1458   Altman, G.W. et al. "Automation of Computer Panel
        Wiring," Transactions of the AIEE 79, Part 1 (1960):
        118-125.

        The authors describe packaging in the pre-LSI era.
        They relate the example of the transistorized IBM
        1400 and 7000.

1459   Breuer, M.A. "Recent Developments in Automated Design
        and Analysis of Digital Systems," Proceedings of
        the IEEE 60 (1972): 12-27.

        This includes a detailed bibliography on recent
        trends in design automation.

1460   Carmody, P. et al. "An Interactive Graphics System for
        Custom Design," Proceedings of the 17th Design
        Automation Conference, Minneapolis (1980): 430-489.

        They discuss the use of interactive processing, using
        graphics and alphanumeric terminals, in automated
        design applications not limited just to the design
        of high technology hardware.

1461   Case, P.W. et al. "The Recording, Checking and Printing
        of Logic Diagrams," Proceedings of the Eastern Joint
        Computer Conference, Philadelphia (1958): 108-118.

        IBM used techniques described in this article in the
        1950s to generate design documentation for parts.

1462   Case, P.W. et al. "Solid Logic Design Automation,"
        IBM Journal of Research and Development 8 (1964):
        127-140.

        The authors describe how they did design automation
        at IBM in the early 1960s.

1463   Donath, W.E. and Lesser, J. LAGER, A Language for the
       Digital Transcription of Design Patterns. Research
       Report RC 1730. Yorktown Heights, N.Y.: IBM Thomas
       J. Watson Research Center, 1966.

       The language was used for FET-based technology of
       the 1960s.

1464   Grace, F.E. "Planning for Automated Artwork," Proceed-
       ings of the 2nd National Conference of the Association
       for Precision Graphics, Los Angeles (1968), Section 6.

       This is a description of a tool to design FET techno-
       logy for the IBM 1620 and 1130 class computers.

1465   Jephson, J.S. et al. "A Three-Value Computer Design
       Verification System," IBM Systems Journal 8 (1969):
       178-188.

       The subject is a computer design simulator of the
       1960s to help detect and handle logic circuit hazards
       and race conditions.

1466   Knuth, Donald E. Mathematics and Computer Science:
       Coping With Finiteness (Stan-CS-76-541). Stanford:
       Stanford University, Computer Science Department,
       February 1976.

       This important figure in the history of programming
       langues discusses how only computers can deal effec-
       tively with finite numbers.

1467   Lee, C.Y. "An Algorithm for Path Connection and Its
       Applications," IRE Transactions, Computers EC-10
       (1961): 346-365.

       This scientist, from Bell Labs, describes an SLT
       packaging technique used in the late 1950s by some
       designers of computers.

1468   Levit, A.D. "ADL, An Automated Drafting Language,"
       Proceedings of the 2nd National Conference of the
       Association for Precision Graphics, Los Angeles
       (1968): Section 5.

       The author describes a language used to help design
       FET-based computers of the mid-1960s.

1469   Preiss, R.J. "The Use of Fault Location Tests in
       Prototype Bring-Up," Proceedings of the IFIP Congress
       New York (1965): 511-517.

       This is a description of testing methods for computer
       components, using software, during the 1960s.

1470   Van Cleemput, W.M. Computer-Aided Design of Digital
       Systems: A Bibliography. Woodland Hills, Ca.: Computer
       Science Press, 1976-1979. 4 vols.

       This is the only bibliography in the subject.

DEUCE

1471   Denison, S.J.M.   "Further DEUCE Interpretative Programs
        and Some Translating Programs," in R. Goodman (ed),
        Annual Review in Automatic Programming 1 (New York:
        127-145.

        This is a detailed, technical review of the DEUCE,
        an early British computer of the 1950s and about
        which there is little information.

1472   Haley, A.C.D.   "DEUCE: A High-Speed General-Purpose
        Computer," Proceedings of the IEEE 103B, Supp. 1-3
        (1956): 165-173.

        The DEUCE was an early commercial British computer
        (circa 1955), which used mercury delay lines. The
        author provides a technical description of the
        system.

Digital Computer Technology

1473   Alt, Franz L.   "Development of Automatic Computers,"
        in Lowell H. Hattery and George P. Bush (eds),
        Electronics in Management (Washington, D.C.: The
        University Press of Washington, D.C., 1956): 15-21.

        In the 1950s Alt worked for the U.S. National Bureau
        of Standards and was a recognized expert on computers.
        In this article he provides a management overview of
        computer technology as it existed in 1955-1956.

1474   Amdahl, Gene M.   "The Logical Design of an Intermediate
        Speed Digital Computer" (Unpublished Ph.D. disserta-
        tion, University of Wisconsin, 1952).

        The author was a major developer of the S/360 at
        IBM and the founder of a company after his name,
        that sold computers in the 1970s and 1980s.

1475   Arnold, Robert R. et al. Introduction to Data Process-
        ing. New York: John Wiley & Sons, Inc., 1966.

        This is a textbook introduction to data processing
        technology, its equipment, applications and manage-
        ment as of the early to mid-1960s. It includes a
        short history of computing equipment (pp.15-31).

1476   Bolhms, Hans.   "Pebbles to Bytes," Equinox 21 (May-
        June 1985): 42-51.

        This overview from the abacus to integrated chips
        includes a photograph of "Dirty Gerty," the first
        transistorized computer made in Canada, and perhaps
        the only published photograph on the device. Other
        useful illustrations are included.

1477   Booth, A.D. and Booth, K.H.V. Automatic Digital Calcu-
        lators. 2nd Ed. London: Butterworths, 1956.

This offers a short review of the history of computer technology in addition to a much longer description of contemporary devices of the mid-1950s. The authors were active participants in the development of computer technology in Great Britain during the 1940s and early 1950s.

1478   Booth, A.D. et al. "Principles and Progress in the Construction of High Speed Digital Computers," Quarterly Journal of Mechanical and Applied Mathematics 2 (1949): 182-197.

They review the state of the art as of the late 1940s, a period of much activity in the field both in Great Britain and in the United States.

1479   Burks, Arthur W. "Super-Electronic Computing Machine," Electronic Industries 5, No. 7 (July 1946): 62.

Burks played a key role in the design of electronic digital computers, making any comments by him of significance to historians. In this brief piece he reflects thoughts at the very dawn of the computer.

1480   Carr, John W., III and Perlis, Alan J. "A Comparison of Large-Scale Calculators," Control Engineering 3 (February 1956): 84-96.

This is a technical treatise on the characteristics and performance of large computers as of the mid-1950s.

1481   Ceruzzi, Paul E. Reckoners: The Prehistory of the Digital Computer, From Relays to the Stored Program Concept, 1939-1945. Westport, Conn.: Greenwood Press, 1983.

This is a balanced and useful history written by an historian. It surveys the ENIAC, ASCC (Mark I), Zuse machines and work done at Bell Laboratories.

1482   Chapin, N. An Introduction to Automatic Computers. Princeton, N.J.: Van Nostrand, 1955.

The book briefly covers the evolution of calculators and, in considerable detail, the development of computer technology during the 1940s and 1950s.

1483   Computerworld Staff. Celebrating the Computer Age. Supplement to Computerworld, November 3, 1986.

This very large supplement has a section on the history of computers and many short articles by such historically important individuals as Berkeley, Noyce, Bell others on Babbage, Hollerith, Atanasoff, Mauchly, Eckert, von Neumann, Watson and Hopper.

1484   Data Processing Management Association. Principles of Automatic Data Processing. Park Ridge, Ill.: Data Processing Management Association, 1965.

This short DPMA publication reflected its role in educating the public, and many within the new data processing industry, about the subject and on how best to use this technology.

1485   Davis, H.M. "Mathematical Machines," Scientific American 180 (April 1949): 28-30.

This fit into a genre of articles which appeared in the late 1940s introducing the new technology of computers to the American public.

1486   Eckert, W.J. and Jones, R. Faster, Faster. New York: McGraw-Hill Book Co., Inc., 1955.

Two well known computer scientists describe the technology and its features as of the mid-1950s.

1487   Engineering Research Associates. High-Speed Computing Devices. New York: McGraw-Hill, 1950; Reprinted at Los Angeles: Tomash Publishers, 1983, with introduction by Arnold Cohen.

This is a major encyclopedic work on technology of computers as of the late 1940s.

1488   Engel, L. "Electronic Calculators; Brainless But Bright," Harper 206 (April 1953): 84-90.

This is one example of many such articles typical of the 1950s describing digital computers and their use in general, non-technical terms.

1489   Forrester, J.W. "Digital Computers: Present and Future Trends," Review of Electronic Digital Computers (Philadelphia: AIEE/IRE, 1951): 109-113.

This MIT engineer, at the time of publication, was involved in leading the development of Whirlwind, and thus was particularly well informed on trends which he describes, particularly those in the United States.

1490   Fahnestock, James D. Computers and How They Work. New York: Ziff-Davis Publishing Co., 1959.

This is an introduction to computer technology as of late second generation computers.

1491   Gregory, R.H. and Van Horn, R.L. Automatic Data-Processing Systems. London: Chatto & Windus, 1960.

Although not a thorough survey, this 705-page book nonetheless represents a detailed snapshot of data processing of the 1950s from many perspectives. It is particularly useful for British views and developments.

1492   Hackney, R.W. and Jessitope, C.R. Parallel Computers. Philadelphia: Heyden & Son, 1981.

The focus is on parallelism in large computers and
how that is accomplished. Chapter One has an historical survey of computers from Babbage to the
ILLIAC IV. The book also comments on machines of
the 1950s.

1493   Halacy, Daniel S. Computers, the Machines We Think
        With. New York: Harper & Row, 1962.

        This is a general introduction to computers. It is
        also useful for appreciating machines of the late
        1950s and very early 1960s.

1494   Hamilton, A. "Brains That Click," Popular Mechanics
        91 (March 1949): 162-167.

        Hamilton frequently wrote on computers in their
        early years. This article is typical of his work
        of describing this new technology for the general
        reader.

1495   Ivall, T. "50 Years of Computer Science," Electronics
        and Wireless World 92, No. 1609 (November 1986): 52-
        62.

        This emphasis is on the development of computer
        technology.

1496   Lagemann, John K. "It All Adds Up," Collier's Magazine
        (May 31, 1947): 22-23, passim.

        This describes digital computing for the general
        public in the United States.

1497   Last, J. "Digital Calculating Machines," The Charted
        Mechanical Engineer (December 1962): 572-579.

        This is a brief, contemporaneous overview of second
        generation computers.

1498   Locke, E.L. "Modern Calculators," Astounding Science
        Fiction 52, No. 5 (January 1949): 87-106.

        This is a popularized description of digital comput-
        ing of the late 1940s: technology and applications.

1499   Lubkin, Samuel. "Decimal Point Location in Computing
        Machines," Mathematical Tables and Other Aids to
        Computation 3, No. 21 (January 1948): 44-50.

        Lubkin's paper was a technical discourse concerning
        digital electronic computers.

1500   MacLaughlan, Lorne. "Electrical Mathematicians,"
        Astounding Science Fiction 53, No. 3 (May 1949): 93-
        108.

        Focus is on digital computers and upon how thy could
        be used.

1501   Malik, R. "Only Begetters of the Computer," New
        Scientist 16 (July 1970): 138-139.

        He reviews some of the mechanical monsters of the
        1940s and 1950s. The author was a European journa-
        list specializing in the data processing industry.

1502   Mann, Martin. "Want to Buy a Brain?," Popular Science
        154, No. 5 (May 1949): 148-152.

        The "brain" was the digital computer which is des-
        cribed for the first time by this magazine. It
        would publish many more articles on computers in the
        next 30 years. This article appeared at about the
        same time as other similar pieces were being publish-
        ed by other widely read American periodicals.

1503   McCulloch, W.S. and Pfeiffer, J. "Of Digital Computers
        Called Brains," Scientific Monthly 69 (December
        1949): 368-376; "Corrections," Ibid. 70 (February
        1950): 140.

        This was a well written yet early article on the
        subject and is narrative in form.

1504   Murray, F.J. Mathematical Machines, 1: Digital Comput-
        ers. New York: Columbia University Press, 1961.

        This is an important, early publication on all kinds
        of computer equipment, both processors and peripherals
        as of the late 1950s.

1505   Murray, F.J. The Theory of Mathematical Machines. New
        York: King's Crown Press, 1948.

        This is the second and full edition of his survey
        on computer technology of the late 1940s.

1506   O'Neal, R.D. "Photographic Methods for Handling Input
        and Output Data," in Proceedings of a Symposium on
        Large-Scale Digital Calculating Machinery (Cambridge,
        Mass.: Harvard University Press, 1948): 260-266.

        The author reviews how this could be done with digi-
        tal computers, using the I/O equipment available to
        him in the late 1940s.

1507   Pantages, A. "Computing's Early Years," Datamation 13,
        10 (October 1967): 60-65.

        This is a short report of the "Historical Session"
        at the 1967 session of the National ACM Conference
        in which a number of early computer pioneers parti-
        cipated.

1508   Patterson, George W. et al. (eds). Theory and Techniques
        for Design of Electronic Digital Computers: Lectures
        Given at the Moore School 8 July 1946-31 August 1946.
        2 vols. Philadelphia: The University of Pennsylvania,

Moore School of Electrical Engineering, 1947; Reprint Cambridge, Mass.: MIT Press, 1985, edited by Martin Campbell-Kelly and Michael R. Williams.

1509   These are 20 lectures covering all aspects of digital computers, delivered at the home of ENIAC. These sessions were influential on many early computer builders.

1510   Randell, Brian. "Digital Computers: Origins," in A. Ralston and C.L. Meek (eds), Encyclopedia of Computer Science (New York: Petrocelli/Charter, 1976): 486-490.

This article provides details on the ENIAC and EDVAC projects.

1511   Rees, M. "Computers: 1954," Science Monthly 79 (August 1954): 118-124.

This reviews quickly existing computer projects in summary fashion.

1512   Richards, R.K. Arithmetic Operations in Digital Computers. New York: D. Van Nostrand Co., Inc., 1955.

This is a serious, 384-page book on data processing technology of the early to mid-1950s. It describes how computers operated at that time and thus is a useful period piece for second generation equipment.

1513   Richards, R.K. Digital Computer Components and Circuits. Princeton, N.J.: Van Nostrand, 1957.

Chapter 1 reviews the history of electronic components and circuits.

1514   Richards, R.K. Electronic Digital Systems. New York: Wiley, 1966.

This continues the theme of his previous books; this time it is a reflection of technology of the 1960s.

1515   Ridenour, L.N. "Mechanical Brains," Fortune 39 (May 1949): 108-110ff.

The author was a frequent comentator on computers in their earliest period. This was one of many he wrote introducing the technology to the American public. This article carried out that objective primarily for business people.

1516   Rosen, S. "Digital Computers: History," in A. Ralston and C.L. Meek (eds), Encyclopedia of Computer Science (New York: Petrocelli/Charter, 1976): 474-486.

The focus is on computers built from the 1940s through the 1960s.

1517   Stibitz, George R.   "Should Automatic Computers Be
        Large or Small?" Mathematical Tables and Other Aids
        to Computation 2, No. 20 (October 1947): 362-364.

        The short article is concerned with digital devices
        made by the inventor, primarily relay computers, at
        Bell Labs in the late 1930s and 1940s.

1518   Stibitz, George R. and Larrivee, Jules A. Mathematics
        and Computers. New York: McGraw-Hill Book Co., 1957.

        Stibitz was the father of a series of Bell Labs
        computers in the 1930s and 1940s. This book is on
        applied mathematics and contains a brief history of
        computers, with a survey of the technology as of the
        mid-1950s. It has a detailed bibliography particu-
        larly useful on publications of the mid-1950s.

1519   Stiffler, W.W. (ed). High-Speed Computing Devices.
        New York: McGraw-Hill, 1950.

        This focuses on the design of computers and related
        devices. It is a good review of technology circa
        1949 and contains a detailed bibliography on the
        subject.

1520   Thornton, J.E.   "Parallel Operation in the Control
        Data 6600," Proceedings FJCC 26, Part 2 (1964): 33-
        40.

        Besides being a series of technical comments on the
        CDC 6600 processor, it reflects leading edge computer
        design of the early 1960s.

1521   Tumbleson, Robert C. "Calculating Machines," Federal
        Science Progress (June 1947): 3-7.

        This is a brief discussion of digital computational
        devices of the 1940s.

1522   UNESCO. Information Processing: Proceedings of the
        International Conference on Information Processing,
        UNESCO, Paris 15-20 June 1959. London: Butterworths,
        1960.

        These are the proceedings of one of the more famous
        DP conferences of the 1950s of an international type.
        It contains dozens of technical papers by both Ameri-
        can and European scientists and engineers.

1523   Wilkes, Maurice V. Automatic Digital Computers. New
        York: John Wiley, 1956.

        This distinguished computer science reviews computer
        technology and software of the 1950s.

1524   Wilkes, Maurice V. "Digital Computers: Early," in A.
        Ralston and C.L. Meek (ed), Encyclopedia of Computer
        Science (New York: Petrocelli/Charter, 1976): 490-495.

He focuses attention on developments of the 1940s
with an illustrated account of the Mark I, Bell
Labs' Model V, and the ENIAC.

1525   Williams, Bernard O.   "Computing With Electricity, 1935-
        1947" (Unpublished Ph.D. dissertation, University of
        Kansas, 1984).

        This is a general history of computers of the 1930s
        and 1940s.

1526   Withington, F.G.   "Five Generations of Computers,"
        Harvard Business Review 52 (1974): 99-103.

        This is a history of the five generations of
        computers, along with a discussion of their economic
        worth over the previous 30 years.

1527   Woodger, M. et al. "The Foundations of Computer
        Engineering," Radio and Electrical Engineering 45,
        No. 10 (1975): 598-602.

        This is the transcript of a discussion regarding the
        origins of the concept of the stored program.

1528   Wulforst, Harry.   Breakthrough to the Computer Age.
        New York: Scribners, 1982.

        This is a history for the general reader, taking
        the story from the ENIAC of the 1940s to the early
        1950s with the IBM 701.

Digital Computers

1529   Beard, M. and Pearcey, T.   "An Electronic Computer,"
        Journal of Scientific Instruments 29 (October 1952):
        305-311.

        They describe the Australian CSIRO Mark I computer.

1530   Beard, M. and Pearcy, T.   "The Genesis of an Early
        Stored-Program Computer: CSIRAC," Annals of the
        History of Computing 6, No. 2 (April 1984): 106-115.

        This is the story of an early vacuum tube stored
        program computer. Both authors worked on this
        Australian machine which they describe.

1531   Blachman, Nelson.   "Czechoslovak Automatic Digital
        Computer, SAPO," European Scientific Notes, No.
        13-7 (July 1, 1959): 150-151; Reprinted in Annals of
        the History of Computing 2, No. 4 (October 1980):
        293-294.

        This reviews the work of Svoboda in the 1950s and
        about Czechoslovakian computing.

1532   Carr, J.W., III et al. "A Visit to Computation Centers
        in the Soviet Union," Communications of the ACM 2, No.
        6 (1959): 8-20.

This is a useful, very early survey of Soviet computing projects, along with a description of data
centers and computer scientists.

1533   Clark, W.A.   "The Lincoln TX-2 Computer Development,"
        Proceedings WJCC (1957): 143-145.

        This describes the TX-2 computer, built in the
        1950s. The TX project helped train a generation of
        engineers who later went on to build mini-computers,
        especially at DEC.

1534   Clark, W.A. and Molnar, C.E.   The LINC: A Description
        of the Laboratory Instrument Computer," Annals of
        the New York Academy of Science 115 (July 1964) 653-
        668.

        This description of LINC was one of the early narra-
        tives of a project involving the use of 12-bit
        computers. It was done at the Lincoln Laboratory
        at MIT, beginning in 1960. The machine's functions
        were first demonstrated in 1962.

1535   "Fast Student; ORDVAC," Time 59 (January 28, 1952):42.

        This was an early, non-technical, public announce-
        ment of the existence and functions of ORDVAC.

1536   Gotlieb, C.C.   "FERUT—The First Operational Electronic
        Computer in Canada," in CIPS Proceedings, Session 84,
        May 9-11, 1984 (Calgary: Information Processing
        Society, 1984): 313-317.

        This is a description of the features and functions
        of the system. It was used, for example, to help
        develop the St. Lawrence Seaway, and was housed at
        the University of Toronto.

1537   Humphrey, Watts S.   "MOBIDIC and Fieldata," Annals of
        the History of Computing 9, No. 2 (1987): 137-182.

        This is the most complete review available on the
        U.S. Army Signal Corps project of the 1950s. It is
        an illustrated and highly detailed account.

1538   Jo, K. et al. "Memoirs of the Pilot Model of Its Vacuum
        Tube Digital Computer" (In Japanese) BIT (Tokyo) 4,
        No. 2 (1972): 113-117.

        They discuss computer projects at Osaka University
        undertaken after 1946.

1539   Johnston, R.F.   "The University of Toronto Model Elec-
        tronic Computer," Proceedings of ACM Meeting at
        University of Toronto (September 1952): 154-160.

        The University of Toronto built an early digital
        computer, described here; it was one of many such
        projects at this school.

1540   Karin, Sidney and Smith, Norris Parker. The Super-
        computer Era. Boston: Harcourt Brace Jovanovich,
        Publishers, 1987.

        This is a general introduction to the subject for
        non technical audiences. It contains references to
        the history of the subject.

1541   Kjellberg, G. and Neovius, G. "The BARK, A Swedish
        General Purpose Relay Computer," Mathematical Tables
        and Other Aids to Computation 5 (1951): 29-34.

        This describes a computer built in 1950 at the Royal
        Institute of Technology at Stockholm.

1542   Okazaki, B. "The First Electronic Computer in Japan:
        The Birth of FUJIC and Its Death," (In Japanese) BIT
        (Tokyo) 3, No. 12 (1971): 1091-1097.

        The author describes his role in building this
        computer, which he started in 1952 and had completed
        in March, 1956.

1543   Pearcey, Trevor. "An Automatic Computer in Australia,"
        Mathematical Tables and Other Aids to Computation 6
        (1952): 167-172.

        He describes the CSIRAC (also known as the CSIRO
        Mark I), the first stored program computer built in
        Australia and done between 1947 and 1951. Only one
        copy of the machine was ever built.

1544   Pfeiffer, J.E. "Brains and Calculating Machines,"
        American Scholar 19, No. 1 (January 1950): 21-30.

        A typical period piece in that it surveys the status
        of computer technology and describes its uses for the
        general reader.

1545   Pfeiffer, J.E. "The Machine That Plays Gin Rummy,"
        Science Illustrated 4, No. 3 (March 1949): 46-48,
        passim.

        He describes the workings of a digital computer and
        speculates on that technology's potential.

1546   "Super Superbrain; Oracle," Science Digest 34 (Novem-
        ber 1953): 32.

        This is a brief comment on the Oracle about which
        little was published.

1547   Zemanek, Heinz. "Die arbeiten an elektronischen
        rechenmaschinen und informationsverarbeitungsmaschi-
        nen am Institut für NTF der TH Wien," Nachrichtentech-
        nische Facherberichte 4 (1956): 56-59.

        He describes an all transistor computer in the process
        of being built—the first in Austria called MAILÜFTERL.

1548   Zworykin, V.K. et al. "Letter-Reading Machine,"
        Electronics 22, No. 6 (June 1949): 80-86.

        The authors describe a device which attached to a
        digital computer, vintage 1948.

                              EDSAC

1549   Brooker, R.A. and Wheeler, D.J. "Floating Operations
        on the EDSAC," Mathematical Tables and Other Aids
        to Computation 7 (1953): 37-47.

        They focus on EDSAC's programming capabilities of
        the 1950s, in an era when programming was done with-
        out benefit of higher level languages.

1550   "The Design of a Practical High Speed Computing Machine.
        The EDSAC," Proceedings of the Royal Society (London)
        195A (1948): 274-279.

        This is a short description of the architecture of
        the EDSAC.

1551   Elliott, W.S. "The Present Position of Automatic
        Computing Machine Development in England," Proceedings
        of a Second Symposium on Large Scale Digital Calcu-
        lating Machinery. 13-16 September 1949. Annals of the
        Computation Laboratory of Harvard University 26
        (Cambridge, Mass.: Harvard University Press, 1951):
        74-80.

        In addition to reviewing various projects then under-
        way in Great Britain, it contains comments on the
        EDSAC.

1552   Gill, S. "Maurice V. Wilkes," in A. Ralston and C.L.
        Meek (eds), Encyclopedia of Computer Science (New
        York: Petrocelli/Charter, 1976): 1558-1559.

        This is an illustrated biography of one of the most
        important of the early British computer scientists.

1553   Hartree, D.R. "Automatic Calculating Machines," The
        Mathematical Gazette 34 (December 1950): 241-252.

        He focuses on the EDSAC's technical features.

1554   Hartree, D.R. The Calculation of Atomic Structure.
        New York: John Wiley & Sons, Inc., 1957.

        He includes a description of his use of the EDSAC.

1555   Naur, Peter. "Impressions of the Early Days of Pro-
        gramming," BIT 20, No. 4 (October 1980): 414-425.

        Naur relates his experience in learning how to use
        the EDSAC at Cambridge University and about his work
        in astronomical research with the machine.

1556   Wheeler, D.J.   "Program Organization and Initial Ordeal
          for the EDSAC," Proceedings of the Royal Society
          (London) A, No. 202 (August 22, 1950): 573-589.

          This is a key paper because it details the first and
          second forms of program representation and loading
          for the EDSAC.

1557   Wilkes, Maurice V. "Computers, Then and Now," Journal
          of the ACM 15, No. 1 (1968): 1-7.

          This is a short survey from 1946, when the Moore
          School conducted a class in computing, forward.

1558   Wilkes, Maurice V. "The Design of a Practical High-
          Speed Computing Machine," Proceedings of the Royal
          Society (London) A, No. 195 (1948): 274-279.

          He describes plans for the construction of the EDSAC.

1559   Wilkes, Maurice V. "Early Computer Development at
          Cambridge: The EDSAC," Radio and Electrical Engineer-
          ing 45, No. 7 (1975): 332-335.

          He surveys the origins of the Mathematical Laboratory
          at Cambridge, of his taking classes at the Moore
          School in 1946, the development of the EDSAC and
          about programming that computer. He includes a
          large number of photographs of the EDSAC taken in
          1951.

1560   Wilkes, Maurice V. "Early Programming Developments in
          Cambridge," in N. Metropolis et al.(eds), A History
          of Computing in the Twentieth Century (New York:
          Academic Press, 1980): 497-501.

          This short, yet informative, article covers his role
          in the design of the EDSAC at the Mathematical Labora-
          tory at Cambridge University, 1946-1950.

1561   Wilkes, Maurice V. "EDSAC," in A. Ralston and C.L.
          Meek (eds), Encyclopedia of Computer Science (New
          York: Petrocelli/Charter, 1976): 523-524.

          Its architect describes the features, functions and
          history of the EDSAC.

1562   Wilkes, Maurice V. "The EDSAC Computer," Review of
          Electronic Digital Computers. Joint AIEE-IRE Computer
          Conference, 10-12 December 1951 (New York: American
          Institute of Electrical Engineering, 1952): 79-83.

          He describes what it was like working with the EDSAC
          and discusses such issues as servicing it and running
          diagnostics.

1563   Wilkes, Maurice V. "Electronic Calculating-Machine
          Development in Cambridge," Nature (October 1, 1949):
          557-558.

This is an illustrated narrative of the EDSAC and
about its use in solving differential equations during the late 1940s.

1564   Wilkes, Maurice V. Memoirs of a Computer Pioneer.
       Cambridge, Mass.: MIT Press, 1985.

       These are important memoirs on the early history of
       digital computing. Wilkes recounts his work, first
       with radios, then later with computers, from the
       1930s down to the 1980s. It is an essential source
       on British computing.

1565   Wilkes, Maurice V. "Programme Design for a High-Speed
       Automatic Calculating Machine," Journal of Scienti-
       fic Instruments 26 (1949): 217-220.

       He reviews computers and programming techniques of
       the 1940s with special reference to the EDSAC exper-
       ience.

1566   Wilkes, Maurice V. et al. "Experience With Marginal
       Checking and Automatic Routing of the EDSAC,"
       Convention Record of IRE, Part 7, Electronic Comput-
       ers (March 1953): 66-71.

       One of Wilkes' concerns with the EDSAC was to make
       it easier to use than previous or contemporary
       digital computers. This article focuses on some of
       his concerns and experiences with the use of EDSAC.

1567   Wilkes, Maurice V. and Renwick, W. "An Ultasonic
       Memory Unit for the EDSAC," Electronic Engineering
       20, No. 245 (July 1948): 208-213.

       This is a technical description of the memory compon-
       ents in the EDSAC and hence a snapshot of such
       technology as of the late 1940s.

1568   Wilkes, Maurice V. and Renwick, W. "The EDSAC,"
       Mathematical Tables and Other Aids to Computation 4
       (April 1950): 61-65.

       This is a formal description of its features and
       use.

1569   Wilkes, Maurice V. and Renwick, W. "The EDSAC,"
       Report of a Conference on High Speed Automatic Calcu-
       lating Machines, 22-25 June 1949 (Cambridge: Univer-
       sity Mathematical Laboratory, January 1950): 9-11;
       Reprinted in Brian Randell (ed), The Origins of Digi-
       tal Computers: Selected Papers (New York: Springer-
       Verlag, 1982): 417-421.

       This reviews the design and programming characteris-
       tics of the EDSAC.

1570   Wilkes, Maurice V. and Renwick, W. "The EDSAC, An
       Electronic Calculating Machine," Journal of

Scientific Instruments 26 (December 1949): 385-391.

1571   Worsley, B.H.   "The EDSAC Demonstration," Report of a
        Conference on High Speed Automatic Calculating
        Machines, 22-25 June 1949 (Cambridge: University
        Mathematical Laboratory, January 1950): 12-16;
        Reprinted in Brian Randell (ed), The Origins of
        Digital Computers: Selected Papers (New York: Spring-
        er-Verlag, 1982): 423-429.

        This describes a demonstration made by W. Renwick of
        EDSAC. It includes flow diagram and programs used.

1572   Zeluff, V.   "EDSAC," Electronics 22 (October 1949):
        124.

        This includes two photographs of the EDSAC with a
        short description of the system.

                            EDVAC

1573   Eckert, J.P.   "A Preview of a Digital Computing
        Machine," in C.C. Chambers (ed), Theory and Techniques
        for the Design of Electronic Digital Computers. Lec-
        tures Delivered 8 July-31 August 1946 (Philadelphia:
        Moore School of Electrical Engineering, University of
        Pennsylvania, 1947): 10.1-10.26.

        This is a discussion of plans for the EDVAC and
        offers an explanation of how decisions were made
        regarding its design.

1574   "EDVAC Replaces ENIAC," The Pennsylvania Gazette
        (Philadelphia: University of Pennsylvania) 45, No. 8
        (April 1947): 9-10.

        This non-technical piece briefly describes the
        EDVAC.

1575   Electronic Control Company. A Tentative Instruction
        Code for a Statistical Edvac. Philadelphia: Electron-
        ic Control Company, May 7, 1947.

        This is a 19-page technical treatise, making it one
        of the first programming manuals.

1576   Huskey, H.D.   "EDVAC," in A. Ralston and C.L. Meek
        (eds), Encyclopedia of Computer Science (New York:
        Petrocelli/Charter, 1976): 534-535.

        This is a short description and history of the EDVAC
        by a major figure in the history of early computing.

1577   Koons, Florence and Lubkin, Samuel. "Conversion of
        Numbers From Decimal to Binary Form in the EDVAC,"
        Mathematical Tables and Other Aids to Computation 3
        No. 26 (April 1949): 427-431.

        They describe work done on the EDVAC at the Moore

School of Electrical Engineering, home of ENIAC, the
predecessor to the EDVAC.

1578   Mauchly, J.W. "Preparation of Problems for EDVAC-Type
        Machines," Proceedings of a Symposium on Large Scale
        Digital Calculating Machinery, 7-10 January 1947.
        Annals of the Computation Laboratory of Harvard Univer-
        sity 16 (Cambridge, Mass.: Harvard University Press,
        1948): 203-207; Reprinted in Brian Randell (ed), The
        Origins of Digital Computers: Selected Papers (New
        York: Springer-Verlag, 1873): 393-397.

        This important article reflected the general concerns
        of those developing computers. He describes the
        EDVAC, then under construction, offering technical
        details and a review of the pros and cons in options
        considered. It also discusses clearly the experience
        gained in programming the device.

1579   "Mercury Memory Tanks in New EDVAC Computer," Electron-
        ics 20 (May 1947): 168, 172, 176.

        This is a technical review of the delay line memory
        used with the EDVAC.

1580   "Minutes of 1947 Patent Conference, Moore School of
        Electrical Engineering, University of Pennsylvania,"
        Annals of the History of Computing 7, No. 2 (January
        1985): 100-116.

        This is introduced by Nancy Stern, noted historian
        of the ENIAC and other projects at the Moore School.
        The conference was held to resolve patent concerns
        regarding EDVAC. The minutes depict how the issue
        was resolved.

1581   Sharpless, T.K. The Pilot Model of EDVAC. (First Meet-
        ing of the Eastern Association for Computing Machin-
        ery, Columbia University, New York, September 15,
        1947-Brief Summary of Talk). File No. 6, Association
        for Computing Machinery, New York (22 September 1947).

        This is a 2-page summary of talks about an experi-
        mental device called Shadrach, used for testing parts
        of the EDVAC.

                              ENIAC

1582   Alt, F.L. "Archaeology of Computers—Reminiscences,
        1945-1947," Communications of the ACM 15, No. 7
        (1972): 693-694.

        Alt recalls work done with the ENIAC and also about
        techniques used for setting up programs on function
        tables.

1583   "An Historical Event—ENIAC," Data Systems Design 1,
        3 (March 1964): 26-27.

The discussion concerns the patent debate over the ENIAC.

1584   "Answers by ENY; Electronic Numerical Integrator and Computer, ENIAC," Newsweek 27 (February 18, 1946): 76.

This was one of the first widely published accounts of the ENIAC available to the American public.

1585   Brainerd, J.G. "Genesis of the ENIAC," Technology and Culture 17, No. 3 (July 1976): 482-488.

This was written by the project leader on ENIAC. He reviews carefully the Moore School project, how it got organized and started, taking the story from the 1930s through the 1940s.

1586   Brainerd, J.G. and Sharpless, T.K. "The ENIAC," Electrical Engineering 67, No. 2 (February 1948): 163-172.

They discuss both how the system worked and review some details of its history.

1587   Burks, A.W. "Electronic Computing Circuits of the ENIAC," Proceedings of the IRE 35 (1947): 756-767.

He describes the electronic characteristics and design features of the ENIAC.

1588   Burks, A.W. "From ENIAC to the Stored-Program Computer: Two Revolutions in Computers," in N. Metropolis et al. (eds), A History of Computing in the Twentieth Century (New York: Academic Press, 1980): 311-344.

This is an excellent article covering the ENIAC, EDVAC, IAS, Whirlwind, EDSAC, UNIVAC I and other processors during the 1940s and 1950s. The author was involved in the development of computers during those decades.

1589   Burks, A.W. "The Logic of Programming Electronic Digital Computers," Industrial Mathematics 1 (1950): 36-52.

This is an early account of programming instructions for digital computers; particular emphasis is on the ENIAC.

1590   Burks, A.W. "Super Electronic Computing Machine," Electronics Industry (July 1946): 62-67, 96.

He describes programs of and a demonstration of the ENIAC; illustrated with photographs and diagrams, including some on programming instructions.

1591   Burks, A.W. and Burks, A.R. "The ENIAC: First General-Purpose Electronic Computer," Annals of the History of Computing 3, No. 4 (October 1981): 310-399.

This is a major review of the ENIAC's functions,
history, and historical significance. The article
is also well illustrated.

1592   Butler, M. "A Historical Background," Nuclear News
        (April 1968): 26-30.

        This is on the evolution of digital systems and, in
        particular, on the ENIAC and IAS system for a non-tech-
        nical audience.

1593   Charney, J.G. and Fjörtoft, R. and Von Neumann, John.
        "Numerical Integration of the Barotropic Vorticity
        Equation," Tellus 2 (1950): 237-254.

        This describes von Neumann's efforts to do weather
        forecasting on the ENIAC.

1594   Clippinger, R.F. A Logical Coding System Applied to
        ENIAC. B.R.L. Report No. 673. Aberdeen, Md.:
        Ballistic Research Laboratories, September 29,
        1948.

        This 48-page document describes how the ENIAC could
        be used in the 1940s by describing its coding con-
        ventions.

1595   Costello, John. "He Changed the World," The Washing-
        tonian (December 1983): 82-100.

        This is on John W. Mauchly, containing many personal
        details, such as about his high school days in Chevy
        Chase (suburb of Washington, D.C.), and his first
        wife (Mary Walel).

1596   Costello, John. "The Little Known Creators of the
        Computers," Nation's Business 59, No. 12 (December
        1971): 56-62.

        These are memoirs of Mauchly, Eckert and the develop-
        ment of the ENIAC.

1597   Eames, C. and Eames, R. A Computer Perspective.
        Cambridge, Mass.: Harvard University Press, 1973.

        This is a profusely illustrated history of computing
        since the 1890s which also contains a great deal of
        material on the ENIAC and other machines of its era.

1598   "Electronic Calculator: ENIAC," Scientific American
        174 (June 1946): 248.

        This briefly describes the functions of the ENIAC.

1599   Eckert, J. Presper, Jr. "The ENIAC," in N. Metropolis
        et al. (eds), A History of Computing in the Twentieth
        Century (New York: Academic Press, 1980): 525-539.

This was written by one of the main architects of
the ENIAC, offering a general overview of his role.

1600   Eckert, J.Presper, Jr.   "In the Beginning and to What
        End," Computers and Their Future (Lalndudno: Richard
        Williams and Partners, 1970): 3/4-3/25.

        He provides a history of the ENIAC, how he and John
        Mauchly developed the concept of the stored program
        and applied it to both the ENIAC and EDVAC.

1601   Eckert, J. Presper, Jr.   "Thoughts on the History of
        Computing," Computer (December 1976): 58-65.

        This is a rambling discussion over a variety of data
        processing issues, including stories of experiences
        with ENIAC and disputes with von Neumann.

1602   Eckert, J. Presper, Jr., Mauchly, John W., Goldstine,
        Herman H., Brainerd, J.G. Description of the ENIAC
        and Comments on Electronic Digital Computing Machin-
        es. Contract W/670/ORD 4926. Moore School of Electri-
        cal Engineering, University of Pennsylvania, Phila-
        delphia (November 30, 1945).

        This document was written by four giants in the
        history of computer technology. It contains a large
        number of details and issues concerning reliability,
        availability, and service. The paper is very tech-
        nical but does reflect the nature of their thinking
        as of late 1945 on the subject of general purpose
        digital computers.

1603   "Electronic Calculator: ENIAC," Scientific American
        174 (June 1946): 248.

        This is a description of the ENIAC for the serious
        general reader in the United States.

1604   "Electronic Computer Known as the ENIAC," Mechanical
        Engineering 68 (June 1946): 560-561.

        This a short review of the ENIAC, complete with one
        photograph.

1605   "ENIAC: At the University of Pennsylvania," Time 47
        (February 25, 1946): 90.

        This major publicity came on the occasion of the
        ENIAC's public debut as a digital computer.

1606   Fegley, Kenneth and Warren, S. Reid, Jr. "Elogue: John
        Grist Brainerd (1904-1988)," Annals of the History
        of Computing 10, No. 4 (1989): 360-365.

        This detailed obituary is about the scientist best
        known for heading up the team that built the ENIAC
        at the University of Pennsylvania in the 1940s.

1607   Gardner, W.D.   "Will the Inventor of the First Digital
        Computer Please Stand Up?," _Datamation_ 20, No. 2
        (February 1974): 84, 88-90.

        This article was written as a result of Judge Larson's
        ruling on the ENIAC patent suit. It discusses Atana-
        soff and includes an interview with him.

1608   Goldstine, Herman H.   "Early Electronic Computers," in
        S. Fernbach and Taub, A.H. (eds), _Computers and Their
        Role in the Physical Sciences_ (New York: Gordon and
        Breach, 1970): 51-102.

        The ENIAC, EDVAC, and IAS computers are described in
        considerable detail with reliance on the author's
        records. It includes comments on his personal role
        and that played by von Neumann.

1609   Goldstine, Herman H. and Goldstine, A.   "The Electronic
        Numerical Integrator and Computer (ENIAC)," _Mathema-
        tical Tables and Other Aids to Computation_ 2, No. 15
        (1946): 97-110.

        This is a good description of the ENIAC and about its
        programming.

1610   Gray, H.J.   _Digital Computer Engineering._   Englewood
        Cliffs, N.J.: Prentice Hall, Inc., 1963.

        It has a chapter on the ENIAC and EDVAC, how they
        worked, and comments about von Neumann.

1611   Hartree, D.R.   _Calculating Machines—Recent and Pros-
        pective Developments._   Cambridge: Cambridge Universi-
        ty Press, 1947.

        This is a lecture, primarily focusing on the ENIAC.

1612   Hartree, D.R.   "The ENIAC, An Electronic Calculating
        Engine," _Nature_ 157 (1946): 527; 158 (1946): 500-506.

        He briefly describes the ENIAC.

1613   Hoffleit, D.   "A Companion of Various Computing Machines
        Used in the Reduction of Doppler Observations,"
        Mathematical Tables and Other Aids to Computation 3
        (1949): 373-377.

        This is a comparison between IBM's relay calculator,
        the ENIAC, and Bell Laboratory's computer in terms of
        actual performance, an early such article that would,
        in years to come, be a frequent publication for each
        generation of machine.

1614   Hughes, T.P.   "ENIAC: Invention of a Computer," _Tech-
        nikgeschichte_ 42 (1975): 148-165.

        This is based on primary materials to tell the story
        of the ENIAC. It begins in July, 1944 and continues

it down through the patent lawsuit of the 1960s. It
is detailed and balanced.

1615   Huskey, H.D. "ENIAC," in A. Ralston and C.L. Meek
        (eds), Encyclopedia of Computer Science (New York:
        Petrocelli/Charter, 1976): 540-541.

        This is a short, illustrated history of the ENIAC.

1616   Jo, K. Mathematical Machines and Instruments. Tokyo:
        Zoshindo Book Co., 1947. (In Japanese).

        The first half of the book is devoted to digital
        equipment and to their history. This publication is
        also one of the earliest Japanese accounts of the
        ENIAC.

1617   "John Mauchly Dies," The Charles Babbage Institute
        Newsletter 2, No. 1 (January 31, 1980): 1,4.

        This is a formal obituary notice of one of the key
        developers of the ENIAC.

1618   Johnson, L.R. System Structure in Data, Programs, and
        Computers. Englewood Cliffs, N.J.: Prentice Hall,
        1970.

        This book contains many details about the EDVAC and
        ENIAC, circa 1945-1955.

1619   Larson, E.R. Findings of Fact, Conclusions of Law and
        Order for Judgement. File No. 4-67 Civ. 138, Honey-
        well Inc. vs. Sperry Rand Corporation and Illinois
        Scientific Developments, Inc. U.S. District Court,
        District of Minnesota, Fourth Division (19 October
        1973).

        This is the Judge's findings concerning the validity
        of the ENIAC patent. He concludes that Eckert and
        Mauchly did not event the automatic digital computer.
        The 319-page document, like the law suit, generated
        vast quantities of information on the ENIAC and on
        the early history of computing.

1620   Ledger, Marshall. "The Case of the ENIAC's Muddled
        History," Pennsylvania Gazette (October 1982): 30-
        35; (November 1982): 29-33; Letters (February 1983):
        3-4; (April 1983): 8; (May 1983): 6-8; (June 1983):
        12.

        This is a narrative history of the ENIAC with over-
        statements about the significance of the project.

1621   Mauchly, John W. "Amending the ENIAC Story," Datamation
        25, No. 11 (1979): 217-219.

        This is a letter to the editor in which he offers
        background material on the evolution of the ENIAC
        and argues that his ideas were developed long before

von Neumann first visited the Moore School of Electrical Engineering in late 1944.

1622   Mauchly, John W. "The ENIAC," in N. Metropolis et al. (eds), A History of Computing in the Twentieth Century (New York: Academic Press, 1980): 541-550.

The historical survey is more important by the fact that Mauchly was one of ENIAC's developers. He also defends the development of the stored program notion.

1623   Mauchly, John W. "Mauchly on the Trials of Building the ENIAC," IEEE Spectrum 12, No. 4 (April 1975): 70-76.

These are his recollections of work done on ENIAC.

1624   Mauchly, John W. "Mauchly: Unpublished Remarks," Annals of the History of Computing 4, No. 3 (July 1982): 245-256.

This consists of letters and comments on his work in the 1930s and 1940s.

1625   Mauchly, Kathleen R. "John Mauchly's Early Years," Annals of the History of Computing 6, No. 2 (April 1984): 116-138.

This covers the period while he was at Ursinus College (1933-41), about his dealings with John V. Atanasoff, and later at the Moore School. The author was Mauchly's wife.

1626   Maynard, M.M. "J. Presper Eckert," A. Ralston and C.L. Meek (eds), Encyclopedia of Computer Science (New York: Petrocelli/Charter, 1976): 521.

This is a short biography of the co-developer of the ENIAC.

1627   "Robot Calculator; ENIAC, All-Electronic Device," Business Week (February 16, 1946): 50ff.

Like other widely-read periodicals of the 1940s, this one provided brief, but important, coverage of the public unveiling of the ENIAC.

1628   Rose, A. "Lightning Strikes Mathematics: ENIAC," Popular Science 148 (April 1946): 83-86.

This is a non-technical description of the first fully operational electronic digital computer in the United States.

1629   Stern, Nancy. "Computers: From ENIAC to UNIVAC," IEEE Spectrum 18, No. 12 (December 1981): 61-69.

She focuses on the role of Eckert and Mauchly as businessmen moving a high technology product from

lab to market and across multiple projects from the
mid-1940s to early 1950s.

1630   Stern, Nancy. From ENIAC to UNIVAC: An Appraisal of
        the Eckert-Mauchly Computers. Bedford, Mass.: Digi-
        tal Press, 1981.

        This is a very complete, and well-researched, study
        of the various computer projects of Eckert and
        Mauchly. It is a major monograph on early computing
        history.

1631   Stern, Nancy. "John William Mauchly: 1907-1980,"
        Annals of the History of Computing 2, No. 2 (April
        1980): 100-103.

        This is an illustrated biography/obituary.

1632   Stern, Nancy. "Who Invented the First Electronic
        Digital Computer?," Abacus 1, No. 1 (1983): 7-15.

        She reviewed the controversy and voted for Eckert
        and Mauchly over Atanasoff as the developers of the
        first such machine.

1633   Tabor, L.P. "Brief Description and Operating Charac-
        teristics of the ENIAC," Proceedings of a Symposium
        on Large Scale Digital Calculating Machinery, 7-10
        January 1947. Annals of the Computation Laboratory
        of Harvard University 16 (Cambridge, Mass.: Harvard
        University Press, 1948): 31-39.

        Tabor provides a technical and contemporary explana-
        tion of the design of the ENIAC, reasons for the
        EDVAC, and problems associated with the earlier
        system.

1634   Tonik, Albert B. "Herman Lukoff, 1923-1979," Annals
        of the History of Computing 2, No. 3 (July 1980):
        196-197.

        This is an obituary/biography with phtograph. He
        worked for the Eckert-Mauchly team on the UNIVAC.

1635   Tropp, H.S. "John W. Mauchly," in A. Ralston and C.L.
        Meek (eds), Encyclopedia of Computer Science (New
        York: Petrocelli/Charter, 1976): 871-873.

        This is a biography of a co-developer of the ENIAC
        and UNIVAC.

1636   Von Neumann, John. First Draft of a Report on the
        EDVAC. Contract No. W-670-ORD-492. Moore School of
        Electrical Engineering. Philadelphia, Pa.: University
        of Pennsylvania, June 30, 1945.

        This is an important paper in the history of computing
        because it was the basis of much computer design.

1637   "War Department Unveils 18,000-Tube Robot Calculator;
        ENIAC," Electronics 19 (April 1946): 308, 310, 312,
        314.

        This reviews the ENIAC, its application to ballistics
        and other uses; illustrated.

1638   Weik, M.H. "The ENIAC Story," American Ordnance Assoc-
        iation (January-February 1961): 3-7.

        This is an early history of the ENIAC with particu-
        lar attention on its role with the Research Division
        of the U.S. Army from the late 1930s/early 1940s
        forward.

1639   Wulforst, Harry. Breakthrough to the Computer Age.
        New York: Scribners, 1982.

        This book contains material on the evolution of all
        of the Eckert/Mauchly projects from ENIAC to UNIVAC.
        The writer is an ex-Sperry Corporation public rela-
        tions employee.

                        Harvard Mark Series

1640   "According to Mark IV," Time 64 (August 9, 1954): 68-
        69.

        This was the last major processor built by Aiken at
        Harvard.

1641   Aiken, H.H. "Proposed Automatic Calculating Machine,"
        IEEE Spectrum (August 1964): 62-69.

        This is a previously unpublished paper of November
        4, 1937 that previews the development of calculating
        devices from Pascal to Babbage, and then describes a
        machine using punch card technology. This machine
        eventually became the Mark I.

1642   Aiken, H.H. and Hopper, G.M. "The Automatic Sequence
        Controlled Calculator," Electrical Engineering 65
        (1946): 384-391, 449-454, 522-528.

        This is a short history of calculating machines but
        with primary focus on how the Automatic Sequence
        Controlled Calculator functioned.

1643   Aiken, H.H. and staff of Computation Laboratory. "A
        Manual of Operation for the Automatic Sequence Con-
        trolled Calculator," full volume of Annals of the
        Computation Laboratory of Harvard University 1
        (Cambridge, Mass.: Harvard University Press, 1946).

        The first chapter is a history of calculating devic-
        es, with comments on Babbage, Muller and Torres.

1644   Auerbach, Isaac L. "Howard Aiken," Annals of the

History of Computing 7, No. 4 (October 1985): 354-355.

One of Aiken's students is the author of this article. Auerbach describes how Aiken treated him and reviews the professor's views on Eckert and Mauchly.

1645   Block, R.M. "Mark I Calculator," Proceedings of a Symposium on Large Scale Digital Calculating Machinery, 7-10 January 1947. Annals of the Computation Laboratory of Harvard University 16 (Cambridge, Mass.: Harvard University Press, 1948): 23-30.

This is a description of the Mark I and the uses it was put to during the mid-1940s.

1646   Campbell, R.V.D. "Mark II Calculator," Proceedings of a Symposium on Large Scale Digital Calculating Machinery, 7-10 January 1947. Annals of the Computing Laboratory of Harvard University 16 (Cambridge, Mass.: Harvard University Press, 1948): 13-22.

This describes the Mark II at Harvard, a paper tape controlled calculator, with comments on its various functions.

1647   Cohen, I. Bernard. "Babbage and Aiken: With Notes on Henry Babbage's Gift to Harvard, and to Other Institutions, of a Portion of His Father's Difference Engine," Annals of the History of Computing 10, No. 3 (1988): 171-193.

Cohen explores the extent of Aiken's knowledge of and inspiration from, Charles Babbage for his own work. He includes an inventory of models of Babbage's machines. Cohen concludes that Babbage had a minor influence on Aiken's ideas on computers.

1648   Freeland, Stephen L. "Inside the Biggest Man-Made Brain," Popular Science (May 1947): 95-100.

This is a description of the Mark II relay calculator at Harvard.

1649   Gardner, W.D. "An Wang's Early Work in Core Memories," Datamation (March 1976): 161-164.

The founder of Wang Laboratories worked on static magnetic memories in the 1940s at Harvard for Aiken.

1650   Genet, N. "Got a Problem? Harvard's Amazing New Mathematical Robot," Scholastic 45 (September 18, 1944): 35.

This briefly describes the Harvard Mark I calculator built by Aiken and IBM.

1651   "Giant New Calculator," Science News Letter 46 (August 1944): 111.

This features the Mark I and Aiken's work.

1652   Harrison, J.O., Jr.   "The Preparation of Problems for
       the Mark I Calculator," Proceedings of a Symposium
       on Large Scale Digital Calculating Machinery, 7-10
       January 1947. Annals of the Computation Laboratory
       of Harvard University 16 (Cambridge, Mass.: Harvard
       University Press, 1948): 208-210.

       This describes how to operate the Harvard Mark I
       calculator.

1653   International Business Machines Corporation. IBM
       Automatic Sequence Controlled Calculator. Endicott,
       N.Y.: International Business Machines Corp., 1945.

       This 6-page functional description of IBM's first
       important computer product grew out of the Mark I at
       Harvard.

1654   "Mathematical Robot Presented to Harvard," Time 44
       (August 14, 1944): 72.

       This was one of the first widely distributed articles
       on computers to appear in the U.S. for the general
       public. It describes the Mark I, and IBM's involve-
       ment.

1655   Miller, Frederick G.   "Application of Printing Tele-
       graph Equipment to Large-Scale Calculating Machinery,"
       Proceedings of a Symposium on Large Scale Digital
       Calculating Machinery, 7-10 January 1947. Annals of
       the Computation Laboratory of Harvard University 16
       (Cambridge, Mass.: Harvard University Press, 1948):
       213-222.

       The machine used to do the work was the Harvard Mark
       II, a relay calculator.

1656   Oettinger, Anthony G.   "Retiring Computer Pioneer—
       Howard Aiken," Communications of the ACM 5, No. 6
       (1962): 298-299, 359.

       This is a short biography of the creator of the Mark
       series of calculators at Harvard in the 1940s and
       early 1950s.

1657   "Robot Works Problems Never Before Solved," Popular
       Mechanics 82 (October 1944): 13.

       This describes works and features of the Harvard
       Mark I.

1658   Salton, Gerard.   "Howard Aiken's Children: The Harvard
       Computation Laboratory and Its Students," Abacus 1,
       No. 3 (1984): 28-34.

       This surveys Aiken's 16 Ph.D. students (1948-58),
       some of whom became major figures in the history of
       computing. It was written by one of Aiken's 16.

1659   Staff of the Computation Laboratory (Howard H. Aiken
        and 55 Others). "Description of a Magnetic Drum
        Calculator," Annals of the Computation Laboratory
        of Harvard University 25 (Cambridge, Mass.: Harvard
        University Press, 1952), entire issue.

        This is on one of Aiken's latest Mark calculators; a
        technical description.

1660   Stoll, E.L. "Mark I," in A. Ralston and C.L. Meek
        (eds), Encyclopedia of Computer Science (New York:
        Petrocelli/Charter, 1976): 852-853.

        This is a short, competent and illustrated history
        of the Harvard Mark I.

1661   "Superbrain," Nation's Business 32 (September 1944):
        8.

        This celebrated the existence of the Harvard Mark I.

1662   Torrey, V. "Robot Mathematician Knows All the Answers,"
        Popular Science 145 (October 1944): 86-89.

        This provides a non-technical description of the
        Mark I.

1663   Tropp, H.S. "Howard Aiken," A. Ralston and C.L. Meek
        (eds), Encyclopedia of Computer Science (New York:
        Petrocelli/Charter, 1976): 34-35.

        This is a short, illustrated biography of the builder
        of the Harvard Mark series of machines, with special
        reference to the Mark I.

1664   Williams, M.R. "Howard Aiken and the Harvard Computa-
        tion Laboratory," Annals of the History of Computing
        6, No. 2 (April 1984): 157-162.

        This was the subject of a 1983 Pioneer Day session
        at AFIPS; contains stories of the 1930s and 1940s.

1665   "World's Greatest Machine for Automatic Calculation,"
        Science News Letter 46 (August 19, 1944): 123.

        This is on the Mark I, a narrative with a great deal
        of hyperbole.

                        Grace M. Hopper

1666   Adams, Vickie Porter. "Captain Grace M. Hopper: The
        Mother of COBOL," Infoworld 3, No. 2 (October 5,
        1981): 33.

        This is an interview with Hopper who recounts her
        work with COBOL.

1667   "Biography of Captain Grace Murray Hopper," in Richard
        L. Wexelblat (ed), History of Programming Languages
        (New York: Academic Press, 1981): 5-7.

This is a biography of the first female programmer
in the U.S. and a major force in the development of
COBOL. Pages 7-24 are her memoirs of those experiences.

1668   Gilbert, Lynn and Moore, Goylen (eds). Particular
       Passions: Talks With Women Who Have Shapped Our Lives.
       New York: Potter, 1981.

       This includes an interview with Hopper (pp. 59-64).
       She comments on her days with the Harvard Computation
       Laboratory and at Univak (1940s-50s).

1669   Johnson, Steve. "Grace Hopper—A Living Legend," All
       Hands (September 1982): 2-6.

       This illustrated biography focuses on her naval career
       and includes quotes of a talk she gave in the spring
       of 1982.

1670   Mason, John F. "Grace Hopper: 'It's Rewarding Trying
       to Do Things in a New Way'," Electronic Design 22
       (October 25, 1976): 82-86.

       In addition to being a short biography, this has comm-
       ents on her work at the Harvard Computation Laboratory
       and at Univac.

1671   Tropp, Henry S. "Grace Hopper: The Youthful Teacher of
       Us All," Abacus 2, No. 1 (1984): 7-18.

       This is a biography by a computer scientist on her
       work with particular emphasis on the Mark I and on
       COBOL.

1672   Wetzstein, Cheryl and Forrestal, Linda. "Grace Murray
       Hopper," The World & I (August 1987): 198-205.

       They offer a biography of Hopper which is well
       illustrated on all aspects of her long career.

IAS Computers

1673   Aspray, William. "The Mathematical Reception of the
       Modern Computer: John von Neumann and the Institute
       for Advanced Study Computer," MAA Studies in Mathema-
       tics 26 (1987): 166-194.

       Aspray looks at the relationship between mathematics
       and computing (1945-55) by looking at von Neumann's
       efforts at building the IAS computer.

1674   Bigelow, Julian. "Computer Development at the Institute
       for Advanced Study," in N. Metropolis et al. (eds), A
       History of Computing in the Twentieth Century: A
       Collection of Essays (New York: Academic Press, 1980):
       291-310.

       He surveys the period from the late 1940s through the

early 1950s and includes material on von Neumann's role and computer developments. The author worked at the IAS in the late 1940s.

1675   Elgot, C. and Robinson, A. "Random-Access Stored-Progra-
        mmed Machines, An Approach to Programming Languages,"
        <u>Journal of the Association for Computing Machinery</u> 11
        (1964): 365-399.

        They focus on von Neumann's approach to programming
        languages.

1676   "Faster Computers, At Princeton and Los Alamos," <u>Scien-
        tific American</u> 187 (August 1952): 36ff.

        This is a survey of IAS hardware systems.

1677   Goldstine, Herman H. and von Neumann, John. <u>Planning
        and Coding of Problems for an Electronic Computing
        Instrument</u>, Part 2,1. Princeton: Institute for Advanc-
        ed Study, Princeton University, 1 April 1947; Part 2,
        2 (1948); Part 2, 3 (1948); same publication with
        slightly different title, "Planning and Coding of
        Problems for an Electronic Computing Instrument: Report
        on the Mathematical and Logical Aspects of an Electron-
        ic Computing Instrument," in <u>John von Neumann's
        Collected Works</u>, ed. by A.H. Taub, 5 (London: Pergamon
        1963): 80-235.

        This is a detailed analysis and description of how to
        code for the IAS computer and offers design consider-
        ations for the system.

1678   Gruenberger, F.J. "The History of the JOHNNIAC,"
        <u>Annals of the History of Computing</u> 1, No. 1 (July
        1979): 49-64.

        This is an illustrated, thorough history of the Rand
        JOHNNIAC computer by a user. It was used from 1950
        to 1966.

                Input/Output and Telecommunications

1679   Fitzgerald, E.L. "Computers With Remote Data Input,"
        <u>Proceedings of the Eastern Joint Computer Conference</u>
        (New York: The Institute of Radio Engineers, 1956):
        69-75.

        The author reviews remote data input via telephone
        lines, circa 1955. It was a very early and compre-
        hensive article on the subject.

1680   Gallagher, James D. "Administrative Automation at
        Sylvania: A Case Study—III. The Program in Opera-
        tion," in <u>Administrative Automation Through IDP and
        EDP</u>, Office Management Series No. 144 (New York:
        American Management Association, 1956): 47-67.

        He describes Sylvania's DP communication system of

the mid-1950s for data transmission. The applications involved payroll and customer order entry.

1681   Hosken, J.C. "Survey of Mechanical Printers," Proceed-
        ings of the Eastern Joint Computer Conference: Review
        of Input and Output Equipment (New York: American
        Institute of Electrical Engineers, 1953): 106-112.

        In addition to reviewing existing devices, the author
        concludes that they are fast enough for current sys-
        tems although expensive.

1682   Pike, J.L. and Ainsworth, E.F. "Input-Output Devices
        for NBS Computers," NBS Circular 551 (1955): 109-118.

        This describes peripherals used on the SEAC, SWAC,
        DYSEAC and other processors (8 in total).

                              IBM Devices

1683   Avery, R.W. et al. "The IBM 7070 Data Processing System,"
        Proceedings of the Eastern Joint Computer Conference
        (Philadelphia, December 1958): 165-168.

        This describes IBM's transistorized version of the
        709.

1684   Baer, G.D. "RAMAC," A. Ralston and C.L. Meek (eds),
        Encyclopedia of Computer Science (New York: Petrocelli/
        Charter, 1976): 1191-1192.

        This describes the first system from any vendor that
        used magnetic disk files commercially in the 1950s.
        It includes a photograph of an IBM 305.

1685   Bashe, Charles J., Buchholz, W. and Rochester, N. "The
        IBM 702, An Electronic Data Processing Machine for
        Business," Journal of the ACM 1 (1954): 149-169.

        The authors describe the features and functions of
        the IBM 702 system of the mid-1950s.

1686   Bashe, Charles J. et al. "The Architecture of IBM's
        Early Computers," IBM Journal of Research and
        Development 25, No. 5 (September 1981): 363-375.

        This covers all computers and system architectures
        for the period 1949 to 1964 up to S/360. It includes
        the 701, 702, 709, 7090, 704, TPM, 650, 7070, 1401,
        1440, 1460 and STRETCH.

1687   Bashe, Charles J. et al. "The Design of the IBM 702
        System," Transactions of the AIEEE 74 (1956): 695-
        704.

        This device used binary coded decimal and alphabetic
        symbols for commercial applications.

1688   Bender, R.R. et al. "A Description of the IBM 7074

System," <u>Proceedings of the Eastern Joint Computer Conference</u> (New York, December 1960): 161-171.

This is a technical description of the features and functions of the IBM 7074 system.

1689   "Brain Builders; Model 702 Electronic Data Processing Machine," <u>Time</u> 65 (March 28, 1955): 81-84ff.

This is intended for a non-technical audience with a description of the possible uses of this system.

1690   Curry, Robert B.   "Facilities for a Large Computer Installation," <u>Advanced Management</u> 23, No. 1 (January 1958): 5-11.

The author reviews the physical installation problems experienced in the installation of an IBM 705 at the Southern Railway Company in Atlanta, Georgia.

1691   Grosch, Herbert R.J.   "In Von Braun Country," <u>Annals of the History of Computing</u> 11, No. 1 (1989): 44-48.

Grosch was the president of the Association for Computing Machinery and of the Institute of Aeronautics and Astronautics. He worked for IBM, GE and the U.S. Government. He describes the acquisition and use of an IBM 704 at GE in the 1950s.

1692   Hunter, G.T. and Clark, G.M.   "Electronic Data Processing Machines," 28 (May 1955): 782-793.

The authors survey the features of all of the IBM calculating equipment available at the time. Their review includes both electronic and mechanical devices.

1693   Hurd, Cuthbert C.   "Computer Development at IBM," in N. Metropolis <u>et al.</u>(eds), <u>A History of Computing in the Twentieth Century</u> (New York: Academic Press, 1980): 389-418.

This illustrated account is by an IBM scientist and covers the years 1947 through 1957, from the IBM 701 through STRETCH. It is excellent for both technical details and on decision making in computer development.

1694   Hurd, Cuthbert C.   "Early IBM Computers: Edited Testimony," <u>Annals of the History of Computing</u> 3, No. 2 (April 1981): 163-182.

He essentially covers the same ground as in the previous citation. Since he participated in the development of many IBM systems of the period, his comments are also memoirs; illustrated.

1695   Hurd, Cuthbert C.   "The IBM Card Programmed Calculator," <u>Proceedings of a Seminar on Scientific Computation,</u>

November 1949 (New York: International Business Machines Corporation, 1950): 37-41.

Hurd describes IBM CPC and applications for which it could be used.

1696 "IBM Computers—The Story of Their Development," Data Processing (London) 2, No. 2 (1960): 90-101.

It reviews quickly the Harvard Mark I, SSE, 603 Multiplier, CPC, 628, Tape Processing Machine and others.

1697 "IBM's Might Memory: IBM 305," Business Week (May 14, 1955): 66.

This is a public announcement of the RAMAC system.

1698 Klaas, P. "Northrop Pioneers Computer Technique," Aviation Week (August 3, 1953): 41, 43-45.

Klass describes work done at Northrop Aviation leading to the IBM CPC and on its use at this aviation firm. He also comments on the BINAC.

1699 Lesser, M.L. and Haanstra, J.W. "The RAMAC Data-Processing Machine: System Organization of the IBM 305," Proceedings of the Eastern Joint Computer Conference: New Developments in Computers (New York: American Institute of Electrical Engineering, 1957): 139-146.

This is a technical overview of the first disk storage system available in the data processing industry.

1700 Lesser, M.L. and Haanstra, J.W. "The Random-Access Memory Accounting Machine—I. System Organization of the IBM 305," IBM Journal of Research and Development 1 (1957): 62-71.

This is a formal description of the IBM 305 system by two of its developers.

1701 Lotkin, M. "Remarks on the IBM Relay Calculator," Proceedings Computation Seminar, December 1949 (New York: IBM, 1951): 154-157.

The author describes the connection of two pluggable Sequence Relay Calculators together into a system.

1702 McLaughlin, Richard A. "The IBM 704: 36-Bit Floating-Point Money-Maker," Datamation 16 (August 1975): 46-50.

This was an important technological improvement over earlier processors that went far to propel IBM to a leadership position within the computer industry in the early to mid-1950s. The system's history is recounted.

1703   Morris, Mitchell E.   "Professor RAMAC's Tenure,"
        Datamation 27, No. 4 (April 1981): 195-198.

        Reviews early RAMAC installations of the 1950s and
        the history of this IBM disk storage system.

1704   Nims, P.T.   "The IBM Type 604 Electronic Calculating
        Punch as a Miniature Card-Programmed Electronic Cal-
        culator," Proceedings, Computation Seminar, August
        1951 (New York: IBM Corporation, 1951): 37-47.

        This is one of a number of articles that appeared in
        the late 1940s and early 1950s of users lashing IBM
        calculating and peripheral devices together to make
        computer-like systems to do continuous and faster
        work.

1705   Nordyke, H.W.   "Magnetic Tape Techniques and Perfor-
        mance," Report on AIEE-IRE-ACM Computer Conference
        (March 1953): 90-95.

        The author describes equipment used as part of the
        IBM 701 system.

1706   "On the Frontier; 702, Electronic Calculator," Fortune
        50 (August 1954): 66-67.

        This is one of a number of articles that appeared on
        early IBM processors in the 700 line. The 702 was
        a major entry into the computer market for IBM.

1707   Phelps, B.E.   "Effervescent Years (Letter to the Edi-
        tor)," IEEE Spectrum 11, No. 5 (May 1974): 30-31.

        He describes work at IBM on calculators and computers
        in the 1940s. He describes the work of R. Seeber on
        the Harvard Mark I and later at IBM in the 1940s and
        1950s.

1708   Sheldon, J.W. and Tatum, L.   "The IBM Card Programmed
        Electronic Calculator," Review of Electronic Digital
        Computers. Joint AIEE-IRE Computer Conference, Decem-
        ber 10-12, 1951 (New York: American Institute of
        Electrical Engineers, 1952): 30-36.

        This is an important, technical description of the
        IBM CPC.

1709   Woodbury, W.W.   "The 603-405 Computer," Proceedings of
        a Second Symposium on Large Scale Digital Calculating
        Machinery, 13-16 September 1949. Annals of the Compu-
        tation Laboratory of Harvard University 26 (Cambridge,
        Mass.: Harvard University Press, 1951): 316-320.

        He describes the combined functioning of an IBM 603,
        405, and one 517 punch.

IBM 650

1710   Andree, Richard V. <u>Programming the IBM 650 Magnetic
        Drum Computer and Data-Processing Machine</u>. New York:
        Henry Holt & Co., Inc., 1958.

        This short technical publication describes how to
        operate a very early IBM processor, but one of IBM's
        most popular of the 1950s. It contains materials on
        using IT and For TRANSIT programming.

1711   Bach, G.L. "A Computer for Carnegie," <u>Annals of the
        History of Computing</u> 8, No. 1 (January 1986): 39-41.

        Carnegie was one of the first universities to install
        a 650; its use there is described.

1712   Bemer, R.W. "Nearly 650 Memoirs of the 650," <u>Annals
        of the History of Computing</u> 8, No. 1 (January 1986):
        66-69.

        The author used a 650 at Lockheed Aircraft Corpora-
        tion in the mid-1950s. His illustrated account offers
        details on usage and early programming done at IBM for
        the 650's system.

1713   Galler, Bernard A. "The IBM 650 and the Universities,"
        <u>Annals of the History of Computing</u> 8, No. 1 (January
        1986): 36-38.

        He describes the availability and use of IBM 650s at
        American universities in the 1950s. There were 21
        situations. He also explains IBM's policies of the
        period toward educational institutions.

1714   Gibbons, James. "How Input/Output Units Affect Data-
        Processor Performance," <u>Control Engineering</u> 4 (July
        1957): 97-102.

        While a technical article on system balancing (a
        topic of concern to computer designers for decades)
        it does review the performance of the IBM 650.

1715   Glaser, E.L. "The IBM 650 and the Woodenwheel," <u>Annals
        of the History of Computing</u> 8, No. 1 (January 1986):
        30-31.

        The author explains how memory for the IBM 650
        evolved in the early 1950s. Woodenwheel referred to
        a type of machine design.

1716   Gordon, Barry. "The IBM MDDPM—Some Recollections of
        a Great Machine," <u>Annals of the History of Computing</u>
        8, No. 1 (January 1986): 77-83.

        This is a reprint of a 1955 paper, along with the
        author's recollections of his work with the IBM 650
        in the 1950s. His focus is largely on the machine's
        development.

1717   Haefner, Richard R. "The 650 at Savannah River,"
        <u>Annals of the History of Computing</u> 8, No. 1 (January
        1986): 84-85.

        He describes the use of the 2nd 650 shipped by IBM,
        to the DuPont Savannah River Laboratory, to do simul-
        taneous equations in the 1950s for various scientific
        projects.

1718   Hamilton, F.E. and Kubie, E.C. "The IBM Magnetic Drum
        Calculator Type 650," <u>Journal of the ACM</u> 1 (1954):
        13-20.

        This is a description of an early magnetic drum
        memory of the 1950s, as it was for the IBM 650. The
        article was reprinted in <u>Annals of the History of</u>
        Computing 8, No. 1 (January 1986): 14-19.

1719   Herriot, John G. "Educational Experience with the IBM
        650," <u>Annals of the History of Computing</u> 8, No. 1
        (January 1986): 59-61.

        The author's paper is a history of data processing
        at Stanford University during the 1950s with primary
        attention on the use of an IBM 650.

1720   Hughes, E.S., Jr. "The IBM Magnetic Drum Calculator
        Type 650, Engineering and Design Considerations,"
        <u>Proceedings of the Western Computer Conference</u>, Los
        Angeles, February 1954, pp. 140-154.

        This is a very early description of how the IBM 650
        was conceived and thus contributes to our understand-
        ing of early commercial computer development.

1721   Hughes, E.S., Jr. "The SSEC and Its Carry-Over Effects
        on the IBM Type 650," <u>Annals of the History of Comput-
        ing</u> 8, No. 1 (January 1986): 12-13.

        He argues that the SSEC reinforced the need for stored
        program computers and more advanced components, both
        of which appeared in the IBM 650 processor of 1953.

1722   Hunter, George Truman. "The Solution of Simultaneous
        Equations," <u>Annals of the History of Computing</u> 8,
        No. 1 (January 1986): 86-87.

        This describes applications run on the IBM 650 in
        the mid-1950s.

1723   Hurd, Cuthbert C. "Epilog," <u>Annals of the History of</u>
        <u>Computing</u> 8, No. 1 (January 1986): 89.

        The author helped create the IBM 650 and other IBM
        computers of the 1950s. He describes the signifi-
        cance of the 650.

1724   IBM Corporation. <u>IBM 650 Magnetic Drum Data-Processing</u>
        <u>Machine Manual of Operations</u>. New York: International

Business Machines Corporation, 1957). Multiple
editions throughout late 1950s.

This is the "official" operations guide and description for the IBM 650, IBM's first disk-driven computer.

1725   IBM Corporation. IBM Type 650 Technical Information
        Manual. New York: International Business Machines
        Corporation, 1955.

        This is IBM's earliest description of the 650 system.

1726   Knuth, Donald E. "The IBM 650:An Appreciation From
        the Field," Annals of the History of Computing 8,
        No. 1 (January 1986): 50-55.

        The author reminisces about using a 650 as a student
        at Case Institute of Technology in the 1950s. He
        includes material on how the processor worked and its
        relationship to early software.

1727   Learson, T.V. and Hurd, C.C. "Announcement IBM Letter,"
        Annals of the History of Computing 8, No. 1 (January
        1986): 8-9.

        This reproduces the announcement materials on the
        IBM 650, dated July 1953. This is a good example of
        the kind of publications coming from IBM on new
        products from the 1940s forward. Learson was a sen-
        ior marketing executive, Hurd a senior engineering
        executive.

1728   McCracken, D.D. et al. Programming Business Computers.
        New York: John Wiley and Sons, 1959.

        This 510-page book is a detailed study, based on the
        IBM 650 computer.

1729   Perlis, Alan J. "Two Thousand Words and Two Thousand
        Ideas—The 650 at Carnegie," Annals of the History
        of Computing 8, No. 1 (January 1986): 42-46.

        The author describes Carnegie's experience with a
        650 in the 1950s. It is both autobiographical and
        illustrated.

1730   "Programming Aids and Applications," Annals of the
        History of Computing 8, No. 1 (January 1986): 62-65.

        This is a reprint of lists of topics and attendants
        at a computational class taught by IBM in August,
        1955 on the 650.

1731   Schussel, George. "IBM vs. REMRAND," Datamation 11
        (May 1965): 63-64.

        The article is a survey of the IBM 650 as the company's
        first major business applications computer.

1732   Trimble, George R.   "The IBM 650 Magnetic Drum Calcula-
        tor," Annals of the History of Computing 8, No. 1
        (January 1986): 20-29.

        This is a description of how the 650 evolved, written
        by one of its designers. It is an excellent overview
        of the device and concerning its technology.

                        IBM 701

1733   Amdahl, Gene M.   "Recollections of the 701A," Annals
        of the History of Computing 5, No. 2 (April 1983):
        213-217.

        These are the recollections of a project leader of
        the 1950s working on the IBM 701; illustrated.

1734   Astrahan, M.M. and Rochester, N.   "The Logical Organi-
        zation of the New IBM Scientific Calculator,"
        Proceedings of the ACM (1952): 79-83.

        They describe the 701's design. Both helped to
        design the system for IBM, a product first announced
        in April 1953.

1735   Backus, J.W.   "The IBM 701 Speedcoding System," Journal
        of the Association for Computing Machinery 1 (January
        1954): 4-6.

        Backus, who later became a major figure in the early
        history of programming, describes the 701's programm-
        ing capabilities.

1736   Baker, C.L.   "The 701 at Douglas, Santa Monica,"
        Annals of the History of Computing 5, No. 2 (April
        1983): 187-194.

        This is an illustrated description of how the 701
        was used at Douglas Aircraft in the early 1950s.

1737   Birkenstock, James W.   "Preliminary Planning for the
        701," Annals of the History of Computing 5, No. 2
        (April 1983): 112-114.

        This offers a useful insight into how computers were
        developed in the early 1950s and is fairly typical
        of IBM's experience throughout that decade.

1738   Buchholz, W.   "The System Design of the IBM Type 701
        Computer," Proceedings of the IRE 41 (1953): 1262-
        1275.

        This is a formal description of the IBM 701 for a
        technical audience.

1739   Buslik, W.S.   "IBM Magnetic Tape Reader and Recorder,"
        Report on AIEE-IRE-ACM Computer Conference (March
        1953): 86-90.

This is a description of equipment configured with
the IBM 701 system.

1740   "Computing at Los Alamos Scientific Laboratory with
the 701," Annals of the History of Computing 5, No.
2 (April 1983): 177-184.

This is an early, useful description of scientific
uses put to this IBM system by a user.

1741   Frizzel, C.E. "Engineering Description of the IBM Type
701 Computer," Proceedings, IRE 41 (1953): 1275-1287.

This is a technical description of IBM's electronic
computer: design, features and functions.

1742   Greenstadt, John. "Recollections of the Technical
Computing Bureau," Annals of the History of Computing
5, No. 2 (April 1983): 149-151.

His focus is on the uses of an IBM 701 in the early
1950s.

1743   Grosch, H.R.J. "The 701 at General Electric," Annals
of the History of Computing 5, No. 2 (April 1983):
195-197.

An ex-GE employee describes how the 701 was used at
his company in the early 1980s. GE was a heavy user
of many computer systems in the 1950s for both commercial and scientific applications.

1744   Haddad, J.A. "701 Recollections," Annals of the History of Computing 5, No. 2 (April 1983): 118-123.

Haddad was a computer developer at IBM in the 1950s
and beyond. The article is one of several published
by the Annals describing the uses of this system.

1745   IBM Corporation. Principles of Operation, Type 701
and Associated Equipment. New York: International
Business Machines Corp., 1953.

This is the operating instructions which came with
the IBM 701 system. Such books were used by users
to operate and program computer systems, processor
and peripheral equipment.

1746   Kishi, Tad. "The 701 at the Lawrence Livermore Laboratory," Annals of the History of Computing 5, No. 2
(April 1983): 206-210.

The national laboratories were early users of scientific computers; this article describes one example
of such usage.

1747   Ladd, D.W. and Sheldon, J.W. "The Numerical Solution
of a Partial Differential Equation on the IBM Type
701 Electronic Data Processing Machine," Annals of

the History of Computing 5, No. 2 (April 1983): 142-145.

The authors used the 701 for scientific applications in the 1950s which they describe.

1748   Logue, J.C. et al. "Engineering Experience in the Design and Operation of a Large Scale Electrostatic Memory," Convention Record of the IRE, Part 7, Electronic Computers (March 1953): 21-29.

This is a description of work done in the design and development of the IBM 701.

1749   Mason, Daniel R. "The 701 in the IBM Technical Computing Bureau," Annals of the History of Computing 5, No. 2 (April 1983): 176-177.

IBM continued its tradition of running service bureaus, from tabulating days, with scientific computing services with the 701 processor in the early to mid-1950s.

1750   McClelland, William F. "Activities of the Applied Science Mathematical Committee on the 701," Annals of the History of Computing 5, No. 2 (1983): 125-127.

This computer received considerable attention from engineers and scientists using computers, some of their interest is described here.

1751   McClelland, William F. "A Tracing Program Subordinate to the Given Program," Annals of the History of Computing 5, No. 2 (1983): 127-131.

He describes software/applications on the 701.

1752   McClelland, William F. "Further Developments in Assembly Programs," Annals of the History of Computing 5, No. 2 (April 1983): 132-133.

He describes software development for the IBM 701.

1753   McClelland, William F. "Remarks on Assemblers," Annals of the History of Computing 5, No. 2 (April 1983): 117-118.

He continues the theme of the previous citation, circa 1953.

1754   McClelland, William F. and Pendery, D.W. "701 Installation in the West," Annals of the History of Computing 5, No. 2 (April 1983): 167-169.

Like many similar articles on other processors, this one reflected early interest in installation and performance of early computers.

1755   McCool, Thomas E. "NSA's Defense Calculator (701),

1952-1953," <u>Annals of the History of Computing</u> 5,
No. 2 (April 1983): 186-187.

The author was a user of the IBM 701 and relates his
experiences with it.

1756   Petrie, George W., III. "The 701 in the Washington
        Federal District," <u>Annals of the History of Computing</u>
        5, No. 2 (April 1983): 172-173.

        This continues the series of user views of early
        scientific processors from IBM, the 701 of the early
        1950s.

1757   Phelps, B.E. <u>The Beginnings of Electronic Computation</u>.
        Report TR 00.2259, Systems Development Division.
        Poughkeepsie, N.Y.: IBM Corporation, 9 December 1971.

        The emphasis is on IBM developments up to the announ-
        cement of the 701.

1758   Porter, Randall E. "First Encounter with the 701,"
        <u>Annals of the History of Computing</u> 5, No. 2 (April
        1983): 202-204.

        He describes his role and that of a 701 at the
        Boeing Airplane Company in the early 1950s.

1759   Rochester, Nathaniel. "The 701 Project As Seen By Its
        Chief Architect," <u>Annals of the History of Computing</u>
        5, No. 2 (April 1983): 115-116.

        This is useful for gaining perspective on the signi-
        ficance of the 701 development effort for the industry
        and IBM.

1760   Rosenheim, D.E. "Installation of the First Production
        701," <u>Annals of the History of Computing</u> 5, No. 2
        (April 1983): 146-147.

        Such early experiences with a computer were always
        watched with great interest by both vendor and possible
        users alike as they learned what to do better the
        next time.

1761   Ross, H.D. "The Arithmetic Element of the IBM Type
        701 Computer," <u>Proceedings of the IRE</u> 41 (October
        1953): 1287-1294.

        This describes a major component of the IBM 701 in
        highly technical terms.

1762   Ryckman, George F. "The IBM 701 Computer at the General
        Motors Research Laboratories," <u>Annals of the History
        of Computing</u> 5, No. 2 (April 1983): 210-212.

        His focus is on applications for the processor.

1763   Schlieser, Walter C. "The 701 at Douglas, El Segundo,"

Annals of the History of Computing 5, No. 2 (April
1983): 204-206.

This reflects the experiences of a technical end user
of the 701 in the 1950s.

1764   "The 701 Installation at Lockheed Aircraft," Annals
of the History of Computing 5, No. 2 (April 1983):
184-185.

Lockheed was an early users of not only of the IBM
701 but other processors as well. The 701, however,
made many large-scale modelling and design applications possible due to its increased capacity and
speed over earlier machines.

1765   Smith, R. Blair. "The IBM 701—Marketing and Customer
Relations," Annals of the History of Computing 5,
No. 2 (April 1983): 170-171.

This is a rare article since little has been published on IBM's computer marketing programs of the 1950s
and a great deal on its technology, however.

1766   Stevens, L.D. "Engineering Organization of Input and
Output for the IBM 701 Electronic Data Processing
Machine," Proceedings, Joint AIEE-IRE-ACM Computer
Conference (New York, December 1952): 81-85.

This is a description of how IBM organized I/O gear
in a 701 configuration.

1767   Strong, Jack A. "The 701 at North American Aviation,"
Annals of the History of Computing 5, No. 2 (April
1983): 201.

Although short, it does the same for North American
as, for example, No. 1764 above.

1768   Tillitt, Harley E. "The 701 at the U.S. Navy China
Lake Installation, Inyokern, California," Annals of
the History of Computing 5, No. 2 (April 1983): 198-
200.

This is yet another application survey involving the
IBM 701.

1769   Walters, L.R. "Diagnostic Programming Techniques for
the IBM Type 701," Convention Record of the IRE,
Part 7, Electronic Computers (March 1953): 55-58.

Diagnostics on early computers were crude at best.
Designers of the 701 attempted to enhance them with
programming tolls for this and subsequent machines.

IBM 1401

1770   McCracken, D.D. A Guide to IBM 1401 Programming. New
York: John Wiley & Sons, 1962.

This is a technical guide that discusses the use of
one of IBM's most popular early computers. It is
also the one least studied by historians.

IBM SSEC

1771   Bashe, Charles J. "The SSEC in Historical Perspective,"
       Annals of the History of Computing 4, No. 4 (October
       1982): 296-312.

       This is an illustrated history of the SSEC. He
       argues that this represented the first use of elec-
       trical computation and a stored program design (late
       1940s).

1771   Eckert, W.J. "Electrons and Computation," The Scienti-
       fic Monthly 67, No. 5 (November 1948): 315-323;
       Reprinted in Brian Randell (ed), The Origins of Digi-
       tal Computers: Selected Papers (New York: Springer-
       Verlag, 1982): 223-232.

       This is an illustrated account of the features and
       functions of the IBM Selective Sequence Electronic
       Calculator, and about its possible uses.

1773   Eckert, W.J. "The IBM Pluggable Sequence Relay Calcu-
       lator," Mathematical Tables and Other Aids to Compu-
       tation 3 (1948): 149-161.

       This does the same as his previous article. The
       machine encouraged IBM to increase its R&D in compu-
       tational equipment.

1774   "IBM Selective Sequence Electronic Calculator," Mathe-
       matical Tables and Other Aids to Computation 3 (1948):
       216-217.

       This reports on IBM's dedication of the SSEC on
       January 27-28, 1948.

1775   International Business Machines Corporation. IBM
       Selective Sequence Electronic Calculator. New York:
       IBM Corporation, 1948.

       This is a 16-page description and user guide. It
       includes some history of the device and a photograph
       of 23 people involved in its development.

1776   McPherson, John C. et al. "A Large-Scale, General-Pur-
       pose Electronic Digital Calculator—The SSEC,"
       Annals of the History of Computing 4, No. 4 (October
       1982): 313-326.

       Originally this was written in 1948 but published
       now for the first time. It describes the machine.

1777   "Mental; Selective Sequence Electronic Calculator,"
       New Yorker 31 (August 6, 1955): 16-17.

This is a brief description of the SSEC and its past intended for a general audience.

1778   "Never Stumped; International Business Machines Selective Sequence Electronic Calculator," New Yorker 26 (March 4, 1950): 20-21.

IBM early-on sought out publicity for its major products; this one on the SSEC is typical.

IBM STRETCH

1779   Buchholz, W. (ed). Planning a Computer System (Project Stretch). New York: McGraw-Hill Book Co., Inc., 1962.

This is a book-length account of STRETCH.

1780   Buchholtz, W. "STRETCH," in A. Ralston and C.L. Meek (eds), Encyclopedia of Computer Science (New York: Petrocelli/Charter, 1976): 1359.

This is a brief, illustrated account of the IBM 7030 computer.

1781   Codd, E.F. et al. "Multiprogramming STRETCH: Feasibility Considerations," Communications, ACM 2 (1959): 13-17.

This is an early description of how one team attempted to manage real storage in the 1950s.

1782   Dunwell, S.W. "Design Objectives for the IBM Stretch Computer," Proceedings, Eastern Joint Computer Conference (Boston, Ma., 1959): 20-22.

One of IBM's engineers describes the thinking that went on behind the development of this important computer.

1783   Torrey, V. "Man Versus Computers; FX-1 and Stretch," Science Digest 51 (June 1962): 18-23.

This is an assessment of the system and on its use.

1784   Yasaki, Edward K. "In Focus: Fastest in Its Time," Datamation 28, No. 1 (January 1982): 34-47.

He discusses the IBM STRETCH computer, its evolution, technical innovations and importance to IBM, and finally, its demise.

Institute Blaise Pascal Computer

1785   Couffignal, L. "La Machine de l'Institut Blaise Pascal," Report of a Conference on High Speed Automatic Calculculating Machines, 22-25 June 1949 (Cambridge: University Mathematical Laboratory, January 1950): 56-66; Reprinted in M.R. Williams and Martin Campbell-Kelly (eds), The Early British Computer Conferences

(Cambridge, Mass.: MIT Press, 1989): 60-69.

This is a detailed technical description of the Institute's computer and in particular, about the parallel arithmetic unit then being developed for the system.

1786   Couffignal, L. "Report on the Machine of the Institut Blaise Pascal," <u>Mathematical Tables and Other Aids to Computation</u> 4, No. 32 (1950): 225-229.

This is a progress report on the same machine, now completed.

1787   Pérès, J., L. Brillouin and L. Couffignal. "Les Grandes Machines Mathematiques," <u>Annal. Telecommun.</u> 2, Nos 11-12 (1948): 329-346, 376-385.

This covers such obvious machines as the Mark I, Bush differential analyzer, ENIAC and the Institut machine with comments on how it differed from American machines.

LEO

1788   Gibbs, G.R. "The LEO I," <u>Datamation</u> (May 1972): 40-41.

Gibbs described the first commercially available British computer, 1949-1951.

1789   Kaye, E.J. and Gibbs, G.R. "A Checking Device for Punched Data Tapes," <u>Electronic Engineering</u> 29 (1954): 386-392.

This was one of a series of articles on LEO; this one describes the input/output for the LEO computer.

1790   Lanaerts, E.H. "Operation and Maintenance," <u>Electronic Engineering</u> 29 (1954): 335-341.

This is one of three articles on LEO written by its developers. This one focuses on the use and care of the British system.

1791   Pinkerton, J.M.M. "Operating and Engineering Experience Gained With LEO," in <u>Automatic Digital Computation, Proceedings of a Symposium Held at the National Physical Laboratory, March 25-28, 1953</u> (London: H.M. Stationery Office, 1954): 21-34.

This provides a useful perspective on LEO I by a user.

1792   Pinkerton, J.M.M. and Kaye, E.J. "LEO—Lyons Electronic Office," <u>Electronic Engineering</u> 29 (1954): 284-291.

This is written by two of its developers. They describe one of the earliest British commercial computers.

1793   Simmons, J.R.M. Leo and the Managers. London: Mac-
        donald, 1962.

        This book is on business management of data process-
        ing that relies heavily on the use of British devices
        of the late 1950s and early 1960s.

MANIAC

1794   Anderson, Herbert L. "Metropolis, Monte Carlo and the
        MANIAC," Los Alamos Science 14 (Fall 1986): 96-107.

        He reviews early computing at the Los Alamos National
        Laboratory (1950s) and comments on the work of Nicholas
        Metropolis. The author also worked there.

1795   Anderson, Herbert L. "Scientific Uses of the MANIAC,"
        Journal of Statistical Physics 43 (1986): 731-748.

        He describes the MANIAC, the first computer used at
        the Los Alamos National Laboratory (1950s).

1796   Jungk, Robert. Brighter Than a Thousand Suns. New
        York: Harcourt, Brace and Co., 1958.

        This contains some discussion of the MANIAC machine
        of the early 1950s.

1797   "The MANIAC: A Great Big Toy," Datamation 24, No. 8
        (1978): 80.

        This publishes an interview with N. Metropolis about
        the MANIAC and on the evolution of the stored program
        concept of the 1940s.

1798   Metropolis, N. "The MANIAC," in his A History of
        Computing in the Twentieth Century (New York: Acade-
        mic Press, 1980): 457-464.

        This is written by an early user/developer of the
        MANIAC at Los Alamos, 1948-1960, and includes comments
        on the ENIAC and is illustrated.

1799   Metropolis, N. and Worlton, J. "A Trilogy on Errors
        in the History of Computing," Proceedings U.S.A.-
        Japan Computing Conference, First, Tokyo, October 3-
        5, 1972 (Montvale, NJ: AFIPS, 1972): 683-691; Reprin-
        ted in Annals of the History of Computing 2, No. 1
        (January 1980): 49-59.

        This paper analizes the extent to which the develop-
        ers of early digital computers and relay calculators
        were aware of Babbage's work, discusses the develop-
        ment of the stored program concept, and offers an
        early history of the MANIAC.

Memory Technologies

1800   Allen, C.A. et al. "A 2.18-Microsecond Megabit Core
        Storage Unit," IRE Transactions, Electronic

Computers, EC-10 (1961): 233-237.

This is a technical description of the memory on an
IBM 7070 (7301) processor and for the STRETCH project
(7302 memory), later also used on the 7080 and 7090
in 1958.

1801   Bonyhard, P.I. et al. "Applications of Bubble Devices,"
        IEEE Transactions, Magnetics, MAG-6 (1970): 447-451.

        This reviews work done on bubble memories at Bell
        Laboratories in the late 1960s.

1802   Bradley, E.M. "A Computer Storage Matrix Using Ferro-
        magnetic Thin Films," Journal of the British IRE 20
        (1960): 765-784.

        This surveys the use of such technologies on a
        processor at International Computers and Tabulators,
        Ltd. in 1958, making this one of the first applica-
        tion of such memory.

1803   Constantine, G., Jr. "A Load-Sharing Matrix Switch,"
        IBM Journal of Research and Development 2 (1958):
        204-211.

        The author, working at IBM, describes his creation,
        a load-sharing matrix used to reduce pulse-shape
        distortion in early memory technologies.

1804   Forrester, Jay W. "Digital Information Storage in
        Three Dimensions Using Magnetic Cores," Journal of
        Applied Physics 22 (1951): 44-48.

        Forrester describes the development of magnetic core
        for RAM at MIT in 1950, the first such memory.

1805   Holt, A.W. and Davis, W.W. "Computer Memory Uses
        Conventional C-R Tubes," Electronics (December 1953):
        178-182.

        This describes memory on National Bureau of Standards
        computers of the early 1950s and is a technical dis-
        cussion.

1806   McLaughlin, R.A. "The IBM 704: 36-Bit Floating-Point
        Money-Maker," Datamation 21 (1955): 45-48, 50.

        This technical piece discusses 4096 by 36-bit memory
        used on the IBM 704 beginning in December, 1955.

1807   Merwin, R.E. "The IBM 705 EDPM Memory System," IRE
        Transactions, Electronic Computers, EC-5 (1956): 219-
        223.

        Merwin describes memory on the IBM 705 in 1956, early
        core memory.

1808   Proebster, W.E. "The Design of High-Speed Thin Magnetic

Film Memory," <u>ISSCC Digest of Technical Papers</u> 5, (1962): 38-39.

Proebster describes an 18 432-bit memory developed at IBM's Zurich Laboratory in 1961-1962.

1809   Raffel, J.I. "Operating Characteristics of a Thin Film Memory," <u>Journal of Applied Physics</u> 30 (1959): 605-615.

This surveys the first thin-film memory to be used. It was developed at MIT's Lincoln Laboratory and, very quickly, became a standard type of memory for computers of the 1960s.

1810   Rajchman, J.A. "A Myriabit Magnetic-Core Matrix Memory," <u>Proceedings, IRE</u> 41 (1953): 1407-1421.

At RCA work was done leading to a two-dimensional matrix of transformers reducing the need for vacuum tubes in early memory units (1952-1953).

1811   Rajchman, J.A. "Static Magnetic Matrix Memory and Switching Circuits," <u>RCA Review</u> 13 (1952): 183-201.

This article offers a summary of early work done at RCA by the author on early computer memories and, more specifically, on magnetic core for RAM in the early 1950s.

1812   Remshardt, R. and Baitinger, U.G. "A High Performance Low Power 1048-bit Memory Chip in MOSFET Technology and Its Application," <u>IEEE Journal of Solid-State Circuits</u>, SC-11 (1976): 352-359.

This ultimately 2048-bit chip technology from IBM became available for use in 1971 although it was developed in the late 1960s; that effort is described here.

1813   Rhodes, W.H. <u>et al</u>. "A 0.7-Microsecond Ferrite Core Memory," <u>IBM Journal of Research and Development</u> 5 (1961): 174-182.

This technical article describes IBM's memory for the HARVEST super computer of the early 1960s.

1814   Ridenour, Louis N. "Computer Memories," <u>Scientific American</u> 192 (June 1955): 92-101.

This important American scientist summarizes existing technology and methods for storing data in computers as of the early to mid-1950s.

1815   Shaw, P.W. "Wire Inserting Machine Mechanizer Core Plan Assembly," <u>Automation</u> 5 (1958): 51-54.

Shaw and his research associates at IBM developed a core plane using hollow steel needles described here.

1816   Simkins, Q.W.   "A High Speed Thin Film Memory: Its
        Design and Development," Proceedings of the Fall
        Joint Computer Conference, AFIPS Supplement 27, Part
        2 (1965): 103-106.

        Simkins describes the magnetic film memory that IBM
        used, beginning in February, 1968, on its System 360
        Model 95.

1817   Werner, G.E. et al. "A 110-Nanosecond Ferrite Core
        Memory," IBM Journal of Research and Development 11
        (1967): 153-161.

        This memory was built at IBM in 1966, employing
        ideas first used on the HARVEST computer. It was
        used only for experimental purposes and never went
        into normal production.

1818   Wiedmann, S.K.   "High-Density Static Bipolar Memory,"
        ISSCC Digest of Technical Papers 16 (1973): 56-57.

        This technical description of a computer memory cell
        is one that used lateral pnp loads, important in the
        memory used on the IBM 4300 machines of the late
        1970s.

                              NORC

1819   "Bigger and Better; Naval Ordnance Research Calculator,"
        Scientific American 192 (February 1955): 62.

        This is a description of an early U.S. Navy computer
        and its usage.

1820   Eckert, W.J. and Jones, Rebecca. Faster, Faster, Simple
        Description of a Giant Electronic Calculator and the
        Problem It Solves. New York: International Business
        Machines Corporation, 1955.

        This 160-page publication, by a leading astronomer
        with long experience using punch card equipment,
        reviews the NORC's operations, functions, and use in
        scientific work.

1821   "NORC: What Goes Into An Automatic Product," Automatic
        Control 2 (March 1955): 23-26.

        In addition to a description of NORC, the paper is a
        technical overview of many components used in com-
        puters of the mid-1950s.

1822   Wegstein, Joseph H. and Alexander, Samuel N.   "Programm-
        ing Scientific Calculators," Control Engineering 3
        (May 1956): 89-92.

        The authors detail how to program the NORC and their
        experience with automatic coding.

PEGASUS

1823   Davison, J.F. Programming for Digital Computers.
        London: Business Publications, 1961.

        This technical discussion is a good reflection of
        how to use the Ferranti Pegasus computer.

1824   Elliott, W.S. et al. "The Design Philosophy of Pegasus,
        A Quantity Production Computer," Proceedings of the
        IEE 103B, Supp. 1-3 (1956): 188-196.

        The Ferranti Pegasus was a successful British machine
        of the late 1950s. This is a technical description
        of the computer. It was also called the PEGASUS.

1825   Swann, B.B. "An Informal History of the Ferranti
        Computer Department," (1975), Privately Circulated.

        This is as much a history of the PEGASUS as of the
        British company that made it in the 1950s and early
        1960s.

RAYDAC

1826   Bloch, R.M. "The Raytheon Electronic Digital Computer,"
        Annals of Harvard Computation Laboratory (1951): 50-
        64.

        RAYDAC is described in detail by one of its develop-
        ers.

1827   Bloch, R.M. et al. "General Design Considerations for
        the Raytheon Computer," Mathematical Tables and
        Other Aids to Computation 3, No. 24 (October 1948):
        317-323.

        The authors built computers for the Raytheon Manufac-
        turing Corporation. The describe the RAYDAC, built
        for the U.S. Government and delivered in 1951.

1828   Bloch, R.M. et al. "The Logical Design of the Raytheon
        Computer," Mathematical Tables and Other Aids to
        Computation 3, No. 24 (October 1948): 286-295.

        This is a formal, technical description of Raytheon's
        first computer, built in the late 1940s and early
        1950s, at Waltham, Massachusetts.

1829   Dean, F.R. "Operating Experience With RAYDAC," Report
        on AIEE-IRE-ACM Computer Conference (March 1953):
        77-80.

        This positive analysis appeared two years after the
        machine went into operation.

1830   Gray, W.H. "RAYDAC Input-Output System," Report on
        AIEE-IRE-ACM Computer Conference (March 1953): 70-76.

This article was one of a series of contemporary
pieces to appear on various aspects of the RAYDAC
and describes some innovative work done on peripherals.

1831   Rehler, K.M.   "The RAYDAC System and Its External
        Memory," Report on AIEE-IRE-ACM Computer Conference
        (March 1953): 63-70.

        This is part of a series published on the computer
        and its features. Memory was of great concern to all
        developers in the early 1950s; the issues are des-
        cribed here.

1832   West, C.F. and DeTurk, J.E.   "A Digital Computer for
        Scientific Applications," Proceedings of the IRE 36
        (December 1948): 1452-1460.

        They describe RAYDAC's design and functions.

                    Research and Development

1833   Aloisi, P.   "L'evolution des transistors de puissance,"
        Bulletin des Schweizerischen Elektrotechnischen de
        l'Association Suisse des Electriciens 77 (1986): 1212-
        1217.

        This brief overview of the evolution of the transis-
        tor reflects the international interest in the topic
        for over three decades.

1834   Anderson, James A. and Rosenfeld, Edward (eds). Neuro-
        computing: Foundations of Research. Cambridge, Mass.:
        MIT Press, 1988.

        This is an anthology of 38 historically significant
        papers from the 1950s to the 1980s, and includes
        articles by Warren McCulloch, John von Neumann,
        down to others by David Rumelhart and Terrence Sejnow-
        ski. They deal with such themes as network structure,
        connectivist model, and network operation.

1835   Berkeley, Edmund C.   "Relations Between Symbolic Logic
        and Large-Scale Calculating Machines," Science 112
        (October 6, 1950): 395-399.

        Berkeley was an early commentator on American comput-
        ers. This was one of his earliest of many articles
        on the same theme.

1836   Booth, Andrew D. and Booth, Kathleen H.V.   Automatic
        Digital Calculators. 2nd Ed.   London: Butterworths
        Scientific Publications, 1956.

        Seventeen chapters cover the theory of computers,
        concepts, language and research on the subject,
        written by two leading British computer scientists
        of the period.

1837   Brown, George S. and Campbell, D.P. "Instrument
Engineering, Its Growth and Promise in Process Control," <u>Mechanical Engineering</u> (February 1950): 124-
127.

Brown, a professor at MIT, and Campbell, also of MIT,
described research done on feedback mechanisms in
the 1940s.

1838   Campbell-Kelly, Martin and Williams, Michael R. (eds).
<u>The Moore School Lectures: Theory and Design of</u>
<u>Electronic Computers</u>. Cambridge, Mass.: MIT Press,
1985.

This is a reprint of lectures given in July/August,
1946 at the University of Pennsylvania. It reflects
the state-of-the-art of the times. The lectures were
heard by many engineers who later went on to build
the major digital systems of the 1940s and 1950s.

1839   <u>Computers—Key to Total Systems Control, Proceedings of</u>
<u>the Eastern Joint Computer Conference, Washington,</u>
<u>D.C., December 12-14, 1961</u>, 20. New York: Macmillan
Co., 1961.

This volumes anthologizes papers on all major computer projects of the period 1959-1961. All are very
technical and represent late second generation work.

1840   Couffignal, L. "Traits Caractéristiques de la Calcu-
latrice de la Machine à Calculer Universelle de
l'Institute Blaise Pascal," <u>Proceedings of the 2nd</u>
<u>Symposium on Large-Scale Digital Calculating Machin-</u>
<u>ery, 13-16 September 1949. Annals of the Computation</u>
<u>Laboratory of Harvard University</u> 26 (Cambridge, Mass.:
Harvard University Press, 1951): 374-386.

He discusses how this particular unit works and also
comments on the general state of R&D on the subject.

1841   <u>Data Processing Equipment Encyclopedia</u>. 2 vols: <u>Electro-</u>
<u>mechanical Devices</u> and <u>Electronic Devices</u>. Detroit:
Gille Associates, Inc., 1961.

This set was an early, detailed collection of descriptions on all manner of computational equipment
and technology, circa late 1950s. Updates to this set
appeared into the 1960s.

1842   Davis, Martin. "Mathematical Logic and the Origin of
Modern Computers," in Esther R. Phillips (ed), <u>Stud-</u>
<u>ies in the History of Mathematics</u>, 26 of Studies in
Mathematics (Washington, D.C.: Mathematical Associa-
tion of America, 1987): 137-165.

This covers an important aspect of early computer
systems research.

1843   Dijkstra, E.W. "Invariance and Non-Determirangy," in

C. Hoare and J. Shepherdson (eds), <u>Mathematical
Logic and Programming Languages</u> (Englewood Cliffs,
N.J.: Prentice-Hall, Inc., 1985): 157-165.

This is partially historical when discussing the
proof of correctness for concurrent systems.

1844   Eckert, W.J. "Electrons and Computation," <u>Scientific
Monthly</u> 67 (November 1948): 315-323.

At the time of publication, Eckert was a leading
authority on the use of punch card equipment for
scientific applications. Here he describes recent
uses of electronics in new calculators, primarily
from IBM.

1845   Gardner, W.D. "The Independent Inventor," <u>Datamation</u>
26, No. 10 (1982): 12-22.

This is useful for an understanding of the scientific
problems facing computer scientists of the 1940s and
1950s.

1846   Grabbe, E.M. <u>et al.</u>(eds). <u>Handbook of Automatic Computation and Control</u>, 2: <u>Computers and Data Processing</u>.
New York: John Wiley & Sons, 1959.

At 1093 pages, this was the largest of the early
reference works on DP technology and uses, of the
1950s. It is a gold mine of details on all aspects
of the subject.

1847   Hilton, A.M. <u>Logic, Computing Machines, and Automation</u>.
Cleveland: Meridian, 1963.

Pages 215-233 is a history of the evolution of logic
devices.

1848   Hochhuth, Rolf. <u>Alan Turing: Erzahlung</u>. Hamburg:
Rowohlt Taschenbuch Verlag GmbH, 1987.

Alan Turing's ideas on computing significantly
influenced the design of computers in the 1940s and
1950s with ideas originally developed in the late
1930s.

1849   Lolli, G. <u>La Macchina e le Dimonstrazioni</u>. Bologna:
il Mulino, 1987.

Lolli reviews briefly the history and philosophy of
formalizations in logic; contains a chapter on the
use of computers and formalization.

1850   Luebbert, W.F. "Data Transmission Equipment Concepts
for FIELDATA," in <u>1959 Proceedings of the Western
Joint Computer Conference</u> (New York: Institute of
Radio Engineers, 1959): 189-196.

The author discusses a family of computing technology

supported by the U.S. Army in the 1950s and involving
projects managed by IBM, Philco, Sylvania and Autone-
tics.

1851   Masani, P. et al. "The Wiener Memorandum on the Mecha-
       nical Solution of Partial Differential Equations,"
       Annals of the History of Computing 9, No. 2 (1987):
       183-197.

       Although a technical piece, it is informative for the
       period of the 1940s about Wiener's views concerning
       mathematics and computing. It has various comments
       on his ideas.

1852   Mauchly, J.W. "The Use of High Speed Vacuum Tube
       Devices for Calculating," Privately circulated memo-
       randum, Moore School of Electrical Engineering, Uni-
       versity of Pennsylvania, August, 1942; Reprinted in
       Brian Randell (ed), The Origins of Digital Computers:
       Selected Papers (New York: Springer-Verlag, 1982):
       355-358.

       He argues that computers should be electrical digital
       in design instead of mechanical differential analy-
       zers and then offers suggestions on what the new type
       should look like.

1853   McCann, G.D. and Criner, H.E. "Mechanical Problems
       Solved Electrically," Westinghouse Engineer 6, No.
       2 (March 1946): 49-56.

       They review work done at Westinghouse using an analog
       machine.

1854   McPherson, J.C. "Mathematical Operations with Punched
       Cards," Journal of the American Statistical Associa-
       tion 37, No. 218 (June 1942): 275-281.

       He describes how punch card devices were used for the
       synthesis and analysis of harmonic functions among
       other applications.

1855   Michie, D. "Turing and the Origins of the Computer,"
       New Scientist 85, No. 1195 (1980): 580-583.

       The author worked with Turing during World War II at
       Bletchley Park. This is a technical discussion of
       Turing's contributions and serves as a good introduc-
       tion to the scientist.

1856   Misa, Thomas J. "Military Needs, Commercial Realities,
       and the Development of the Transistor, 1948-1958," in
       Merritt Roe Smith (ed), Military Enterprise and Techno-
       logical Change (Cambridge, Mass.: MIT Press, 1985):
       253-287.

       Misa analyzes the role played by the U.S. Army Signal
       Corps in advancing the study of solid-state electro-
       nics.

1857   Niemann, Ralph A. Dahlgren's Participation in the
        Development of Computer Technology. MP 81-416.
        Dahlgren, Va.: Naval Surface Weapons Center, 1982.

        The author's 42-page booklet reviews his work and
        that of others in mathematics with the Mark I at
        Harvard. It includes illustrated material on the
        use of DP with the Mark II and III, NORC, Stretch,
        CDC 6700 and the CDC Cybe 74, all between 1942 and
        1972.

1858   Phelps, Byron E. "Computer Circuit Design in the
        1940s," Annals of the History of Computing 4, No. 4
        (October 1982): 368-370.

        Much of the discussion is on how it differed between
        the SSEC and the ENIAC and is a technical discourse.

1859   Rajchman, J. "The Selective Electrostatic Storage Tube,"
        RCA Review (March 1951): 53-87.

        He surveys his most important computer-related
        project of his career, work on the Selectron. Due
        to manufacturing difficulties it was hardly used as
        a computer memory, a casualty of early computing.

1860   "Revolution in Robotland; Symposium on Calculating
        Machinery," Newsweek 34 (September 26, 1949): 58.

        This describes a gathering of engineers interested
        in computing in the United States. Such meetings
        began receiving wide attention by the end of the
        1940s.

1861   Richards, R.K. Digital Computer Components and Circuits.
        Princeton, N.J.: D. Van Nostrand, 1957.

        Although a technical treatise, it is a good snapshot
        of second generation technology of the mid-1950s.

1862   Richtmyer, R.D. "The Post-War Computer Development,"
        American Mathematical Monthly 72, No. 2 (1965): 8-
        14.

        The article describes how the stored program computer
        evolved after ENIAC and includes a short description
        of that processor. The author attributes the idea of
        converter code to John von Neumann.

1863   Schantz, Herbert F. The History of Optical Character
        Recognition. Manchester, VT: Recognition Technologies
        Users Association, 1982.

        This short book takes the story of OCR from 1808 to
        the 1980s and is the only history published todate
        on the subject.

1864   Smith, C.E. and Gove, E.L. "An Electromechanical

Calculator for Directional-Antenna Patterns,"
<u>Transactions of the American Society of Electrical
Engineers</u> 62 (1943): 78-82.

They describe a special purpose analog calculating
device built in the early 1940s.

1865   Smith, Charles V.L. <u>Electronic Digital Computers</u>. New
        York: McGraw-Hill Book Co., Inc., 1959.

        This is a detailed description of components used in
        computers and is a very hardware oriented book, circa
        second generation equipment.

1866   Tropp, Henry S. "Origin of the Term <u>Bit</u>," <u>Annals of
        the History of Computing</u> 6, No. 2 (April 1984): 152-
        155.

        He describes the concept of the <u>bit</u> and then its
        history.

1867   Tyler, Arthur W. "Optical and Photographic Storage
        Techniques," <u>Proceedings of a Symposium on Large-Scale
        Digital Calculating Machinery</u> (Cambridge, Mass.:
        Harvard University Press, 1948): 146-150.

        This technical paper reflected a common area of
        research on input/output technologies, work which
        surface in such systems as Whirlwind and SAGE.

1868   Wald, A. <u>Sequential Analysis</u>. New York: John Wiley,
        1947.

        The focus is on technology of the 1940s with comments
        on the Colossus.

1869   Wilkes, Maurice V. "The Genesis of Microprogramming,"
        <u>Annals of the History of Computing</u> 8, No. 2 (April
        1986): 115-126.

        He is attributed as the developer of this notion.
        This publication reprints two articles by him pub-
        lished in 1951-52, along with a retrospective added
        for the <u>Annals</u> reprint.

                        Robots, Pre-1960

1870   "Another New Product for Robot Salesmen," <u>Modern Indus-
        try</u> 13, No. 2 (February 1947).

        This was a very early article on the subject of a
        robotic device for commercial use.

1871   Asimov, I. <u>I, Robot</u>. New York: Del-Ray Books, 1950.

        This is one of the most famous books published on
        robots and in which he defines the "rights" and
        "duties" of robots. It helped publicize the term
        robotics.

1872   "The Automatic Factory," Fortune 34, No. 5 (November
        1946): 160ff.

        This speculative piece discusses the use of robotic
        devices; it is a snapshot of thinking on the subject
        during the 1940s, particularly about their potential.

1873   Berkeley, Edmund C. The Construction of Living Robots.
        New York: E.C. Berkeley, 1952.

        By the early 1950s many were commenting on the sub-
        ject of automation, of which robotics was a major
        part, and the implications for society and the econo-
        my.

1874   Binder, E. "Adam Links Champion Athlete," Amazing
        Stories 14 (July 1940): 28-47.

        This is a piece of science fiction using a robot as
        as a theme, written by an important sci-fi writer
        of the 1930s and 1940s.

1875   Binder, E. "I, Robot," Amazing Stories 13 (January
        1939): 8-18.

        This reflects typical thinking of the 1930s on the
        subject of robots, highly unrealistic and overly
        optimistic on capabilities versus technical realities
        of the time.

1876   Bruinsma, A. Multivibrator Circuits; Introduction to
        Robot Technique. Trans. from German by E. Harker.
        New York: Macmillan, 1960.

        During the 1950s much work was done on basic research
        of robotics; this book reflects that effort.

1877   Bruinsma, A. Practical Robot Circuits: Electronic
        Sensory Organs and Nerve Systems. Trans. from German
        by E. Harker. Eindhoven: Philips, 1959.

        By the late 1950s cybernetic and computing work was
        merging with electrical engineering; this work
        reflects significant research on robotics.

1878   Čapek, Karel. R.U.R. Trans. by Paul Selver. New York:
        Doubleday, Page & Co., 1923.

        This was a Czech play that first introduced the word
        robot to English-reading audiences. The play was a
        great success in 1921 in London. It has been reprint-
        ed many times since then.

1879   Chapuis, Alfred. Les Automates dans les Oeuvres
        d'Imagination. Neuchâtel: Editions du Griffon, 1947.

        This expert on automata also surveys perceptions
        about robots.

1880   Chapuis, Alfred. Les Automates, figures artificielles
        d'hommes et d'animaux; histoire et technique.
        Neuchâtel: Editions du Griffon, 1949.

        This is a classic history of automata from ancient
        times to the early 1900s and is an excellent descrip-
        tion of how they worked.

1881   Chapuis, Alfred. Automates: Machines automatiques et
        Machinisme. Preface de Alphonse Bernoud. Geneva: S.A.
        des Publications Techniques, 1928.

        This is a more technical piece than his previously
        cited works above and covers more modern developments.

1881   Chapuis, Alfred. "Du Goût des Chinois pour les Auto-
        mates," Journal Suisse d'Horlogerie et de Bijouterie
        46 (1921): 154-155.

        This is an early piece by Chapuis on automata and
        robots.

1882   Chapuis, Alfred. The Jacquet-Droz Automatons. Neuchâ-
        tel: History Museum, 1956.

        This describes well-known French automatons and
        automata of the eighteenth century.

1884   Chapuis, Alfred and Droz, Edmond. Automata: A Histori-
        cal and Technological Study. Trans. from French by
        Alec Reid. Neuchâtel: Editions du Griffon, 1958.

        This is a major work on all manner of automata from
        ancient times to the early 1900s; illustrated. It
        covers clocks, automata, mechanical toys, musical
        instruments and other devices.

1885   Chapuis, Alfred and Gelis, E. Le Monde des Automates:
        étude historique et technique. 2 vols. Paris: Blondel
        la Rougery, 1928.

        This is a very detailed history of the subject and
        was the foundation for much of Chapuis' future work
        on the history of the topic.

1886   Cohen, John. Human Robots in Myth and Science. London:
        Allen and Unwin, 1966.

        This is a short history of automata; illustrated.

1887   Diels, Herman. Antike Technik: Sieben Vorträge.
        Leipzig: B.G. Teubner, 1920.

        This describes an early automata device.

1888   Evans, Henry Ridgely. Edgar Allan Poe and Baron von
        Kempelen's Automaton. Kenton, Ohio: International
        Brotherhood of Magicians, 1939.

Kempelen's device of the nineteenth century was
widely seen in both Europe and in North America.

1889   The Famous Chess-Player. London: H. Reynall, 1783 (?).
       This is a description of von Kempelen's automaton.

1890   Florescu, Radu. In Search of Frankenstein. New York:
       Warner Books, 1976.

       Frankenstein was the most widely known fictional
       automata in history; this is a history of the subject.

1891   Freudenthal, Hans. Machines Pensantes. Conference faits
       au Palais de la Decouverte le Mai 1953. Paris: n.p.,
       1953.

       This conference focuses on contemporary work in the
       field of automata and robotics.

1892   Geduld, Harry M. and Gottesman, Ronald (eds). Robots.
       Robots. Robots. Boston: New York: Graphic Society,
       1978.

       This anthology of articles has pieces on robots in
       literature and legend, history, and other essays on
       their functions and role in movies.

1893   Gerber, A. "Goethe's Homunculus," Modern Language
       Notes 12 (1897): 69-79.

       The German philosopher conceived of a thinking
       automata called Homunculus, described here.

1894   Gill, Arthur. Introduction to the Theory of Finite-
       State Machinery. New York: McGraw-Hill, 1952.

       This is a good window into the technology of
       feedback systems/robots of the 1940s and 1950s.

1895   Glut, Donald F. The Frankenstein Legend. Metuchen,
       N.J.: The Scarecrow Press, 1973.

       This is a useful survey of the topic of literature's
       most famous robotic creature.

1896   Goertz, R.C. "Fundamentals of General Purpose Remote
       Manipulators," Nucleonics 10 (November 1952): 36-42.

       He describes a teoperator for handling radioactive
       materials—an early practical robot.

1897   Haas, Walter de. Automaten: die Befreiung des Menschen
       durch die Maschine. Stuttgart: Dieck & Co., 1930.

       This is an early review of practical applications of
       automata and survey of the general subject of robots.

1898   Hatfield, Henry Stafford. Automation: Or the Future
       of the Mechanical Man. London: K. Paul, Trench,
       Trubner & Co., Ltd., 1928.

This is a description and philosophic look, at all kinds of automation of the 1920s.

1899   Held, H.L. Das Gespenst des Golem. Munich: Allgemeine Verlaganstalt, 1927.

1900   J.A. "Automatas, cajas de musica y pajaros mecánicos," Revista de las artes y los oficios, No. 75 (1950): 24-28.

This is a brief survey of old automata.

1901   "The Jacquet-Droz Androids," Scientific American 88 (April 18, 1903): 301-302.

This surveys eighteenth century automata.

1902   Kiaulehn, Walther. "Automaten-Raritaten," Der Türmer (Berlin) (February 1936): 449-452.

This surveys old automata from Europe.

1903   Knips-Hasse, A. Das Automaten-Kabinett. Berlin: E. Bloch, 1893.

This describes an automata device.

1904   Lagemann, John K. "From Piggly Wiggly to Keedoozle," Collier's Magazine 122, No. 18 (October 30, 1948): 20-21, passim.

This is a non-technical discussion of robotics over time, mainly in fiction.

1905   Leaver, E.W. and Borwn, J.J. "Machines Without Men," Fortune 34, No. 5 (November 1946): 165ff.

This is a serious review of robotic devices in American industry as of the late 1940s. Some were quasi-programmable.

1906   Ludwig, Albert. "Homunculi und Androiden," Archiv fur das Studium der neueren Sprachen und Literaturen. Braunschweig, 1918. Band 137, pp. 137-153; Band 138, pp. 141-155; Band 139, pp. 1-25.

This is a description of a set of automata with additional comments on pre-twentieth century robotic devices in general.

1907   "Machines Predict What Happens in Your Plant," Business Week (September 25, 1948): 68-69, passim.

The focus is on the use of computers and robotic devices in American industry.

1908   Maingot, Elaine. Les Automates. Paris: Hachette, 1959.

This is a general overview of automata over many
centuries, with bibliography.

1909   Martin, Henri. "Historique des Automates du Moyen Age
        a la fin du XVIIme siecle," Journal Suisse d'Horlo-
        gerie 32 (1908): 244-248, 316-321, 382-389, 419-422;
        33 (1909): 60-65, 98-103.

        This is a history of early automata, mainly European.

1910   Maskelyne, John N. and Cooke, George A. A Guide to
        Their . . . Entertainment of Modern Miracles. London:
        n.p., 187(?).

        This is a nineteenth century critic of spiritualism
        attacking robotic devices. Cooke also was a lesser
        known critic.

1911   Papp, Desiderius. Der Maschinenmensh. Wien: Stein,
        1925.

        This describes robotic devices and uses.

1912   Paul, Richard P. "The Early Stages of Robotics," IEEE
        Control Systems Magazine 5, No. 1 (February 1985):
        27-31.

        He covers post-World War II developments.

1913   Pease, M.C. "Devious Weapon," Astounding Science Fic-
        tion 53, No. 2 (April 1949): 34-43.

        Pease discusses robotic devices and their potential
        use in defense.

1914   Perregaux, Charles. Les Jaquet-Droz et leurs Automates.
        Neuchâtel: Wolfrath & Sperle, 1906.

        In addition to reviewing the history and function of
        Jaquet-Droz automata, this discusses other devices of
        the 1700s.

1915   Petzoldt, Fritz. Werkzeugeinrichtungen auf Einspindel-
        automaten. Berlin: J. Springer, 1941.

        This is a technical treatise on automata/robotic
        devices and uses.

1916   Racknitz, Joseph F. Ueber den Schachspieler des Herrn
        von Kempelen und dessen Nachbildung. Leipzig:
        Breitkopf, 1789.

        This describes the device made by von Kempelen.

1917   Rosenfeld, B. Die Golemsage und ihre Verwertung in der
        deutschen Literatur. Breslau: Priebatsch, 1934.

        This is a monograph on the Golem automata and its
        role in literature, mainly Jewish legends in German.

1918   Rosenfeld, L.C.   From Beast-Machine to Man-Machine.
       New York: Oxford University Press, 1940.

       This goes from images of mean robotic creatures,
       such as Frankenstein, to the potentials offered by
       modern technology of the 1930s as portrayed in liter-
       ature.

1919   Sabliere, Jean (ed).   De L'Automate a L'Automatisation,
       Textes de Héron d'Alesandre, Salomon de Caus, Camus
       La Lorrain, Jacques de Vaucanson, ... Paris:
       Gauthier-Villars, 1966.

       This is an anthology of papers dealing with ancient
       and early modern period European automata.

1920   Il Segreto del famoso automa che giucava a scacchi.
       Florence: G. Benelli, 1841.

       This describes well-known automata and how they worked.

1921   Shannon, Claude E.   Programming a Computer for Playing
       Chess. Murrat Hill, N.J.: Bell Telephone Laboratories,
       October 8, 1948.

       One of the important pioneers in artificial intelli-
       gence wrote of his early work on chess playing
       designs and how digital computers could be used to
       do the job often relegated to earlier automata.

1922   Shannon, Claude E. and McCarthy, J. (eds). Automata
       Studies. Princeton, N.J.: Princeton University Press,
       1956.

       While claimed by artificial intelligence experts as
       the origins of their field, these papers also concern-
       ed automata and robotic themes in general.

1923   Shelley, Mary W.   Frankenstein. (1818).

       This is the famous horror story which has appeared
       in numerous editions. The most recent useful edition
       is Frankenstein; or The Modern Prometheus, ed. by M.
       K. Joseph (London: Oxford University Press, 1971).

1924   Silberer, Herbert.   "Der Homunculus," Imago 3 (1914):
       37-79.

       This is a lengthy offering on the history of Homuncu-
       lus, an early automata.

1925   Spilhaus, Athelstan.   "Let Robot Work for You," The
       American Magazine (December 1948): 47, passim.

       This is on the use of robotic devices in the U.S.
       and is a non-technical piece.

1926   Steiner, Hugo.   "Der Golem. Prager Phantasien," Jahr-
       buch Deutscher Bibliophilen und Literaturfreunde 5
       (1917): 114.

This is on Golem, an automata in Jewish East European mythology.

1927   Strehl, Rolf. _The Robots Are Among Us_. Trans. from German by Herman Scott. London: Arco Publishers, 1955.

The tradition of automata in German literature and mythology is great. This is an example.

1928   Valtenin, Veit. "Goethes Hommunkulus," _Modern Language Notes_ 13 (1898): 432-443, 462-471.

This surveys Hommunkulus automata.

1929   Willis, Robert. _An Attempt to Analyze the Automation Chess Player of Mr. de Kempelen_. London: J. Booth, 1821.

This device circulated around Europea and North America at various fairs for decades.

1930   Windisch, Karl Gottliev von. _Lettres sur le joueur d'echecs de M. Kempelen_. Basle: Chez l'Editeur, 1783.

The machine was suspected for years to be a hoax. This is an early expose on the subject.

Robots, Post-1960

1931   Asimov, I. _Robots and Empire_. Garden City, N.Y.: Doubleday and Co., 1985.

A leading writer on science and science fiction, discusses the subject of robots in all its aspects.

1932   Beni, Gerrardo and Hackwood, Susan (eds). _Recent Advances in Robotics_. New York: John Wiley & Sons, 1985.

The editors work at Bell Labs. Their book is a survey of current research on robotics but also includes material on the history of robotics in the 20th century. Research projects were all from the 1970s and 1980s.

1933   Burks, Arthur Walter (ed). _Essays on Cellular Automata_. Urbana: University of Illinois Press, 1970.

Biological themes have been part of robotics since the 1950s.

1934   Carroll, Charles Michael. _The Great Chess Automation_. New York: Dover Publications, 1975.

Chess playing has been a recurring theme in automata and artificial intelligence for decades. This is useful for the period of the 1960s and 1970s but also for background in earlier years.

1935   Decade of Robotics. Special Tenth Anniversary Issue
        of The Industrial Robot. New York: Springer-Verlag,
        1983.

        This short book has some historical material, but
        especially for the post 1950 period. It also covers
        the work of Joseph Engelberger, head of Unimation,
        and considered nationally as the father of the modern
        industrial robot.

1936   Ernest, H.A. "A Computer-Controlled Mechanical Hand."
        (Unpublished Sc.D. Thesis, Massachusetts Institute
        of Technology, 1961).

        The author received the first U.S. patent for a
        computer-controlled robot (1961). Work on that
        project is reflected in his dissertation.

1937   Giedion, Siegfried. Mechanization Takes Command. New
        York: W.W. Norton, 1969.

        Part of the discussion is about the modern use of
        robotics in industry.

1938   Ginzburg, Abraham. Algebraic Theory of Automata. New
        York: Academic Press, 1968.

        By the 1960s robots were being developed using much
        the same methods and technologies found in computers.
        This is an example of that process typical of the
        period.

1939   Gisburg, Seymour. An Introduction to Mathematical
        Machine Theory. Reading, Mass.: Addison-Wesley
        Publishing Co., 1962.

        This is an early, technical piece on the modern
        automated machine. Many of the ideas expressed here
        influenced robotic developments in the 1960s.

1940   Hu, Sze-Tsen. Mathematical Switching Circuits and
        Automata. Berkeley: University of California Press,
        1968.

        Like the previous title, this one example of work
        done in which computing technology and robotics
        came together, borrowing from each other.

1941   Korein, J.U. and Ish-Shalom, J. "Robotics," IBM
        Systems Journal 26, No. 1 (1987): 55-95.

        This is an outstanding review of developments in
        robotics, especially during the 1980s; includes a
        detailed bibliography.

1942   Moore, Edward F. (ed). Sequential Machines. Reading,
        Mass.: Addison-Wesley Publishing Co., 1964.

        This is a technical treatise on components and design
        of robotic functions.

1943   Nelson, Raymond John. Introduction to Automata. New
       York: John Wiley & Sons, 1967.

       This is a technical introduction, circa 1960s, to
       subjects that applied to both computers and robotics.

1944   Neumann, John von and Burks, Arthur W. Theory of
       Self-reproducing Automata. Urbana: University of
       Illinois Press, 1966.

       This publishes material developed earlier of a highly
       theoretical nature by two very important pioneers in
       the development of the modern computer and its tech-
       nologies.

1945   Nof, Shimony (ed). Handbook of Industrial Robotics.
       New York: John Wiley & Sons, Inc., 1985.

       This is a detailed review of all aspects of the
       subject as known in the early 1980s. Its 77 chapters
       by 100 authors describe robots, their use, and offer
       case studies. It is an important piece for histor-
       ians of robots.

1946   Pontus-Hulten, K.G. The Machine As Seen At the End of
       the Mechanical Age. Greenwich, Conn.: New York
       Graphic Society, 1968.

       Many of the images are robotic and intelligent.

1947   Prasteau, Jean. Les Automates. Paris: Grund, 1968.

       This is a narrative survey of robots, their history,
       nature and use.

1948   Salomaa, Arto. On Probalistic Automata with One Input
       Letter. Turka, Finland, 1965.

       The author is a prolific writer on the mathematics
       of robotics. This was an early important work of
       his on the subject.

1949   Schuh, J.F. Principles of Automation: What A Robot
       Can and Cannot Do. Princeton, N.J.: Van Nostrand,
       1965.

       This was a widely distributed book for over twenty
       years and, at publication, was very realistic,
       providing a balanced account of the real possibili-
       ties and limits of contemporary robotics.

                              SAGE

1950   Astrahan, M.M. et al. "Logical Design of the Digital
       Computer for the SAGE System," IBM Journal of
       Research and Development 1 (1957): 76-83.

       This is a formal, well organized account on the SAGE.

1951   Astrahan, M.M. et al. "History of the Design of the
        SAGE Computer—The AN/FSQ-7," Annals of the History
        of Computing 5, No. 4 (October 1983): 340-349.

        This is an important, illustrated account of SAGE
        that also offers insight on how early computer systems
        were designed and built.

1952   Benington, Herbert D. "Production of Large Computer
        Programs," Annals of the History of Computing 5,
        No. 4 (October 1983): 350-361.

        This was drafted originally in 1956 and is a descrip-
        tion of programming the SAGE system.

1953   Everett, R.R. et al. "SAGE—A Data-Processing System for
        Air Defense," Proceedings of the Eastern Joint Comput-
        er Conference, Washington, D.C., 1957: 148-155; Reprin-
        ted in Annals of the History of Computing 5, No. 4
        (October 1983): 330-339; illustrated.

        This describes the SAGE system as understood in 1957.
        The authors all worked on the development of SAGE.

1954   Harrington, John V. "Radar Data Transmission," Annals
        of the History of Computing 5, No. 4 (October 1983):
        370-374.

        This is an illustrated account of the role of TP in
        SAGE and includes descriptions of the FST-1 and FST-2
        radar data compression system.

1955   International Business Machines Corporation. The Sage/
        Bomarc Air Defense Weapons Systems. Kingston, N.Y.:
        IBM Corporation, 1959.

        It discusses guided missiles, weapons and air defense
        applications of the 1950s.

1956   Jacobs, John F. "Sage Overview," Annals of the History
        of Computing 5, No. 4 (October 1983): 323-329.

        This is a brief, illustrated history of SAGE by one
        who helped to develop it.

1957   Tropp, Henry S. et al. "A Perspective on SAGE: Discuss-
        ion," Annals of the History of Computing 5, No. 4
        (October 1983): 375-398.

        Discussion was by builders of the SAGE system, held
        on October 26, 1982.

1958   Valley, George E., Jr. "How the SAGE Development
        Began," Annals of the History of Computing 7, No. 3
        (July 1985): 196-226.

        In this memoir the author discusses his role in the
        creation of the SAGE at MIT, a very personable account.

1959   Wieser, C. Robert. "The Cape Cod System," Annals of

the History of Computing 5, No. 4 (October 1983): 362-
369.

This is an illustrated description of the prototype
for SAGE, 1951-53.

SEAC

1960   Cuthill, E.   "Digital Computers in Nuclear Reactor
        Design," in F.L. Alt and M. Rubinoff (eds), Advances
        in Computers (New York: Academic Press, 1964) 5, pp.
        289-348.

        This contains a description of work done at the
        Atomic Energy Commission (AEC) using computers, from
        the early 1950s to the 1960s, with passing comments
        on the SEAC.

1961   Greenwald, S. et al. "SEAC," Proceedings, IRE 41 (1953):
        1300-1313.

        The authors describe the computer built by the U.S.
        National Bureau of Standards between 1948 and 1950.
        This includes a technical description of the system.

1962   Greenwald, S. et al. "SEAC." National Bureau of Standards
        Circular 551 (1955): 5-26.

        Essentially covers the same material is the previous
        publication.

1963   Huskey, H.D.   "SEAC," in A. Ralston and Meek, C.L.
        (eds), Encyclopedia of Computer Science (New York:
        Petrocelli/Charter, 1976): 1239.

        This describes the NBS computer, built in the late
        1940s, and includes a description of its features.

1964   "SEAC Takes Pictures; Standards Electronic Automatic
        Computer," Science News Letter 73 (March 8, 1958):
        151.

        This describes some work done on the SEAC late in its
        life.

1965   "Seeing-Eye Computer; Standards Electronic Automatic
        Computer," Time 71 (March 17, 1958): 61.

        This covers the same material as the previous cita-
        tion and comes after publicity by NBS on the SEAC.

1966   Shupe, P.D., Jr. and Kirsch, R.A.   "SEAC—Review of
        Three Years of Operation," Proceedings of the Eastern
        Joint Computer Conference (1953): 83-90.

        This is a highly technical analysis of the SEAC but
        useful in determining the quality of performance of
        early digital systems.

1967   Slutz, Ralph J. et al. "High-Speed Memory Development

at the National Bureau of Standards," NBS Circular
551 (1955).

He describes the memory that was put on the SEAC, SWAC
and DYSEAC computers in the late 1940s and very early
1950s.

1968   Slutz, Ralph J. "Memories of the Bureau of Standard's
        SEAC," in N. Metropolis et al. (eds), A History of
        Computing in the Twentieth Century (New York: Acade-
        mic Press, 1980): 471-477.

        These are memoir comments by one of the developers
        but they are of limited value for the historian.

1969   U.S. Government, National Bureau of Standards. Computer
        Development (SEAC and DYSEAC) at the National Bureau
        of Standards. NBS Circular 551. Washington, D.C.: U.S.
        Government Printing Office, 1955.

        This volume discusses the technical features of
        computers installed with the help of NBS and include
        the SEAC, SWAC and DYSEAC. It was written by the
        builders of these machines.

1970   Wright, H. et al. "Operational Experience with SEAC,"
        National Bureau of Standards Circular 551 (1955): 119-
        136.

        This article shows that the use of diodes and resis-
        tors as logic elements, coupled with an effective
        maintenance program, made this a very reliable compu-
        ter when compared to earlier machines.

Semiconductors and Chips

1971   Agusta, B. et al. "A 16-Bit Monolithic Memory Analog
        Chip," Journal of Applied Physics 37 (1966): 574-
        579.

        This technical paper described the first monolithic
        integrated circuit to come from IBM, circa mid-1960s.

1972   Augarten, Stan. State of the Art: A Photographic His-
        tory of the Integrated Circuit. Introduction by Ray
        Bradloury. New Haven: Ticknor & Fields, 1983.

        This is a photographic history, beginning with point
        contact transistors from Bell Labs (1947 forward) to
        gallium arsenide chips and Josephson junctions.

1973   Bardeen, John, Brattain, Walter, and Shockley, William.
        Nobel Lectures—Physics, 1942-62. New York: Elsevier,
        1964.

        These three Nobel laureates discuss how they develop-
        ed the transistor and worked on other semiconductors.

1974   Bell, C.G. and Newell, A. Computer Structures: Readings and Examples. New York: McGraw-Hill Book Co., 1971.

Although intended for students of computer science,
it is an excellent reflection of existing technologies of the late 1960s. Issues are discussed by two
very important computer scientists.

1975   Bilous, O. et al. "Design of Monolithic Circuit Chips,"
        IBM Journal of Research and Development 10 (1966):
        370-376.

        The technology discussed in this article appeared in
        IBM's computers in the late 1960s.

1976   Bloch, E. and Galage, D. "Component Progress: Its
        Effect on High-Speed Computer Architecture and Machine
        Organization," Computer 11 (1978): 64-76.

        They argued that chip densities for large computers,
        would have over 1 million circuits by the year 2000.

1977   Bloch, E. and Henle, R.A. "Advances in Circuit Tech-
        nology and Their Impact on Computing Systems,"
        Proceedings of the International Federation of Infor-
        mation Processing Systems Congress (1968): 2: 613-
        628.

        This technical piece is based on research done at
        IBM on semiconductor technology in the mid-1960s.

1978   Bradley, W.E. et al. "Surface Barrier Transistor Com-
        puter Circuits," IRE Convention Record, Part 4,
        Computer Information Theory and Automatic Control
        (1955): 139-145.

        This describes direct-coupled transistor logic
        circuits, the first to use switching properties of
        transistors instead of vacuum tubes in the 1950s.

1979   Branin, F.H., Jr. "Computer Methods of Network Ana-
        lysis," Proceedings, IEEE 55 (1967): 1787-1801.

        This is a description of a tool to help speed up the
        design of bipolar transistors in switching circuits
        for computer chips.

1980   Bylinsky, Gene. The Innovation Millionaires. New York:
        Charles Scribner's, 1976.

        This has a chapter on the work of John Noyce and
        Gordon Moore in their development of semiconductor
        chips.

1981   Davis, E.M. et al. "Solid Logic Technology: Versatile,
        High-Performance Microelectronics," IBM Journal of
        of Research and Development 8 (1964): 102-114.

        They describe SLT in semi-conductors of the early
        1960s as developed at IBM.

1982   Dettmer, Roger. "(G.W.A. Dummer): Prophet of the
        Integrated Circuit," Electronics and Power 30
        (1984): 279-281.

        Very little material has appeared on Dummer's work;
        the article is a useful overview.

1983   Dummer, G.W.A. Electronic Inventions and Discoveries.
        New York: Pergamon Press, 1983.

        In this third edition Dummer includes a discussion
        about transistors, chips and computers in an histori-
        cal context.

1984   Fox, P.E. and Nestork, W.J. "Design of Logic Circuit
        Technology for IBM System/370 Models 145 and 155,"
        IBM Journal of Research and Development 15 (1971):
        384-390.

        This article describes the monolithic systems tech-
        nology (MST) that so improved the price/performance
        of S/370 computers of the 1970s.

1985   Gupta, Amar and Toong, Hoo-min (eds). Advanced Micro-
        processors. New York: IEEE Press, 1983.

        This is a collection of 41 papers published between
        1971 and 1983 on microprocessors. The earliest deals
        with the Intel 4004 (a computer on a chip) and con-
        tinues through four generations of components.

1986   Hellerman, L. and Racite, M.P. "Reliability Techniques
        for Electronic Circuit Design," IRE Transactions,
        Reliability, Quality Control, RQC-14 (1958): 9.

        This briefly describes the statistical design of
        diode-transistor circuits to reduce cost by better
        performance tolerances. The work was done in the late
        1950s.

1987   Henle, R.A. and Hill, L.O. "Integrated Computer Cir-
        cuits—Past, Present, and Future," Proceedings of the
        Institute of Electrical and Electronic Engineers 54
        (December 1966): 1852-1853.

        This is an early review of ICs, originally designed
        for the Stretch computer of the late 1950s and early
        1960s at IBM.

1988   IBM Journal of Research and Development 24, No. 2 (1980).

        This is an extra issue and was devoted entirely to
        the discussion of Josephson computer technology which,
        in the late 1970s, was once again seen as a new wave
        of semiconductor technology. By the late 1980s it
        was seen to be more of a 21st century opportunity.

1989   Jones, M.E. et al. "Semiconductors: The Key to Computa-
        tional Plenty," Proceedings of the IEEE 70 (1982):

1380-1409.

This is a history of semiconductors. The authors all
did developmental work in the field, covering the
1950s through the 1970s.

1990   Leach, T.J. "Automated Assembly of Alloy-Junction
        Transistors," Electronics 33 (1960): 57.

        This describes IBM's mechanized manufacturing of
        germanium disk sub-assemblies of the late 1950s and
        early 1960s.

1991   Malvino, Albert Paul. Digital Computer Electronics,
        An Introduction to Microprocessors. New York: McGraw-
        Hill, 1983.

        This is not only a good snapshot of the technology
        of microprocessors of the early 1980s, but also is
        an important technical description of computers.

1992   Mead, Carver and Conway, Lynn. Introduction to VLSI
        Systems. Reading, Mass.: Addison-Wesley, 1980.

        This good text reflects computer hardware technology
        of the late 1960s, particularly for mini-computers.

1993   Miller, B. "Microcircuitry Production Growth Outpaces
        Applications," Aviation Week 81 (November 16, 1964):
        76-77ff.

        That problem appeared cotinuously in the 1960s and
        beyond at regular intervals. The process, and its
        effects, are first identified in this article.

1994   Millman, Jacob. Micro-electronics, Digital and Analog
        Circuits and Systems. New York: McGraw-Hill, 1979.

        This was the Bible on chips for many years. It also
        discusses the evolution of chip technology and pro-
        duction methods. It is a highly technical treatise,
        however.

1995   Morse, Stephen P. et al. "INTEL Microprocessors—8008
        to 8086," Computer 13, No. 10 (October 1980): 42-60.

        This is on the history of the Intel processors during
        the decades of the 1960s and 1970s.

1996   National Geographic Society. Those Inventive Americans.
        Washington, D.C.: National Geographic Society, 1971.

        This is a popularized account of the development of
        the transistor and includes biographies of the key
        inventors.

1997   Nelson, R.R. "The Link Between Science and Invention:
        The Case of the Transistor," in The Role and Direction
        of Inventive Activity—Economic and Social Factors

Princeton, N.J.: Princeton University Press for U.S.
Bureau of Economic Research, 1962, pp. 549-583.

The author describes how development problems were
solved, making this technology practical to use.

1998   Noyce, Robert N. "Hardware Prospects and Limitations,"
        in Michael Dertouzos and Joel Moses (eds), The
        Computer Age: A Twenty-Year View (Cambridge, Mass.:
        MIT Press, 1979): 321-337.

        The chairman of the board of Intel Corporation, and
        a major developer of the semiconductor IC, surveys
        the growth in capacity and cost changes since the
        1950s.

1999   Noyce, Robert N. and Hoff, Marcian E., Jr. "A History
        of Microprocessor Development at Intel," IEEE Micro
        1 (February 1981): 8-21.

        This covers the period 1969-1970s and also discusses
        the origins of the company and its activities.

2000   Queisser, Hans. The Conquest of the Microchip. Cambrid-
        ge, Mass.: Harvard University Press, 1988.

        The author was part of Shockley's team in the 1950s
        and helped in the development of the chip. This is
        a useful survey from 1900 to the 1980s and offers
        a great deal of material on European developments
        not available in other publications.

2001   Reid, T.R. The Chip: How Two Americans Invented the
        Microchip and Launched a Revolution. New York: Simon
        and Schuster, 1984.

        This is a non-technical, popular history of the work
        of Jack Kilby and Robert Noyce.

2002   Roberts, D.H. "Silicon Integrated Circuits: A Personal
        View of the First 25 Years," Electronics and Power
        30 (1984): 282-284.

        This is a short memoir covering the period from the
        late 1950s.

2003   Schofman, J. "The Dutch Contribution to Barrier-Layer
        Semiconductors in the Pre-Germanium Era," Janus 69
        (1982): 1-28.

        This is a rare piece on European developments in the
        1950s and 1960s.

2004   Scientific American. Microelectronics. New York: W.H.
        Freeman, 1977.

        This is a review of the nature of chips and includes
        an article by Robert Noyce.

2005   Sedore, S.R. "SCEPTRE: A Program for Automatic Network

Analysis," IBM Journal of Research and Development 11 (1967): 627-637.

The piece of software described here is of the mid-1960s and was used to shorten the development cycle for bipolar transistors in switching circuits. The use of software was a standard feature of semiconductor manufacturing throughout the 1960s and after.

2006   Shockley, William. Electrons and Holes in Semiconductors, With Applications to Transistor Electronics. New York: Van Nostrand, 1950.

This was the first book to appear on chip technology and was written by one of the inventors/developers of this technology. It is a semenal work in data processing.

2007   Stern, L. "Science of Vanishing Electronics; Integrated Circuits," Science Digest 55 (June 1964): 44-47.

This reports on the status of ICs as of 1964 with recent developments in a new generation in this technology.

2008   Streetman, B. Solid State Electronic Devices. Englewood Cliffs, N.J.: Prentice-Hall, Inc., 1980.

Although a technical publication, it offers an excellent survey of semiconductors and solid-state physics of the 1970s. Thus it is useful for seeing the progression of significant developments that began in the early 1960s with new generations, for example, of ICs.

2009   Trigg, George L. Landmark Experiments in 20th-Century Physics. New York: Crane, Russak, 1975.

This includes a discussion of the invention of the transistor of the late 1940s and about its use in the 1950s.

2010   Wallmark, V.T. "Is There a Minimum Size in Integrated Circuits?," Physics Technology 10 (1979): 62-67.

The author expressed the opinion that by the year 2000 circuits per chips could exceed one million. It is a useful article for measuring expectations in the 1970s for this technology.

2011   Weeks, W.T. et al. "Algorithms for ASTAP—A Network-Analysis Program," IEEE Transactions, Circuit Theory, CT-20 (1973): 628-634.

ASTAP was the best software tool available in the early to mid-1970s for use in designing bipolar transistors. It defined the characteristics of these components. The original notion of having such software tools first came up in the 1960s.

2012   Yourke, H.S. "Millimicrosecond Transfer Current Switch-
        ing Circuits," IRE Transactions, Circuit Theory CT-4
        (1957): 236.

        The author describes circuit improvements in computers
        of the late 1950s, all pre-ASLT, however.

Storage Equipment

2013   Bloch, E. "The Engineering Design of the Stretch
        Computer," Proceedings, Eastern Joint Computer Con-
        ference (Boston, 1959): 48-58.

        This paper describes the logic technology of IBM's
        Stretch computer of the late 1950s, using new techno-
        logy for circuit components and cards. Comments on
        storage are included.

2014   Brillouin, Leon N. "Electromagnetic Delay Lines,"
        Proceedings of a Symposium on Large-Scale Digital
        Calculating Machinery (Cambridge, Mass.: Harvard
        University Press, 1948): 110-124.

        This describes the technology of very early memories
        and, hence, storage for digital computers of the
        1940s.

2015   Codd, E.F. et al. "Multiprogramming STRETCH: Feasibili-
        ty Considerations," Communications, ACM 2, No. 11
        (November 1959): 13-17.

        The size of memory and quantity of storage were
        always considerations in early machines. This article
        describes a leading-edge technological development
        of the late 1950s.

2016   Committee on New Recording Means and Computing Devices,
        Society of Actuaries. Current Status of Magnetic
        Tapes As a Recording and Data Processing Medium.
        Chicago: Society of Actuaries, 1955.

        A great deal of controversy existed in the early to
        mid-1950s about whether it was better for data to be
        on tape or on some other magnetic or paper medium.
        This concludes that it was better and cheaper to keep
        data on tape as opposed to punch cards.

2017   Forrester, Jay W. "High-Speed Electrostatic Storage,"
        Proceedings of a Symposium on Large-Scale Digital
        Calculating Machinery (Cambridge, Mass.: Harvard
        University Press, 1948): 125-129.

        Forrester, father of Whirlwind and already at MIT,
        reports on early work done with the new computer's
        memory.

2018   Haeff, Andrew V. "The Memory Tube and Its Application
        to Electronic Computation," Mathematical Tables and
        Other Aids to Computation 3, No. 24 (October 1948):
        281-286.

Considerable amounts of research was being done in
the late 1940s on computer memories. This article
reports on some of that work during a period when
basic technological options were just beginning to
be explored.

2019   Henle, R.A.   "High-Speed Transistor Computer Circuit
        Design," <u>Proceedings of the Eastern Joint Computer
        Conference</u> (1956): 64-66.

        Henle reviews briefly transistorized storage being
        developed at IBM for Stretch in the mid-1950s.

2020   King, G.W.   "Information; Its Storage and Handling in
        Automatic Control Systems," <u>Scientific American</u> 187
        (September 1952): 132-142ff.

        It is a useful survey of the situation as of the
        early 1950s.

2021   Kornei, Otto. "Survey of Magnetic Recording,"
        <u>Proceedings of a Symposium on Large-Scale Digital
        Calculating Machinery</u> (Cambridge, Mass.: Harvard
        University Press, 1948): 223-237.

        He reviews various off-line data storage devices and
        their associated technologies, circa 1947-48.

2022   Lesser, M.L. and Haanstra, J.W.   "The Random-Access
        Memory Accounting Machine—I. System Organization of
        the IBM 305," <u>IBM Journal of Research and Develop-
        ment</u> 1 (1957): 62-71.

        This is a first description of the IBM 305 RAMAC
        system. It is a detailed description of the first
        movable head disk drives commercially available. The
        introduction of the IBM 305 and 650 was a major
        technological event in the DP industry.

2023   Moore, Benjamin L.   "Magnetic and Phosphor Coated
        Discs," <u>Proceedings of a Symposium on Large-Scale
        Digital Calculating Machinery</u> (Cambridge, Mass.:
        Harvard University Press, 1948): 130-132.

        This line of research became important during the
        1950s. This was an early paper on the subject.

2024   Mulvany, R.B. and Thompson, L.H.   "Innovations in Disk
        File Manufacturing," <u>IBM Journal of Research and
        Development</u> 25, No. 5 (September 1981): 711-723.

        Very little has been written on the history of
        computer products' manufacturing. This surveys the
        subject of IBM equipment, beginning with the 350
        (1957) and goes to the 3370 of the early 1980s.

2025   Noyes, T. and Dickinson, W.E.   "The Random-Access
        Memory Accounting Machine—II. The Magnetic-Disk
        Random-Access Memory," <u>IBM Journal of Research and
        Development</u> 1 (1957): 72-75.

This is a formal description of the IBM 350 disk file,
the first production model of a movable-head disk
drive.

2026   Peterson, W.W.   "Addressing for Random Access Storage,"
         IBM Journal of Research and Development 1 (1957): 130-
         146.

         The author describes the first generalized indexing
         systems available for disk technology that made it
         possible to use disk drives as random access memory
         in the 1950s.

2027   Rajchman, Jan A.   "The Selectron—A Tube for Selective
         Electrostatic Storage," Mathematical Tables and Other
         Aids to Computation 2, No. 20 (October 1947): 359-361
         and frontpiece.

         Today the author is recognized as one of the pioneers
         in developing computer memory technology while at
         RCA. This surveys his early work in the field.

2028   Sharpless, T. Kite.   "Mercury Delay Lines as a Memory
         Unit," Proceedings of a Symposium on Large-Scale Digi-
         tal Calculating Machinery (Cambridge, Mass.: Harvard
         University Press, 1948): 103-109.

         Sharpless was one of the senior engineers on the ENIAC
         project at the Moore School of Electrical Engineering.
         She and others continued R&D there into the late
         1940s, some of which is reviewed in this article.

2029   Sheppard, C. Bradford.   "Transfer Between External and
         Internal Memory," Proceedings of a Symposium on Large-
         Scale Digital Calculating Machinery (Cambridge, Mass.:
         Harvard University Press, 1948): 267-273.

         The author was an engineer on the EDVAC in the 1940s
         and thus was on the leading edge of much computer
         development when he wrote the article. The material
         reviews work done on the EDVAC.

2030   Walsh, J.L.   "IBM Current Mode Transistor Logical Cir-
         cuits," Proceedings of the Western Joint Computer
         Conference, Los Angeles, California (1958): 34-36.

         Walsh briefly discusses transistors made at IBM for
         use in Stretch and which would be used in IBM's
         computers of the late 1950s (7090 and 7094).

2031   Welsh, H.F. and Lukoff, H.   "The Uniservo-Tape Reader
         and Recorder," Proceedings of the Joint AIEE-IRE-ACM
         Computer Conference, New York, December 10-12, 1952,
         pp. 47-53.

         They describe the early use of metal tape for digital
         magnetic recording.

2032   Williams, F.C.   "Cathode Ray Storage," in M.V. Wilkes
        (ed), <u>Report On A Conference On High Speed Automatic
        Computing Machines, July 22-25, 1949</u> (Cambridge, Mass.:
        The University Mathematical Laboratory): <u>passim</u>.

        The Williams Tube was a widely used form of memory
        in the period of the late 1940s and early 1950s.
        This historically important article describes the
        device.

2033   Wolf, M.E.   "The R&D Bootleggers: Inventing Against
        The Odds," <u>IEEE Spectrum</u> 12 (1975): 38-45.

        The author describes the effort it took within IBM
        to get direct access products designed, built, and
        introduced in the late 1950s.

2034   Yourke, H.S.   "Millimicrosecond Transistor Current
        Switching Circuits," <u>IRE Transactions, Circuit Theory</u>
        CT-4 (1957): 236-240.

        The switch was made originally for the IBM Stretch
        computer but was later also used in the IBM 7090 and
        7094 processors.

Christopher Strachey

2035   Alton, J. <u>et al</u>. <u>Catalogue of the Papers of Christo-
        pher Strachey (1916-1975)</u>. Oxford: Contemporary
        Scientific Archives Centre, 1980.

        This 200-page book describes his extensive collection
        of papers housed at the Bodleian Library.

2036   Barron, D.W.   "Christopher Strachey: A Personal Reminis-
        cence," <u>Computer Bulletin</u>, Ser.2 (1975): 5, 8-9.

        This is on the work of the British computer scientist
        with programming languages.

2037   Campbell-Kelly, Martin.   "Christopher Strachey, 1916-
        1975: A Biographical Note," <u>Annals of the History of
        Computing</u> 7, No. 1 (January 1985): 19-42.

        This is an illustrated biography of the man who work-
        ed on logic designs for computers and programming
        languages in the period 1950s-1970s, and especially
        on denotational semantics.

2038   Clarke, S.H.L.   "The Elliott 400 Series and Before,"
        <u>Radio and Electronic Engineer</u> 45, No. 8 (1975): 415-
        421.

        The Elliott 400 was a British computer of the 1950s
        and early 1960s with which Strachey was associated.

2039   Scott, D.S.   "An Appreciation of Christopher Strachey
        and His Work," in J.E. Stoy (ed), <u>Denotational
        Semantics: The Scott-Strachey Approach to Programming</u>

Language Theory (Cambridge, Mass.: MIT Press, 1977):
xiv-xxx.

Although often remembered for his work in programming
languages, Strachey was active in other aspects of
computer science, including the logic design of
computer hardware in Great Britain.

2040   Strachey, Christopher. "Systems Analysis and Programm-
        ing," Scientific American 25, No. 3 (1966): 112-124."

He was already a highly regarded computer scientist
before he wrote this article in which we see a good
expression of his views.

2041   Strachey, Christopher and Milne, R.E. A Theory of
        Programming Language Semantics. London: Chapman and
        Hall, 1976.

This was published after Strachey's death, yet is a
good summation of his work.

2042   Strachey, Christopher and Wilkes, M.V. "Some Proposals
        for Improving the Efficiency of Algol 60," Communica-
        tions, ACM 4, No. 11 (1961): 488-491.

Two important British scientists, both with programming and hardware achievements to their credit,
comment on a European-based programming language.

SWAC

2043   Blanch, Gertrude and Rhodes, Ida. "Table-Making at the
        National Bureau of Standards," In B.K.P. Scaife (ed),
        Studies in Numerical Analysis, Papers in Honor of
        Cornelius Lanczos (New York: Academic Press, 1974):
        1-6.

The article is useful in understanding the work of
the NBS after World War II when it began to acquire
and build computers, like SWAC and SEAC.

2044   Huskey, Harry D. "The National Bureau of Standards
        Western Automatic Computer (SWAC)," Annals of the
        History of Computing 2, No. 2 (April 1980): 111-121.

Huskey surveys the pre-1949 role of NBS, adds material on its work with UCLA on SWAC (1948-49). He
was involved and offers an illustrated history based
on primary material and includes bibliography.

2045   Huskey, Harry D. "SWAC," in A. Ralston and Meek, C.L.
        (eds), Encyclopedia of Computer Science (New York:
        Petrocelli/Charter, 1976): 1382-1383.

This is a shorter version of the previous citation
but with greater focus on the actual machine.

2046   Huskey, Harry D. "The SWAC: The National Bureau of

Standards Western Automatic Computer," In N. Metropolis et al. (eds), A History of Computing in the Twentieth Century (New York: Academic Press, 1980): 419-
431.

He covers work done in the period 1948-1954 with an
illustrated account. It is particularly useful for
a technical description of the system.

2047   Huskey, Harry D. et al. "The SWAC—Design Features and
        Operating Experience," Proceedings, IRE 41, No. 10
        (1953): 1294-1299.

        Unlike his other publications, this was contempora-
        neous with the project between NBS and UCLA.

2048   Lowan, A.N. "The Computation Laboratory of the National
        Bureau of Standards," Scripta Mathematica 15 (1949):
        33-63.

        The author describes the agency established by the
        NBS and was the brain child of John H. Curtiss. It
        was an early and important user of computers and
        advised various U.S. Government agencies on the topic.

2049   "Mark of Progress," Time (September 4, 1950): 56.

        This is a brief announcement of and description of
        SWAC.

2050   "Talking ZEPHYR," Newsweek (June 13, 1949): 52.

        Refers to the SWAC project with UCLA.

2051   U.S. National Bureau of Standards. "National Bureau of
        Standards Western Automatic Computer—Recent Develop-
        ments and Operating Experience," NBS Technical News
        Bulletin 37, No. 10 (October 1953): 145-150.

        This is a technical piece that suggests what the
        levels of reliability and ease of use were for SWAC
        and, for that matter, of other machines of the early
        1950s.

                            UNIVAC

2052   Allen, W. and Smith. G.E. "Univac and Univac Scienti-
        fic," Instruments and Automation 28 (June 1955): 960-
        969.

        This is a technical description of the first two
        Univac computers. They were the machines that receiv-
        ed so much public attention in the early 1950s in the
        U.S.A.

2053   Eckert, J. Presper, Jr., Mauchly, John W. and Weiner,
        J.R. "An Octal System Automatic Computer," Electrical
        Engineering 68, No. 4 (April 1949): 335.

Eckert and Mauchly were the creators of the modern
electronic digital computer and the Univac in particular. They wrote this piece while designing the
UNIVAC I.

2054   Eckert-Mauchly Computer Corporation. The Univac System.
        Philadelphia: Eckert-Mauchly Computer Corporation,
        1948.

        This is an early description of the features of the
        Univac then under construction and about the BINAC
        too.

2055   Erxleben, A. "From Surplus A Bargain Computer; Univac,"
        Popular Mechanics 18 (June 1963): 42-44.

        This was written at the end of the life of the early
        Univac machines as they were being retired.

2056   Heiser, Donald H. "Management Experience in the Census
        Bureau," in Lowell H. Hatterly and George P. Bush
        (eds), Electronics in Management (Washington, D.C.:
        The University Press of Washington, D.C., 1956): 139-
        156.

        He shares the experience had by the U.S. Bureau of
        the Census in managing the UNIVAC I installation from
        1951 to 1956.

2057   Hopper, Grace Murray. "The Education of a Computer,"
        Annals of the History of Computing 9, Nos. 3-4 (1988):
        271-281.

        Originally published in 1952, this article reflects
        her thinking about computer design while she was
        involved with developing software for the UNIVAC
        series in the early 1950s.

2058   Kopp, Robert. "Experience on the Air Force UNIVAC,"
        Proceedings Eastern Computer Conference, Joint I.R.E.-
        A.I.E.E.-A.C.M., December 8-10, 1953 (Washington,
        D.C., 1954): 62-66.

        Kopp reviews the creation of and experience with
        a maintenance staff responsible for a UNIVAC I. It
        is very useful for understanding how reliable this
        machine was.

2059   Lukoff, Herman. From Dits to Bits: A Personal History
        of The Electronic Computer. Forest Grove, Oregon:
        Robotics Press, 1979.

        His memoirs go from before ENIAC through Sperry Univac.
        It contains material on his student days at the Moore
        School and about EDVAC, BINAC, UNIVAC I and LARC.

2060   Maynard, M.M. "UNIVAC I," in A. Ralston and Meek, C.L.
        (eds), Encyclopedia of Computer Science (New York:
        Petrocelli/Charter, 1976): 1440-1441.

This describes the UNIVAC I and tells its history very briefly.

2061   Snyder, Frances E. and Livingston, Hubert M. "Coding
        of a Laplace Boundary Value Problem for the UNIVAC,"
        Mathematical Tables and Other Aids to Computation 3,
        No. 25 (January 1949): 341-350.

        This is a technical paper by an end user of the mach-
        ine and written early in its history. The authors
        worked with the BINAC.

University of Manchester Mark Series

2062   "A Calculating Machine With a Memory," Illustrated
        London News (June 25, 1949): 831-833.

        It includes photographs of the Manchester computer
        with some brief comments on the Mark I.

2063   Buckingham, R.A. "Atlas," A. Ralston and Meek, C.L.
        (eds), Encyclopedia of Computer Science (New York:
        Petrocelli/Charter, 1976): 137-139.

        The Atlas was the third computer built at the Univer-
        sity of Manchester (1960s).

2064   Campbell-Kelly, Martin. "Programming the MARK I: Early
        Programming Activity at the University of Manchester,"
        Annals of the History of Computing 2, No. 2 (1980):
        130-168.

        This is an illustrated account covering the period
        1946 to 1954 and is a very complete paper on the
        topic.

2065   Drath, P. "The Relationship Between Science and
        Technology: University Research and the Computer
        Industry, 1945-1962." (Unpublished Ph.D. disserta-
        tion, Victoria University of Manchester, 1973).

        The author describes computers built by Ferranti and
        this university's electrical engineering department
        between 1945 and 1962. He includes a background
        chapter on British computing during World War II.

2066   Halsbury, Earl of. "Ten Years of Computer Develop-
        ment," Computer Journal 1, No. 4 (1959): 153-159.

        This is primarily on British computer developments
        and particularly, at Manchester and at Cambridge. It
        also comments on World War II and Colossus.

2067   Kilburn, T. A Storage System for Use With Binary
        Digital Computing Machines. Manchester: University
        of Manchester, 1947; Reprinted, 1978.

        It describes work done just after World War II.

2068   Kilburn, T.   "The University of Manchester Universal
        High-Speed Digital Computing Machine," Nature
        (London) 164 (October 22, 1949): 684-687.

        This was one of the first articles to appear in Great
        Britain on a British digital computer.

2069   Kilburn, T. et al. "A Transistor Digital Computer With
        A Magnetic-Drum Store," Proceedings of the IEE 103B,
        Supp. 1-3 (1956): 390-406.

        They discuss work done at Manchester on two transistor
        computers (1953-55).

2070   Kilburn, T. and Piggot, L.S.   "Frederick Calland Will-
        iams, 1911-1977," Biographical Memoirs of Fellows of
        the Royal Society 24 (1978): 583-604.

        This is an obituary/biography of a scientist involved
        in early computing at the University of Manchester in
        the 1940s and 1950s.

2071   Lavington, Simon H.   "Computer Development at Manchester
        University," in N. Metropolis et al. (eds), A History
        of Computing in the Twentieth Century (New York: Acade-
        mic Press, 1980): 433-443.

        This is an illustrated account covering the period
        1949-1959 and adds much to our understand of the roles
        played by Tom Kilburn and Frederick C. Williams with
        the Mark I.

2072   Lavington, Simon H. Early British Computers. Maynard,
        Mass.: Digital Press, 1980.

        This short book is an essential source on the subject
        covering the period 1930-1955 with discussions about
        Colossus, EDSAC, Pilot ACE, Mark I, Leo and other
        machines.

2073   Lavington, Simon H.   "The Early Days of British Comput-
        ers," Electronics and Power (November-December 1978):
        827-832; (January 1979): 40-45.

        This is an illustrated history for the period 1945-
        1955 and covers the same material as his other
        publications.

2074   Lavington, Simon H.   "A Golden Era Rich in Talent,"
        Computing (August 11, 1977): 19.

        He argues that such a period existed in British comput-
        ing between 1945 and 1951.

2075   Lavington, Simon H.   A History of Manchester Computers.
        Manchester: N.C.C. Publications, 1975.

        This 44-page booklet summarizes the five computer
        projects at Manchester between 1946 and 1975. It

relies heavily on primary material and focuses on
the roles played by Williams, Kilburn, M.H.A. Newman,
A. Turing and others and is well illustrated.

2076   Lavington, Simon H.   "The Manchester Mark I and Atlas:
        A Historical Perspective," Communications, ACM 21, No.
        1 (1978): 4-12.

        He discusses the historical significance of these
        machines for British computing (1940s-1950s).

2077   Pollard, B.W.   "The Design, Construction, and Perfor-
        mance of a Large-Scale General-Purpose Digital Compu-
        ter," Report on AIEE-IRE Computer Conference (Feb-
        ruary 1952): 62-70.

        The author focuses on the University of Manchester
        digital computer of the late 1940s and work done in
        the early 1950s.

2078   Robinson, A.A.   "Multiplication in the Manchester Univer-
        sity High-Speed Digital Computer," Electronic Engineer-
        ing 25 (January 1953): 6-10.

        Robinson was an early user of British digital machines
        and thus his comments are useful for appreciating
        their effectiveness, particularly for the period of
        the late 1940s and early 1950s.

2079   Williams, Frederick C.   "Early Computers at Manchester
        University," The Radio and Electronic Engineer 45,
        No. 7 (1975): 327-331.

        The author was a major force behind the development
        of much early technology, including the Williams Tube
        and MADAM machine. These are his memoirs of the late
        1940s and early 1950s.

2080   Williams, Frederick C. and Kilburn, Tom.   "Electronic
        Digital Computers," Nature 162 (September 1948): 487;
        Reprinted in Brian Randell (ed), The Origins of Digital
        Computers: Selected Papers (New York: Springer Verlag,
        1982):415-416.

        They describe the machine at the Royal Society
        Computing Machine Laboratory.

2081   Williams, Frederick C. and Kilburn, Tom.   "The University
        of Manchester Computer Machine," Joint AIEE-IRE Comput-
        er Conference, December 10-12, 1952 (Philadelphia,
        1952): passim.

        They discuss MADAM and its features. The paper was
        also published in Review of Electronic Digital Comput-
        ers (February 1952): 57-61.

                            John von Neumann

2082   Aspray, William.   "The Mathematical Reception of the

Modern Computer: John von Neumann and the Institute
for Advanced Study Computer," in Esther R. Phillips
(ed), <u>Studies in the History of Mathematics</u> 26 of
Studies in Mathematics (Washington, D.C.: Mathematical Association of America, 1987): 166-194.

Aspray, at the time of this writing, was involved in
researching the life and work of von Neumann for a
full-length biography. Work on the IAS machine was a
critical phase and the article an important overview of the subject.

2083   Birkhoff, G. <u>et al</u>. Memorial papers on John von
Neumann, <u>Bulletin of the American Mathematical Socie-
ty</u> 64, No. 3, Pt.2 (1958).

The entire issue was devoted to von Neumann and was
published as a result of his death.

2084   Blair, C. ¼Passing of a Great Mind," <u>Life</u> (February
25, 1957): 89, 90, 93, 94, 96, 101, 102, 104.

This is a detailed obituary of von Neumann.

2085   Bochner, S. "John von Neumann," <u>National Academy of
Sciences Biographical Memoirs</u> 32 (1957): 438-457.

This is an obituary/biography and an analysis of his
work.

2086   Burks, A.W., Goldstine, H.H. and Neumann, John von.
<u>Preliminary Discussion of the Logical Design of an
Electronic Computing Instrument Part 1, Vol. 1</u>.
Princeton, N.J.: Institute for Advanced Study, 28
June, 1946, 2nd ed. 2 September, 1947; Reprinted in
A.H. Taub (ed), <u>John von Neumann: Collected Works</u>
(Oxford: Pergamon, 1963), 5, pp. 34-79.

This is one of the best known documents to be published on computers. It details the architecture of a
computer, as essentially adopted by the computer
industry at large for the next forty years. It was
the basis for the design of a parallel binary device
called the IAS Computer.

2087   Goldstine, Herman H. and Wigner, E.P. "Scientific
Work of J. von Neumann," <u>Science</u> 125 (1957): 683-684.

This is a biography and analysis of his work by two
very enthusiastic admirers.

2088   Goldstine, Herman H. and Neumann, John von. "On the
Principles of Large Scale Computing Machines," in
A.H. Taub (ed), <u>John von Neumann: Collected Works</u>
(Oxford: Pergamon Press, 1963), 5, pp. 1-32.

This is an excellent source on von Neumann's views
on computer design as of 1946, particularly on the
concept of the stored program.

2089   Halmos, P.R.   "The Legend of John von Neumann," Ameri-
        can Mathematical Monthly 80 (1973): 382-394.

        In addition to being an important participant in the
        development of the modern computer, von Neumann was
        a very important mathematician of this century. This
        is a useful biography on him.

2090   Heims, Steve J.   John von Neumann and Norbert Wiener:
        From Mathematics to the Technologies of Life and
        Death. Cambridge, Mass.: MIT Press, 1980.

        The author focus on the issues of confronting respon-
        sibility by scientists and thus is not a biography.
        He is concerned with the arms race and atomic bombs.
        There is almost nothing here on computers; however,
        some biographical data is included.

2091   Huskey, H.D.   Review of H.H. Goldstine's The Computer
        From Pascal to von Neumann, Science 180 (May 11,
        1973): 580-590.

        He reviews the heated argument over who developed
        the concept of the stored program while analyzing
        the book.

2092   Knuth, D.E.   "Von Neumann's First Computer Program,"
        Computer Surveys 2, No. 4 (1970): 247-260.

        This is a review of a sort program von Neumann wrote
        in 1945 for use in what eventually became the EDVAC.
        The article comments on both ENIAC and EDVAC as well.

2093   Stern, Nancy.   "John von Neumann's Influence on Elec-
        tronic Digital Computing, 1944-1946," Annals of the
        History of Computing 2, No. 4 (October 1980): 349-362.

        Stern documents his role with ENIAC and EDVAC.

2094   Taub, A.H. (ed). John von Neumann: Collected Works,
        1903-1957. 6 vols. Oxford: Pergamon Press, 1961-63.

        This is the most complete collection of his papers
        to be published and they include considerable amounts
        of material on computers, particularly volume 5.

2095   Todd, J.   "John von Neumann and the National Accounting
        Machine," SIAM Review 16, No. 4 (1974): 526-530.

        This discusses mathematical work done by von Nuemann
        using a calculating machine.

2096   Tropp, H.S.   "John von Neumann," in A. Ralston and
        Meek, C.L. (eds), Encyclopedia of Computer Science
        (New York: Petrocelli/Charter, 1976): 1451-1453.

        This is a short, illustrated biography.

2097   Ulam, Stanislaw.   "John von Neumann, 1903-1957,"

Bulletin, American Mathematical Society 64 (1957): 1-49.

This is a detailed biography and technical discourse on his work in mathematics, logic and computers on the occasion of his death. The paper was also reprinted in Annals of the History of Computing, 4, No. 2 (April 1982): 157-181.

2098   Ulam, Stanislaw. Review of Computer and the Brain by John von Neumann, Scientific American 198 (June 1958): 127-128ff.

It is also a dialogue on the ideas in the book. Both the book and the review were published shortly after von Neumann's death.

2099   Neumann, John von. Collected Works. 6 vols. Oxford: Pergamon Press, 1961-63.

These were edited by A.H. Taub and represent a major source on von Neumann.

2100   Neumann, John von. The Computer and the Brain. New Haven: Yale University Press, 1958.

These were a series of lectures delivered late in his life in which he compares and contrasts computers to brains.

2101   Neumann, John von. "The NORC and Problems in High-Speed Computing," Annals of the History of Computing 2, No. 3 (July 1981): 274-279.

The IBM NORC calculator of the 1950s is the subject of this paper, originally written in 1954.

2102   Neumann, John von. Papers of John von Neumann on Computing and Computer Theory. Ed. by William Aspray and Arthur Burks. Cambridge, Mass.: MIT Press, 1987.

This very large book constitutes the best collection of von Neumann's papers on computing and includes a biography.

2103   Neumann, John von. "The Principles of Large-Scale Computing Machines," Annals of the History of Computing 3, No. 3 (July 1981): 263-273.

This is a semenal paper on computer architecture, originally dated May 15, 1946. This publication includes a forward by Nancy Stern (pp. 263-64). The Annals republished the paper in 10, No. 4 (1989): 243-256.

2104   Neumann, John von. Theory of Self-Reproducing Automata. Urbana: University of Illinois Press, 1966.

This has material on the logic of a computer.

2105   Neumann, John von and Goldstine, Herman H. "Numerical
        Inverting of Matrices of High Order," <u>Bulletin, Ameri-</u>
        <u>can Mathematical Society</u> 53 (1947): 1021-1099.

        This is one of the first modern papers to be published
        on numerical analysis and thus contributed to the
        solution of large groups of linear algebraic problems
        at the dawn of the age of computers.

2106   Vonneuman, Nicholas A. <u>John von Neumann—As Seen By</u>
        <u>His Brother</u>. Meadowbrook, Penn.: Privately printed,
        undated (late 1980s?).

        He reviews von Neumann's childhood and young adult-
        hood as background to his work and views. The author
        announced his intent to expand this publication at
        some future date.

                            WHIRLWIND

2107   Ackley, J.N. "Whirlwind I," in A. Ralston and Meek,
        C.L. (eds), <u>Encyclopedia of Computer Science</u> (New
        York: Petrocelli/Charter, 1976): 1456-1457.

        This is a short history of the MIT project of the
        1940s and early 1950s.

2108   Cole, R.B. "Whirlwind One: Speediest Electro-Brain,"
        <u>Science Digest</u> 31 (March 1952): 92.

        Although brief, it was one of the first published
        accounts of this military project at MIT.

2109   Evans, Christopher. "Conversation: Jay W. Forrester,"
        <u>Annals of the History of Computing</u> 5, No. 3 (July
        1983): 297-301.

        This interview with the creator of Whirlwind was
        held in 1972; illustrated.

2110   Everett, Robert R. <u>Digital Computing Machine Logic</u>.
        Memorandum M-63. Cambridge, Mass.: Massachusetts
        Institute of Technology, Servomechanisms Laboratory,
        March 19, 1947.

        This paper is on coding (programming) at an early
        stage of Whirlwind's design.

2111   Everett, Robert R. "WHIRLWIND," in N. Metropolis <u>et</u>
        <u>al.</u>(eds), <u>A History of Computing in the Twentieth</u>
        <u>Century</u> (New York: Academic Press, 1980): 365-384.

        This covers the period 1945-1952 and is written by
        a participant in the MIT project; illustrated.

2112   Forrester, Jay W. "Data Storage in Three Dimensions
        Using Magnetic Cores," <u>Journal of Applied Physics</u>
        20 (1951): 44-48.

        The memory developed for Whirlwind was the subject of

much interest in computer science circles. In this
paper Forrester described memory that represented a
significant improvement over older ones in reliability.

2113   Mattill, J.   "Economics vs. Innovation: How Whirlwind
       Almost Lost," Technology Review 80 (February 1978):
       26.

       This discussed the very large expense of the Whirlwind
       project and adds details about its long history.

2114   Redmond, Kent C. and Smith, Thomas M.   Project Whirlwind:
       The History of a Pioneer Computer. Maynard, Mass.:
       Digital Press, 1980.

       This is the most complete history of the Whirlwind
       project available. It is based on primary research
       and is illustrated.

2115   Smith, T.M.   "Project Whirlwind: An Unorthodox Develop-
       ment Project," Technology and Culture 17, No. 3 (July
       1976): 447-464.

       The project was massive, involved hundreds of people
       and was very expensive. This is an overview of the
       project.

                    World War II: British Role

2116   Beesly, P.   Very Special Intelligence: The Story of the
       Admiralty's Operational Intelligence Centre, 1939-
       1945. London: Hamish Hamilton, 1977.

       This is on the British use of deciphering methods to
       understand German coded messages. It discusses
       computers and Bletchley Park.

2117   Bennet, Ralph.   Ultra in the West. London: Hutchinson,
       1979.

       This describes how the British deciphered German
       coded messages during World War II.

2118   Bertrand, Gustav.   Enigma ou la Plus Grande Enigme de
       la Guerre 1939-1945. Paris: Librairie Plon, 1973.

       This tells the story of Enigma and deciphering of
       German code.

2119   Brown, A. Cave.   Bodyguard of Lies. New York: Harper &
       Row, 1975.

       This is a massive study of espionage operations by
       the Allies during World War II. This includes
       comments on A. Turing and British computers.

2120   Bundy, William P.   "Some of My Wartime Experiences,"
       Cryptologia 11 (April 1987): 65-77.

> Bundy was an American working at Bletchley Park dur-
> ing the war. He offers little not available in other
> publications..

2121   Calvocoressi, P. "The Ultra Secrets of Station X,"
        Sunday Times (November 24, 1974): 33-34.

> This discusses work done at Bletchley Park to translate
> German coded messages for the Allies. The author
> mentions the use of "prototype computers" to help in
> the process, offering new details not available before.

2122   Campbell, D. "Why Is Britain's Wartime Code-Breaking
        Still Secret?," New Scientist 73 (February 17, 1977):
        402.

> The answer involves the use of British computers and
> work done by Alan Turing.

2123   Clarke, William F. "Bletchley Park, 1941-1945,"
        Cryptologia 12 (April 1988): 90-97.

> These are excerpted papers of the author at Churchill
> College, Cambridge University, describing World War
> II experiences at the British Government Code and
> Cypher School. It was originally drafted in the
> 1950s.

2124   Cunningham, L.B.C. and Hynd, W.R.B. "Random Processes
        in the Problems of Air Warfare," Supplement to the
        Journal of the Royal Statistical Society 8, No. 2
        (1946): 62-85.

> They describe a relay computer derived from the
> designs of Shire and Runcorn; illustrated.

2125   Deavours, Cipher A. "The Black Chamber: La Methode
        des Batons," Cryptologia 4, No. 4 (October 1980):
        240-247.

> He reviews French cryptoanalysts' method for discover-
> ing ways to use Enigma, a tool of the Allies.

2126   Deavours, Cipher A. et al. Cryptology: Yesterday, Today,
        and Tomorrow. Norwood, Mass.: Artech House, 1987.

> This has three sections: historical, mechanical and
> mathematical. It contains six articles on World War
> II.

2127   Deavours, Cipher A. and Reeds, J. "The Enigma, Part I:
        Historical Perspectives," Cryptologia 1, No. 4 (Octo-
        ber 1977): 381-391.

> This is an illustrated account of how the Enigma
> cipher machine worked. Others are described which
> were also used during World War II.

2128   Erskine, Ralph. "From the Archives: GC and CS Mobilizes
        'Men of the Professor Type'," Cryptologia 10, No. 1
        (January 1986): 50-59.

This contains three letters, written in 1939, by
Alastair Denniston, of the British Government's
Code and Cypher School, containing a list and short
biographies of new hires for Bletchley Park. They
went on to develop early computers in Britain.

2129   Garlinski, Jozef. The Enigma War. New York: Charles
       Scribner's Sons, 1979.

       This is a history of cryptography, primarily about
       how the Allies broke German codes. The author was
       involved in the process during this war.

2130   Garlinski, Josef. Intercept: Secrets of the Enigma
       War. London: Dent, 1979.

       This is the English edition of the book cited before.

2131   Golombek, H. and Hartson, W. The Best Games of C.H.O.D.
       Alexander (With a Memoir By Sir Stuart Milner-Barry).
       London: Oxford University Press, 1976.

       This has material on work done at Bletchley Park.

2132   Good, I.J. "Early Work on Computers at Bletchley,"
       Annals of the History of Computing 1, No. 1 (July
       1979): 38-48.

       He recalls work done during World War II and contains
       many thumbnail sketches of people involved.

2133   Good, I.J. Good Thinking: The Foundations of Probabi-
       lity and Its Applications. Minneapolis: University
       of Minnesota Press, 1983.

       This reprints 23 of his papers and his introduction
       adds much biographical data. Good was a cryptoanalyst
       at Bletchley Park during World War II. He later worked
       with Turing.

2134   Good, I.J. "Pioneering Work on Computers at Bletchley,"
       in N. Metropolis et al. (eds), A History of Computing
       in the Twentieth Century: A Collection of Essays (New
       York: Academic Press, 1980): 31-46.

       This is an excellent article on British work during
       World War II, particularly on decoding and computer
       developments.

2135   Good, I.J. "Some Future Social Repercussions of Comput-
       ers," International Journal of Environmental Studies
       1 (1970): 67-79.

       It contains remarks about World War II developments
       (1943) and about Turing's involvement.

2136   Hay, I. The Post Office Went to War. London: HM
       Stationery Office, 1946.

Much British intelligence work, involving the early
use of computers, was under the control of the Post
Office.

2137   Hinsley, F.H. et al. British Intelligence in the Second
        World War. 4 vols. London: Her Majesty's Stationery
        Office, 1979-1988. Published in USA by New York:
        Cambridge University Press. Vols are counted as 1,
        2, and 3 Part I and II.

        This is a major study on the subject. It is based
        on British archives and has much material on Bletchley
        Park, some on British computers, and considerable
        amounts of discussion concerning code breaking. For
        a detailed review of volume 2 (which has material on
        Enigma), see Annals of the History of Computing 7,
        No. 2 (April 1985): 187-189.

2138   "Intelligence Services During the Second World War,"
        special issue of Journal of Contemporary History
        (April 1987).

        It contains some discussion of activities at Bletchley
        Park.

2139   Johnson, B. The Secret War. London: BBC, 1978.

        This reviews British intelligence work at Bletchley
        Park.

2140   Jones, R.V. "The Secret War (Letter to the Editor),"
        New Scientist 73 (February 24, 1977): 480.

        The author worked with Turing in 1939 on a code
        deciphering device.

2141   Jones, R.V. The Wizard War. New York: Coward, McCann
        and Geoghegen, 1978.

        This is a full treatment of the subject of British
        intelligence work at Bletchley Park during World War
        II.

2142   Kahn, D. The Code Breakers. New York: Macmillan, 1967.

        The author, an expert on cryptoanalysis, offers a
        history of work done at Bletchley Park.

2143   Kahn, David. "Cryptology Goes Public," Foreign Affairs
        58, No. 1 (1979): 141-159.

        He discusses Ultra in World War II but also current
        issues involving cryptology.

2144   Kahn, David. "The Ultra Conference," Cryptologia 3,
        No. 1 (1979): 1-8; Reprinted in American Committee on
        the History of the Second World War, Newsletter No. 22
        (Fall 1979): 34-42.

        This reviews a German conference held in November,

1978, on British and German cryptologists of World War II.

2145   Kahn, David. "The Ultra Secret," The New York Times Book Review (December 29, 1974): 5.

He reviews Wintherbotham's book (cited below) and criticizes his description of how Enigma was broken. Kahn also mentions that Colossus was built to solve machine ciphers.

2146   Kahn, David. "Why Germany Lost the Code War," Cryptologia 6, No. 1 (January 1982): 26-31.

He argues that the Allies did a better job on code breaking, using computers in the process.

2147   Kozaczuk, Wladyslaw. Enigma: How the German Cipher Was Broken and How It Was Read By the Allies in World War II. Edited and trans. by Christopher Kasparek. Frederick, Md.: University Publishers of America, 1984. Originally published as W Kregu Enigmy (Warsaw, 1979).

Although intended to be a study of the role played by the Poles, it contains material on the British.

2148   Kosaczuk, Wladyslaw. "Enigma Solved," Cryptologia 6, No. 1 (January 1982): 38-39.

This is his view of how the Allies broke the German code in World War II.

2149   Kozaczuk, Wladyslaw. "The War of Wits," Poland 6 (1975): 34-35, No. 7 (1975): 32-34.

He discusses British computers and intelligence activities during the war.

2150   Kruh, Louis. "The Slidex RT Code," Cryptologia 8, No. 2 (April 1984): 163-171.

He describes one of 20 codes used by the Allies in Operation Overlord (invasion of Normandy, June, 1944). For additional comments see Annals of the History of Computing 7, No. 2 (April 1985): 191.

The code was used in 1944.

2151   Lewin, R. Ultra Goes to War: The Secret Story. New York: McGraw-Hill, 1979.

Its focus is on British intelligence during the war and on Bletchley Park. It is well done.

2152   Luebbert, W.F. and Stoll, E.L. "Colossus and the Ultra Secret," Abacus (June 1977): 10-21.

This describes German cipher devices and Bletchley

Park's code breaking efforts. This is well illustrated.

2153   Lynch, A.C. <u>The Secret Digital Computers of 1943</u>.
       London: Professional Group 57, IEE, July 1978.

       This describes the Heath Robinson and Colossus
       machines and the use of photo-electric paper tape
       readers for these computers.

2154   Michie, D. "The Bletchley Machines," in. Brian Randell
       (ed), <u>Origins of Digital Computers</u> (Berlin: Springer-
       Verlag, 1973): 327-328.

       This is an early account of Bletchley Park's acti-
       vities.

2155   Michie, D. "The Disaster of Alan Turing's Buried
       Treasure (Letter to the Editor)," <u>Computer Weekly</u>
       (March 3, 1977): 10.

       This is a humorous review of Turing's work at Bletch-
       ley Park.

2156   Michie, D. "Machines That Play and Plan," <u>Science
       Journal</u> (October 1968): 83-88.

       This is a brief review of Michie's World War II work
       at Bletchley Park, with comments on Turing.

2157   Millington, R. "What Did You Do in the War Daddy?,"
       <u>Computing</u> (June 3, 1976): 10.

       This is a short account about minor digital and
       analog calculators in Britain during World War II
       and includes those for TRE for cryptoanalysis.

2158   Milner-Barry, S. "C.H.O.'D. Alexander—A Personal
       Memoir," <u>The Best Games of C.H. O.'D. Alexander</u>.
       Ed. by H. Golombek and W. Hartston (Oxford: Oxford
       University Press, 1976): 1-9.

       This is a short account of Bletchley Park and Enigma
       (sometimes called ENIGMA).

2159   Morris, Christopher. "Ultra's Poor Relations," <u>Intelli-
       gence and National Security</u> 1, No. 1 (January 1986):
       111-122.

       The author provides a first-hand account of how the
       Allies broke the Germany navy's hand ciphers during
       World War II.

2160   Muggeridge, M. <u>Chronicles of Wasted Time</u>. Part 2: <u>The
       Infernal Grove</u>. London: Collins, 1973.

       Bletchley Park's machines are described; in particu-
       lar Colossus.

2161   Stevenson, W. <u>A Man Called Intrepid</u>. New York: Harcourt
        Brace & Co., 1976.

        This is on British intelligence with material on
        the work done at Bletchley Park.

2162   Todd, J. and Sadler, D.H. "Admiralty Computing Ser-
        vice," <u>Mathematical Tables and Other Aids to Compu-
        tation</u> 2, No. 19 (July 1947): 289-297.

        The article is a summary of a paper, from July,
        1944, on a range finder performance computer under
        development.

2163   Welchman, Gordon. <u>The Hut Six Story: Breaking the
        Enigma Codes</u>. New York: McGraw-Hill, 1982.

        These memoirs are an important addition to the
        literature on British intelligence. He discusses
        Turing, Bletchley Park, computation processes, and
        describes many of the people involved.

2164   Whiting, C. <u>The Battle for Twelveland</u>. London: Corgi,
        1975.

        Whiting describes Anglo-American intelligence and
        includes a short chapter on Enigma. He claims the
        British post office had a computer at Bletchley
        Park by February, 1940.

2165   Winterbotham, F.W. <u>The Ultra Secret</u>. London: Weiden-
        feld and Nicolson, 1974.

        This is another narrative history of how the British
        broke German codes and ciphers in World War II. He
        too implies the British had a computer doing the
        job by 1940 at Bletchley Park.

2166   Winton, John. <u>Ultra at Sea</u>. London: Leo Cooper, 1988.

        The book is useful for understanding the use of
        Ultra intelligence data by the Allies at sea during
        World War II.

2167   Zorpette, G. "Breaking the Enemy's Code: British
        Intelligence and the Colossus Computer," <u>IEEE
        Spectrum</u> (September 1987): 47-51.

        The article specifically deals with Colossus about
        which little is known. This piece adds little that
        is new but does explain how it was applied against
        the German Geheimschreiber codes during the war.

                    World War II: German Role

2168   Atha, Robert. "'Bombe!' 'I Could Hardly Believe It',"
        <u>Cryptologia</u> 9, No. 4 (October 1985): 332-336.

        Atha describes how he maintained key-finding aids

for the German Enigma cipher machines in the posse-
ssion of the U.S. Navy. He details the mechanics of
the German device.

2169   Dreyer, H.J. and Walther, A.   "Der Rechenautomat IPM,"
       Entwicklung Mathematischer Instrumente in Deutschland
       1939 bis 1945 (Darmstadt: Institute für Praktische
       Mathematik, Technische Hochschule, 19 August 1946):
       11-15; Reprinted in Brian Randell, The Origins of
       Digital Computers: Selected Papers (New York: Spring-
       er-Verlag, 1982): 155-157.

       They describe briefly a tape controlled calculator
       destroyed by Allied bombs while being built in
       Darmstadt. Randell's reprint is in English.

2170   Jensen, W.   "Hilfsgeräte der Kryptographie" (Unpublish-
       ed Ph.D. dissertation, Technischen Hochschule,
       Munich, 1952) but later withdrawn.

       Jensen describes various devices, all using photo-
       electric tape readers and electromagnetic relays for
       cryptographic activities in Germany during World
       War II.

2171   Kahn, David.   "The Geheimschreiber," Cryptologia 3,
       No. 4 (October 1979): 210-214.

       He reprints an Allied interrogation report of April
       1945 which describes varioys cryptographic devices
       used by the Germans. The article includes one photo-
       graph of a device.

2172   Rohrbach, J.   "Chiffrierverfahren der neuestren Zeit,"
       Archiv der Elektrischen Ubertragung 2 (December
       1948): 362-369.

       It contains a short passage explaining the operation
       of the Geheimschreiber.

2173   Rohrbach, J.   "Mathematische und maschinelle Methoden
       beim chiffrieren und dechiffrieren," FIAT Review of
       German Science, 1939-1946: Applied Mathematics
       (Weisbaden: Office of Military Government for Germany,
       1948): 233-257.

       Pages 247-49 discuss German cryptoanalysis and
       devices used during World War II.

2174   Rohwehr, J.   "Notes on the Security of the German
       Decoding Systems" (Trans by A.J. Barker), Appendix
       10 in The Critical Convoy Battles of March 1943
       (London: Ian Allan, 1977): 229-244.

       He uses an unpublished manuscript on Enigma and
       other devices.

2175   Rohrbach, Hans.   "Report on the Decipherment of the
       American Strip Cipher O-2 by the German Foreign

Office (Marburg 1945)," Cryptologia 3, No. 1 (January 1979): 16-26.

The author and his group were captured by the U.S. Army in April, 1945. The report is based on their interogation of their efforts to decipher Allied codes during the war.

2176   Schreyer, H. "Das Röhrenrelais und seine Schaltung-stechnik" (Unpublished Ph.D. dissertation, Techn. Hochschule, Berlin, 1941).

The author worked with electrical valves and applied them in switching circuits.

2177   Walther, A. and Dreyer, H.-J. "Geräte für Beliebige Rechenzwecke," Entwicklung Mathematischer Instrumente in Deutschland, 1939-1945. Ber. A3. Darmstadt: Inst. Prakt. Math., August 19, 1946.

They describe Zuse's work on calculators but also projects at the Institute for Practical Mathematics at Darmstadt during World War II.

2178   Walther, A. and Dreyer, H.-J. "Mathematische Maschinen und Instrumente. Instrumentelle Verfahren." FIAT Review of German Science, 1939-1946: Applied Mathematics, Part 1 (Weisbaden: Office of Military Government for Germany, Field Information Agency, 1948): 129-165.

It contains a very short discourse on computers: Zuse's and Dreyer's.

2179   Wolfgang, Mache. "Geheimschreiber," Cryptologia 10, No. 4 (October 1986): 230-247.

The author reviews the Siemens and Halske T52 teleprinter online cipher machine and the Lorenz SZ40 and 42 cipher attachments used during World War II, particularly by the British at Bletchley Park.

World War II: Polish Role

2180   Andrew, Christopher and Dilks, David (eds). The Missing Dimension: Governments and Intelligence Communities in the Twentieth Century. London: Macmillan, 1984.

This contains several articles that offer new material on Polish code breaking, about Enigma, and British intelligence during World War II.

2181   Calvocoressi, P. "The Secrets of Enigma," The Listener 97, No. 2492 (January 20, 1977): 70-71, No. 2493 (January 27, 1977): 112-114, No. 2494 (February 3, 1977): 135-137.

This is a good review of the Enigma cipher machine

used to break German codes during the war. Useful
details are provided on Polish devices that, by 1939,
could be characterized as "somewhat primitive, special
purpose, electromechanical, not electronic computer."

2182   Deavours, C.A. "The Black Chamber," Cryptologia 4,
        No. 3 (July 1980): 129-132.

        He surveys Polish devices from 1928 to 1940 and how
        they worked.

2183   Dickson, D.A. "Enigma—The Ultra Secret," Journal of
        the Royal Signals Institute 13, No. 4 (Apring 1978):
        22-23.

        This is on Polish efforts regarding Enigma when a
        captured Enigma devise was given to the Royal
        Signals Museum.

2184   Kasparek, Christopher and Woytak, Richard. "In Memo-
        riam: Marian Rejewski," Cryptologia 6, No. 1 (Janua-
        ry 1982): 19-25.

        Rejewski worked with Enigma machines in the 1930s
        and 1940s and it was he who was the first to break
        German codes that made it possible for the Allies
        to read confidential Axis messages throughout World
        War II.

2185   Kozaczuk, Władysław. Bitwa o Tajemnice. Warsaw:
        Książka i Wiedza, 1967.

        This is a history of Polish code breaking with
        Enigma during World War II.

2186   Kozaczuk, Władysław. "Enigma Wie Der Code Faschisten
        Genackt Wurde," Horizont 8 (1975): 41-49.

        Reviews efforts by Polish cryptoanalysts in France
        and in Poland to crack Enigma, the German system
        for encoding secret messages.

2187   Kozaczuk, Władysław. W Kregu Enigmy. Warsaw: Ksiazka
        i Wiedza, 1979.

        This is an expanded edition of his 1967 book on
        Polish code breaking and Enigma.

2188   Kozaczuk, Władysław. Wojna w Eterze. Warsaw: Wydawnic-
        twa Radia i Telewizji, 1977.

        Yet another study on Enigma by Poland's leading
        expert on World War II intelligence activities.

2189   Kozaczuk, Władysław. Złamany Szyer. Warsaw: Wydannic-
        two MON, 1976.

        This adds more material on Enigma and Polish efforts
        during World War II.

2190   Marinkowić, Ilija. "Enigma" do Pabjede. Zagreb: n.p.,
       1977.

       This is a history of Polish code breaking and Enigma.

2191   Rejewski, Marian. "An Application of the Theory of
       Permutations in Breaking the Enigma Cipher," Appli-
       cationes Mathematique 16, No. 4 (1980): 543-559.

       The author was the individual who actually broke the
       Enigma code for the Allies and, in this article,
       explains how.

2192   Rejewski, Marian. "How Polish Mathematicians Deciph-
       ered the Enigma," Annals of the History of Comput-
       ing 3, No. 3 (July 1981): 213-234.

       These are the memoirs of the author's role and that
       of the Polish Cipher Bureau, 1932-39, working on
       Enigma military codes and machines. It is an illus-
       trated and technical paper.

2193   Rejewski, Marian. "Mathematical Solution of the
       Enigma Cipher," Cryptologia 6, No. 1 (January 1982):
       1-18.

       This covers similar material to the previous cita-
       tion but with greater emphasis on the technical
       features of his early work on Enigma.

2194   Rejewski, Marian. "Remarks on Appendix 1 to British
       Intelligence in the Second World War, by F.H.
       Hinsley," Cryptologia 6, No. 1 (January 1982): 74-
       83.

       He critiques to clarify the Polish role in the
       Enigma story. See citation 2137 for Hinsley's
       publication.

2195   Saccho, L. Manuel de Cryptographie. Trans from Italian
       to French by J. Bres. Paris: Payot, 1951.

       This is a review of the use of computer-like devices
       in code breaking during World War II.

2196   Strumph-Wojtkiewicz, Stanisław. Sekret Enigmy. Warsaw:
       Iskry, 1978.

       This is a narrative history of how the Poles broke
       German Enigma codes and learned to use the machine.

2197   Welchman, Gordon. "From Polish Bomba to British Bombe:
       The Birth of Ultra," Intelligence and National Sec-
       urity 1, No. 1 (January 1986): 71-110.

       This surveys the joint Polish-British effort to
       break Enigma codes.

2198   Woytak, Richard. "A Conversation with Marian

Rejewski," <u>Cryptologia</u> 6, No. 1 (January 1982): 50-
60.

The discussion is on the role he played in breaking
the Enigma code and that of other Poles during the
1930s and early 1940s.

World War II: U.S. Role

2199   Crawford, P.O., Jr. "Automatic Control by Arithmeti-
        cal Operations" (Unpublished M.Sc. Thesis, Massachu-
        setts Institute of Technology, 1942).

        He explains the design for a calculating device for
        operating and controlling antiaircraft gun fire.
        MIT did a great deal of work on such feedback systems
        during the war that required computer-like devices.

2200   Eckert, W.J. "The IBM Pluggable Sequence Relay Calcu-
        lator," <u>Mathematical Tables and Other Aids to Calcu-</u>
        <u>lation</u> 3 (1948): 149-161.

        This is a programming description of a device that
        was built originally during World War II for the
        Aberdeen Proving Ground and installed in December,
        1944.

2201   Farago, Ladislas. <u>The Broken Seal: "Operation Magic"</u>
        <u>and the Secret Road to Pearl Harbor</u>. New York: Random
        House, 1967.

        Farago surveys the work of the U.S. Navy's crypto-
        analysis organization in the 1930s and early 1940s
        relative to the Japanese and ultimately, to Pearl
        Harbor.

2202   Feynman, R.P. "Los Alamos From Below—Reminscences of
        1943-1945," <u>Engineering and Science</u> 39, No. 2
        (January-February 1976): 13-20.

        These are humorous memoirs that mention how punched
        card devices were used to help develop the atomic
        bomb.

2203   Lewin, Ronald. <u>The American Magic: Codes, Ciphers,</u>
        <u>and the Defeat of Japan</u>. London: Farrar, Straus
        Giroux, 1982.

        The author provides considerable details on British
        and American cryptoanalysis during World War II.

2204   Lovell, C.A. "Continuous Electrical Computation,"
        <u>Bell Laboratories Record</u> 25 (March 1947): 114-118.

        The author describes a 1940 Bell Labs analog device,
        precursor of the M-9 gun director, which became the
        U.S. Army's main fire control mechanism for large
        antiaircraft guns in World War II.

2205   MacEwan, D. and Beevers, C.A.   "A Machine for the
        Rapid Summation of Fourier Series," Journal of Scien-
        tific Instruments 19 (October 1942): 150-156.

        They describe a special purpose machine for calcula-
        tions in the use of Fourier Synthesis in crystallo-
        graphy.

2206   Metropolis, Nicholas and Nelson, E.C.   "Early Comput-
        ing at Los Alamos," Annals of the History of Comput-
        ing 4, No. 4 (October 1982): 348-357.

        Los Alamos National Laboratory worked on many war
        related problems, including the development of the
        atomic bomb, and were quick to rely on the use of
        advanced computational devices.   Both authors worked
        there during World War II; many of their publications
        are cited in this article.

2207   Novick, David et al. Wartime Production Controls. New
        York: Columbia University Press, 1949.

        The war called forth the need to apply business
        applications of punch card equipment to manage
        war related controls.

2208   Rajchman, J.A.   Report on Electronic Predictors for
        Anti-Aircraft Fire Control. Camden, N.J.: Research
        Laboratories, RCA Manufacturing Co., Inc., 1942.

        The author announced that tentative designs had been
        completed.   Similar work was also underway at MIT.

2209   Rajchman, J.A. et al. Report on the Development of
        Electronic Computer.   Camden, N.J.: Research Labora-
        tories, RCA Manufacturing Co., Inc., 1941.

        In addition to being a useful, 68-page account of
        R&D at RCA, it is also one of the earliest uses of
        the term "electronic computer".

2210   Rees, Mina.   "The Mathematical Sciences and World War
        II," American Mathematical Monthly 87, No. 8 (Octob-
        er 1980): 607-621.

        Rees recruited mathematicians to work on war-related
        projects, which she describes, some of which were on
        computational projects such as von Neumann and the
        Moore School, ENIAC and so forth.

2211   Stibitz, G.R.   "Introduction to the Course on Electron-
        ic Computers," in C.C. Chambers (ed), Theory and
        Techniques for the Design of Electronic Digital
        Computers: Lectures Delivered 8 July-31 August 1946
        (Philadelphia: Moore School of Electrical Engineer-
        ing, University of Pennsylvania, 1947): 1.1-1.19.

        He offers a brief review of computer development
        activities during World War II.

2212   Ulam, Stanislaw. *Adventures of a Mathematician*. New
        York: Scribners, 1976.

        This is the autobiography of an applied mathematician
        who worked on the atomic bomb at Los Alamos and with
        John von Neumann.

                         Zuse Computers

2213   Bauer, Friedrich L. *Between Zuse and Rutishauser*.
        The Early Development of Digital Computing in Central
        Europe. Munich: Institut für Informatik, Technische
        Universitat, 1976; Reprinted in N. Metropolis *et al*.
        (eds), *A History of Computing in the Twentieth Cen-*
        tury (New York: Academic Press, 1980): 505-524.

        This is an illustrated account of Zuse's computers
        and software (Plankalkul) during the years of the
        1930s-1950s.

2214   Bauer, Friedrich L. and Wössner, H. "The 'Plankalkul'
        of Konrad Zuse: A Forerunner of Today's Programming
        Languages," *Communications, ACM* 15, No. 7 (1972):
        678-685.

        Zuse developed this language for use on his computer
        and the article compares it to others.

2215   Ceruzzi, Paul E. "The Early Computers of Konrad Zuse,
        1935 to 1945," *Annals of the History of Computing*
        3, No. 3 (July 1981): 241-262.

        This is a detailed, balanced account on Zuse and on
        his contributions; excellent introduction to the
        subject.

2216   Czauderna, Karl-Heinz. *Konrad Zuse, der Weg zu seinem*
        Computer Z3. Report 120, Gesellschaft für Mathematik
        und Datenverarbeitung. Munich: R. Oldenbourg, 1979.
        Variation published as *Konrad Zuse—der Weg zu seinem*
        Computer Z3 und dessen Verwirklichung. Augsburg:
        Fachbereich Elektrotechnik der Fachhochschule, 1978.

        These publications cover the Z1, Z2, Z3 and includes
        memoir material by those who worked with him and
        illustrations.

2217   Desmonde, W.H. and Berkling, K.J. "The Zuse Z3,"
        Datamation 12, No. 9 (1966): 30-31.

        This is a brief review of one of Zuse's later mach-
        ines and on the man's overall contributions.

2218   Dreyer, H.J. and Walther, A. "Das Rechengerät von
        Zuse," *Entwicklung Mathemastischer Instrumente in*
        Deutschland 1939 bis 1945 (Darmstadt: Institut für
        Proktische Mathematik Technische Hochschule, August
        19, 1946): 4-10.

This surveys Zuse's programmable calculators and their uses from 1939 to 1945.

2219   Gebhardt, Friedrich (ed). Skizzen aus den Anfangen der Datenverarbeitung. Munich: R. Oldenbourg Verlag, 1983.

This 99-page book is a general collection of papers on German computing in the 1930s and 1940s.

2220   Golbach, W. and Schneider, R. "Beschreibung der Rechenanlage Zuse Z3," Zuse Forum 2, No. 4 (September 1963): 19-31.

This recounts how the Deutsches Meseum in Munich rebuilt the Z3 computer; illustrated.

2221   Lyndon, R.C. "The Zuse Computer," Mathematical Tables and Other Aids to Computation 2, No. 20 (1947): 355-359.

He surveys the Z4 computer which was then under construction.

2222   Schreyer, H. "Rechnische Rechenmaschine," dated October 15, 1939, first published in Brian Randell, The Origins of the Digital Computer: Selected Papers (New York: Springer Verlag, 1982): 171-173.

Randell's version is in English. The paper does describe Zuse's work and potential applications.

2223   Speiser, A.P. "The Relay Calculator Z4," Annals of the History of Computing 2, No. 3 (July 1980): 242-245.

This is a history of the Z4 machine of the late 1940s and early 1950s; illustrated.

2224   Stiefel, E. "La Machine à Calculer Arithmétique Z4 de l'Ecole Polytechnique Federale à Zurich," Les Machines a Calculer et la Pensée Humaine. Collog. Internaille du CNRS Paris, 8-13 January 1951 (Paris: Editions du CNRS, 1953): 33-40.

Z4's performance capabilities are described.

2225   Stucken, H. "Programmgesteuerte Rechenmaschinen in Deutschland," Phys. Blätter 6 (1950): 166-170.

This is a review of Zuse's efforts to develop program controlled computers in the 1930s and 1940s.

2226   Zemanek, H. "Konrad Zuse," in A. Ralston and Meek, C.L. (eds), Encyclopedia of Computer Science (New York: Petrocelli/Charter, 1976): 1463-1464.

This is a short, illustrated biography of Zuse.

2227   Zuse, Konrad.   Der Computer—Mein Lebenswerk. Munich:
       Verlag Moderne Industrie, 1970; Reprinted by Berlin:
       Springer Verlag, 1984; Italian edition L'Elaborate
       Nasce in Europa: Un secolo di calcolo automatico
       (Milan: Etas Libri, 1975).

       These are the memoirs of Germany's foremost computer
       scientist of the 1930s and 1940s. It includes many
       technical details about the various Z computers.

2228   Zuse, Konrad.   "Die ersten programmgesteuerten Relais-
       Rechenmaschinen," in M. Graef (ed), 350 Jahre
       Rechenmaschinen (Munich: Carl Hanser, 1973): 51-57.

       Zuse reviews his work on the Z3 and Z4 primarily.

2229   Zuse, Konrad.   "Die Mathematischen Voraussetzungen für
       die Entwicklung logistischkombinativer Rechenmaschi-
       nen," Z. Angew. Math. Mech. 29 (1949): 36-37.

       This is an early report by Zuse on his machines and
       is especially useful in understanding his views on
       programming.

2230   Zuse, Konrad.   "Entwicklungslinien einer Rechengerate-
       Entwicklung von der Mechanik zur Elektronik," in W.
       Hoffman (ed), Digitale Informationswalder (Braunsch-
       weig: Vieweg, 1962): 508-532; Partial reprint in
       Brian Randell, The Origins of the Digital Computer:
       Selected Papers (New York: Springer Verlag, 1982):
       175-190.

       This is an important paper on Zuse's computer,
       particularly on the Z3, which was running in 1941,
       and the Z4, which was installed at the Zurich ETH
       in 1950. Randell has reproduced illustrations and
       diagrams in his English translation.

2231   Zuse, Konrad.   "German Computer Activities," in
       Computers and Their Future (Llandudno: Richard
       Williams and Partners, 1970): 6/3-6/17.

       He concentrates on his work and on those of Schreyer
       and Dirks, fellow engineers who worked with him in
       the 1930s and 1940s.

2232   Zuse, Konrad.   "Installation of the German Computer
       Z4 in Zurich 1950," Annals of the History of
       Computing 2, No. 3 (July 1980): 239-241.

       There is in this article many personal memoirs. For
       another version of the installation of a Z computer
       see No. 2220 above.

2233   Zuse, Konrad.   The Plankalkul, Report 106. Gesillschaft
       für Mathematik und Datenverarbeitung. Bonn: Gesill-
       schaft für Mathematik und Datenverarbeitung, 1976.

       Zuse wrote this originally in 1945 as an exposition

on his idea for an algorithmic language. The 1976
publication includes material from 1972 by Zuse on
his work of the 1930s and 1940s.

2234   Zuse, Konrad. "Programmgesteuerte Rechenmaschinen in
       Deutschland," Z. Angew. Math. Mech. 30 (1950): 292-
       293.

       It is primarily a description of his computers.

2235   Zuse, Konrad. "Uber Programmgesteuerte Rechengeräte
       für Industrielle Verwendung," Probleme der Entwick-
       lung Programmgesteuerster Rechengeräte und Integrier-
       anlagen (Aachen: Mathematisches Institut, Technische
       Hochschule, 1953): 55-75.

       He describes a number of Z computers.

2236   Zuse, Konrad. "Some Remarks on the History of Computing
       in Germany," in N. Metropolis et al, (eds), A History
       of Computing in the Twentieth Century (New York:
       Academic Press, 1980): 611-627.

       This is an illustrated account covering mainly 1934
       to 1948, and his Z computers, his role, and their
       features.

2237   Zuse, Konrad. Verfahren zur selbsttatigen Durchfuhrung-
       en mit Hilfe von Rechmaschinen. German patent applica-
       tion Z23624 (11 April 1936); Partially reprinted in
       Brian Randell, The Origins of the Digital Computer:
       Selected Papers (New York: Springer Verlag, 1982):
       163-170.

       He describes an electromagnetic programmable calcu-
       lator which used punched cards and floating point
       binary number representation. Randell's reprint is
       in English translation with diagrams.

2238   Zuse, Konrad. "The Working Program-Controlled Comput-
       er of 1941," Honeywell Computer Journal 6, No. 2
       (1972): 49-58.

       This is a partial reprint and translation of his 1962
       article. See No. 2230 above.

6

Hardware, 1960s–1980s

Computers developed since the early 1960s have been the least studied by scholars concerned with the history of computing, as the period when they first appeared has not yet taken on an historical definition. Contemporary materials generally describe devices and technologies and are less analytical or historical. As yet, this material adds little to our appreciation of computing's history. However, those important surveys that have been produced, and the historical/memoir materials that have been published, are cited below.

In this period there has been an extraordinary burst in the acquisition of hardware systems, which we have come to associate with the "computer revolution" or the "age of data processing." It is in this period that the computer has become ubiquous. The era is better covered by application briefs (Chapter 8) and the numerous surveys of the industry at large (Chapter 9), and least of all by histories of hardware. The one exception is the subject of micro computers which is acquiring a literature of its own. The only publications included here are those that have an historical bent. There are hundreds of user manuals and some 150 PC magazines alone published worldwide, but none have been included in this bibliography.

The material in this chapter is organized by device types. IBM equipment has received the greatest amount of publicity and is, therefore, well represented in this chapter. Depending on who's statistics are cited, IBM mainframes, for example, populated anywhere from 65 to 80 percent of all medium to large data centers in the United States in the 1960s. That decreased to perhaps the 60th percentile by the late 1980s as computing was diffused across all parts of organizations. Historians should find the predominance of literature on IBM equipment useful. For all hardware announcements after 1969, an excellent contemporary source to consult is ComputerWorld, the industry's voluminous weekly newspaper. The periodicals section in Chapter 1 suggests other sources on the period as well.

Data Entry

2239   Alrich, John C.   "Keypunch Replacement Equipment,"
        Datamation 16, No. 6 (June 1970): 79-89.

        Alrich compares prices and performance of data entry
        equipment from 22 vendors which were available in
        1970, presenting a great deal of information.

2240   Caray, Robert F.   "A History of Keyed Data Entry,"
        Datamation 16, No. 6 (June 1970): 73-76.

        He begins with key punches, goes to the Sperry-Rand
        Unityper, down to Mohawk Data Sciences Corporation's
        key-to-tape converter of 1965, and through key-to-
        disk devices available in 1970.

2241   Goldberg, Adele (ed).   A History of Personal Worksta-
        tions. New York: ACM Press and Reading, Mass.: Addi-
        son-Wesley Publishing Co., 1988.

        This reprints a group of papers on the subject from
        a conference held in January, 1986. It contains a
        great deal of illustrated material from the 1950s on
        but is devoid of any serious discussion of either of
        the most popular workstations of the 1980s: Apple
        and IBM micro computers.

2242   IBM Corporation.   Installation Manual—Physical Plann-
        ing Unit Record Data Processing Equipment. White
        Plains, N.Y.: International Business Machines Corp.,
        February 1961.

        This is a 24-page document that explains how to
        install punched card data entry equipment (EAM).
        The equipment described continued to be used all
        through the 1960s.

2243   IBM Corporation.   An Introduction to IBM Punched Card
        Processing. White Plains, N.Y.: Data Processing Divi-
        sion, International Business Machines Corp., 1960.

        A 20-page description, it includes a short history
        of EAM equipment, current applications, how to code
        data, and uses of card input. A glossary is included.

2244   McLaughlin, R.A.   "Alphanumeric Display Terminal Sur-
        vey," Datamation 19, No. 11 (November 1973): 71-92.

        Over 100 CRTs available in 1973 are surveyed, with
        descriptions of their functions, prices, and uses.

2245   Mills, Peter.   "Before and After at Occidental's Medi-
        care Administration," Datamation 19, No. 3 (March
        1973): 54-56.

        He discusses productivity of operators before (using
        keypunch equipment) and after (using key-to-disk).
        Productivity went up 40 percent in 6 weeks.

2246   Nelson, David L. and Bell, C. Gordon. "The Evolution
        of Work Stations," IEEE Circuits and Devices Maga-
        zine 2, No. 4 (July 1986): 12-16.

        Bell helped to develop minis and real-time processors
        yet this article focuses on work stations only.

2247   Reagan, F.H. "Should OCR Be Your Data Input Medium?,"
        Computer Decisions 3, No. 6 (June 1971): 19-23.

        Reagan surveys existing OCR devices as of 1971,
        from 23 vendors.

2248   U.S. Department of the Navy, Navy Management Office,
        Data Processing Systems Division. Source Data
        Automation Equipment Guide. Washington, D.C.: U.S.
        Government Printing Office, March 1961.

        This 91-page publication has sections on automatic
        typing equipment, transaction recording devices,
        optical scanners, punched tag/ticket and card punch
        machines, embossers and intercouplers. All of these
        items are of the period 1960-61.

Digital Computers

2249   Adler, Irving. Thinking Machines; A Layman's Introduc-
        tion to Logic, Boolean Algebra, and Computers. New
        York: The John Day Co., 1961.

        This computer science book appeared late in second
        generation computing. Some of the components des-
        cribed in this book appeared in machines of the
        1960s.

2250   "AEC Is First Customer for Control Data 6600," Aviation
        Week 79 (September 2, 1963): 85.

        The CDC 6600 was an important scientific/engineering
        processor of the 1960s, described in this article.

2251   Ashenhurst, Robert L. (ed). "Special 25th Anniversary
        Issue," Communications, ACM 26, No. 1 (January
        1983).

        This reprints major papers published between 1960 and
        1978, 21 in all. For details see Annals of the History
        of Computing 5, No. 3 (July 1983): 313-14.

2252   Barnes, G. et al. "The ILLIAC IV Computer," IEEE Trans-
        actions, Computers C-17 (August 1968): 746-757.

        This is a functional description of an early super
        computer, the ILLIAC IV, built in the 1960s.

2253   Bell, C. Gordon. "RISC: Back to the Future," Datamation
        32 (June 1, 1986): 96-108.

        He describes research on reduced instruction set

computer (RISC) architectures of the 1970s and 1980s which appeared in commercial micro computers by the late 1980s. One widely used example was the IBM RT/PC.

2254   Bell, C. Gordon et al. "A New Architecture for Mini-computers—The DEC PDP-11," Conference Proceedings AFIPS SJCC (1970): 36: 657-675.

This is a functional description of one of the most important, widely used mini computers of the early 1970s.

2255   Bellman, R. "Is Science Big Enough to Cope With Society?," Saturday Review 48 (June 5, 1965): 43-44.

It contains material on the status and role of digital computers in 1964-65.

2256   Bishop, Peter. Fifth Generation Computers: Concepts, Implementation, and Uses. New York: Halstead, 1986.

This contains a brief history of computer concepts since Babbage, then a review of contemporary technology, and finally describes the notion of a fifth generation of computers coming. It was an early publication to address the subject.

2257   Boyce, Jefferson. Digital Computer Fundamentals. Englewood Cliffs, N.J.: Prentice-Hall, Inc., 1977.

This is a serious, technical introduction to computers and their technology, circa fourth generation. It is a useful reflection of thinking in the mid-1970s.

2258   "Building Another Giant: Control Data 7600," Business Week (December 7, 1968): 38.

Building on the success of earlier machines, such as the CDC 6600, for engineers and scientists, the firm produced the 7600. The event is noted here; it does not contain a technical description of the processor.

2259   Campbell, R. "How the Computer Gets the Answer," Life 63 (October 27, 1967): 60-72.

This is a popularized account of digital computing in the mid-1960s and how they were being employed in the United States.

2260   Cashman, Michael. "Products of Their Time," Datamation 28, No. 10 (September 1982): 127-134.

Cashman offers a quick survey of DP product announcements over the period 1957-1982.

2261   "Computer Hardware Continues to Lead Programming Abili-
        ty," Aero Technology 21 (March 25, 1968): 60.

        As did many articles of the 1960s and 1970s, this
        one recorded how the advances in hardware continued
        to surpass those in programming and in software in
        general.

2262   "Computer That Grows With You; DEC's PDP-6," Business
        Week (March 14, 1964): 56ff.

        This is essentially an announcement of the new PDP
        mini computer with some description of its features
        and functions.

2263   Datapro Research Corporation. Datapro 70. The EDP
        Buyer's Bible. Delran, N.J., 1970—.

        Published under different, yet similar titles, this
        publication has continued to appear down to the
        present. It is a major source of information on
        devices available in the market and with such details
        as features, functions, costs, performance, compari-
        sons, vendors' addresses and services.

2264   Davis, R.M. "Evolution of Computers and Computing,"
        Science 195 (March 18, 1977): 1096-1102.

        The focus is on developments during the 1970s and
        anticipated changes in subsequent years in both
        hardware and software.

2265   Fields, Craig. About Computers. Cambridge, Mass.:
        Winthrop, 1973.

        This is a description of fourth generation technology
        early in its development.

2266   Giloi, W.K. "Die Entwicklung der Rechnerarchitektur
        von der von-Neumann-Maschine bis zu den Rechnern der
        'funften Generation'," Elektronische Rechenanlangen
        26, No. 2 (1984): 55-70.

        Contemporary technology is compared to what is appear-
        ing in fifth generation devices.

2267   Gonick, Larry. The Cartoon Guide to Computer Science.
        New York: Barnes & Noble, 1983.

        This funny book describes computers and includes
        some historical perspectives.

2268   Gruenberger, Fred (ed). "18 Symposia," Popular Comput-
        ing 1, No. 44 (1976): 4-7.

        He describes various exchanges of ideas by computer
        scientists from 1958 to the mid-1970s on their
        work and technology.

2269   Gruenberger, Fred (ed). Fourth Generation Computers.
       Englewood Cliffs, N.J.: Prentice-Hall, Inc., 1970.

       Computers changed dramatically in the 1960s and
       those changes are reflected in this book.

2270   Gumpert, G. "The Rise of Mini-Computer," Journal of
       Communication 20 (September 1970): 280-290.

       The mini came into its own in the 1960s. This is a
       useful survey of activities leading to the introduc-
       tion of more specialized, smaller processors,
       particularly in the second half of the 1960s.

2271   "Harris-Intertype Computers Made Especially for Type
       Composition," Publishers Weekly 185 (April 6, 1964):
       62-65.

       Composition equipment early-on acquired computing
       capability, a trend that became increasingly evident
       in other industrial machines, particularly in the
       1970s. This article describes early developments
       within the publishing industry.

2272   Hollingdale, S.H. and Toothill, G.C. Electronic Com-
       puters. Baltimore: Penguin, 1965.

       The authors explain the nature of computer hardware
       late in second generation and early third. They
       also offer details on their use in the 1960s.

2273   Hord, R. Michael. The ILLIAC IV: The First Super-
       computer. Rockville, Md.: Computer Science Press,
       1982.

       This is a technical description of the first large
       array processor. It was operational between 1975
       and 1981. The book has little history and no index
       to its 350 pages.

2275   IBM Corporation. Introduction to IBM Data Processing
       Systems. New York: IBM Corporation, June, 1960.

       It offers fundamental concepts and operational
       principles, citing various IBM machines for examples.

2276   Irwin, Wayne C. Digital Computer Principles. New York:
       D. Van Nostrand Co., Inc., 1960.

       This is targeted at a reader with no knowledge of
       computers of the early 1960s and was used throughout
       the decade. It is a technical description with no
       history.

2277   Kidder, Tracy. The Soul of a New Machine. Boston:
       Atlantic-Brown, 1981.

       This very successful, widely-read book is a history
       of the development of the Data General MV/8000 mini.

It is particularly useful for appreciating how crash
projects in the DP world are conducted.

2278   Knight, K.E. "Changes in Computer Performance: A His-
        torical Review," Datamation 12, No. 9 (1966): 40-
        54.

        Knight describes increases in capacity of processors
        versus declining costs for hardware in the 1960s.
        His work on the costs of computing has influenced
        significantly the work of economists looking at the
        data processing industry and its products.

2279   Lehmann, N. Joachim. "Die analytische Machine—Grund-
        lagen einer Computer-Analytik," Sitzungsber. Sachs.
        Akad. Wiss. Leipzig. Math-Natur. Kl. 118 (1985): 64
        pp.

        This is a general description of the technology and
        its principles.

2280   Levy, H.M. and Eckhouse, R.H., Jr. Computer Programm-
        ing and Architecture: The VAX-11. Bedford, Mass.:
        Digital Press, 1980.

        This technical description also provides background
        on the history of the VAX series, the outgrowth of
        DEC's PDP minis of the 1970s.

2281   McCauley, Carole Spearin. Computers and Creativity.
        New York: Praeger Publishers, 1974.

        Already by the 1970s the impact of digital computers
        on people and society was receiving considerable
        attention. The relationship of technology to actions
        within modern society had become important.

2282   Muroga, Saburo. "Elementary Principle of Parametron,"
        Datamation 4 (October 1958): 31-34.

        The article is a description of the development and
        first use of a parametron-based computer which was
        built for the University of Tokyo in the mid-1950s
        but which continued in operation deep into the 1960s.

2283   Patterson, D.A. and Séquin, C.H. "A VLSI RISC," IEEE
        Computer 15, No. 9 (September 1982): 8-21.

        RISC technology was developed in the 1970s and came
        into its own during the 1980s. This is a description
        of RISC.

2284   Pennington, Ralph H. Introductory Computer Methods and
        Numerical Analysis. New York: Macmillan Co., 1965.

        This is vintage 1960s views of hardware technology.

2285   Russell, R.M. "The CRAY-1 Computer System," Communica-
        tions, ACM 21, No. 1 (January 1978): 63-72.

CRAY super computers were very popular in the late 1970s and throughout the 1980s. They were the most widely used of this kind of processor in the United States. This describes an early model.

2286   Schoenfeld, R.L. and Milkman, N. "Digital Computers in the Biological Laboratory," Science 146 (October 9, 1964): 190-198.

This is much an application brief as it is a statement about the practicalness of digital computing and analog devices in laboratories by the mid-1960s.

2287   Schultz, Louise. Digital Processing: A System Orientation. Englewood Cliffs, N.J.: Prentice-Hall, Inc., 1963.

Women writers on DP were rare in the early 1960s. Schultz offers a technical review of the subject of computers, circa early to mid-1960s, and on how to use that family of machines.

2288   Spencer, Donald D. How Computers Work. Rochelle Park, N.J.: Hayden Book Co., Inc., 1974.

The author of many books on data processing provides a general overview of computers for the general reader. The material is based on technology of the early 1970s, circa fourth generation.

2289   Thomas, Shirley. Computers. New York: Holt, Rinehart & Winston, Inc., 1965.

By this period many books were appearing in print on the nature and use of computer technology. This is a typical example of this type of publication.

2290   Thornton, James E. "The CDC 6600 Project," Annals of the History of Computing 2, No. 4 (October 1980): 338-348.

This is system development history in a practical form. The CDC 6600, developed in 1964, was an important machine of the period. The author offers details on it and on design management; illustrated.

2291   Turn, R. Computers in the 1980s. New York: Columbia University Press, 1974.

This reflects technological possibilities from the perspective of how computer scientists felt in the early 1970s.

2292   Werkheiser, A.H. "Control Data Corporation 6000 Series," in A. Ralston and Meek, C.L. (eds), Encyclopedia of Computer Science (New York: Petrocelli/Charter, 1976): 362-363.

This is a history of the system, 1964-1970.

Hardware Technology

2293   Balkovie, M.D. et al. "High-Speed Voiceband Data
       Transmission Performance on the Switched Telecommu-
       nications Network," Bell System Technical Journal
       50, No. 4 (April 1971): 1349-1384.

       This relates the results of a survey conducted in
       1969-70 to measure error rates on over 1500 calls
       totalling 700 hours.

2294   Bard, Yonathan and Sauer, Charles H. "IBM Contribu-
       tions to Computer Performance Modeling," IBM Journal
       of Research and Development 25, No. 5 (September
       1981): 562-570.

       This is a history of methods of simulation and
       measurement, 1960s and 1970s.

2295   Barden, W. "Analog-to-Digital Conversion," Electrical
       World 79 (May 1968): 49-52.

       The focus is on input/output equipment of the 1960s
       to perform this conversion.

2296   Barnes, G.H. et al. "The Illiac IV Computer," IEEE
       Transactions C-17, 8 (August 1968): 746-767.

       This is as much a technical description of the
       system's components as it is of the ILLIAC IV.

2297   Bartree, Thomas C. Digital Computer Fundamentals. New
       York: McGraw-Hill Book Co., Inc., 1960.

       This is a detailed, general introduction to the
       technology of computers, from basic principles to
       complex issues. The intended audience was the DP
       professional.

2298   Bobeck, A.H. and Scovil, H.E.D. "Magnetic Bubbles,"
       Scientific American 224, No. 6 (1971): 78-90.

       This technology was given high hopes as being signi-
       ficant in the early 1970s. It is described along
       with the basis of that hope.

2299   Bouknight, W.J. "The Illiac IV System," Proceedings,
       IEEE (April 1972): 369-379.

       This is a functional description of the super
       computer and of the technology with which it was
       made.

2300   Bukstein, E. "Computer Input-Output Equipment,"
       Electrical World 75 (November 1964): 52-54ff.

       More than just a description of I/O equipment, it
       also discusses fundamental technologies involved.

2301   Campbell-Kelly, Martin. "Data Communications at the
        National Physical Laboratory (1965-1975)," <u>Annals
        of the History of Computing</u> 9, Nos. 3-4 (1988): 221-
        247.

        NPL did considerable work on packet switching in
        data communications with computers. This offers
        insight on British telecommunications in the 1960s
        not available elsewhere.

2302   Colton, Bruce. "The Advanced Flexible Processor,
        Array Architecture," in Peter Lykos and Isaiah
        Shavitt (eds), <u>Supercomputers in Chemistry</u> (Wash-
        ington, D.C.: American Chemical Society, 1981): 245-
        267.

        This is a brief history of the Flexible Processor
        (FP) at Control Data Corporation in 1972 and on the
        Advanced Flexible Processor (AFP).

2303   "Computer Gets Faster Running Mate; Linking Microform
        Techniques to Computer," <u>Business Week</u> (June 8,
        1968): 84-85.

        This was a line of technological R&D that enjoyed
        a momentary, if hardly successful attention.

2304   Dauer, Frederick William. "On the Mechanics and
        Design of Impact Printing Devices" (Unpublished Ph.D.
        dissertation, University of Colorado, 1981).

        Although a technical paper, it contains much material
        on the history of such devices.

2305   Davis, E.M. <u>et al</u>. "Solid Logic Technology: Versatile,
        High-Performance Microelectronics," <u>IBM Journal of
        Research and Development</u> 8 (1964): 102-114.

        This represents the first description of IBM's use
        of SLT, used to integrate semiconductor and resistor
        components, replacing the SMS printed circuit package
        cards of the early 1960s.

2306   Diebold, John. "What's Ahead in Information Technolo-
        gy," <u>Harvard Business Review</u> 43 (September 1965):
        76-82.

        Since Diebold was such a highly regarded commentator
        on data processing in the U.S., his views on the
        future of such technology were important. He explains
        what new applications will be possible and the evolu-
        tion of technology in positive terms.

2307   Dorf, Richard C. <u>Introduction to Computers and Comput-
        er Science</u>. San Francisco: Boyd and Fraser, 1972.

        This book, over 600 pages long, was written by an
        electrical engineer. Dorf presents a detailed tech-
        nical survey of contemporary technology based on early
        fourth generation developments.

2308   Gaggioni, H.P. "The Evolution of Video Technologies,"
        IEEE Communication Magazine 25, No. 11 (November
        1987): 20-36.

        This describes methods for improving color video
        and their economic effects. There is included some
        discussion of computer video (1970s-80s).

2309   Galton, Antony. "Temporal Logic and Computer Science:
        An Overview," in Antony Galton (ed), Temporal Logics
        and Their Application (Orlando, Fla.: Academic Press,
        1987): 1-52.

        Although intended for a technical audience, his
        overview provides historical perspective and details.

2310   Gebhardt, Friedrich (ed). Skizzen aus den Anfangen
        der Datenverarbeitung. Munich: R. Oldenbourg
        Verlag, n.d. (1970s?).

        This is a collection of historical essays and
        includes contributions by Konrad Zuse, Helmut T.
        Schreyer and Wilfried de Beauclair on early comput-
        ing in Central Europe (1930s-1960s).

2311   Heiserman, D. L.   "Large-Scale Integration," Electri-
        cal World 82 (December 1969): 37-40ff.

        By the end of the 1960s, the story of integrated
        circuits, compaction of components, and so forth
        was an important development in hardware packaging.
        Part of that story is narrated here.

2312   "Information Acquisition and Display," Duns Review 86,
        Pt. 2 (September 1965): 153-155ff.

        The use of technology to accomplish the job is sur-
        veyed in this article intended for a business audien-
        ce.

2313   Johnson, David S. "The Geneology of Theoretical
        Computer Science: A Preliminary Report," SIGACT
        News 16, No. 2 (Summer 1984): 36-49.

        The author reviews the evolution of theoretical
        computer science, covering the genesis of over 500
        research efforts.

2314   Lancaster, D. "Logic Demon; Duplicating the Logic
        Functions of Giant Electric Computers," Popular
        Electronics 25 (December 1966): 41-45.

        This was one of a series of articles published in
        this magazine reporting on computer science in the
        1960s.

2315   Meacham, Alan D. and Thompson, Van B. (eds). Data
        Processing Library Series. Detroit: American Data
        Processing, Inc., 1962.

They produced a series of volumes intended to cover all aspects of the subject. Four were published by the end of 1962, consisting of articles by experts on specific topics.

2316   Noyce, Robert N. "Large Scale Integration: What is Yet to Come?," Science 195 (1977): 1102-1106.

One of the creators of the computer chip argues that further miniaturization, capacity, and price performance would come and then described these prospects. In hindsight he was very correct.

2317   Noyce, Robert N. and Hoff, Marcian E., Jr. "A History of Microprocessor Development at Intel," IEEE Micro 1 (February 1981): 8-21.

Chip technology developments of the 1970s is reviewed by a leading figure in the industry with help from Hoff.

2318   Olson, C. Marcus. "The Pure Stuff: A Memoir (On Producing Pure Silicon)," American Heritage of Invention and Technology 4, No. 1 (Spring/Summer 1988): 58-63.

Integration of components was, by the 1980s, recognized as one of the major technological events of the twentieth century, and that made inexpensive and practical computers possible.

2319   Pearce, G.F. "Amateur Scientist," Scientific American 218 (June 1968): 122-126.

The article is on analog computing.

2320   Pierce, W.H. "Redundancy in Computers: Extra Parts to Suppress Errors," Scientific American 210 (February 1964): 103-106, 152.

The strategy of building into computers redundant circuits and other functions was done as an effective way of reducing down time. That strategy is explained and illustrated.

2321   "Process-Control Computers," Fortune 71 (April 4, 1965): 223-224.

This describes the application of computers, primarily analog, to various manufacturing and processing applications in the 1960s.

2322   Queisser, Hans. The Conquest of the Microchip. Cambridge, Mass.: Harvard University Press, 1988.

This is a history of the transistor and microchips with considerable focus on the physics of crystals and its current state-of-the-art. The author worked in Silicon Valley for a while. He also offers many details on German developments.

2323   Rhea, J.   "Industry Moving Into Fourth Generation;
         Super-Scale Computers," <u>Aero Technology</u> 21 (June 17,
         1968): 25-28.

         In reasonably lay terms he explains the process lead-
         ing to the evolution of computer design as later
         seen in the 1970s.

2324   Roberts, Lawrence G.   "The Evolution of Packet Switch-
         ing," <u>Proceedings of the IEEE</u> 66 (November 1978):
         1307-1313.

         Packet switching networks began to develop in the
         1960s. This article has material on the role played
         by professors and engineers at MIT.

2325   Schantz, Herbert F.   <u>The History of OCR</u>. Manchester,
         Vermont: Recognition Technologies Users Association,
         1982.

         This is a book-length history of the subject with
         comments on its role in the 1980s.

2326   Schechter, Bruce.   <u>The Path of No Resistance: The
         Story of the Revolution in Superconductivity</u>. New
         York: Simon & Schuster, 1989.

         This recounts the 1986 breakthrough achieved by Alex
         Müller and George Bednorz in creating a superconduc-
         tive compound. The story is taken down through 1987
         in which he reviews the work of other scientists all
         attempting to make superconductors that operated at
         increasingly higher temperatures.

2327   Sienkiewicz, J.M.   "Flip-Flop Circuits," <u>Popular
         Mechanics</u> 14 (March 1961): 59-62.

         Such circuits were common features of computers of
         the late 1950s and early 1960s with home-made devices
         using them throughout the 1960s. The technology of
         the period is explained.

2328   Sienkiewicz, J.M.   "How to Understand and Make a Flip-
         Flop Computer," <u>Popular Mechanics</u> 14 (April 1961):
         72-75ff.

         This continues the discussion from the previous
         article.

2329   Triebwasser, S.   "Large-Scale Integration and the
         Revolution in Electronics," <u>Science</u> 163 (January 31,
         1969): 429-434.

         The author describes the process of miniaturization
         of electrical circuits in computers.

2330   Ulsh, H.B.   "Current Ideas in the Philosophy of Testing
         Electrical Contacts," <u>IEEE Transactions, Parts, Matter,
         Packaging</u> PMP-2 (1966): 68-70.

The author argues that gold plating was used in
computing, particularly SMS packaging, for reasons
of reliability and performance, beginning in 1959.
It was a way of controlling corrosion in components.

2331   U.S. National Bureau of Standards. Means of Achieving
       Interchangeability of Computer Peripherals. Federal
       Information Processing Systems Report by the Center
       for Computer Science and Technology. Washington,
       D.C.: U.S. Government Printing Office, May 1972.

       In addition to recommendations, this report has
       information on the number and value of peripherals
       used by the U.S. Government as of March 31, 1972.

2332   Watson, W.J. "The TI ASC: A Highly Modular and Flex-
       ible Super Computer Architecture," Proceedings of
       AFIPS (1972): 221-228.

       This is a technical piece, vintage early 1970s, on
       computer architecture.

2333   Wiedmann, S.K. "Advancements in Bipolar VLSI (Very
       Large Scale Integration) Circuits and Technologies,"
       IEEE Journal of Solid-State Circuits SC-29 (1984):
       282-291.

       VLSI became standard fare in large computers in the
       late 1970s and throughout the 1980s. This is a
       technical paper with useful historical information.

2334   Winograd, S. "How Fast Can Computers Add?," Scientific
       American 219 (October 1968): 93-100.

       This is a survey of computer design as of the mid-
       1960s.

2335   Zeidler, H.M. et al. Patterns of Technology in Data
       Processing and Data Communications. Stanford Research
       Report 7379B-4, February 2969, in U.S. Department of
       Commerce Clearinghouse Document PB 183 612, vol. 1.

       This is one of seven SRI reports for the FCC on the
       subject. Surveys the cost of computers, software,
       terminals, and data communications. It contains a
       great deal of information and bibliography.

                  IBM Hardware and Technology

2336   Bode, Richard. The Computer Age: The Evolution of IBM
       Computers. Armonk, N.Y.: IBM Corporation, 1979.

       This is a 13-page pamphlet, originally an article in
       Think magazine in 1976. It covers developments from
       the 1950s to 1976; well illustrated.

2337   Brear, Scott. "Evolution of the IBM 3270," Computer-
       world (January 21, 1985): ID/13, ID/15-ID/16.

This is a brief history of the DP industry's most
widely used cathode ray terminal (CRT), from 1965 to
1985.

2338   Hopkins, M.E. "A Perspective on the 801/Reduced
       Instruction Set Computer," IBM Systems Journal 26,
       No. 1 (1987): 107-121.

       Hopkins describes work done at IBM on an experimen-
       tal mini computer, begun in 1976, and its implica-
       tions for the design of systems in the 1980s.

2339   Hsiao, M.Y. et al. "Reliability, Availability, and
       Serviceability of IBM Computer Systems: A Quarter
       Century of Progress," IBM Journal of Research and
       Development 25, No. 5 (September 1981): 453-465.

       This is a history of RAS from 1956 to 1980 with a
       survey of design intentions, technologies, functions
       on IBM computers and I/O from the IBM 650 down to
       1981.

2340   Leeson, Daniel N. and Dimitry, Donald L. Basic Pro-
       gramming Concepts and the IBM 1620 Computer. New
       York: Holt, Rinehart and Winston, Inc., 1962.

       This is a thorough survey of the computer and about
       its use.

2341   Peck, Tracy G. "Worldwide Systems Engineering," IBM
       Systems Journal 24, Nos. 3-4 (1985): 182-188.

       Peck describes the role of the IBM Systems Engineer
       from 1960 to 1985. The IBM SE was as common a feature
       of a data center as an IBM computer. They advised
       customers on usage, capacity, education, and appli-
       cation development.

2342   Svigals, J. "IBM 7070 Data Processing System,"
       Proceedings of the Western Joint Computer Conference
       (San Francisco, March 1959): 222-231.

       The IBM 7070 was in use until the mid-1960s before
       newer products, such as the IBM 360 began replacing
       the older machines. This is a description.

2343   Taylor, R.L. "Low-End General-Purpose Systems," IBM
       Journal of Research and Development 25, No. 5 (Sep-
       tember 1981): 429-440.

       This is a history of IBM processors from the S/3
       (1969) to 1980, with comments on the S/32, S/34, S/38,
       and technical evolutions in design and packaging of
       each.

2344   Wilkes, Maurice V. "Historical Perspective—Computer
       Architecture," AFIPS Conference Proceedings, Fall
       Joint Computer Conference 41 (1972): 971-976.

       He comments frequently on IBM magnetic storage from

the 1950s through the 1960s and the company's impact
technologically.

IBM Printers

2345   Elzinga, C.D. et al. "Laser Electrophotographic Print-
        ing Technology," IBM Journal of Research and Develop-
        ment 25, No. 5 (September 1981): 767-773.

        They detail the development of non-impact printers
        at IBM during the 1960s and 1970s. It has illustra-
        tions of the IBM 3800 and IBM 6670.

2346   IBM Corporation. IBM 1403 Field Engineering Manual:
        Theory of Operation. Armonk, N.Y.: IBM Corporation,
        1973.

        This publication went through many editions. The
        IBM 1403 and, in particular the IBM 1403 N series
        were the most popular systems printers of the 1960s
        and 1970s in the DP industry.

2347   Mayadas, A.F. et al. "The Evolution of Printers and
        Displays," IBM Systems Journal 25, Nos. 3-4 (1986):
        399-416.

        This overviews such equipment from IBM since the
        1940s. The authors illustrate how previous develop-
        ments influenced current products. It is illus-
        trated with charts.

2348   Nickel, T.Y. and Kania, F.J. "Printer Technology in
        IBM," IBM Journal of Research and Development 25,
        No. 5 (September 1981): 755-765.

        It begins with the IBM 1403 and goes down through
        the IBM 3211 (1950s-1980).

2349   Pennington, K.S. and Crooks, W. "Resistive Ribbon
        Thermal Transfer Printing: A Historical Review and
        Introduction to a New Printing Technology," IBM
        Journal of Research and Development 29 (1985): 449-
        458.

        The article contains material on IBM printers as far
        back as the 1940s.

IBM SNA and Teleprocessing

2350   Gentle, Edgar C., Jr. Data Communications in Business.
        New York: American Telephone and Telegraph Co., 1965.

        This is as much a book on how to use TP as it is a
        description of the technology as of the 1960s for
        the transmital of information (data) as opposed to
        just conversations by telephone.

2351   Jaffe, J.M. et al. "SNA Routing: Past, Present, and
        Possible Future," IBM Systems Journal 22, No. 4

(1983): 417-434.

While a technical paper on IBM's networking approach,
it does provide a brief review of its evolution since
the early 1970s.

2352   Jarema, David R. and Sussenguth, Edward H.   "IBM Data
       Communications: A Quarter Century of Evolution and
       Progress," IBM Journal of Research and Development
       25, No. 5 (September 1981): 391-404.

       This is both history and a technical survey from TP
       that was point-to-point batch transmissions down to
       networking (SNA and so forth), from the 1960s through
       the 1970s.

2353   Lewin, Leonard. Telecommunications: An Interdiscipli-
       nary Text. Norwood, Mass.: Artech House, 1986.

       This is a contemporary introduction to telecommuni-
       cations. It includes material on computer networks
       and data communications, circa 1970s and 1980s.

2354   Morgan, P.F.A. "Highlights in the History of Tele-
       communications," Telecommunications Journal 53
       (1986): 138-149.

       This adds material on telecommunications of data
       from computers across telephone lines.

2355   Rosenberg, Art. "Time-Sharing: A Status Report,"
       Datamation 12, No. 2 (1966): 66-77.

       This is a very informed report coming when time-shar-
       ing was becoming widely accepted. It describes the
       increasing number of dedicated time-sharing systems
       being developed within the U.S.

2356   Scherr, A.L. "Structures for Networks of Systems,"
       IBM Systems Journal 26, No. 1 (1987): 4-12.

       While the thrust of the paper is on anticipated
       developments, it does cover evolution of networking
       of computer systems, primarily of the 1970s.

2357   Strauss, William. "The Westinghouse Telecomputer
       Center; A Preview for Managers," Industrial Manage-
       ment Review 6 (1965): 65-69.

       Strauss describes a very large teletype system oper-
       ated out of Westinghouse in Pittsburg, Pennsylvania,
       supporting several hundred locations. By 1960s'
       standards, that was a very large network.

2358   Sundstrom, R.J. and Schultz, G.D. "SNA's First Six
       Years: 1974-1980," Fifth International Conference on
       Computer Communication (Amsterdam: North-Holland
       Publishing Co., 1980): 578-585.

       The authors, both IBM engineers, describe the

evolution of the features of IBM's Systems Network
Architecture.

2359   Sundstrom, R.J. et al. "SNA: Current Requirements and
        Direction," IBM Systems Journal 26, No. 1 (1987):
        13-36.

        The article traces the evolution of IBM's SNA from
        its announcement in 1974 to the present and is the
        most complete account of the important subject as
        of this date.

IBM System/360

2360   Amdahl, Gene M. et al. "Architecture of the IBM System
        /360," IBM Journal of Research and Development 8
        (1964): 87-101.

        Amdahl is joined by G.A. Blaauw and F.P. Brooks, Jr.,
        in describing the system that they managed through
        design, clearly IBM's most successful product upt to
        that point.

2361   Brooks, F.P. and Iverson, K.E. Automatic Data Process-
        ing. System/360 Edition. New York: John Wiley, 1969.

        Published late in the life of the IBM S/360, the
        book is a useful technical review of the family of
        computers.

2362   "Computer System Mixes Science, Business Tasks; System/
        360," Science News Letter 85 (April 18, 1964): 248.

        This was published within days of IBM introducing
        the family of new computers and is an initial des-
        cription of the very large announcement of some 250
        products: hardware (computers and new peripherals),
        operating systems, programming languages, and some
        other software aids.

2363   Conti, Carl J. et al. "Structured Aspects of the System
        /360 Model 85, I—General Organization," IBM Systems
        Journal 7 (1968): 2-14.

        The authors described the use of cache memory of a
        360 Model 85. Conti became a senior IBM executive
        responsible, throughout the 1980s, for developing
        all of IBM's high end processors, sequels to 360.

2364   Crawford, F.R. Introduction to Data Processing.
        Englewood Cliffs, N.J.: Prentice-Hall, Inc., 1968.

        Crawford, of IBM, cites the use of the 360 to des-
        cribe the use of computers. It has a chapter on the
        history of computing (pp. 15-42). Historical refer-
        ences appear throughout the book on all aspects of
        data processing technology, both hardware and soft-
        ware.

2365   "Do-All Thinkmachine: System/360," Time 83 (April 17,
        1964): 117.

This was _Time_ magazine's account of IBM's announcement of the S/360 family of computers. All major
business journals published an account of the system.

2366   Evans, Bob O. "System/360: A Retrospective View,"
        Annals of the History of Computing 8, No. 2 (April
        1986): 155-179.

        The author lead IBM's technical efforts to develop
        S/360. This is a major publication on the most
        important computer built up to that time (1960s) by
        any vendor.

2367   Falkoff, A.D. et al. "A Formal Description of System/
        360," _IBM Systems Journal_ 3, Nos. 2-3 (June 1964):
        198-262.

        This was IBM's full, technical description of its
        most important product of the 1960s, and an early
        account of the system by an engineer involved in its
        development. Co-authors were also IBMers.

2368   Gifford, David and Spector, Alfred. "Case Study: IBM's
        System/360-370 Architecture," _Communications, ACM_
        30, No. 4 (April 1987): 291-307.

        One of the few articles ever published to look at
        IBM's major announcements of the 1960s and 1970s as
        one historical continuum of technological change.

2369   Hellerman, Herbert et al. "The SPREAD Discussion Con-
        tinued," _Annals of the History of Computing_ 6, No.
        2 (April 1984): 144-151.

        This includes biographies of key IBM engineers on
        the project, along with their views on the origins
        of and evolution of S/360.

2370   "IBM Unwraps Its Billion-Dollar Gamble; System/360
        Data Equipment," _Business Week_ (April 11, 1964): 67-
        68ff.

        This was one of the first published announcements of
        the System 360, announced by IBM on April 7.

2371   Liptay, J.S. "Structural Aspects of the System/360
        Model 85, II—The Cache," _IBM Systems Journal_ 7
        (1968): 15-21.

        He described how monolithic semiconductor memory
        could be used in a buffered cache memory system and
        how it was employed on a System 360 Model 85 in the
        mid 1960s.

2372   "Now System 360," _Newsweek_ 63 (April 20, 1964): 91-
        93.

        Newsweek's article illustrated IBM's care in assuring
        that all the major magazines covered the announcement.

2373   Padegs, A.   "System/360 and Beyond," IBM Journal of
        Research and Development 25, No. 5 (September 1981):
        377-390.

        Padegs recounts the evolution of computer architec-
        tures at IBM beginning with the S/360 down to 1981.
        He offers details on why things were done, particu-
        larly regarding overall architectural strategic
        decisions.

2374   Patrick, Robert L.   "The Seed of Empire," Datamation
        30, No. 7 (May 15, 1984): 30-34.

        While on the history of S/360, it also includes
        material on the SPREAD Report.

2375   Platz, E.F.   "Solid Logic Technology Computer Circuits
        —Billion Hour Reliability Data," Microelectronics
        and Reliability (Elmsford, N.Y.: Pergamon Press,
        1969): 8, p. 59.

        The author explains the characteristics of early IBM
        high-speed integrated circuits of the late 1960s as
        used in S/360.

2376   Pugh, E.W.   "Device and Array Design for a 120-Nano-
        second Magnetic Film Main Memory," IBM Journal of
        Research and Development 11 (1967): 169-178.

        Pugh describes memory array technology he worked on
        for IBM in the mid-1960s for the S/360 family of
        computers.

2377   Pugh, E.W.   Memories That Shaped an Industry: Decisions
        Leading to IBM System/360.   Cambridge, Mass.: MIT
        Press, 1984.

        This is a book-length account of the development of
        the S/360 in the form of memoirs by an engineering
        manager on the project.

2378   Schussel, G.   "IBM vs. RemRand," Datamation (May 1965):
        54-66.

        This offers some insight on competition for the S/360
        family just as IBM began to ship the computer to
        customers in quantity.

2379   Solomon, M.B.   "Economies of Scale and the IBM System/
        360," Communications, ACM 9, No. 6 (June 1966): 435-
        440.

        This suggests instruction timings and cost to execute
        three types of problems on 5 models of S/360: Model
        30, 40, 50, 65, and 75.

2380   "SPREAD Report: The Origins of the IBM System/360
        Project," Annals of the History of Computing 5, No.
        1 (January 1983): 4-44.

This reprints the actual report with an introduction
by B.O. Evans. The report was written in 1961 and
recommended the creation of what became known as the
System 360 family of computers. This is a major
document in the history of modern computers.

2381   Wise, T.A. "I.B.M.'s $5,000,000,000 Gamble; System/360
        Computer," Fortune 74 (September 1966): 118-123ff,
        (October 1966): 139ff.

        This was the first detailed analysis of the S/360
        story to be published. It also offers material on
        the acceptance of the product within the data process-
        ing world.

                        IBM System/370

2382   Ayling, J.K. "Monolithic Main Memory is Taking Off,"
        1971 IEEE International Convention Digest 14 (1971):
        70-71.

        Ayling described memory in IBM's S/370 Models 135
        and the earlier 145. The 145 was introduced on Sep-
        tember 23, 2970, the 135 on March 8, 1971. IBM was
        the first vendor to ship commercially applied semi-
        conductor main memory.

2383   Case, R.P. and Padegs, A. "Architecture of the IBM
        System/370," Communications, ACM 21, No. 1 (January
        1978): 73-96.

        This is a formal description of IBM's large computer
        family of the 1970s by two of its developers.

2384   Irwin, J.W. et al. "The IBM 3803/3420 Magnetic Tape
        Subsystem," IBM Journal of Research and Development
        15 (1971): 391-400.

        This is a description of the control/switch unit for
        the IBM 3420 family of tape drives which had new
        technologies and introduced with the S/370 computers.

2385   Phillips, W.B. "A Systems Approach to Magnetic Tape
        Drive Design," Proceedings of the IEEE International
        Convention (New York, March 24-27, 1969): 273-274.

        He describes the technology incorporated in the IBM
        2401 Models 4 and 5 tape drives and developments
        since 1966.

2386   Rodriguez, J.A. "An Analysis of Tape Drive Technology,"
        Proceedings of IEEE 63 (1975): 1153-1159.

        He analyzed the technology in the IBM 3420, first
        shipped in 1973, and subsequently the most widely
        used tape system in the DP industry during the 1970s
        and early 1980s.

2387   Stevens, L.D. "The Evolution of Magnetic Storage,"
        IBM Journal of Research and Development 25, No. 5
        (September 1981): 663-675.

The author provides a history of tape and disk drives from IBM from 1953 to 1980. Four phases of development are identified: events from 1953 to 1962, 1963 to 1966, 1967 to 1980, and major developments anticipated in subsequent years.

Memory Technologies

2388   Berry, J.R. "Miniature World of Micro-circuits," Popular Mechanics 124 (September 1965): 120-123.

This is a brief overview of the situation as of the mid-1960s, reflecting significant advances in miniaturization in electronics over the previous five years.

2389   Gardner, W. David. "An Wang's Early Work in Core Memories," Datamation 22 (March 1976): 161-164.

Wang worked at Howard Aiken's laboratory at Harvard University on ferrite core memories in the late 1940s and started Wang Laboratories in 1951 to build and sell computer memories.

2390   Getler, M. "IC Lines Increase, Prices Decrease; Use of Integrated Circuitry," Missiles and Rockets 16 (April 5, 1965): 32-33ff.

This documents recent developments and examples where new ICs were being put to use.

2391   Harding, William E. "Semiconductor Manufacturing in IBM, 1957 to the Present: A Perspective," IBM Journal of Research and Development 25, No. 5 (September 1981): 647-658.

This is a rare piece in that little has been published on the history chip manufacturing. It goes from germanium-based transistors to VLSI silicon, 1957-1980.

2392   Hazen, Robert M. The Breakthrough: The Race for the Superconductor. New York: Summit Books, 1988.

Hazen recounts recent research on superconductivity (late 1980s), including his own work and describes the meeting of the American Physical Society, March 18, 1987, called the "Woodstock of Physics."

2393   Hittinger, W.C. and Sparks, M. "Microelectronics," Scientific American 213 (November 1965): 56-64.

This is a very good overview of developments over the previous several years.

2394   Houston, G.B. "Trillion-Bit Memories," Datamation 19, No. 10 (October 1973): 52-58.

Houston has written a history of various types of computer storage with data on access times vs.

capacities, cost vs. capacities, capacities vs.
times.

2395   "Integrated-Circuit Industry," Electrical World 74
        (November 1965): 38-40.

        This is an early discussion of who was making this
        technology, volumes and roducts.

2396   Keyes, R.W. "The Evolution of Digital Electronics
        Towards VLSI," IEEE Journal of Solid-State Circuits
        SC-14 (1979): 193-201.

        This is a history of semiconductor technology from
        the 1960s through the 1970s.

2397   Keyes, R.W. and Nathan, M.I. "Semiconductors at IBM:
        Physics, Novel Devices, and Materials Science," IBM
        Journal of Research and Development 25, No. 5 (Sep-
        tember 1981): 779-792.

        This is on the physics of semiconductors and materi-
        als, 1950s-70s: electrons, inversion layers, injec-
        tion lasers, electroluminescence, Gunn effect,
        MESFETS, solar cells and so forth.

2398   Lancaster, D. "Integrated Circuits: What's Available?,"
        Electrical World 74 (November 1965): 47-49.

        The subject was timely given the large number of
        developments in the period 1962-65.

2399   Leedham, C. "Chip Revolutionizes Electronics," New
        York Times Magazine (September 19, 1965): 56-57ff.

        Leedham has published an article for the general
        public on recent developments with chips, an early
        article on the subject targeted at a non-technical
        audience.

2400   Matick, R.E. "Impact of Memory Systems on Computer
        Architecture and System Organization," IBM Systems
        Journal 25, Nos. 3-4 (1986): 274-305.

        The author argues that memory influenced systems
        more than any other component and offers evidence
        over a period of decades.

2401   "Micro Electronics, State of the Art: Integrated Cir-
        cuits Improving in Quality, Dropping in Cost,"
        Missiles and Rockets 14 (February 3, 1964): 50-52ff.

        This is one of many published in the mid-1960s,
        documenting significant and recent changes in ICs.

2402   Mims, Forrest M., III. Siliconnections: Coming Age in
        the Electronics Era. New York: McGraw-Hill, 1985.

        Offers some history of chip development.

2403   Pugh, E.W. et al. "Solid State Memory Development in
       IBM," IBM Journal of Research and Development 25,
       No. 5 (September 1981): 585-602.

       Written by an IBM engineer involved in the process,
       he surveys IBM memory developments since the 1950s
       through the 1970s, and speculates on developments in
       the 1980s. This is illustrated, detailed, technical
       and has a good bibliography.

2404   Rymaszewski, E.J. et al. "Semiconductor Logic Techno-
       logy at IBM," IBM Journal of Research and Develop-
       ment 25, No. 5 (September 1981): 603-616.

2405   Seraphim, D.P. and I. Feinberg. "Electronic and Packag-
       ing Evolution in IBM," IBM Journal of Research and
       Development 25, No. 5 (September 1981): 617-629.

       Packaging of semiconductors into computer components
       is discussed from the IBM 1400 series through the
       IBM 3081; illustrated.

                          Micro Computers

2406   Bradbeer, Robin. The Personal Computer Book. 2nd ed.
       Aldershot, U.K.: Gower, 1982.

       This is one of dozens of such publications to appear
       by the early 1980s cataloging equipment types while
       describing the technology in general terms.

2407   "Buying Computers By the Dozen; Desk-Sized Monrobot
       XI," Business Week (July 20, 1963): 45-46.

       This describes an ancient predecessor to the desk-top
       micro of the 1970s.

2408   Chposky, James and Leonsis, Ted. Blue Magic: The
       People, Power and Politics Behind the IBM Personal
       Computer. New York: Facts on File Publications, 1988.

       This is a history of how IBM came to market with a
       micro computer, written by two journalist/free lance
       writers. It relies heavily on interviews with par-
       ticipants.

2409   Dunkley, Christopher. Television Today and Tomorrow:
       Wall-to-Wall Dallas? New York: Viking, 1985.

       While an assessment of micros in the home of the
       future, he does describe the use of such equipment
       in the early to mid-1980s.

2410   "Early Small Computers," Annals of the History of
       Computing 11, No. 1 (1989): 53-54.

       The author describes a micro computer called the
       Kenbak, built in 1971.

2411   Freiberger, Paul and Swaine, Michael. Fire in the

<u>Valley: The Making of the Personal Computer</u>. New York: Osborne/McGraw-Hill, 1984.

This is an important, early history of the subject that contains a great amount of detail, covering the period 1975-1983; illustrated.

2412   Frude, Neil. <u>The Intimate Machine: Close Encounters With the New Computers</u>. New York: New American Library, 1983.

The author is a psychologist who describes the characteristics of PC hackers of the 1970s and early 1980s and then comments on PC users in general.

2413   Garr, Doug. <u>Woz: The Prodigal Son of Silicon Valley</u>. New York: Avon, 1984.

This is a biography of Steve Wozniak and an account of the early days of Apple.

2414   Glossbrenner, Alfred. <u>The Complete Handbook of Personal Computer Communications</u>. New York: St. Martins Press, 1983.

This was one of the first books to appear on PCs in a networked environment. During the 1980s that trend of networking such machines became widespread.

2415   Gupton, James, Jr. <u>Getting Down to Business with Your Microcomputer</u>. Northridge, Cal.: Source Books, 1979.

This was an early, widely distributed "how to" book that described the technology, its uses, and gave advice on the subject.

2416   Henry, G.G. "IBM Small-System Architecture and Design —Past, Present, and Future," <u>IBM Systems Journal</u> 25, Nos. 3-4 (1986): 321-333.

While the emphasis is on the IBM RT personal computer, its historical antecedents are well documented.

2417   IBM Corporation. <u>Produce Announcement. The IBM Personal Computer</u>. White Plains, N.Y.: IBM Corporation, August 12, 1981.

This was the initial "Blue Letter" announcing the IBM PC1 and offers the initial technical description, pricing, and terms and conditions of sale.

2418   Layer, Harold A. "Microcomputer History and Prehistory —An Archaeological Beginning," <u>Annals of the History of Computing</u> 11, No. 2 (1989): 127-130.

He lists 45 microcomputers, essentially of the 1970s, with brief descriptions of each.

2419   Littman, Jonathan. "The First Portable Computer," <u>PC World</u> (October 1983): 294-300.

He argues that Paul Friedle, of IBM at Palo Alto, made SCAMP in 1972, which was the predecessor of the IBM 5100 and the grandfather of the IBM PC (5150).

2420   Lutus, Paul. "Cottage Computer Programming," in Steve Ditlea (ed), Digital Deli (New York: Workman Publishing, 1984): 81-83.

This constitutes the illustrated memoirs of a PC programmer (1976-84) and includes comments on cottage programming in general.

2421   Nickerson, Raymond S. Using Computers: The Human Factors of Information Systems. Cambridge, Mass.: Bradford Books/MIT Press, 1986.

This is an example of a growing body of literature on the role of micros on people and their applications which appeared throughout the 1980s.

2422   Nilles, Jack M. Exploring the World of the Personal Computer. Englewood Cliffs, N.J.: Prentice-Hall, Inc., 1982.

He describes how the PC is making it possible for people to do more of their jobs at home now and into the future. He offers evidence of that trend drawn from the late 1970s and early 1980s.

2423   Osborne, Adam. An Introduction to Microcomputers. 3 vols. Berkeley, Cal.: Osborne/McGraw-Hill, 1982.

These volumes are not only an important, detailed source on the technical aspects of the topic, but historically significant as well because the author was the first to market micros on a national basis in the United States in the 1970s.

2424   O'Shea, Tim and Self, John. Learning and Teaching With Computers. Brighton, U.K.: Harvester, 1983.

This was one of the first publications to describe the application of micro computers in education.

2425   Papert, Seymour. Mindstorms: Children, Computers and Powerful Ideas. New York: Basic Books, 1980.

The author, an MIT professor, argues that LOGO language was useful in teaching childred about computers in the 1970s. It offers much material on childrens' contacts with computers.

2426   Perry, Tekla S. and Wallich, Paul. "Design Case History: The Commodore 64," IEEE Spectrum 22, No. 3 (March 1985): 48-58.

The Commodore 64 was an early, popular American micro computer. Its creation is described in this article.

2427   Press, Larry. "The ACM Conference on the History of
       Personal Workstations," Abacus 4, No. 1 (Fall 1986):
       65-70.

       The author reports on the first major conference ever
       held on the subject. Proceedings were subsequently
       published. It contains material, however, on micro
       computers.

2428   Press, Lawrence. The IBM PC and Its Applications. New
       York: John Wiley & Sons, 1984.

       Part of the first chapter and Appendix B is on the
       history of the PC. The entire book, however, is
       useful for a source on the technical features of
       early models and for a description of their uses.

2429   Rose, Frank. West of Eden: The End of Innocence at
       Apple Computer. New York: Viking, 1989.

       This is a general history of the company with empha-
       sis on the period of the late 1980s, after Apple had
       become a major corporation.

2430   Rothman, David H. The Silicon Jungle. New York:
       Ballantine Books, 1985.

       This poorly organized memoir of a USA Today reporter
       focuses on his initial use of a Kaypro micro comput-
       er. He also includes a history of Kaypro and Word-
       star software.

2431   Schneider, Ben Jr. My Personal Computer and Other
       Family Crises. New York: Macmillan, 1985.

       By the early 1980s, books began to appear on the
       effects of PCs on people, particularly psychological
       influences. This book is an early example of this
       type of publication.

2432   Sculley, John, with John A. Byrne. Odyssey: Pepsi to
       Apple . . . The Journey of a Marketing Impressario.
       New York: Harper & Row, 1987.

       Sculley was the chief executive officer at Apple
       Computers in the late 1980s. It contains many
       details about the departure of Steve Jobs from the
       firm and then about the revitalization of Apple.

2433   Solomon, Les. "Solomon's Memory," in Steve Ditlea (ed),
       Digital Deli (New York: Workman Publishing, 1984):
       36-41.

       These are the memoirs of the editor of Popular
       Electronics of the mid-1970s. He reviews the early
       history of micro computers.

2434   Swann, Peter. "A Decade of Microprocessor Innovation:
       An Economist's Perspective," Microprocessors & Micro-
       systems 11 (January/February 1987): 49-59.

This is one of the few reviews of early micro computing from an economic point of view rather than functional. It also discusses that portion of the data
processing world that manufactured such machines.

2435   "10 Years of Byte: Special Anniversary Supplement,"
        Byte (September 1985): 197-222.

        This has important data on the history of Byte (1970s)
        and on the early history of micro computers.

2436   Thacker, C.P. et al. Alto: A Personal Computer. Palo
        Alto, Cal.: Xerox Corporation, 1979.

        This is a functional description of an early, widely
        distributed micro computer.

2437   Warren, J. "Personal and Hobby Computing: An Overview,"
        IEEE Computer 10, No. 3 (March 1977): 10-22.

        The article was written just as micro computers were
        becoming widely available in the U.S. market but
        yet not fully understood by DP professionals at large.

                 Storage Equipment: DASD & Tape

2438   Bachman, C.W. "The Evolution of Storage Structures,"
        Communications, ACM 15 (1972): 628-634.

        He describes the role of blocking factors in logical
        records as an important way to continue improving
        the efficiency of data rates on magnetic storage
        devices.

2439   Bachman, C.W. and Williams, S.B. "A General Purpose
        Programming System for Random Access Memories," AFIPS
        Conference, Proceedings of the Fall Joint Computer
        Conference 26 (1964): 411-422.

        They discuss software which made better use of disk
        storage in the early years of DASD (1963-64 in par-
        ticular).

2440   Gagliardi, U.O. "Trends in Computer System Architec-
        ture," Proceedings, IEEE 63 (1975): 858-862.

        An important discussion point in this general over-
        view is magnetic storage, such as memory and DASD,
        in the 1970s.

2441   Grossman, Carol P. "Evolution of the DASD Storage
        Control," IBM Systems Journal 28, No. 2 (1989): 196-
        226.

        This is a technical history (1950s-1980s) on control
        units for DASD and cache storage with the focus on
        how improvements came in performance, function and
        reliability.

2442   Haughton, K.E. "An Overview of Disk Storage Systems,"
        Proceedings, IEEE 63 (1975): 1148-1152.

        This is a general introduction to DASD of the 1970s
        with emphasis on technical developments over time.

2443   Hoagland, A.S. "A High Track-Density Servo-Access
        System for Magnetic Recording Disk Storage," IBM
        Journal of Research and Development 5 (1961): 287-
        296.

        It is a discussion of a track-following feedback
        control system a decade before it appeared in the
        IBM 3350 DASD of the 1970s.

2444   Hoagland, A.S. "Storage Technology: Capabilities and
        Limitations," Computer 12, No. 5 (1979): 12-18.

        The survey focuses on the period of the 1970s,
        offering a useful, balanced analysis.

2445   Mee, C.D. "A Comparison of Bubble and Disk Storage
        Technologies," IEEE Transactions, Magnetics MAG-12
        (1976): 1-6.

        Disk was the standard and Bubble the great hope of
        the future.

2446   Modern Data Services, Inc. Market Survey: IBM Compa-
        tible Disk, Tape, and Core Storage. Framingham,
        Mass.: Modern Data Services, Inc., 1972.

        This contains the results of a survey of 1,215 IBM
        S/360 and S/370 users offering data on tape and disk
        used, and about memory acquired for computers.

2447   Poland, C.B. "Advanced Concepts of Utilization of
        Mass Storage," Proceedings, IFIPS Congress 65, No.
        1 (1965): 249-254.

        The author discusses recent (1960s) trends in system
        software that made DASD more usable in the first
        major period of disk usage.

2448   Rude, A.F. and Ward, M.J. "Laser Transducer Systems
        for High-Accuracy Machine Positioning," Hewlett-Pack-
        ard Journal 27 (1976): 2-6.

        The authors discuss the use of a laser interferometer
        and a grinder spindle used in the manufacture of
        disk products. Literature on disk manufacturing's
        history is limited so the article sheds light on
        activities during the 1970s.

2449   Turnburke, V.P., Jr. "Sequential Data Processing
        Design," IBM Systems Journal 2 (1963): 37-48.

        The author describes a process for handling files on
        tape in batch mode and recent experiences which were
        reflected in subsequent tape drive products.

Storage Equipment: IBM Products

2550   Aron, J.D. "Information Systems in Perspective," ACM
        Computing Surveys 1 (1969): 213-236.

        Aron focuses on recent advances in file indexing
        which made DASD more useful in the era of the S/360.

2551   Brown, D.T. et al. "Channel and Direct Access Device
        Architecture," IBM Systems Journal 11 (1972): 186-
        199.

2552   Buchholz, Werner. "File Organization and Addressing,"
        IBM Systems Journal 2 (1963): 86-111.

        An important early computer scientist at IBM reviews
        indexing on DASD devices of the 1960s.

2553   Buslik, W.S. "IBM Magnetic Tape Recorder," Proceedings
        of the Joint AIEE-IRE-ACM Computer Conference, New
        York, December 10-12, 1952, pp. 86-99.

        This describes the IBM 726 tape drive, announced in
        1952, the first made by the company.

2554   Carothers, J.D. et al. "A New High Density Recording
        System: The IBM 1311 Disk Storage Drive With Inter-
        changeable Disk Packs," AFIPS Conference Proceedings,
        Fall Joint Computer Conference 24 (1963): 327-340.

        Describes a machine that had removable disk packs.

2555   Dodd, G.G. "Elements of Data Management," ACM Comput-
        ing Surveys 1 (1969): 117-132.

        Dodd reviews how this was done by OS/360, complete
        with device independence in the 1960s.

2556   Engh, James T. "The IBM Diskette and Diskette Drive,"
        IBM Journal of Research and Development 25, No. 5
        (September 1981): 701-707.

        These were products introduced between 1967 and 1980.

2557   Harker, J.M. et al. "A Quarter Century of Disk File
        Innovation," IBM Journal of Research and Development
        25, No. 5 (September 1981): 677-689.

        This survey goes from the 1950s to 1981, from the
        350 to the 3380; illustrated.

2558   Harris, J.P. et al. "Innovations in the Design of
        Magnetic Tape Subsystems," IBM Journal of Research
        and Development 25, No. 5 (September 1981): 691-699.

This is a history of such systems from 1949 to 1980.
It takes the story from the IBM 726 tape drive through
the IBM 3420 and IBM 8809; illustrated.

7

Programming Languages

The history of programming languages dates back to the 1940s with their Golden Age coming in the late 1950s and early 1960s—so far. In that latter period, they became higher level languages, many of which remain in use over three decades later. This chapter contains the growing body of literature providing both histories of languages and surveys of them. The number of articles on programming languages is in the thousands. The list below focuses on descriptive materials on major languages through the late 1970s. It includes many of the original or "official" descriptions, surveys of multiple languages, and historical material and memoirs. The latter have paid considerable attention to languages.

Most historical materials on these languages are memoir in nature because they were written by the developers themselves. However, in recent years an increasing number of book-length anthologies of histories and whole issues of journals have been devoted to languages or to a combination of machines and programming languages. Bibliographies are also being published on the subject. As this bibliography goes to press, Jean Sammet's important book, <u>Programming Languages: History and Fundamentals</u> (1969), is being rewritten as three different ones, with one dedicated to the history of languages. Archival collections concerning languages are continuously receiving attention, particularly from the Charles Babbage Institute.

While the total number of higher level languages may exceed two thousand, this chapter concerns only the most widely used in the United States. Some attention has been paid to materials on developments outside the United States. The reader interested in programming languages should also consult the previous two chapters, since many discussions of hardware also include surveys of programming languages for specific machines. The subject of languages is currently a fast-growing sub-field in the historical literature of computing. Many of the original technical papers for these languages explain how they came about, their early uses, and their evolution. Thus they represent significant contemporary sources for the study of their history. All widely used languages have been documented and their history at least briefly chronicled.

General Descriptions

2559   Adams, Charles W. "Small Problems on Large Computers,"
        Proceedings of the ACM Meeting in Pittsburg (May
        1952): 99-102.

        Adams discusses, for the first time, a floating point
        address notation (originally conceived by C.V. Wilkes).
        The assembler described here was the classic structure
        of those to follow for two decades.

2560   Aho, Alfred V. "Translator Writing Systems: Where Do
        They Stand?," Computer 13 (1980): 9-14.

        Aho wrote an excellent summary of a class of compil-
        ers that created arithmetic instructions, eliminated
        redundant computation, thereby reducing accesses to
        memory.

2561   Albers, Donald J. and Steen, Lynn A. "A Conversation
        with Don Knuth," Annals of the History of Computing
        4, No. 3 (July 1982): 257-274.

        This is an illustrated, qutobiographical piece on
        the work of an important specialist on programming
        languages (1960s-80s).

2562   Allen, F.E. "The History of Language Processor Tech-
        nology in IBM," IBM Journal of Research and Develop-
        ment 25, No. 5 (September 1981): 535-548.

        The discussion surveys compilers, interpreters,
        assemblers, and macro systems from 1953 to 1980.

2563   Backus, John W. "Can Programming Be Liberated From the
        von Neumann Style? A Functional Style and Its Algebra
        of Programs," Communications, ACM 21 (1978): 613-641.

        This pioneer in the development of programming lan-
        guages of the 1950s comments on functional programm-
        ing in the 1970s, a period of little development in
        the field.

2564   Backus, John W. "Programming in America in the 1950s
        —Some Personal Impressions," in N. Metropolis et al.
        (eds), A History of Computing in the Twentieth Cen-
        tury: A Collection of Essays (New York: Academic
        Press, 1980): 125-136.

        Backus, the father of Fortran, discusses this and
        other early programming issues.

2565   Balzer, Robert. "A 15 Year Perspective on Automatic
        Programming," IEEE Transactions on Software Engineer-
        ing SE-11 (November 1985): 1257-1268.

        This is a progress report on advances and limitations
        of higher level languages.

2566   Barton, R.S. "Programming Languages and Computer
         Design: A Case History," High-Level Languages, Info-
         tech State of the Art Report No. 7 (N.C.: Infotech
         Information, Ltd., 1972): 363-374.

         The author offers an early perspective on British
         programming activities.

2567   Bemer, R.W. "The Status of Automatic Programming for
         Scientific Problems," Proceedings of the Fourth
         Annual Computer Applications Symposium, Armour
         Research Foundation 1957, pp. 107-117.

         This is a very early history of programming languages
         with focus on the 1950s.

2568   Bemer, R.W. "Survey of Modern Programming Techniques,"
         The Computer Bulletin (1961): 127-135.

         This contains material on two IBM universal compilers
         of the 1960s: XTRAN and SLANG. XTRAN is well describ-
         ed in detail.

2569   Bennett, J.M. and Glennie, A.E. "Programming for High-
         Speed Digital Calculating Machines," in B.V. Bowden
         (ed), Faster Than Thought (London: Pitman, 1953): 101-
         113.

         This is a useful introduction to the early programm-
         ing efforts evident in the late 1940s and at the start
         of the 1950s.

2570   Bobrow, D.G. (ed). Symbol Manipulation Languages and
         Techniques, Proceedings of the IFIP Working Confer-
         ence on Symbol Manipulation Languages. Amsterdam:
         North-Holland Publishing Co., 1968.

         This is a review of formal algebraic manipulation
         languages of the 1960s.

2571   Böhm, C. "Calculatrices digitales du dechiffrage des
         formules logico-mathématiques par la machine même
         dans la conception du programme," Annali di mat. pura.
         applique Series 4, 37 (1954): 5-47.

         Written by a student of Rutishauser, this is on his
         own work on problem solving software.

2572   Campbell-Kelly, Martin. "Programming the EDSAC: Early
         Programming Activity at the University of Cambridge,"
         Annals of the History of Computing 2, No. 1 (1980):
         7-36.

         The author covers activities between 1949 and 1952
         with a well researched, illustrated, technical report.

2573   Cantrell, H.N. "Where Are Compiler Languages Going?,"
         Datamation 8, No. 8 (August 1962): 25-28.

         The question was critical at the start of the 1960s

as new languages emrged, such as ALGOL and COBOL,
and just before the announcement of IBM's S/360 with
its new operating systems.

2574   Cheatham, T.E., Jr. "The Introduction of Definitional
       Facilities into Higher Level Programming Languages,"
       Proceedings, FJCC 29 (1966): 623-637.

       This article reflected views of the mid-1960s toward
       the development of higher level languages coming
       right after an important spurt of development in the
       late 1950s/early 1960s.

2575   Chorofas, D.N. Programming Systems for Electronic
       Computers. London: Butterworth, 1962.

       The book is a survey of the purpose and structure of
       ALGOL, FORTRAN and COBOL. It gives a short history
       of each along with an explanation on how to use them.

2576   Cunningham, J.F. "Conference on Data Systems Langua-
       ges (CODASYL)," in A. Ralston and C.L. Meeks (eds),
       Encyclopedia of Computer Science (New York: Petro-
       celli/Chester, 1976): 350.

       This brief article reviews the history, organization
       and mission of CODASYL, the industry group dedicated
       to standardizing computer languages, covering the
       period 1958-1975.

2577   d'Agapeyeff, A. et al. "Progress in Some Commercial
       Source Languages," in R. Goodman (ed), Annual Review
       in Automatic Programming (New York: Pergamon Press,
       1963): 277-298.

       Its focus is on commercial application languages of
       the early 1960s. It also explains the emergence of
       the concept of using English-like languages.

2578   Dantzig, George. "Reminiscences About the Origin of
       Linear Programming," in Arthur Schlissel (ed),
       Essays in the History of Mathematics, Memoirs of the
       American Mathematical Society No. 298 (Providence,
       R.I.: American Mathematical Society, 1984): 1-11.

       It is a useful history of linear programming with
       comments on some of the key individuals involved
       over the period 1950-1980.

2579   Dijkstra, Edsger W. "A Programmer's Early Memoirs,"
       in N. Metropolis et al. (eds), A History of Computing
       in the Twentieth Century (New York: Academic Press,
       1980): 563-573.

       His memoirs are of 1951-59 and he discusses types of
       programming available then and documents his role in
       Holland.

2580   Dijkstra, Edsger W. "On the Design of Machine Indepen-
       dent Programming Languages," in R. Goodman (ed),

Annual Review in Automatic Programming (New York: Pergamon Press, 1963) 3: 27-42.

One of the important developers of software in the 1950s and 1960s looks at the desire of the time to create languages that were independent of any particular computer, that is, were universal and could function on any computer.

2581   Dorfman, Robert. "The Discovery of Linear Programming," *Annals of the History of Computing* 6, No. 3 (July 1984): 283-295.

This is a history of linear programming. The author argues that it was discovered three times by three different people, all in the period 1939-1947.

2582   Fenves, S.J. "Problem-Oriented Languages for Man-Machine Communication in Engineering," *Proceedings of the IBM Scientific Computing Symposium on Man-Machine Communication* (White Plains, N.Y.: Data Processing Division, IBM Corporation, 1966): 43-56.

This discusses programming for civil engineering, contains material on COGO and STRESS, and about their uses in the mid-1960s.

2583   Gorn, S. "Handling the Growth by Definition of Mechanical Languages," *Proceedings, SJCC* 30 (1967): 213-214.

This speculates on the future of languages and is useful in appreciating the expectations of many in the late 1960s.

2584   Greibach, S.A. "Formal Languages: Origins and Directions," *Annals of the History of Computing* 3, No. 1 (January 1981): 14-41.

This is a survey of the origins of the theory of formal languages and automata with Turing and others in the 1930s, down through the 1960s. It is illustrated, detailed, and balanced.

2585   Halpern, M.I. "Foundations of the Case for Natural-Language Programming," *Proceedings, FJCC* 29 (1966): 639-649.

Halpern, like many of his peers in the 1960s, was defining how a natural or human-like language could become the basis of a programming language.

2586   Halpern, M.I. "Machine Independence: Its Technology and Economics," *Communications, ACM* 8, No. 12 (December 1965): 782-785.

He deals with issues related to conversion and compatibility of programs as seen in the early 1960s.

2587   Hoare, Charles Antony Richard. "The Emperor's Old
        Clothes," (1980 Turing Award Lecture, ACM'80, Nash-
        ville, October 27, 1980), Communications, ACM 24,
        No. 2 (February 1981): 75-83.

        These are his memoirs of developing languages from
        1960 forward with advice on how to manage such
        projects.

2588   Hopper, Grace M. "Automatic Programming: Present
        Status and Future Trends," Mechanisation of Thought
        Processes, National Phys. Lab. Symposium 10, 1958:
        155-200.

        This is a detailed survey from the perspective of
        the 1950s by a major leader in the development of
        higher level programming languages.

2589   Hopper, Grace M. "Computer Software," in Computers
        and Their Future (Llandudno: Richard Williams and
        Partners, 1970): 7/3-7/26.

        She describes the evolution of programming techniques
        from the 1940s forward. She was active in computer
        science developments throughout the period.

2590   Hopper, Grace M. "The Education of a Computer,"
        Proceedings of the ACM (1952): 243-249.

        She reports on the use of compilers on UNIVAC I.

2591   Hopper, Grace M. and Mauchly, John W. "Influence of
        Programming Techniques on the Design of Computers,"
        Proceedings, IRE 41 (1953): 1250-1254.

        Two of the most influential pioneers in modern
        computing speculate on language development in the
        1950s.

2592   Horowitz, Ellis (ed). Programming Languages: A Grand
        Tour. Rockville, Md.: Computer Science Press, Inc.,
        1983, 1985, 1987.

        This is a collection of 30 important articles on
        major languages. Although technical papers, they
        offer an historical record of programming languages.

2593   Jeenel, Joachim. Programming for Digital Computers.
        New York: McGraw-Hill Book Co., Inc., 1959.

        This is an introductory text on basic ideas at the
        start of the Golden Age of programming, reflecting
        1950's knowledge.

2594   Kahrimanian, H.G. "Analytical Differentiation by a
        Digital Computer," Symposium on Automatic Programm-
        ing for Digital Computers (Washington, D.C.: Office
        of Naval Research, Department of the Navy, 1954): 6-
        14.

The author describes an early use and motivation for, digital computers to do formal algebraic manipulation with software.

2595   Knuth, Donald E. The Art of Computer Programming. 3 vols. Reading, Mass.: Addison-Wesley, 1968.

This is a classic in the field of programming. It surveys how programming was done in the 1960s.

2596   Knuth, Donald E. "A History of Writing Compilers," Computers and Automation 11 (1962): 8-14.

This early account is on the evolution of language processors of the 1950s.

2597   Knuth, Donald E. and Pardo, Luis Trabb. "The Early Development of Programming Languages," in N. Metropolis et al. (eds), A History of Computing in the Twentieth Century: A Collection of Essays (New York: Academic Press, 1980): 197-274.

This is an excellent review of developments from the 1930s through the 1950s.

2598   Knuth, Donald E. and Pardo, Luis Trabb. "The Early Development of Programming Languages," Encyclopedia of Science and Technology (ed. by J. Belzer et al.) (New York: Marcel Dekkler, Inc., 1977): 419-493.

This covers the same material as their previous publication.

2599   Kowalski, Robert A. "The Early Years of Logic Programming," Communications, ACM 31 (January 1988): 38-43.

The author offers a history of logic programming in Edinburgh and Marseilles in the 1970s.

2600   Landin, P.J. "The Next 700 Programming Languages," Communications, ACM 9, No. 3 (March 1966): 157-166.

There was a great deal of concern regarding future developments, especially about user friendliness and data bases. This article is a good reflection of those concerns as of the mid to late 1960s.

2601   Leeds, H.D. and Weinberg, G.M. Computer Programming Fundamentals. New York: McGraw-Hill, 1961.

While a text, it relied heavily on the IBM 7090 as the basis for describing programming and its characteristics.

2602   Licklidier, J.C.R. "Languages for Specialization and Application of Prepared Procedures," Information System Sciences: Proceedings of the Second Congress (Washington, D.C.: Spartan Books, 1965): 177-187.

Argues the case for having specialiez languages.

2603   Locke, W.N. and Booth, A.D. Machine Translation of
       Languages. Cambridge, Mass.: MIT Technology Press,
       1955.

       This is a survey of programming languages of the
       early 1950s and how they functioned.

2604   Lucas, Peter. "Formal Semantics of Programming
       Languages: VDL," IBM Journal of Research and Develop-
       ment 25, No. 5 (September 1981): 549-561.

       This includes material on the history of PL/I and
       about the Vienna Definition Language (VDL), 1964-69.

2605   Lucas, Peter. "On the Formalization of Programming
       Languages: Early History and Main Approaches," in D.
       Bjorner and C.B. Jones (eds), The Vienna Development
       Method: The Meta-Language (New York: Springer-Verlag,
       1978): 1-23.

       Although a technical article, it contains an histo-
       rical review of language definition and the work of
       such people as Backus, Dijlastra, John McCarthy,
       Strachey, Knuth and others.

2606   MacDonald, N. "Computer Programming Languages in Use
       in Business—A Survey," Computers and People 24,
       No. 10 (October 1975): 22-25.

       This reflects a survey of 57 users.

2607   MacLennan, Bruce J. Principles of Programming Langua-
       ges: Design, Evaluation, and Implementation. New
       York: Holt, Rinehart & Winston, 1983.

       This is an introductory text to computer science yet
       contains historical entries in eight chapters on
       major languages, such as FORTRAN and ALGOL, with
       statements about their technical significance.

2608   McCracken, Daniel D. et al. Digital Computer Programm-
       ing. New York: John Wiley & Sons, Inc., 1957.

       This introduction to computing for the novice appear-
       ed at the sunset of low level languages. Revised edi-
       tion in 1959 began to reflect the rapid changes that
       came in the late 1950s.

2609   McGee, W.C. "The Formulation of Data Processing
       Problems for Computers," in F.L. Alt and M. Rubinoff
       (eds), Advances in Computers (New York: Academic
       Press, 1963): 4: 1-52.

       This is an important survey of programming languages
       of the period, especially for business applications.

2610   McGee, W.C. "Generalization: Key to Successful Electron-
       ic Data Processing," Journal of the ACM 5, No. 1
       (January 1959): 1-23.

This surveys trends in the development of programming languages suitable for business applications in
the late 1950s.

2611   McGee, W.C. and Tellier, H. "A Re-Evaluation of Generalization," Datamation 6, No. 4 (July-August 1960):
25-29.

This continues the theme of the author's previous
articles.

2612   Mittman, B. "Development of Numerical Control Programming Languages in Europe," Proceedings, ACM 22nd National Conference (1967): 479-482.

Mittman reviewed work done to develop specialized
languages to do machine tooling (N/C type) in Europe
during the 1960s. The application made it possible
to direct equipment what to cut, bend, fold or make.

2613   Narasimhan, R. "Programming Languages and Computers:
A Unified Metatheory," in F.L. Alt and M. Rubinoff
(eds), Advances in Computers (New York: Academic
Press, 1967): 8: 188-245.

By this publication date, computer scientists were
attempting to provide a coherent strategy for the
development of both computers and programming languages in a coordinated form.

2614   Newman, M.H.A. "General Principles of the Design of
All-Purpose Computing Machines," Proceedings of the
Royal Society of London A, No. 195 (1948): 271-274.

This is on the importance of stored program concepts
and the value of conditional branching in programming languages.

2615   Nolan, J. "Analytical Differentiation on a Digital
Computer" (Unpublished M.A. thesis, MIT, May 1953).

He describes an early attempt to use digital computers
to do formal algebraic manipulation.

2616   Orchard-Hays, William. "History of Mathematical
Programming Systems," Annals of the History of Computing 6, No. 3 (July 1984): 296-312.

Linear programming as a computational science is
described. This includes illustrations and comments
about the author's role with George Dantzig and work
at Rand Corporation in the 1950s.

2617   Pantages, A. "Languages in the Sixties," Datamation
11, No. 11 (November 1965): 141-142.

This was the report on the SHARE-JUG workshop on
programming languages. It offers comments on trends
and as yet unsatisfied requirements.

352 Bibliographic Guide

2618 Perlis, Alan J. et al. Software Metrics. Cambridge,
      Mass.: MIT Press, 1981.

      While the book is on current technology, it also
      contains a 404-item annotated bibliography covering
      the period 1967-1980 (pp. 271-399).

2619 Peterson, R.M. "Automatic Coding at G.E.," Automatic
      Coding, Franklin Institute Monograph No. 3 (Phila-
      delphia: Franklin Institute, 1957): 3-16.

      This reports on programming activities at GE in the
      1950s. GE did many leading edge user-oriented
      activities in data processing in the 1950s and was
      watched by many other corporations for trends.

2620 Philippaks, A.S. "Programming Language Use," Datama-
      tion 19, No. 10 (October 1973): 109-114.

      A study was done in 1972 and a questionnaire was
      returned by 164 users. The study was on the amount
      of effort it took to use various types of programm-
      ing languages.

2621 Pomeroy, J.W. "A Guide to Programming Tools and Tech-
      niques," IBM Systems Journal 11, No. 3 (1972): 234-
      254.

      This is a good survey of software technologies and
      methods as of the late 1960s and early 1970s.

2622 "The RAND Symposium: 1962, Pt. 1," Datamation 8, No.
      10 (October 1962): 25-32; Pt 2 in Ibid. No. 11
      (November 1962): 23-30.

      This is a description of early programming languages
      and in particular their characteristics as of the
      late 1950s and early 1960s.

2623 Raphael, B. "Aspects and Applications of Symbol
      Manipulation," Proceedings, ACM 21st National Con-
      ference (1966): 69-74.

      This is an introductory paper on the use of symbolic
      manipulation, useful in string and list languages.

2624 Raphael, B. et al. "A Brief Survey of Computer Language
      for Symbolic and Algebraic Manipulation," in D.G.
      Bobrow (ed), Symbol Manipulation Languages and Tech-
      niques, Proceedings of the IFIP Working Conference on
      Symbol Manipulation Languages (Amsterdam: North-Holl-
      and Publishing Co., 1968): 1-54.

      Besides describing string and list processing lan-
      guages, the authors also describe their uses.

2625 Reinfeld, Nyles V. and Vogel, William R. Mathematical
      Programming. Englewood Cliffs, N.J.: Prentice-Hall,
      Inc., 1958.

Their focus is on the application of programming languages to business problems and on the benefits of mathematical programming.

2626   Reynolds, C.H. "What's Wrong With Computer Programming Management?," in G.F. Weinwurm (ed), On the Management of Computer Programming (Philadelphia: Auerbach, 1971): 35-42.

This is a good reflection on programming management problems, frustrations and concerns of the late 1960s and early 1970s.

2627   Rice, R. et al. "Promising Avenues for Computer Research," Proceedings, FJCC 27, Pt. 2 (1965): 85-100.

The thrust of and value of this article lies with software and the author's reflections on concerns of the 1960s for software. These writers wanted programming and software tools to do special applications.

2628   Richards, R.K. Arithmetic Operations in Digital Computers. Princeton, N.J.: D. Van Nostrand Co., Inc., 1955.

The author, an IBM engineer, prepared a detailed, technical treatise on programming in its very early days and about the use of computers as of the early 1950s. This is one of the first publications on the operations of digital computers to appear in the United States.

2629   Ridgeway, Richard K. "Compiling Routines," Proceedings of the ACM Meeting at Toronto (September 1952): 1-3.

This was one of the first, if not earliest, technical articles to appear describing the idea of a program compiler—a basic concept that still remained key in the late 1980s.

2630   Rosen, S. (ed). Programming Systems and Languages. New York: McGraw-Hill, 1967.

This was a well distributed, highly respected anthology of papers on the topic of programming languages and their use.

2631   Rosen, S. "Programming Systems and Languages, A Historical Survey," Proceedings, Spring Joint Computer Conference (1964): 1-16.

This is a very early publication on trends in the development of programming languages, with primary focus on the 1950s.

2632   Rosin, Robert F. "Supervisory and Monitor Systems," Computing Surveys 1, No. 1 (1969): 37-54.

Although a technical paper, it includes a chronological narrative from the early 1950s to the late
1960s which includes such topics as job-by-job
processing prior to 1956, batch systems of the mid-
1950s and other topics associated with programming
languages.

2633   Rutishauser, H. et al. Programmgestuerte Digitale
       Rechengerate (Elektronische Rechenmaschinen). Mitt.
       Aus dem Inst.f. Angewandte Mathematik an der E.T.H.
       Zurich 2 (1951).

       This is on the design and programming of digital
       computers in Europe; particularly useful for early
       European programming.

2634   Ruyle, A. et al. "The Status of Systems for On-line
       Mathematical Assistance," Proceedings, ACM 22nd Nat-
       ional Conference (1967): 151-167.

       They compare AMTRAN, Culler-Fried, Lincoln Reckoner
       and MAP to each other.

2635   Sammet, Jean E. "An Annotated Descriptor Based Bib-
       liography on the Use of Computers for Non-Numerical
       Mathematics," Computing Review 7, No. 4 (July-August
       1966): B1-B31.

       This is a survey of formal algebraic manipulation
       languages; it has less bibliography and more narra-
       tive description.

2636   Sammet, Jean E. "Formula Manipulation by Computer,"
       in F.L. Alt and M. Rubinoff (eds), Advances in Com-
       puters (New York: Academic Press, 1967): 47-102.

       She surveys available languages to do formal algebraic
       manipulations.

2637   Sammet, Jean E. "History of IBM's Technical Contribu-
       tions to High Level Programming Languages," IBM
       Journal of Research and Development 25, No. 5 (1981):
       520-534.

       The topics include APL, Fortran, GPSS, PL/I, Commer-
       cial Translator, CPS, FORMAC, QUIKTRAN, and SCRATCH-
       PAD, all covering the period 1950s-1970s.

2638   Sammet, Jean E. Programming Languages: History and
       Fundamentals. Englewood Cliffs, N.J.: Prentice-Hall,
       Inc., 1969.

       This nearly 800 page book is a classic on the subject
       and the most complete history of programming langua-
       ges, down through the 1960s.

2639   Sammet, Jean E. "Programming Languages: History and
       Future," Communications, ACM 15 (1972): 601-610.

       This is more history than futures, 1950s-1970s.

2640   Sammet, Jean E.   "Revised Annotated Descriptor Based
        Bibliography on the Use of Computers for Non-Numeri-
        cal Mathematics," in D.G. Bobrow (ed), Symbolic Mani-
        pulation Languages and Techniques, Proceedings of the
        IFIP Working Conference on Symbol Manipulation Langua-
        ges (Amsterdam: North-Holland Publishing Co., 1968):
        358-484.

        This is an updated version of her 1966 publication
        on the subject (No. 2635).

2641   Sammet, Jean E.   "Roster of Programming Languages—
        1968," Computers and Automation 17, No. 6 (June 1968):
        120-123; "1969" Ibid., 18, No. 7 (June 1969): 3-8;
        "1970" Ibid. 19, No. 6B (November 1970): 6-11, 21;
        "1971" Ibid. 20, No. 6B (June 1971): 6-13; "1971"
        Ibid. 21, No. 6B (August 1972): 2-11; "Roster of
        Programming Languages for 1973," ACM Computing Reviews
        15 (1974): 147-160; "1974-1975" Communications, ACM
        19 (1976): 655-669; "1976-1977" ACM SIGPLAN Notices 13
        (1978): 56-85.

        These articles listed currently existing higher-level
        languages, predominantly in the U.S., which had been
        implemented. It was the most complete inventory of
        existing languages produced in the late 1960s and
        throughout most of the 1970s.

2642   Sammet, Jean E.   "Software History," in A. Ralston and
        E.D. Reilly, Jr. (eds), Encyclopedia of Computer
        Science and Engineering (New York: Van Nostrand
        Reinhold Co., 1983): 1353-1359.

        This is a brief history of key programming languages,
        operating systems, and data handling software, 1950s-
        1980.

2643   Sammet, Jean E.   "Survey of Formula Manipulation,"
        Communications, ACM 9, No. 8 (August 1966): 555-569.

        This surveys existing languages to do formal algebra-
        ic manipulations in the 1960s.

2644   Sammet, Jean E.   "The Use of English As a Programming
        Language," Communications, ACM 9, No. 3 (March 1966):
        228-230.

        She argues that English could and should be the basis
        for a programming language, a common sentiment among
        some programmers and language developers.

2645   Sanderson, P.C.   Computer Languages: A Practical Guide
        to the Chief Programming Languages. New York: Philo-
        sophical Library, Inc., 1970.

        This survey competes nicely with Sammet's (No. 2638).

2646   Shaw, C.J.   Theory, Practice, and Trend in Business
        Programming. Santa Monica, Cal.: System Development

Shaw reviews various languages designed to solve
business problems in the early 1960s. Besides
describing their features, he compares their functions.

2647   Sibley, R.A. "The SLANG System," Communications, ACM
       (1961): 75-84.

       Sibley describes a very early universal compiler
       developed by IBM.

2648   Sojka, Deborah and Dorn, Philip H. "Magic Moments in
       Software," Datamation 27, No. 9 (Special Report,
       August 25, 1981): 7-15.

       A chronology of milestones in software is printed
       but should be used with caution due to errors.

2649   Steel, T.B., Jr. "Beginnings of a Theory of Information
       Translation," Communications, ACM 7, No. 2 (February
       1964): 97-103.

       Steel is talking about programming languages.

2650   Thomas, Walker H. "Fundamentals of Digital Computer
       Programming," Proceedings of the IRE 41 (October
       1953): 1245-1249.

       The author demonstrates basic programming techniques
       very early in the history of programming languages
       and even of digital computers.

2651   Wegner, P. Programming Languages, Information Struc-
       tures, and Machine Organization. New York: McGraw-
       Hill, 1968.

       This is very much a vintage 1960s publication on
       programming languages of the period.

2652   Weinwurm, G.F. (ed). On the Management of Computer
       Programming. Philadelphia: Auerbach, 1971.

       The author describes programming techniques as they
       were at the end of the 1960s and as practised in the
       early 1970s.

2653   Wells, Mark B. "Reflections on the Evolution of
       Algorithmetic Language," in N. Metropolis et al.
       (eds), A History of Computing in the Twentieth
       Century: A Collection of Essays (New York: Academic
       Press, 1980): 275-287.

       Wells looks back on developments in the 1960s and
       perhaps comments based on his own experiences in the
       period.

2654   Wexelblat, R.L. (ed). History of Programming Languages,
       ACM Monograph Series. New York: Academic Press, Inc.,
       1981.

This is an important, general history of programming
languages and is a basic reference work on all aspects of the subject.

2655   Wilkes, Maurice V. et al. The Preparation of Programs
        for an Electronic Digital Computer. Reading, Mass.:
        Addison-Wesley, 1951; 2nd Ed., 1957; Reprinted with
        an introduction by Martin Campbell-Kelly (Los Angeles:
        Tomash Publishers, 1982).

        This was an early, important book on programming in
        the late 1940s as practised on the EDSAC.

2656   Willey, E.L. et al. Some Commercial Autocodes—A Com-
        parative Study," A.P.I.C. Studies in Data Processing
        No. 1 (London: Academic Press, 1961).

        The authors describe eight languages from the period
        1960/61 used for business applications: FLOW-MATIC,
        IBM Commercial Translator, COBOL, FACT, CODEL, ELLIOTT
        and NEBULA and SEAL.

2657   Wirth, N. "On the Design of Programming Languages,"
        IFIP Congress 74 (Amsterdam: North-Holland Publishing
        Co., 1974): 386-393; Reprinted in Ellis Horowitz (ed),
        Programming Languages: A Grand Tour (Rockville, Mad.:
        Computer Science Press, Inc., 1987): 23-30.

        Wirth focuses on the technical experiences he had
        with programming langues since the early 1950s.

2658   Zemanek, H. "Formalization—History, Present and
        Future," Programming Methodology: Lecture Notes in
        Computer Science 23 (New York: Springer-Verlag,
        1975): 477-501.

        Zemanek is mot interested here in programming language
        architecture between the 1950s and the 1970s.

                        Specific Languages

2659   The A-2 Compiler System. Philadelphia: Remington-Rand,
        Inc., 1955.

        This is a description of the first automatic coding
        system that could be characterized as compilers (A-0,
        and A-1).

2660   Adams, C.W. and Laning, J.H., Jr. "The M.I.T. Systems
        of Automatic Coding: Comprehensive, Summer Session
        and Algebraic," Symposium on Automatic Programming
        for Digital Computers (Washington, D.C.: Office of
        Naval Research, Department of the Navy, 1954): 40-
        68. The authors describe an algebraic coding system
        of 1952/1953 at MIT while working on the Whirlwind
        computer. It was probably the first system in the
        U.S. in which a user could write mathematical express-
        ions in a notation similar to normal format.

2661   Arden, Bruce W. "GAT: An early Compiler and Operating

358   Bibliographic Guide

System," <u>Annals of the History of Computing</u> 8, No.
1 (January 1986): 56-58.

This compiler was completed in 1958 and was developed at the University of Michigan; a technical memoir.

2662   Arden, Bruce W. <u>et al</u>. "MAD at Michigan," <u>Datamation</u>
       7, No. 12 (December 1961): 27-28.

       MAD was a programming language, described here by
       its developers, that ran on an IBM 704 (1959-61).
       It was useful for running problems quickly in an
       academic environment.

2663   Backus, John W. "The IBM 701 Speedcoding System,"
       <u>Journal of the ACM</u> 1 (1954): 4-6.

       This is a description of IBM's first automatic code
       to simplify programming, written by the project
       leader responsible for its development.

2664   Backus, John W. "The Syntax and Semantics of the
       Proposed International Algebraic Language of the
       Zurich ACM-GAMM Conference," <u>Proceedings of the First
       International Conference on Information Processing,
       UNESCO, Paris, 1959</u> (London: Butterworth, Munich: R.
       Oldenbourg, 1960): 125-132.

       This was one of the most important papers ever
       published on programming. The author introduced
       here the Backus notation (BNF), which defined how a
       programming language could be defined more rigorously.

2665   Backus, John W. and Herrick, H. "IBM 701 Speedcoding
       and Other Automatic Programming Systems," <u>Symposium
       on Automatic Programming for Digital Computers</u>
       (Washington, D.C.: Office of Naval Research, Depart-
       ment of the Navy, 1954): 106-145.

       Backus headed IBM's 701 Speed Coding project in 1953.
       He describes the software.

2666   Baecker, Harry D. "An Early Example of Microprogramm-
       ing," in <u>CIPS Proceedings</u>, Session 84, May 9-11,
       1984 (Calgary, Alberta: Canadian Information Process-
       ing Society, 1984): 318-322.

       This discusses coding on a Dutch computer called the
       STANTEC ZEBRA, of which 30 were made.

2667   Balke, K.G. and Carter, G.L. "The COLASL Automatic
       Coding Language," <u>Symbolic Languages in Data Process-
       ing</u> (New York: Gordon and Breach, 1962): 501-537.

       COLASL was a scientific computing language created at
       Los Alamos for production oriented work (1961-62).

2668   Bernick, M.D. <u>et al</u>. "ALGY—An Algebraic Manipulation
       Program," <u>Proceedings, WJCC</u> 19 (1961): 389-392.

They describe Algy, the earliest language to appear
for the purpose of doing formal algebraic manipulation. It came out in the late 1950s and ran on a
Philco 2000 computer.

2669   Blackwell, F.W. "An On-Line Symbol Manipulation
        System," Proceedings, ACM 22nd National Conference
        (1967): 203-209.

        This is a description of LOLITA, an extension to the
        Culler-Fried system, a list processing language. It
        was used to process strings of symbols in the 1960s.

2670   Bradford, D.H. and Wells, M.B. "MADCAP II," in R.
        Goodman (ed), Annual Review in Automatic Programming
        (New York: Pergamon Press, 1961): 2: 115-140.

        MADCAP II was a numerical scientific problem solving
        language used at Los Alamos National Laboratory on
        the MANIAC II.

2671   Brooker, R.A. "Some Technical Features of the Manches-
        ter Mercury AUTOCODE Programme," Mechanisation of
        Thought Processes, National Physical Laboratory
        Symposium 10 (1958): 201-229.

        AUTOCODE was an early (1950s) programming language.

2672   Brown, S.A. et al. "A Description of the APT Language,"
        Communications, ACM 6, No. 11 (November 1963): 649-
        658.

        This is a machine tool language developed at MIT in
        the 1950s. It was one of the first of its kind of
        specialized programming tools.

2673   Brown, W.S. "A Language and System for Symbolic Alge-
        bra on a Digital Computer," Proceedings of the IBM
        Scientific Computing Symposium on Computer-Aided
        Experimentation (White Plains, N.Y.: Data Processing
        Division, IBM Corporation, 1966): 77-114.

        This is a formal description of Bell Labs' language
        to do formal algebraic manipulations, called ALTRAN,
        circa mid-1960s.

2674   Brown, W.S. et al. "The ALPAK System for Nonnumerical
        Algebra on a Digital Computer," Bell System Technical
        Journal 42, No. 5 (September 1963): 2081-2119; 43,
        No.2 (March 1964): 785-804; 43, No. 4, Pt. 2 (July
        1964): 1547-1562.

        They describe ALPAK, which served as the basis of
        ALTRAN.

2675   Busch, K.J. "TELSIM, A User-Oriented Language for
        Simulating Continuous Systems at a Remote Terminal,"
        Proceedings, FJCC 29 (1966): 445-463.

        It did digital simulations of block diagrams in 1960s.

2676   Cameron, S.H. et al. "DIALOG: A Conversational Programm-
        ing System With a Graphical Orientation," Communica-
        tions, ACM 10, No. 6 (June 1967): 349-357.

        This on-line language was developed at the Illinois
        Institute of Technology, ran on a UNIVAC 1105 and
        on an IBM 7094, both in the 1960s.

2677   Cheatham, T.E., Jr. "The TGS-II Translator Generator
        System," Proceedings of the IFIP Congress 65 (Wash-
        ington, D.C.: Spartan Books, 1966): 592-593.

        TGS-II was a compiler writing language developed at
        the Massachusetts Computer Associates, Inc. It was
        also called TRANDIR software.

2678   Christensen, C. AMBIT: A Programming Language for
        Algebraic Symbol Manipulation. Report No. CA-64-4-R.
        Wakefield, Mass.: Computer Associates, Inc., October
        1964.

        This is a general description of AMBIT, a minor list
        processing language of the early 1960s.

2679   Christensen, C. "On the Implementation of AMBIT, A
        Language for Symbol Manipulation," Communications,
        ACM 9, No. 8 (August 1966): 570-573.

        This list processing language is described by the
        developer.

2680   Chu, Y. "An ALGOL-Like Computer Design Language,"
        Communications, ACM 8, No. 10 (October 1965): 607-
        615.

        The system was never implemented, but was designed
        to simulate digital systems.

2681   Clapp, L.C. and Kain, R.Y. "A Computer Aid for Symbol-
        ic Mathematics," Proceedings, FJCC 24 (November 1963):
        509-517.

        This describes the first attempt to develop a formal
        algebraic manipulation language, called Magic Paper.
        It was never fully implemented.

2682   Clippinger, R.F. "FACT—A Business Compiler: Descrip-
        tion and Comparison with COBOL and Commercial Trans-
        lator," in R. Goodman (ed), Annual Review in Automatic
        Programming (New York: Pergamon Press, 1961): 2: 231-
        292.

2683   Conway, R.W. and Maxwell, W.L. "CORC—The Cornell
        Computing Language," Communications, ACM 6, No. 6
        (June 1963): 317-321.

        Developed at Cornell University to run on a Burroughs
        220 and a CDC 1604, CORC was intended to teach students.
        It had a powerful facility for correcting errors in
        the compiler.

2684   Conway, R.W. et al. "CLP—The Cornell List Processor,"
        Communications, ACM 8, No. 4 (April 1965): 215-216.

        The language was implemented at Cornell University
        in the mid-1960s.

2685   Cramer, M.L. and Strauss, J.C. "A Hybrid-Oriented
        Interactive Language," Proceedings, ACM 21st National
        Conference (1966): 479-488.

        They describe a way to do digital simulation of block
        diagrams, used in the design of computer systems.

2686   Desautels, E.J. and Smith, D.H. "An Introduction to
        the String Manipulation Language SNOBOL," in S.
        Rosen (ed), Programming Systems and Languages (New
        York: McGraw-Hill, 1967): 419-454.

        The language was developed at Bell Labs in the early
        1960s as an improvement over COMIT.

2687   Engelman, C. "MATHLAB—A Program for On-Line Machine
        Assistance in Symbolic Computations," Proceedings,
        FJCC 27, Pt. 2 (November 1965): 117-126.

        The language was developed in 1964 to do formal
        algebraic manipulations. Engelman developed the
        language while at MITRE Corporation.

2688   Feldman, J.A. "A Formal Semantics for Computer Langua-
        ges and Its Application in a Compiler-Compiler,"
        Communications, ACM 9, No. 1 (January 1966): 3-9.

        The Formal Semantic Language (FSL) was an early and
        effective language with which to express semantics.

2689   Feldman, J.A. "TALL—A List Processor for the Philco
        2000 Computer," Communications, ACM 5, No. 9 (Septem-
        ber 1962): 484-485.

        Feldman describes an early string and list version
        of IPL-V.

2690   Feurzeig, Wallace. "The LOGO Lineage," in Steve
        Ditlea (ed), Digital Deli (New York: Workman Publi-
        shing, 1984): 158-161.

        These are the illustrated memoirs of an eraly LOGO
        user. He discusses how the language developed from
        1966 to the 1970s.

2691   Gawlik, H.J. "MIRFAC: A Compiler Based on Standard
        Mathematical Notation and Plain English," Communica-
        tions, ACM 6, No. 9 (September 1963): 545-547.

        The language was used to solve numerical scientific
        problems.

2692   Geschke, C.M. et al. "Early Experience with MESA,"
        Communications, ACM 20, No. 8 (1977): 540-552.

MESA was a programming language implemented in the
1960s. Its functions are described here by its developers.

2693   Goldfinger, R. "New York University Compiler System,"
        Symposium on Automatic Programming for Digital Com-
        puters, Navy Mathematical Computing Advisory Panel,
        13-14 May 1954 (Washington, D.C.: Office of Naval
        Research, 1954): 30-33.

        This language allowed for interpretive algebraic
        coding, typical of many scientific and mathematical
        problem-solving exercises of the day.

2694   Gordon, Geoffrey. "The Development of the General
        Purpose Simulation System (GPSS)," in Richard L.
        Wexelblat (ed), History of Programming Languages
        (New York: Academic Press, 1981): 403-426; dialogue
        about the paper, 426-437.

        This is a history of GPSS by a developer/user, cover-
        ing activities between 1960 and 1968. For many years
        GPSS was one of the more widely used simulation
        languages, particularly for telecommunications.

2695   Graham, R.M. "Ada—The Billion-Dollar Language,"
        Abacus 1, No. 2 (1984): 7-21.

        This reviews the evolution and features of Ada, a
        language that was strongly supported by the U.S.
        Department of Defense in the 1980s.

2696   Grems, M. and Porter, R.E. A Digest of the Boeing Air-
        plane Company Algebraic Interpretive Coding System.
        Seattle, Wash.: Boeing Airplane Company, July 1955.

        This is the only detailed description available of
        BACAIC, a very early numerical scientific language.

2697   Grosch, Herbert R.J. "Ada's First Stirring," Annals
        of the History of Computing 11, No. 1 (1989): 54.

        This has anecdotes on the origins of Ada computing
        language in the mid-1970s.

2698   Guzman, A. and McIntosh, H.V. "CONVERT," Communica-
        tions, ACM 9, No. 8 (August 1966): 604-615.

        They describe the use of pattern-matching to LISP
        with a system called CONVERT.

2699   Hoare, C.A.R. and Wirth, N. "An Axiomatic Definition
        of the Programming Language PASCAL," ACTA Informati-
        ca 2 (1973): 335-355.

        The authors provided an early description of PASCAL,
        a language intended for scientific computing; it was
        popular in the 1970s.

2700   IBM Corporation. General Information Manual: IBM

Commercial Translator. White Plains, N.Y.: IBM Corporation, 1959, 1960.

This describes the functions and use of an early IBM language intended for use in commercial applications (1958-64) on the IBM 709, 7070, and 7090.

2701   IBM Corporation. Speedcoding System for the Type 701 Electronic Data Processing Machines. New York: IBM Corporation, 1953.

This is a description of IBM's first automatic code for simplifying programming.

2702   Kapps, C.A. "SPRINT: A Direct Approach to List-Processing Languages," Proceedings, SJCC 30 (1967): 677-683.

SPRINT was a minor list processing language that was relatively machine independent, however.

2703   Katz, C. "GECOM: The General Compiler," Symbolic Languages in Data Processing (New York: Gordon and Breach, 1962): 495-500.

Katz describes a business programming language for the GE-225. The author was head of the design group and he characterized GECOM as a "compiling technique" rather than as a new language.

2704   Klerer, M. and May, J. "A User-Oriented Programming Language," Computer Journal 8, No. 2 (July 1965): 103-109.

This was a programming language developed for use on the GE-225 and GE-235 at Columbia University. It was used in numerical scientific problem solving.

2705   Knowlton, K.C. "A Programmer's Description of L^6," Communications, ACM 9, No. 8 (August 1966): 615-625.

This language was developed at Bell Laboratories in 1965.

2706   Landy, B. and Needham, R.M. "Software Engineering Techniques Used in the Development of the Cambridge Multi-Access System," Software 1, No. 2 (April 1971): 167-173.

This is an example of how programming was done on a major project in the 1960s.

2707   Leslie, H. "The Report Program Generator," Datamation 13, No. 6 (June 1967): 26-28.

RPG was one of the most widely used report generators of the 1960s and 1970s and was considered a language by many users. This is a very early description of RPG.

2708   Marks, Shirley L. "JOSS—Conversational Computing for

the Nonprogrammer," Annals of the History of Computing 4, No. 1 (January 1982): 35-52.

JOSS (JOHNNIAC Open-Shop System) was developed by
the RAND Corporation, 1963-80s. In the 1960s it was
an early attempt at on-line programming; illustrated.

2709   McClure, R.M. "A Programming Language for Simulating
       Digital Systems," Journal of the ACM 12, No. 1 (Janua-
       ry 1965): 14-22.

       This software was described as a specialized language
       called "Language for Simulating Digital Systems."

2710   McGinn, L.C. "A Matrix Compiler for UNIVAC," Automa-
       tic Coding, Journal of the Franklin Institute, Mono-
       graph No. 3, Philadelphia, Pa. (April 1957): 71-83.

       This was a very early specialized language to do
       operations on matrices and also using arithmetic
       functions on these and transposition.

2711   McLure, R.M. "TMG—A Syntax Directed Compiler,"
       Proceedings, ACM 20th National Conference (1965):
       262-274.

       The author describes the compiler used in the early
       1960s to develop ALTRAN, a Bell Labs programming
       language for formal algebraic manipulations.

2712   Metze, G. and Seshu, S. "A Proposal for a Computer
       Compiler," Proceedings, SJCC 28 (1966): 253-263.

       This is a language designed to write other languages
       primarily for simulating digital systems.

2713   Miller, E.R. and Jones, J.L. "The Air Force Breaks
       Through the Communications Barrier," UNIVAC Review
       (Winter 1959): 8-12.

       This is on the use of AIMACO by the U.S. Air Force in
       the late 1950s for business-oriented programming
       problems.

2714   Mooers, C.N. and Deutsch, L.P. "TRAC, A Text Handling
       Language," Proceedings, ACM 20th National Conference
       (1965): 229-246.

       Written by its developers, TRAC was a language for
       handling unscructured text interactively in the early
       1960s.

2715   Morissey, J.H. "The QUIKTRAN System," Datamation 11,
       No. 2 (February 1965): 42-46.

       An IBM developer describes a dialect of FORTRAN with
       powerful debugging capabilities.

2716   Morris, A.H., Jr. The FLAP Language—A Programmer's
       Guide. Dahlgren, Va.: U.S. Naval Weapons Lab, 1967.

The language was used for many years at the Dahlgren
facility to do formal algebraic manipulations. The
publication describes how to use it and for what
applications.

2717   Mullery, A.P. et al. "ADAM—A Problem-Oriented Symbolic
        Processor," Proceedings, SJCC 23 (1963): 367-380.

        The authors proposed that a new, higher level language
        be developed. They describe such a language and the
        hardware needed to support it.

2718   Myers, Edith D.   "(Jean D. Ichbiah): The Spirit Behind
        ADA (Programming Language)," Datamation 32, No. 7
        (April 1, 1986): 101.

        This is a narrative description of ADA, a programming
        language developed for the U.S. military.

2719   Nygaard, Kristen and Dahl, Ole-Johan.   "The Development
        of the SIMULA Languages," in Richard L. Wexalblat
        (ed), History of Programming Lnaguages (New York:
        Academic Press, 1981): 439-480; dialogue about the
        paper, 480-492.

2720   "OMNITAB on the 90," Datamation 9, No. 3 (March 1963):
        54.

        The language was developed at the National Bureau of
        Standards for use on with its IBM 7090/94. It mimicked
        a desk calculator more than functioned as a programm-
        ing language.

2721   Orgel, S. Purdue Compiler: General Description. West
        Lafayette, Indiana: Purdue Research Foundation, 1958.

        This 33-page document describes a language implemented
        only at Purdue in the 1950s.   ˋ

2722   Parnas, D.L.   "A Language for Describing the Functions
        of Synchronous Systems," Communications, ACM 9, No.
        2 (February 1966): 72-76.

        Parnas describes an extension of ALGOL, called SFD.

2723   Perlis, A.J. and Samelson, K.   "Preliminary Report—
        International Algebraic Language," Communications,
        ACM 1 (1958): 8-22.

        This is a technical description of IAL, an early
        attempt (1950s) to develop a universal language,
        later called ALGOL.

2724   Perlis, A.J. and Smith, J.N.   A Mathematical Language
        Compiler. Automatic Coding Monograph No. 3 (Philadel-
        phia: Franklin Institute, 1957): 87-102.

        This is abrief description of the Internal Transla-
        tor, a compiler the authors developed for use on the
        IBM 650.

2725   Peterson, H.E. et al. "MIDAS—How It Works and How It's
       Worked," Proceedings, FJCC 26 (1964): 313-324.

       On a language to do digital simulation of block
       languages in the early 1960s and includes an assess-
       ment of performance.

2726   Quatse, J.T. "Strobes—Shared Time Repair of Big Elec-
       tronic Systems," Proceedings, FJCC 27, Pt. 1 (1965):
       1065-1071.

       The language was Shared Time Repair Of Big Electron-
       ic Systems to communicate with hardware during
       repairs. It was developed in the early 1960s.

2727   Remington Rand. The A-2 Compiler System. Philadelphia:
       Remington Rand, 1955.

       A-2 ran on the UNIVAC I for numerical and scientific
       computing. This is the user's manual for the A-2.

2728   Reynolds, J.C. "An Introduction to the COGENT Programm-
       ing System," Proceedings, ACM 20th National Conference
       (1965): 422-436.

       Describes a list processing language than ran on a
       CDC 3600 and a CDC 3800 in the early 1960s.

2729   Rice, J.R. and Rosen, S. "NAPSS—A Numerical Analysis
       Problem Solving System," Proceedings, ACM 21st Nation-
       al Conference (1966): 51-56.

       The Numerical Analysis Problem Solving System was an
       early attempt at a higher level language, easy to
       use for numerical scientific problems.

2730   Rochester, Nathaniel. "Symbolic Programming," IRE
       Transactions, Electronic Computers, EC-2 (1953): 10-
       15.

       The author describes NR9003, the first symbolic
       assembly program developed at IBM to run on a 701.
       Rochester was an IBM engineering manager and wrote
       the software that tested the 701.

2731   Roos, D. "An Integrated Computer System for Engineer-
       ing Problem Solving," Proceedings, FJCC 27, Pt. 2
       (1965): 151-159.

       ICES was a specialized languages developed at MIT
       for applications in civil engineering. By the mid-
       1960s, over 300 organizations used it.

2732   Roos, D. ICES Systems Design. 2nd Ed., revised.
       Cambridge, Mass.: MIT Press, 1967.

       This is a user's guide to ICES.

2733   Ross, Douglas T. "Origins of the APT Language for

Automatically Programmed Tools," in Richard L. Wexelblat, History of Programming Languages (New York: Academic Press, 1981): 279-338; dialogue about the paper, 338-366.

APT during the years 1956-60 was developed by MIT for the U.S. Air Force and is a precursor to CAD/CAM software.

2734   Sammet, Jean E.   "A Method of Combining ALGOL and COBOL," Proceedings, WJCC 19 (1961): 379-387.

She wanted GECOM's features in ALGOL and COBOL rather than have GE's language be a rival to COBOL. It was an issue at the start of the 1960s as COBOL was being launched.

2735   Scheff, B.H.   "A Simple User-Oriented Compiler Source Language for Programming Automatic Test Equipment," Communications, ACM 9, No. 4 (April 1966): 258-266.

Describes the Depot Installed Maintenance Automatic Test Equipment for testing hardware and was a highly specialized language called DIMATE.

2736   Scheff, B.H.   "Bypassing Professional Programmers," Datamation 12, No. 10 (October 1966): 65-81.

DIMATE is again described by Scheff.

2737   Schlaeppi, H.P.   "A Formal Language for Describing Machine Logic, Timing, and Sequencing (LOTIS)," IEEE Transactions, Electronic Computers EC-13, No. 4 (August 1964): 439-448.

Not to be confused with LOTUS, a popular spread sheet package of the 1980s, LOTIS was a machine logic software of the 1960s, described in this article.

2738   Schlesinger, S. and Sashkin, L.   "POSE: A Language for Posing Problems to a Computer," Communications, ACM 10, No. 5 (May 1967): 279-285.

This is a minor language being described by its developers.

2739   Sperry Rand Corporation.   UNICODE—Automatic Coding for UNIVAC Scientific Data Automation System 1103 or 1105. Philadelphia: Sperry Rand Corporation, 1958, 1959.

This was Sperry's answer to IBM's FORTRAN programming language for numerical and scientific computing.

2740   Sutherland, I.E.   Sketchpad: A Man-Machine Graphical Communication System. Technical Report No. 296. Lexington, Mass.: MIT Lincoln Laboratory, January 1963.

Sketchpad was a minor list processing language of the early 1960s.

2741   Taylor, A.   "The FLOW-MATIC and MATH-MATIC Automatic Programming Systems," in R. Goodman (ed), Annual Review in Automatic Programming (New York: Pergamon Press, 1960): 1: 196-206.

He describes two business-oriented languages of the late 1950s.

2742   "Towards a Formal Description of Ada," in D. Bjorner (ed), Lecture Notes in Computer Science (New York: Springer-Verlag, Inc., 1980): 98.

ADA was developed as a language for U.S. military use in the 1980s.

2743   Walker, D.E.   "SAFARI, An On-line Text-Processing System," Proceedings of the American Documentation Institute Annual Meeting (Washington, D.C.: Thompson Book Co., 1967): 4: 144-147.

The system described here is of an early online word processor/text editing package developed at MITRE Corporation. It also did linguistic and logical processing to structure information.

2744   Walter, R.A.   "A System for the Generation of Problem-Oriented Languages," Proceedings of the 5th National Conference, The Computer Society of Canada (May-June 1966): 351-355.

The language described was STRUDL, used for civil engineering in the 1960s.

2745   Wells, M.B.   "Recent Improvements in MADCAP," Communications, ACM 6, No. 11 (November 1963): 674-678.

MADCAP was used on the MANIAC II computer.

2746   Wirth, N.   "PL360, A Programming Language for the 360 Computers," Journal of ACM 15 (1968): 37-74.

PL/360 had some features of a high level language but was not machine independent. The system called out was the IBM S/360 family of computers.

2747   Wirth, N.   "The Programming Language PASCAL," ACTA Informat. 1 (1971): 35-63.

PASCAL was an up-and-coming scientific language in the 1970s. This is an early description of it.

2748   "Wolontis-Bell Interpreter," Annals of the History of Computing 8, No. 1 (January 1986): 74-76.

This is a reprint of a 1955 paper by V.M. Wolontis of Bell Labs on a floating-point decimal interpretive system that ran on an IBM 650.

2749   Wrubel, Marshal H. _A Primer of Programming for Digital
        Computers_. New York: McGraw-Hill Book Co., Inc., 1959.

        The book is based on the use of an IBM 650 with focus
        on programming. It has a great deal of material on a
        language called SOAP.

2750   Yowell, E.C. "A Mechanized Approach to Automatic Cod-
        ing," _Automatic Coding, Journal of the Franklin Insti-
        tute_, Monograph No. 3 (Philadelphia: Franklin Insti-
        tute, April 1957): 103-111.

        This describes the first known case of a computer
        being constructed with programming language order
        code; it became the NCR 304.

                              ALGOL

2751   "ACM Committee on Programming Languages and GAMM
        Committee on Programming, Report on the Algorithmic
        Language ALGOL," in A.J. Perlis and K. Samelson (eds),
        Numerical Mathematics (1959): 41-60.

        This is on the birth of ALGOL.

2752   Anderson, J.P. "A Computer for Direct Execution of
        Algorthmic Languages," _Proceedings, EJCC_ 20 (1961):
        184-193.

        Proposes the design of a computer to support the use
        of ALGOL 60.

2753   Bemer, R.W. "A Politico-Social History of Algol,"
        Annual Review in Automatic Programming (New York:
        Pergamon Press, 1969): 5: 151-238.

        This is an important publication, taking the story
        from conception of ALGOL through its early life. It
        is also funny.

2754   "Biography of Alan J. Perlis," in Richard L. Wexelblat
        (ed), _History of Programming Languages_ (New York:
        Academic Press, 1981): 171.

        He was a pioneer in the development of ALGOL.

2755   "Biography of John McCarthy," in Richard L. Wexelblat
        (ed), _History of Programming Languages_ (New York:
        Academic Press, 1981): 197.

        Although better known for his work with artificial
        intelligence, McCarthy was also involved with ALGOL.

2756   "Biography of Peter Naur," in Richard L. Wexelblat (ed),
        History of Programming Languages (New York: Academic
        Press, 1981): 172.

        Naur was a major figure in the development of ALGOL.

2757   Feldman, J.A.   "A Formal Semantics for Computer Langua-
        ges and Its Application in a Compiler-Compiler,"
        Communications, ACM 9, No. 1 (January 1966): 3-9.

        This is a general description of Formula ALGOL.

2758   "General Panel Discussion: Is A Unification of ALGOL-
        COBOL, ALGOL-FORTRAN Possible? The Question of One
        or Several Languages," Symbolic Languages in Data
        Processing (New York: Gordon and Breach, 1962): 833-
        849.

        Part of the debate, at that time, was over the issue
        of universal languages and whether to support one or
        the other, or both.

2759   Iturriaga, R.   "Contributions to Mechanical Mathema-
        tics" (Unpublished Ph.D. dissertation, Carnegie
        Institute of Technology, 1967).

        This was written by one of the developers of Formula
        ALGOL, offering a description of the language.

2760   Naur, Peter.   "The European Side of the Last Phase of
        the Development of ALGOL60," in Richard L. Wexelblat
        (ed), History of Programming Languages (New York:
        Academic Press, 1981): 92-170.

        The period covered goes from the 1950s through 1962
        and was written by a father of ALGOL.

2761   Perlis, Alan J.   "The American Side of the Development
        of Algol," in Richard L. Wexelblat (ed), History of
        Programming Languages (New York: Academic Press,
        1981): 139-170.

        He covers the period 1956-1960s. The author was a
        major player in the development of ALGOL.

2762   Perlis, Alan J. and Iturriaga, R.   "An Extension to
        ALGOL for Manipulating Formulae," Communications,
        ACM 7, No. 2 (February 1964): 127-130.

        Written by the two creators of Formula ALGOL, they
        offer a short description of this multipurpose
        language.

2763   Weber, H.   "A Microprogrammed Implementation of EULER
        on the IBM System/360 Model 30," Communications, ACM
        10, No. 9 (September 1967): 549-558.

        Weber describes how microprogramming on a computer
        was done to improve the efficiency of an ALGOL
        language called EULER. It was an early instance of a
        digital computer being modified to run more efficient-
        ly for a particular language.

2764   Zemanek, H.   "Die algorithmische Formelsprache ALGOL,"
        Elektronische Rechnanlagen 1 (1959): 72-79, 140-143.

        This is on the birth of ALGOL and early features.

APL

2765   "Biography of Adin D. Falkoff," in Richard L. Wexelblat
        (ed), History of Programming Languages (New York:
        Academic Press, 1981): 691.

        This is an illustrated, one paragraph biography of
        an important developer of APL.

2766   "Biography of Kenneth E. Iverson," in Richard L. Wexel-
        blat (ed), History of Programming Languages (New York:
        Academic Press, 1981): 691.

        This is a short, illustrated biography of an APL
        developer.

2767   Falkoff, Adin D. and Iverson, Kenneth E. "The Design
        of APL," IBM Journal of Research and Development 17,
        No. 4 (July 1973): 324-334.

        Two developers of the language provide a description
        of it.

2768   Falkoff, Adin D. and Iverson, Kenneth E. "The Evolu-
        tion of APL," in Richard L. Wexelblat (ed), History
        of Programming Languages (New York: Academic Press,
        1981): 661-674; Discussion of the paper, 674-690.

        The period is 1961-68 primarily and is written by
        its developers as a technical retrospective.

2769   Falkoff, Adin D. et al. "A Formal Description of Sys-
        tem/360," IBM Systems Journal 3, Nos. 2-3 (June
        1964): 198-262.

        This was the first formal technical description of
        S/360 but it also included comments on APL.

2770   Iverson, Kenneth E. A Programming Language. New York:
        John Wiley & Sons, 1962.

        This was the first book-length study of APL, written
        by one of its developers.

2771   Iverson, Kenneth E. "Formalism in Programming Langua-
        ges," Communications, ACM 7, No. 2 (February 1964):
        80-88.

        The father of APL reviews his ideas for the language,
        a tool that only came into its own a decade later.

2772   Iverson, Kenneth E. "Programming Notation in System
        Design," IBM Systems Journal 2 (June 1963): 117-128.

        This was an early description of APL.

2773   Katz, J.H. and McGee, W.C. "An Experiment in Non-Proced-
        ural Programming," Proceedings, FJCC 24 (1963): 1-13.

        The describe a language with many APL-like features.

2774   McDonnell, E.E.   "The Socio-Technical Beginnings of
       APL," ACM SIGPLAN/STAPL 10 (December 1979): 13-18.

       This offers a good description of the design deci-
       sions made and on the early history of APL.

2775   Prager, W.   An Introduction to APL. Boston: Bacon,
       1971.

       This is a description of how to use the language,
       published at the dawn of its popularity.

2776   Way, T.J.   "APL After Twenty-Five Years," IBM Research
       Highlights (August 1979): 3-6.

       The focus is mainly on the origins and evolution of
       APL in its early years (1950s-1960s).

                              BASIC

2777   "Biography of Thomas E. Kurtz," in Richard L. Wexelblat
       (ed), History of Programming Languages (New York:
       Academic Press, 1981): 549.

       This individual helped to develop BASIC, a major
       programming language.

2778   Kemeny, John G. and Kurtz, Thomas E.   Back to BASIC.
       The History, Corruption and Future of the Language.
       Reading, Mass.: Addison-Wesley, 1985.

       This is the history of one of the most widely used
       programming languages between 1965 and 1985, written
       by its two developers.

2779   Kemeny, John G. and Kurtz, Thomas E.   "Bringing Up
       BASIC," in Steve Ditlea (ed), Digital Deli (New
       York: Workman Publishing, 1984): 155-157.

       This is a short, illustrated history of BASIC.

2780   Kurtz, Thomas E.   "BASIC," in Richard L. Wexelblat (ed),
       History of Programming Languages (New York: Academic
       Press, 1981): 515-537; Dialogue on paper, 536-549.

       The history covers in detail the period 1956-71 and
       includes details on the role of Dartmouth College
       and General Electric.

2781   Lee, J.   "The Formal Definition of the Basic Language,"
       Computer Journal 15 (1972): 32-41.

       This is a description of BASIC as it was in the early
       1970s and as it worked on a large computer.

2782   Mather, D.G. and Waite, S.V.F. (eds), BASIC. 6th ed.
       Hanover, NH: University Press of New England, 1971.

       This is a standard text on BASIC.

COBOL

2783 Bemer, Robert W. "A View of the History of COBOL," Honeywell Computer Journal 5, No. 3 (1971): 130-135.

Bemer was involved in the creation of COBOL. He tells his story, covering the period 1959-60.

2784 "Biography of Jean E. Sammet," in Richard L. Wexelblat (ed), History of Programming Languages (New York: Academic Press, 1981): 277.

This is a short biography of an IBMer active in the development of COBOL and a noted authority on the history of programming languages.

2785 Clippinger, Richard F. "Comments on the Meeting of October 14, 1959," Annals of the History of Computing 7, No. 4 (October 1985): 327-328.

This was the session that decided to try and design COBOL based on the Honeywell Business Compiler. The author argues little was accomplished at the meeting.

2786 Conner, Richard L. "Cobol, Your Age Is Showing," Computerworld, May 14, 1984, pp. ID/7-ID/18.

This is a history and analysis of COBOL. It is critical of its capabilities in the mid-1980s.

2787 Cowan, Roydan A. "Is Cobol Getting Cheaper?," Datamation 10 (June 1964): 46-50.

The author compares COBOL on 23 different systems, offering data on costs and speed of operation.

2788 Cunningham, Joseph F. "COBOL and CODASYL Revisited," Annals of the History of Computing 7, No. 4 (October 1985): 310-312.

The author describes the use of COBOL in the U.S. Air Force during the early 1960s.

2789 Fimple, M.D. "FORTRAN vs. COBOL," Datamation 10, No. 8 (August 1964): 34, 39-40.

This was published at the time COBOL was just beginning to be widely accepted as a business-oriented language.

2790 Humby, E. "Rapidwrite," in R. Goodman (ed), Annual Review of Automatic Programming (New York: Pergamon Press, 1963): 299-310.

This is a description of a programming language related to COBOL.

2791 Jones, John L. "Viewpoint and Reminiscences of the Chairman of CODASYL," Annals of the History of Computing 7, No. 4 (October 1985): 313-315.

Jones was one of the leading advocates for COBOL, and chairman of the task force set up in 1960-61 working on its development.

2792   Lee, J.A.N. and Sammet, Jean E. "Early Meetings of the Conference on Data Systems Languages, Minutes of Meetings May 28-29, 1959, July 7, 1959, January 7-8, 1960, February 12, 1960," Annals of the History of Computing 7, No. 4 (October 1985): 316-325.

These are the minutes of the Short Range Committee meetings. It was this group that initially created COBOL.

2793   Lee, J.A.N. and Sammet, Jean E. "Meetings of the Inter-mediate-Range Committees," Annals of the History of Computing 7, No. 4 (October 1985): 329-341.

This reproduces notes from crucial meetings held on October 8, 9, and 14, 1959 on COBOL.

2794   Phillips, Charles A. COBOL, Report to Conference on Data Systems Language, Including Revised Specifications for a Common Business Oriented Language for Programming Electronic Digital Computers. Washington, D.C.: U.S. Department of Defense, June 1961.

The author, of the U.S.D.O.D. reported on the development of the language, initially in April 1960. This report includes revisions made into 1961.

2795   Phillips, Charles A. "Recollections on the Early Days of COBOL and CODASYL: Reminiscences (Plus a Few Facts)," Annals of the History of Computing 7, No. 4 (October 1985): 304-310.

He was considered by some observers as the midwife at the birth of COBOL because he chaired the language's development committee.

2796   Sammet, Jean E. "Brief Summary of the Early History of COBOL," Annals of the History of Computing 7, No. 4 (October 1985): 288-303.

This illustrated article is a brief history and includes details on the author's role.

2797   Sammet, Jean E. "The Early History of Cobol," in Richard L. Wexelblat (ed), History of Programming Languages (New York: Academic Press, 1981): 199-243; dialogue on paper, 243-276.

This is a major history of COBOL.

2798   Sammet, Jean E. and Garfunkel, Jerome. "Summary of Changes in COBOL, 1960-1985," Annals of the History of Computing 7, No. 4 (October 1985): 342-347.

This traced changes in the language during its first 25 years.

2799   Shneiderman, Ben. "The Relationship Between COBOL and
        Computing Science," Annals of the History of Comput-
        ing 7, No. 4 (October 1985): 348-352.

        The author analyzes the rocky relations between
        COBOL proponents and computer scientists. The author
        supports the value of COBOL.

2800   Strong, Jack A. "The Tale of the Near Demise of COBOL
        at Birth," Annals of the History of Computing 7,
        No. 4 (October 1985): 326-327.

        Strong was a member of the CODASYL Executive Committ-
        ee that early-on took on the task of discussing the
        potential benefits of a COBOL-like language.

2801   "Time to Switch to COBOL?," EDP Analyzer 1, No. 11
        (December 1963): 1-11.

        This appeared just as Cobol was becoming recognized
        as a major business-oriented programming language.

2802   U.S. Department of Defense. COBOL: Initial Specifica-
        tions for a Common Business Oriented Language. Wash-
        ington, D.C.: U.S. Government Printing Office, April,
        1960.

        This is the first published account of COBOL, written
        by the Short-Range Committee which designed the lan-
        guage between June and December, 1959.

2803   U.S. Department of Defense. COBOL-1961: Revised Speci-
        fications for a Common Business Oriented Language.
        Washington, D.C.: U.S. Government Printing Office,
        1961.

        The revised standard specifications was used by COBOL
        users from 1961 forward in developing their own
        versions.

2804   Whitmore, A.J. "COBOL At Westinghouse," Datamation 8,
        No. 4 (April 1962): 31-32.

        This was written by a very early user of COBOL.

                                COMIT

2805   Guzman, A. and McIntosh, H.V. "CONVERT," Communications,
        ACM 9, No. 8 (August 1966): 604-615.

        This has many ideas drawn from COMIT, used in CONVERT
        and LISP.

2806   Hilton, W.R. and Hillman, D.J. The Structure of LECOM.
        Bethlehem, Pa.: Lehigh University, Center for the
        Information Sciences, June, 1966.

        A COMIT-based system is described which ran on a GE-
        225. It was a string and list programming language.

2807   Stone, P.J. and Hunt, E.B. "A Computer Approach to
        Content Analysis: Studies Using the General Inquirer
        System," Proceedings, SJCC 23 (1963): 241-256.

        This is a discussion of the use of COMIT, an early
        string and list processing language developed at MIT
        in 1957.

2808   Yngve, V.H. "COMIT," Communications, ACM 6, No. 3
        (March 1963): 83-84.

        He describes COMIT's features.

2809   Yngve, V.H. "COMIT as an IR Languaguage," Communica-
        tions, ACM 5, No. 1 (January 1962): 19-28.

        The author was one of its developers describing its
        features.

                              FORMAC

2810   Bond, E.R. et al. "FORMAC—An Experimental FORmula
        MANipulation Compiler," Proceedings, ACM 19th Nation-
        al Conference (1964): K2.1-K2.1-11.

        The authors describe an early language designed to
        do formal algebraic manipulations. FORMAC is an
        extension to FORTRAN and on an IBM 7090/94.

2811   Duby, J.J. "Sophisticated Algebra on a Computer—
        Derivatives of Witt Vectors," in D.G. Dobrow (ed),
        Symbol Manipulation Languages and Techniques, Proceed-
        ings of the IFIP Working Conference on Symbol Manipu-
        lation Languagues (Amsterdam: North-Holland Publish-
        ing Co., 1968): 71-85.

        This is a description of the functions and use of
        FORMAC as described by the head of the development
        team for the language.

2812   Howard, J.C. "Computer Formulation of the Equations
        of Motion Using Tensor Notation," Communications, ACM
        10, No. 9 (September 1967): 543-548.

        Describes the use of FORMAC as a programming language.

2813   Neidleman, L.D. "An Application of FORMAC," Communica-
        tions, ACM 10, No. 3 (March 1967): 167-168.

        This covers similar ground as the previous citation.

2814   Sammet, Jean E. "Formula Manipulation by Computer," in
        F.L. Alt and M. Rubinoff (eds), Advances in Computers
        (New York: Academic Press, 1967): 8: 47-102.

        Essentially this an article on how to use FORMAC as
        a formal algebraic manipulation language.

2815   Sammet, Jean E. and Bond, E. "Introduction to FORMAC,"
        IEEE Transactions, Electrical Computers EC-13, No. 4
        (August 1964): 386-394.

This is a description of the language's features.

2816   Tobey, R.G.   "Eliminating Monotonous Mathematics with
       FORMAC," Communications, ACM 9, No. 10 (October
       1966): 742-751.

       This explains the benefits of FORMAC as a formal
       algebraic manipulation language. The author was a
       developer of the language at IBM.

                              FORTRAN

2817   Allen, Frances E.   "A Technological Review of the Early
       FORTRAN Compilers," Annals of the History of Comput-
       ing 6, No. 1 (January 1984): 22-27.

       These are the illustrated memoirs of an IBMer, cover-
       ing mid to late 1950s.

2818   Allen, Frances E.   "A Technological Review of the
       FORTRAN I Compiler," AFIPS Conference Proceedings 51
       (1981): 805-809.

       The author speculated on the impact FORTRAN would
       have on future compilers.

2819   Backus, John W.   "Automatic Programming: Properties
       and Performance of FORTRAN Systems I and II," Mecha-
       nisation of Thought Processes, National Physical
       Laboratory Symposium 10, 1958 (London: H.M. Station-
       ery Office, 1959): 231-255.

       The father of FORTRAN evaluates the language's
       performance.

2820   Backus, John W.   "The History of FORTRAN I, II, and
       III," in Richard L. Wexalblat (ed), History of Pro-
       gramming Languages (New York: Academic Press, 1981):
       25-45; Reprinted in Annals of the History of Comput-
       ing 1, No. 1 (1979): 21-37.

       This is a history and full statement of his views
       about FORTRAN.

2821   Bashkow, T.R. et al. "System Design of a FORTRAN
       Machine," IEEE Transactions, Electrical Computers EC-
       16, No. 4 (August 1967): 485-499.

       They argue the case for developing a computer
       specifically designed to run FORTRAN. In 1967 this
       was still the most widely used such tool for scien-
       tific computing.

2822   Bemer, Robert W.   "Computing Prior to FORTRAN," AFIPS
       Conference Proceedings 51 (1982): 811-816; Reprinted
       in Annals of the History of Computing 6, No. 1 (Jan-
       uary 1984): 16-18.

       These are memoirs of the 1930s and 1940s and on the
       significance of FORTRAN.

2823   "Biography of John Backus," in Richard L. Wexelblat
        (ed), <u>History of Programming Languages</u> (New York:
        Academic Press, 1981): 74.

        This is a short, illustrated biography of the father
        of FORTRAN and an early, important contributor to
        the standardization of programming's notation of the
        1950s and 1960s.

2824   Bright, Herbert S.   "Early FORTRAN User Experience,"
        <u>Annals of the History of Computing</u> 6, No. 1 (January
        1984): 28-31.

        This describes use at Westinghouse laboratory; illus-
        trated.

2825   Bright, Herbert S.   "FORTRAN Comes to Westinghouse-
        Bettis, 1957," <u>Annals of the History of Computing</u>
        1, No. 1 (July 1979): 72-74.

        This covers the same material as the previous cita-
        tion.

2826   Davidson, Charles.   "The Emergence of Load-and-Go
        Systems for FORTRAN," <u>Annals of the History of
        Computing</u> 6, No. 1 (January 1984): 35-37.

        The experiences of the University of Michigan and
        University of Wisconsin are included in the account.

2827   Goldberg, Richard.   "Register Allocation in FORTRAN I,"
        <u>Annals of the History of Computing</u> 6, No. 1 (January
        1984): 19-20.

        These are memoirs on how the compiler evolved in its
        early days (1950s).

2828   Greenfield, Martin N.   "History of FORTRAN Standardi-
        zation," <u>AFIPS Conference Proceedings</u> 51 (1982): 817-
        824.

        This history is broken into periods: 1962-66, 1967-
        70, 1971-78, 1978 to present.

2829   Greenfield, Martin N.   "The Impact of FORTRAN Standardi-
        zation," <u>Annals of the History of Computing</u> 6, No. 1
        (January 1984): 33.

        His focus is on the impact of FORTRAN standardization
        that made it easier for many people to use the lan-
        guage.

2830   Heising, William P.   "The Emergence of Fortran IV From
        Fortran II," <u>Annals of the History of Computing</u> 6,
        No. 1 (January 1984): 31-32.

        These are memoirs on the evolution of Fortran from
        the IBM 701 days forward.

2831   Hemmes, David A.   "FORTRANSIT Recollections," <u>Annals</u>

of the History of Computing 8, No. 1 (January 1986):
70-73.

He describes the first compiler which permitted
source code to compile on more than one computer.
It was a subset of FORTRAN and appeared in 1957.

2832   Hughes, Robert A. "Early FORTRAN at Livermore,"
       Annals of the History of Computing 6, No. 1 (January
       1984): 30-31.

       FORTRAN was used in nuclear research in the 1950s.

2833   Lee, J.A.N. "An Annotated Bibliography of FORTRAN,"
       Annals of the History of Computing 6, No. 1 (January
       1984): 49-58.

       This is a detailed bibliography covering the period
       1954-78.

2834   Lee, J.A.N. "Pioneer Day, 1982," *Annals of the History
       of Computing* 6, No. 1 (January 1984): 7-14.

       He reivews the NCC session on the history of FORTRAN
       at which John Backus and Robert W. Bemer spoke.

2835   Leeson, Daniel N. "IBM FORTRAN Exhibit and Film,"
       Annals of the History of Computing 6, No. 1 (January
       1984): 41-48.

       This illustrated article was on the exhibit celebrat-
       ing the 25th anniversary of FORTRAN, one of the long-
       est used programming languages. The full text of the
       film is included.

2836   McCraken, Daniel D. "The Early History of FORTRAN
       Publications," *Annals of the History of Computing* 6,
       No. 1 (January 1984): 33-34.

       He describes a number of publications, including his
       of 1961, *A Guide to FORTRAN Programming* (New York:
       John Wiley, 1961).

2837   McPherson, John C. "Early Computers and Computing
       Institutions," *Annals of the History of Computing* 6,
       No. 1 (January 1984): 15-16.

       This offers background on why FORTRAN-like software
       was needed in the 1930s and 1940s.

2838   Melbourne, A.J. and Pugmire, J.M. "A Small Computer
       for the Direct Processing of FORTRAN Statements,"
       Computer Journal 8, No. 1 (April 1965): 24-27.

       They describe a proposed machine which woould never
       be built to support FORTRAN by using micro-programs.

2839   Nutt, Roy. "Compiler Techniques Available in 1954,"
       Annals of the History of Computing 6, No. 1 (January
       1984): 20-22.

This brief, illustrated review is of non-Fortran
software with comments on the effect they had on the
design of FORTRAN.

2840   Rosenblatt, Bruce. "The Successors to FORTRAN—Why
        Does FORTRAN Survive?," Annals of the History of
        Computing 6, No. 1 (January 1984): 39-40.

        These are memoirs of FORTRAN at Standard Oil. The
        answer to the question was that it was available
        which generated libraries of programs and subroutines
        quickly and because it was very adaptable.

2841   Sakoda, James M. "A Dynamic Storage Allocation Lan-
        guage—DYSTAL," Annals of the History of Computing
        6, No. 1 (January 1984): 37-38.

        These are the memoirs of Sakoda's work with FORTRAN
        from the 1950s into the 1970s.

2842   Sakoda, James M. "DYSTAL: Non-numeric Applications of
        FORTRAN," AFIPS Conference Proceedings 51 (1982):
        825-830.

        This is a history of DYSTAL, a list processing
        language related to FORTRAN.

2843   Tropp, Henry S. "FORTRAN Anecdotes," Annals of the
        History of Computing 6, No. 1 (January 1984): 59-64.

        He offers a variety of stories on FORTRAN and reprints
        comments of others published in a variety of places.

Human-Like Languages

2844   Bobrow, D.G. "Syntactic Analysis of English by Com-
        puter—A Survey," Proceedings, FJCC 24 (1963): 365-
        387.

        The author surveyed various efforts to make human
        languages, such as English, a programming device.

2845   Fraser, J.B. "The Role of Natural Language in Man-
        Machine Communication," in D. Walker (ed), Information
        System Science and Technology (Washington, D.C.:
        Thompson Book Co., 1967): 21-28.

        By the 1960s the nature of a language that looked
        like English was an attractive topic for computer
        scientists. This one puts forth the case that it
        could be the basis of a programming language.

2846   Halpern, M.I. "Foundations of the Case for Natural-
        Language Programming," Proceedings, FJCC 29 (1966):
        639-649.

        Argues that English could be the basis of a programm-
        ing language and why.

2847   Kirsch, R.A. "Computer Interpretation of English Text and Picture Patterns," <u>IEEE Transactions, Electronic Computers</u> EC-13, No. 4 (August 1964): 365-376.

The author describes an early attempt to develop a software tool that served as a bridge between English-like text and machine level language.

2848   Sammet, Jean E. "The Use of English as a Programming Language," <u>Communications, ACM</u> 9, No. 3 (March 1966): 228-230.

She argues the case for having English or "natural" languages as programming languages.

2849   Simmons, R.F. "Answering English Questions by Computer: A Survey," <u>Communications, ACM</u> 8, No. 1 (January 1965): 53-69.

This is a snap shot of various attempts to produce English-like programming languages in the U.S. in the early 1960s.

2850   Simmons, R.F. "Natural-Language Processing," <u>Datamation</u> 12, No. 6 (June 1966): 61-72.

Simmons reviews current efforts underway (mid-1960s) to develop human-like programming languages.

2851   Tabory, R. and Peters, P.S., Jr. <u>Can One Instruct Computers in English? A Feasibility Study Concerning the Use of English in User/Computer Communication</u>. TM 48.67.003, Federal Systems Division. Cambridge, Mass.: IBM Corporation, October 1967.

There were many such publications that appeared in the 1960s looking at how and why to make English a programming language.

2852   Thompson, F.B. "English for the Computer," <u>Proceedings</u>, <u>FJCC</u> 29 (1966): 349-356.

This describes one project to produce English-like programming tools.

2853   Weizenbaum, J. "Contextual Understanding by Computers," <u>Communications, ACM</u> 10, No. 8 (August 1967): 474-480.

This important scientist, noted for his work on artificial intelligence, discusses the possibility of English-like programming languages.

IDS

2854   Bachman, C.W. "Software for Random Access Processing," <u>Datamation</u> 11, No. 4 (April 1965): 36-41.

The author describes IDS, which was GE's programming language for business applications on the GE-225. The was in charge of the language's development team.

2855   Bachman, C.W. and Williams, S.B. "A General Purpose
        Programming System for Random Access Memories,"
        Proceedings, FJCC 26, Pt. 1 (1964): 411-422.

        This describes IDS.

2856   General Electric Corporation. Introduction to Integra-
        ted Data Store. Phoenix, Arizona: Computer Depart-
        ment, General Electric, April 1965.

        This publication presents IDS as an extension of
        COBOL for GE users.

                                    IPL

2857   Chapin, N. "An Implementation of IPL-V on a Small
        Computer," Proceedings, ACM 19th National Conference
        (1964): D1.2-1-D1.2-6.

        He describes the development and use of an important
        and early list processing language.

2858   Newell, A. and Simon, H.A. "The Logic Theory Machine
        —A Complex Information Processing System," IRE
        Transactions, Information Theory IT-2, No. 3 (Septem-
        ber 1956): 61-79.

        This was the initial paper that introduced IPL-V. It
        is very important because IPL introduced the idea of
        list processing in computer languages.

2859   Newell, A. et al. (eds). Information Processing Lang-
        uage-V Manual. 2nd Ed. Englewood Cliffs, N.J.: Pren-
        tice-Hall, Inc., 1965.

        This is a user's manual for IPL-V, the earliest string
        and list programming language. It offers details on
        features and initial use of IPL.

                                    JOSS

2860   Baker, Charles L. "JOSS—Johnniac Open-Shop System,"
        in Richard L. Wexelblat (ed), History of Programming
        Languages (New York: Academic Press, 1981): 495-
        508; Dialogue on paper, 508-513.

        This was RAND Corporation's language, written by a
        developer/user, covering the period 1960-67.

2861   "Biography of Charles L. Baker," in Richard L. Wexel-
        blat (ed), History of Programming Languages (New York:
        Academic Press, 1981): 512-513.
        Baker helped to develop JOSS, and worked with the
        JOHNNIAC and other early machines.

2862   Bryan, G.E. and Smith, J.W. JOSS Language. Santa
        Monica, Cal.: RAND Corporation, 1967. (RM-5377-PR).

        This describes JOSS II with some history.

2863   Shaw, J.C.   JOSS: A Designer's View of an Experimental
       On-line Computing System.   Santa Monica, Cal.: RAND
       Corporation, August 1964.   (P-2922).

       This was written by the man many called the father
       of JOSS. JOSS was the first widely-known interactive
       programming language developed in the U.S.

2864   Shaw, J.C.   JOSS: Experience With an Experimental
       Computing Service for Users at Remote Typewriter
       Consoles. Santa Monica, Cal.: RAND Corporation, May
       1965.   (P-3149).

       The creator of JOSS describes its use in remote,
       interactive computing. It involved users at RAND
       located at various U.S. Air Force bases in the U.S.

JOVIAL

2865   "Biography of Jules I. Schwartz," in Richard L. Wexel-
       blat (ed), History of Programming Languages (New
       York: Academic Press, 1981): 401.

       The father of JOVIAL is featured in a brief biogra-
       phy.

2866   Clark, E.R.   "On the Automatic Simplification of
       Source-Language Programs," Communications, ACM 10,
       No. 3 (March 1967): 160-165.

       This is a description of the features of JOVIAL.

2867   Coffman, E.G., Jr.   A Brief Description and Comparison
       of ALGOL and JOVIAL. FN-5618. Santa Monica, Cal.:
       System Development Corporation, June 1961.

       This is a discussion of two general purpose langua-
       ges which, in 1960-61, were potential rivals to
       become the most widely endorsed language used by the
       U.S. military.

2868   Hogan, Michael Olin.   "The History of JOVIAL." (Unpub-
       lished M.S. Thesis, California State University,
       Northridge, 1983).

       JOVIAL's history began in 1958 at the RAND Corpora-
       tion. This account takes the story down to the 1970s.
       JOVIAL was used with SAGE, ALGOL, and CLIP.

2869   Klein, S.   "Automatic Paraphrasing in Essay Format,"
       Mechanical Translation 8, Nos 3-4 (June, October
       1965): 68-83.

       Klein describes a text processing application using
       JOVIAL.

2870   Marsh, D.G.   "JOVIAL in Class," in R. Goodman (ed),
       Annual Review in Automatic Programming (New York:
       Macmillan, 1964): 4: 167-181.

This contains an early description of JOVIAL's use.

2871   Schwartz, Jules I. "The Development of JOVIAL," in
       Richard L. Wexelblat (ed), History of Programming
       Languages (New York: Academic Press, 1981): 369-388;
       Dialogue on paper, 388-400.

       These are the memoirs of JOVIAL's developer. It is
       a detailed, technical paper with details on the SAGE
       project for the U.S. military.

2872   Shaw, C.J. A Comparative Evaluation of JOVIAL and
       FORTRAN IV. N-21169. Santa Monica, Cal.: System
       Development Corporation, January 1964.

       Shaw compares JOVIAL to the DP industry's most
       widely used language for scientific and mathematical
       programming.

2873   Shaw, C.J. "JOVIAL—A Programming Language for Real-
       Time Command Systems," in R. Goodman (ed), Annual
       Review in Automatic Programming (New York: Pergamon
       Press, 1963): 3: 53-119.

       This is an annotated description of JOVIAL.

2874   Shaw, C.J. "A Specification of JOVIAL," Communications,
       ACM 6, No. 12 (December 1963): 721-736.

       This is a general survey of the language's features.

2875   Shaw, C.J. "System Development Corporation's Procedure
       -Oriented JOVIAL," Datamation 7, No. 6 (June 1961):
       28-32.

       This describes a very early version of JOVIAL.

2876   U.S. Air Force. Standard Computer Programming Language
       for Air Force Command and Control System. CED 2400,
       Air Force Manual AFM 100-24. Washington, D.C.: U.S.
       Government Printing Office, June 1967.

       This is a user's manual for JOVIAL.

                              LISP

2877   Abrahams, P.W. et al. "The LISP2 Programming Language
       and System," Proceedings, FJCC 29 (1966): 661-676.

       This surveys the objectives and features of LISP2,
       a multi-purpose high level language developed in the
       early 1960s.

2878   Allen, John. Anatomy of LISP. New York: McGraw Hill,
       1978.

       This is a complete and useful survey of the language.

2879   Bastian, A.L. et al. "On the Implementation and Usage of a Language for Contract Bridge Bidding," <u>Symbolic Languages in Data Processing</u> (New York: Gordon and Breach, 1962): 741-758.

They focus on the use of LISP 1.5, an early yet important list language developed for use in artificial intelligence.

2880   Berger, M. "NTT Builds a Lisp Machine for Japan," <u>Electronics</u>, October 30, 1986, pp. 44-47.

Artificial intelligence represented a major research initiative in Japan during the 1970s and 1980s. This describes some use of LISP in Japan.

2881   Berkeley, Edmund C. and Bobrow, Daniel (eds). <u>The Programming Language LISP, Its Operation and Applications</u>. Cambridge, Mass.: Information International, Inc., 1964; MIT Press, 1966.

This is a detailed, useful survey of the language. LISP was first developed at MIT for use in AI.

2882   McCarthy, John. "A History of LISP," in Richard L. Wexelblat (ed), <u>History of Programming Languages</u> (New York: Academic Press, 1981): 173-185; Dialogue on paper, 185-197.

This is a useful history of the language, covering largely from 1956 through 1958, its very early stages.

2883   McCarthy, John <u>et al. LISP 1 Programmer's Manual</u>. Cambridge, Mass.: MIT Computation Center and Research Laboratory of Electronics, 1960.

This is a very early user's guide; many would be published over the next 30 years.

2884   Woodward, P.M. "List Programming," in L. Fox (ed), <u>Advances in Programming and Non-Numerical Computation</u> (New York: Pergamon Press, 1966): 29-48.

This is a tutorial chapter focusing on LISP 1.5.

List Processors

2885   Abrahams, P.W. "List-Processing Languages," in M. Klerer and G.A. Korn (eds), <u>Digital Computer User's Handbook</u> (New York: McGraw-Hill, 1967): 1/239-1/257.

This is a useful overview of a whole class of programming languages under development in the 1960s.

2886   Bobrow, D.G. (ed). <u>Symbol Manipulation Languages and Techniques, Proceedings of the IFIP Working Conference on Symbol Manipulation Languages</u>. Amsterdam: North-Holland Publishing Co., 1968.

This is an excellent and detailed source on list languages.

2887   Bobrow, D.G. and Raphael, B. "A Comparison of List
        Processing Languages," Communications, ACM 7, No. 4
        (April 1964): 231-240.

        For the historian, this is a useful overview of
        list processing languages early in their development
        offering reasons for their need.

2888   Gray, J.C. "Compound Data Structure for Computer
        Aided Design; A Survey," Proceedings, ACM 22nd
        National Conference (1967): 355-365.

        Gray surveys string and list languages of the mid-
        1960s.

2889   Roberts, L.G. "Graphical Communication and Control
        Languages," in Information System Sciences: Proceed-
        ings of the Second Congress (Washington, D.C.: Spar-
        tan Books, 1965): 211-217.

        This describes a minor list processing language.

2890   Satterthwait, A.C. "Programming Languages for Compu-
        tational Linguistics," in F.L. Alt and M. Rubinoff
        (eds), Advances in Computing (New York: Academic
        Press, 1966): 209-238.

        They discuss the role of string and list processing
        languages.

2891   Wilkes, Maurice V. "Lists and Why They Are Useful,"
        Proceedings, ACM 19th National Conference (1961):
        F1-1-F1-5.

        One of Britain's greatest computer scientists explains
        the importance of such languages just as their devel-
        opment got underway.

                                META

2892   Oppenheim, D.K. and Haggerty, D.P. "META 5: A Tool to
        Manipulate Strings of Data," Proceedings, ACM 21st
        National Conference (1966): 465-468.

        This was a language developed by a group from ACM
        as a series of syntax-directed compiling systems.

2893   Schneider, F.W. and Johnson, G.D. "META-3—A Syntax-
        Directed Compiler-Writing Compiler to Generate
        Efficient Code," Proceedings, ACM 19th National
        Conference (1964): D1.5-1-D1.5-8.

        The article is a description of an important compiler
        writer.

2894   Schorre, D.V. "META-II—A Syntax-Oriented Compiler
        Writing Language," Proceedings, ACM 19th National
        Conference (1964): D1.3-1-D1.3-11.

        This was based on Backus's notation, an ACM project.

NELIAC

2895   Halstead, M.H. Machine-Independent Computer Programm-
        ing. Washington, D.C.: Spartan Books, 1962.

        This was written by one of the developers of NELIAC,
        an ALGOL-based language for numerical scientific
        programming of the early 1960s. It was used mainly
        by the U.S. Navy; the account is very complete.

2896   Huskey, H.D. et al. "NELIAC—A Dialect of ALGOL,"
        Communications, ACM 3, No. 8 (August 1960): 463-468.

        This was written by developers of the language, done
        for the U.S. Navy between 1958 and 1960.

2897   Johnsen, R.F., Jr. Implementation of NELIAC for the
        IBM 704 and IBM 709 Computers. San Diego, Cal.:
        U.S. Navy Electronics Laboratory, TM-428, September
        1960.

        This is a description of how NELIAC was used by the
        U.S. Navy.

2898   Masterson, K.S., Jr. "Compilation for Two Computers
        with NELIAC," Communications, ACM 3, No. 11 (Novem-
        ber 1960): 607-611.

        This is an early publication on NELIAC's features.

2899   Singman, D. et al. "Computerized Blood Banks Control,"
        Journal of the AMA 194 (November 1965): 583-586.

        This describes a civilian application using NELIAC.

PACT I

2900   Baker, Charles L. "The PACT I Coding System for the
        IBM Type 701," Journal of the ACM 3 (1956): 272-278.

        This is a technical description of a very early
        compiling system written by one of its developers
        in 1954-55.

2901   Derr, J.I. and Luke, R.C. "Semi-Automatic Allocation
        of Data Storage on PACT I," Journal of the ACM 3
        (1956): 299-308.

        This is a description of one of the more important
        features of this innovative compiler of the mid-
        1950s.

2902   Greenwald, I.D. and Martin, H.G. "Conclusions After
        Using the PACT I Advanced Coding Technique," Journal
        of the ACM 3 (1956): 309-313.

        The author affirms the value of programming languages
        while suggesting further avenues of research .

2903   Hemstead, Gus and Schwartz, Jules I. "FACT Loop
        Expansion," Journal of the ACM 3 (1956): 292-298.

The technical article was one of a series on this
early compiling system, one of the first to emphasize
storage optimization as well.

2904   Melahn, Wesley S. "A Description of a Cooperative Ven-
        ture in the Production of an Automatic Coding Sys-
        tem," Journal of the ACM 3 (1956): 266-271.

        PACT I ran on an IBM 701, initially in 1954. Its
        performance is reviewed here.

2905   Miller, Robert C. and Oldfield, Bruce. "Producing
        Computer Instructions for the PACT I Compiler,"
        Journal of the ACM 3 (1956): 288-291.

        This is an important description of how the language
        was developed in the 1950s with lessons on what was
        happening with other language development projects.

2906   Mock, Owen R. "Logical Organization of the PACT I
        Compiler," Journal of the ACM 3 (1956): 279-287.

        This is a description of the technical features of
        PACT I.

2907   Steel, T.B., Jr. "PACT IA," Journal of the ACM 4
        (1957): 8-11.

        This is a visionary piece, presaging programming
        concepts employed in the late 1950s and throughout
        the 1960s.

PL/I

2908   Bates, F. and Douglas, M.L. Programming Languages/One.
        Englewood Cliffs, N.J.: Prentice-Hall, Inc., 1967.

        This is a complete explanation of the early version
        of PL/I (pronounced PL one).

2909   "Biography of George Radin," in Richard L. Wexelblat
        (ed), History of Programming Languages (New York:
        Academic Press, 1981): 599.

        Radin, an IBM Fellow, was a developer of the PL/I.

2910   Burkhardt, W.H. "PL/I: An Evaluation," Datamation 12,
        No. 11 (November 1966): 31-39.

        This is an early overview of PL/I as a multi-purpose
        programming language that just got its start in the
        1960s.

2911   Dodd, G.G. "APL—A Language for Associative Data
        Handling in PL/I," Proceedings, FJCC 29 (1966): 677-
        684.

        Described a possible use for PL/I for which the
        language had not been designed.

2912   McCracken, D.D. "The New Programming Language,"
        Datamation 10, No. 7 (July 1964): 31-36.

        This is a general description of PL/I.

2913   Radin, George. "The Early History and Characteristics
        of PL/I," in Richard L. Wexelblat (ed), History of
        Programming Languages (New York: Academic Press,
        1981): 551-575; Dialogue on paper, 575-597.

        This is an important history of the language, writt-
        en by one of its developers.

2914   Weinberg, G.M. PL/I Programming Primer. New York:
        McGraw-Hill, 1966.

        This is an early book-length description of PL/I
        and how to use it.

                        Query Languages

2915   Barlow, A.E. and Cease, D.R. "Headquarters, U.S. Air
        Force Command and Control System Query Language,"
        Information System Sciences: Proceedings of the
        Second Congress (Washington, D.C.: Spartan Books,
        1965): 57-76.

        This query language (473L) was developed in the early
        1960s.

2916   Bennett, E. et al. "AESOP: A Prototype for On-Line
        User Control of Organizational Data Storage, Retriev-
        al and Processing," Proceedings, FJCC 27, Pt. 1
        (1965): 435-455.

        This early online query package was one of many
        developed at MITRE Corporation running on the STRETCH
        (IBM 7030) system. It used a CRT and light pen, one
        of the first to do so.

2917   Bobrow, D.G. "A Question-Answering System for High
        School Algebra Word Problems," Proceedings, FJCC 26,
        Pt. 1 (1964): 591-614.

        This is a functional description of STUDENT.

2918   Bryant, J.H. and Semple, P., Jr. "GIS and File Manage-
        ment," Proceedings, ACM 21st National Conference
        (1966): 97-107.

        GIS was a query language developed in the mid-1960s.

2919   Climenson, W.D. "RECOL—A Retrieval Command Language,"
        Communications, ACM 6, No. 3 (March 1963): 117-122.

        RECOL was developed in the U.S. as a query language.

2920   Connors, T.L. "ADAM—A Generalized Data Management
        System," Proceedings, SJCC 28 (1966): 193-203.

        ADAM was developed at MITRE Corporation in the 1960s.
        This one ran on STRETCH (IBM 7030).

2921   Cooper, W.S.   "Fact Retrieval and Deductive Question-
        Answering Information Retrieval Systems," Journal
        of the ACM 11, No. 2 (April 1964): 117-137.

        This describes an early query language. It was
        developed by the author at IBM.

2922   Craig, J.A. et al. "DEACON: Direct English Access and
        CONtrol," Proceedings, FJCC 29 (1966): 365-380.

        This package was developed at General Electric,
        beginning in 1963. By 1968 it was no longer in use.

2923   "Discussion—The Pros and Cons of a Special IR Langua-
        ge," Communications, ACM 5, No. 1 (January 1962):
        8-10.

        This is a useful, if short, review of query languages
        of the early 1960s.

2924   Dixon, P.J. and Sable, J.D. "DM-1, A Generalized Data
        Management System," Proceedings, SJCC 30 (1967):
        185-198.

        This is a functional description of an early query
        tool.

2925   Green, B.F. et al. "BASEBALL: An Automatic Question-
        Answer," Proceedings, WJCC 19 (1961): 219-224.

        This was one of the first query tools (1959) to be
        developed. It was written in IPL-V as a list process-
        or of data.

2926   Grems, M. "A Survey of Languages and Systems for
        Information Retrieval," Communications, ACM 5, No.
        1 (January 1962): 43-46.

        This survey is of early query languages and covers
        a wide range of software tools.

2927   Meadow, C.T. and Waugh, D.W. "Computer Assisted
        Interrogation," Proceedings, FJCC 29 (1966): 381-394.

        Reviews a query language typical of the mid-1960s.

2928   Nelson, D.B. et al. "GIM-1, A Generalized Information
        Management Language and Computer System," Proceed-
        ings, SJCC 30 (1967): 169-173.

        This is the only known publication on GIM.

2929   Raphael, B. "A Computer Program Which Understands,"
        Proceedings, FJCC 26, Pt. 1 (1964): 577-589.

        This variant was an attempt to develop an English-
        like query tool.

2930   Savitt, D.A. et al. "ASP: A New Concept in Language
        and Machine Organization," Proceedings, SJCC 30

(1967): 87-102.

This article is a description of the features and use
of ASP, a query language.

2931   Simmons, R.F.   "Answering English Questions by Comput-
       er: A Survey," Communications, ACM 8, No. 1 (January
       1965): 53-69.

       This reflects an early desire to use English. This
       package has English-like phrases but no structured
       data base against which to make queries. It was
       called Protosynthex.

2932   Simmons, R.F.   "Natural-Language Processing," Datama-
       tion 12, No. 6 (June 1966): 61-72.

       Simmons surveys research by many in developing
       query languages in the mid-1960s; well done.

2933   Simmons, R.F. et al. "An Approach Toward Answering
       English Questions From Text," Proceedings, FJCC 29
       (1966): 357-363.

       This reviews work done by the authors to do file/data
       queries.

2934   Slagle, J.R.   "Experiments with a Deductive Question-
       Answering Program," Communications, ACM 8, No. 12
       (December 1965): 792-798.

       The author reflects research typical of the early
       1960s on data query software tools.

2935   Spitzer, J.F. et al. "The COLINGO System Design Philo-
       sophy," Information Systems Sciences: Proceedings of
       the Second Congress (Washington, D.C.: Spartan Books,
       1965): 33-47.

       This ran on an IBM 1401 and was developed at the
       MITRE Corporation in the early 1960s.

2936   Steil, G.P., Jr.   "File Management on a Small Computer:
       The C-10 System," Proceedings, SJCC 30 (1967): 199-
       212.

       This was as much an artificial query language as it
       was a data management system; developed at MITRE.

2937   Summit, J.A. et al. "DIALOG—An Operational, On-Line
       Reference Retrieval System," Proceedings, ACM 22nd
       National Conference (1967): 51-56.

       DIALOG was a very early online data query package.

SNOBOL

2938   "Biography of Ralph E. Griswold," in Richard L. Wexel-
       blat (ed), History of Programming Langues (New York:

Academic Press, 1981): 660.

Griswold was involved in the development of SNOBOL
programming language as a major proponent and
designer.

2939   Boehm, E.M. and Steel, T.B., Jr. "The SHARE 709 Sys-
        tem: Machine Implementation of Symbolic Programming,"
        Journal of the ACM 6 (1959): 134-140.

        They described the frustrations of trying to imple-
        ment SHARE 709 and about its inferior quality.

2940   Bratman, Harvey and Boldt, Ira V., Jr. "THE SHARE 709
        System: Supervisory Control," Journal of the ACM 6
        (1959): 152-155.

        This early language processor, described in technical
        terms, had new functions for the mid-1950s. This is a
        good account of such functions as SQUOZE.

2941   Digri, Vincent J. and King, Jane E. "The SHARE 709
        System: Input-Output Translation," Journal of the
        ACM 6 (1959): 141-144.

        There is a painful description of how modules of
        SQUOZE decks were located into this early language.

2942   Farber, D.J. et al. "SNOBOL, A String Manipulation
        Language," Journal of the ACM 11, No. 1 (January
        1964): 21-30.

        This was the first publication to describe SNOBOL.
        The authors are its developers at Bell Laboratories.

2943   Forte, A. SNOBOL3 Primer; An Introduction to the
        Computer Programming Language. Cambridge, Mass.:
        MIT Press, 1967.

        This is on how to use the features of SNOBOL as of
        the mid to late 1960s.

2944   Greenwald, Irwin D. and Kane, Maureen. "The SHARE
        709 System: Programming and Modification," Journal
        of the ACM 6 (1959): 128-133.

        They describe source-level debugging capabilities
        in this early language processor.

2945   Griswold, Ralph E. "A History of the SNOBOL Programm-
        ing Language," in Richard L. Wexelblat (ed), History
        of Programming Languages (New York: Academic Press,
        1981): 601-645; Dialogue on paper, 645-659.

        This is an important account of SNOBOL of the 1960s.

2946   Mock, Owen and Swift, Charles J. "The SHARE 709 Sys-
        tem: Programmed Input-Output Buffering," Journal of
        the ACM 6 (1959): 145-151.

This was a language processor for an IBM 709/7090/
7094.

2947   Shell, Donald L.   "The SHARE 709 System: A Cooperative
        Effort," Journal of the ACM 6 (1959): 123-127.

        This is a description of its features.

Soviet Programming

2948   Ershov, Andrei Petrovich.   "Automatic Programming in
        the Soviet Union," Datamation 5, No. 4 (1959): 14-20.

        The author is the leading spokesmen on Soviet comput-
        ing for the period 1950s-1970s.

2949   Ershov, Andrei Petrovich.   The British Lectures.
        Philadelphia: Heyden and Son, 1980.

        This 57-page document consists of lectures he gave
        on his work and on Soviety data processing from 1950
        to 1980. It is useful for a quick survey of Soviet
        projects and computer scientists.

2950   Ershov, Andrei Petrovich.   Programming Programme for
        the BESM Computer. London: Pergamon, 1959.

        This short book covers Soviet programming on their
        BESM computer of the 1950s.

2951   Ershov, Andrei Petrovich.   "The Work of the Computing
        Center of the Academy of Sciences of the USSR in
        the Field of Automatic Programming," Mechanisation
        of Thought Processes, National Physical Laboratory
        Symposium 10, 1958: 257-278.

        This is an early Soviet report on projects in the
        USSR.

2952   Ershov, Andrei Petrovich and Shura-Bura, Mikhail R.
        "The Early Development of Programming in the USSR,"
        in N. Metropolis et al. (eds), A History of Computing
        in the Twentieth Century: A Collection of Essays (New
        York: Academic Press, 1980): 137-196.

        This is on Russian developments from about 1948
        through 1963. Both authors were involved in various
        Soviet computing projects during the period.

Time-Sharing Languages and Systems

2953   Auroux, A. et al. "DIAMAG: A Multi-Access System for
        On-Line ALGOL Programming," Proceedings, SJCC 30
        (1967): 547-552.

        This extended ALGOL to online usage on an IBM 7044.
        It describes DIAMAG programming.

2954   Bequaert, F.C.   "RPL: A Data Reduction Language,"
        Proceedings, SJCC 30 (1967): 571-575.

RPL was hardly used but was intended for application with remote job entry processing.

2955   Coffman, E.G. et al. "A General-Purpose Time-Sharing System," Proceedings, SJCC 25 (1964): 397-411.

This was an early effort to develop a time-sharing system.

2956   Corbato, F.J. et al. "An Experimental Time-Sharing System," Proceedings, SJCC 21 (1962): 335-344.

The article is a description of MIT's CTSS system, developed in the 1950s by students; written by its chief developer.

2957   Corbato, F.J. et al. The Compatible Time-Sharing System: A Programmer's Guide. Cambridge, Mass.: MIT Press, 1963.

This was the first full length study, and user's guide, on CTSS, MIT's time-sharing system of the late 1950s and early 1960s.

2958   Fano, R.M. "Project MAC," Encyclopedia of Computer Science and Technology (New York: Marcel Dekker, 1979): 12: 339-360.

This details the history of Project MAC by its first director, a project at MIT in the 1950s in time-sharing.

2959   Feingold, S.L. "PLANIT: A Flexible Language Designed for Computer-Human Interaction," Proceedings, FJCC 31 (1967): 545-552.

PLANIT was a time-sharing system of the 1960s described by its developer.

UNCOL

2960   Bratman, H. "An Alternate Form of the 'UNCOL Diagram'," Communications, ACM 4, No. 3 (March 1961): 142.

This language was never implemented but is described. Many languages were designed in the 1960s that were never implemented, this is one example.

2961   Conway, M.E. "Proposal for an UNCOL," Communications, ACM 1, No. 10 (October 1958): 5-8.

It was intended to bridge the gap between machine code and higher level languages of the late 1950s.

2962   Steel, T.B., Jr. "UNCOL: The Myth and the Fact," in R. Goodman (ed), Annual Review in Automatic Programming (New York: Pergamon Press, 1961): 2: 325-344.

This discusses the problem of bridging higher level languages to machine code.

2963   Strong, J. _et al_. "The Problem of Programming Communi-
        cation with Changing Machines: A Proposed Solution,"
        Communications, ACM 1, No. 8 (August 1958): 12-18;
        "Part 2," _Ibid_., No. 9 (September 1958): 9-16.

        This is the case for a universal language, called
        UNCOL (UNiversal Computer Oriented Language). It
        was written by its chief architects.

8

Software and Applications

The history of applications and software products has barely been touched on by historians. The exceptions, and there are only a few, include the use of computers in space exploration, data bases, and operating systems. But applications in particular, the reason why organizations acquired data processing in the first place, have received no attention to speak of. Applications represent the single largest gap in our knowledge of the history of computing and data processing. Although the bibliography below has very few entries on the history of applications and software, it attempts to pull together relevant materials of use to historians.

Because the subject of application software is terra incognita, citations below are overwhelmingly contemporary and sporadic at best. What they have in common is that they were readily available materials as of their date of publication. Thus one can assume these must have had some influence. Ironically, the volume of publications describing software packages and their use run into the tens of thousands just in English alone! At best, therefore, the purpose one could hope for below is to suggest the kind of literature there is on the subject.

Historically, publications on applications have appeared in several sources. Beginning in the early 1950s, some indigenous to an industry carried articles on the particular uses computers were put to in their world. By the late 1960s, these journals were also carrying articles on software packages and their uses and, by the early 1970s, advertisements by software vendors. Industry specific journals represent the single largest source of materials on uses. A second body of publications consists of articles published by journals in the office equipment or data processing industry. Finally, there were numerous books published on the uses of computers in business, medicine, liberal arts, education, and so forth since the 1950s. None of these materials has been studied by historians. Little of it has been captured in bibliographies intended for scholars.

General Descriptions

2964   Abbott, Russell J. "Knowledge Abstraction," <u>Communica-</u>
        <u>tions, ACM</u> 30 (August 1987): 664-671.

        The author includes comments on the history of soft-
        ware abstraction.

2965   "Adding Power; Multiprogramming and Multiprocessing
        Computers," <u>Forbes</u> 102 (November 1, 1968): 26-27.

        Besides a description of computers, this offers
        comments on how they were being used in the late
        1960s.

2966   Bodlaender, H.L. <u>Distributed Computing: Structure and</u>
        <u>Complexity</u>. CWI Tract 43. Amsterdam: Centrum voor
        Wiskunde en Informatica, 1987.

        Although a technical piece, it contains an histori-
        cal overview of the subject.

2967   Brooks, Frederick P., Jr. <u>The Mythical Man-Month:</u>
        <u>Essays on Software Engineering</u>. Reading, Mass.:
        Addison-Wesley Publishing Co., 1975, 1978.

        This is perhaps the best known of the early books
        on the development of software. It remained in print
        into the 1990s. Brooks was the manager at IBM respon-
        sible for many crucial developments on the S/360.

2968   Denicoff, Marvin. "Sophisticated Software: The Road to
        Science and Utopia," in Michael Dertouzos and Joel
        Moses (eds), <u>The Computer Age: A Twenty-Year View</u>
        (Cambridge, Mass.: MIT Press, 1979): 367-391.

        This reviews past achievements in software and includ-
        es material on time-sharing, networking, AI, software
        and file systems, 1950s-1970s.

2969   Derk, Molisa Diane Harris. "The Complexity Trap:
        Some Effects of Complexity on the Historical
        Development of Software" (Unpublished M.A. Thesis,
        University of Oklahoma, 1985).

        The author discusses the evolution of assemblers,
        compilers, operating systems, and is well researched.

2970   Galler, Bernard A. "Thoughts on Software Engineering,"
        <u>Annals of the History of Computing</u> 11, No. 2 (1989):
        132-133.

        He summarizes some of the issues that worried comput-
        er scientists of the 1960s about how best to develop
        complex software.

2971   Gries, David. "My Thoughts on Software Engineering in
        the Late 1960s," <u>Annals of the History of Computing</u>

11, No. 2 (1989): 133.

Gries describes his role at a 1968 software conference hosted by NATO in Garmisch, Germany.

2972   Joint Users Group. Computer Programs Directory. New
       York: Macmillan Publishing Co., 1971; revisted ed.,
       1974.

       These were two early, annotated inventories of soft-
       ware packagages available in the United States. They
       described functions, costs, availability, what systems
       they ran on, and degree of documentation.

2973   Kurtz, Thomas E. "The Computer and Information Systems
       Program at Dartmouth College (CIS)," Annals of the
       History of Computing 11, No. 2 (1989): 143.

       CIS (1979-88) was software and curriculum. He offers
       an explanation of why it was terminated after genera-
       ting 121 graduates.

2974   Lilley, Dorothy and Trice, Ronald W. A History of
       Information Science, 1945-1985. New York: Academic
       Press, 1989.

       It focuses on the relationships of information scien-
       ce and various technologies to library science.

2975   Naur, P. and Randell, B. (eds). Software Engineering
       —Report on a Conference Sponsored by the NATO
       Science Committee, Garmisch, Germany, 7 to 11 Octo-
       ber, 1968. Brussells: NATO Scientific Affairs Div.

       Software engineering was of growing concern in the
       1960s. This was a major conference on the subject.
       For a review of the conference see Annals of the
       History of Computing 11, No. 2 (1989): passim.

2976   Perlis, Alan. "Twenty Year Retrospective: The NATO
       Software Engineering Conferences," Annals of the
       History of Computing 11, No. 2 (1989): 132.

       Perlis describes conferences held in the 1960s and
       the issues discussed at these. He participated in
       many software engineering projects of the period.

2977   Ross, Doug. "The NATO Conferences From the Perspective
       of An Active Software Engineer," Annals of the Histo-
       ry of Computing 11, No. 2 (1989): 133-141.

       This is particularly useful for details on U.S.
       software engineering efforts of the 1950s and 1960s.

2978   Shaw, Mary. "Remembrances of a Graduate Student,"
       Annals of the History of Computing 11, No. 2 (1989):
       141-143.

       She was at Carnegie Mellon and describes the impact

on herself and software engineers in general in the
U.S. caused by the 1968 NATO conference on software
(1960s-1970s).

2979   Yourdon, E. Classics of Software Engineering. New York:
       Yourdon Press, 1979.

       This is a collection of seminal programs being
       described that involves both applications and pro-
       gramming, circa 1950s-70s.

2980   Yourdon, E. Papers of the Revolution. New York: Your-
       don Press, 1982.

       This is a continuation of the theme of his earlier
       book (No. 1979).

2981   Wasserman, Anthony I. and Belady, L.A. "Software Engi-
       neering: The Turning Point," IEEE Computer (1978):
       30-41.

       The writers cover developments from 1968 to 1978
       with a survey of the origins of software engineering.

2982   Welky, Larry. "The Origins of Software," Datamation
       26, No. 12 (December 1980): 127-130.

       This is a history of the software industry (1960s-
       1970s). U.S. sales in 1969 were $25 million, in
       1979 they reached $1 Billion.

                    Applications, 1930s-1940s

2983   Allen, E.E. "Machine Accounting and Check-signing at
       Binghampton," American City 50 (November 1935): 52.

       The Comptroller describes the use of Burroughs
       equipment by his city government.

2984   Berkeley, Edmund C. "Electronic Machinery for Handling
       Information, and Its Uses in Insurance," Transactions
       of the Actuarial Society of America 48 (May 1947):
       36-52.

       Written by an early DP consultant who writes a des-
       cription of computer possibilities in the 1940s.

2985   Berkeley, Edmund C. "Electronic Sequence Controlled
       Calculating Machinery and Applications in Insurance,"
       Proceedings of 1947 Annual Conference, Life Office
       Management Association (New York: Life Office Manage-
       ment Association, 1947): 116-129.

       This describes early use of computers in insurance.

2986   Burroughs Adding Machine Company. Budgetary Control
       Through Modernized Mechanical Methods. Detroit:
       Burroughs Adding Machine Company, 193(?).

       This is an illustrated application brief.

2987   "Business Machines and Tax Rates," _American City_ 50
        (December 1935): 7.

        Calls attention to growing use of equipment by cities.

2988   "Cities Are Adopting Modern Office Practice," _American_
        City 51 (June 1936): 101.

        This covers activities in various cities using data
        processing equipment.

2989   Curry, Haskell B. and Wyatt, Willa A. _A Study of In-_
        _verse Interpolation of the Eniac._B.R.L. Report No.
        615. Aberdeen, Md.: Ballistic Research Laboratories,
        August 19, 1946.

        This surveys uses made of the ENIAC.

2990   Dudley, Homer. "The VOCODER," _Bell Laboratories Record_
        18, No. 4 (December 1939): 122-126.

        This describes the Voice Operation Demonstrator put
        on display at the New York World's Fair of 1939. It
        was an analyzer and synthesizer of human speech.

2991   Dudley, Homer _et al._ "A Synthetic Speaker," _Journal of_
        the Franklin Institute 227 (June 1939): 739-764.

        This is a more detailed account of the material in
        the previous citation concerning the VOCODER.

2992   "Electrical Bookkeeping and Accounting; 32d National
        Business Show, New York City," _American City_ 50
        (November 1935): 55-56.

        At the major office appliance show of the year new
        devices were introduced; their applications described.

2993   Gill, S. "A Process for the Step-by-Step Integration
        of Differential Equations in an Automatic Digital
        Computing Machine," _Proceedings of the Cambridge_
        Philosophical Society 47 (1951): 96-108.

        This describes early scientific/mathematical uses of
        digital computers in Great Britain.

2994   Hoffleit, Dorrit. "A Comparison of Various Computing
        Machines Used in Reduction of Doppler Observations,"
        Mathematical Tables and Other Aids to Computation 3,
        No. 25 (January 1949): 373-377.

        The author describes the application as well.

2995   Kimball, George E. and Morse, Philip M. _Methods of_
        Operations Research. New York: John Wiley, 1951.

        This was a very early publication on operations
        research relying on the use of linear programming.

2996   Leaver, E.W. and Brown, J.J. "Machines Without Men,"
        Fortune 34 (November 1946): 192-204.

        It focuses on the use of commercial electronics.

2997   Leontief, Wassily W. "Computational Problems Arising
        in Connection with Economic Analysis of Interindus-
        trial Relationships," Proceedings of a Symposium on
        Large-Scale Digital Calculating Machinery (Cambridge,
        Mass.: Harvard University Press, 1948): 169-175.

        This describes early uses of computers in the 1940s.

2998   Lotkin, Max. Inversion on the Eniac Using Osculatory
        Interpolation. B.R.L. Report No. 632. Aberdeen, Md.:
        Ballistic Research Laboratories, July 15, 1947.

        This 42-page report reviews problem solving on ENIAC.

2999   Lowan, Arnold N. "The Computation Laboratory of the
        National Bureau of Standards," Scripta Mathematica
        15, No. 1 (March 1949): 33-63.

        Much of the discussion is about the kinds of problems
        being solved at the NBS using digital computing.

3000   Matz, Adolph. "Electronics in Accounting," Accounting
        Review 21, No. 4 (October 1946): 371-379.

        This is an early piece on the use of computers in a
        commercial environment.

3001   McCoskey, Joseph F. and Trefathen, Florence N. (eds).
        Operations Research for Management. Baltimore: The
        Johns Hopkins Press, 1954.

        This is a collection of case histories on OR.

3002   McPherson, James L. "Applications of High-Speed
        Computing Machines to Statistical Work," Mathematical
        Tables and Other Aids to Computation 3, No. 22 (April
        1948): 121-126.

        This was an early definition of applications for
        digital computers and in highly technical terms.

3003   Mitchell, Herbert F., Jr. "Inversion of a Matrix of
        Order 38," Mathematical Tables and Other Aids to
        Computation 3, No. 23 (July 1948): 161-166.

        This is on early problem solving in mathematics using
        a digital computer.

3004   Nebeker, Frederik. "The 20th-Century Transformation
        of Meteorology" (Unpublished Ph.D. dissertation,
        Princeton University, 1989).

        He offers a great deal of information on the use of
        computational equipment in the study of meteorology
        from the late 1800s forward.

3005   "Old Field Fortune Teller: Electronic Oil Pool Analy-
        zer," Popular Mechanics 86 (September 1946): 154.

        This application relied on the use of analog devices.

3006   Parnell, R. "Regarding Taxpayers as Customers and
        Going After Business; A Story of Mechanization, Newark,
        N.J.," American City 50 (July 1935): 50, 52.

        The Director of Revenue and Finance for Newark des-
        cribes his use of office equipment.

3007   "Pedro the Voder: A Machine That Talks," Bell Laborato-
        ries Record 17, No. 6 (February 1939): 170-171.

        This is on a voice simulator built at Bell and
        displayed at the New York World's Fair in 1939.

3008   Potter, Ralph et al. Visible Speech. New York: D. Van
        Nostrand Co., 1947.

        It includes a discussion of how machines in the 1930s
        and 1940s were used to imitate voices.

3009   "Revolutionizing the Office," Business Week No. 1030
        (May 28, 1949): 65-72.

        The article was an early one on using computers in
        office applications.

3010   Ridenour, Louis N. et al. Bibliography in an Age of
        Science. Urbana: University of Illinois Press, 1951.

        This 90-page focuses on library research and how data
        processing equipment was being used and would be.

3011   Tarski, Alfred. A Decision Method for Elementary
        Algebra and Geometry. Report R-109. Santa Monica,Ca.:
        RAND Corporation, August 1, 1948.

        This 60-page document reviews how to solve problems
        in mathematical logic using a digital calculator at
        RAND Corporation in the 1940s.

3012   Trefethen, Florence N. "A History of Operations
        Research," in Joseph F. McCloskey and Florence N.
        Trefethen (eds), Operations Research for Management
        (Baltimore: The Johns Hopkins University Press, 1954):
        3-35.

3013   "Weather Under Control," Fortune (February 1948): 106-
        111, passim.

        Describes weather forecasting in the late 1940s using
        computers.

3014   "Whiz at Figures; Machines Practical for Insurance
        Companies," Business Week (May 17, 1947): 20.

        This is an application brief on electronic machines.

3015   Zworykin, V.K. Outline of Weather Proposal. Princeton,
        N.J.: Radio Corporation of America Research Laborator-
        ies, October 1945.

        This 11-page document discusses computer use in weath-
        er forecasting, a very early such publication.

                          Applications, 1950s

3016   American Association of Collegiate Registrars and
        Admissions Officers, Committee on Machine Equipment.
        Office Machine Equipment. Chicago: American Associa-
        tion of Collegiate Registrars and Admissions Officers,
        1959.

        This 82-page publication also describes applications.

3017   American Management Association. Advances in EDP and
        Information Systems. AMA Management Report No. 62.
        New York: American Management Association, 1961.

        This consists of a series of papers presented at the
        AMA's 7th Annual Data Processing Conference, March
        1961. Issues include management, economics of DP,
        functions and uses and applications' cost studies.

3018   American Management Association. Data Processing Today:
        A Progress Report. AMA Management Report No. 46. New
        York: Finance Division, American Management Associa-
        tion, 1960.

        This is a useful overview of late 1950s applications
        of computers, management issues and technological
        considerations. Includes Chrysler's role with DP.

3019   Astin, A.V. "Statement /on automation/," in Automation
        and Technological Change; Hearings, Joint Committee
        on the Economic Report, Congress of the United States
        . . . October 14-18, 1955 (Washington, D.C.: U.S.
        Government Printing Office, 1955): 571-589.

        Testimony reviews government scientific applications
        and the state-of-the-art of computer technology.

3020   Bank Management Commission. Automation of Bank Operat-
        ing Procedures. New York: American Bankers Associa-
        tion, 1955.

        The pamphlet describes the requirement for computers
        and details applications for checking and savings
        account management. ABA was very aggressive in endors-
        ing computing in the 1950s.

3021   Becker, Esther. The Office in Transition; Meeting the
        Problems of Automation. New York: Harper, 1957.

        Discusses the use of computers in commercial environ-
        ments and impact on management and personnel.

3023   Bell, W.D. A Management Guide to Electronic Computers.

New York: McGraw-Hill Book Co., Inc., 1957.

It includes a contemporary description of the American Airlines reservation system as it was in the 1950s.

3024   Benson, Bernard S. "Cut Research and Development Costs,"
        Automatic Control 3 (October 1955): 22-26.

        All the examples cited involve data reduction tech-
        niques in aircraft design of the early 1950s.

3025   Berkeley, Edmund C. The Computer Revolution. Garden
        City, N.Y.: Doubleday, 1962.

        This widely distributed book describes applications,
        role and structure of computers, and impact on
        society.

3026   Bishop, John F. "Analogue or Digital Control?,"
        Automatic Control 1 (December 1954): 16-18.

        This summarizes the pros and cons of each as applied
        to the control of plant processes in the early 1950s.

3027   Bradshaw, Thornton F. and Newman, Maurice S. "The
        Evolutionary Trend from Manual Methods to Computers,"
        Special Report No. 3 (New York: American Management
        Association, 1955): 17-38.

        This may well have been the first important survey
        conducted on applications of computers in the U.S.

3028   "Brain; Univac on Election Night," New Yorker 32
        (November 17, 1956): 44-45.

        Describes the use of a UNIVAC to predict outcome.

3029   Brown, Arthur and Peck, Leslie G. "How Electronic
        Machines Handle Clerical Work," Journal of Accountancy
        99 (January 1955): 31-37.

        They compare payroll applications done manually, on
        punched card equipment, and then with computers to
        illustrate the differences as experienced by one
        manufacturing company.

3030   Brown, Robert G. Statistical Forecasting for Inventory
        Control. New York: McGraw-Hill Book Co., 1959.

        Describes inventory control systems of the 1950s.

3031   Brown, R. Hunt. Office Automation—Integrated and
        Electronic Data Processing. New York: Automation
        Consultants, Inc., 1955-1961.

        This included monthly update newsletters on new
        equipment and applications.

3032   Buckingham, Walter. Automation, Its Impact on Business and People. New York: Harper & Row, 1961.

Based on his testimony before U.S. congressional
committees on automation, covering office and
industrial applications and implications.

3033   Burgess, Robert W. "Statement /on automation7," in
        Automation and Technological Change: Hearings, Joint
        Committee on the Economic Report, Congress of the
        United States . . . October 14-18, 1955 (Washington,
        D.C.: U.S. Government Printing Office, 1955): 78-82.

        He describes the experience of the U.S. Bureau of
        the Census with computers and includes general
        commentary on automation.

3034   Burton, Alfred J. Electronic Computers and Their
        Business Applications. London: E. Benn, 1960.

        This is a useful introduction to applications of
        the late 1950s and computers of the period.

3035   "Business Week Reports to Readers on Computers,"
        Business Week (June 21, 1958): 68-72ff.

        Does the same as the previous citation.

3036   Calhoun, Everett S. The Challenge of Electronic Equip-
        ment to Accountants. Stanford, Ca.: Stanford Research
        Institute, 1953.

        This 13-page booklet describes how computers could be
        used in accounting early in the computer era.

3037   "Can Control Devices Solve Common Problems Facing
        Industry and Business?," Automatic Control 2 (May
        1955): 14-17.

        Yes; this describes how in order processing, inven-
        tory control, materials handling and in retail.

3038   Canning, Richard G. "Cost Reduction Through Electronic
        Production Control," Mechanical Engineering 75 (Novem-
        ber 1953): 887-890.

        Historically significant because this was an early
        description of computers at work on orders and
        production scheduling.

3039   Canning, Richard G. Electronic Data Processing for
        Business and Industry. New York: John Wiley & Sons,
        Inc., 1956.

        This is a typical second generation guide to applica-
        tions of computers.

3040   Carr, John W., III. and Perlis, Alan J. "Small-Scale
        Computers as Scientific Calculators," Control
        Engineering 3 (March 1956): 99-104.

They analyzed features of digital computers of the
period and how they might be used in scientific study.

3041   Carroll, Phil. Cost Control Through Electronic Data
       Processing. New York: Society for the Advancement
       of Management, 1958.

       This 32-page booklet describes management issues
       and problems which could be addressed with computers
       and recommends applications with examples.

3042   Casey, Robert S. et al. (eds). Punched Cards. New York:
       Reinhold Publishing Co., 1958.

       This 2nd edition is an authoritative resource on
       electronic accounting machines covering all aspects
       of the subject, including business applications.

3043   Chapin, Ned. "Can Computers Cut Your Costs?," Automa-
       tion 3 (March 1956): 45-51.

       This was a typical example of a rapidly growing body
       of literature evident in 1954-55 on how to cost jus-
       tify DP. Chapin wrote extensively on the subject in
       the 1950s, setting standards followed by many U.S.
       companies.

3044   Churchman, C.West et al. Introduction to Operations
       Research. New York: John Wiley & Sons, Inc., 1957.

       This very long book (645 pages) was a major guide to
       OR and computing as of the late 1950s.

3045   Clippinger, Richard F. "Economics of the Digital
       Computer," Harvard Business Review 33, No. 1 (January
       -February 1955): 77-88.

       Reviews how computers were being used in mid-1950s
       and describes their cost justification and uses.

3046   Colburn, Dorothy. "The Computer As An Accountant,"
       Automatic Control 1 (December 1954): 19-21.

       She describes how to use electronic equipment to
       record, arrange, process and print information in
       accounting; a period piece on batch processing.

3047   "The Computer Age," Business Week (April 7, 1956): 52-
       68.

       Many applications are described in refineries, office
       applications, central processing of statistical data,
       and role of service bureaus for smaller firms.

3048   "Computer Figures Census," Science News Letter 59 (June
       23, 1951): 389.

       It discusses the U.S. census of 1950.

3049   "Computer Runs Refinery Unit for Texaco," Business Week
       (April 4, 1959): 44-45.

This describes one of the earliest computer-controlled facilities. It was established at the Texaco Poly-
merization Plant, Port Arthur, Texas. Includes evidence of benefits.

3050   Computer Use Report. N.C.: N.P., 1959.

Surveys use of DP in 14 applications in U.S. with
data on why used and justifications with information
on acceptance and rejection in 20 industries.

3051   "Computers Start to Run the Plants," Business Week
(November 5, 1960): 50-52.

Recites cases of process and manufacturing uses.

5052   Controllers Institute Research Foundations, Inc.
Business Electronics Reference Guide. New York:
Controllers Institute Research Foundation, Inc.,
I (1955), II (1956), III (1956), IV (1958).

Includes hardware and software descriptions.

5053   Courtney, Peggy (ed). Business Electronics Reference
Guide. New York: Controllership Foundation, Inc.,
1958.

Same publication as No. 5052. Volume 4 describes 383
company and government DP installations in the U.S.
Describes what was installed and applications while
presenting products from 34 U.S. and non-U.S. vendors.

5054   Data Processing Annual, vol. 3, Punched Card and
Computer Applications and Reference Guide. N.C.,
Michigan: Gille Associates, Inc., 1961.

Gille became American Data Processing, Inc., soon
after publication. The book is a discussion of punched cards and computer applications, hardware and
forms with 26 case studies, bibliography, and equipment comparisons.

3055   Data Processing by Electronics. New York: Haskins and
Sells, 1955.

This explains how to use computers to process records.
It was intended for a non-technical audience.

3056   Dempewolff, R.F. "Count Off, Americans," Popular Mechanics 93 (February 1950): 106-110.

Reviews intended use of computers in U.S. census, 1950.

3057   Diebold, John. Automation: The Advent of the Automatic
Factory. Princeton: D. Van Nostrand Co., Inc., 1952.

This is an early, widely distributed volume on the
subject. It is a useful gauge of the optimism felt
for future automation in the 1950s.

3058   Diebold, John. "Automation—The New Technology,"
        <u>Harvard Business Review</u> 32 (November-December 1953):
        63-71.

        He explains the nature of automation, including
        computerization, and why its benefits.

3059   Dimond, T.L. "Devices for Reading Handwritten Charac-
        ters," <u>Proceedings of the Eastern Joint Computer
        Conference: Computers with Deadlines to Meet</u> (New
        York: The Institute of Radio Engineers, 1958): 232-
        237.

        This reflected ongoing interest since the 1930s on
        developing equipment to handle interpretation of
        handwritten numbers and words.

3060   Draper, A.E. "Fast Predictors: Computers and the U.S.
        Presidential Elections," <u>Annals of the History of
        Computing</u> 10, No. 3 (1988): 209-212.

        He describes the use of a UNIVAC to predict the
        results of the U.S. elections in 1952.

3061   "Electronic Eggheads; Can Automation Help Balance the
        U.S. Budget?," <u>Newsweek</u> 47 (January 9, 1956): 21-23;
        Reprinted as "Uncle Sam's Electronic Beaurocrats,"
        <u>Science Digest</u> 39 (April 1956): 11-15.

        The subject of U.S. Government accounting and
        computer automation early-on became a major issue.

3062   Eppert, Ray P. "Automation Is an Asset in Banking,"
        <u>Automation</u> 2 (November 1955): 57-61.

        Banks discovered the benefits of computing during
        the 1950s; benefits of computers are described.

3063   "Erma-Electronic Bookkeeper," <u>Research for Industry</u> 7
        (October 1955): 1-12.

        This is on bookkeeping for checking accounts at Bank
        of America in the 1950s; system called ERMA.

3064   Evans, Arthur D. <u>Engineering Data Processing System
        Design</u>. New York: D. Van Nostrand Co., 1960.

        This was an early volume on the subject of CAD.

3065   Evans, Lawrence B. "Impact of the Electronics Revolu-
        tion on Industrial Process Control," <u>Science</u> 195
        (March 18, 1977): 1146-1151.

        Feedback and continuous process control using comput-
        ers is explained from the 1950s to the 1970s.

3066   Fairbanks, Ralph W. "Electronics in the Modern Office,"
        <u>Harvard Business Review</u> 30, No. 5 (September-October
        1952): 83-98.

This was the first article published by the HBR on commercial uses of computers, recognition of their impact anticipated on business, a process underway.

3067   Fernbach, Sidney. "Scientific Uses of Computers," in Michael Dertouzos and Joel Moses (eds), The Computer Age: A Twenty-Year View (Cambridge, Mass.: MIT Press, 1979): 146-160.

Reviews use of computers since 1950s and speculates on future uses. This was written by a scientist and one time director of the computer center at Lawrence Livermore Laboratory.

3068   Fieldler, E.R. and Kennedy, D.R. "A Survey of Users of the IBM 650 Computer," Computers and Automation (October 1957): 10, 28.

Surveys 81 users as of 1956 on what was installed, applications, and number of programmers employed.

3069   Furlong, B. "Can You Trust the Weatherman?," Natural History 65 (September 1956): 345-351ff.

Describes recent improvements in weather forecasting some of which involved use of computers.

3070   Gerosa, L.E. "New York City's Payroll Turned Out by Univac," American City 72 (January 1957): 104-105.

This is an application brief involving UNIVAC.

3071   Gillespie, Cecil M. Accounting Systems, Procedures and Methods. 2nd Ed. Englewood Cliffs, N.J.: Prentice-Hall, Inc., 1961.

This edition includes extensive material on data processing equipment and uses in accounting.

3072   Grabbe, Eugene M. (ed). Automation in Business and Industry. New York: John Wiley & Sons, 1957.

This was the largest reference work to-date on DP applications and technology and as such a good mirror of the subject circa mid-1950s.

3073   Grabbe, Eugene M. "Data Processing Systems: How They Are Used," Control Engineering 2 (December 1955): 40-45.

Surveys how computers developed and their prospects and concludes with discussion of their use in science, business and process control.

3074   Gregory, Robert H. "Computers and Accounting Systems," Accounting Research 6 (January 1955): 38-48.

This is an early piece on using computers. Readers are cautioned to do systems analysis in detail before installing this new equipment.

3075   Gustafson, P.   "What Computers Can Do For You," <u>Nations
       Business</u> 44 (October 1956): 40-43ff.

       Hundreds of articles such as this one appeared in the
       1950s for mass public exposure in the United States.

3076   Haines, Roger W.   "Computer-Based Environmental Control
       Systems: Their History and Development," <u>Energy
       Engineering</u> 83, No. 2 (1986): 11-17.

       This is a very usable history of the subject.

3077   Harris, W.B.   "Electronic Business," <u>Fortune</u> 55 (June
       1957): 136-139.

       This describes business uses of computers in U.S.A.

3078   Harrison, Thomas J. <u>et al</u>. "Evolution of Small Real-
       Time IBM Computer Systems," <u>IBM Journal of Research
       and Development</u> 25, No. 5 (September 1981): 441-451.

       Covers many types of applications and industries
       from the 1950s to 1980 and about how they evolved.

3079   Hattery, Lowell H.   "Electronic Computers and Personnel
       Administration," <u>Personnel Administration</u> 19 (March-
       April 1956): 7-13.

       He surveys impact of electronics on personnel issues.
       Argues that computers have not created significant
       unemployment, reflecting an issue of concern in the
       1950s.

3080   Hermann, P.J. <u>et al</u>. "Basic Applications of Analog
       Computers," <u>Instruments and Automation</u> 29 (March
       1956): 464-469.

       This overviews some applications in engineering.

3081   Hermann, Cyril C. and Magee, J.F.   "'Operations Resear-
       ch' for Management," <u>Harvard Business Review</u> 32, No.
       4 (July-August 1953): 100-112.

       The authors worked for MIT and Arthur D. Little
       respectively. They introduced the subject as a new
       scientific method of management.

3082   Hetter, F.L. <u>et al</u>. "Logistics Application in the
       Aviation Supply Office," in Lowell H. Hattery and
       George P. Bush (eds), <u>Electronics in Management</u>
       (Washington, D.C.: The University Press of Washington,
       D.C., 1956): 80-91.

       Three naval officers describe their experience with
       an IBM 701 and IBM 702 in the mid-1950s.

3083   Higgins, John A. and Glickauf, Joseph S.   "Electronics
       Down to Earth," <u>Harvard Business Review</u> 32, No. 3
       (March-April 1954): 97-104.

This article focuses on operating characteristics of first generation computers, their economic advantages and anticipated usages in business.

3084   Hoch, Saul. "Logistics Application in the Air Force," in Lowell H. Hattery and George P. Bush (eds), Electronics in Management (Washington, D.C.: The University Press of Washington, D.C., 1956): 67-79.

A user surveys U.S. Air Force experience with computers, describing use and results of the early 1950s.

3085   "How a Computer Takes Over," Business Week (July 24, 1954): 58-62.

This is on the use of electronic digital computers in insurance industry for commercial applications.

3086   "How One Company Utilizes a Medium-Size Electronic Digital Computer," Management Methods (September 1955): 44-45.

All-State Insurance Company's utilization of a computer for commercial applications is described.

3087   Howell, Frank S. "Using a Computer to Reconcile Inventory Count to Books," N.A.C.A. Bulletin 38 (June 1956): 1223-1233.

This details an application not well done on punched card equipment but made easier with computers, a gendre of applications made possible in the 1950s.

3088   Hurni, M.L. "Decision Making in the Age of Automation," Harvard Business Review 34, No. 5 (September-October 1955): 49-58.

Preaches the gospel of technology applied to decision-making scientifically with computers.

3089   "IBM Opens Way to New Market," Business Week (September 15, 1956): 43-46.

Its business was largely driven by the introduction of computers suitable for commercial applications, such as the IBM 650.

3090   International Business Machines Corporation. Machine Functions. New York: International Business Machines Corporation, 1957.

This 31-page publication explains available electric accounting machines and sample applications explained.

3091   Integrated Data Processing and Computers. Working Documents. Paris: OECD, 1961.

This is a collection of European papers on American DP installations. They include reviews of Associated

Grocers of New Hampshire, Inc., Service Bureau
Corporation, Dennison Manufacturing Co., Chesapeake
& Ohio Railway Co. It includes questionnaire used.

3092   Kaplan, Bonnie. "Computers in Medicine, 1950-1980: The
       Relationship Between History and Policy" (Unpublished
       Ph.D. dissertation, University of Chicago, 1984).

       This is a useful history of one set of applications.

3093   Komons, Nick A. Science and the Air Force: A History
       of the Air Force Office of Scientific Research.
       Arlington, Va.: Historical Division, Office of Infor-
       mation, U.S. Air Force, 1966.

       This contains a great deal on computer projects from
       the 1940s through the early 1960s.

3094   Klingman, Herbert F. (ed). Electronics in Business.
       New York: Controllership Foundation, 1955.

       This contains an extensive annotated bibliography on
       commercial applications, seminars, classes, equip-
       ment, and location of major U.S. data centers.

3095   Kruse, Benedict. "Electronic Brain Keeps Tabs on
       11,500 Rexall Stores," American Business 24 (December
       1954): 41-44.

       This compares applications before computers at the
       Rexall chain with comments on the impact of computers
       on the way the company was run.

3096   Kuhnel, A.H. "Industrial Uses of Special Purpose Com-
       puters," Instruments and Automation 28 (July 1955):
       1108-1113.

       This describes process control and industrial produc-
       tion from the late 1940s to mid-1950s.

3097   Langman, A.W. "Television; Election Returns and
       Computing Machines," Nation 183 (November 3, 1956):
       374-376.

       TV returns that year in the U.S. also included the
       use of computers to predict the outcome.

3098   Lassing, Lawrence P. "Computers in Business," Scienti-
       fic American 190 (January 1954): 21-25.

       The cases studied were Remington Rand's inventory
       management at John Plain Company, use of IBM 701s at
       Douglas Aircraft for engineering, and at Monsanto
       Chemical, UNIVAC at GE, all useful application briefs.

3099   Ledley, R.S. "Digital Electronic Computers in Bio-
       medical Science," Science 130 (November 6, 1959):
       1225-1234; Reply with rejoinder by R.G. Hoffman,
       Ibid. 131 (February 19, 1960): 472ff.

This is an early article on the use of computers in medicine and discussion about their potential uses.

3100   Lehmer, Derrick H. et al. "An Application of High-Speed Computing to Fermat's Last Theorem," Proceedings National Academy of Science, USA 40 (1954): 25-33.

Lehmer, of Berkeley, did research on number theoretical conjectures, using SWAC at UCLA.

3101   Love, Albert G. et al. Tabulating Equipment and Army Medical Statistics. Washington, D.C.: Office of the Surgeon General, Department of the Army, 1958.

The U.S. Army had been collecting such data since the 1880s and had, in fact, been an even earlier user of punch card equipment than most U.S. Government agencies of the late 1800s.

3102   Lucas, E.D. "Automatic Production Inventory Control," Control Engineering 2 (September 1955): 68-73.

Inventory control became a major computer-based application in the late 1950s. This one describes the experience of a gas utility company managing materials and supplies.

3103   Lybrand, Ross Bros. & Montgomery. Survey of Benefits Resulting From the Use of Electronic Data Processing Equipment. New York: Lybrand, Ross Bros. & Montgomery, 1959.

The consulting firm reports on a May, 1959 survey it did on the use of DP: personnel displacement, improved management control, reduced expenses due to faster billing, and on improved competitive positions with 11 case studies. Nine were in manufacturing, and one each in railroads and airplanes.

3104   "A Magnetic Drum Speeds Stock Transactions," Automatic Control 2 (January 1955): 26.

This describes an electronic quotation service at the Toronto Stock Exchange in the early 1950s.

3105   Malcom, Donald G. and Rowe, Alan J. (eds). Management Control Systems. New York: John Wiley & Sons, Inc., 1960.

Papers presented at a symposium hosted by the Systems Development Corporation in Santa Monica, Cal., July 1959, are published. These application descriptions.

3106   Martin, E. Wainright, Jr. Electronic Data Processing: An Introduction. Hanewood, Ill.: Richard D. Irwin, Inc., 1961.

The author taught at the University of Indiana. His book was aimed at business managers on applications.

414   Bibliographic Guide

3107   Martin, William L.   "A Merchandise Control System,"
        <u>Proceedings of the Western Joint Computer Conference:
        Trends in Computers—Automatic Control and Data Pro-
        cessing</u> (New York: American Institute of Electrical
        Engineers, 1954): 184-191.

        The topic is inventory control for a mail order firm.
        Benefits are described for the application.

3108   McPherson, James L. <u>et al</u>. "Information Processing in
        Social and Industrial Research," <u>Scientific Monthly</u>
        76 (February 1953): 100-108.

        Written at the dawn of the first generation of com-
        puters, the authors describe the use of digital
        processors in economic analysis, accounting, and in
        management.

3109   Meacham, Alan D. and Thompson, Van B. (eds). <u>Computer
        Applications Service</u>. Detroit: American Data Process-
        ing, Inc., 1962.

        20 applications are described in detailed along with
        available data processing equipment.

3110   Mendelssohn, Rudolph C. "Machine Methods in Employment
        Statistics," <u>Monthly Labor Review</u> 78 (May 1955): 567-
        569.

        Describes use of a small computer on large statisti-
        cal problems.

3111   Mitchell, Herbert F., Jr. "Electronic Computers in
        Inventory Control," <u>Proceedings of the Conference on
        Operations Research in Production and Inventory Con-
        trol, January 20-22, 1954</u> (Cleveland, Ohio: Case
        Institute of Technology, 1954): 61-67.

        The application was at the John Plain Company and
        at GE in Louisville, Kentucky.

3112   Noble, David F.   <u>Forces of Production: A Social History
        of Industrial Automation</u>. New York: Alfred Knopf,
        1984.

        This very important book is a history of computer-
        based automatic machine tools (numerical control)
        from its earliest days at MIT (1940s). It includes
        the role of the U.S. Air Force (1950s). Argues that
        computers made it possible to shift control of pro-
        duction from skilled labor to managers and programm-
        ers, and not for economic but control reasons.

3113   Noe, Jerre D. "Data Processing Systems: How They
        Function," <u>Control Engineering</u> 2 (October 1955): 70-
        77.

        Although technical, this offers a comparison between
        manual and DP systems solving business, scientific
        and control problems.

3114   Noe, Jerre D. Electronics in Financial Accounting.
        Stanford, Cal.: Stanford Research Institute, 1955.

        This 29-page publication provides an early overview
        on computer uses in accounting and about ERMA.

3115   "Office Robots," Fortune 45 (January 1952): 82-87ff.

        Focus is on accounting/office applications.

3116   Osborn, Roddy F. "GE and UNIVAC: Harnessing the High-
        Speed Computer," Harvard Business Review 32, No. 4
        (July-August 1954): 99-107.

        Osborn was the business procedures manager at GE and
        was responsible for installing the first computer in
        the U.S. for commercial applications. He reviews the
        experience and describes the value of computers for
        business in general. It was an important article.

3117   Piper, W.W. and Prener, J.S. "Hartree-Fock Wave Func-
        tions for Mn^{+4}," Physical Review 100 (1955): 1250.

        They describe the use of an IBM 650 at GE Research
        Laboratory in 1955 to study quantum mechanics.

3118   Price, George R. "Mathematics, Computers and Your
        Health," Think 26, No. 2 (February 1960): 18-23.

        This is an illustrated story of computers in medicine.

3119   Pyre, Magnus. Automation: Its Purpose and Future. New
        York: Philosophical Library, 1957.

        Surveys where it is being done, effects, and possible
        future from the vantage point of the mid-1950s. It
        includes applications in accounting, military, manu-
        facturing, transportation and processing.

3120   Remington Rand Univac. The General Electric Company
        Sales Analysis Application. New York: Remington Rand
        Univac, 1957.

        This application brief describes the first commercial
        use of a computer, UNIVAC, installed at GE's Appliance
        and Television Receiver Division in the early 1950s.

3121   Report Committee, Society of Actuaries. A New Record-
        ing: Means and Computing Services. Chicago: Society
        of Actuaries, 1952.

        This was a very early report on the use of computers
        to process insurance records in the U.S.

3122   "Revolution in Office Work," U.S. News & World Report
        46 (May 4, 1959): 66-71.

        Describes the rapid acceptance and use of computers
        in the U.S. for commercial applications in the previ-
        ous, particularly in banking.

3123   Ross, R.R.   "Application of Electronic Data Processing
        to Billing and Accounting," Workshop for Management
        (Greenwich, Conn.: Management Publishing Co., 1956):
        354-360.

        These applications are described and how to install
        explained. They were widely adopted by data centers.

3124   Salveson, M.E. and Canning, R.G.   "Automatic Data
        Processing in Larger Manufacturing Plants," Proceed-
        ings of the Western Computer Conference (New York:
        The Institute of Radio Engineers, 1953): 65-73.

        Production control for a plant with 1,000 workers is
        described: use, costs, and benefits.

3125   Say, M.G.A. et al. (eds).   Analogue and Digital Comput-
        ers. New York: Philosophical Library, 1960.

        Focus is on the design and use of both types of
        computers and their application.

3126   Schmidt, C.W. and Bosak, R.   "Production Scheduling
        and Labor Budgeting with Computers," Electronic Data
        Processing in Industry: A Casebook of Management
        Experience (New York: American Management Associa-
        tion, 1955): 206-214.

        This describes work underway at Lockheed's Georgia
        Division to implement these applications.

3127   Sheean, G.M.   "A Univac Progress Report," Systems 20
        (March-April 1956): 334.

        This reports on GE's use of a UNIVAC, the first
        acquired for commercial applications: payroll account-
        ing and scheduling.

3128   Shiskin, Julius.   "An Application of Electronic Com-
        puters to Economic-Series Analysis," The Analysts
        Journal (May 1955): 35-37.

        Describes work done on a UNIVAC at the U.S. Bureau
        of the Census. The user describes how the application
        was done on the computer.

3129   Shiskin, Julius.   Electronic Computers and Business
        Indicators. Occasional Paper No. 57. Princeton, N.J.:
        Princeton University Press for the National Bureau
        of Economic Research, Inc., 1957.

        He describes how to use computers for economic
        analysis.

3130   Shiskin, Julius.   "Seasonal Computations on Univac,"
        The American Statistician 9 (February 1955): 19-23.

        He describes statistical analysis as an application
        on the UNIVAC I computer.

3131   Simmons, J.R.M. LEO and the Managers. London: Macdon-
        ald & Co., Ltd., 1962.

        An early user of LEO, a British computer, describes
        its application (1953-1960s) for payroll initially
        for 17,000 employees then other uses.

3132   Smillie, K.W. "Velvet Gloves and Latin Squares: Mem-
        ories of Some Early Computing in Canada," CIPS
        Proceedings. Session 84, May 9-11, 1984 (Calgary,
        Alberta: Canadian Information Processing Society,
        1984): 323-326.

        The author describes his experience using an NCR
        102A in Ottawa. Velvet Gloves was the code name for
        an air-to-air guided missile designed in Canada.

3133   "Special Report on Computers," Business Week (June 21,
        1958): 68-92.

        This was extensive coverage on computers for its
        time for such a general U.S. audience. It is a good
        reflection of second generation computing costs and
        uses, as of 1958.

3134   Slater, R.E. "Electronic Data-Processing in an Insur-
        ance Company," Pioneering in Electronic Data-Process-
        ing. Proceedings of the Second Annual AMA Electronics
        Conference, February 27-29, 1956. Special Report No.
        9 (New York: American Management Association, 1956).

        The author reviews use of a UNIVAC I by the John
        Hancock Mutual Life Insurance Company.

3135   Spinning, H.M. "Calculation of Crude-Oil Run Tickets
        by Electronics," The Oil and Gas Journal 51 (February
        1953): 70-71ff.

        This industry became a major user of computers. This
        article was one of the first to describe uses of
        computers in the oil business, describing a tracking
        system for crude oil from gaugers' tickets to royalty
        payments.

3136   Steen, Lynn Arthur (ed). Mathematics Today: Twelve
        Informal Essays. New York: Springer-Verlag, 1978.

        Contains material on development of weather predic-
        tion with computers; illustrated.

3137   Steier, Henry P. "Airlines Plan Expanded Uses of
        Reservisors," American Aviation 19 (August 1, 1955):
        27-28.

        This describes early use of computers for airline
        reservations.

3138   Stickney, George F. "Treasury Department Check Recon-
        ciliation Project," in Lowell H. Hattery and George
        P. Bush (eds), Electronics in Management (Washington,

D.C.: The University Press of Washington, D.C.,
1956): 92-98.

He surveys use, justification and plans for computerization of the management of over 350 million
checks drawn annually on the U.S. Treasury.

3139   "Underwood's Electronic Brain; Elecom 125," American
City 71 (December 1956): 19.

More than a description of a machine, how it was
used by a city government is included.

3140   U.S. Congress, House Committee on Post Office and Civil
Service. Use of Electronic Data Processing Equipment.
Washington, D.C.: U.S. Government Printing Office,
1959.

These are hearings held on June 5, 1959 on their use
by the U.S. Government and has material on the Census
Bureau.

3141   U.S. Congress, House Subcommittee on Automation and
Energy Resources, Joint Economic Committee. New Views
on Automation, Papers Submitted to the Subcommittee
. . . . 86th Cong., 2nd Sess. Washington, D.C.: U.S.
Government Printing Office, 1960.

Papers by experts describe various types of uses in
banking, technology, management. Contributors include
Walter Buckingham, Vannevar Bush, John Diebold, James
P. Mitchell, Ralph J. Cordiner, A.R. Zipf, and Walter
P. Reuther. The volume is over 600 pages in length.

3142   U.S. Congress, House Subcommittee on Census and Government Statistics of the Committee on Post Office and
Civil Service. Report on the Use of Electronic Data
Processing Equipment in the Federal Government, Hearings Before . . . . 86th Cong., 2nd Sess. Washington,
D.C.: U.S. Government Printing Office, August 31,
1960.

This is a comprehensive survey on the use of computers
as of 1960 and is a major source on installed applications.

3143   U.S. Congress, House Subcommittee on Unemployment and
the Impact of Automation of the Committee on Education and Labor. Impact of Automation on Employment.
Hearings Before . . . . 87th Cong., 1st. Sess. Washington, D.C.: U.S. Government Printing Office, April
1961.

This 793 page document is a mine of information on
the subject as applied to the U.S.

3144   U.S. Congress, House Subcommittee on Census and
Government Statistics of the Committee on Post Office
and Civil Service. Use of Electronic Data-Processing

Hearings Before . . . . Washington, D.C.: U.S.
Government Printing Office, 1959.

Includes material on the management of such equipment.

3145   U.S. Congress, House Subcommittee on Economic Stabili-
        zation of the First Joint Economic Committee. Automa-
        tion and Recent Trends. Hearings Before 85th
        Cong., 1st Sess. Washington, D.C.: U.S. Government
        Printing Office, November 1957.

        These were very early hearings on data processing,
        surveying uses in banks and other financial institu-
        tions. Roger W. Bolz, editor of Automation Magazine,
        testified. Contains material on magnetic ink charac-
        ter recognition application.

3146   U.S. Congress, House Subcommittee on Economic Stabili-
        zation of the Joint Economic Committee. Instrument
        and Automation. Hearings Before . . . . 84th Cong.,
        2nd Sess. Washington, D.C.: U.S. Government Printing
        Office, 1956.

        This was an early study of the role played by instru-
        ments and automatic controllers in automation. Sys-
        tems engineering and automation receive considerable
        attention by Albert F. Sperry who testified.

3147   U.S. Department of Labor, Bureau of Labor Statistics.
        Impact of Office Automation in the Insurance Industry.
        Washington, D.C.: U.S. Government Printing Office,
        1966.

        Offers considerable volume of data and argues that
        this industry in the U.S. was an early and extensive
        user of data processing equipment.

3148   Van Auken, K.G., Jr. "The Introduction of an Electronic
        Computer in a Large Insurance Company," Automation and
        Technological Change, Hearings Before the Subcommittee
        on the Economic Stabilization of the Joint Committee on
        on the Economic Report. 84th Cong., 1st Sess. (Washing-
        ton, D.C.: U.S. Government Printing Office, 1955):
        290-300.

        He explains the rationale and then describes uses.

3149   Watson, R.E. Iron Series Hartree-Fock Calculations.
        Cambridge, Mass.: MIT Solid State and Molecular Theory
        Group, 1959.

        Watson describes calculations done on the WHIRLWIND.

3150   Westin, Alan and Baker, Michael A. Databanks in a Free
        Society: Computers, Record-Keeping and Privacy. New
        York: Quadrangle, 1972.

        This is a detailed compendium of cases in the use of
        computers in the U.S., 1950s-1960s.

3151   Woodbury, David O. Let ERMA Do It. New York: Harcourt,
        Brace, & Co., 1955.

        ERMA was the most widely-known banking application
        of the 1950s in the U.S.; described.

3152   Workshop for Management. Proceedings of the Eighth
        Annual Systems Meeting. New York: Systems and
        Procedures Association of America, Management Maga-
        zines, Inc., Book Division, 1956.

        Its focus is on general management techniques, use
        and operation of computers, and operations research.
        It includes case studies and material on applications
        and management using such systems as IBM 702, 705,
        and UNIVAC.

                        Applications, 1960s

3153   Allen, J.R. "Current Trends in Computer-Assisted
        Instruction," Computers and Humanities 7, No. 1 (Sep-
        tember 1972): 47-55.

        Application descriptions reach back into the 1960s.

3154   American Institute of Certified Public Accountants.
        Accounting and the Computer. New York: American Insti-
        tute of Certified Public Accountants, 1966.

        This is a selection of articles published between
        1962 and 1966 on accounting applications in the
        Journal of Accountancy and Management Services.

3155   Anderson, John. "Who Really Invented the Video Game?,"
        Creative Computing (October 1982): 190-196.

        This is a history of its development in 1958 by Willy
        Higinbotham at Brookhaven National Laboratory. It was
        tennis on an oscilloscope; illustrated.

3156   "Automating Chores in the Office; Business Equipment
        Exposition at New York's Coliseum," Business Week
        (October 30, 1965): 104ff.

        Covers all manner of equipment not just computers.

3157   Awad, Elias M. Business Data Processing, 2nd Ed.
        Englewood Cliffs, N.J.: Prentice-Hall, Inc., 1968.

        In addition to describing hardware, it describes
        commercial applications using computers and cards.

3158   Bacon, M.L., Jr. "State Computer Analyzes City Traffic;
        Green Bay, Wis.," American City 79 (December 1964):
        84-85.

        This is a common use of computers, to manage traffic.

3159   Barnett, J. "Computer-Aided Design and Automated
        Working Drawings," Architectural Record 138 (October
        1965): 85ff.

CAD applications came into their own in the 1960s. This is a good introduction to the subject.

3160   Barnett, M.P. and Kelley, K.L. "Computer Editing of Verbal Texts, Pt. 1. The ES1 System," American Documentation 14, No. 2 (April 1963): 99-108.

Describes an early word-processing package called ES1, a batch system.

3161   Berkwitt, G.J. "March of the Blue-Collar Computers; Computerized Process Control," Duns Review 91 (January 1968): 63-64ff.

Process control applications are described.

3162   Berkwitt, G.J. "Up-Tight in Software," Duns Review 92 (October 1968): 73-74ff.

Continues the theme of the previous citation.

3163   Bitzer, M.D. "Nursing in the Decade Ahead. Computers Have Entered Our Lives," American Journal of Nursing 70 (October 1970): 2117-2118.

This surveys computers and nursing from 1960s onward.

3164   Bloom, Steve. "The First Golden Age," in Steve Ditlea (ed), Digital Deli (New York: Workman Publishing, 1984): 327-332.

This is a history of video games from 1972 to 1978 in the U.S. Reviews Space Invaders, Pac-Man, Donkey Kong, along with the people and equipment involved.

3165   Boos, William. "HONE: The IBM Marketing Support System," IBM Systems Journal 24, Nos. 3-4 (1985): 189-199.

He describes the evolution and features of one of the largest online systems in the world. It was used by IBM's salesmen from 1970 onward.

3166   Booz, Allen and Hamilton. Study of the Interdependence of Computers and Communications Services. New York: Booz, Allen and Hamilton, 1968.

Prepared for the Business Equipment Manufacturer's Association, contains compilation of applications.

3167   "Boundless Age of the Computer; With Editorial Comment," Fortune 69 (March 1964): 97-98, 100-111ff; (April 1964): 153-156ff; (June 1964): 112-116ff; 70 (August 1964): 124-126ff; (October 1964): 120-121ff.

This is an important survey of all aspects of computing with emphasis on the uses to which such technology was put by the mid-1960s.

3168   Brewer, Donald W. The Impact of the Electronic Computer

Upon the Production Control Function. Rock Island,
Ill.: U.S. Management Engineering Training Agency,
1968.

Process and manufacturing applications are described.

3169   Brooks, F.P. and Iverson, K.E. Automatic Data Processing. New York: John Wiley & Sons, 1963.

This was one of the first publications to teach
methodically DP techniques, including how to organize
data files and sort type; a minor classic.

3170   Buckingham, W. "White-Collar Automation," Nation 194
(January 6, 1962): 10-12.

These included office applications and simulation.

3171   Bukstein, E. "Scientific Computers," Electronic World
73 (March 1965): 34-35ff.

This describes scientific uses of computers in U.S.A.

3172   Bundy, R.F. "Computer-Assisted Instruction: Where Are
We?," Education Digest 34 (September 1968): 5-8.

CAI came into initial form in the 1960s, described.

3173   Bunker, D.L. "Computer Experiments in Chemistry,"
Scientific American 211 (July 1964): 100-108.

Chemical engineering relied on computers by the 1960s
with their applications described here.

3174   Burton, A.G. and Mills, R.J. Electronic Computers and
Their Business Applications. London: Benn, 1960.

This contains descriptions of such common applications as payroll, general ledger, and accounts
receivables and inventory management.

3175   California State, Intergovernmental Board on EDP. Survey
of EDP Activities in State and Local Government—1970.
Sacramento: State of California, 1971. No. E1490-59.

This reviews status and plans for state and local
governments in California in 128 locations.

3176   Canning, R.G. Electronic Data Processing for Business
and Industry. New York: John Wiley and Sons, 1956.

This was an early, important, and well done introduction to the subject of DP and on its uses.

3177   Case, P.W. et al. "Design Automation in IBM," IBM Journal of Research and Development 25, No. 5 (September
1981): 631-646.

They survey the evolution of this application from
1958 to 1980, particularly for semiconductor designs.

3178   Chartrand, Robert Lee. Computers in the Service of
        Society. New York: Pergamon Press, 1972.

        Includes some history of computer applications from
        the 1940s to the 1970s from a series of seminars.

3179   "Computer-Based Terminal System to Handle Department
        Cable Flow," Department of State Bulletin 53 (October
        18, 1965): 645.

        The system managed diplomatic communications between
        consular and embassy locations with Washington, D.C.

3180   "Computer Time Sharing Goes On the Market; Service of
        Keydata Corporation, Boston," Business Week (December
        4, 1965): 116.

        This describes an early commercial use of cooperative
        processing in which numerous users employed the same
        computer and for a fee.

3181   "Computers and the College Store," Publishers Weekly
        187 (June 14, 1965): 62-64.

        Essentially inventory and retail applications as
        applied to book stores are described.

3182   "Computers Feed Many Mouths; MIT's Project MAC," Business
        Week (February 1, 1964): 54-55.

        Project MAC was MIT's campus-wide time sharing sys-
        tem.

3183   Cooke, Geoffrey. Technology and Employment in the Lon-
        don Clearing House. London: Banking Information Ser-
        vice, 1986.

        This is a case study on the use of computers in the
        British financial community in the 1970s and 1980s.

3184   Cooley, W.W. and Glaser, R. "Computer and Indivisualiz-
        ed Instruction," Science 166 (October 31, 1969): 574-
        582.

        Describes the use of computers in CAI education before
        the advent of the micro computer.

3185   Coombs, James H. et al. "Markup Systems and the Future
        of Scholarly Text Processing," Communications, ACM
        30, No. 11 (November 1987): 933-947.

        Surveys text processing methods up to the mid-1970s.

3186   Corbató, F.J. et al. "Multics—The First Seven Years,"
        AFIPS Proceedings SJCC 40 (1972): 571-583.

        This is on programming large projects in the 1960s;
        done at MIT.

3187   Cornwall, Hugo. The New Hacker's Handbook. London:
        Century, 1986.

        This is a British "how to" book for hackers.

3188   Diamond, J.J. A Report on Project GROW: Philadelphia's
        Experimental Program in Computer Assisted Instruction.
        Philadelphia, Pa.: Philadelphia School District, 1969.

        This reports on one of the first, major such projects
        in the United States.

3189   Diebold, John. "Application of Information Technology,"
        Annals of the American Academy of Political and Social
        Science 340 (March 1962): 38-45.

        Diebold, already well recognized as an expert on auto-
        mation, comments on future trends in data processing.

3190   Duckworth, E. A Guide to Operational Research. London:
        Methuen, 1962.

        This was a very lucid, early book on the subject as
        of the early 1960s.

3191   Eckert, James B. and Wyland, Robert R., II. "Automation
        at Commercial Banks," Federal Reserve Bulletin 48,
        No. 11 (November 1962): 1408-1420.

        This is an inventory of recent application trends in
        the U.S. banking industry.

3192   Edward, Perry and Broadwell, Bruce. Data Processing.
        Belmont, Cal.: Wadsworth, 1979.

        It includes discussion of many application areas.

3193   Ehrle, Raymond A. "Decision-Making in An Automated
        Age," Personnel Journal 42, No. 10 (November 1963):
        492-494.

        This addresses the interactive and data handling
        abilities of computers to provide "what if" simula-
        tion of decision options.

3194   Elliott, C. Orville and Wasley, Robert S. Business
        Information Processing Systems. Homewood, Ill.:
        Irwin, 1965.

        This is a broad study of applications and equipment
        as of the early 1960s.

3195   Fano, R.M. and Corbató, F.J. "Time-Sharing on Comput-
        ers," Scientific American 215 (September 1966): 128-
        136, 312.

        Besides a general discussion of the subject, they
        include comments on systems at MIT.

3196   Flatt, H.P. "Computer Modeling in Energy and the
        Environment," IBM Journal of Research and Develop-
        ment 25, No. 5 (September 1981): 571-580.

        This describes IBM's role in managing air pollution,
        solar energy, plasma physics, coal gasification, and
        energy conservation with computers in the 1960s and
        1970s.

3197   Freed, Roy N. Computers and Law: A Reference Work.
        4th ed. Boston: N.p., 1973.

        This is on law effecting computers and is a compen-
        dium of cases, applications and sources of informa-
        tion--a major source on the subject.

3198   Freedman, A. "Office Automation in the Insurance In-
        dustry," Monthly Labor Review 88 (November 1965):
        1313-1319.

        Written at a time when insurance companies were moving
        toward computerized applications quickly.

3199   Friis, William. "A 20-Year Retrospective on Teller
        Terminals," ABA Banking Journal 74 (April 1982): 71,
        75-76, 78.

        The period covered is from 1962 to 1982, and surveys
        hardware and applications for automated teller ter-
        minals used by U.S. banks.

3200   Fukuchi, F.K. "How Computers Are Used," Science Digest
        57 (March 1965): 58-62.

        Focus is on scientific uses, circa early 1960s.

3201   Gallagher, J.D. Management Information Systems and
        the Computer. New York: American Management Associa-
        tion, 1961.

        Reviews two major U.S. DP projects, one at Sylvania
        and the other at American Air Lines, both of the 1950s.

3202   Garrity, J.T. "Top Management and Computer Profits,"
        Harvard Business Review 41 (July 1963): 6-8ff.

        The article consists of cases in the use of computers
        in industrial applications and why.

3203   Gasparski, Wojciech W. "In Two Thousand Years Later:
        From Vitruvius to Systems Engineering," in F.R.
        Pichler and R. Trappl (eds), Progress in Cybernetics
        and Systems Research 6 (New York: Hempishee Publishing,
        1982): 273-283.

        Compares Marcus Vitruvius Polio's work on design
        methods to what is done today with some material on
        methodologies of the 1960s and 1970s.

3204   Geller, I. "Master Machines of Retailing," Duns

<u>Review</u> 94 (October 1969): 107-109.

Describes retail applications and machines (point-of-sale terminals) of the 1960s.

3205   Gilimore, K. "Electronics in Banking; MICR and ERMA,"
        <u>Electrical World</u> 69 (April 1963): 29-32ff.

These are good examples of how the banking industry applied computer-related technology to specific applications.

3206   "Giving the Facts Fast; Warranty Protection System,"
        <u>Business Week</u> (November 20, 1965): 126ff.

A commercial application relying on computerized data management, described and with benefits.

3207   Glass, Robert L. (ed). <u>Computing Catastrophes</u>. Seattle:
        Computing Trends, 1983.

Eighteen incidents illustrate dependence on computers and impact of such events.

3208   Gleason, G.T. "Computer Assisted Instruction: Prospects
        and Problems," <u>Education Digest</u> 33 (March 1968): 14-17.

This is a good introduction to CAI applications.

3209   Goodman, Edith H. "Computer Use Survey," <u>Data Process-
        ing</u> 4, No. 8 (August 1962): 9-12.

This is one of several important surveys done in the early 1960s on what applications had been implemented in the U.S.

3210   Green, Anthony. "C(omputer) A(ided) E(ngineering) in
        Historical Perspective," <u>Electronics and Power</u> 29
        (1983): 81.

This is a brief survey of CAI applications.

3211   Hamilton, Adrian. <u>The Financial Revolution</u>. London:
        Viking, 1986.

Surveys trends, reviews TP, EFT, ATMs, credit cards as part of the account of changes in banking.

3212   Hamming, Richard W. <u>Computers and Society</u>. New York:
        McGraw-Hill Book Co., 1972.

The author, of Bell Telephone Labs, described computers as of 1970 and their use in business, science, and education in non-technical terms.

3213   Harris, E. <u>et al</u>. "Can A Computer Teach? With Study-
        Discussion Program," <u>PTA Magazine</u> 62 (April 1968):
        7-10.

In addition to discussing the application, the
authors include a bibliography on the topic.

3214   Hayes, R.M. and Becker, J. Handbook of Data Process-
        ing for Libraries. New York: Becker and Hayes, Inc.,
        1970.

        This is comprehensive, well-prepared, covering all
        types of library applications, existing installations
        and costs and benefits as of the late 1960s.

3215   Head, Robert V. Real-Time Business Systems. New York:
        Holt, Rinehart & Winston, Inc., 1964.

        He describes this class of applications with cases.

3216   Hearle, Edward F. and Mason, Raymond J. A Data Process-
        ing System for State and Local Governments. Englewood
        Cliffs, N.J.: Prentice-Hall, Inc., 1963.

        This short book surveys all kinds of public sector
        applications for computers as of the early 1960s.

3217   Hein, L.W. Introduction to Electronic Data Processing
        for Business. New York: Van Nostrand, 1961.

        This introduces basic applications as of late 1950s.

3218   Herman, F. and Skillman, S. Atomic Structure Calcula-
        tions. Englewood Cliffs, N.J.: Prentice-Hall, Inc.,
        1963.

        Describes their use of an IBM 7090 at RCA's labora-
        tories at Princeton, N.J.

3219   Hockey, Susan. A Guide to Computer Applications in
        the Humanities. Baltimore: The Johns Hopkins Univer-
        sity Press, 1981.

        On the use of, terminology and technology of compu-
        ters in humanities; includes a bibliography.

3220   International Data Corporation. Computer Applications
        and Their Implementation. Santa Monica: IDC, 1969.

        Surveys over 2000 computer users in the U.S., show-
        ing installed applications by industry, programming
        languages in use, manpower, and expenses.

3221   "In So Far As . . . Attempt to See If Computers Can
        Evaluate Essay Style," Newsweek 65 (April 5, 1965):61.

        The application is in education.

3222   Irwin, T. "Electronic Eyes Are Watching Your Tax
        Returns; Revolutionary Operation Called Automatic
        Data Processing," Popular Mechanics 125 (March 1966):
        94-98ff.

In the 1960s U.S. Internal Revenue Service began to
develop computerized applications; this is an early
report on the project.

3223   Kallios, A.E. and Stempel, J.S. The Application of
EDP to the Purchasing Function. Management Bulletin
No. 83. New York: American Management Association,
1966.

This became an early application to be computerized.

3224   Kaplan, Bonnie Mae. "Computers in Medicine, 1950-
1980: The Relationship Between History and Policy"
(Unpublished Ph.D. dissertation, University of Chicago, 1983).

This is on research and teaching in U.S. hospitals
and on medical computing's impact on medical culture.

3225   Kaufman, Felix. Electronic Data Processing and Auditing. New York: Ronald Press Co., 1961.

Describes the impact of DP on accounting and auditing
and describes standard uses of computers in these
fields.

3226   Kemeny, John G. Man and Computer. New York: Charles
Scribner's Sons, 1972.

This collection of lectures were delivered by the
creator of BASIC.

3227   Kemeny, John G. and Kurtz, T.E. "Dartmouth Time-Sharing," Science 162 (October 11, 1968): 223-228.

They developed a system for teaching students about
computing; they describe the application.

3228   Klein, W.H. "Computer's Role in Weather Forecasting,"
Weatherwise 22 (October 1969): 195-201ff.

By the late 1960s this application was over twenty
years old. Recent developments are discussed.

3229   Knowlton, K.C. "A Computer Technique for Producing
Animated Movies," Proceedings, SJCC 25 (1964): 67-
87.

The author describes software he used to make movies.

3230   Kompass, E.J. "A Survey of On-Line Control Computer
Systems," Control Engineering (January 1972): 52-56.

Surveys over 100 computer installations using this
technology for process/manufacturing control.

3231   Kozmetsky, G. and Kircher, P. Electronic Computers
and Management Control. New York: McGraw-Hill, 1956.

This became one of the most widely read books on why

and how to use DP in business; it preceeded hundreds
of other books on the same subject.

3232   Lander, L.B. "Techniques for Decision-Making Control,"
        Proceedings, The Computing and Data Processing Society
        of Canada (Toronto: University of Toronto Press, 1963).

        This was a relatively new application area in the
        early 1960s, but one that grew all through the 1960s.

3233   Landreth, Bill. Out of the Inner Circle. Bellvue,
        Washington: Microsoft Press, 1985.

        This American "how to" book was written by a highly
        experienced computer hacker on the subject.

3234   Ledley, R.S. et al. "BUGSYS: A Programming System for
        Picture Processing—Not for Debugging," Communications,
        ACM 9, No. 2 (February 1966): 79-84.

        Described software that could be used to do analysis
        of photomicrographs of neuron dendrites in the early
        1960s.

3235   Lessing, L. "Transistorized M.D.; Systems for Monitor-
        ing Patients," Fortune 68 (September 1963): 130-134ff.

        This is a very early article on the subject.

3236   Leveson, J.H. (ed). Electronic Business Machines.
        London: Heywood, 1959.

        Contains advice on how to manage, install and pay
        for DP, and describes applications.

3237   Levy, David. 1975 U.S. Computer Chess Championship.
        Woodland Hills, Ca.: Computer Science Press, 1976.

        Provides a good survey of the application.

3238   Levy, M.P. et al. "Role of the Computer in Engineering
        Practice," Architectural Record 134 (August 1963):
        158-161.

        By the early 1960s computers were beginning to play
        a major role in complex engineering applications.

3239   Levy, Steven. Hackers: Heroes of the Computer Revolu-
        tion. New York: Doubleday, 1984.

        This describes who they were and then offers a series
        of stories of true incidents of the 1970s and 1980s.
        It offers comments on their characteristics and is
        well researched.

3240   Li, David H. Accounting, Computers, Management Infor-
        mation Systems. New York: McGraw-Hill, 1968.

        This covers both applications and implementation as
        of the mid-1960s.

3241   Lipperman, Lawrence L.   Advanced Business Systems. AMA
        Research Study No. 86. New York: American Management
        Association, 1968.

        This describes applications, their benefits, costs
        and how best to implement with cases and examples.

3242   Logsdon, Tom. The Robot Revolution. New York: Simon
        and Schuster, Inc., 1984.

        This includes a history of robots (pp. 33-55) and
        then describes their application today and future.

3243   Longo, L.F. "SURGE: A Recoding of the COBOL Merchan-
        dise Control Algorithm," Communications, ACM 5, No.
        2 (February 1962): 98-100.

        Describes a fixed format form for resolving inventory
        level projections.

3244   "Lot of Little Users Share a Big Computer," Business
        Week (August 7, 1965): 61-63.

        "Cooperative use" was the phrase employed in the
        1960s for either time-sharing on a system or work
        done through a service bureau, both described here.

3245   Manchester, H. "Here Comes the Electronic Tax Collec-
        tor," Readers Digest 80 (March 1962): 165-168.

        Describes computer applications at the U.S. IRS.

3246   Marti, John and Zeilinger, Anthony. Micros and Money.
        London: Policy Studies Institute, 1982.

        Surveys the use of micros and applications in the
        financial industry in Great Britain during the 1980s
        with some data on the 1970s.

3247   Martin, John Henry and Friedberg, Ardy. Writing to
        Read. New York: Warner Books, 1986.

        Describes IBM's software to teach young children how
        to read using micro computers. It was a widely used
        software package in the late 1980s; includes its
        development.

3248   McCarthy, E. Rerome et al. Integrated Data Processing
        Systems. New York: John Wiley & Sons, Inc., 1966.

        This is as much a description of applications and
        data management as it is of DP technology.

3249   McRae, T.W. The Impact of Computers on Accounting.
        New York: John Wiley & Sons, Inc., 1964.

        This constituted the largest and earliest, set of
        commercial applications brought onto computers in
        the 1950s and 1960s.

3250   Metcalfe, R.M. and Boggs, D.R.   "Ethernet: Distributed
       Packet Switching for Local Computer Networks,"
       Communications, ACM 19 No. 7 (July 1976): 395-404.

       This is a formal description of Xerox's local area
       network offering of the 1970s, still available in
       the 1980s.

3251   Miller, Robert W.   "How to Plan and Control with PERT,"
       Harvard Business Review 40, No. 2 (March-April 1962):
       93-104.

       PERT was a useful batch system for planning such
       activities as the volume of transactions on a tele-
       phone line for optimal use and managing the tasks of
       a complex project.

3252   Moeser, K.S.   "Future Possibilities of Decision Making
       and Control," Proceedings, The Computing and Data
       Processing Society of Canada. Toronto: University of
       Press, 1963.

       What-if analysis with computers just came into use
       in this period; possibilities are discussed.

3253   Morris, Derrick and Sumner, F.H.   "An Appraisal of the
       ATLAS Supervisor," Proceedings, ACM (1967): 67-75.

       This technical, quantitative analysis reviews ATLAS
       in 1966 and how it performed; a confusing paper.

3254   Morrison, Richard J. et al. Work Measurement in Machine
       Accounting: Controls, Incentives, Scheduling and Cost-
       ing Procedures. New York: Ronald Press, 1963.

       The authors review available accounting and office
       equipment and their uses as of the early 1960s.

3255   Mumford, G.S.   "Computer-Controlled Telescope," Sky &
       Telescope 36 (September 1968): 157.

       An early application of computers to data gathering
       from a telescope is described.

3256   Myers, C.A. (ed). The Impact of Computers on Management.
       Cambridge, Mass.: MIT Press, 1967.

       The focus is on management in general: their ability
       to make decisions differently, impact on organizations
       and cost structures in the 1960s.

3257   National Retail Merchants Association. A Comparative
       Report on Data Processing Equipment in Member Stores
       of the National Retail Merchants Association (1956-
       1958). New York: Retail Research Institute of the
       National Retail Merchants Association, 1959.

       This 16-page report reviews uses and equipment for
       point-of-sale transactions as of the late 1950s.

3258   Nett, R. _et al_. _Introduction to E.D.P._ Chicago: Free
        Press, 1959.

        It contains discussion on selection and training of
        DP personnel, along with application briefs.

3259   New York Academy of Sciences. _Computers in Medicine_
        and Biology. New York: New York Academy of Sciences,
        1964.

        This reviews just applications in these two fields.

3260   O'Brien, J.A. _The Impact of Computers on Banking_.
        Boston: Bankers Publishing Co., 1968.

        Describes applications, cost comparisons, organiza-
        tion; a major work on the subject.

3261   Olsen, P.F. and Orrange, R.J. "Real-Time Systems for
        Federal Applications: A Review of Significant Tech-
        nological Developments," _IBM Journal of Research and_
        Development 25, No. 5 (September 1981): 405-416.

        The period is 1956-1980, the subject is application
        work at the Federal Systems Division of IBM on mili-
        tary systems and technical developments.

3262   O'Shea, Tim and Self, John. _Learning and Teaching with_
        Computers: Artificial Intelligence in Education.
        Englewood Cliffs, N.J.: Prentice-Hall, Inc., 1983.

        Contains a chapter on the history of computers in
        education and a detailed bibliography.

3263   O'Toole, T. "White-Collar Automation," _Reporter_ 29
        (December 5, 1963): 24-27.

        Describes office applications.

3264   Phister, Montgomery, Jr. "Qutron II: An Early Multi-
        programmed Multiprocessor for the Communication of
        Stock Market Data," _Annals of the History of Comput-_
        ing 11, No. 2 (1989): 109-126.

        This is the only history available of the stock
        quotation software used from the early 1960s to the
        1980s. It had over 72,000 users; illustrated.

3265   Pierce, J.R. "Transmission of Computer Data," _Scienti-_
        fic American 215 (September 1966): 144-150ff, 312.

        This describes how telecommunications was done and
        gave examples of applications.

3266   "Process-Control Computers," _Fortune_ 71 (April 1965):
        223-224.

        Describes specialized equipment and their uses in
        manufacturing, processing, and refinery installa-
        tions.

3267   Putnam, Arnold D. "Integrated Information and Control
        Systems," Computer-Based Management for Information
        and Control. Management Bulletin No. 30. New York:
        American Management Association, 1963.

        Describes their nature, how to manage, with examples.

3268   Rajan, Amin. New Technology and Employment in Insur-
        ance, Banking and Building Societies. Aldershot, U.K.:
        Gower, 1984.

        Focus is on applications of computers in Great
        Britain's insurance industry in the 1970s and 1980s.

3269   Research Institute of America. Computers in Business—
        An RIA Survey of Users and Non-Users. New York: RIA,
        April 1969.

        RIA surveyed 2,422 organizations about how they did
        or, did not, use computers, explaining reasons, costs
        and number and type of applications.

3270   Richardson, Dennis W. Electric Money: Evolution of an
        Electronic Funds-Transfer System. Cambridge, Mass.:
        MIT Press, 1970.

        This banking application is explained in detail.

3271   Riche, R.W. and Alliston, J.R. "Impact of Office Auto-
        mation in the Internal Revenue Service," Monthly
        Labor Review 86 (April 1963): 388-393.

        Discusses U.S. IRS's early use of computers in tax
        collection and management.

3272   Rider, B.M. "The 1969 Automation Survey," Banking
        (October-November 1969): 61-65, 75-78.

        Survey results of a study done by the American
        Bankers Association involving 4,885 banks are present-
        ed with details on what was automated and why.

3273   Robertson, W. "Challenge to the Brokers; Instinct Sys-
        tem," Fortune 79 (April 1969): 67-68ff.

        Describes investment management automation.

3274   Roman, Daniel D. "The PERT System: An Appraisal of
        Program Evaluation Review Technique," The Journal of
        the Academy of Management 5, No. 1 (April 1962): 57-
        65.

        PERT became a popular management tool in the 1960s;
        described.

3275   Rosenfeld, Azriel. "Computer Vision Research at the
        University of Maryland: A 20-Year Retrospective,"
        Pattern Recognition 17 (1984): 373-375.

        This is on an R&D project for computer usage in science.

3276   Rosin, R.F.   "Determining a Computing Center Environ-
       ment," Communications, ACM 8, No. 7 (July 1965): 463-
       468.

       Surveys over 10,000 jobs ruon on an IBM 7090 at the
       University of Michigan.

3277   Rule, James B.   Private Lives and Public Surveillance:
       Social Control in the Computer Age.   London: Allen
       Lance, 1973.

       Discusses the role of security and privacy as social
       and legal issues growing out of new applications.

3278   "Rx for Hospitals: Computers; Information System at
       Massachusetts General Hospital and Missouri Medical
       Center," Business Week (May 15, 1965): 142ff.

       Medical uses of computers are described along with
       what hardware.

3279   Sadowski, Randall P.   "History of Computer Use in
       Manufacturing Shows Major Need Now Is for Integra-
       tion," Industrial Engineering 16, No. 3 (March 1984):
       34-36, 38, 40, 42.

       The response is to growth of systems that could not
       share data, a common problem of the late 1970s/1980s.

3280   Salverson, Melvin E.   "Computers for Decision Making,"
       Computer-Based Management for Information and Control.
       Management Bulletin No. 30.   New York: American
       Management Association, 1963.

       This was one of a series of AMA reports on new uses
       for computers; this one was on simulation of options.

3281   Sanders, Donald H.   Computers in Business, An Introduc-
       tion. New York: McGraw-Hill, 1968.

       This survey of applications is in response to vast
       expansion in use of computers in the mid-1960s.

3282   Sawits, M.   "Model for Branch Store Planning," Harvard
       Business Review 45 (July 1967): 140-143.

       Its basis was the experience of Federated Department
       Stores, Inc., in the early 1960s using a computer to
       model options in decisions.

3283   Schneider, Ben Ross.   Travels in Computerland; or,
       Incompatibilities and Interfaces: A Full and True
       Account of the Implementation of the London Stage
       Information Bank.   Reading, Mass.: Addison-Wesley,
       1974.

       This is a witty tale of an historian using a computer
       to research the stage's calendar, 1600-1800.

3284   "School Scheduling By Computer; Generalized Academic
       Simulation Programs," School and Society 93 (March
       6, 1965): 143ff.

       Scheduling is described, an early use of computers
       for the management of schools and colleges.

3285   Sell, Peter S. Expert Systems. New York: John Wiley
       & Sons, 1985.

       This 112-page monograph has some history of expert
       systems although its primary focus is on descriptions
       of such applications and about their construction.

3286   Shade, Michael J. Plastic Money: Evolution and Impact
       of a Point-of-Sale Electronic Funds Transfer System.
       New Brunswick, N.J.: Rutgers University Press, 1973.

       This was a new use for computers in the 1970s, some
       background on the 1960s is provided.

3287   "Sharing the Comp ter's Time," Time 86 (November 12,
       1965): 104.

       This describes "cooperative use" or time-sharing in
       a service bureau environment.

3288   Shea, Stevens L. "Computer-Based Management Informa-
       tion Systems," Computer-Based Management for Infor-
       mation and Control. Management Bulletin No. 30. New
       York: American Management Association, 1963.

       This describes the applications involved.

3289   Smith, Leland. "Editing and Printing Music by Comput-
       er," Journal of Music Theory 17 (1973): 292-309.

       This describes a novel use of computers, one that
       would become very common during the 1980s.

3290   Spencer, Ralph D., Jr. "Computers for Decision Making
       and Control," Proceedings, The Computing and Data
       Processing Society of Canada. Toronto: University of
       Toronto Press, 1963.

       This became a series of new applications by the early
       1960s which are partially described here and why.

3291   Stella, M. "Speech Synthesis," in F. Fallside and W.
       Woods (eds), Computer Speech Processing (Englewood
       Cliffs, N.J.: Prentice-Hall, 1985): 421-460.

       It offers a history of speech synthesis and a survey
       of then available speech synthesis techniques.

3292   Suppes, Patrick. "Past, Present and Future Educational
       Technologies," Developing Mathematics in Third World
       Countries (New York: North-Holland, 1979): 53-66.

       It goes from writing to computers with details on the

author's work at Stanford University in 1963 on CAI.

3293   Sverson, Arthur L.   "Management Systems and the Excep-
       tion Principle," Systems and Procedures Journal 15,
       No. 4 (July-August 1964): 44-51.

       The exception principle was to produce computer
       generated reports with data only on situations out
       of the norm rather than the results of all transac-
       tions of one type. It became a common design feature
       by the 1970s.

3294   Swets, J.A. and Feurzeig, W.   "Computer-Aided Instruc-
       tion," Science 150 (October 29, 1965): 572-576.

       The concept is described with examples of use.

3295   Taussig, John N.   EDP Applications for the Manufactur-
       ing Function. AMA Research Study No. 77. New York:
       American Management Association, 1966.

       This is a very useful introduction to the subject.

3296   Taylor, J.W. and Dean, N.J.   "Managing to Manage the
       Computer; Summary of Survey," Harvard Business Review
       44 (September 1966): 98-110.

       Booze, Allen & Hamilton surveyed U.S. companies to
       see how they used computers in the 1960s.

3297   Teicholz, E.D.   "Architecture and the Computer,"
       Architectural Forum 129 (September 1968): 58-61.

       The use of computers to help design buildings was a
       new application in the 1960s described here.

3298   "Telecommunication," Duns Review 88 Pt. 2 (September
       1966): 149-150ff.

       The use of TP in business applications is described.

3299   Tomayko, James E.   "IBM Computers and the Election of
       1960," Annals of the History of Computing 10, No. 3
       (1988): 213-216.

       Describes how IBM machines were used to track and
       predict the results of the U.S. national elections
       of 1960.

3300   U.S. Department of the Navy, Special Projects Office,
       Bureau of Naval Weapons. PERT Instruction Manual and
       Systems and Procedures for the Program Evaluation
       System. Washington, D.C.: U.S. Government Printing
       Office, 1960.

       This is the original user guide for the use of PERT,
       a project management package developed as part of the
       POLARIS submarine program.

3301   U.S. Office of Technology Assessment. Effects of

Information Technology on Financial Services. Washington, D.C.: U.S. Government Printing Office, 1984.

Done at the request of the U.S. Congress, it covers the activities of U.S. banks (1960s-80s).

3302   U.S. Office of Technology Assessment. Selected Electronic Funds Transfer Issues. Privacy, Security, and Equity: Background Paper. Washington, D.C.: U.S. Government Printing Office, 1982.

Covers U.S. issues for the period 1967-1982.

3303   Van Dam, Andries. "Computer Graphics Comes of Age" Communications, ACM 27, No. 7 (July 1984): 638-648.

This is an interview with Van Dam who discusses how the application evolved from SAGE days to the present.

3304   Walters, E.S. and Wallace, V.L. "Further Analysis of a Computing Center Environment," Communications, ACM 10, No. 5 (May 1967): 267-272.

This continues the work of R.F. Rosin (No. 3276) on work run on an IBM 7090 at the University of Michigan.

3305   Weiss, B. and Laties, V.G. "Reinforcement Schedule Generated by an On-Line Digital Computer," Science 148 (April 30, 1965): 658-661.

Process control application is described.

3306   Wells, W.D. "Computer Simulation of Consumer Behavior," Harvard Business Review 41 (May 1963): 93-98.

This time it was done with a computer.

3307   "Western Union Hums with Data; Computer Data-Transmission," Business Week (February 20, 1965): 150-152.

This is a telecommunications application brief.

3308   Wise, W.R. "Electronic Draftsman," Electrical World 74 (July 1965): 70-71.

This describes engineering CAD applications.

3309   Yelavich, B.M. "Customer Information Control System— An Evolving System Facility," IBM Systems Journal 24 Nos. 3-4 (1985): 264-278.

This is about CICS, one of the most widely used application sub-systems in the industry, made by IBM.

Artificial Intelligence

3310   Anderson, Alan Ross (ed). Mind and Machines. Englewood Cliffs, N.J.: Prentice-Hall, Inc., 1964.

Includes contributions by Alan Turing on computer capabilities to think.

3311   Bernstein, Jeremy. "Profiles: Marvin Minsky," The New
       Yorker, December 14, 1981, pp. 50-126.

       This is a biography of Minsky and about his work in
       AI at MIT, 1940s-1970s.

3312   Bloomfield, Brian. "Epistemology for Knowledge Engin-
       eers," CC-1A 3, No. 4 (1986): 305-320.

       Represents a summary of arguments in favor of expert
       systems.

3313   Bloomfield, Brian (ed). The Question of Aritificial
       Intelligence: Philosophical and Sociological Pers-
       pectives. London: Croom Helm, 1988.

       This is a multi-disciplinary collection of papers on
       AI with a bent toward philosophical issues.

3314   Block, C. The Golem: Legends of the Ghetto of Prague.
       New York: Rudolf Steiner Press, 1925.

       This is a survey of stories of a robotic creature
       that had AI qualities from the Middle Ages.

3315   Boden, Margaret A. Artificial Intelligence and Natural
       Man. New York: Basic Books, 1977.

       Catalogs various AI projects of the 1970s and argu-
       ments in favor of such research.

3316   Cohen, John. Human Robots in Myth and Science. London:
       Allen and Unwin, 1966.

       It is an historical review down to the 1950s.

3317   Dreyfus, Hubert L. What Computers Can't Do. New York:
       Harper & Row, 1972.

       This is an important work, written by a professor at
       Berkeley (university of California), he attacked the
       field of AI.

3318   Ebbinghaus, Hermann. Memory. Translated by H.A. Rogers
       and Clara E. Bussenius. New York: Dover Publications,
       1964.

       Originally published in 1885 as Über das Gedächtnis,
       this book reflected the modern psychological study
       of memory, a subject area as precursor of AI.

3319   Feigenbaum, E.A. and Feldman, Julian. Computers and
       Thought. New York: McGraw-Hill, 1963.

       This is a sampling of papers by members of the AI
       community and includes A. Turing's essay, "Computing
       Machinery and Intelligence."

3320   Firschein, Oscar. Artificial Intelligence. Information
       Techology Series 6. Reston, Va.: AFIPS Press, 1984.

This is a collection of AI papers presented at conferences between 1964 and 1980.

3321   Fodor, Jerry A. _The Language of Thought_. New York:
        Crowell, 1975.

        Fodor suggested that a human's mind is a computer.

3322   Fowler, Roger. _Understanding Language: An Introduction
        to Linguistics_. London: Routledge & Kegan Paul, 1974.

        This has some historical perspective and is a side-
        avenue of AI.

3323   Gardner, Howard. _The Mind's New Science: A History of
        the Cognitive Revolution_. New York: Basic Books,
        Inc., 1985.

        This is an excellent history from the revolt against
        behaviorism through Turing, von Neumann and Wiener
        down through the early years of computers. It also
        describes parallel developments in cognitive sciences.

3324   George, F.H. _Automation, Cybernetics and Society_.
        Philadelphia: Philosophical Society, 1959.

        Set in a social context, this is a good survey of
        the subject as of the late 1950s.

3325   Gordon, Howard. _The Mind's New Science: A History of
        the Cognitive Revolution_. New York: Basic Books, 1985.

        Contains historical data on AI, linguistics, neuro-
        science, psychology, philosophy and andanthropology.
        Includes a good bibliography.

3326   Grabiner, Judith V. "Computers and the Nature of Man:
        A Historian's Perspective on Controversies About
        Artificial Intelligence," _Bulletin of the American
        Mathematical Society_ New Series 15, No. 2 (October
        1986): 113-126.

        AI was a field riddled with false promises and con-
        stantly with controversy. These are reviewed.

3327   Haack, Stephanie. "A Brief History of Artificial In-
        telligence," in Steve Ditlea (ed), _Digital Deli_
        (New York: Workman Publishing, 1984): 231-233.

        She argues that people always were in search of AI
        and that much progress had been made in the develop-
        ment of this field of study. Includes historical notes.

3328   Herder, Johann Gottfried von. _J.G. Herder on Social
        and Political Culture_. Ed. by F.M. Barnard. Cambridge:
        Cambridge University Press, 1969.

        This collection of material includes his "Essay on
        the Origin of Language" which deals with the debate
        in the 18th century on "artificial language."

3329   Kemeny, J.G.   "Man Viewed as a Machine," Scientific
       American 192 (April 1955): 58-67.

       This mechanistic view is an early piece on AI by the
       individual who later developed BASIC programming lan-
       guage.

3330   Lamb, John.   "In Pursuit of AI,"   Datamation 30, No. 6
       (May 1, 1984): 139-140.

       This is a biography of Donald Mitchie and about AI
       at the Turing Institute. Mitchie also worked on the
       Colossus computer during World War II.

3331   Leithauser, Brad.   "The Space of One Breath," New York-
       er (March 9, 1987): 41-73.

       In this well-written article on the 1986 Fifth World
       Computer Chess Championship in Cologne, is a history
       of computer chess.

3332   McCorduck, Pamela.   Machines Who Think. San Francisco:
       W.H. Freeman, 1979.

       This is a very good history of AI with focus on moti-
       vations of computer scientists working in the field;
       covers 1950s to 1970s.

3333   McCulloch, Warren S.   Embodiments of Mind. Cambridge,
       Mass.: MIT Press, 1988.

       A collection of reprinted writings of his, the physio-
       logical psychiatist, who worked on physiological
       aspects of neural network theory and on the theory
       of automata, reviews his ideas.

3334   Meltzer, B. (ed).   Machine Intelligence. New York:
       American Elsevier, 1969.

       The subject is cybernetics and education.

3335   Miller, G.A.   "The Magical Number Seven, Plus or Minus
       Two: Some Limits on Our Capacity for Processing In-
       formation," Psychological Review 63 (1956): 81-97.

       This was one of the earliest articles to suggest
       humans thought like computers, even calling the brain
       a storage device.

3336   Minsky, Marvin.   Computation: Finite and Infinite Mach-
       ines. Englewood Cliffs, N.J.: Prentice-Hall, Inc.,
       1967.

       One of the giants of AI writes on the subject in
       general terms.

3337   Minsky, Marvin.   "Computer Science and the Representa-
       tion of Knowledge," in Michael Detouzos and Joel Moses
       (eds), The Computer Age: A Twenty-Year View (Cambridge,
       Mass.: MIT Press, 1979): 392-421.

This is his version of AI's history: intents, issues
and results since the 1950s.

3338   Minsky, Marvin (ed). Semantic Information Processing.
        Cambridge, Mass.: MIT Press, 1968.

        This series of articles by various scientists working
        on AI reflects activities of the 1960s.

3339   Minsky, Marvin. "Steps Toward Artificial Intelligence,"
        Proceedings of the IRE 49 (1961): 8-30.

        This critical piece reflects his views on AI, a
        semenal article by Minsky.

3340   Minsky, Marvin and Papert, Seymour. Perceptions.
        Cambridge, Mass.: MIT Press, 1968.

        This discussion of AI is on vision-type intelligent
        devices. It was an early work on Minsky's interest
        in robotics.

3341   Newell, A. and Simon, H.A. "Computer Simulation of
        Human Thinking," Science 134 (December 22, 1961):
        2011-2017; Reply with rejoinder by M. Taube, Ibid.
        136 (April 13, 1962): 195-196ff.

        This was at the heart of AI's role and mission.

3342   Newell, Allen and Simon, Herbert A. Human Problem
        Solving. Englewood Cliffs, N.J.: Prentice-Hall, Inc.,
        1972.

        A better understanding of how the human brain did
        that would allow AI to progress to a similar pattern
        of behavior, the subject and intent of this work.

3343   Pratt, Vernon. Thinking Machines: The Evolution of
        Artificial Intelligence. New York: Basil Blackwell,
        Inc., 1987.

        This is an illustrated history of AI, taking the
        story from the 17th century down to von Neumann
        computers.

3344   Raphael, Bertram. The Thinking Computer: Mind Inside
        Matter. San Francisco: W.H. Freeman, 1976.

        Builds the case for AI, vintage 1970s.

3345   Reichart, Jasia. Robots: Fact, Fiction, and Prediction.
        New York: Viking Press, 1978.

        This illustrated account is a popular history of
        robots with AI intermixed.

3346   Rheingold, H. Tools for Thought: The People and Ideas
        Behind the Next Computer Revolution. New York: Simon
        and Schuster, 1985.

        Details role of MIT and of the U.S. Government in AI.

3347   Richards, P.I. "On Game-Learning Machines," Science
        Monthly 74 (April 1952): 201-205.

        This describes computer use of chess-playing games.

3348   Ritchie, David. The Binary Brain: Artificial Intelli-
        gence in the Age of Electronics. Boston: Little,
        Brown and Company, 1984.

        Describes the evolution of computers, how human
        minds work, and then how the two will join together.
        It includes history of artificial intelligence.

3349   Robins, R.H. A Short History of Linguistics. Blooming-
        ton: Indiana University Press, 1967.

        Linguistics influenced scientists working on AI. This
        book offers a history that serves as good background
        to a branch of AI.

3350   Rose, Frank. Into the Heart of the Mind: A Quest for
        Artificial Intelligence. New York: Harper & Row,
        1984.

        This is as much a survey of how computers were being
        applied to leading edge applications in the 1960s-
        1980s, as it was on AI.

3351   "Runner-Up; Chess Playing Computer, 704," New Yorker
        34 (November 29, 1958): 43-44.

        This describes computer chess-playing in 1958; 704
        refers to the computer used to perform the tasks.

3352   Sagan, Carl. The Dragons of Eden: Speculations on the
        Evolution of Human Intelligence. New York: Ballatine
        Books, 1977.

        This popularizer of serious scientific thought, a
        professor of astronomy, wrote that computers repre-
        sented an advancement of the human brain.

3353   Samuel, A.L. "Artificial Intelligence: A Frontier of
        Automation," Annals of the American Academy of Poli-
        tical and Social Science 340 (March 1962): 10-20.

        By the early 1960s AI's potential were being written
        about in all manner of publications, including in
        political science.

3354   Shannon, Claude. "A Chess-Playing Machine," Scientific
        American 182 (February 1950): 48-51.

        A major figure in AI and information theory poses
        some of the fundamental questions on AI while des-
        cribing the characteristics of a chess-playing mach-
        ine using computers.

3355   Shannon, Claude. The Mathematical Theory of Communica-
        tion. With W. Weaver. Urbana: University of Illinois
        Press, 1949.

This was the first major work on the subject of information theory in modern times. This important work illustrated how data on a line could be quantifiably measured and analyzed. It was the book that most launched information theory as a subject for study. It was based on research done at Bell Laboratories on communication problems.

3356   Shannon, Claude and McCarthy, John. Automata Studies.
        Annals of Mathematical Studies 34. Princeton: Princeton University Press, 1956.

        Edited by two important figures in the early history of AI and information theory, these are the proceedings of a conference held at Dartmouth College in the summer of 1956, one of the first held on AI. The publication is a crucial piece of AI history.

3357   Simon, Herbert. The Sciences of the Artificial.
        Cambridge, Mass.: MIT Press, 1969.

        A strong proponent of AI articulates his views. He thinks of man as a processor of information.

3358   Simon, Herbert and Newell, Allen. "Information Processing Language V on the IBM 650," Annals of the History of Computing 8, No. 1 (January 1986): 47-49.

        Two leading AI experts reviewed their early work with IPL-V at Carnegie in the 1950s.

3359   Simons, G.L. Introducing Artificial Intelligence.
        New York: John Wiley & Sons, 1985.

        This is a non-technical survey of AI and includes history, philosophical implications and current issues.

3360   Taube, Mortimer. Computers and Common Sense: The Myth of Thinking Machines. New York: Columbia University Press, 1961.

        The author attacked the fundamental ideas and hopes of those working on AI. His was one of the earliest attacks on the general field of AI.

3361   Tomeski, Edward Alex and Klahr, Michael. "How Artificial Intelligence Has Developed," Journal of Systems Management 6 (May 1986): 6-10.

        This is primarily on U.S. developments since the 1940s.

3362   Trakhtenbrot, B.A. "A Survey of Russian Approaches to Perebor (Brute-Force Search) Algorithms," Annals of the History of Computing 6, No. 4 (October 1984): 384-400.

        This is on Soviet research on AI; the author is a specialist in the theory of automata.

3363   Trask, M. The Story of Cybernetics. London: Studio
        Vista, 1971.

        This is an historical account of computers down to
        and including AI.

3364   Tropp, H. "Norbert Wiener," in A. Ralston and C.L.
        Meek (eds), Encyclopedia of Computer Science (New
        York: Petrocelli/Charter, 1976): 1557-1558.

        This is an illustrated biography of a great mathe-
        matician and proponent of AI.

3365   Verity, John W. "Where It All Began," Datamation 30,
        No. 2 (December 1, 1984): 153-154.

        This is a short biography of Claude Shannon and
        about his work in information theory.

3366   Waldrop, M.M. Man-Made Minds: The Promise of Artificial
        Intelligence. New York: Walker, 1987.

        This is a survey of AI for the general reader with
        an historical overview.

3367   Wang, H. "Games, Logic and Computers," Scientific
        American 213 (November 1965): 98-104ff.

        Games and AI were bound together in the late 1950s
        and early 1960s; this explains much activity of the
        period in computerizing chess and other thinking
        games.

3368   Warrick, Patricia S. The Cybernetic Imagination in
        Science Fiction. Cambridge, Mass.: MIT Press,1985.

        This is a history of science fiction's treatment of
        artificial intelligence.

3369   Weizenbaum, Joseph. Computer Power and Human Reason:
        From Judgment to Calculation. New York: W.H. Freeman
        and Co., 1976.

        This is an outstanding book on the impact of comput-
        ers and on the scientific relationship to man's
        rationality and self image. The author taught at MIT
        and developed SLIP.

3370   Weizenbaum, Joseph. "ELIZA—A Computer Program For
        the Study of Natural Language Communication Between
        Man and Machine," Communications, ACM 9, No. 1 (Jan-
        uary 1965): 36-45.

        This important paper in the field of AI described a
        language that simulated discussions between patient
        and psychoanalyst.

3371   Whorf, Benjamin. Language, Thought, and Reality. Ed.
        by J.B. Carroll. Cambridge, Mass.: MIT Press, 1956.

        It was the first semenal book to contain the argument

that human language influenced one's view of the
world. It encouraged the study of linguistics and
programming languages.

3372   Wiener, Norbert. Cybernetics. 2nd ed. Cambridge, Mass.:
        MIT Press, 1961.

        This is a classic in the field of AI, first published
        in 1948. It gave definition to the new field.

3373   Wiener, Norbert. "Cybernetics; New Field of Study
        Looks Into Processes Common to Nervous Systems and
        Mathematical Machines," Scientific American 179
        (November 1948): 14-19.

        This paper explained his notion of cybernetics, and
        introduced the word. It was the case for AI before
        it was called that.

3374   Wiener, Norbert. God and Golem, Inc. Cambridge, Mass.:
        MIT Press, 1966.

        This is one of his later works on the subject of AI.

3375   Wiener, Norbert. The Human Use of Human Beings. New
        York: Avon Books, 1969.

        All through the 1960s Wiener continued to discuss
        human thinking, the structure of nervous systems and
        role in information theory and handling.

3376   Wiener, Norbert. I Am a Mathematician. Garden City,
        N.Y.: Doubleday, 1956.

        This is the second volume of his autobiography. This
        focuses on his career and how he helped to establish
        the field of cybernetics.

3377   Wiener, Norbert. "Machines Smarter Than Men?," U.S.
        News & Library 56 (February 24, 1964): 84-86.

        He answers the question with No.

3378   Wiener, Norbert. Norbert Wiener: Collected Works. Ed.
        by P. Masani. 4 vols. Cambridge, Mass.: MIT Press,
        1976-1986.

        This is a large collection of his papers with commen-
        taries. Volume 4 is on cybernetics; the first three
        are on mathematics, physics and philosophy.

3379   Wiener, Norbert. "Revolt of the Machines; Summary of
        Address," Time 75 (January 11, 1960): 32.

        Argues that computers could be the greatest threat
        to man's ascendency by outgrowing his control.

3380   Wiener, Norbert. "Some Moral and Technical Consequen-
        ces of Automation," Science 131 (May 6, 1960): 1355-
        1358; Discussion, 132 (August 26, 1960): 555-557,
        741-742.

This series offered up a discussion of the moral
and technical consequences of automation in general
and not just about AI.

3381   Winograd, Terry. <u>Understanding Natural Language</u>. New
       York: Academic Press, 1972.

       The monograph describes SHRDLU, a simulated robot.
       The book was influencial on AI scientists.

3382   Yates, Frances. <u>The Art of Memory</u>. Chicago: University
       of Chicago Press, 1966.

       This is a study of various mnemonic systems that
       have existed from ancient times through the Renai-
       ssance.

Computer-Aided Design (CAD)

3383   Gray, J.C. "Compound Data Structure for Computer
       Aided Design; A Survey," <u>Proceedings, ACM 22nd Nation-
       al Conference</u> (1967): 355-365.

       Surveys early CAD software used, for example, to
       design parts of machines.

3384   Ross, D.T. "A Generalized Technique for Symbol Mani-
       pulation and Numerical Calculation," <u>Communications,
       ACM</u> 4, No. 3 (March 1961): 147-150.

       Describes work done since 1959 at MIT on <u>A</u>utomated
       <u>E</u>ngineering <u>D</u>esign (AED), a CAD package.

3385   Ross, D.T. "The Automated Engineering Design (AED)
       Approach to Generalized Computer-Aided Design,"
       <u>Proceedings, ACM 22nd National Conference</u> (1967):
       367-385.

       This is a detailed description of AED, which had
       been under development at MIT since 1959.

3386   Ross, D.T. and Rodriguez, J.E. "Theoretical Founda-
       tions for the Computer-Aided Design System," <u>Proceed-
       ings, SJCC</u> 23 (1963): 305-322.

       In addition to being a formal description of AED,
       the article mirrors early development issues concern-
       ing CAD/CAM software in general.

3387   Stotz, R.H. "Man-Machine Console Facilities for
       Computer-Aided Design," <u>Proceedings, SJCC</u> 23 (1963):
       323-328.

       The author reviews issues concerning CAD software
       as of the early 1960s.

Data Base Management Systems (DBMS)

3388   Carmichael, J.W.S. "History of the ICL Content-Address-
       able File Store (CAFS)," <u>ICL Technical Journal</u> 4
       (November 1985): 352-357.

CAFS was better known in Europe than in American computer circles in the 1980s.

3389   Chamberlin, D.D. "A Summary of User Experience with the SQL Data Sublanguage," Proceedings of the International Conference on Data Bases (Aberdeen, Scotland: British Computer Society and University of Aberdeen, 1980): 181-203.

This helps understand DB developments of the 1970s.

3390   Chamberlin, D.D. and Boyce, R.F. "SEQUEL—A Structured English Query Language," Proceedings of the ACM SIGFIDET Workshop on Data Description, Access, and Control (New York: Association for Computing Machinery, 1974): 249-264.

SEQUEL was a general purpose query language that had DBMS features common to many systems of the 1970s.

3391   Czarnik, B. et al. "ZETA: A Relational Data Base Management System," Proceedings of the ACM Pacific 75 Regional Conference (New York: Association for Computing Machinery, 1975): 21-25.

This early relational data base was developed at the University of Toronto; a technical description.

3392   The Data Bases Market. New York: Frost & Sullivan, 1977.

This is a market survey for DBMS packages.

3393   Emerson, E.J. "DMS 1100 User Experience," in D.A. Jardine (ed), Data Base Management Systems (Amsterdam: North-Holland Publishing Co., 1974): 35-46.

DMS was Univac's DBMS software of the 1970s.

3394   Fry, J.P. and Sibley, E.H. "Evolution of Data-Base Management Systems," Computing Surveys 8, No. 1 (March 1976): 7-42.

This is the only survey available on DB and file management software covering the period from the 1950s to the mid-1970s.

3395   Held, G. et al. "INGRES—A Relational Data Base System," Proceedings of the National Computer Conference (Montvale, N.J.: AFIPS Press, 1975): 409-416.

This is a technical description of an early relational DBMS, developed at the University of California, Berkeley.

3396   Hutt, A.T.F. "History of the CAFS Relational Software," ICL Technical Journal 4 (November 1985): 358-364.

See also No. 3388 for more details on CAFS.

3397   McGee, W.C.   "Data Base Technology," IBM Journal of
       Research and Development 25, No. 5 (September 1981):
       505-519.

       This surveys the role IBM played in the development
       of DBMS from the 1950s through the 1970s. States
       that the term data base came into existence in 1964.

3398   McGee, W.C.   "The Information Management System IMS/VS,"
       IBM Systems Journal 16 (1977): 84-168.

       This was an important, formal technical description
       of IBM's DB and data communications subsystem of
       the 1970s and early 1980s.

3399   Neufeld, M. Lynne and Cornog, Martha.   "Database
       History: From Dinosaurs to Compact Discs," Journal
       of the American Society for Information Science 37,
       No. 4 (1986): 183-190.

       This is a very brief survey of major file handling
       methods and software from the 1940s to the 1980s.

3400   Peterson, W.W.   "Addressing for Random-Access Storage,"
       IBM Journal of Research and Development 1 (1957):
       130-146.

       This was one of the first technical papers on data
       structuring and on hashing as a method frequently
       used in the 1960s.

3401   Schubert, R.F.   "Basic Concepts in Data Base Management
       Systems," Datamation 18 (1972): 42-47.

       This is a relatively non-technical review of DB
       designs at the dawn of the 1970s, the decade that
       saw the appearance of numerous DBMS.

3402   Tsichritzis, D.C. and Klug, A."The ANSI/X3/SPARC DBMS
       Framework: Report of the Study Group on Data Base
       Management Systems," Information Systems 3 (1978):
       173-192.

       This was a semantic data base of the 1970s; the
       article is a technical description of its features.

3403   Weiss, H.M.   "The ORACLE Data Base Management System,"
       Mini-Micro System 13 (1980): 111-114.

       ORACLE was an early relational DBMS.

3404   Whitney, V.K.M. "RDMS: A Relational Data Management
       System," Proceedings, Fourth International Symposium
       on Computer and Information Sciences (COINS IV) (New
       York: Plenum Press, 1972): passim.

       This technical description concerns a DBMS developed
       by General Motors.

Discrete Simulation

3405   Crane, Diana. "Computer Simulation: New Laboratory
        for the Social Sciences," in Morris H. Philipson
        (ed), Automation: Implications for the Future (New
        York: Vintage Books, 1962): 339-354.

        Crane describes how computers were and could be used
        in support of social science topics.

3406   Dahl, O. and Nygaard, K. "SIMULA—An Algol-Based
        Simulation Language," Communications, ACM 9, No. 9
        (September 1966): 671-682.

        Described SIMULA, developed in 1965 and ran on a
        UNIVAC 1107.

3407   Dimsdale, B. and Markowitz, H.M. "A Description of the
        SIMSCRIPT Language," IBM Systems Journal 3, No. 1
        (1964): 57-67.

        This was a software modeling package developed at
        RAND Corporation.

3408   Efron, R. et al. "A General Purpose Digital Simulator
        and Examples of Its Application, Pts. I, II, III, and
        IV," IBM Systems Journal 3, No. 1 (1964): 21-56.

        This is a technical description of GPSS, originally
        developed to model telecommunication networks.

3409   Gordon, G. "A General Purpose Systems Simulation
        Program," Proceedings, EJCC 20 (1961): 87-104.

        The father of GPSS describes the program.

3410   Gordon, G. "A General Purpose Systems Simulator,"
        IBM Systems Journal 1 (September 1962): 18-32.

        He describes the features and use of GPSS.

3411   Greenberger, M. and Jones, M.M. "On-Line Simulation
        in the OPS System," Proceedings, ACM 21st National
        Conference (1966): 131-138.

        This is a short description of OPS, developed at
        MIT in the early 1960s.

3412   Greenberger, M. et al. On-Line Computation and Simula-
        tion: The OPS-3 System. Cambridge, Mass.: MIT Press,
        1965.

        This is the fullest description of the features and
        uses for OPS, a very early online simulator.

3413   Herscovitch, H. and Schneider, T.H. "GPSS III—An
        Expanded General Purpose Simulator," IBM Systems
        Journal 4, No. 3 (1965): 174-183.

        Describes a later version of a widely used tool.

3414   Jones, M.M.   "On-Line Simulation," Proceedings, ACM
       22nd National Conference (1967): 591-599.

       He describes OPS-4.

3415   Kiviat, P.J.   "Development of New Digital Simulation
       Languages," Journal of Industrial Engineering 17,
       No. 11 (November 1966): 604-609.

       This surveys languages of the mid-1960s.

3416   Knuth, D.E. and McNeley, J.L.   "A Formal Definition of
       SOL," IEEE Transactions, Electrical Computers EC-13,
       No. 4 (August 1964): 409-414.

       Describes an ALGOL-like modeling package.

3417   Knuth, D.E. and McNeley, J.L.   "SOL—A Symbolic Language
       for General-Purpose Systems Simulation," IEEE Trans-
       actions, Electrical Computers EC-13, No. 4 (August
       1964): 401-408.

       See previous citation; same theme.

3418   Krasnow, H.S.   "Computer Languages for System Simula-
       tion," in M. Klerer and G.A. Korn (eds), Digital
       Computer User's Handbook (New York: McGraw-Hill,
       1967): 1-258-1-277.

       This is an excellent survey of the strengths and
       weaknesses of languages for discrete simulation such
       as DYNAMO, GPSS, SIMSCRIPT, SOL, MILITRAN, SIMULA
       and OPS.

3419   Markowitz, H.M. et al. SIMSCRIPT—A Simulation Programm-
       ing Language. Englewood Cliffs, N.J.: Prentice-Hall,
       Inc., 1963.

       This is the earliest book-length description of a
       language to do computerized simulations; developed
       at RAND Corporation.

3420   Reitman, J.   "The User of Simulation Languages—The
       Forgotten Man," Proceedings, ACM 22nd National Con-
       ference (1967): 573-579.

       This is a useful survey of programming languages to
       do simulations of the 1960s.

3421   Teichroew, D. and Lublin, J.F.   "Computer Simulation—
       Discussion of the Technique and Comparison of Lan-
       guages," Communications, ACM 9, No. 10 (October
       1966): 723-741.

       A useful snapshot of the tools that were available
       in the 1960s.

Graphics

3422   Corbin, H.S. and Frank, W.L.   "Display Oriented

Computer Usage System," Proceedings, ACM 21st
National Conference (1966): 515-526.

DOCUS used push button displays, several languages,
and ran on a CDC 1604B.

3423   Hurwitz, A. et al. "GRAF: Graphic Additions to FORTRAN,"
       Proceedings, SJCC 30 (1967): 553-557.

       Provided graphic display outlet for Fortran
       problems.

3424   Roberts, L.G. "Graphical Communication and Control
       Languages," Information System Sciences: Proceedings
       of the Second Congress (Washington, D.C.: Spartan
       Books, 1965): 211-217.

       This is a survey of available graphic tools of the
       early 1960s.

3425   Schwinn, P.M. "A Problem Oriented Graphic Language,"
       Proceedings, ACM 22nd National Conference (1967):
       471-477.

       GL was used to display data.

3426   Skinner, F.D. "Computer Graphics—Where Are We?,"
       Datamation 12, No. 5 (May 1966): 28-31.

       This is a useful snapshot of graphic software of
       the 1960s.

3427   Sutherland, I.E. "Computer Graphics; Ten Unsolved
       Problems," Datamation 12, No. 5 (May 1966): 22-27.

       Surveys issues related to the development of graphics
       software in the mid-1960s.

3428   Van Dam, A. and Evans, D. "A Compact Data Structure
       for Storing, Retrieving and Manipulating Line Draw-
       ings," Proceedings, SJCC 30 (1967): 601-610.

       Originally run on an IBM 7040 under MULTILANG, the
       software was called PENCIL, a simple data structure
       graphic language.

3429   Wexelblat, R.L. and Freedman, H.A. "The MULTILAND
       On-Line Programming System," Proceedings, SJCC 30
       (1967): 559-569.

       This describes PENCIL that ran under MULTILANG.

       Management of Data Processing, 1940s-1950s

3430   Acker, R.D. "Personnel and Training Needs," in Lowell
       H. Hattery and George P. Bush (eds), Electronics in
       Management (Washington, D.C.: Yniversity Press of
       Washington, D.C., 1956): 119-123.

       Surveys the effort to build a staff at Metropolitan
       Life Insurance Company.

3431   American Management Association. The Changing Dimen-
        sions of Office-Management—Technical and Managerial
        Trends in Administrative Operations. Management
        Report No. 41. New York: American Management Assoc-
        iation, 1960.

        This is an anthology of 25 papers delivered at the
        AMA's 1959 Annual Office Management Conference and
        range from automation to operations research with
        case studies.

3432   American Management Association. Electronic Data
        Processing in Industry—A Case Book of Management
        Experience. Special Report No. 3. New York: Ameri-
        can Management Association, 1955.

        Twenty representatives of U.S. companies described
        their experiences at AMA's Electronics Conference,
        March 1955. Topics included evolution of DP, planning,
        equipment and uses; includes glossary of terms.

3433   American Management Association. Electronics in Action
        —The Current Practicality of Electronic Data Process-
        ing. Special Report No. 22. New York: American
        Management Association, 1957.

        Thirteen papers are presented by U.S. companies from
        AMA's third Annual Electronics Conference and Exhibit,
        February 1957. Topics included feasibility studies,
        applications, and prospects. Others were selection
        and training problems, operations research.

3434   American Management Association. Establishing an
        Integrated Data Processing System Blueprint for a
        Company Program. Special Report No. 11. New York:
        American Management Association, 1956.

        Sixteen papers and four cases are from an AMA confer-
        ence held in February-March 1956. Topics included
        installation efforts and management of people.

3435   American Management Association. The Impact of Comput-
        ers on Office Management. New York: American Manage-
        ment Association, December 1954.

        Focus is on methods as influenced by DP on people
        management.

3436   American Management Association. Keeping Pace With
        Automation—Practical Guides for the Company Execu-
        tive. Special Report No. 7. New York: American
        Management Association, 1956.

        Thirteen papers are from the AMA Conference on Auto-
        mation, October 1955. Topics included computers,
        factory automation, and cases.

3437   American Management Association. Pioneering in Elec-
        tronic Data Processing—Company Experience With
        Electronic Computers. Special Report No. 9. New York:

American Management Association, 1956.

Eleven papers are from the AMA conference Electronics
at Work, February 1956. Topics included feasibility
studies, personnel, applications; 11 companies presented.

3438   Anthony, Robert N. (ed). Proceedings, Automatic Data
        Processing Conference, September 8-9, 1955, Harvard
        University, Graduate School of Business, 1956.
        Cambridge, Mass.: Harvard University Graduate School
        of Business, 1956.

        These papers deal with basic principles, centraliza-
        tion vs. decentralization, applications, operations
        research, and include case studies.

3439   Anthony, Robert N. and Schwartz, Samuel. Office Equip-
        ment: Buy or Rent? Boston: Management Analysis
        Center, Inc., 1957.

        Discusses financial considerations influencing
        decisions of the mid-1950s in the U.S. as second
        generation computers shipped in quantity.

3440   Bagby, Wesley S. "Deciding Upon an Electronic Data-
        Processing System," The Controller 24 (May 1956):
        216-221.

        By reviewing how an insurance company cost-justified
        its acquisition of a computer, one sees what factors
        were used in the mid-1950s; payback was 5-6 years.

3441   Bagby, Wesley S. "The Human Side of Electronics,"
        Proceedings of the Second Annual AMA Electronics
        Conference: Pioneering in Electronic Data Processing.
        Special Report No. 9. New York: American Management
        Association, February 27-29, 1956.

        Bagby comments on his experience in installing the
        first computer at Pacific Mutual in 1953 and about
        how employee morale was preserved.

3442   Becker, Esther R. and Murphy, Eugene F. The Office in
        Transition. New York: Harper & Brothers, 1957.

        Describes punch cards, computers, DP and how to
        develop applications, their design and programming.

3443   Beer, Stafford. Cybernetics and Management. New York:
        John Wiley & Sons, 1959.

        Services as a lucid survey for non-technical readers.

3444   Bekker, John A. "Automation: Its Impact on Management,"
        Advanced Management Journal 24, No. 12 (December
        1959): 20-24.

        Management is defined as all managers, not just those
        in data processing.

3445   Bell, William D. A Management Guide to Electronic
        Computers. New York: McGraw-Hill Book Co., 1957.

        More than just a description of hardware, this tells
        how they were being configured and used in 11 cases.

3446   Berkeley, Edmund C. and Wainwright, Lawrence. Comput-
        ers: Their Operation and Applications. New York:
        Reinhold Book Corporation, 1956.

        While a general introduction, it covers their use
        as of the mid-1950s and comments on the IBM 700s.

3447   Bittel, Lester R. et al. (eds). Practical Automation.
        New York: McGraw-Hill Book Co., Inc., 1957.

        They surveyed organizational issues associated with
        the installation of a computer system; excellent.

3448   Bright, James R. Automation and Management. Boston:
        Harvard Business School, Division of Research, 1958.

        Surveys management problems and issues related to
        automated manufacturing; includes 13 U.S. cases that
        had leading edge applications in 1954.

3449   Burroughs Corporation. Burroughs Data Processing Guide.
        Pasadena: Electrodata Division, Burroughs Corpora-
        tion, 1960.

        This manual describes operating procedures to make
        effective use of its products.

3450   Bush, George P. "Cost Considerations," in Lowell H.
        Hattery and George P. Bush (eds), Electronics in
        Management (Washington, D.C.: University Press of
        Washington, D.C., 1956): 101-111.

        Identifies sources of expenses associated with install-
        ing computers in the early to mid-1950s and shares
        what early users have discovered.

3451   Canning, Richard G. Electronic Data Processing for
        Business and Industry. New York: John Wiley & Sons,
        1956.

        Provides advice on how to use and select DP solutions
        with cost justification.

3452   Canning, Richard G. Installing Electronic Data Process-
        ing Systems. New York: John Wiley & Sons, Inc.,
        1957.

        This is a tactical guide with numerous case studies.

3453   Chapin, Ned. Automatic Computers: A Systems Approach
        for Business. Princeton: D. Van Nostrand Co., Inc.,
        1957.

        Offers cost justification, operational advice.

3454   Chapin, Ned. An Introduction to Automatic Computers.
        New York: D. Van Nostrand Co., Inc., 1955; 2nd ed.,
        1959.

        Chapin's overview of computer concepts was one of
        the best of the early books and was widely read by
        management concerned with data processing.

3455   Clippinger, Richard F. "Economics of the Digital
        Computer," Harvard Business Review 33 (January-
        February 1955): 77-78.

        While based on first generation technology, focus is
        on potential uses of computers in business applica-
        tions, costs and benefits. It includes a list of
        computer service bureaus of the period.

3456   Conway, B. et al. Business Experience with Electronic
        Computers: A Synthesis of What Has Been Learned From
        Electronic Data Processing Installations. New York:
        Controllers Institute Research Foundation, Inc.,
        1959.

        Included subjects are experiences with acquisition
        decisions, introduction to DP systems the first
        time, conversion from other systems and methods,
        management of DP systems, relations with vendors.

3457   Controllers Institute Research Foundation, Inc. A
        Case Study in Planning at Port of New York Authority.
        New York: Controllers Institute Research Foundation,
        Inc., 1956.

        This involved computerization at the Port.

3458   Controllers Institute Research Foundation, Inc. Apprais-
        ing the Economics of Electronics in Business. New
        York: Controllers Institute Research Foundation, Inc.,
        1956.

        This offers suggestions on how to address the issue
        of cost justification and financing data processing.

3459   Craig, Harold F. Administering a Conversion to Electron-
        ic Accounting. Boston: Harvard University, Graduate
        School of Business Administration, 1955.

        This is a cost study of an insurance company's exper-
        ience in moving to punch card accounting and reflects
        a very early experience with EDP (1950s).

3460   Curry, Robert B. "Preparing Employees for the Change-
        over," in Lowell H. Hattery and George P. Bush (eds),
        Electronics in Management (Washington, D.C.: Univer-
        sity Press of Washington, D.C., 1956): 124-138.

        This is an excellent look at the concerns of employ-
        ees when a computer was first installed in early
        1950s, with suggestions on how best to manage the
        issue.

3461   Curtiss, John H.   "Teamwork in a Computations Labora-
        tory," in George P. Bush and Lowell H. Hattery (eds),
        Teamwork in Research (Washington, D.C.: American
        University Press, 1953): 165-168.

        Describes experiences at the U.S. National Bureau of
        Standards computation lab, emphasizing the importance
        of teamwork in complex projects.

3462   Dale, Ernest.   "Centralization Versus Decentralization,"
        Advanced Management Journal 20, No. 6 (June 1955):
        11-16.

        The debate whether to keep all computing in one data
        center or distribute computing to many locations has
        its pros and cons, discussed here in an early article
        on the topic.

3463   Data Processing Manning Survey. Published by Systems
        and Procedures Association, reprinted in Datamation
        4, No. 2 (March-April 1958): 31-33.

        Presents results of survey on DP job descriptions,
        titles, salaries all from the New York area, 1957.

3464   Dichter, Ernest.   Why They Don't Buy Computers: A
        Motivational Research Study Conducted for Modern
        Office Procedures. Cleveland: Modern Office Procedur-
        es, 1960.

        This is a 54-page catalog of why people do not use
        computers, why and how some do, and who makes the
        decision to acquire them.

3465   Dreher, Carl.   Automation: What It Is, How It Works,
        Who Can Use It.   New York: W.W. Norton and Co., Inc.,
        1957.

        Includes cartoons on automation; a light survey.

3466   EDP—The First Ten Years. New York: McKinsey and Co.,
        Inc., 1961.

        This consists of 43 short articles by McKinsey's
        employees on lessons for management. Topics include
        DP in transition, information systems, management.

3467   Electronic Data Processing Conference, Selected Papers,
        May 14-15, 1959. University, Alabama: University of
        Alabama Extension News Bulletin, 1959.

        The 38-page publication discusses "Profitable Utili-
        zation of Computers in Banking," "Electronic Data
        Processing and the Numerically Controlled Milling
        Machine," "Selecting and Training Personnel for Com-
        puter Work."

3468   Elliott, J.D.   "EDP—Its Impact on Jobs, Procedures
        and People," Journal of Industrial Engineering 9,
        No. 5 (September-October 1958): 407-410.

The author, Director of Control Data Processing at
Detroit Edison, described the first computer installa-
llation there and effects on staffs; an early publication by a DP manager.

3469   Frese, Walter. "Organizational Effects," in Lowell H.
        Hatterly and George P. Bush (eds), Electronics in
        Management (Washington, D.C.: University Press of
        Washington, D.C., 1956): 157-162.

        This is one of the earliest articles to discuss the
        effect of computers on organizational structures and
        processes; based on experience within the U.S. Govern-
        ment in the early to mid-1950s.

3470   Gallagher, James D. "Administrative Automation at
        Sylvania," Administrative Automation Through IDP
        and EDP. Office Management Series No. 144. New York:
        American Management Association, 1956.

        This described Sylvania's first installation and its
        effects on management.

3471   Gallagher, James D. Management Information Systems and
        the Computer. New York: American Management Associa-
        tion, Inc., 1961.

        Describes how businesses were using computers most
        efficiently and about management's role. Surveys
        uses at American Airlines and at Sylvania Electric
        Products, Inc.

3472   Gammon, William Howard. "The Automatic Handling of
        Office Paper Work," Public Administration Review
        (1954): 63-73.

        Surveys publications of the early 1950s on the
        management of computing.

3473   Gammon, William Howard. "Evaluating and Selecting
        Equipment," in Lowell H. Hattery and George P. Bush
        (eds), Electronics in Management (Washington, D.C.:
        University Press of Washington, D.C., 1956): 38-50.

        This is a well-done reflection of managerial concerns
        of the mid-1950s.

3474   General Electric Company. The Next Step in Management:
        An Appraisal of Cybernetics. New York: General
        Electric Company, 1952.

        An internal GE publication, it reviews role of com-
        puters, applications, and management as of 1952.

3475   Gotlieb, J.N. and Hume, P. High-Speed Data Processing.
        New York: McGraw-Hill Company, Inc., 1958.

        Surveys the history of computers, programming and
        other DP issues. Cost justifications are included.

3476   Grabbe, Eugene M. et al. Handbook of Automation, Com-
        putation, and Control. 3 vols. New York: John Wiley
        & Sons, Inc., 1958-60.

        Covers all aspects of the topic. Vol. 1 is primarily
        on mathematics and control functions, 2 on DP tech-
        nology, 3 on systems and components with focus on
        systems engineering.

3477   Gregory, Robert H. and Van Horn, Richard L.   Automatic
        Data-Processing Systems: Principles and Procedures.
        San Francisco: Wadsworth Publishing Co., Inc., 1960.

        Reflects DP technology as of the late 1950s, manage-
        ment and acquisition patterns.

3478   Gregory, Robert H. and Van Horn, Richard L.   Business
        Data Processing and Programming. Belmont, Cal.:
        Wadsworth Publishing Co., 1963.

        This surveys equipment, systems design, programming
        and applications. Both authors worked at RAND Cor-
        poration; includes bibliography and list of widely
        read DP journals of the early 1960s.

3479   Guest, Leon C., Jr.   "Administrative Automation at
        Sylvania: A Case Study—I. Centralized Data Process-
        ing—Decentralized Management," in Administrative
        Automation Through IDP and EDP. Office Management
        Series No. 144 (New York: American Management Asso-
        ciation, 1956): 28-37.

        Sylvania, a highly decentralized firm, wanted to
        reverse the trend toward increasing numbers of cleri-
        cal staff and thus created a centralized DP center
        but run with decentralized management.

3480   Guest, Leon C., Jr.   "Centralized Data Processing for
        Decentralized Management," Systems Magazine 20, No.
        5 (September-October 1956): 6-7.

        Carries on the same theme as the previous citation.

3481   Hamming, R.W.   "Controlling the Digital Computer,"
        Science Monthly 85 (October 1957): 169-175.

        This is as much an article about its use and manage-
        ment as it is about its development scientifically.

3482   Haskens and Sells.   Data Processing by Electronics: A
        Basic Guide for the Understanding and Use of a New
        Technique. New York: Haskens and Sells, May 1955.

        Summarizes functional characteristics and costs of
        148 DP systems and covers management issues associa-
        ted with computers.

3483   Hattery, Lowell H.   Executive Control & Data Process-
        ing. Washington, D.C.: Anderson Kramer Associates,
        1959.

This is a manager's guide to data processing.

3484   Hattery, Lowell H. "Management Impact of Electronic
       Systems," in Lowell H. Hattery and George P. Bush
       (eds), Electronics in Management (Washington, D.C.:
       University Press of Washington, D.C., 1956): 3-11.

       Reviews challenges facing managers applying this new
       technology to their organizations, 1950s-1960s.

3485   Hattery, Lowell H. and Bush, George P. (eds). Electron-
       ics in Management. Washington, D.C.: University
       Press, 1956.

       This is a collection of papers presented at the First
       Institute on Electronics in Management held at Ameri-
       can University in November 1955 with focus on manage-
       ment issues and case studies from the 1950s.

3486   Haverstroh, Chadwick J. "The Impact of Electronic Data
       Processing on Administrative Organizations," National
       Tax Journal 14, No. 3 (September 1961): 258-270.

       The article is detailed and a useful reflection of
       both managerial and organizational issues.

3487   Hoos, Ida Russakoff. "When the Computer Takes Over
       the Office," Harvard Business Review 38, No. 4 (July-
       August 1960): 102-112.

       Reflects the concerns and lessons learned in install-
       ing computers in 19 organizations for the first time.

3488   Hunter, G. Truman. "A Management Forecast," in Lowell
       H. Hattery and George P. Bush (eds), Electronics in
       Management (Washington, D.C.: University Press of
       Washington, D.C., 1956): 174-183.

       This IBMer looked out at the future for management
       issues involving computers and in the process dis-
       cussed concerns of many managers in the new industry
       of 1955-56.

3489   International Business Machines Corporation. Super-
       vision of an Electronic Data Processing Machine
       Installation, 702-705. Customer Assistance Bulletin
       No. 2. New York: International Business Machines
       Corporation, March 1957.

       IBM reviews what a DP organization should look like
       and offers job descriptions, circa second generation
       era.

3490   Jacobson, Arvid E. (ed). Proceedings of the First
       Conference on Training Personnel for the Computing
       Machine Field. Detroit: Wayne University Press, 1955.

       These were papers presented at a conference held at
       Wayne University on manpower requirements and educa-
       tion for DP professionals.

3491   Jones, Gardner M. <u>Electronics in Business</u>. East Lan-
       sing, Mich.: Bureau of Business and Economic Research,
       Michigan State University, 1958.

       The central theme is the organizational consequences
       of DP, and argues that computers are forcing various
       departments to work together due to centralization of
       data required for computer-based applications.

3492   Kaufman, Felix. <u>Electronic Data Processing and Audit-
       ing</u>. New York: The Ronald Press, 1961.

       Written by a computer literate accountant, this
       reflects concerns of accountants during the 1950s
       and 1960s while describing accounting applications.

3493   Klingman, Herbert F. <u>Electronics in Business: A Case
       Study in Planning</u>. New York: Controllership Founda-
       tion, Inc., January 1956.

       This is a discussion of how to plan for an initial
       computer installation, using Port of New York Author-
       ity as the base case.

3494   Knox, Frank M. <u>Integrated Cost Control in the Office</u>.
       NOMA Series in Office Management. New York: McGraw-
       Hill Book Co., Inc., 1958.

       This well-known author of management books surveys
       the office of the late 1950s/early 1960s stressing
       human relations as crucial rather than the use of
       technology or specific methods of management.

3495   Kozmetsky, George and Kirsher, Paul. <u>Electronic Com-
       puters and Management Control</u>. New York: McGraw-Hill
       Book Co., Inc., 1956.

       Emphasis is on applications in business, experience
       with initial uses, impact on management, control and
       selection of devices.

3496   Kruisinga, H.J. <u>The Balance Between Centralization
       and Decentralization in Managerial Control</u>. Leiden:
       H.E. Stenfert Kroese N.V., 1954.

       Computers made possible either alternative, igniting
       considerable debate on the issue.

3497   Laubach, Peter B. <u>Company Investigations of Automatic
       Data Processing</u>. Boston: Harvard University, Graduate
       School of Business Administration, 1957.

       Surveys how various companies conducted feasibility
       studies in the early 1950s for new computers.

3498   Lazarro, Victor (ed). <u>Systems and Procedures, A Hand-
       book for Business and Industry</u>. Englewood Cliffs,
       N.J.: Prentice-Hall, Inc., 1959.

       Covers systems analysis, charting, auditing, measure-
       ments, forms control, records management, DP equipment
       selection and DP personnel.

3499   Leavitt, Harold J. and Whisler, Thomas J.   "Management
        in the 1980's," Harvard Business Review 35, No. 6
        (November-December 1958): 41-49.

        This attempted to define trends in management that
        included the use of computers.

3500   Levenson, J.H. (ed).   Electronic Business Machines.
        New York: Philosophical Library, 1960.

        This is a series of lectures delivered at Dundee Tech-
        nical College on computers with attention paid to how
        they worked, the measurement of their value, effective-
        ness, and applications.

3501   Lipstreu, Otis.   "Organizational Implications of Auto-
        mation," The Journal of the Academy of Management 3,
        No. 2 (August 1960): 119-125.

        Experiences of the 1950s suggests that changes were
        significant due to all manner of automation.

3502   Mann, Floyd C. and Williams, Lawrence K.   "Observations
        on the Dynamics of a Change to Electronic Data Process-
        ing Equipment," Administrative Science Quarterly 5,
        No. 2 (September 1960): 217-256.

        With equipment becoming more reliable and less expen-
        sive, more was being used.

3503   Massie, Joseph L.   "Automatic Horizontal Communication
        in Management," The Journal of the Academy of Manage-
        ment 3, No. 2 (August 1960): 87-92.

        This was made possible by the advent of new technolo-
        gies, such as the computer.

3504   Meagher, George E.   "Decentralization of Operations,"
        Proceedings of the 1961 Annual Conference of the Life
        Office Management Association (New York, 1961): 82-87.

        Reviews the effects of a DP decentralization decision
        at Prudential Life Insurance Company.

3505   Mellinger, Harry K. (ed).   A Guide for Business Systems
        Analysis. Willow Grove, Pa.: Philco Corporation, 1960.

        Describes how to develop a computer application based
        on the experience at Middletown Air Material Area,
        Olmsted Air Force Base, Pennsylvania.

3506   National Industrial Conference Board. Management's
        Role in Electrical Data Processing. Conference Board
        Reports No. 92. New York: National Industrial Confer-
        ence Board, 1959.

        Focuses on how to organize for and implement second
        generation computing with examples.

3507   Nett, Robert and Hetzler, Stanley A. An Introduction
        to Electronic Data Processing. Chicago: Free Press
        of Glencoe, 1959.

It includes a review of management issues, such as
training and organization in data processing.

3508   Neuschel, Richard F. Management by System. New York:
        McGraw-Hill Book Co., Inc., 1960.

        Includes a chapter on integrated management reporting
        systems, and discusses DP feasibility studies, con-
        cepts and applications; revised version of 1950 ed.

3509   Neuschel, Richard F. Streamlining Business Proceedures.
        New York: McGraw-Hill Book Co., 1950.

        This became a classic on systems during the 1950s,
        written at the dawn of the computer.

3510   Neuchel, Richard F. What Top Management Needs to Know
        About Electronic Data Processing. New York: McKinsey
        & Co., n.d. (late 1950s).

        This 10-page publication describes problems, justifi-
        cations, avoidable mistakes and guidelines for manage-
        ment based on experiences gained in the 1950s.

3511   Nichols, Frederick G. Commercial Education in the High
        School. New York: D. Appleton-Century, 1933.

        This Harvard professor included material on the use
        of business machines of the 1920s and 1930s with
        comments similar to many made in the 1950s.

3512   Optner, Stanford, L. Systems Analysis for Business
        Management. Englewood Cliffs, N.J.: Prentice-Hall,
        Inc., 1960.

        He offers a general theory and observations on systems
        analysis for the development of business applications.
        Includes 10 case studies on how companies handled
        computers in the 1950s.

3513   Organization for European Economic Cooperation. Inte-
        grated Data Processing and Computers; A Report of A
        Group of European Experts, European Productivity
        Agency, Organization for European Economic Coopera-
        tion. Paris: OEEC, November 1960.

        This 77-page document was a byproduct of a European
        visit to the U.S. in April-June 1960 on how best to
        do installations and when to use service bureaus. It
        also comments on the role of government.

3514   Place, Irene. Administrative Systems Analysis. Ann
        Arbor, Mich.: Bureau of Business Research, School of
        Business Administration, University of Michigan, 1957.

        This 83-page document is a useful description of the
        role played by systems analysts in the 1950s; survey
        results included.

3515   Postley, John A. Computers and People: Business Activi-
        ty in the New World of Data Processing. New York:

McGraw-Hill Book Company, Inc., 1960.

The author, from RAND Corporation, surveyed impact
of computers as of the late 1950s, on business, end
users, applications and its industry at large.

3516   Price Waterhouse & Co. The Auditor Encounters Electron-
        ic Data Processing. New York: Price Waterhouse &
        Co., n.d. (late 1950s).

        Surveys auditing in DP systems with suggestions on
        how to maintain an "audit trail" in systems, using
        a payroll application to illustrate the process.

3517   Proceedings of the First Conference on Training Perso-
        nnel for the Computing Machine Field. Wayne Univer-
        sity, Detroit Michigan, June 22-23, 1954.

        This was one of the first conferences held on the
        subject in the U.S.

3518   Proceedings of the Life Office Automation Forum, 1959.
        New York: Life Office Management Association, 1959.

        Topics included purchase vs. rent, programming and
        feasibility studies in the insurance industry. LOMA
        conferences annually included discussions about
        computing issues beginning with the conference of
        1957 in Washington, D.C.

3519   Rigby, F.D. "Electronic Computers for Navy Business,"
        Research Reviews (May 1955): 1-5.

        Summarizes experiences in tailoring a DP system to
        fit logistic and business applications for the U.S.
        Navy; the study sponsored by the ONR.

3520   Scott, James T. "Procedural Changes for Electronic
        Systems," in Lowell H. Hattery and George P. Bush
        (eds), Electronics in Management (Washington, D.C.:
        University Press of Washington, D.C., 1956): 112-118.

        This user described management issued involved when
        switching to a c omputer system in the 1950s.

3521   Shultz, George P. and Whisler, Thomas L. (eds). Manage-
        ment Organization and the Computer. Chicago, Ill.:
        University of Chicago Press, 1960.

        Eleven papers are presented from a seminar hosted by
        the Graduate School of Business Administration of
        the University of Chicago and the McKinsey Foundation
        in February 1959. It has 4 sections: "Information:
        Technology and Management Organization," "Technical
        Developments and Their Use by Management," "Organiza-
        tion: Concepts and Problems," "Information Technology:
        Experience in Five Companies."

3522   Simmons, Leo C. "Executive Problems and Opportunities
        Arising Out of Automatic Systems," in Lowell H.
        Hatterly and George P. Bush (eds), Electronics in
        Management (Washington, D.C.: University Press of

Washington, D.C., 1956): 163-173.

Reviews experience of the U.S. Steel Corporation with computers in the early 1950s.

3523   Simon, Herbert A. "Management by Machine," Management Review 49, No. 11 (November 1960): 12-19.

Reviews its possibilities for the 1960s.

3524   Smith, J. Sanford. The Management Approach to Electronic Digital Computers. London: MacDonald and Evans, Ltd., 1957.

This is typical of many such publications of the period; directed toward non-DP management.

3525   Smith, Robert M. "Is This a Blue-print for Tomorrow's Offices?," Office Management (August 1955): 12-14ff.

Describes the installation of foffice applications at Sylvania Electric in the mid-1950s.

3526   Solo, Myron B. "Selecting Electronic Data Processing Equipment," Datamation (November-December 1958): 28-32.

Describes how the County of Los Angeles did it in the 1950s, with financial examples.

3527   Sperry Rand, Remington Rand UNIVAC. UNIVAC Educational Series. New York: Remington Rand UNIVAC, Division of Sperry Rand, 1959.

This is a set of 3 excellent booklets on applications, programming, and an annotated bibliography.

3528   Sperry Rand, Remington Rand UNIVAC. UNIVAC's Real "MACOY". New York: Remington Rand UNIVAC, Division of Sperry Rand, 1960.

This 12-page publication advises on programming, recruitment of personnel, training, site preparation, delivery and installation of computers.

3529   Starbuck, William H. "Computing Machines: Rent or Buy?," The Journal of Industrial Engineering 9, No. 4 (July-August 1958): 254-258.

This is a detailed analysis of the topic and is a good window into second generation computer economics.

3530   Stieber, Jack. "Automation and the White-Collar Worker," Personnel 34, No. 3 (November-December 1957): 8-18.

The automation includes computing.

3531   Stilian, G.M. "Impact of Automation on the Manufacturing Executive's Job," Management Review 47, No. 4 (March 1958): 19-23.

The discussion goes beyond computing to N/C machines and shop floor automation.

3532   Strengthening Management for the New Technology. Ameri-
        can Management Association General Management Series
        No. 178. New York: American Management Association,
        Inc., November 1955.

        This is a series of papers presented at the General
        Management Conference of the AMA, May 23-25, 1955.

3533   Systems and Procedures Association. The Systems Man
        and EDP. Detroit: Systems and Procedures Association,
        1960.

        This is an 8-page report on the impact of DP on SPA
        member companies in the U.S. Contains results of a
        survey on the tasks of the systems analyst along
        with the role of 15 vendors.

3534   Thompson, T.R. "Special Requirements for Commercial
        or Administrative Applications," in Automatic Digital
        Computation; Proceedings of a Symposium Held at the
        National Physical Laboratory on March 25-28, 1953
        (London: Her Majesty's Stationery Office, 1954): 85-
        101.

        Cites examples of clerical and mathematical applica-
        tions and discusses hardware needs for these.

3535   Thurston, Philip H. Systems and Procedures. Responsi-
        bility. Boston: Division of Research, Graduate School
        of Business Administration, Harvard University, 1959.

        He describes the opinions of systems analysts and
        operators regarding their work in the late 1950s.

3536   "27 Companies Evaluate the Impact of New Data Process-
        ing Techniques," Dunn's Review and Modern Industry
        (October 1955): 77-90.

        Suggests what one had to do in order to install DP
        systems in the early 1950s.

3537   United Nations. Handbook on Data Processing Methods,
        Part 1, Provisional Edition. Prepared jointly by the
        Statistical Office of the United Nations, New York,
        and the Statistics Division, Food and Agriculture
        Organization of the United Nations. Rome: United
        Nations, 1959.

        Reviews the basics of DP, offering information on
        installing DP equipment in the late 1950s.

3538   U.S. Congress, Subcommittee on Census and Government
        Statistics of the Committee on Post Office and Civil
        Service, House of Representatives. 86th Cong., 2nd
        Sess. Office Automation and Employee Job Security.
        Hearings before the Subcommittee . . . . . Washington,

D.C.: U.S. Government Printing Office, March 2 and 4,
1960.

Reviews problems experienced by U.S. Government agencies in setting up DP shops in the 1950s and includes
excellent material on general worker forces, such as
at the U.S.Veterans Administration.

3539   U.S. Department of Agriculture. Planning for Automatic
Data Processing. Commodity Stabilization Service
Operating Procedure. Washington, D.C.: U.S. Department
of Agriculture, 1960.

Carl Barnes, of CSS, directed the preparation of this
study, a "how to" based on lessons learned in the
1950s.

3540   U.S. Department of the Air Force. Management of Data
Processing Equipment. A.F. Manual 171-9. Washington,
D.C.: Statistical Services, Department of the Air
Force, June 1, 1958.

The U.S.A.F. was, in the late 1950s, the world's
largest user of computers. This publication is an
excellent guide, reflecting this service's experience
with data processing and computers.

3541   U.S. Department of the Army. Introduction to Automatic
Data Processing. Washington, D.C.: U.S. Department of
the Army, April 1958.

This early U.S.A. publication on DP covers most
aspects in an introductory manner along with management tips and cost justification.

3542   U.S. Department of Labor, Bureau of Labor Statistics.
Adjustments to the Introduction of Office Automation.
Bulletin No. 1276. Washington, D.C.: U.S. Government
Printing Office, May 1960.

This is a useful introduction to issues of the 1950s
and sizing of the acceptance of computers in U.S.A.

3543   U.S. Department of Labor. Occupations in Electronic
Data Processing. Washington, D.C.: U.S. Employment
Service, Department of Labor, January 1959.

This provides occupational descriptions for 13 jobs
that range from "coding clerk" to analysts, programmers to tape librarians.

3544   U.S. Department of the Navy. Data Processing in Navy
Management Information Systems. Washington, D.C.:
Office of the Secretary, Department of the Navy, April
16, 1959.

Known as the Navy's "Gray Book" on DP, offering advice,
particularly on personnel matters.

3545   "UCLA to Train Computer Technicians," Business Week

(November 24, 1956): 116.

University of California—Los Angeles had a long and
early association with computers; this describes its
computer training program.

3546   Wallace, Edward L. Management Influence on the Design
        of Data Processing Systems: A Case Study. Boston:
        Division of Research, Graduate School of Business
        Administration, Harvard University, 1961.

        Surveys the failure of Bremfort Company to use com-
        puters effectively, describing why. This is an unus-
        ual survey since most described why they were success-
        ful.

3547   Wallace, Frank. Appraising the Economics of Electronic
        Computers. New York: Controllership Foundation, Inc.,
        1956.

        This accountant argues, as did most in the 1950s, that
        computers should be justified on the basis of reduced
        clerical costs; explains how to do the analysis.

3548   Weber, C. Edward. "Change in Managerial Manpower with
        Mechanization of Data-Processing," Journal of Busi-
        ness 32, No. 2 (April 1959): 151-163.

        Relates experiences of several U.S. organizations
        with emphasis on effects upon employees with the
        introduction of computers.

3549   Weber, Philip H. Determining Salaries for Computer
        Personnel. Chicago: Research Bureau of Management
        and Business Automation, 1960.

        Includes a salary and position survey done in 1960.

3550   Weinberg, Edgar. Adjustments to the Introduction of
        Office Automation. Bulletin No. 1276, Bureau of
        Labor Statistics, U.S. Department of Labor. Washing-
        ton, D.C.: U.S. Government Printing Office, May, 1960.

        See No. 3542 for a variation in the citation.

        Management of Data Processing, 1960s-1970s

3551   Allen, P. "Danger Ahead! Safeguard Your Computer,"
        Harvard Business Review 46 (November 1968): 97-101.

        An early article on physical security of systems.

3552   American Foundation on Automation and Employment, Inc.
        Automation and the Middle Manager. New York: American
        Foundation on Automation and Employment, 1966.

        Automation is primarily computer-based.

3553   Angus, Anne Denny. The Computer People. London: Faber
        and Faber, 1970.

In addition to discussion of applications and their
management, as known in Great Britain, is a chapter
on ICT in the 1960s (pp. 164-193).

3554   Association for Systems Management. Business Systems.
       Cleveland: Association for Systems Management, 1970.

       This is an early college text reflecting thinking of
       the 1960s.

3555   Auditor General, Comptrolleger, Department of the Air
       Force. Guide for Auditing Automatic Data Processing
       Systems. Washington, D.C.: U.S. Government Printing
       Office, November 1961.

       This was a widely-used volume and reflects early con-
       cerns with the audability of applications.

3556   Avots, Ivars. "The Management Side of PERT," Califor-
       nia Management Review 4, No. 24 (Winter 1962): 16-27.

       This describes specific experience using PERT.

3557   Baumes, Carl G. Administration of Electronic Data
       Processing. Business Policy Study No. 98. New York:
       National Industrial Conference Board, Inc., 1961.

       124 companies were researched on the management of
       data centers, covering all aspects of a DP manager's
       job; excellent for late 1950s and early 1960s.

3558   Berkwitt, George. "Middle Managers vs. The Computer,"
       Duns Review 88 (November 1966): 40-42, 107-110.

       Argues that many executives were resisting use of
       computers and gives many examples of why.

3559   Boehm, Barry. Software Engineering Economics. Englewood
       Cliffs, N.J.: Prentice-Hall, Inc., 1981.

       This surveys the "sociology" of programmers: their
       work habits and behavior.

3560   Boehm, George A.W. "The Decision-Making Potential of
       Computers," Computer-Based Management for Information
       and Control. Management Bulletin No. 30. New York:
       American Management Association, 1963.

       The effect on management was reviewed as well.

3561   Borchardt, Rudolph. "The Catalyst in Total Systems,"
       Systems and Procedures Journal 14, No. 3 (May-June
       1963): 16-30.
       This describes management issues.

3562   Brabb, George J. and Hutchins, Earl B. "Electronic
       Computers and Management Organization," California
       Management Review 6, No. 1 (Fall 1963): 33-43.

This technology causes changes to vertical and horizontal structures and to decision-making.

3563   Breakville, Frank. "Future of Computers," Best's Insurance News-Life Edition 66, No. 8 (December 1965): 34-35.

While mainly in the insurance industry, the effects on management generally are a reflection of the thinking of the 1960s.

3564   Brown, Warren B. "Systems, Boundaries, and Information Flow," Academy of Management Journal 9, No. 4 (December 1966): 318-327.

This is very much on organizational issues.

3565   Bueschel, Richard T. EDP and Personnel. Management Bulletin No. 86. New York: American Management Association, 1966.

Useful for defining job positions of the 1960s and typical management issues.

3566   Bull, G.M. "B.Sc. In Computer Science—10 Years Experience," IFIP Second World Computer Conference on Computers in Education, September 1-5, 1975 (Marseilles, France): 347-350.

This is on British experience.

3567   Cisler, Walker L. "Management's View of the Systems Function," Systems and Procedures Journal 16, No. 4 (July-August 1965): 16-20.

This is a DP view of the subject.

3568   Courtney, V.A. "Computer Operation," Best's Insurance News-Life Edition 66, No. 9 (January 1966): 32-35.

Recounts his experience in the 1960s.

3569   Cross, Hershner et al. Computers and Management: The 1967 Leatherbee Lectures. Boston: Graduate School of Business Administration, Harvard University, 1967.

The authors were all business executives who discussed the impact of computers on their organizations in the 1960s.

3570   Dale, Ernest. The Decision-Making Process in the Commercial Use of High-Speed Computers. Cornell Studies in Policy and Administration. Ithaca, N.Y.: Graduate School of Business and Public Administration, Cornell University, 1964.

How applications and usage were decided upon in the 1960s is the subject.

3571   Daniel, D. Ronald. "Measure Your EDP Progress: A

'5,000-Mile' Checkup," <u>The Management Review</u> 50, No.
3 (March 3, 1961): 21-26.

He comments on the growth of computer usage in the
U.S. and its characteristics.

3572   Dearden, John.   "Computers: No Impact on Divisional
        Control; Excerpts From the Impact of Computers on
        Management," <u>Harvard Business Review</u> 45 (January
        1967): 99-104.

        He argues that computers did not affect senior manage-
        ments ability to control business functions.

3573   Dearden, John.   "How to Organize Information Systems,"
        <u>Harvard Business Review</u> 43 (March 1965): 65-73.

        Based on the experiences of various U.S. companies.

3574   DeMillo, R. <u>et al</u>. "Social Processes and Proofs of
        Theorems and Programs," <u>Communications, ACM</u> 22, No.
        5 (1979): 271-280.

        They challenge the notion that programming's documen-
        ted remains can tell us about the nature of a pro-
        grammer's behavior.

3575   Dunlop, John T. <u>Automation and Technological Change</u>.
        Englewood Cliffs, N.J.: Prentice-Hall, Inc., 1965.

        This covers the subject broadly with many comments
        on the use of computers in the American economy.

3576   Esser, Herbert J.   "The Computer—A Challenge to the
        Personnel Profession," <u>Personnel Journal</u> 44, No. 6
        (June 1965): 292-294.

        The first such article to be published on the subject.

3577   Finerman, A. (ed).   <u>University Education in Computer
        Science</u>. New York: Academic Press, 1969.

        This is a series of papers presented at SUNY, Stony
        Book, N.Y. in 1967 on American programs in graduate
        and academic projects; research included.

3578   Fischbach, J.W.   "Data Processing for the Business
        Community," <u>California Management Review</u> 4, No. 1
        (Fall 1961): 35-50.

        Case studies of experiences are presented.

3579   Flock, L.R.   "Seven Deadly Dangers in EDP," <u>Harvard
        Business Review</u> 40 (May 1962): 88-96.

        All were management related and grounded in case
        studies.

3580   Garrity, John T.   <u>Getting the Most Out of Your Computer</u>.
        New York: McKinsey and Company, Inc., 1963.

This is advice to management by a consulting firm.

3581   Golembiewski, Robert T.   "Innovation and Organization
        Structure," Personnel Administration 27, No. 5
        (September-October 1961): 3-4.

        This is less about personnel than about organization
        as affected by technological introductions.

3582   Gorn, S.   "The Computer and Information Science: A New
        Basic Discipline," SIAM Review 5, No. 2 (1963): 150-
        155.

        Published at the peak of academic debate on whether
        DP was a new discipline or not.

3583   Gorn, S.   "Information Science and the Management of
        Information Processing Professionals," Proceedings
        of the 1965 Fall Conference and Business Exposition,
        Data Processing Management Association, November 3-5,
        1965 (Dallas, Texas): 441-444.

        Argues that this was a new field, different from
        either mathematics or engineering.

3584   Greenbaum, Joan M.   In the Name of Efficiency: Manage-
        ment Theory and Shop Floor Practice in Data Process-
        ing Work. Philadelphia: Temple University Press, 1979.

        Describes the DP department and how to run it.

3585   Greenwood, Frank and Danziger, Erwin M.   Computer Sys-
        tems Analysis. Management Bulletin No. 90. New York:
        American Management Association, 1967.

        They describe the function as practised in the 1960s.

3586   Haines, G. et al. "The Computer As A Small-Group Member,"
        Administrative Science Quarterly 6, No. 3 (December
        1961): 360-374.

        Haines and co-authors describe data processing organi-
        zations.

3587   Hamm, B.C. and Greer, T.V.   "Automation and the Growth
        of Functional Authority," Personnel 40, No. 6 (Novem-
        ber-December 1963): 53-57.

        Decentralization of information and responsibility is
        the theme of the article.

3588   Hattery, L.H.   "Organizing for Data Processing Systems,"
        Advanced Management Journal 26, No. 3 (March 1961):
        23-25ff.
        Useful as a reflection of practises in early 1960s.

3589   Higginson, M. Valliant.   Managing with EDP. AMA Research
        Study No. 71. New York: American Management Associa-
        tion, 1965.

This publication focuses on the use of DP as decision-making tools for management.

3590 Hockman, John. "An Integrated Management Information System," Systems and Procedures Journal 14, No. 1 (January-February 1963): 40-42.

This was an ideal sought after and elaborated upon all during the 1960s and 1970s, described here.

3591 "How to Spend the Computer Budget; Buy, Rent, or Lease," Business Week (June 1, 1968): 100ff.

Based on U.S. tax and accounting practises of the 1960s.

3592 "Implications of a Systems Approach to Organization and Management," Personnel Journal 44, No. 2 (February 1965): 78-79.

This continues a discussion begun in the 1950s and extended down to the present.

3593 "Information Processing; With Yardsticks of Management Performance," Forbes 101 (January 1, 1968): 47-49; Ibid., 103 (January 1, 1969): 176ff.

Focus is on the measurement financially of a manager's performance using computers to help in the 1960s.

3594 Johnson, John E. "Using the Computer for Better Management," Computer-Based Management for Information and Control. Management Bulletin No. 30. New York: American Management Association, 1963.

This is an application brief directed toward management based on late 1950s and early 1960s experiences.

3595 Johnson, Richard A. et al. "Systems Theory and Management," Management Science 10, No. 2 (January 1964): 367-384.

By the mid-1960s quite a body of literature was developing on the subject; this reflects the issues.

3596 Kobrin, C.L. "Computer: Its Impact on Management," Iron Age 189, No. 10 (March 8, 1962): 65-72.

Describes how it was becoming considerable and why.

3597 Kraft, Philip. "Job Content, Fragmentation and Control in Computer Software Work," Industrial Relations 25 No. 2 (1986): 184-196.
Kraft has studied programmers and their work.

3598 Kraft, Philip. Programmers and Managers: The Routinization of Computer Programming in the United States. New York: Springer-Verlag, 1977.

This is a major study of work flows in DP shops.

3599   Kraft, Philip. "The Routinizing of Computer Programm-
        ing," Sociology of Work and Occupation 6, No. 2
        (1979): 139-155.

        Essentially restates his position from his book on
        the same topic.

3600   Krout, A.J. "How EDP is Affecting Workers and Organi-
        zations," Personnel 39, No. 4 (July 1962): 38-50.

        This is not limited just to DP workers of the early
        1960s and late 1950s.

3601   Leavitt, Harold J. "Dealing with Management of Obso-
        lence," Computer-Based Management for Information and
        Control. Management Bulletin No. 30. New York: Ameri-
        can Management Association, 1963.

        Obsolence is of equipment, applications and procedures.

3602   Lee, Hak Chong. The Impact of Electronic Data Process-
        ing Upon Patterns of Business Organization and Admin-
        istration. Albany, N.Y.: School of Business, State
        University of New York at Albany, 1965.

        The effects were clearly evident by the early 1960s.
        This is one of many publications to describe the
        process at work in the U.S.

3603   Loseke, D.R. and Sonquist, J.A. "The Computer Worker
        in the Labor Force," Sociology of Work and Occupations
        6, No. 2 (1979): 156-183.

        This is a useful analysis of a workforce that came
        into its own only in the late 1950s/early 1960s.

3604   "Lots of New Jobs in Computers; Careers in Electronic
        Data Processing," Changing Times 19 (August 1965):
        21-23.

        Defines such positions as programmer, systems anal-
        yst and computer operator as of the 1960s.

3605   Lott, Richard W. Basic Data Processing. Englewood
        Cliffs, N.J.: Prentice-Hall, Inc., 1967.

        A useful source that describes how application deve-
        lopment took place in the 1960s.

3606   Lucas, Henry C., Jr. and Turner, Jon A. "A Corporate
        Strategy for the Control of Information Processing,"
        Sloan Management Review 23, No. 3 (Spring 1982): 25-
        36.

        Suggestions based on experiences of the 1970s.

3607   Malcolm, D.G. and Rowe, A.J. "An Approach to Computer-
        Based Management Control Systems," California

Management Review 3, No. 3 (Spring 1961): 4-16.

Their focus is on management structure and controls.

3608   "Management Control in Real Time," _Systems_ 6, No. 6
       (September 1965): 26-28.

       Computers were making it possible to know how things
       were happening as they took place, making it possible
       to make changes quickly in a timely fashion.

3609   Mann, Floyd C. and Williams, Lawrence K. "Some Effects
       of the Changing Work Environment in the Office,"
       Journal of Social Issues 18, No. 3 (1962): 90-101.

       Computers created more deadlines than before existed.
       Deadlines were now more important than before.

3610   Marschak, Jacob. "Economics of Inquiring, Communicat-
       ing, and Deciding," _American Economic Review_ 58, No.
       2 (1968): 1-8.

       A fascinating view economically of our response to
       more information with which to manage organizations.

3611   Mathews, M.V. "Choosing A Scientific Computer for Ser-
       vice," _Science_ 161 (July 5, 1968): 23-27; "Discussion,"
       Ibid. 161 (August 30, 1968): 844-845; _Ibid._ 162
       (November 8, 1968): 620.

       Besides being focused on scientific applications, the
       notion of what was more manegable is included.

3612   McCullough, David. _The Great Bridge_. New York: Simon
       & Schuster, 1972.

       For the historian of DP it is useful for understand-
       ing the impact of great technological complexity and
       change on the management of a large project.

3613   McGill, Donald A.C. _Punched Cards: Data Processing for
       Profit Improvement_. New York: McGraw-Hill Book Co.,
       1962.

       This "how to" book was directed at DP managers of the
       early 1960s; contains 10 case studies of DP centers.

3614   McManus, G.J. "Are Computers Taking Over Management's
       Functions?," _Iron Age_ 187, No. 13 (March 30, 1962):
       69-71.

       Computers were determined here as not taking over,
       helping and with examples from the early 1960s.

3615   Melitz, P.W. "Impact of Electronic Data Processing on
       Managers," _Advanced Management Journal_ 26, No. 4
       (April 1961): 4-6.

       Carries on the same theme as the previous citation.

3616   "Middle Management and Technological Change," _Management
       Review_ 52, No. 10 (October 1963): 55.

As with other articles of the early 1960s, many were identifying the initial effects of computers.

3617   Myers, Charles A. (ed). The Impact of Computers on Management. Cambridge, Mass.: MIT Press, 1967.

This reprints 9 papers from a conference on the subject covering such issues as organizational control, economic environments, real-time systems, computers and profit centers, and integrated manufacturing.

3618   Myers, Gibbs. "What the Future Holds," Systems and Procedures Journal 15, No. 5 (September-October 1964): 14-18.

Myers calls up a common view of the time, that more computers would be used in creative ways.

3619   Nolan, Richard L. "Managing the Crisis in Data Processing," Harvard Business Review 57, No. 2 (March-April 1979): 115-126.

Now a minor classic, he defines various stages in the evolution of DP: organization, applications, technology, and administration.

3620   Nolan, Richard L. Managing the Data Resource Function. St. Paul: West Publishing Co., 1974.

This collection of papers deal with DP management issues.

3621   "Only One of Three Pays for Itself," Business Week (April 13, 1963): 152-156.

Discusses the cost effectiveness of data processing.

3622   Orlicky, Joseph. The Successful Computer System: Its Planning, Development, and Management in a Business Enterprise. New York: McGraw-Hill Book Co., 1969.

Intended for the DP manager of the late 1960s with discussion on project management, feasability studies, and application development.

3623   Popkin, Gary and Pike, Arthur. Introduction to Data Processing. Boston: Houghton Mifflin, 1977.

Besides explaining the technology, it discusses management issues.

3624   Pryor, H. "How to Pick A Computer," Science Digest 57 (April 1965): 75-79.

Reflected practise of the period.

3625   Raffaele, J.A. "Automation and the Coming Diffusion of Power in Industry," Personnel 39, No. 3 (May-June 1962): 29-39.

In part it was caused by the use of computers.

3626   Reif, William E. Computer Technology and Management
        Organization. Iowa City: Bureau of Business and
        Economic Research, University of Iowa, 1968.

        Surveys literature on the subject and then impact
        on a manufacturing company.

3627   Rico, Leonard. The Advance Against Paperwork; Comput-
        ers, Systems, and Personnel. Ann Arbor: Bureau of
        Industrial Relations, University of Michigan, 1967.

        This 330-page book contains many experiences drawn
        from the 1960s.

3628   Sanders, Donald H. Computers in Business: An Introduc-
        tion. New York: McGraw-Hill Book Co., 1963.

        This is a college text with some history, and includ-
        es a lengthy discussion of the use and management of
        DP as of the early 1960s and late 1950s; includes
        illustrations, bibliography and glossary.

3629   Schwitter, Joseph P. "Computer Effect Upon Management
        Jobs," Journal of the Academy of Management 8, No. 3
        (September 1965): 233-237.

        A rare study of the effect of computers only partially
        mentioned in other studies.

3630   Sheeham, Robert. "A Red Umbrella in a High Wind,"
        Fortune (August 1965): 140ff.

        Reviews the significant commitment to computers made
        by Travelors Insurance Company, describing the effects
        on it and the industry.

3631   Somers, Gerald G. et al. (eds). Adjusting to Technologi-
        cal Change. New York: Harper and Row, 1963.

        Focus is on labor and automation, a subject of major
        concern in the early 1960s.

3632   Svec, Fred J. Organizational Placement of the Computer
        Systems Designer. Rock Island, Ill.: U.S. Army Manage-
        ment Engineering Training Agency, 1968.

        While describing U.S. military practise, the subject
        at large was explored as of the 1960s.

3633   U.S. Civil Service Commission. A Study of the Impact
        of Automation on Federal Employees. Washington, D.C.:
        U.S. Government Printing Office, 1964.

        This was one of many studies on the subject since the
        U.S. Government was an extensive user of computers.

3634   U.S. Department of Labor, Bureau of Labor Statistics.
        Impact of Office Automation in the Internal Revenue
        Service. Bulletin No. 1364. Washington, D.C.: U.S.
        Government Printing Office, July 1963.

IRS was an early user of computers; applications and management practises are reviewed.

3635   U.S. Department of Labor, Bureau of Labor Statistics. Implications of Automation and Other Technological Developments. Bulletin No. 1319. Washington, D.C.: U.S. Government Printing Office, February 1962.

The subject was frequently studied by U.S. agencies in the 1950s and early 1960s as it affected the American at large and through case studies.

3636   Vergin, Roger C. and Grimes, Andrew J. "Management Myths and EDP," California Management Review 7, No. 1 (Fall 1964): 59-70.

Organizational and justification issues are major themes of the period and the article reflects common opinions of the early 1960s.

3637   Weinberg, Gerald M. The Psychology of Computer Programming. New York: Van Nostrand Reinhold, 1971.

In this useful, early study of the subject, he shows how to study programs to understand programmers and their work.

3638   Weiner, J.B. "SDS: It's Real-Time Management," Duns Review 92 (September 1968): 114-116.

This is as much on time-sharing and the interest in it as about SDS.

3639   Weinwrum, G.F. "Computer Management Control Systems Through the Looking Glass," Management Science 7, No. 4 (July 1961): 411.

The issues are management of organizations, circa 1960.

3640   "When the Music Stops," Forbes 102 (July 15, 1968): 18-19.

Discusses leasing and renting of computer equipment.

3641   "Where Centralization is Paying Off," Systems 6, No. 1 (January 1965): 22-24.

It includes examples of centralization, mid-1960s.

3642   Whistler, Thomas J."The Manager and the Computer," Journal of Accountancy (January 1965): 27-32.

More than the title suggests, accountancy is part of the discussion.

3643   Wu, Margaret. Introduction to Computer Data Processing. New York: Harcourt Brace Jovanovich, 1975.

Besides describing hardware of the 1970s, it describes its use and management.

Office Applications

3644   American Management Association. Electronics in the
        Office: Problems and Prospects. Office Management
        Series No. 131. New York: American Management Asso-
        ciation, 1952.

        Surveys use of computers in accounting and small
        office applications at the start of the 1950s.

3645   American Management Association. A New Approach to
        Office Mechanization: Integrated Data Processing
        Through Common Language Machines. New York: American
        Management Association, 1954.

        Describes office applications at U.S. Steel Corp.

3646   American Management Association. The Impact of Computers
        on Office Management: Experience in Computer Applica-
        tion. Office Management Series No. 136. New York:
        American Management Association, 1954.

        Focuses on how to install applications doing clerical
        work on insurance and payroll files.

3647   August, Kendall. "Office Technology: The Big Leap For-
        ward," Duns Review 84, Pt. 2 (September 1964): 118-
        119, 157-159, 163-164, 166, 168-170.

        Shows examples of integrated systems of the 1960s.
        This issue of Duns Review has several articles on DP.

3648   Brown, R. Hunt. Office Automation. New York: Automation
        Consultant, Inc., 1955.

        This is a comprehensive manual on what to install for
        which applications in accounting, science, all first
        generation activity.

3649   Fairbanks, Ralph W. Successful Office Automation.
        Englewood Cliffs, N.J.: Prentice-Hall, Inc., 1956.

        Describes existing office applications in detail.

3650   Hoos, Ida Russakoff. Automation in the Office. Washing-
        ton, D.C.: Public Affairs Press, 1961.

        Useful for understanding offfices of the late 1950s.

3651   Levin, Howard S. Office Work and Automation. New York:
        John Wiley & Sons, Inc., 1956.

        Levin details common applications, many on office.

3652   Machung, Anne. "From Psyche to Technic: Politics of
        Office Work" (Unpublished Ph.D., University of Wiscon-
        sin, Madison, 1983).

        Studies secretaries and word processors covering all
        of the twentieth century in the U.S.

3653   Milward, George E. (ed). <u>Organization and Methods</u>. New
        York: St. Martin's Press, Inc., 1959.

        Includes material on 7 basic clerical operations and
        computing equipment to work on these of the 1950s.

3654   "Office Automation," <u>Duns Review</u> (October 1955): 54-114.

        This is a major review of the status as of the mid-
        1950s in the U.S. with many examples.

3655   Office of Technology Assessment, U.S. Congress. <u>Automa-
        tion of America's Offices</u>. Washington, D.C.: U.S.
        Government Printing Office, December 1985.

        Analyzes possible trends during 1985-95, including
        social and economic, and impact of U.S. Government.

3656   "Office: The Great Information Revolution; Symposium,"
        <u>Duns Review</u> 82, Pt. 2 (September 1963): 94-100ff.

        Useful for measuring expectations in the 1960s.

3657   <u>Report of the United States Government Delegates to a
        Meeting of the International Labor Organization. The
        Fifth Session of the Advisory Committee on Salaried
        Employees and Professional Workers. Cologne, Germany.
        November 23, December 4, 1959</u>. Washington, D.C.: U.S.
        Government Printing Office, 1959.

        Includes observations on an international committee's
        study on "The Effects of Mechanization on Automation
        in Offices."

3658   Rothberg, H.R. "Study of the Impact of Office Automa-
        tion in the IRS," <u>Monthly Labor Review</u> 92 (October
        1969): 26-30.

        Contains many details typical of numerous offices of
        the 1960s, not just unique to IRS.

3659   Smith, Georgina M. <u>Office Automation and White Collar
        Employment</u>. New Brunswick, N.J.: Institute of Manage-
        ment and Labor Relations, Rutgers The State University,
        n.d. (1960?).

        Studies employment as influenced by DP and other tech-
        nologies as of about 1960; an M.A. thesis originally.

3660   Stallard, John J. <u>et al. The Electronic Office: A Guide
        for Managers</u>. New York: Dow-Jones Irwin, 1983.

        An excellent reflection of the issues, applications
        and justification/costs of office automation, late
        1970s and early 1980s.

3661   Steffens, John. <u>The Electronic Office: Progress and
        Problems</u>. London: Policy Studies Institute, 1983.

        Gives mixed reviews for the benefits of office automa-
        tion in the late 1970s and early 1980s.

3662   Strassman, Paul A. Information Payoff: The Transforma-
        tion of Work in the Electronic Age. New York: Free
        Press, 1985.

        Focus is on office automation during the 1980s.

3663   Terry, George R. Office Automation. Homewood, Ill.:
        Dow-Jones-Irwin, Inc., 1966.

        Surveys trends in automation and experiences, 1960s.

3664   U.S. Department of Labor, Bureau of Labor Statistics.
        Adjustments to the Introduction of Office Automation.
        Bulletin No. 1276. Washington, D.C.: U.S. Government
        Printing Office, May 1960.

        On the advance of automation in the U.S., primarily
        covers the period 1950-60 and on office workers.

3665   U.S. Department of Labor, Bureau of Labor Statistics.
        Automation and Employment Opportunities for Office
        Workers. Occupational Outlook Series, Bulletin No.
        1241. Washington, D.C.: U.S. Government Printing
        Office, 1958.

        Has much material on job types as of the 1950s.

3666   U.S. Office of Records Management. Estimating Paper
        Work Costs. National Archives and Records Service.
        Washington, D.C.: U.S. Government Printing Office,
        1969.

        This is a thorough study of the costs of paper work
        as of the 1960s.

3667   Van Deusen, Edmund. "The Coming Victory Over Paper,"
        Fortune 52 (October 1955): 130-132.

        Describes computers usable for bookkeeping in banks
        and offices, arguing they would come to dominate.

                        Operating Systems

3668   AT&T Bell Laboratories. UNIX System Readings and Appli-
        cations. 2 vols. Englewood Cliffs, N.J.: Prentice-
        Hall, Inc., 1987.

        This is a major collection of materials on AT&T's
        important operating system.

3669   Auslander, M.A. et al. "The Evolution of the MVS Oper-
        ating System," IBM Journal of Research and Develop-
        ment 25, No. 5 (September 1981): 471-482.

        This history of MVS starts with older operating
        systems of the late 1950s through the 1970s.

3670   Belady, L.A. et al. "The IBM History of Memory Manage-
        ment Technology," IBM Journal of Research and Develop-
        ment 25, No. 5 (September 1981): 491-503.

Describes the evolution of memory management aspects of IBM operating systems, such as virtual memory.

3671   Bender, G. et al. "Function and Design of DOS/360 and TOS/360," IBM Systems Journal 6 (1967): 2-21.

Describes two IBM operating systems for the S/360.

3672   Clark, W.W. "The Functional Structure of OS/360, Part III: Data Management," IBM Systems Journal 5 (1966): 30-51.

Included are descriptions of BTAM, QTAM, TCAM, RTAM, XTAM and VTAM.

3673   Corbató, F.J. and Vyssotsky, V.A. "Introduction and Overview of the MULTICS System," Proceedings, Fall Joint Computer Conference (AFIPS) 27 (1965): 185-196.

This second generation system was developed at MIT as part of Project MAC as a programming tool.

3674   Corbató, F.J. et al. "An Experimental Time-Sharing System," Proceedings, Spring Joint Computer Conference (AFIPS) 21 (1962): 335-344.

Describes MIT's student's time sharing system.

3675   Cragun, Donald W. "Convergence Effort Combines 4.2 with UNIX System V," Computer Technology Review 6 (February 13, 1987): 14-23.

Deals with the history of UNIX and U.S. Government's (DARPA) support for UNIX R&D at University of California, Berkeley in the 1980s.

3676   Creasy, R.J. "The Origin of the VM/370 Time-Sharing System," IBM Journal of Research and Development 25, 5 (September 1981): 483-490.

This is a technical history of the IBM VM/370 operating system from 1964 to about 1974.

3677   Denning, P.J. "Third Generation Computer Systems," Computing Surveys 3, No. 4 (December 1971): 175-216.

This excellent article offers a comparative analysis of operating systems of the 1960s.

3678   Denning, P.J. "Virtual Memory," Computing Surveys 2 (1970): 153-189.

Describes the concept and its appearance in the 1960s.

3679   Derk, Molissa Diane Harris. "The Complexity Trap: Some Effects of Complexity on the Historical Development of Software" (Unpublished M.A. Thesis, University of Oklahoma, Norman, 1985).

Historical examples come from assemblers, compilers, and operating systems with a description of how they reduced programming efforts, 1950s-1970s.

3680   Fotheringham, J.   "Dynamic Storage Allocation in the
        ATLAS Computer, Including an Automatic Use of a Back-
        ing Store," Communications, ACM 4 (1961): 435-436.

        This describes software on the British super computer.

3681   Jones, William J.   "MGDPS and DSDPS—Two Stages of an
        Early Operating System," Annals of the History of
        Computing 11, No. 2 (1989): 99-108.

        Recollections of a GE operating system developed to
        help process missile test data from the Atlas missile,
        1957-1959.

3682   Kiely, S.C. "An Operating System for Distributed
        Processing—DPPX," IBM Systems Journal 18 (1979):
        507-525.

        DPPX was the operating system announced in 1978 for
        the IBM 8100 distributed processing computer.

3683   Lett, A.S. and Konigsford, W.L.   "TSS/360: A Time-Shared
        Operating System," Proceedings, Fall Joint Computer
        Conference (AFIPS) 33, Part I (1968): 15-28.

        This is a formal description of an IBM operating sys-
        tem for the S/360 computer; IBM's first VS SCP.

3684   Margolis, Phil.   "The History of UNIX," The DEC Profess-
        ional 5 (February 1986): 18-19.

        Describes evolution of UNIX of the 1960s and 1970s
        and its implementation on DEC equipment, such as the
        PDP-7.

3685   Mastrogiovanni, Amy P.   "Operating Systems: Some Reflec-
        tions After a Meeting in Chicago," Annals of the His-
        tory of Computing 10, No. 3 (1988): 195-209.

        Reviews Pioneer Day at the NCC Conference, June 17,
        1987, which included a discussion of operating sys-
        tems of the 1950s and 1960s.

3686   McFadyen, J.H.   "Systems Network Architecture: An
        Overview," IBM Systems Journal 15 (1976): 4-23.

        This early, formal statement of IBM's SNA, describes
        a bedrock telecommunications architecture, 1970s-80s.

3687   Mealey, G.H.   "The Functional Structure of OS/360, Part
        I: Introductory Survey," IBM Systems Journal 5 (1966):
        3-11.

        This was IBM's major operating system of the 1960s.

3688   Parmelee, R.P. et al. "Virtual Storage and Virtual
        Machine Concepts," IBM Systems Journal 11 (1972): 99-
        130.

        Describes VM suitable for interactive computing.

3689   Ritchie, Dennis. "Evolution of the UNIX Time-Sharing
        System," Microsystems 5 (October 1984).

        One of its developers describes its function and
        history.

3690   Rosen, Saul. "Programming Systems and Languages,
        1965-1975," Communications, ACM 15, No. 7 (July 1972):
        591-600.

        Surveys languages in wide use between 1965 and 1975
        and contains details on operating systems.

3691   Rosin, R.F. "Supervisory and Monitor Systems," Comput-
        ing Surveys 1, No. 1 (March 1969): 37-54.

        Surveys evolution of operating systems, 1950s-1968.

3692   Scherr, A.L. "Functional Structure of IBM Virtual
        Storage Operating Systems Part II: OS/VS-2 Concepts
        and Philosophies," IBM Systems Journal 12 (1973):
        382-400.

        Describes the features and development of MVS, IBM's
        largest operating system of the 1970s.

3693   Tanenbaum, Andrew S. Operating Systems: Design and
        Implementation. Englewood Cliffs, N.J.: Prentice-Hall,
        Inc., 1987.

        Although a text on design of operating systems, it
        contains material on their history.

3694   Weizer, N. "A History of Operating Systems," Datama-
        tion 27, No. 1 (January 1981): 119-126.

        This is one of only a few articles on the subject,
        beginning with rudimentary elements in the 1940s and
        continuing down to about 1980.

3695   Wheeler, E.F. and Ganek, A.G. "Introduction to Systems
        Application Architecture," IBM Systems Journal 27,
        No. 3 (1988): 250-263.

        This is a formal statement of SAA, the design archi-
        tecture IBM used for software and systems in the very
        late 1980s and into the 1990s. The entire issue of
        the journal is devoted to SAA.

3696   Witt, B.I. "The Functional Structure of OS/360, Part
        II: Job and Task Management," IBM Systems Journal 5
        (1966): 12-29.

        This was one of a series of technical papers describ-
        ing the operating systems of the S/360 computers of
        the 1960s.

                          Operations Research

3697   Acer, John W. Business Games: A Simulation Technique.
        Iowa City: Bureau of Labor and Management, State

University of Iowa, 1960.

Describes business games and concludes with an evaluation of their future potential.

3698   Ackoff, Russell L. A Comprehensive Bibliography on
       Operations Research. New York: John Wiley & Sons,
       Inc., 1958.

       Over 3,000 references are presented, current through
       1957, through the first decade of OR.

3699   American Management Association. Operations Research—
       A Basic Approach. Special Report No. 13. New York:
       American Management Association, 1956.

       Reprints 8 papers presented at an AMA seminar held
       in January and March 1956. Describes OR applications
       in resource allocation, production distribution,
       plant scheduling, aircraft maintenance and engineering.

3700   Andlinger, Gerhard R. et al. Operations Research—
       Challenge to Modern Management. Boston: Graduate
       School of Business Administration, Harvard Universi-
       ty, 1954.

       Surveys why one would use OR, includes its history
       and uses as of the early 1950s, and potential.

3701   Batchelor, James H. Operations Research: An Annotated
       Bibliography. St. Louis, Mo.: St. Louis University
       Press, 1959.

       This 866-page publication cites 4,195 titles.

3702   Beveridge, W.I.B. The Art of Scientific Investigation.
       New York: W.W. Norton Co., 1951.

       Surveys how scientific discoveries are made with
       discussion of experimentation, chance, hypothesis,
       difficulties and strategies, all OR themes.

3703   Branbury, J. and Maitland, J. (eds). Proceedings of the
       Second International Conference on Operational Re-
       search. New York: John Wiley & Sons, Inc., 1961.

       The conference was held in Aix-en-Provence, 1960. In
       810 pages it covers all aspects of OR and contains
       many case studies of current uses in industry, govern-
       ment, and in the military.

3704   Bross, Irwin D.F. Design for Decision. New York: The
       MacMillan Co., 1953.

       This is an early aid to statistical decision-making
       and includes a history of decision-making.

3705   Cabell, R.W. and Phillips, A. Problems in Basic Opera-
       tions Research Methods for Management. New York: John
       Wiley & Sons, 1961.

       Discusses all aspects of OR, with example, circa 1960.

3706   Chorfas, Dimitris N. <u>Operations Research for Industrial</u>
        <u>Management</u>. New York: Reinhold Publishing Corp., 1958.

        Intended for advanced users of OR and covers all
        aspects of the subject as known in the late 1950s.
        Includes case studies, management issues, and game
        theories.

3707   Churchman, C. West. <u>Prediction and Optimal Decision</u>.
        Englewood Cliffs, N.J.: Prentice-Hall, Inc., 1961.

        Focuses on the relationship between problems of value
        and those of fact and uses examples from the late
        1950s to show how they are handled with OR.

3708   Churchman, C. West <u>et al</u>. (eds). <u>Introduction to Opera-</u>
        <u>tions Research</u>. New York: John Wiley & Sons, Inc.,
        1957.

        This 655-page book includes a history of OR back to
        World War II; this was a basic text in the 1950s.

3709   Churchman, C. West. and Verhulst, M. (eds). <u>Management</u>
        <u>Sciences, Models, and Techniques</u>. 2 vols. Paris: Insti-
        tute of Management Science, 1959.

        These are conference papers on all aspects of OR.

3710   Croxton, F.E. and Cowden, D.J. <u>Applied General Statis-</u>
        <u>tics</u>. Englewood Cliffs, N.J.: Prentice-Hall, Inc.,
        1955.

        This is an early text such as used in OR work.

3711   Deming, W. Edwards. <u>Sample Design in Business Research</u>.
        New York: John Wiley & Sons, 1960.

        Focus is on uses of statistics in business with
        OR applications, circa late 1950s.

3712   Flagle, Charles D. <u>et al</u>. <u>Operations Research and Sys-</u>
        <u>tems Engineering</u>. Baltimore, Md.: The Johns Hopkins
        University Press, 1960.

        A collection of papers on OR that reflects thinking
        on the role of computers and information theory.

3713   Garvin, Walter W. <u>Introduction to Linear Programming</u>.
        New York: McGraw-Hill Book Co., 1960.

        Describes the theory of linear programming and how
        it is applied.

3714   Gass, Saul I. <u>Linear Programming</u>. New York: McGraw-Hill
        Book Co., 1958.
        This was the first textbook on the subject.

3715   Greene, Jay and Sisson, Roger L. <u>Dynamic Management</u>
        <u>Decision Games</u>. New York: John Wiley & Sons, Inc.,
        1959.

They describe how to use decision games to solve
business problems; includes 7 games of the 1950s.

3716   Hertz, David B. The Theory and Practice of Industrial
       Research. New York: McGraw-Hill Book Co., Inc., 1950.

       This very early book on OR includes a history of the
       application and surveys its status as of 1949.

3717   Hildebrand, F.B. Introduction to Numerical Analysis.
       New York: McGraw-Hill Book Co., Inc., 1956.

       This is a technical volume on how to do OR.

3718   Holt, C.C. et al. Planning Production, Inventories, and
       Work Force. Englewood Cliffs, N.J.: Prentice-Hall,
       Inc., 1960.

       In addition to examples, the benefits of OR is
       detailed.

3719   Luce, R. Duncan and Raiffa, Howard. Games and Decisions:
       Introduction and Critical Survey. New York: John Wiley
       & Sons, Inc., 1957.

       Surveys the Behavioral Models Project at the Bureau of
       Applied Social Research, Columbia University, and
       includes an extensive bibliography.

3720   McDonald, John. Strategy in Poker, Business, and War.
       New York: W.W. Norton & Co., Inc., 1950.

       This is a very early description of OR and theory of
       games for the general reader; illustrated.

3721   McKean, Roland N. Efficiency in Government Through
       Systems Analysis. New York: John Wiley & Sons, Inc.,
       1958.

       Describes how OR was being used with two case studies
       on water resource management.

3722   McKinsey, J.C.C. Introduction to the Theory of Games.
       New York: McGraw-Hill Book Co., 1952.

       This is an early publication surveying mathematical
       theory of games of chance and strategy, the kind of
       approach that launched OR.

3723   Metzger, Robert W. Elementary Mathematical Programming.
       New York: John Wiley & Sons, Inc., 1958.

       This is a useful snapshot on linear programming.

3724   Miller, David W. and Starr, Martin K. Executive Decisions
       and Operations Research. Englewood Cliffs, N.J.: Pren-
       tice-Hall, Inc., 1960.

       They describe executive decision-making, circa 1950,
       and include a bibliography.

3725   Morse, Philip M. and Kimball, George E. Methods of Oper-
        ations Research. New York: Technology Press of MIT and
        John Wiley & Sons, Inc., 1952.

        This is useful for appreciating the early history of
        OR in the U.S. and includes actual cases of usage.

3726   Operations Research. Conference Board Reports No. 82.
        New York: National Industrial Conference Board, 1957.

        This is a 20-page look at how OR could be used to
        solve problems in business.

3727   Richards, Max D. and Greenlaw, Paul S. Management Deci-
        sion Making. Homewood, Ill.: Richard D. Irwin, Inc.,
        1966.

        This is on OR as practised in the 1960s.

3728   U.S. Civil Service Commission. Operations Research Ana-
        lyst. Announcement No. 193B. Washington, D.C.: U.S.
        Civil Service Commission, 1959.

        This 6-page report describes the role of OR analysts
        in the U.S. Government.

3729   Vance, Stanley. Management Simulation. New York: McGraw-
        Hill Book Co., 1960.

        Focuses on top management decision-making with cases.

3730   Vazsonyi, Andrew. Scientific Programming in Business
        and Industry. New York: John Wiley & Sons, 1958.

        This is a clear explanation of linear programming
        and OR from the period of the 1950s, with applications.

3731   Von Neumann, John and Morgenstern, Oskar. Theory of
        Games and Economic Behavior. Princeton, N.J.: Prince-
        ton University Press, 1944.

        This is an historically important book on the use of
        games theory to solve complex problems. It became a
        basic text for early OR. A 1947 edition served as a
        widely-used source on OR.

                            Space Exploration

3732   Braun, W. von and Ordway, F.I. History of Rocketry and
        Space Travel. 3rd ed. New York: Thomas Y. Crowell Co.,
        1975.

        Includes the role of computers, 1950s-1960s.

3733   Cooper, A.E. and Chow, W.T. "Development of On-Board
        Space Computer Systems," IBM Journal of Research and
        Development 20 (1976): 5-19.

        Describes an on-board IBM system for astronomical
        observations in the 1960s and 1970s.

3734   Ezell, E.C. and Ezell, L.N. The Partnership: A History
        of the Apollo-Soyuz Test Project. Washington, D.C.:
        National Aeronautics and Space Administration, 1978.

        Includes discussions about the role of computers,
        1970s.

3735   Green, C.M. and Lomask, M. Vanguard, A History. Wash-
        ington, D.C.: National Aeronautics and Space Admin-
        istration, 1970.

        DP and space programs, 1957-early 1960s, are describ-
        ed as part of an "official" history.

3736   Grimwood, J.M. Project Mercury, A Chronology. Washing-
        ton, D.C.: National Aeronautics and Space Adminis-
        tration, 1963.

        This is suggestive of amny uses put to DP in the
        late 1950s and early 1960s.

3737   Hacker, B.C. and Grimwood, J.M. On the Shoulders of
        Titan, A History of Project Gemini. Washington, D.C.:
        National Aeronautics and Space Administration, 1977.

        Includes discussion about how computers were used by
        NASA in the 1960s.

3738   Holder, W.G. and Siuru Jr., N.D. Skylab, Pioneer Space
        Station. Chicago: Rand McNally & Co., 1974.

        Includes discussion of the role DP played in the 1960s
        and early 1970s on this project.

3739   James, S.E. "Evolution of Real-Time Computer Systems
        for Manned Spaceflight," IBM Journal of Research and
        Development 25, No. 5 (September 1981): 417-428.

        This is a good overview of NASA and IBM's role in
        using computers for space explorations from the mid-
        1950s to 1980.

3740   Koppes, Clayton R. JPL and the American Space Program:
        A History of the Jet Propulsion Laboratory, 1936-1976.
        New Haven: Yale University Press, 1982.

        This monograph is on rocketry and JPL with discussion
        about the use of many technologies, including DP.

3741   Mazlish, Bruce (ed). The Railroad and the Space Program:
        An Exploration in Historical Analogy. Cambridge, Mass.:
        MIT Press, 1965.

        This is useful for patterns of institutional response
        to a high-technology field of major proportions.

3742   Schneck, Paul B. (ed). "Spacial Section on Computing in
        Space," Communications, ACM 27, No. 9 (September 1984):
        901-936.

Includes 3 articles on NASA and software developed during the 1960s and 1970s.

3743   Tomayko, James E. Computers in Spaceflight: The NASA Experience. Encyclopedia of Computer Science and Technology, 18, Supp. 3. New York: Encyclopedia of Computer Science and Technology, 1987.

This is the most complete history of the subject, covering events from 1957 to 1987.

3744   Tomayko, James E. "NASA's Manned Spacecraft Computers," Annals of the History of Computing 7, No. 1 (January 1985): 7-18.

Argues that NASA's contribution to computing was in software verification and fault tolerance rather than in using leading edge technology.

Storage and Retrieval Methods

3745   Charles Bruning Company, Inc. Basic Microfilm Indexing and Filing Techniques. Mount Prospect, Ill.: Charles Bruning Co., Inc., 1959.

This 20-page booklet describes basic methods in use in the 1950s. By the 1960s these were being applied to DP systems.

3746   Controllership Foundation, Inc. Corporate Records Retention. Vol. 1. New York: Controllership Foundation, Inc., 1958.

This was the first of 3 guides published by this organization on legal requirements of the U.S. Government on this subject. Many of these practises drove the demand for computerized record keeping.

3747   Hattery, Lowell H. and McCormick, Edward M. (eds). Information Retrieval Management. Detroit: American Data Processing, Inc., 1962.

This is a collection of papers presented at the Fourth Institute on Information Storage and Retrieval, held at the American University, Washington, D.C., February 1962. Included was discussion of the role being played by data processing.

3748   IBM Corporation. An Introduction to Information Retrieval. White Plains, N.Y.: International Business Machines, Inc., 1960.

This 16-page publication describes the process and how it began.

3749   Mitchell, William E. Records Retention. Syracuse, N.Y.: Ellsworth Publishing Co., 1959.

Illustrates basic issues about record retention.

3750   National Science Foundation. Nonconventional Technical

Information Systems in Current Use. No. 2 Washington,
D.C.: National Science Foundation, September 1959.

This 66-page report describes then in use applications incorporating new management methods for data
storage. A supplement was published in March 1960.

3751   Odell, M.K. and Strong, E.P. _Records Management and
Filing Operations_. New York: MacGraw-Hill Book Co.,
1947.

This was a standard and major reference on the subject
in the 1940s and 1950s. It also addresses the issue
of data on punched cards.

3752   Tomeski, Edward A. _et al_. (eds). _The Clarification,
Unification and Integration of Information Storage
and Retrieval_. New York: Management Dynamics, 1961.

This consists of 8 papers presented at a symposium
in New York on February 23, 1961, on machine readable
files.

3753   U.S. Congress, Senate. _Documentation, Indexing, and
Retrieval of Scientific Information. A Study of Fede-
ral and Non-Federal Science Information Processing
and Retrieval Programs, Prepared by the Staff of the
Committee of Government Operations, U.S. Senate, 86th
Cong., 2nd Sess_. Washington, D.C.: U.S. Government
Printing Office, June 1960.

Describes trends in information gathering technologies of the late 1950s and early 1960s at various
U.S. Government agencies.

Word Processing

3754   Bishop, D.A. _et al_. "Development of the IBM Magnetic
Tape SELECTRIC Composer," _IBM Journal of Research and
Development_ 12 (1968): 380-398.

Describes a product which combined magnetic tape
transport units with SELECTRIC composers, a basic
piece of magnetic tape products of IBM of the 1960s.

3755   Buehner, W.L. "Application of Ink Jet Technology to a
Word Processing Output Printer," _IBM Journal of Research and Development_ 21 (1977): 2-9.

Reviews technical features of a high-quality printing
system, as available on the IBM OS/6 word processor
announced in January 1977.

3756   Johnson, D.S. "Automatic Typewriter Application," _The
Office_ 67 (1968): 69-76.

This is one of the first articles to appear on "word
processing" using DP technology instead of typewriters.

3757   May, F.T. "IBM Word Processing Developments," _IBM Journal of Research and Development_ 25, No. 5 (September
1981): 741-753.

Covers developments at IBM from 1964 to 1980 in the development of products and applications for word processing.

3758   Poppel, H.L.   "The Automated Office Moves In," <u>Datamation</u> 25 (1979): 73-77.

This is typical of hundreds of such articles to appear in the 1970s on the marriage of data processing with word processing and about it expanding role. As such it is a good period piece.

3759   Wohl, A.   "A Review of Office Automation," <u>Datamation</u> 26 (1980): 116-119.

This is a good snap-shot of word processing and DP's role at the start of the new decade.

3760   Zisman, M.D.   "Office Automation: Revolution or Evolution?," <u>Sloan Management Review</u> 19 (1978): 1-16.

This article presents the business case for word processing and examples of what had been done.

9

Information Processing Industry

This chapter's citations survey the information processing industry, its institutions, major vendors, national activities, and collections of biographies. While the majority
of these materials deal with the post-World War II era, some
cover a broader period. Most of the publications were written
by journalists, government analysts, and economists. A few
were written by historians. The majority are contemporary,
but these are also full of useful information on the history
of the industry. They also reflect the growing activity in
Europea and Asia.

The industry in postwar America represents the fastest
growing body of literature on computing's economic activity.
Historians have begun to focus on company histories, while
biographical collections are now in vogue. Industry surveys
are predominantly economic. Studies of the impact of computers on society are beginning to rival the output of economists, although not their thoroughness. The major antitrust
lawsuits of the 1970s in the United States flushed out an
enormous amount of material from company records, making them
public and usable. A number of publications of the late
1970s and early 1980s used this new body of data to describe
events, particularly of the 1960s.

Publications on the contemporary period are best used in
conjunction with those listed in earlier chapters on programming languages, software, applications, and hardware.

Despite the growing volume of publications, very few
articles and books rely on a thorough and critical examination of archival materials. An impressive amount, however,
has grown out of interviews of participants, particularly
biographical publications. These, therefore, represent significant primary materials on the period. Many of the economic
surveys are well done, thorough, and useful, and most government publications provide mountains of raw data on the topic.

Little attempt has been made to include news articles
from magazines unless they are obviously major contributions
to the history of data processing. However, what is included
helps to define the issues of the industry in terms useful to
historians.

AFIPS

3761   Armer, Paul et al. "Reflections on a Quarter-Century:
        AFIPS Founders," Annals of the History of Computing
        8, No. 3 (July 1986): 225-256.

        Summarizes retrospectives from July 1984 and is
        anecdotal, informative and illustrated.

3762   Auerbach, I.L. "American Federation of Information
        Processing Societies (AFIPS)," in Anthony Ralston
        and Chester L. Meek (eds), Encyclopedia of Computer
        Science (New York: Petrocelli/Charter, 1976): 56-57.

        Describes the mission and activities of AFIPS and
        its history from 1961 to 1975. Ralston was its
        president in 1975.

3763   Auerbach, I.L. "Harry H. Goode, June 30, 1909-October
        30, 1960," Annals of the History of Computing 8, No.
        3 (July 1986): 257-260.

        This biography/obituary is of a man who helped to
        organize AFIPS.

3764   "Brief Histories of AFIPS and Its Constituent Socie-
        ties," Annals of the History of Computing 8, No. 3
        (July 1986): 219-224.

        This is a collection of paragraph-length briefs on
        each.

3765   Carlson, Walter M. "Why AFIPS Invested in History,"
        Annals of the History of Computing 8, No. 3 (July
        1986): 270-274.

        Describes AFIPS' role from 1961 to document the his-
        tory of DP and includes personal recollections.

3766   "Perspectives on a Quarter-Century: AFIPS Presidents,"
        Annals of the History of Computing 8, No. 3 (July
        1986): 275-302.

        Memoirs of AFIPS presidents are presented, 1961 on-
        ward.

3767   Rector, Robert W. "Personal Recollections on the First
        Quarter-Century of AFIPS," Annals of the History of
        Computing 8, No. 3 (July 1986): 261-269.

        Rector was involved extensively with AFIPS and offers
        much new evidence on its activities.

3768   Ware, Willis H. "AFIPS in Retrospective," Annals of
        the History of Computing 8, No. 3 (July 1986): 303-
        310.

        Ware was AFIPS' first chairman. He contrasts what
        it was supposed to be with what it became.

Asia

3768   Cheatham, T.E., Jr. et al. "Computing in China: A
       Travel Report," Science 182 (October 12, 1973): 134-
       140.

       This reports on developments in China in the 1970s.

3769   Garner, Harvey L. "Computing in China, 1978," IEEE
       Computer 12, No. 3 (1979): 81-96.

       This is a broad view of China's computer projects
       with materials on both the 1960s and 1970s. Argues
       that China was very behind the West on computing.

3770   Grieco, Joseph M. Between Dependency and Autonomy.
       India's Experience with the International Computer
       Industry. Berkeley: University of California Press,
       1984.

       This is a thorough discussion of India's DP industry
       of the 1960s and 1970s and is useful for appreciat-
       ing computing in the developing world.

3771   Williams, W.R. (ed). Looking Back to Tomorrow. Well-
       ington, New Zealand: New Zealand Computer Society,
       1985.

       This is a collection of essays on DP in New Zealand
       since about 1960.

AT&T

3772   Coll, Steve. The Deal of the Century: The Breakup of
       AT&T. New York: Atheneum, 1986.

       This is based on interviews, court documents and
       published materials. Argues that it was in AT&T's
       best interests to abandon local telephone service in
       the 1980s.

3773   Danielian, N.R. AT&T: The Story of Industrial Conquest.
       New York: Vanguard Press, 1939.

       This is a general history of the company and about
       telephones.

3774   Goulden, Joseph C. Monopoly. New York: G.P. Putnam's
       Sons, 1968.

       This is a hostile survey of post-World War II AT&T
       by a journalist.

3775   Stone, Alan. Wrong Number: The Breakup of AT&T. New
       York: Basic Books, Inc., 1989.

       Although a political history of the breakup of AT&T
       in the early 1980s, it offers perspective on company
       rivals versus public interests at work.

3776   Tunstall, Jeremy. Communications Deregulation: The
        Unleashing of America's Communication Industry. New
        York: Basil Blackwell, 1986.

        Includes a survey of AT&T's breakup in the early
        1980s and its impact on the U.S. TP and DP worlds.

3777   Tunstall, W. Brooke. Disconnecting Parties: Managing
        the Bell System Break Up—An Inside View. New York:
        McGraw-Hill, 1985.

        This is the only memoir on AT&T's breakup published
        in the 1980s.

ACM

3778   Alt, Franz L. "Fifteen Years ACM," Communications,
        ACM 30, No. 10 (October 1987): 850-857.

        Reviews early days of ACM (late 1940s-early 1960s).

3779   Auerbach, Isaac L. "Association for Computing Machin-
        ery (ACM)," in Anthony Ralston and Chester L. Meeks
        (eds), Encyclopedia of Computer Science (New York:
        Petrocelli/Charter, 1976): 128-129.

        Surveys mission, activities and history of ACM from
        1947 to 1975. ACM was the oldest of the more impor-
        tant organizations within the DP industry.

3780   Cochran, Anita. "ACM: The Past 15 Years, 1972-1987,"
        Communications, ACM 30, No. 10 (October 1987): 866-
        872.

        This was one of several 40th anniversary articles
        published by this issue of Communications.

3781   Feckzo, Linda. "Making Computer History for 40 Years,"
        Communications, ACM 30, No. 10 (October 1987): 849.

        Does much the same as Cochran in No. 3780.

3782   Revens, Lee. "The First 25 Years: ACM, 1947-1962,"
        Communications, ACM 30, No. 10 (October 1987): 860-
        865.

        The author was actively involved with ACM in the
        period under discussion.

3783   Weiss, Eric. "Commentaries on the Past 15 Years,"
        Communications, ACM 30, No. 10 (October 1987): 880-
        883.

        Like the others above, this is a memoir of the ACM.

Bell Laboratories

3784   Alt, F.L. "A Bell Telephone Laboratories' Computing
        Machine," Mathematical Tables and Other Aids to
        Computing 3 (1948): 1-13, 69-84.

Describes Bell's 5th relay computer, its first
general purpose programmed computer; contrasted
with ENIAC as well.

3785   Andrews, E.G. "A Review of the Bell Labs Digital
        Computer Developments," Proceedings, Joint AIEE-
        IRE Computer Conference, Philadelphia, December
        10-12, 1951 (New York: American Institute of Elec-
        trical Engineers, 1952): 101-105.

        Surveys the development of relay computers at Bell
        in the late 1940s and early 1950s.

3786   Andrews, E.G. "The Bell Computer, Model VI," Proceed-
        ings of a Second Symposium on Large Scale Digital
        Calculating Machinery, 13-16 September 1949. Annals
        of the Computation Laboratory of Harvard University
        26 (Cambridge, Mass.: Harvard University Press,
        1951): 20-31.

        This is an illustrated description of the Model VI.

3787   Andrews, E.G. "Telephone Switching and the Early Bell
        Laboratories Computers," Bell System Technical Jour-
        nal 42 (1963): 341-353; reprinted in Annals of the
        History of Computing 4, No. 1 (January 1982): 13-19.

        This is a history and a description of early Bell
        computers, 1940s-1950s.

3788   Andrews, E.G. and Box, H.W. "Use of Relay Digital
        Computer," Electrical Engineering 69 (1950): 158-163.

        Used the Model V and describes how it was programmed
        at Bell Labs.

3789   Andrews, E.G. and Dode, H.W. "Use of the Relay Digital
        Computer," Annals of the History of Computing 4, No.
        1 (January 1982): 5-13.

        Reprints No. 3788 and includes an introduction.

3790   Atherton, W.A. From Compass to Computer. San Francisco:
        San Francisco Press, 1984.

        This is a memoir that discusses, in part, work done
        at Bell Labs in the 1940s.

3791   Bell Telephone Laboratories. Facts About Bell Labs.
        12th Ed. Murray Hill: Bell Telephone Laboratories,
        1982.

        This brief review highlights activities at the lab.

3792   Bernstein, Jeremy. Three Degrees Above Zero. Bell
        Labs in the Information Age. New York: Charles Scrib-
        ner's Sons, 1984.

        This is an illustrated history of Bell Labs.

3793 Booth, A.D. "Relay Computers," Report of a Conference
      on High Speed Automatic Calculating Machines, 22-25
      June 1949 (Cambridge, England: University Mathematical
      Laboratory, January 1950): 17-21.

      Surveys Model I through V from Bell Labs, Mark I
      from Harvard and Booth's Automatic Relay Computer.

3794 Braun, Ernest and MacDonald, Stuart. Revolution in
      Miniature: The History and Impact of Semiconductor
      Electronics. Cambridge: Cambridge University Press,
      1978; 2nd ed., 1983.

      This is an excellent history of semiconductors with
      considerable materials on Bell Labs from the 1940s
      to the 1970s. Second edition takes the story down
      to the date of publications and with revisions of
      earlier chapters.

3795 Bromley, Allan G. "Origins of Antiaircraft Analog
      Computers," Annals of the History of Computing 6,
      No. 2 (April 1984): 163-164.

      Describes the development of the M-9 by Bell Labs
      during World War II.

3796 Brooks, John. Telephone: The First Hundred Years.
      New York: Charles Scribners, 1975.

      Includes some details on the role of Bell Labs.

3797 Cesareo, O. "The Relay Interpolator," Bell Laborator-
      ies Record 23 (December 1946): 457-460.

      Describes what eventually became a Bell Labs comput-
      er, focusing on its military applications.

3798 "Complex Computer Demonstrated," Bell Laboratories
      Record 19, No. 2 (October 1940): v-vi.

      This is a very early report from Bell on the use of
      relay calculators, intended to improve telephone
      service.

3799 "Development of the Electric Director," Bell Laborator-
      ies Record 22, No. 5 (January 1944): 225-230.

      Describes defense-related research on fire control
      mechanisms at Bell Labs during World War II.

3800 "Electrical Gun Director Demonstrated," Bell Laborator-
      ies Record 22, No. 4 (December 1943): 157-167.

      Describes Bell's early fire control mechanism.

3801 Fagen, M.D. (ed). A History of Engineering and Science
      in the Bell System: The Early Years (1875-1925).
      Murray Hill, N.J.: Bell Telephone Laboratories, 1975.

This is a history of R&D in information and telephonic technologies down to the creation of Bell Labs.

3802   Higgins, W.H.C. et al. "Defense Research at Bell Labs," Annals of the History of Computing 4, No. 3 (July 1982): 218-236.

This is an illustrated and detailed account, 1925-75.

3803   Hoddeson, Lillian H. "The Emergence of Basic Research in the Bell Telephone System, 1875-1915," Technology and Culture 22 (July 1981): 512-544.

This sheds light on the use of technology in message switching and on the management of early R&D.

3804   Hoddeson, Lillian H. "The Entry of the Quantum Theory of Solids into the Bell Telephone Laboratories, 1925-40: A Case Study of the Industrial Application of Fundamental Science," Minerva 18 (Autumn 1980): 422-447.

This line of research led ultimately to the use of silicon and hence to the transistor at Bell Labs.

3805   Hoddeson, Lillian H. Multidisciplinary Research in Mission-Oriented Laboratories: The Evolution of Bell Laboratories' Program in Basic Solid-State Physics Culminating in the Discovery of the Transistor, 1935-1948. Urbana: University of Illinois Press, 1978.

This is an excellent history of Bell Labs and on the development of the transistor.

3806   Hoddeson, Lillian H. "The Roots of Solid-State Research at Bell Labs," Physics Today 30 (March 1977): 23-30.

This studies activities primarily of the 1930s at Bell Labs.

3807   Holbrook, B.D. Bell Laboratories and the Computer From the Late '30s to the Middle '60s. Computing Science Technical Report No. 36. Murray Hill, N.J.: Bell Laboratories, 1975.

This is a useful history of the subject.

3808   Holbrook, B.D. and Brown, W. Stanley. A History of of Computing Research at Bell Laboratories (1937-1975). Computing Science Technical Report No. 99. Murray Hill, N.J.: Bell Telephone Laboratories, 1982.

Also contains a chronology, 1854-1975.

3809   Hollcroft, T.R. "The Summer Meeting in Hanover," American Mathematical Society Bulletin 46 (1940): 861.

Bell Labs exhibited a processor functioning in a TP mode from Hanover, N.H. to Murray Hill.

3810   Juley, J. "The Ballistic Computer," Bell Laboratories
        Record 24 (1947): 5-9.

        Reviews Bell's Model III computer and activities of
        the 1940s.

3811   La Porte, Deirdre and Stibitz, George R. "Eligue: E.
        G. Andrews, 1898-1980," Annals of the History of
        Computing 4, No. 1 (January 1982): 4-5.

        An illustrated obituary, E.G. Andrews helped build
        computers at Bell Labs between 1943 and 1959.

3812   Loveday, E. "George Stibitz and the Bell Labs Relay
        Computer," Datamation (September 1977): 80-85.

        Discusses his leadership role in the 1930s and 1940s.

3813   Mabon, Prescott C. Mission Communications: The Story
        of Bell Laboratories. Murray Hill, N.J.: Bell Tele-
        phone Laboratories, 1975.

        This is a general history of the Bell Labs.

3814   Morgan, S.P. "Minicomputers in Bell Laboratories
        Research," Bell Laboratories Record 51 (July-August
        1973): 194-201.

        This is a history of their uses at Bell Laboratories
        in the 1960s and early 1970s.

3815   Pierce, John R. Musical Sound. New York: Scientific
        American Books, 1983.

        Bell Labs had techniques in the 1950s for making
        computer-based music; a history of the project.

3816   Price, G. Baley. "Award for Distinguished Service to
        Dr. Thornton Carl Fry," American Mathematical Monthly
        89, No. 2 (Fall 1982): 80-83.

        This is a biography and analysis of Fry's work on
        computers at Bell Labs between the 1930s and 1950s.

3817   "Relay Computer for the Army," Bell Laboratories Record
        26, No. 5 (May 1948): 208-209.

        This describes Bell's relay computer for the U.S.
        Army in the 1940s.

3818   Smits, F.M. (ed). A History of Engineering and Science
        in the Bell System: Electronics Technology (1925-1975).
        Indianapolis: AT&T Bell Laboratories, 1985.

        Contains details on the early history of relay comput-
        ers and other computer-related projects.

3819   Stevenson, M.G. "Bell Labs: A Pioneer in Computing
        Technology," Bell Laboratories Record 51, No. 11
        (1973): 344-351.

It reviews the early relay computers. For additional
details and later developments see the same publication, 52, No. 1 (1974): 13-20; 52, No. 2 (1974): 55-
63.

3820   Stibitz, George R. "Automatic Computing Machinery,"
        Annals of the History of Computing 4, No. 2 (April
        1982): 140-142.

        Reprints memos of 1947 and 1950 by the author on
        what DP could do.

3821   Stibitz, George R. "Computer," in Brian Randell (ed),
        The Origins of Digital Computers: Selected Papers
        New York: Springer-Verlag, 1982): 247-252.

        This was written in 1940 while at Bell Labs. It is
        an early description of how a computer might function
        with binary decimal number representation.

3822   Stibitz, George R. "Early Computers," in N. Metropolis
        et al.(eds), A History of Computing in the Twentieth
        Century (New York: Academic Press, 1980): 479-483.

        Describes sporadic incidents at Bell Labs covering
        the period 1938-1945.

3823   Stibitz, George R. "The Organization of Large Scale
        Calculating Machinery," Proceedings of a Symposium
        on Large Scale Digital Calculating Machinery, 7-10
        January 1947. Annals of the Computation Laboratory
        of Harvard University 16 (Cambridge, Mass.: Harvard
        University Press, 1948): 91-100.

        Discusses the need for better program specifications,
        index registers, and so forth.

3824   Stibitz, George R. "The Relay Computers at Bell Labs,"
        Datamation 13, No. 4 (April 1967): 35-44 and 13, No.
        5 (May 1967): 45-49.

        These are memoirs of his work at Bell Labs on comput-
        ers, particularly in the 1940s.

3825   Stibitz, George R. and Larrivee, J.A. Mathematics and
        Computers. New York: McGraw-Hill, 1957.

        This is a short review of desk top calculators and
        has material on Bell Labs' relay computers.

3826   Tropp, Henry S. An Inventory of the Papers of George
        Robert Stibitz Concerning the Invention and Develop-
        ment of the Digital Computer. Dartmouth, N.H.: Dart-
        mouth College, 1973.

        Includes a short biography of Stibitz.

3827   U.S. Navy Department. Computer Mark 22 Mod.0: Develop-
        ment and Description. Report No. 178-45. Washington,

D.C.: U.S. Navy Department, December 6, 1945.

This publication describes a relay computer built by
Bell Labs for the U.S Navy.

3828   Warren, C.A. et al. "Military Systems Engineering and
        Research," in M.D. Fagen (ed), A History of Engineer-
        ing and Science in the Bell System, II: National Ser-
        vice in War and Peace (1925-1975) (Murray Hill, N.J.:
        Bell Telephone Laboratories, 1978): 625-636; variation
        of same in Annals of the History of Computing 4, No.3
        (July 1982): 236-244.

        Describes early transistor projects at Bell Labora-
        tories (1940s-1950s).

3829   Williams, S.B. "Bell Telephone Laboratories' Relay
        Computing System," Proceedings of a Symposium on
        Large Scale Digital Calculating Machinery, 7-10 Jan-
        uary 1947. Annals of the Computation Laboratory of
        Harvard University 16 (Cambridge, Mass.: Harvard Uni-
        versity Press, 1948): 40-68.

        This is a good description of the Model V computer
        and work done at Bell Labs on it; illustrated.

3830   Williams, S.B. "A Relay Computer for General Applica-
        tion," Bell Laboratories Record 25 (February 1947):
        49-54.

        This is a general review of Bell Labs' Model V com-
        puter by a developer of the system.

                    Biographies and Memoirs

3831   Addison, J.W. "Eloge: Alfred Tarski, 1901-1983," Annals
        of the History of Computing 6, No. 4 (October 1984):
        335-336.

        This is an illustrated obituary of a major logician
        from the University of California at Berkeley.

3832   Applied Computer Research. Directory of Top Computer
        Executives. Phoenix, Arizona: Applied Computer Resear-
        ch, 1978, 1980, 1981, 1982, 1983.

        This is a listing with addresses and so forth.

3833   Aspry, William F., Jr. "From Mathematical Constructi-
        vity to Computer Science: Alan Turing, John von Neu-
        mann, and the Origins of Computer Science in Mathema-
        tical Logic" (Unpublished Ph.D. dissertation, Univer-
        sity of Wisconsin, Madison, 1980).

        This is a major study of their concepts for computers
        and is a detailed, technical study, 1930s-1940s.

3834   Auerbach, Isaac L. "Eloge: Dov Chevion, 1917-1983,"
        Annals of the History of Computing 7, No. 1 (January
        1985): 4-6.

Chevion was very active in fostering computing in
Israel; an obituary.

3835   Auerbach, Isaac L. "Eloge: Niels Ivar Bech, 1920-1975,"
        Annals of the History of Computing 6, No. 4 (October
        1984): 332-334.

        This is an illustrated obituary of a Danish computer
        builder.; active period was in the 1960s.

3836   "Authors," IBM Journal of Research and Development 25,
        No. 5 (September 1981): 833-846.

        Includes short biographies of contributors to this
        issue of the journal; most were pioneers in the
        development of IBM hardware and software, 1950-1980.

3837   Berkeley, Edmund C. Who's Who in the Computer Field.
        Newtonville, Mass.: Berkeley Enterprises, 1963.

        This was one of the first such compendiums on the
        data processing community in the U.S.

3838   "Biography of Douglas T. Ross," in Richard L. Wexel-
        blat (ed), History of Programming Languages (New
        York: Academic Press, 1981): 367.

        Ross worked with software development in the 1950s
        and 1960s.

3839   "Biography of Geoffrey Gordon," in Richard L. Wexel-
        blat (ed), History of Programming Languages (New
        York: Academic Press, 1981): 437.

        Gordon was a consulting systems engineer at IBM who
        developed GPSS, a modeling programming language.

3840   Blum, J. et al. "Eloge: Walter W. Jacobs, 1914-1982,"
        Annals of the History of Computing 6, No. 2 (April
        1984): 100-105.

        Jacobs worked on computing projects for the U.S.
        military in the 1940s and 1950s; illustrated.

3841   Brown, George H. And Part of Which I Was; Recollec-
        tions of a Research Engineer. Princeton, N.J.: Angus
        Cupar Publishers, 1982.

        Brown was a research executive at RCA who led many
        of his company's early computer projects.

3842   Brown, Gordon S. "Harold L. Hazen, 1901-1980," Annals
        of the History of Computing 3, No. 1 (January 1981):
        4-12.

        Hazen was a leading computer engineer at MIT in the
        1920s and beyond; illustrated obituary.

3843   Bryden, D.J. "George Brown, Author of the Rotula,"

Annals of Science 28 (1972): 1-29.

This is a serious biography and description of his device for addition, using a single carry wheel.

3844   Caddes, Carolyn. *Portraits of Success, Impressions of Silicon Valley Pioneers*. Palo Alto, Ca.: Tioga Publishing Co., 1986.

Contains illustrated biographies of 61 people; its strength are the photographs.

3845   Computer Consultants Ltd. *Who is Related to Whom in the Computer Industry*. New York: Pergamon Press, 1966, 1969.

This is a directory of the industry and of some of its leaders.

3846   Cortada, James W. *Historical Dictionary of Data Processing: Biographies*. Westport, Conn.: Greenwood Press, 1987.

Provides over 150 biographies of key individuals in the history of computing and data processing.

3847   Curtis, Kent K. et al. "John Pasta, 1918-1981: An Unusual Path Toward Computer Science," *Annals of the History of Computing* 5, No. 3 (July 1983): 224-238.

This is an obituary, biography with an illustration.

3848   "Daniel L. Slotnick, 1931-1985," *Annals of the History of Computing* 8, No. 1 (January 1986): 90.

This is an obituary notice of a computer science professor from the University of Illinois; developed the Illiac IV in the 1960s.

3849   de Bakker, J.W. and Van Vliet, J.C. (eds). *Algorithmic Languages*. Amsterdam: North-Holland, 1981.

Contains a discussion of the work of Adriaan van Wijngaarden at the Mathematical Centre in Amsterdam, 1942-1981.

3850   Debus, Allen G. *World Who's Who in Science*. Chicago: Marquis—Who's Who, Inc., 1968.

Includes some biographies of computer scientists.

3851   "Edmund Callis Berkeley," *Annals of the History of Computing* 10, No. 3 (1988): 216-217.

This is an obituary of ACM's founder and publisher of *Computers and People*; lived 1908-1988.

3852   Evans, Christopher. *Pioneers of Computing*. (Audiocassettes). London: Science Museum, 1970—in progress).

These are 1 hour long taped interviews with major
figures in computing. For a survey of contents see
Annals of the History of Computing 3, No. 4 (October
1981): 417-420.

3853   Feynman, Richard P. "Los Alamos From Below," Annals
of the History of Computing 10, No. 4 (1989): 343-345.

Feynman recalls his work at Los Alamos National Laboratory with calculators and computers in the 1940s.

3854   Frenkel, Karen A. "Alan L. Scherr, Big Blue's Time-
Sharing Pioneer," Communications, ACM 30 (October
1987): 825-826.

Describes IBM's first successful time-sharing tool:
TSO and the role played by Scherr.

3855   Gani, J. (ed). The Making of Statisticians. New York:
Springer-Verlag, 1982.

These are memoirs of various individuals including
R.L. Anderson, D.J. Finney and Tosio Kitagawa.

3856   Gleiser, Molly. "The First Man to Compute the Weather,"
Datamation 26, No. 6 (1980): 180-182, 183.

This is a biography of Lewis Fry Richardson (1881-
1953). He used mathematics in weather prediction
and employed the ENIAC at Aberdeen Proving Ground,
1950.

3857   Grath, Robert W. The IBM Alumni Directory. Dallas:
Privately Printed, 1970s (?).

Contains over 2,500 names of ex-IBMers and where they
worked; various editions published.

3858   "Herbert Samuel Bright," Annals of the History of
Computing 10, No. 3 (1988): 217-218.

This is the obituary of the founder/president of
Computation Planning, Inc. He was a cryptographer.

3859   Jaffe, B. Michelson and the Speed of Light. Garden City:
Doubleday, 1960.

Albert A. Michelson (1852-1931) was an American
physicist who'w work contributed to the early research leading to electronic computing.

3860   "James L. Buie," Annals of the History of Computing 11,
No. 1 (1989): 49.

Buie developed the transistor-to-transistor logic
type of ICs (1960s); worked at TRW, Inc.

3861   Katz, Howard. "Tribute to the Pioneers: Microcomputing
Founders Talk About the Good Old Days," Computek 1,
No. 1 (eptember-October 1984): 38-42.

19 pioneers participated and involved all the major developers of the 1970s and early 1980s.

3862   Kingery, R.A. et al.(eds). Men and Ideas in Engineering: Twelve in History From Illinois. Urbana: University of Illinois Press, 1967.

Contains a biography of Louis Nicot Ridenour, Jr., one of the developers of ORDVAC and ILLIAC machines.

3863   Leaders in American Science. Nashville: Who's Who in American Education, Inc., 1953-1969; 8 volumes.

This is an important biographical source; illustrated.

3864   "Lewis Winner," Annals of the History of Computing 11, No. 1 (1989): 50.

Obituary of the person most responsible for organizing the IEEE's annual solid state circuit conference for 31 years. It was the most important such conference held in the computer industry.

3865   Loomis, F.W. "Louis Nicot Ridenour, Jr., " Physics Today 12 (September 1959): 18-21.

Obituary notice for the American physicist who worked on the ORDVAC and ILLIAC.

3866   Malik, R. "Only Begetters of the Computer," New Scientist 4 (1970): 138-139.

Interviews J.P. Eckert, Grace M. Hopper and Konrad Zuse.

3867   Mednick, Barbara K. "A Few Good Men From UNIVAC," Tech Minnesota 2, No. 4 (September 1988): 407, 12-13.

Interviews David Lundstrom, author of a book by the same title on UNIVAC Division, Sperry Rand and about CDC; illustrated.

3868   Milligan, Margaret. "Data Processing Digest: Thirty Years Before the Masthead," Annals of the History of Computing 7, No. 3 (July 1985): 245-250.

This is a memoir of the Data Processing Digest and her role from 1954 to 1985.

3869   Morse, Marston. "George David Birkhoff and His Mathematical Work," Bulletin of the American Mathematical Society 52 (1946): 357-391.

Contains a detailed analysis and life of Birkhoff. Useful for understanding his work on topography and early computational projects at Harvard University.

3870   "Morton Michael Astrahan," Annals of the History of Computing 11, No. 1 (1989): 49.

This is the obituary notice for an IBM veteran
engineer who developed the I/O interrupt and was the
first chairman of the IRE Professional Group on Electronic Computers; worked in the period 1950s-1970s.

3871   Nagler, J.W.   "In Memoriam Gustav Tauschek," Blätter
        für Technikgeschichte 26 (1966): 1-14.

        Covers his work with bookkeeping machines, punched
        card devices and character recognition units.

3872   Nash, C. "The Birth of a Computer," Byte (February
        1985): 177ff.

        This is an interview with James H. Wilkinson.

3873   "Neil D. Macdonald," Annals of the History of Computing
        10, No. 3 (1988): 217.

        This was Edmund C. Berkeley's pseudonym for second
        editor of Computers and People.

3874   Oblonsky, Jan G.   "Antonin Svoboda, 1907-1980," Annals
        of the History of Computing 2, No. 4 (October 1980):
        284-292.

        Svoboda was a computer scientist in Checkoslovakia.

3875   Phillips, E.W.   "Presentation of Institute Gold Medals
        to Mr. Wilfred Perks and Mr. William Phillips, 23
        November 1964," Journal of the Institute of Actuaries
        91, No. 1 (No. 388) (1965): 19-21.

        Sheds light on Phillips' work on computing in 1936.

3876   Phillips, Norman A.   "Eloge: Jule G. Charney, 1917-
        1981," Annals of the History of Computing 3, No. 4
        (October 1981): 308-309.

        A good source on his work with computers in advancing
        the study of weather prediction, 1950-1980s.

3877   Pine, Carol and Mundale, Susan.   Self-Made: The Stories
        of Twelve Minnesota Entrepreneurs. Minneapolis: Dorn
        Books, 1982.

        Chapter Six is a biography of William C. Norris,
        founder of CDC.

3878   "Rita Goldberg Minker," Annals of the History of Comput-
        ing 11, No. 1 (1989): 50.

        Minker was a mathematician and early programmer at
        Bell Labs and at RCA where she worked on the BIZMAC.

3879   Ritchie, David.   The Computer Pioneers. New York: Simon
        and Schuster, 1986.

        Based on interviews, covers all the major figures,
        such as Stibitz, Zuse, Aiken, Atanasoff, Mauchly.

3880   Rosenberg, Jerry M. The Computer Prophets. London:
        Macmillan Co., 1969.

        Contains biographies from Blaise Pascal down to the
        present.

3881   Seitz, F. and Taub, A.H. "Louis N. Ridenour, Physicist
        and Administrator," Science 131 (1 January 1960): 20-
        21.

        This is an obituary notice.

3882   Shook, Robert L. "Francis G. ("Buck") Rodgers," in his
        The Greatest Salespersons. What They Say About Sell-
        ing (New York: Harper & Row, 1978): 55-73.

        This is a biography and survey of the views of IBM's
        corporate vice president for marketing in the late
        1970s to early 1980s.

3883   Slater, Robert. Portraits in Silicon. Cambridge, Mass.:
        MIT Press, 1987.

        This covers 34 people active in the 1950s to late
        1980s with interviews of most; an uncritical study.

3884   Sorenson, Charles E. My Forty Years with Ford. New York:
        Norton, 1950.

        These are the memoirs of Ford Motor Company's most
        important production expert; sheds light on attitudes
        and activities concerning all manner of automation.

3885   Spencer, Donald D. Famous People of Computing: A Book
        of Posters. Ormond Beach, Fla.: Camelot Publishing
        Co., 1982.

        Contains 37 drawings and short biographies; very
        inaccurate, poor quality illustrations.

3886   Sveistrup, Poul et al. (eds). Niels Ivar Bech—en epoke
        i edb-udviklingen i Danmark. Copenhagen: DATA, 1976.

        This is a memorial volume dedicated to Bech, the lead-
        ing Danish computer designer who headed Regnecentra-
        len during the 1960s.

3887   "Thanks for the Memories," Datamation 28, No. 10
        (September 1982): 27-52.

        These are short biography of industry giants: Seymour
        Cray, Lester L. Kilpatrick, Ruth M. Davis, Jay W.
        Forrester, Frank R. Lautenberg, J. Prespert Eckert,
        John W. Mauchly, Dan McGurk, William Shockley, Max
        Palevsky, Gene M. Amdahl, William Rogers and others.

3888   Todd, John. "John Hamilton Curtiss, 1909-1977," Annals
        of the History of Computing 2, No. 2 (April 1980): 104-
        110.

Curtiss headed the Applied Mathematics Division of the National Bureau of Standards, 1946-53, and helped launch SEAC and SWAC.

3889   Tropp, Henry S. "The Effervescent Years: A Retrospective," IEEE Spectrum 11, No. 2 (1974): 70-79.

This is on American computing based on interviews with Stibitz, Aiken, Atanasoff, Eckert, Mauchly, von Neumann and people at NCR and IBM.

3890   Tropp, Henry S. "The 20th Anniversary Meeting of the Association for Computing Machinery: 30 August 1967," Annals of the History of Computing 9, Nos. 3-4 (1988): 249-270.

This is the transcript of the meeting which involved recollections of the 1940s to the 1960s of computing pioneers on their work; it is not on the ACM.

3891   Tropp, Henry S. "Wallace J. Eckert," in Anthony Ralston and Chester L. Meeks (eds), Encyclopedia of Computer Science (New York: Petrocelli/Charter, 1976): 521-522.

This is a biography with a statement of his historical significance to computing's past.

3892   Voth, Ben. A Piece of the Computer Pie. Houston: Gulf, 1974.

Memoir material on the 1960s and 1970s reflected here.

3893   Weiss, Eric A. "Obituaries: George H. Brown," Annals of the History of Computing 10, No. 2 (1988): 140-141.

Brown was an early radio engineer (1930s), eventually became RCA's vice president of research and engineering who retired in 1972; lived 1918-1987.

3894   Weiss, Eric A. "Obituaries: Richard P. Freynman," Annals of the History of Computing 10, No. 2 (1988): 141-142.

Feynman (1918-1988) won a Nobel Prize for reconstructing quantum mechanics and electrodynamics after World War II.

3895   Who's Who in Computers and Data Processing 1971. A Biographical Dictionary of Leading Computer Professionals. 5th ed. New York: Quadrangle Books, 1971.

By the third edition it was a 3 volume compendium.

3896   Wilkinson, J.H. "Some Comments from a Numerical Analyst" (1970 Turing Award Lecture), Journal of the ACM 18, No. 2 (1971): 137-147.

These are memoirs about computing in the 1950s-1960s.

3897   Wolfe, Tom. "The Tinkerings of Robert Noyce," <u>Esquire</u>
        (December 1983): 346-374.

        This is an excellent biography; illustrated.

3898   Worthy, James. <u>William C. Norris: Portrait of a Maver-</u>
        <u>ick</u>. Cambridge, Mass.: Ballinger, 1987.

        This is a full biography of CDC's founder.

3899   Yarmish, Rina J. and Grinstein, Louise S. "Brief Notes
        on Six Women in Computer Development," <u>The Journal of</u>
        <u>Computers in Mathematics and Science Teaching</u>, Part I
        (Winter 1982); Part II (Spring 1983).

        Topics include Ada Lovelace, Grace M. Hopper, among
        others.

3900   Young, Jeffrey S. <u>Steve Jobs: The Journey is the Reward</u>.
        Glenview, Ill.: Scott, Foresman and Company, 1988.

        This is a biography of Apple Computer's founder.

3901   Zemanek, Heinz. "V.M. Glushkov, 1923-1982," <u>Annals of</u>
        <u>the History of Computing</u> 4, No. 2 (April 1982): 100-
        101.

        This is an obituary notice for an important Soviet
        computer scientist; illustrated.

3902   Zientara, Marguerite <u>et al</u>. <u>The History of Computing:</u>
        <u>A Biographical Portrait of the Visionaries Who Shap-</u>
        <u>ed the Destiny of the Computer Industry</u>. Framingham,
        Mass.: CW Communications, 1981.

        This is a collection of short biographies of all the
        major figures in computing from Pascal to the present.

                              Burroughs

3903   Barrus, Clara. <u>John Burroughs, Boy and Man</u>. Garden
        City, N.Y.: Doubleday, Page & Co., 1922.

        This is a full length biography.

3904   Coleman, John S. <u>The Business Machine: With Mention</u>
        <u>of William Seward Burroughs, Joseph Boyer, and Others</u>
        <u>—Since 1880</u>. New York: Newcomen Society, 1949.

        This senior Burroughs executive described the early
        history of his company in lauditory terms.

3905   Dijkstra, Edsger W. <u>Selected Writings on Computing: A</u>
        <u>Personal Perspective</u>. New York: Springer-Verlag, 1982.

        These are his trip reports, 1973-80s, and about his
        views while a Burroughs Research Fellow.

3906   Gleiser, Molly. "William S. Burroughs," <u>Computer Deci-</u>
        <u>sions</u> (March 1978): 34-36.

This short biography also describes his development
of a practical adding machine in the 1880s.

3907   Macdonald, Ray W. Strategy for Growth: The Story of
        Burroughs Corporation. New York: Newcomen Society
        in North America, 1978.

        The author was chairman and chief executive officer
        of Burroughs; this is a short history of his firm.

3908   Morgan, B. Total to Date: The Evolution of the Adding
        Machine; The Story of Burroughs. London: Burroughs
        Machines, 1953.

        This is a short history of the company from the 1880s.

Canada

3909   Bleackley, B.J. and LePrairie, J. Entering the Comput-
        er Age. The Computer Industry in Canada: The First
        Thirty Years. Agincourt, Ontario: Book Society of
        Canada, 1982.

        This is the most complete account available on the
        subject and is illustrated.

3910   Booth, Ian J.M. and Booth, Andrew D. "Computer Devel-
        opment at Saskatoon, 1962-1972," CIPS Proceedings,
        Session 84, May 9-11, 1984 (Calgary, Alberta: Cana-
        dian Information Processing Society, 1984): 331-334.

        These are memoirs of the constructors of the M2 Com-
        puter at the University of London; M3 at Saskatoon
        in 1964.

3911   Burleson, D.L. "School Technology: Canadian Style;
        International Conference on Communications Media in
        Education," Senior Scholastic 93 (October 25, 1968):
        14.

        Canadian schools were early users of DP; that inter-
        est is reflected in this article.

Company Histories

3912   Baum, Claude. The Systems Builders; The Story of SDC.
        Santa Monica, Cal.: Systems Development Corporation,
        1981.

        This celebrates the firm's 25th anniversary and serves
        as an institutional history down to merger with the
        Burroughs Corporation.

3913   Bender, Eric. "The House That 123 Built," Computer-
        world, July 15, 1985, pp. ID/10-11, 13-15, 18-20.

        This is a survey of LOTUS Inc, largest vendor of
        micro computer spreadsheet software of the early
        1980s.

3914   Bolt, Beranek, and Newman, Inc. <u>A History of ARPANET:</u>
        <u>The First Decade</u>. Report 4799. Washington, D.C.:
        DARPA, April 1981.

        This is a history of an early packet switching tele-
        communications package and the organizations that
        developed it.

3915   <u>A Century of Progress; The General Electric Story,</u>
        <u>1876-1978</u>. Schenectady, N.Y.: Hall of History Foun-
        dation, 1981.

        This is an illustrated history in chronological order
        and is not a critical analysis of GE.

3916   Cohen, Scott. <u>ZAP! The Rise and Fall of Atari</u>. New
        York: McGraw-Hill, 1984.

        Relying on interviews, the author describes the his-
        tory of the micro computer company from 1972 to its
        decline in the 1980s.

3917   Computer Sciences Corporation. <u>CSC News</u>, 15, No. 3
        (April 1984): 1-32.

        The entire issue is devoted to the history of CSC
        (1959-84), one of the largest software firms in the
        U.S. during the period.

3918   Dataproducts Corporation. <u>The First 20 Years of Data-</u>
        <u>products</u>. Woodland Hills, Cal.: Dataproducts Corpora-
        tion, 1982.

        This is a brief, chronological history; illustrated.

3919   Delmont, J. "ERA: Control Data's Forerunner in a
        Gloomy Glider Factory," <u>Contact</u> (July 1976): 3-6.

        ERA's history is described, 1946-1955.

3920   Dorfman, D. "Move Over Horatio Alger; Apple Computer
        and Amdahl Corporation," <u>Esquire</u> 89 (June 6, 1978):
        9-11.

        This is on the rise of these two firms in the 1970s.

3921   "Electronic Eating; J. Lyons & Co., Ltd.," <u>Business</u>
        <u>Week</u> (June 30, 1956): 126.

        Provides brief details on an early British computing
        company.

3922   Forman, Richard L. <u>Fulfilling the Computer's Promise:</u>
        <u>The History of Informatics, 1962-1982</u>. Woodland Hills,
        Cal.: Informatics General Corporation, 1985.

        This is a massive history of one of the oldest soft-
        ware firms in the industry.

3923   Forman, Richard L. "Tales in Peripheral Enterprise:
       The Rise of Dataproducts Corporation in the Computer
       Industry, 1962-1972" (Inpublished M.A. thesis, Uni-
       versity of California, Santa Barbara, 1980).

       In the 1970s Dataproducts was the largest manufac-
       turer of computer printers.

3924   Gibson, Weldon B. SRI: The Take-Off Days. Los Altos,
       Ca.: Kaufmann, 1980.

       This is an institutional history.

3925   Graham, Margaret. RCA and the Videodisc: The Business
       of Research. Cambridge: Cambridge University Press,
       1986.

       This describes videodisc development in the U.S.
       during the 1970s and early 1980s.

3926   Grigsby, J. "Cooling Off a Hot Concept; Itel Corp.,"
       Forbes 120 (December 15, 1977): 57-59.

       Offers a survey of its activities throughout the
       1970s as a leasing company and prvider of other
       services.

3927   Hewlett-Packard Company. Hewlett-Packard: A Company
       History. Palo Alto, Ca.: Hewlett-Packard Co., 1983.

       This illustrated pamphlet offers a brief history of
       the company which dates back to the 1930s.

3928   Hogan, Thom. "Apple: The First Ten Years," A+ Magazine
       5, No. 1 (January 1987): 43, 44, 46.

       This is a short history of the microcomputer firm.

3929   "Hooking Them Up," Time 91 (May 31 1968): 68-69.

       Describes the services of Computer Sciences Corp.

3930   Kahaner, Larry. On the Line: The Men of MCI—Who Took
       on AT&T, Risked Everything and Won! New York: Warner
       Books, 1986.

       This is a history of MCI by a reporter based on
       interviews and publicly available documents.

3931   Kaye, Glynnis Thompson (ed). A Revolution in Progress:
       A History of Intel to Date. Santa Clara: Intel Corp.,
       1984.

       This 51-page publication is an illustrated history
       of the company (1968-84) and catalogs its products.

3932   Lanzarotta, Sandy. "Datamation—The Early Days,"
       Datamation 28, No. 10 (September 1982): 157-160.

       Surveys the history of an industry favorite magazine.

3933   Littman, Jonathan. Once Upon a Time in Computerland:
        The Amazing Billion-Dollar Tale of Bill Millard. Los
        Angeles: Price Stern Sloan, Inc., 1987.

        This is a well written company history with a great
        deal about the microcomputer market in the U.S.A.

3934   Lundstrom, David E. A Few Good Men From Univac. Cam-
        bridge, Mass.: MIT Press, 1987.

        This is a memoir of an employee about Control Data
        Corporation (CDC), particularly of the 1960s.

3935   McKenna, Regis. The Regis Touch. Reading, Mass.:
        Addison-Wesley, 1985.

        The author describes how he set images for companies
        with details on Intel's effectiveness during the
        1970s and 1980s.

3936   Mettler, Reuben F. The Little Brown Hen That Could:
        The Growth Story of TRW, Inc. New York: Newcomen
        Society in North America, 1982.

        The author was chairman and chief executive officer
        at TRW at the time of publication; a history of TRW.

3937   Norberg, Arthur L. "Computing in the 21st Century: A
        Charles Babbage Institute Symposium," Annals of the
        History of Computing 10, No. 2 (1988): 127-132.

        Held in September 1986 to celebrate the 40th anniver-
        sary of ERA's founding, his article contains material
        on the company and on the industry at large.

3938   Norris, William. "Entrepreneurism: The Past, Present,
        and Future of Computing in the U.S.A.," Computer
        Museum Report 1 (Spring 1987): 12.

        Describe's CDC's initial marketing strategy, 1960s.

3939   Osborne, Adam and Dvorak, John. Hyper-growth: The Rise
        and Fall of Osborne Computer Corporation. Berkeley:
        Idthekkethan Publishing Co., 1984.

        These are Osborne's personal views on how his company
        rose and fell.

3940   Raimondi, Donna. "From Code Busters to Mainframes: The
        History of CDC," Computerworld, July 15, 1985, pp. 93,
        98-99.

        This is an illustrated history of CDC with interviews
        of key company executives.

3941   Raleigh, Lisa. "Woz on the Last 10 Years," A+ Magazine
        5, No. 1 (January 1987): 38-41.

        Steve Wozniak helped developed the Apple microcomputer.

3942   Scott, Otto J. The Creative Ordeal: The Story of
        Raytheon. New York: Atheneum, 1974.

        Raytheon participated in a number of U.S computer
        projects during the 1940s and 1950s as a defense
        contractor for the U.S. Government.

3943   The Story of the American Totalisator Co. Towson, Md.:
        American Totalisator Co., 1961 (?).

        This describes the origins and functions of the
        totalisator and the company that sold it.

3944   "Successful Stripling; Nixdork," Time 91 (May 17,
        1968): 91-92.

        This describes the work and products of Nixdorf, a
        European word processing provider of the 1960s.

3945   "Texas Instruments: Big Opportunities in Small Packa-
        ges," Forbes 103 (March 1, 1969): 32-34ff.

        This is an analysis of TI's products of the 1960s
        and marketing programs, particularly for chips.

3946   Texas Instruments, Inc. 50 Years of Innovation: The
        History of Texas Instruments. Dallas: Texas Instru-
        ments, Inc., 1980.

        This is an illustrated company history full of infor-
        mation on all facets of TI's history.

3947   Tomash, Erwin. "The Start of an ERA: Engineering Re-
        search Associates, Inc., 1946-1955," in N. Metropolis
        et al. (eds), A History of Computing in the Twentieth
        Century (New York: Academic Press, 1980): 485-495.

        Tomash was present at the creation of ERA and comments
        on other organizations as well, such as CDC and UNIVAC.

3948   TRW Inc. The Little Brown Hen That Could. Cleveland,
        Ohio: TRW Inc., n.d. (circa 1980s).

        This illustrated pamphlet details history from 1901
        to the early 1980s.

3949   Uttal, B. "Gene Amdahl Takes Aimes at IBM," Fortune
        96 (September 1977): 106-110.

        This is a contemporary account of Amdahl's plans to
        market plug compatible computers against IBM.

3950   Wang, An with Linden, Eugene. Lessons: An Autobiography.
        Reading, Mass.: Addison-Wesley Publishing Co., Inc.,
        1986.

        Wang reflects on his early work at the Harvard Compu-
        tational Laboratory, upon his development of computer
        memories in the late 1940s and about Wang Laboratories.

3951   West, James L. Tandy Corporation: "Start on a Shoe
        String". New York: The Newcomen Society in North
        America, 1968.

        This is a history of the company that, in fact, began
        as a supplier of shoe repair products and includes
        details on Radio Shack stores back to 1969.

Corporations and Economics

3952   Bain, Joe S. Barriers to New Competition. Cambridge,
        Mass.: Harvard University Press, 1956; Reprinted 1970.

        He describes barriers, their characteristics and con-
        sequences for manufacturing firms with comments on
        management style and role in innovation.

3953   Einhorn, Henry A. Enterprise Monopoly in the United
        States: 1899-1958. New York: Columbia University
        Press, 1969.

        Speaks to the general issue of monopolistic behavior
        in the United States.

3954   National Industrial Conference Board. Mergers in Busi-
        ness. New York: National Industrial Conference Board,
        1929.

        Mergers were very common in the office appliance
        industry in its early years; the features of such
        mergers in the U.S. are described.

3955   Noble, David F. America by Design: Science, Technology,
        and the Rise of Corporate Capitalism. New York: Knopf,
        1977.

        This is a major work sheding light on how technology
        emerged through the economy into products brought to
        market.

3956   Reich, Leonard S. The Making of American Industrial
        Research: Science and Business at GE and Bell, 1876-
        1926. New York: Cambridge University Press, 1986.

        This is a comparative analysis of R&D at GE and at
        AT&T's Bell Labs with a description of these evolved
        and influenced their parent companies.

3957   Scherer, F.M. Industrial Market Structure and Economic
        Performance. Chicago: Rand McNally, 1970.

        This is useful for appreciating the U.S. situation
        in the 20th century in which the DP industry function-
        ed.

3958   Sobel, Robert. The Entrepreneurs: Explorations Within
        the American Business Tradition. New York: Weybright
        and Talley, 1974.

        The tradition was a strong one in data processing.

3959   Stevens, William (ed). <u>Industrial Combinations and</u>
        <u>Trusts</u>. New York: Macmillan, 1914.

        While less specific on office appliance companies,
        it details how trusts were done, a pattern evident
        even, for example, at C-T-R, the precursor to IBM.

3960   Waterman, Robert H., Jr. <u>The Renewal Factor: How the</u>
        <u>Best Get and Keep the Competitive Edge</u>. New York:
        Bantom Books, 1987.

        He focuses on change and how to do it well, citing
        examples from many firms including H-P and IBM.

3961   Wilkins, Mira. <u>The Emergence of Multinational Enter-</u>
        <u>prise</u>. Cambridge, Mass.: Harvard University Press,
        1970.

        Useful for understanding a process also at work with-
        in the U.S. data processing industry.

3962   Wilkins, Mira. <u>The Maturing of Multinational Enter-</u>
        <u>prise</u>. Cambridge, Mass.: Harvard University Press,
        1974.

        Useful for appreciating a process evident in the
        office appliance industry in part, as with type-
        writers and adding machines at various times.

                    Digital Equipment Corporation (DEC)

3963   "A Q and A with DEC's President Ken Olsen," <u>Computer-</u>
        <u>world</u> (June 7, 1982): 10-11.

        DEC celebrated its 25th anniversary in August 1982.
        Olsen was DEC's first president and only CEO up to
        that time.

3964   Olsen, Kenneth H. <u>Digital Equipment Corporation: The</u>
        <u>First Twenty-Five Years</u>. New York: Newcomen Society
        of North America, 1983.

        This is the founder's view of the company's origins
        and development all through the 1960s and 1970s.

3965   Raimondi, Donna. "Through the Years with DEC," <u>Comput-</u>
        <u>erworld</u> (October 14, 1985): 87, 95-96.

        This is a product and company history of DEC, 1957-
        1985.

3966   Rifkin, Glenn and Harrar, George. <u>The Ultimate Entre-</u>
        <u>preneur: The Story of Ken Olsen and Digital Equipment</u>.
        Chicago: Contemporary Books, 1988.

        This is a full length biography of Olsen and history
        of DEC written by two journalists associated with
        <u>Computerworld</u>.

Data Processing Industry

3967   American Federation of Information Processing Societies.
       The State of the Information Processing Industry.
       New York: AFIPS Press, 1966.

       This is based on interviews and secondary sources.
       It is a review of personnel, salaries, hardware,
       installations, applications, and has a bibliography.

3968   "Antitrusters Score Patent Victory in AT&T Case,
       Settle with IBM," Business Week (January 28, 1956):
       160.

       These were major events in the history of the indus-
       try; the account is contemporary.

3969   Archbold, Pamela and Verity, John. "A Global Industry:
       The Datamation 100," Datamation 31, No. 11 (June 1,
       1985): 36-182.

       This summarizes activities of the top 100 companies
       in the DP industry with data on sales, volumes, prof-
       its. This was the first such survey by the magazine
       and has been published ever since on a yearly basis.

3970   Arthur D. Little, Inc. and White, Weld & Co, Research
       Department. The Electronic Data Processing Industry:
       Present Equipment, Technological Trends, Potential
       Markets. New York: White, Weld & Co., 1956.

       This is a very early survey of the DP industry once
       it was selling and installing computers.

3971   "As Time Goes By," Datamation 28, No. 10 (September
       1982): 65-124.

       This is a general history of the industry from 1957
       to 1982 covering many aspects of its development.

3972   Association of Data Processing Service Organizations.
       Annual ADAPSO Industry Report. New York: Quantum
       Science Corporation, 1967—present.

       Focus is on the U.S. data processing industry.

3973   Barquin, R.C. "Computation in Latin America," Datama-
       tion 20, No. 3 (March 1974): 73-78.

       Details are given on every Latin American country,
       giving details on how many computers there were per
       million people and per billions of dollars of GNP as
       of 1972 and 1973.

3974   "Battle of the Computer Marketeers," Fortune 71 (Jan-
       uary 1965): 171-172.

       This is on vendors in the U.S. DP industry of the
       mid-1960s.

3975   Bell, W.D.   "Employment in the Computing Field," Radio
        and TV News 58 (September 1957): 40-41ff.

        Surveys emerging career paths in data processing as
        they seemed in the late 1950s.

3976   Bello, F.   "War of the Computers," Fortune 60 (October
        1959): 128-133ff.

        This is an analysis of the DP industry at the end of
        the 1950s in the U.S.

3977   "Bendix Gives Up on Computers; Sale of Computer Divi-
        sion to CDC," Business Week (March 9, 1963): 36.

        Retirement from the computer field happened with
        many firms; this was an early one explained here.

3978   Billings, Thomas H. and Hogan, Richard C.   A Study of
        the Computer Manufacturing Industry in the United
        States. Springfield, Va.: Reproduced by National
        Technical Information Service, 1970.

        This is full of information and data about the U.S.
        industry of the 1960s; an important early study.

3979   Boggs, Raymond L. and Solomon, Lewis I. The U.S. Comput-
        er Industry: A Strategic Analysis, 1980-1982. Welles-
        ley, Mass.: Venture Development Corporation, 1981.

        This is an economic analysis of opportunities and
        realities.

3980   Bower, Richard S.   "Market Changes and the Computer
        Services Industry," Bell Journal of Economics 4, No.
        2 (Autumn 1973): 539-590.

        This is an extensive study of costs and profitability
        in the computer services business which is judged to
        be competitive in the early 1970s.

3981   Brock, Gerald W.   The U.S. Computer Industry: A Study
        of Market Power. Cambridge, Mass.: Ballinger Publish-
        ing Co., 1975.

        This is as much a history as an economic analysis.
        He suggests that IBM be broken up into several firms
        and uses data generated by various antitrust lawsuits
        against the industry giant.

3982   Burck, G.   "Computer Industry's Great Expectations,"
        Fortune 78 (August 1968): 92-97ff.

        This is useful for appreciating what was happening in
        the U.S. industry in the late 1960s.

3983   Burnett, Ed.   "Computers in Use: Analyzed by Standard
        Industrial Classification: 1974 Compared with 1968,"
        Computers and People 24, Nos. 5-7 (May, June and July
        1975).

He compares the number of locations with computers
by major SIC codes, looking at 24,500 cites in 1975
versus 17,600 in 1968.

3984   Burnett, Ed.   "Computers in Use, Analyzed by Standard
        Industrial Classification," Computers and Automation
        (September 1969): 43-48.

        Burnett conducted one of the largest such surveys to
        date to compute how many establishments there were
        per computer in each major industry in the U.S.

3985   Carroll, John M.   "Electronic Computers for the Busi-
        nessman," Electronics 28 (June 1955): 122-131.

        Surveys 38 cites with descriptions of installed
        computers, prices, and activities in the U.S.

3986   Computer and Business Equipment Manufacturers Associa-
        tion. Computer and Business Equipment Marketing and
        Forecast Data Book. Hasbrouck Heights, N.J.: Hayden
        Book Co., 1985.

        Offers data on what kinds of computers were install-
        ed in the U.S., their market shares by vendor, and
        defines future opportunities; a snapshot of the 1970s
        and early 1980s in the U.S. industry.

3987   Computer and Technology Information, Inc. The Finan-
        cial Structure of the Computer Industry. Newport
        Beach, Cal.: Computer and Technology Information,
        Inc., 1970.

        This is a 27-page overview as of the late 1960s.

3988   "Computers Go Commercial by Degrees," Business Week
        (November 21, 1953): 68-70ff.

        Surveys a strend that began in the early 1950s and
        became significant by mid-decade. It identifies the
        applications that made possible the expansion of the
        computer business into commercial fields.

3989   "Computers: The Booming State of the Art," Newsweek 72
        (August 19, 1968): 68-70.

        Informative analysis of what was happening in the
        U.S. DP industry in the late 1960s.

3990   Computerworld. The Age of MIS. Farmingham, Mass.: IDG
        Communications, 1987.

        This illustrated supplement to the newspaper reviews
        all aspects of the DP industry between 1967 and 1987.

3991   Cortada, James W. Historical Dictionary of Data
        Processing: Organizations. Westport, Conn.: Greenwood
        Press, 1987.

        This offers histories of over 160 organizations in
        the industry.

3992   Daoust, Charles F. and McEntee, Angelina P. World
        Trade in Adding Machines, Calculators, Cash Regis-
        ters, 1953-1959. Washington, D.C.: U.S. Department
        of Commerce, 1960.

        This 27-page publication contains an enormous amount
        of statistical data on volumes, primarily concerning
        U.S. exports.

3993   Davis, Ruth M. "Evolution of Computers and Computing,"
        Science 195 (March 3, 1977): 1096-1102.

        Identifies the historical elements constituting the
        world of computers in 1976.

3994   Dean, Neal J. "The Computer Comes of Age," Harvard
        Business Review (January-February 1968): 83-91; Re-
        printed in John Dearden et al. (eds), Managing Com-
        puter-Based Information Systems (Homewood, Ill.:
        Richard D. Irwin, Inc., 1971): 610-622.

        This Booze, Allen & Hamilton study of 108 companies
        reveals trends on how DP was managed, spent on it,
        and for what in the mid to late 1960s.

3995   Dertouzos, Michael and Moses, Joel (eds). The Computer
        Age: A Twenty-Year View. Cambridge, Mass.: MIT Press,
        1979.

        Twenty-two essays survey prospects for users, trends
        in computer usage, discuss socioeconomic effects,
        and changes expected in technology, covering the
        period between the early 1970s and deep into 1990s.

3996   Diebold, John. "Congressional Testimony," in Morris
        H. Philipson (ed), Automation: Implications for the
        Future (New York: Vintage Books, 1962): 12-76.

        Reprints his testimony from the 1950s on the case
        for using computers.

3997   Diebold, John (ed). The World of the Computer. New
        York: Random House, 1973.

        This is a wealth of information on various uses of
        computers and about the industry supplying machines.

3998   Dorfman, Nancy S. Innovation and Market Structure:
        Lessons from the Computer and Semiconductor Indus-
        tries. Cambridge, Mass.: Ballinger Books, 1987.

        She focuses on the role played by large, established
        companies and small start-up firms in driving tech-
        nological changes, primarily in the U.S.

3999   EDP Idea Finder, Data Processing Digest, 1957-1959.
        Los Angeles, Cal.: Canning, Sisson and Associates,
        Inc., 1960.

This 656-page book is a collection of articles on DP issues published between 1957 and 1959 and is a useful reflection of the period. It is well indexed and cross referenced.

4000   Ernst, D. <u>The Global Race in Micro-Electronics</u>. Frankfurt: Campus, Verlag, 1983.

This is an economic analysis of trends and actions taking place in the late 1970s and early 1980s.

4001   Evans, B.O. "Computers and Communications," in Michael Dertouzos and Joel Moses (eds), <u>The Computer Age: A Twenty-Year View</u> (Cambridge, Mass.: MIT Press, 1979): 338-366.

The father of the IBM S/360 reviews the evolution of computers, their costs and economic impact and volumes sold. He does the same for telecommunications and concludes with implications for the 1980s.

4002   Fahey, Michael. "Open Is As Open Does," <u>Network World</u> 4 (July 20, 1987): 37-40.

Fahey describes the trend for industry-wide technical standards emerging in the 1980s.

4003   "$5-Billion World Market for Computers; Special Report," <u>Business World</u> (February 19, 1966): 110-114.

This is as much a snapshot of the "computer industry" of the mid-1960s as it was an opportunity statement.

4004   Fleck, G. (ed). <u>A Computer Perspective</u>. Cambridge, Mass.: Harvard University Press, 1973.

Intended for a general audience, this includes an illustrated history of computing and its industry.

4005   Forester, Tom. <u>High-Tech Society</u>. Cambridge, Mass.: MIT Press, 1987.

This is a fact filled survey of the technology, uses and events in the world of computers covering all major nations and the industry during the 1970s and first half of the 1980s; excellent survey.

4006   Frielink, A.B. (ed). <u>Economics of Automatic Data Processing</u>. Amsterdam: North-Holland Publishing Co., 1965.

4007   Fulton, J.F. and Flanders, R.B. "Employment and Occupational Outlook in Electronics," <u>Monthly Labor Review</u> 86 (September 1963): 1026-1032.

This focuses only on U.S. job opportunities and the situation as of the early 1960s.

4008   Freeman, C. <u>et al</u>. "Research and Development in Electronic Capital Goods," <u>National Institute Economic</u>

<u>Review</u> 34 (November 1965): 40-91.

Summarizes the origins of computer technology and
the early growth of the DP industry in the U.S.

4009   Gilchrist, Bruce. "Manpower Statistics in the Infor-
        mation Processing Field," <u>Computers and Automation</u>
        (September 1969): 24-27.

        Offers data on employment in the DP industry for
        the 1960s in the U.S.

4010   Gilchrist, Bruce and Weber, R.E. <u>Numerical Bias in</u>
        <u>the 1970 U.S. Census Data on Computer Occupations</u>.
        Montvale, N.J.: AFIPS Press, 1974.

        Compares and reconciles data from U.S. Bureau of the
        Census and the U.S. Bureau of Labor Statistics for
        occupations of programmer, systems analyst, computer
        operators and keypunch operators for the years
        1969-1973.

4011   Gilchrist, Bruce and Weber, R.E. "Sources of Trained
        Computer Personnel—A Quantitative Survey," <u>AFIPS</u>
        <u>Conference Proceedings</u> 40 (1972): 633-679.

        They survey all manner of schools and universities,
        estimating how many graduates have come from this
        source into the DP industry since 1965 in the U.S.

4012   Gilchrist, Bruce and Weber, R.E. (ed). <u>The State of</u>
        <u>the Computer Industry in the United States</u>. Montvale,
        N.J.: AFIPS Press, 1973.

        This is a statistical snapshot of the industry as
        of 1971 and projections to 1976. Includes some data
        on the late 1960s.

4013   Gilchrist, Bruce and Wessel, Milton. <u>Government Regu-</u>
        <u>lation of the Computer Industry</u>. Washington, D.C.:
        AFIPS, 1972.

        Surveys regulations from the 1950s to 1971.

4014   Gilder, George. <u>Microcosm: The Quantom Revolution in</u>
        <u>Economics and Technology</u>. New York: Simon & Schuster,
        1989.

        Looks at the history and prospects of the U.S. micro-
        electronics industry, arguing that the U.S. will
        continue to be world leaders in this technology.

4015   Greenberger, Martin (ed). <u>Computers and the World of</u>
        <u>the Future</u>. Cambridge, Mass.: MIT Press, 1966 ed.

        This is a collection of papers on present and antici-
        pated computing trends.

4016   Greenberger, Martin (ed). <u>Computers, Communications</u>

and the Public Interest. Baltimore: Johns Hopkins
University Press, 1971.

This is a good introduction to public policy issues
of the 1960s and 1970s concerning these technologies
in the U.S.

4017   Greenfield, H.I. "An Economist Looks at Data Process-
        ing," Computers and Automation (October 1957): 18-23.

        Explains why the need for more DP has been rising
        in the 1950s but also why computers have not yet
        influenced clerical productivity in the U.S.

4018   Groppelli, A.A. "The Growth Process in the Computer
        Industry" (Unpublished Ph.D. dissertation, New York
        University, 1970).

        This is a quantitative analysis of the industry with
        emphasis on the role of IBM; contains much industry
        census data covering the period 1940s-1960s.

4019   "Growing Market in Used Computers," Business Week
        (September 8, 1962): 49-50ff.

        This is an early article on a trend that became, in
        time, a significant one within the industry.

4020   "Growing Wildly Without a Blueprint; The Data-Process-
        ing and Communications Industries in the 1970s,"
        Business Week (December 6, 1969): 192ff.

        This continues the magazine's analysis of trends in
        the U.S. DP industry of the late 1960s.

4021   Gruenberger, Fred J. "A Short History of Digital
        Computing in Southern California," Computing News
        (1958): 145.23-145.31; Reprinted in Annals of the
        History of Computing 2, No. 3 (July 1980): 246-252.

        These are memoirs of Los Angeles (1942-57) and the
        furthance of DP on the U.S. West Coast.

4022   Halamka, John D. Espionage in the Silicon Valley.
        Berkeley: SYBEX, 1984.

        This is a short collection of stories on the subject
        in California, circa 1970s and 1980s.

4023   Hamblen, J.W. Inventory of Computers in United States
        Higher Education: 1969-1970. Washington, D.C.: Office
        of Computing Activities, National Science Foundation,
        March 1972.
        This is a survey of computer population and uses.

4024   Hanson, Dirk. The New Alchemists: Silicon Valley and
        the Microelectronics Revolution. Boston: Little-Brown,
        1982.

This has some history of computers and data processing in general; some of the factual material is sus-
pect. Intended for the general reader.

4025   Harmon, J. Alvin. The International Computer Industry.
        Cambridge, Mass.: Harvard University Press, 1971.

        This is a history of the industry in the U.S., Europe
        and in Japan.

4026   Hershman, A. "Boom In Used Computers?," Duns Review
        90 (December 1967): 63-64.

        By the late 1960s there was an active market for
        used computers; that market is described here.

4027   "How the High-Fliers Take Off," Business Week (November
        22, 1969): 112-114ff.

        Describes companies within the U.S. industry.

4028   Industry Marketing Stattistics Program, Computer and
        Business Equipment Manufacturers Association. The
        Computer and Business Equipment Industry Marketing
        Data Book. Washington, D.C.: The Association, 1983.

        Surveys the U.S. industry as of the early 1980s with
        data on volumes and size.

4029   Information Industry Market Place. 4 vols. New York:
        R.R. Bowker, 1980.

        This is a major survey of the U.S. industry with a
        large quantity of statistical information on volumes
        and sizes.

4030   International Data Corporation (IDC). Annual Industry
        Survey, 1966—present.

        IDC's survey of the DP industry is widely-read. It
        reviews product types, people, applications, and
        industry segments, such as service bureaus, vendors.

4031   International Data Corporation (IDC). The Growth
        Potential of the Computer Industry in Massachusetts.
        Newtonville, Mass.: IDC, 1970.

        This analysis was prepared for the Massachusetts
        Department of Commerce and Development and includes
        data on activities of the 1960s and suggests what
        should be done in the 1970s. The state developed a
        significant computer presence during these two decades.

4032   Irwin, Manley R. "The Computer Utility: Market Entry
        in Search of a Public Policy," Journal of Industrial
        Economics 17, No. 3 (July 1969): 239-252.

        Argues that the FCC regulations restricted innovative
        entrants into the industry during the 1960s, parti-
        cularly in telecommunications.

4033   Juliussen, Egil et al. Computer Industry Almanac.
        Dallas: Computer Industry Almanac, 1987.

        This is a massive, 750 page compendium listing firms,
        their financial rankings, products, industry organiza-
        tions and so forth for 1985-86 for both the U.S. and
        Europe. A subsequent edition was published for 1987-88.

4034   Katz, Barbara Goody and Philips, Almarin. "The Comput-
        er Industry," in Richard R. Nelson (ed), Government
        and Technical Progress: A Cross-Industry Analysis
        (New York: Pergamon Press, 1982): 162-232.

        This is a useful survey of the industry's features
        as of the late 1970s.

4035   Kendrick, John W. Postware Productivity Trends in the
        United States, 1948-1969. New York: National Bureau
        of Economic Research, 1973.

        This very important economic analysis contains data
        on volumes shipped and analysis of the office equip-
        ment and computer industries at large. Continues his
        work of the same title, published 1961.

4036   Kendrick, John W. Productivity Trends in the United
        States. New York: National Bureau of Economic Research,
        1961.

        He includes specific material on office equipment and
        computing products through 1958.

4037   Klass, P.J. "Survey Shows Size of Computer Market,"
        Aviation Week 70 (February 16, 1959): 71ff.

        This was a report on an early economic snapshot of
        the U.S. DP industry.

4038   Klein, H.E. "Computers for Everybody!," Duns Review 78
        (December 1961): 42-46.

        Klein surveys U.S. data processing service bureaus of
        the early 1960s.

4039   Klingman, Herbert F. (ed). Electronics in Business: A
        Descriptive Reference Guide. 2nd Ed. New York: Con-
        trollership Foundation, Inc., July 1955.

        Contains information on bibliography, conferences,
        seminars, training programs, surveys of equipment and
        costs, applications and lists 13 commercial computer
        centers in the U.S.

4040   Lampe, David R. The Massachusetts Miracle: High Tech-
        nology and Economic Revitalization. Cambridge, Mass.:
        MIT Press, 1988.

        This is an economic review of high technology indus-
        tries in Massachusetts in the 1970s and 1980s, includ-
        ing data processing.

4041   Lecht, Charles P. The Wave of Change: A Techno-Econo-
       mic Analysis of the Data Processing Industry. New
       York: Advanced Computer Techniques Corporation, 1977.

       His is a high level economic survey of the DP indus-
       try in historical perspective.

4042   Lee, Wayne J. (ed). The International Computer Indus-
       try. Washington, D.C.: Applied Library Resources,
       1971.

       This is an economic narrative covering the industry
       in the U.S., Europea and in Asia.

4043   Lerner, Eric J. "Technology and the Military: DOD's
       Darpa at 25," IEEE Spectrum (August 1983): 72-73.

       This describes the role of the U.S. Department of
       Defense's R&D funding organization (Defense Advanced
       Research Projects Agency), which played a major role
       in funding work on computers, 1958-82.

4044   Lias, Edward J. "A History of General Purpose Computer
       Uses in the United States: 1954 to 1977 and Likely
       Future" (Unpublished Ph.D. dissertation, New York
       University, 1978).

       He comments on utilization, impact on society and
       role in the U.S. Its quality does not compare to that
       of the better economic studies published on the same
       theme.

4045   Lions, J. "The Australian Computer Journal: Twenty
       Years On," The Australian Computer Journal 19, No. 4
       (1987): 185-189.

       The article and the journal are a good source on
       computing activities in Australia.

4046   Lutze, Stephen Christian. "The Formation of the Inter-
       national Computer Industry, 1945-50" (M.A. thesis,
       University of California, Santa Barbara, June 1979).

       This is a very useful study that is well documented
       on the early phases of the computer's introduction
       into the U.S. economy.

4047   Macdonald, N. "Computing Service Survey," Computers
       and Automation 7, No. 7 (July 1958): 9-12.

       Surveys companies offering computer services with
       data on size, age and processors used as of the late
       1950s in the U.S.

4048   Mahoney, Eileen. "Negotiating the New Information
       Technology and National Development: The Role of the
       Intergovernmental Bureau for Informatics" (Unpub-
       lished Ph.D. dissertation, Temple University, 1986).

       Covers the period 1946-61 of the International Compu-
       tation Centre.

4049   "Making A Market in Old Computers," Business Week
        (November 16, 1968): 179-180.

        Reports on the sale of used computers in the U.S.

4050   Malone, Michael S. The Big Score: The Billion-Dollar
        Story of Silicon Valley. New York: Doubleday, 1985.

        This is a very useful survey of data processing
        firms in California including on H-P, Fairchild,
        Intel, Advanced Micro Devices, National Semiconduc-
        tor among others; based largely on interviews and
        published material.

4051   Management and Business Automation Magazine. "EDP Jobs
        and Salaries," published annually since 1959.

        This is a major source on the topic as applied to
        the U.S. industry throughout the 1960s and 1970s.

4052   McClellan, Stephen T. The Coming Computer Industry
        Shakeout: Winners, Losers, and Survivors. New York:
        John Wiley and Sons, 1984.

        Surveys the U.S. industry by company, providing some
        history, current situation, and forecast through the
        early 1990s.

4053   McLaughlin, John F. Mapping the Information Business.
        Cambridge, Mass.: Program on Information Resources
        Policy, Harvard University, 1980.

        This is an important source on all aspects of infor-
        mation handling, not just computers and associated
        products, in the U.S.

4054   McLaughlin, R.A. "A Survey of 1974 DP Budgets,"
        Datamation 20, No. 2 (February 1974): 52-57.

        The survey on U.S. data centers, was taken on the
        verge of significant increases in spending on DP,
        and covers all phases of the budgeting process in
        181 U.S. and 13 Canadian installations. He published
        other such surveys in Datamation (February 1973): 61-
        63; (March 1975): 63-74; (February 1976): 52-58.

4055   "The Mechanization of Work," Scientific American 247
        (September 1982).

        The entire issue is devoted to the subject with a
        great deal of information on the use of computers
        in the U.S.A.

4056   Miller, B. "Avionics Demands Spur Microcircuit Sales,"
        Aviation Week 79 (December 23, 1963): 63-65ff.

        Military flight demands encouraged miniaturization
        of electronics; the article explores the issues as
        of the early 1960s.

4057   Mowshowitz, A. The Conquest of Will. Reading, Mass.:
       Addison-Wesley Publishers, 1976.

       Contains material on the evolution of the DP industry
       in the 1960s and 1970s.

4058   National Academy of Sciences. International Develop-
       ments in Computer Science. Washington, D.C.: National
       Academy Press, 1982.

       Describes developments in technology over the previous
       several years and identifies trends evident at time
       of publication.

4059   Noll, Roger G. "Regulation and Computer Services," in
       Michael Dertouzos and Joel Moses (eds), The Computer
       Age: A Twenty-Year View (Cambridge, Mass.: MIT Press,
       1979): 254-284.

       Surveys developments in public policy in the U.S.
       since the 1960s with particular attention to AT&T
       and the role of the FCC. Sees a trend toward more
       regulation; in fact it was the opposite.

4060   Pantages, Angeline. "Deja Vu on a Decade," Datamation
       28, No. 10 (September 1982): 56-62.

       Written by an editor of Datamation, it is a survey
       and memoir of 1972-1979.

4061   Peters, Thomas J. and Waterman, Robert H., Jr. In Search
       of Excellence: Lessons From America's Best-Run Com-
       panies. New York: Harper & Row, 1982.

       Contains a great deal about the corporate cultures
       of Apple Computers, DEC, IBM, H-P, Intel, ITT, Lanier,
       Litton, Motorola, NCR, STC, Tandem, TI, TRW, United
       Technologies, Wang, Western Electric, and Westing-
       house. Millions of copies of the book were sold in
       the 1980s.

4062   Phillips, John Patrick. "Patterns of Price and Com-
       petition in the Computer Industry" (Unpublished
       Ph.D. dissertation, University of Illinois, 1971).

       It is useful in large part for the 1950s and 1960s.

4063   Phister, Montgomery,Jr. Data Processing Technology
       and Economics. Santa Monica, Cal.: Santa Monica
       Publishing, 1976.

       This contains a massive amount of data on all aspects
       of data processing costs from the 1940s to the early
       1970s, primarily U.S.

4064   Phister, Montgomery, Jr. Data Processing Technology
       and Economics, 1975-1978 Supplement. Santa Monica,
       Cal.: Santa Monica Publishing Co., 1979.

       Updates the previous edition with data on the 1970s.

4065   Porat, Marc Uri. The Information Economy: Definition
        and Measurement. Washington, D.C.: Office of Tele-
        communications, U.S. Department of Commerce.

        Assumes that a growing number of workers in the U.S.
        work with information as their primary task and then
        measures that; includes data on data processing.

4066   Pullen, E. and Simko, R. "Our Changing Industry,"
        Datamation (January 1977): 49.

        Contains brief comments on the U.S. industry, 1970s.

4067   Richard J. Barber Associates. The Advanced Research
        Projects Agency, 1958-1974. Alexandria, Va.: Defense
        Technical Information Center, 1975.

        This is the agency's "official" history and details
        its role in funding R&D projects in the U.S.

4068   Riley, Robert. "A Case Study of a Differential Mono-
        poly: The Computer Time-Sharing Industry" (Unpublish-
        ed Ph.D. dissertation, University of Cincinnati,
        1970).

        This is a detailed study of the service bureau piece
        of the U.S. DP industry.

4069   Rogers, Everett M. and Larsen, Judith K. Silicon
        Valley Fever: Growth of High-Technology Culture. New
        York: Basic Books, 1984.

        Describes Silicon Valley in detail with material on
        Apple, Intel, and other firms.

4070   Rosen, S. A Quarter Century View. New York: Associa-
        tion of Computing Machinery, 1971.

        This is a serious of observations on the U.S. indus-
        try by a long-time observer of its activities.

4071   Rubin, Michael Rogers and Huber, Mary Taylog. The
        Knowledge Industry in the United States, 1960-1980.
        Princeton, N.J.: Princeton University Press, 1986.

        They argue that "knowledge industries" made up 29
        percent of the U.S.GNP in 1958, 34 percent in 1980.

4072   Rurak, Marilyn. The American Computer Industry in Its
        International Competitive Environment. Washington,
        D.C.: U.S. Department of Commerce, 1976.

        In effect, this is a market survey of the U.S. DP
        industry of the 1970s.

4073   Salerno, Lynn M. Computer Briefing: The Concise Update
        on the Latest Developments. New York: John Wiley,
        1986.

        It is a useful introduction to social and economic

issues of the early 1980s concerning data processing.
It also is an update on trends in DP technology.

4074   Sanders, Donald H. Computers and Management in a Chang-
        ing Society. New York: McGraw-Hill, 1974.

        It contains a general history of the DP industry.

4075   Sanders, James. Information Market Place, 1978-79. An
        International Directory of Information Products and
        Services. New York: R.R. Bowker, 1978.

        This is set up as a directory on both European and
        American firms.

4076   Schelberg, W.V. "Development of the Computer Industry
        and Patents," in E. Takats (ed), Proceedings I.A.P.I.
        P. International Conference on Correlation Between
        the Protection of Industrial Property and Industrial
        Development, Hungary 28 September-2 October 1970 (N.
        c.: OMKDK, 1971): 201-208.

        Reviews important patents in the history of digital
        computers and their role in the development of market-
        able products.

4077   Sharpe, William F. The Economics of Computers. New
        York: Columbia University Press, 1969.

        This is a highly technical and detailed study of
        pricing and selling patterns for computers of the
        1960s and affects on the industry's economics.

4078   Silberman, Amichai. "The Rise of the Digital Computer
        Technological Community in the U.S." (Unpublished
        Ph.D. dissertation, University of Wisconsin, Madison,
        1986).

        This is a major source on DP organizations since
        World War II and is a sociological analysis of their
        formation, mission and history.

4079   Skinner, Wickham and Rogers, David C.D. Manufacturing
        Policy in the Electronics Industry: A Casebook of
        Major Production Problems. Homewood, Ill.: Richard
        D. Irwin, Inc., 1968.

        Emphasis is more on electronics than computers but
        with a sense of the experiences vendors in the DP
        industry faced in the 1960s.

4080   Smolin, Ronald P. (ed). Computer Industry: A Directory
        and Ranking of Public Companies. Philadelphia, Pa.:
        AIIS, 1985.

        The rankings and data are on U.S. firms in the DP
        industry.

4081   "Software Gap, A Growing Crisis for Computers; Shortage

of Programmers," Business Week (November 5, 1966):
126-128.

This was one of many such articles to call out the
lack of programmers in the U.S. during the 1960s
and 1970s as the industry grew rapidly.

4082   Sojka, Deborah. "The Old Clothes of Advertising,"
       Datamation 28, No. 10 (September 1982): 137-153.

       Reproduces 21 advertisements from Datamation, 1957
       to 1982 on DP products in the U.S.

4083   Soma, John T. The Computer Industry: An Economic-Legal
       Analysis of Its Technology and Growth. Lexington,
       Mass.: Lexington Books, 1976.

       Focus is on the U.S. DP industry, with emphasis on
       legal implications and issues, 1960s and 1970s.

4084   Sprague, Richard E. "A Western View of Computer His-
       tory," Communications, ACM 15 (July 1972): 686-694.

       This is a history of computer activities in Califor-
       nia in the 1940s and 1950s, particularly in support
       of defense projects.

4085   Stoneman, Paul. Technological Diffusion and the Com-
       puter Revolution: The U.N. Experience. Cambridge:
       Cambridge University Press, 1976.

       This economic study surveys such topics as cross-
       border marketing, international patent licensing,
       and the global industry, circa early 1970s.

4086   Szuprowicz, B. "Computers: Shake-Out in Time Sharing?"
       Duns Review 93 (April 1969): 87-88ff.

       The author describes recent developments in the
       service bureau business in the U.S., circa 1960s.

4087   Thomas, David. Knights of the New Technology. The
       Inside Story of Canada's Computer Elite. Toronto:
       Key Porter Books, 1983.

       This surveys Canada's industry, major firms and
       leaders, primarily of the 1970s and early 1980s.

4088   Tigre, Paulo Bastos. Technology and Competition in
       the Brazilian Computer Industry. New York: St.
       Martin's Press, 1983.

       This is an economic analysis of Latin America's
       largest DP market, circa 1970s.

4089   The Time Sharing Computer Services Market. New York:
       Frost & Sullivan, 1975.

       This is a U.S. market survey on service bureaus.

4090   "Time Sharing Zooms Through the Ceilling," <u>Business
        Week</u> (June 22, 1968): 121-123.

        Describes service bureau work in the U.S. in the
        1960s.

4091   Tomeski, E.A. <u>The Computer Revolution</u>. London: Macmi-
        llan Co., 1970.

        Reflects the views of the 1960s on the impact of
        DP on society and with a statement of its signifi-
        cance.

4092   Tuck, Jay. <u>High-Tech Espionage: How the KGB Smuggles
        Nato's Strategic Secrets to Moscow</u>. London: Sidgwick
        & Jackson, 1986.

        This is the only book available on KGB efforts in
        the U.S. dealing with data processing. Estimates
        that 20,000 agents are at work, many in Silicon
        Valley.

4093   "Under IBM's Umbrella; Competition in Computer Indus-
        try," <u>Forbes</u> 102 (July 15, 1968): 17-19.

        Characterizes IBM's position within the industry as
        dominant but with competitive activity evident.

4094   U.S., Bureau of International Commerce. <u>Electronic
        Data Processing Equipment, Peripheral Devices and
        Software</u>. Washington, D.C.: U.S. Government Print-
        ing Office, 1970.

        This is a market survey as of 1969 with much tabular
        data on volumes.

4095   U.S., Bureau of the Census. <u>Historical Statistics of
        the United States, Colonial Times to 1970</u>. 2 vols.
        Washington, D.C.: U.S. Government Printing Office,
        1975.

        Various editions and revisions have appeared over
        the past three decades. It is the major statistical
        summary on the U.S. economy with data on office and
        computer sales throughout the 20th century.

4096   U.S., Civil Service Commission. <u>Occupations of Federal
        White Collar Workers</u>. Washington, D.C.: Bureau of
        Manpower Information Systems, 1968.

        This edition listed DP professions for the years
        1958-68 with populations and salaries. This annual
        publication first began appearing in 1954.

4097   U.S. Department of Commerce. <u>The Computer Industry</u>.
        Washington, D.C.: U.S. Government Printing Office,
        April 1983.

        Discusses the state of the industry as of early 1983
        in the U.S., Europe and Japan.

4098   U.S. Department of Commerce. <u>Global Market Survey:</u>
       <u>Computers and Related Equipment</u>. Washington, D.C.:
       U.S. Government Printing Office, 1973.

       Describes the opportunity and recent volumes.

4099   U.S., Federal Trade Commission. <u>Industrial Corporation</u>
       <u>Reports: Business Machines and Typewriter Manufactur-</u>
       <u>ing Corporations</u>. Washington, D.C.: U.S. Government
       Printing Office, 1941.

       This is a good source for statistical data on the
       U.S. office appliance industry of the 1930s.

4100   U.S. House of Representatives, Committee on Post Office
       and Civil Service, 86th Congress, 2nd Session. <u>Report</u>
       <u>on the Use of Electronic Data-Processing Equipment in</u>
       <u>the Federal Government</u>. Washington, D.C.: U.S. Govern-
       ment Printing Office, 1960.

       This surveyed the largest collection of computer users
       in the world, circa 1960. They had 20 percent of all
       computers installed that were built in the U.S. as
       measured by sales value.

4101   U.S. Senate. <u>Hearings Before the Subcommittee on Anti-</u>
       <u>trust and Monopoly of the Committee on the Judiciary</u>
       <u>in the Industrial Reorganization Act—S1167 (Part 7—</u>
       <u>Computers), United States Senate</u>. Washington, D.C.:
       U.S. Government Printing Office, 1974.

       These hearings took place at the same time that the
       U.S. Government had suid IBM for violating antitrust
       laws.

4102   U.S. Senate, Committee on the Judiciary. <u>The Computer</u>
       <u>Industry. Hearings Before the Subcommittee on Anti-</u>
       <u>trust and Monopoly, July 23-26, 1974</u>. Washington,
       D.C.: U.S. Government Printing Office, 1974.

       Continues the theme of the previous citation; much
       of this testimony hostile toward IBM.

4103   U.S., General Services Administration. <u>Inventory of</u>
       <u>Automatic Data Processing Equipment in the United</u>
       <u>States Government</u>. Washington, D.C.: General Services
       Administration, 1975.

       The inventory is as of 1974/1975 and is significant.

4104   U.S., National Commission on Technology, Automation,
       and Economic Progress. <u>Technology and the American</u>
       <u>Economy</u> 1 (February 1966): 3-4.

       A brief survey of rate of change in U.S. technology.

4105   Van Tassel, Dennie. <u>The Compleat Computer</u>. Chicago:
       Science Research Associates, 1976.

       Comments on the U.S. industry of the early 1970s.

4106   Wallace, Bob. "COS, MAP/TOP Groups Establish Bridge
        Council," Network World 4 (February 9, 1987): 2-52.

        Reviews actions of the Manufacturing Automation Pro-
        tocol group which joined with Corporation for Open
        Systems to set technical standards across the industry.

4107   Waters, Marie B. Worldwide Directory of Computer Com-
        panies, 1973-1974. Orange, N.J.: Academic Media,
        1973.

        This is a 633-page directory on the DP industry.

4108   Webbink, Douglas W. The Semiconductor Industry: A Sur-
        vey of Structure, Conduct and Performance. Washing-
        ton, D.C.: Federal Trade Commission, 1977.

        This was one of the first, thorough economic surveys
        of this subsector of the information processing in-
        dustry worldwide, circa 1960s and 1970s.

4109   Weik, Martin H. A Survey of Domestic Electronic Digital
        Computing Systems. Aberdeen Proving Ground, Md.:
        Ballistics Research Laboratory, 1955.

        This is an important, early source on the population
        of computers in the United States.

4110   Weil, Ulric. Information Systems in the 80's: Products,
        Markets, and Vendors. Englewood Cliffs, N.J.: Prentice-
        Hall, Inc., 1982.

        This is an analysis of major vendors, often a chapter
        each, with data on who they are, what they sell and
        their business prospects with considerable amounts
        of data on the period of the 1970s and early 1980s.

4111   Wells, John Varick. "The Origins of the Computer Indus-
        try: A Case Study in Radical Technological Change"
        (Unpublished Ph.D. dissertation, Yale University,
        1978).

        Covers the period from the 1920s to the 1950s; chro-
        nology included (pp. 265-278).

4112   Westin, Alan F. Data Banks in a Free Society. New York:
        Quadrangle Books, 1972.

        Surveys how data privacy in computer systems was
        handled between 1969 and 1971.

4113   Westin, Alan F. (ed). Information Technology in a
        Democracy. Cambridge, Mass.: Harvard University
        Press, 1971.

        This is a survey of social/political issues.

4114   "When EDP Goes Back to the Experts; Facilities Manage-
        ment Companies," Business Week (October 18, 1969):114.

FM firms were not new to the office appliance industry but were different when, in the 1960s, they
existed with computer services.

4115   White, P.T. "Behold the Computer Revolution," National
        Geographic 138 (November 1970): 593-633.

        Reviews the technology, its industry, and uses as of
        the late 1960s.

4116   Whiteside, Thomas. Computer Capers. Tales of Electron-
        ic Thievery, Embezzlement, and Fraud. New York: T.Y.
        Crowell Co., 1978.

        Contains stories on computer crimes and about how it
        was being stopped in the U.S.

4117   Wilson, John W. The New Ventures: Inside the High-
        Stakes World of Venture Capital. Reading, Mass.:
        Addison, Wesley, 1985.

        While an excellent survey on the roles played by
        venture capitalists in the U.S. in the 1970s and
        1980s, it cites examples of their work in data
        processing, e.g., Lotus 1-2-3 and with microcomputer
        firms.

4118   Withington, Frederick G. The Computer Industry, 1969-
        1974. Cambridge, Mass.: Arthur D. Little, 1969.

        Offers data on the industry, machines, people, and
        volumes in the U.S. for the period.

4119   "World Boom in Computers, and a Challenge to U.S.,"
        U.S. News and World Report 68 (March 9, 1970): 78-81.

        This analyzes the growth of DP worldwide and the
        marketing of products from Europe and Japan.

                    Data Processing Organizations

4120   Armer, Paul. "SHARE—A Eulogy to Cooperative Effort,"
        Annals of the History of Computing 2, No. 2 (April
        1980): 122-129.

        Reprints a presentation he made in 1956; a forward
        offers a brief history.

4121   Auerbach, Isaac L. "American Society for Information
        Science (ASIS)," in Anthony Ralston and Chester L.
        Meek (eds), Encyclopedia of Computer Science (New
        York: Petrocelli/Charter, 1976): 57-58.

        Describes the mission, activities and history of ASIS.

4122   Auerbach, Isaac L. "Association for Educational Data
        Systems (AEDS)," in Anthony Ralston and Chester L.
        Meeks (eds), Encyclopedia of Computer Science (New
        York: Petrocelli/Charter, 1976): 130.

AEDS is described from its inception (1962) to 1975.

4123   Auerbach, Isaac L. "Association Française Pour La
       Cybernetique Economique et Technique (AFCET)," in
       Anthony Ralston and Chester L. Meeks (eds), Encyclo-
       pedia of Computer Science (New York: Petrocelli/Char-
       ter, 1976): 130-131.

       AFCET's history is reviewed, 1969-1975.

4124   Auerbach, Isaac L. "British Computer Society (BCS),"
       in Anthony Ralston and Chester L. Meeks (eds),
       Encyclopedia of Computer Science (New York: Petro-
       celli/Charter, 1976): 185-187.

       BCS came into existence in 1957 and is a major
       British computer/data processing organization.

4125   Auerbach, Isaac L. "Institute of Electrical and Elec-
       tronics Engineers—Computer Society (IEEE-CS)," in
       Anthony Ralston and Chester L. Meeks (eds), Encyclo-
       pedia of Computer Science (New York: Petrocelli/
       Charter, 1976): 711-712.

       Reviews its role from 1953 to 1975.

4126   Auerbach, Isaac L. "Society for Computer Simulation
       (SCS)," in Anthony Ralston and Chester L. Meeks (eds),
       Encyclopedia of Computer Science (New York: Petro-
       celli/Charter, 1976): 1281-1282.

       Surveys its history from 1956 to 1975.

4127   Auerbach, Isaac L. "Society for Industrial and Applied
       Mathematics (SIAM)," in Anthony Ralston and Chester
       L. Meeks (eds), Encyclopedia of Computer Science (New
       York: Petrocelli/Charter, 1976): 1282-1283.

       This is a history of SIAM from 1952 to 1975.

4128   Auerbach, Isaac L. "The Start of IFIP—Personal
       Recollections," Annals of the History of Computing
       8, No. 2 (April 1986): 180-192.

       This illustrated article is a key publication on
       IFIP (International Federation for Information Pro-
       cessing), covering the years 1955 to the early 1960s.

4129   Data Processing Management Association. This Is DPMA.
       Park Ridge, Ill.: DPMA, 1983.

       This describes the mission and history of DPMA, 1949
       to 1983.

4130   Harris, F.H. "Institute for Certification of Computer
       Professionals (ICCP)," in Anthony Ralston and Chester
       L. Meeks (eds), Encyclopedia of Computer Science
       (New York: Petrocelli/Charter, 1976): 710-711.

       Surveys ICCP from 1973 to 1975.

4131   IEEE. A Centennial Guide to Electrical Engineering
        History for the IEEE. New York: Center for the His-
        tory of Electrical Engineering, 1983.

        This includes histories of the American Institute of
        Electrical Engineers (AIEE), the Institute of Radio
        Engineers (IRE), and their merger into the IEEE.

4132   Korzeniowski, Paul. "NCC Past to Present: A Barometer
        of Industry Progress," Computerworld (July 8, 1985):
        Preview/8.

        This is a history of NCC from its creation in 1973
        to 1985. It was the U.S. DP industry's biggest com-
        puter exhibit and conference.

4133   Lees, R.B. History of USE Inc: 1955-1980. Bladensburg,
        Md.: USE Inc., 1980.

        This is an illustrated history of the Univac users
        group.

4134   Mahoney, Eileen. "Negotiating the New Information
        Technology and National Development: The Role of the
        Intergovernmental Bureau for Informatics" (Unpublish-
        ed Ph.D. dissertation, Temple University, May 1986).

        This is a major source on the International Computa-
        tion Centre from 1946 to 1961.

4135   "The Way It Was: A Glance Book," DM 14, No. 7 (July
        1976): 36-44.

        This is an illustrated history of DPMA (1951-76).

4136   Zemanek, H. (ed). A Quarter Century of IFIP. Amster-
        dam: North-Holland, 1986.

        These are the proceedings of the 25th anniversary
        deliberations of IFIP, Munich, March 27, 1985. He
        reports on the event in "A Quarter Century of IFIP,"
        Abacus 3, No. 2 (1986): 28-33, 57.

                              Europe

4137   Alexander, S.N. "European Experience with Electronic
        Computers," in Lowell H. Hattery and George P. Bush
        (eds), Electronics in Management (Washington, D.C.:
        University Press of Washington, D.C., 1956): 22-30.

        An American government official surveys building and
        use of computers of the 1950s in Britain, France,
        Germany, Holland and elsewhere.

4138   Berenyi, I. "Computers in Eastern Europe," Scientific
        American 223 (October 1970): 102-108.

        The subject covers the 1960s across all Eastern Europe.

4139   Bruijn, W.N. de. Computers in Europe, 1966.Amsterdam:
        Automatic Information Processing Research Center, 1966.

Surveys installations by country from 1955 to 1965.

4140   Bruijn, W.N. de. "Recent Developments in the European
        Market," Datamation 13, No. 12 (December 1967): 25-
        26.

        Details the number of installations of computers by
        country between 1965 and 1967.

4141   Computer Consultants, Ltd. Computers in Europe.
        Llandudno, Wales: Computer Consultants, Ltd., 1971.

        This is an important, detailed study of installa-
        tions and uses of data processing.

4142   Computer Consultants, Ltd. European Computer Survey.
        London: Pergamon Press, 1968.

        This is an important survey of the DP industry in
        Europe: installations, vendors and uses.

4143   "Computer Sales Soar in Europe," Business Week (April
        28, 1962): 63-64ff.

        Describes in large part U.S. sales to Europe.

4144   Connolly, J. History of Computing in Europe. New York:
        IBM World Trade Corp., 1967.

        This is a detailed history from Hollerith punch card
        days to the present with much material both on IBM
        and other vendors: their products, installations,
        organizations and by all countries.

4145   Council of Europe. The Computer Industry in Europe:
        Hardware Manufacturing. Doc. 2893. Brussels: Council
        of Europe, January 15, 1971.

        Surveys the DP industry in Europe, arguing that IBM
        dominates it. Describes what has been done to estab-
        lish national computer companies and recommends a
        united resistance to American imports.

4146   Datamation. "Datamation's International Computer Cen-
        sus," Datamation 8, No. 8 (August 1962): 46-48.

        Catalogs systems installed in the U.S., Benelux,
        France, Germany, Britain, Italy, Scandanavia as of
        July 1962 by vendor and by machine type.

4147   Dosi, Giovanni. Industrial Adjustment and Policy: II;
        Technical Change and Survival: Europe's Semiconductor
        Industry. Brighton, U.K.: Sussex European Research
        Center, 1981.

        This is an economic analysis, particularly useful
        for events of the 1960s and 1970s.

4148   European Economic Community. L'Industrie électronique
        des pays de la communauté et les investissements

Américains. Collection Etudes, Serie Industrié, No.
1. Brussels: European Economic Community, 1969.

EEC studied the size and role of the industry in
Europe and the activities of local governments in
support of national firms in the 1960s.

4149   García Santesmases, José. "Early Computer Developments
       in Madrid," Annals of the History of Computing 4, No.
       1 (January 1982): 31-34.

       Describes computing at the University of Madrid in
       the 1950s and 1960s.

4150   Hu, Y.S. The Impact of U.S. Investments in Europe: A
       Case Study of the Automotive and Computer Industries.
       New York: Praeger, 1973.

       Argues that the U.S. industry was more effective in
       claiming greater market share in the 1960s than local
       European vendors.

4151   Jequier, Nicolas. "Computers," in Raymond Vernon (ed),
       Big Business and the State: Changing Relations in
       Western Europe (Cambridge, Mass.: Harvard University
       Press, 1974): 195-228.

       Surveys the industry in Europe which he argues was
       dominated by U.S. firms in the 1960s and early 1970s.

4152   Kranakis, Eda. "Early Computers in the Netherlands,"
       CWI Quarterly 1 (1988): 61-84.

       This is a useful survey on Dutch activities where
       computing was an active field since the early 1950s.

4153   Lee, Wayne J. The International Computer Industry.
       Washington, D.C.: Applied Library Resources, Inc.,
       1971.

       Has data on the use of computers in different coun-
       tries.

4154   Mackintosh, Ian. Sunrise Europe: The Dynamic of Infor-
       mation Technology. Oxford: Basil Blackwell, 1986.

       Describes the discussion going on in Europe in the
       1980s concerning its computer industry's competi-
       tive posture.

4155   Malik, Rex. "The Real Time Club," Annals of the History
       of Computing 11, No. 1 (1989): 51-52.

       The author was a European computer journalist in the
       1960s and 1970s. He describes a group that met in-
       formally to focus on real time computing in Europe.

4156   Marczyński, R.W. "The First Seven Years of Polish
       Digital Computers," Annals of the History of Comput-
       ing 2, No. 1 (January 1980): 37-48.

This is an illustrated account of work done by the
author, 1946-59.

4157   Oblonsky, Jan G.   "The Development of the Research
        Institute of Mathematical Machines in Prague," Infor-
        mation Processing Machines 10 (1964): 15-24; Reprin-
        ted in Annals of the History of Computing 2, No. 4
        (October 1980): 294-298.

        Concerns Svoboda's work with computers in the 1950s
        and 1960s.

4158   O.E.C.D. Gaps in Technology—Electronic Computers.
        Paris: O.E.C.D., 1969.

        Argues that it is crucial for a local DP industry to
        exist and that currently IBM dominated it.

4159   O.E.C.D. Impact des entreprises multinationales sur les
        potentiels scientifiques et techniques nationaux.
        Industrie des ordinateurs et de l'informatique. Pre-
        pared by A. Michalet and M. Delapierre. Paris: O.E.C.
        D., 1977.

        Surveys European computer developments from the 1950s
        into the 1970s and the development of a European
        computer industry.

4160   "Philips Takes the Plunge; European Computer Market,"
        Business Week (June 22, 1968): 105.

        This announces that one of Europe's largest electron-
        ics firms is entering the computer business and why.

4161   Salton, G.   "Automated Information Processing in West-
        ern Europe," Science 144 (May 8, 1964): 626-632.

        Describes trends evident in the early 1960s.

4162   Schwarz, H.R.   "The Early Years of Computing in Swit-
        zerland," Annals of the History of Computing 3, No.
        2 (April 1981): 121-132.

        This is an illustrated account, beginning with 1950
        and the Z-4 then about the ERMETH, down to 1962.

4163   Sharp, Margaret (ed). Europe and the New Technologies.
        London: Frances Pinter, 1985.

        Contains an assessment of Europe's computer science
        capabilities and role in the 1970s and 1980s.

4164   Siekman, P.   "Now It's the Europeans versus I.B.M.,"
        Fortune 80 (August 15, 1969): 86-91ff.

        Describes growing resistance to IBM in Europe and
        response to the development of local DP companies.

4165   Svoboda, Antonin.   "From Mechanical Linkages to Electron-
        ic Computers: Recollections from Czechoslovakia," in

N. Metropolis et al. (eds), *A History of Computing in the Twentieth Century* (New York: Academic Press, 1980): 579-586.

This is an illustrated memoir of 1937-1954 and about the SAPO computer.

4166   "Taking the Hard Sell to Eastern Europe; Incomex 66 Exhibit in Czechoslovakia," *Business Week* (June 4, 1966): 34-36.

Contains comments on computing there in the 1960s.

4167   Von Weiher, S. and Goetzeler, H. *The Siemens Company: Its Historical Role in the Progress of Electrical Engineering*. Munich: Bruckmann, 1984.

This is a company history, contains material on its role with computers, and data processing activities in Germany during the 1970s and 1980s.

4168   "Why GE Is Joining Olivetti; Hopes to Get European Computer Market," *Business Week* (September 12, 1964): 140ff.

Creating partnerships was common in the industry; this was an early important example described here.

4169   Zemanek, H. "Computer Prehistory and History in Central Europe," *Proceedings 1976 National Computer Conference AFIPS Conference Proceedings* 45 (Montvale, N.J.: AFIPS Press, 1976): 15-20.

This is primarily on Austrian automata, punched cards and the work of Otto Schäffler.

France

4170   Bellan, Bertrand et al. *L'Industrie en France*. Paris: Flammarion for the Centre de Recherche en Économie Industrielle, 1983.

Contains material on the size, nature and activities of the DP industry in France during the 1970s and early 1980s.

4171   "Bull at the Alter; Deal with Machines Bull," *Fortune* 70 (September 1964): 59-60ff.

Describes the early relations between GE and Bull.

4172   Bransten, T.R. and Brown, S.H. "Machines Bull's Computer Crisis; France's Proud Business Machine Firm," *Fortune* 70 (July 1964): 154-155.

At the time the firm was not considered competitive. This is a survey of its activities in the 1960s.

4173   France, Commissariat General du Plan. *V Plan 1966-1970: Electronique*. Paris: La Documentation Française, 1966.

Surveys who acquired French output and the plans to
encourage the development of a local computer industry in France.

4174   France, Ministère de l'Industrie et de la Recherche.
        Composant électronique. Paris: La Documentation Fran-
        çaise, 1976.

        This contains a great deal of material on semiconduc-
        tor activities in France during the 1960s and 1970s.

4175   "French Computer Industry Faces Dilemma," Aviation
        Week 86 (May 29, 1967): 317-319.

        This is a useful contemporary discussion of what
        role the French DP industry should play.

4176   "Gallic Thrust at IBM; Iris, All-French Computer,"
        Business Week (October 5, 1968): 77.

        This is valuable as a contemporary statement of
        French concern that IBM would dominate the local DP
        industry.

4177   "Gamma Invasion; Compagnie des Machines Bull," Fortune
        59 (April 1959): 78ff.

        More than a discussion of the Gamma series of comput-
        ers, this surveys the role of Machines Bull and on
        the French DP industry.

4178   Gandouin, Jacques. Correspondance et rédaction admin-
        istratives. Paris: A. Colin, 1966.

        Has material on office equipment, telecommunications,
        and on the French postal system of the 1960s.

4179   Jublin, Jacques and Quatrepoint, Jean-Michel. French
        Ordinateurs—de l'affaire Bull a l'assassinat du Plan
        Calcul. Paris: Editions Alain Moreau, 1976.

        This is a detailed study of the French computer busi-
        ness. Although not well documented, it is the only
        useful narrative of events of the 1950s and 1970s
        currently available.

4180   Le Bolloch, C. "L'intervention de l'Etat dans l'Indus-
        trie Eléctronique en France de 1974 à 1981" (Unpub-
        lished Ph.D. dissertation, Université de Rennes I,
        VER de Sciences Economiques, 1983).

        Focus is on French government actions taken to bol-
        ster a national computer industry in the 1970s.

4181   Lorenzi, Jean-Hervé and Le Boucher, Eric. Mémoires
        Volées. Paris: Editions Ramsay, 1979.

        Describes the French industry of the 1960s and 1970s
        and the role played by the French government to support
        a local industry.

4182   Pottier, C. and Touati, P.Y.   "Concurrence internion-
        ale et localisation de l'industrie des semi-conduc-
        teurs en France," EEE 24 (1981): whole issue.

        Contains data on French semiconductor production in
        the 1960s and 1970s.

4183   Poulain, Pierre. Éléments foundamentaux de l'informa-
        tique. 2nd ed. Paris: Dunod, 1968. 2 vols.

        Describes the use of data processing quipment and
        other related devices available in France during
        the 1950s and 1960s, with examples.

4184   Samuel, Arthur L.   "Computers with European Accents,"
        1957 Proceedings of the Western Joint Computer Con-
        ference (New York: Institute of Radio Engineers,
        1957): 14-17.

        Includes discussion of the French CUBA computer of
        the late 1950s and its use in French defense.

4185   Truel, J.L.   "Structuration en filière et politique
        industrielle dans l'électronique: une comparison
        internationale," Revue d'Economie Industrielle No.
        23, I° trim. (1983): 293-303.

        This is on European government policies aimed at
        fostering local high-technology industries and in-
        cludes material on French activities of the 1970s
        and early 1980s.

4186   Walsh, J.   "France: First the Bomb, Then the Plan
        Calcul," Science 156 (May 12, 1967): 767-770.

        Describes the French plan to foster a national DP
        industry.

4187   Wierzynski, G.H.   "G.E.'s $200-Million Ticket to
        France," Fortune 75 (Jun 1, 1967): 92-95.

        Narrates the merger of GE and Machines Bull DP
        activities in Europe.

                              Germany

4188   Breitenacher, M. et al. Elekstrotechnische Industrie.
        Munich: IFO-Institut für Wirtschaftsforschung, 1974.

        Focus is on the German semiconductor/computer indus-
        try of the 1960s and 1970s.

4189   Federal Republic of Germany, Bundersministerium für
        Forschung und Techbologie (BMFT). Informationstech-
        nik. Bonn: BMFT, 1984.

        Discusses German data processing industry of the
        1970s and 1980s.

4190   Haake, Rolf. Einführung in die Informations- und

Dokumentationstechnik unter besonderer Berücksichti-
gung der Lochkarten. Leipzig: Bibliographisches
Institute, 1965.

Surveys office equipment and punch card systems
available in Germany during the early 1960s and is
illustrated.

4191   Kloten, N. et al. Der EDV-Market in der Bundes Repub-
lik Deutschland. Tübingen: Mohr, 1976.

Details the structure and size of the German computer industry of the 1970s.

4192   Lehmann, N.J. "Bericht über den Entwurf eines Kleinen
Rechenautomaten an der Technischen Hockschule Dresden," Ber. Math. Tagung (January 1953): 262-270.

Narrates post-World War II developments at the Technische Hoshschule Dresden (1948-1950s).

4193   Lewicki, A. Einführung in die Mikroelektronik. Munich:
R. Oldenburg, 1966.

Reviews early German semiconductor activities.

4194   Rösner, A. Die Wettbewerbverhältnisse auf der Markt
fur elektronische Datenverarbeitungsanlagen in der
BRD. Berlin: Duncker-Humblot, 1978.

This is a survey of the German electronics world of
the 1970s with considerable attention paid to the
computer market.

4195   Stibic, Vladimir. Wege von der Mechanisierung zur
Automatisierung der Verwaltungsarbeit. Berlin: Verlag
Die Wirtschaft, 1962.

This lengthy publication surveys office and DP equipment available in Germany in the late 1950s and early
1960s; includes a bibliography of German sources.

4196   "Successful Stripling; Nixdorf," Time 91 (May 17, 1968):
91-92.

This is an early American account of Nixdorf and of
its activities.

4197   Walther, Alwin. "German Computing," Datamation 6
(September 1960): 27ff.

This is an early article surveying the German computer industry of the 1950s and describes the activities
of Zuse, Brown Bovieri Mannheim and Siemens.

4198   "Wunderkind Sprints in Computers," Business Week (November 2, 1968): 76ff.

Comments on the West German industry of the 1960s.

Great Britain

4199   Booth, Andrew D. "Computers in the University of Lon-
        don, 1945-1962," in N. Metropolis et al (eds), A
        History of Computing in the Twentieth Century (New
        York: Academic Press, 1980): 551-561.

        This is a memoir of activities involving ARC, APEX,
        MAC, and the M3; illustrated.

4200   Bowden, Lord. "The Language of Computers," American
        Scientist 58 (January-February 1970): 43-53.

        Offers material on the Ferranti computer firm.

4201   Campbell-Kelly, M. "ICL Company Research and Develop-
        ment, Part I, 1904-1959," ICL Technical Journal 5
        (May 1986): 2-17.

        This is a history of ICL's origins.

4202   "Computer Giants Wed in Britain; International Computers
        & Tabulators, Ltd., and English Electric Computers,
        Ltd.," Business Week (March 30, 1968): 62.

        This was a major event in the history of British
        data processing; this is a contemporary account.

4203   Dickson, K. "The Influence of Ministry of Defense
        Funding on Semiconductor Research and Development in
        the United Kingdom," Research Policy 12, No. 2
        (1973): 113-120.

        British agencies attempted to bolster their industry
        in the 1970s with little effect. This is a descrip-
        tion of the effort in its early stages.

4204   Edwards, D.B.C. "Computer Developments in Great Bri-
        tain," Computers and Their Future (llandudno: Richard
        Williams and Partners, 1970): 1/1-1/21.

        Focus is on events at Manchester University and about
        the Williams tube of the 1940s and 1950s.

4205   Great Britain. Integrated Data Processing and Comput-
        ers. London: H.M. Stationery Office, 1960.

        This is an OEEC study reviewing the state of Britain's
        DP industry as of 1959; thorough and critical.

4206   Great Britain, Treasury, Organisation and Methods Divi-
        sion. Machines and Appliances in Government Offices.
        Rev. ed. London: H.M. Stationery Office, 1954.

        This is a small, illustrated study on British comput-
        ing of the early 1950s.

4207   Greene, C.A. Everard. The Beginnings: Reminiscences
        of C.A. Everard Greene. London: The British Tabulat-
        ing Machine Co., 1936.

The author was the chief executive officer of BTM in
the early 20th century; these are his memoirs.

4208   Hendry, John. "Prolonged Negotiations: The British
        Fast Computer Project and the Early History of the
        British Computer Industries," Business History 26
        (November 1984): 286-300.

        Argues that the history of British computing in the
        1960s and 1970s is very much a story of firms con-
        solidating and of joint projects, some of which began
        in the 1950s and are described here.

4209   Hendry, John. "The Teashop Computer Manufacturer: J.
        Lyons, Leo and the Potentials and Limits of High-
        Tech Diversification," Business History 29 (1987):
        66-72.

        This is a history of the first British company to
        market computers. Its first product was Leo.

4210   Hills, J. Information Technology and Industrial Poli-
        cy. London: Croom Helm, 1984.

        Focus is primarily on British events and government
        attitudes toward this technology in the 1970s and
        1980s.

4211   Kraus, Jerome. "The British Electron-Tube and Semi-
        conductor Industry, 1935-62," Technology and Culture
        9, No. 4 (October 1968): 544-561.

        This well-researched article includes material on
        radio, television, microelectronics and an overview
        of the British electronics industry.

4212   Locksley, Gareth. A Study of the Evolution of Concen-
        tration in the U.K. Data Processing Industry with
        Some International Comparisons. Luxumbourg: Office
        for Official Publications of the European Communi-
        ties, 1983.

        This was one of a series of publications on Europe's
        competitiveness in the world economy.

4213   Miller, Harry. The Way of Enterprise: A Study of the
        Origins, Problems and Achievements in the Growth of
        Post-War British Firms. London: Andre Deutsch, 1963.

        Contains a history of Elliott-Automation, Ltd. (pp.
        25-29) and comments on the structure of British firms
        in general.

4214   Moonman, Eric (ed). British Computers and Industrial
        Innovation: The Implications of the Parliamentary
        Select Committee. London: Geoerge Allen and Unwin,
        1971.

        This comments on the British computing industry of
        the 1960s.

4215   Ross-Skinner, J. "British Computers: We Will Survive;
        International Computers, Ltd.," Duns Review 94
        (December 1969): 62-64ff.

        This is more an analysis of IC's activities in the
        late 1960s than a survey of its history.

4216   Schnee, J. "Government Programs and the Growth of
        High-Technology Industries," Research Policy 7 (1978):
        2-24.

        Discusses the British computer market from the 1950s
        to the mid-1970s and the role of the U.K. Government.

4217   United Kingdom, Civil Service Department. Computers
        in Central Government Ahead. Management Study 2.
        London: H.M. Stationery Office, 1971.

        Whilt eht thrust is on the future, this does catalog
        computers then in use within the British government
        and their applications.

4218   United Kingdom, Department of Employment. Computers in
        Offices, 1972. London: H.M. Stationery Office, 1972.

        Includes data on what was installed and for what
        uses, and impact on people.

4219   United Kingdom, House of Commons, Select Committee on
        Science and Technology. Session 1969-70, United King-
        dom Computer Industry. 2 vols. London: H.M. Station-
        ery Office, 1970.

        The subject is the DP industry's prospects in the
        1970s in Britain what the government's role should
        be. Includes testimony from many segments of Britain's
        DP industry.

4220   United Kingdom, House of Commons, Select Committee on
        Science and Technology. Session 1970-71, The Pros-
        pects for the UK Computer Industry in the 1970s,
        Fourth Report. 3 vols. London: H.M. Stationery Office,
        1971.

        Continues the work of the previous citation; recommends
        more pro-active government role, particularly in R&D.

4221   Williams, N. "Early Computers in Europe," Proceedings
        1976 National Computing Conference. AFIPS Conference
        Proceedings 45 (Montvale, N.J.: AFIPS Press, 1976):
        21-29.

        Contains material on the development of LEO.

4222   Womersley, J.R. "Scientific Computing in Great Bri-
        tain," Mathematical Tables and Other Aids to Comput-
        ing 2 (1946): 110-117.

        This is on the use of commercial devices for scienti-
        fic applications in Great Britain.

Honeywell

4223   "Challenging the Jolly Grey Giant: Honeywell Competes
       with IBM," Time 99 (January 3, 1972): 62-63.

       Describes Honeywell's marketing efforts in the U.S.

4224   "GE and Honeywell Test Their Match," Business Week
       (May 30, 1970): 30-31.

       Describes their plans to work together in the 1970s.

4225   Henkel, Tom. "Research Acquistions Tell Honeywell's
       Tale," Computerworld (September 9, 1985): 95, 98-99.

       This is a general history of the firm.

4226   Honeywell Inc., Plaintiff vs. Sperry Rand Corporation
       and Illinois Scientific Developments, Inc., Defen-
       dants File No. 4-67. Civ. 138. Minnesota. Minneapo-
       lis, Minn.: U.S. District Court, District of Minne-
       sota, 1973.

       This has a wealth of information on both companies
       from the 1950s into the 1970s.

4227   Spencer, Edson W. Honeywell After 100 Years. New York:
       Newcomen Society of the United States, 1985.

       The author was chairman and chief executive officer
       of the company in the 1980s; an illustrated history.

IBM

4228   "Another Great Divide; Major Lawsuits Against IBM,"
       Forbes 103 (February 1, 1969): 15-17.

       Describes lawsuits brought on by competitors in U.S.
       courts in the 1960s.

4229   Bakis, H. IBM: une multinational regionale. Grenoble:
       Université de Grenoble, 1977.

       Focus is on IBM in Europe's semiconductor and DP
       industries of the 1970s.

4230   Barratt, G.M. (ed). IBM Hursley: The First 25 Years—
       A Festschrift. Hursley, U.K.: IBM Corporation, 1983.

       This is a collection of 14 papers (1961-83), all
       technical, on activities of the lab, such as SCAMP
       and PL/1.

4231   Belden, T.G. and Belden, M.R. The Lengthening Shadow:
       The Life of Thomas J. Watson. Boston: Little, Brown
       & Co., 1962.

       This is the first major biography on Watson, the
       founder of IBM.

4232   Beman, L. "IBM's Travails in Lilliput," _Fortune_ 88
        (November 1973): 148-150.

        Describes IBM's antitrust problems of the early
        1970s.

4233   Bigelow, R.P. "U.S. Versus IBM: An Exercise in Futi-
        lity," _Abacus_ 1, No. 2 (1984): 42-55.

        The author is a lawyer and survey's the major case
        and argues in favor of IBM.

4234   Brennan, J.F. _The I.B.M. Watson Laboratory at Colum-
        bia University: A History_. Armonk, N.Y.: IBM Corp.,
        1971.

        Based on the lab's archives and taped interviews,
        this is a 68-page history from the 1930s to 1970
        with special emphasis on the development of the IBM
        610 Autopoint Computer.

4235   Burck, G. "Assault on Fortress I.B.M.," _Fortune_ 69
        (June 1964): 112-116ff.

        The commentary is on competitive pressures.

4236   "Computer Sales Soar in Europe," _Business Week_ (April
        1962): 63-64ff.

        Much of the story is about IBM's successes in Europe.

4237   DeLamarter, Richard T. _Big Blue: IBM's Use and Abuse
        of Power_. New York: Dodd, Mead & Co., 1986.

        This hostile account of IBM argues that it has a
        stranglehold on the DP industry, using data on the
        1960s to generalize on the 1980s weakly.

4238   Dixon, J.M. "IBM Thinks Twice; Building Policies,"
        Architectural Forum 124 (March 1966): 32-39.

        IBM was a major landlord with hundreds of facilities
        in the U.S. during the twentieth century; its practi-
        ses on real estate are described.

4239   Doherty, W.J. and Pope, W.G. "Computing As a Tool for
        Human Augmentation," _IBM Systems Journal_ 25, Nos.
        3-4 (1987): 306-320.

        Describes the growth in the use of computing at the
        IBM Thomas J. Watson Research Center, Yorktown Heights,
        N.Y. since 1968.

4240   Drucker, Peter F. "Thomas Watson's Principles of Mod-
        ern Management," _Esquire_ (December 1983): 194-202.

        The author, a leading authority on business manage-
        ment, offers a very incorrect but positive biography
        of Thomas J. Watson.

4241   Engelbourg, Saul. International Business Machines: A
        Business History. New York: Arno, 1976.

        Originally written as a dissertation, with same tit-
        le, for Columbia University, 1954. It covers the
        period of Thomas J. Watson, 1914-1954.

4242   Fisher, Franklin M. et al. Folded, Spindled, and
        Mutilated: Economic Analysis and U.S. vs. IBM.
        Cambridge, Mass.: MIT Press, 1983.

        This is the most definitive study of the IBM anti-
        trust suit of the 1970s available.

4243   Fisher, Franklin M. et al. IBM and the U.S. Data Pro-
        cessing Industry: An Economic History. New York:
        Praeger, 1983.

        This is a 500-plus page history of many companies
        in the U.S. industry, not just about IBM. Covers the
        period from the late 1940s to 1980.

4244   Foy, N. The I.B.M. World. London: Methuen, 1974;
        Published in U.S. as The Sun Never Sets on IBM. The
        Culture and Folklore of IBM World Trade. New York:
        William Morrow and Co., 1975.

        This is a short history of IBM's operations in
        Europe down to the early 1970s.

4245   Gould, Heywood. Corporation Freak. New York: Tower
        Publications, 1971.

        This is a short description of IBM since the 1960s.

4246   Grosch, H.R.J. "The Way It Was 1957: A Vintage Year,"
        Datamation 18 (September 1977): 77-78.

        Argues that IBM was investing heavily in R&D, creat-
        ing a new level of sophistication in the market.

4247   Hochman, S. "Spy in the Computer Factory; A Visit to
        the Watson Research Center in Ossining, N.Y.," Look
        33 (March 4, 1969): 22.

        Describes the facility and its mission.

4248   "Impact of Two Historic Antitrust Decrees," Business
        Week (February 4, 1956): 26-27.

        The 1956 decree fundamentally influenced all market-
        ing at IBM down to the present. The other involved
        AT&T.

4249   "IBM: A Special Company," Think 55, No. 5 (September
        1989): entire issue.

        This is an illustrated history of IBM on the 75th
        anniversary of Watson, Sr., joining C-T-R.

4250   IBM Corporation. <u>Development of International Business Machines Corporation</u>. New York: IBM Corporation, 1936.

         This is an early history, beginning with Hollerith's tabulators, time recording etc., down to the 1930s.

4251   IBM Corporation. <u>Highlights of IBM History</u>. Armonk, N.Y.: IBM Corporation, 1971.

         This is a chronological history of IBM and of its products.

4252   IBM Corporation. <u>New Methods for Knowing</u>. New York: IBM Corporation, 1960.

         This is an illustrated introduction to the company and to its history and products.

4253   IBM Corporation. <u>Thirty Years of Management Briefings, 1958 to 1988</u>. Armonk, N.Y.: IBM Corporation, 1988.

         These are CEO pronouncements to the management team at large within IBM and reflects the management philosophy of the firm.

4254   "IBM's Growth Power," <u>Duns Review</u> 82 (July 1963): 33-35ff.

         This is a detailed analysis of the firm and of its potential as of the early 1960s.

4255   "International Business Machines Co.'s Robots That Read and Tabulate Reports," <u>News Week</u> 7 (February 8, 1936): 34-35.

         Contains financial data on IBM's performance during the 1930s with analysis.

4256   International Data Corporation. <u>IBM and the Courts: A Six Year Journal</u>. Waltham, Mass.: International Data Corp., March 1973.

         Describes the antitrust suits and the U.S. case against IBM.

4257   Kean, David W. <u>IBM San Jose: A Quarter Century of Innovation</u>. San Jose, Cal.: IBM Corporation, 1977.

         This is a history of the location primarily responsible for disk drive products from the early 1950s forward. Contains material also on the 701, 650, CPC, and NORC; strongest on the 1950s and illustrated.

4258   Killen, Michael. <u>IBM: The Making of the Common View</u>. New York: Harcourt Brace Jevanovich, 1988.

         Describes the decision making process at IBM that led to the announcement of Systems Application Architecture (SAA) in 1987.

4259   "Legacy of Enterprise," <u>Newsweek</u> 48 (July 2, 1956): 60-62.

This announces the death of Thomas J. Watson, head
of IBM.

4260   Maisonrouge, Jacques. Inside IBM: A Personal Story.
        New York: McGraw-Hill, 1988; originally published
        in French by Paris: Editions Robert Laffont, S.A.,
        1985.

        These are the memoirs of a senior IBM executive,
        covering the period 1940s to the early 1980s. He
        began in IBM France and ultimately worked at cor-
        porate headquarters.

4261   Malik, R. And Tomorrow the World: Inside IBM. London:
        Millington, 1975.

        This is a journalist's account of IBM's history
        and current role, with primary focus on Europe.

4262   Manarin, C. "FSD People and Their Part in Building
        the Trident Submarine," FSD Magazine 3 (1979): 2-7.

        FSD is the Federal Systems Division, the organization
        with responsibility of marketing to the U.S. Govern-
        ment within IBM.

4263   McCabe, R. "Women in Data Processing," National Busi-
        ness Woman 38 (September 1959): 6-7.

        Discusses women at IBM.

4264   McKenna, Regis. Who's Afraid of Big Blue? How Compa-
        nies Are Challenging IBM and Winning. Reading, Mass.:
        Addison-Wesley Publishing Co., 1989.

        The book is a description of strategic "errors" made
        by IBM in the 1970s and 1980s and how competitors
        are taking advantage of these, particularly high
        function work station vendors.

4265   McPherson, J.C. "Thomas J. Watson, Sr.," A. Ralston
        and CL. Meeks (eds), Encyclopedia of Computer Science
        (New York: Petrocelli/Charter, 1976): 1455-1456.

        This is a brief, illustrated biography of IBM's
        founder.

4266   Millis, D. Quinn. The IBM Lesson: The Profitable Art
        of Full Employment. New York: Times Books, 1988.

        This Harvard professor argues the case for full
        employment practises and cites how IBM preserved
        its during major reorganizations in the 1980s.

4267   Murphy, T. (ed). "Computer Communications Research at
        IBM Zurich," IBM Research Highlights No. 2 (1985):
        1-6.

        Begins with 1950 and carries through the creation of

the laboratory under Ambros P. Speiser, down to 1985.

4268   "New Answer Men; Systems Engineers," Business Week
        (November 10, 1962): 65-66.

        Describes the creation of the new position of SE at
        IBM, serving customers. The position has remained a
        significant one down through the 1980s.

4269   "1960: The Year Systems Engineering Began," Digest 4,
        No. 3 (May 1985): 7-11.

        The whole issue of DP Digest, an IBM publication,
        is devoted to the 25th anniversary of the IBM SE.
        The article is an illustrated history of the position.

4270   Patterson, W.D. "SR's Businessman of the Year: T.J.
        Watson, Jr.," Saturday Review 50 (January 14, 1967):
        74ff.

        The son of IBM's founder is reviewed, particularly
        IBM's introduction of the S/360.

4271   Phelps, Byron E. "Electronic Computer Developments at
        IBM," Annals of the History of Computing 2, No. 3
        (July 1980): 253-267.

        This is an illustrated history of IBM computer
        development from the IBM 603 (1942) through the
        early machines of the 1950s.

4272   "R&D Landmarks From the Labs and Plants of IBM,"
        Spectrum 2, No. 1 (1985): 23-27.

        This is an illustrated chart of developments from
        1937 to 1984 for processors, storage units, input
        and output equipment and software.

4273   Richardson, Frederick L.W. and Walker, Charles R.
        Human Relations in an Expanding Company; A Study of
        the Manufacturing Departments in the Endicott Plant
        of the International Business Machines Corporation.
        New Haven: Labor and Management Center, Yale Univer-
        sity, 1948.

        This monograph studied personnel practises at IBM's
        oldest U.S. plant, home for all manufacture of punch
        card equipment and R&D at the time.

4274   Rodgers, Francis G. "Buck" and Shook, Robert L. The
        IBM Way. New York: Harper and Row, 1986.

        IBM's Corporate Vice President for marketing during
        the late 1970s and early 1980s described how the
        firm marketed and sold.

4275   Rodgers, William. Think: A Biography of the Watsons
        and I.B.M. New York: Stein and Day, 1969.

        This was an early and better history of the company
        down to the late 1960s.

4276   "Science Research Association Sold to IBM for $62
        Million," Publishers Weekly 184 (December 30, 1963):
        33.

        SRA was the first significant acquisition of IBM
        since the end of World War II and during the 1960s.
        What IBM wanted to do with SRA is explained.

4277   Sheehan, R. "Q. What Grows Faster Than I.B.M.? A.
        I.B.M. Abroad," Fortune 62 (November 1960): 166-170ff.

        Surveys IBM's expansion into Europe during the late
        1950s.

4278   Sheehan, R. "Tom Jr.'s IBM," Fortune 54 (September
        1956): 112-119ff.

        This is one snapshot of IBM several months after the
        death of Watson, Sr., focusing on changes underway.

4279   Sobel, Robert. IBM. Colossus in Transition. New York:
        Times Books, 1981.

        This is the best general history of the company
        written by an historian and taking the story down
        through the 1970s.

4280   "Soldier; T.J. Watson," Time 68 (July 2, 1956): 68ff.

        This is a death notice and biography of IBM's founder
        who died in late June.

4281   "Tackling IBM; Antitrust Suit Filed by Control Data,"
        Time 92 (December 20, 1968): 77-78.

        This was one of the more important suits filed against
        IBM; this is a contemporary account of its initiation.

4282   Tate, Paul and Verity, John. "Under the Gun," Datama-
        tion 30 (September 1, 1984): 42-48.

        They describe the European Community-IBM agreement
        whereby IBM would share technical design details with
        mainframe competitors operating in Europe.

4283   "Thinking Man's Exhibit; IBM Pavilion at World's Fair,"
        Esquire 60 (October 1963): 118-123.

        Describes IBM's exhibit and high profile at this
        particular world's fair.

4284   "Thomas John Watson (1874-1956)," Think 22, No. 7
        (July, August, September 1956).

        The IBM company magazine presented a detailed review
        of the founder and of his company in an illustrated
        report.

4285   Verity, John W. and Schatz, Willie. "Fast Break in
        Armonk," Datamation 31 (January 1985): 68-74.

In reaction to the U.S. Government dropping its antitrust suit against IBM, the authors analyze the significance to the firm.

4286   Watson, Thomas J. "As a Man Thinks". Thomas J. Watson,
        The Man and His Philosophy of Life as Expressed in
        His Editorials. New York: IBM Corporation, 1954. An
        earlier edition was entitled As a Man Thinks (New
        York: IBM Corporation, 1936).

        These were anthologies of editorials, primarily from
        Think magazine.

4287   Watson, Thomas J. Human Relations. New York: IBM Corp-
        oration, 1949.

        These are his views on management issues.

4288   Watson, Thomas J. Men, Minutes and Money. New York:
        IBM Corporation, 1927, 1930, 1934.

        These various editions of over 880 pages were collec-
        tions of his speeches and articles.

4289   Watson, Thomas J., Jr. "The Greatest Capitalist in
        History," Fortune 116, No. 5 (August 31, 1987): 24-
        35.

        IBM's CEO and chairman (1950s-70s) recalls how he
        expanded the company into computers and how it evolv-
        ed. He announced he was writing his memoirs.

4290   Watson, Thomas J., Jr. "Managing Change," MGR. 1, No.
        1 (January 1986): 12-16.

        These are recollections of leadership at IBM and
        his thoughts on the subject of managing change.

4291   Weiner, J.B. "Apostle of Growth: The Unorthodox Mr.
        Watson," Duns Review 84 (November 1964): 33-34.

        In large part reviews the S/360 decision and other
        actions Watson, Jr., took.

4292   "Where IBM Looks For New Growth," Business Week (June
        15, 1968): 88-91.

        Describes some of IBM's actions in a period of enor-
        mous growth for the firm.

4293   Zientara, Marguerite. "The Story of IBM," in Steve
        Ditlea (ed), Digital Deli (New York: Workman Publish-
        ing, 1984): 284-285.

        This is a brief history of the company with focus on
        the role played by Thomas J. Watson, Sr.

Italy

4294   Brezzie, P. La Politica dell'Electronica. Rome: Editori
        Ruiniti, 1980.

The author surveys the Italian semiconductor industry
and the role of the Italian government for the 1970s.

4295   Fast. <u>Rapporto sulla microelettronica nazionale</u>. Milan:
       Fast, 1980.

       Does the same thing as the previous citation.

4296   Italy, Ministero dell'Industria. <u>Programma finalizzato</u>
       <u>Elettronica</u>. Rome: Ministero dell'Industria, 1979.

       This describes government programs to encourage the
       development of a national semiconductor industry in
       the 1970s and 1980s.

4297   Italy, Ministero della Ricerca Scientifica e Tecnolo-
       gica. <u>Programma Nazionale di Ricerca per la Micro-</u>
       <u>elettronica</u>. Rome: Ministero della Ricerca Scienti-
       fica e Tecnologica, 1983.

       Describes the efforts of the Italian government to
       support R&D in microelectronics in the early 1980s.

4298   Pertile, R. <u>L'industria dell'informatica e dei compon-</u>
       <u>enti elettronici: analisi delle prospettive e</u>
       <u>proposte di interveno</u>. Rome: ISPE, 1975.

       Although useful on Europe's semiconductor industry,
       it also offers material on Italy's own activities
       of the 1970s.

4299   Soria, L. <u>Informatica: un'occasione perduta</u>. Turin:
       Einaudi, 1979.

       Describes the Italian data processing world and, in
       particular, the semiconductor industry of the 1970s
       and early 1980s.

                                   Japan

4300   Beika, Minoru. <u>History of the Office Mechanization in</u>
       <u>Japan: From Business Mechanization to the Automation</u>
       <u>of Management</u> (in Japanese). Tokyo: Nippon Keiei
       Shuppankai, 1975.

       Covers the period 1892 to 1970 with focus on admin-
       istrative issues with details on what machines were
       made and used, impact of Hollerith and then computers.
       Includes a bibliography of 350 items, all in Japanese.

4301   Belady, Laszlo A. "The Japanese and Software: Is It
       a Good Match?," <u>Computer</u> 19, No. 6 (June 1986): 57-
       61.

       Surveys Japanese computer industry as part of his
       plenary address at Compcon Spring, 1986.

4302   "Chronological Chart of Digital Computers in Japan,
       Compared to those in Western Countries" (in Japanese)

FUJI 6, No. 4 (1955): 216.

Goes from the relay to the electronic computers (1940-1950s), especially Fujitsu events.

4303   Coran, Carl Louis. "The Role and Significance of MITI
       in the Economic Development of the Japanese Computer
       Industry" (Unpublished M.S. thesis, George Washing-
       ton University, School of Government and Business
       Administration, 1976).

       The Ministry of Trade and Industry (MITI) was the
       single most important organization in launching
       Japan's DP industry during the 1950s and 1960s.

4304   Electrotechnical Laboratory. Guide to ETL, 1983-1984.
       Tokyo: ETL, 1983.

       Describes the organization and mission of ETL which
       became part of MITI in 1952 and a major developer
       of Japanese computers.

4305   Fujitsu Limited. Fujitsu and the Computer Industry in
       Japan. Tokyo: Fujitsu Limited, 1983.

       Describes some of the firms activities in the 1970s
       and early 1980s.

4306   Gresser, Julian. "Japan's Industrial Policy and the
       Development of the Japanese Computer and Telecommu-
       nications Industry," in Subcommittee on Trade of the
       House Committee on Ways and Means, High Technology
       and Japanese Industrial Policy: A Strategy for U.S.
       Policymakers, 96 Cong. 2 sess. Washington, D.C.: U.S.
       Government Printing Office, 1980.

       Reflects concern in the U.S. Government with Japanese
       investments in computer R&D and studies possible
       impact on the U.S. DP industry in the late 1970s and
       early 1980s.

4307   Hatta, A. "A History and Future Trends of Computer
       Architecture at Nippon Electric Company (NEC),"
       Japan Information Processing Society, Computer Archi-
       tecture SIG Newsletter, No. 52 (March 7, 1984): 2 (in
       Japanese).

       Details the role of transistor technology in building
       Japanese computers in the late 1950s and early 1960s.
       NEC's involvement with computers is described.

4308   Helm, Leslie Donald. "The Japanese Computer Industry:
       A Case Study in Industrial Policy" (Unpublished M.A.
       thesis, University of California, Berkeley, 1978).

       This is a useful introduction to the subject for the
       1960s and 1970s.

4309   "The History of Fujitsu's Computers" (in Japanese) FUJI
       6, No. 4 (1955): n.p.

Includes 34 photographs to chronicle developments at this company from 1940 to 1956.

4310   Imai, James K. "Computers in Japan—1969," <u>Datamation</u> 16 (January 1970): 149-150.

Describes the market in Japan in 1968-69: vendors, customers and business volumes.

4311   International Data Corporation. <u>The Impact of Japanese Vendors as Partners and Competitors in the Worldwide Information Technology Market</u>. Framingham, Mass.: IDC, 1981. 2 vols.

This includes profiles of leading Japanese firms, case studies, applications, and assessment of Japan's technologies as of the start of the 1980s.

4312   Ishii, Osamu. "Research and Development on Information Processing Technology at Electrotechnical Laboratory —A Historical Review" (in Japanese) <u>Bulletin of the Electrotechnical Laboratory</u> 45, Nos. 7-8 (1981): <u>passim</u>.

ETL played a significant role in the development of Japanese computer technology in the 1950s and 1960s.

4313   Japan Electronic Industry Development Association (JEIDA) and Japan Electronic Computer Co. (JECC). <u>Japanese Computers</u>. English ed. Latham, N.Y.: Science and Technology Press, 1983.

Includes a chronology of Japanese computers, 1950-82.

4314   Japan Information Processing Center. <u>Computer Market in Japan</u>. Tokyo: JIPDEC, 1979.

This is a major source of statistical data on the Japanese data processing industry of the 1970s.

4315   "Japan's Computer Industry, Wait Till 1980," <u>Forbes</u> 104 (December 15, 1969): 36-37.

Describes Japanese intentions of invading the U.S. DP industry with goods by 1980.

4316   Johnson, Chalmers. <u>MITI and the Japanese Miracle:The Growth of Industrial Policy, 1925-1975</u>. Stanford, Cal.: Stanford University Press, 1982.

This is a very detailed and useful history of MITI and its impact on the Japanese computer world after 1950.

4317   Kimura, Tosaku. "Birth and Development of Computers," in <u>Natural Sciences and Museums</u> 46, No. 3 (1979): special issue on computers (in Japanese).

Contains material on Fujitsu, Toshiba, and Oki from the 1950s forward.

4318   Kobayashi, Koji. Computers and Communications: A Vision of C&C. Cambridge, Mass.: MIT Press, 1986.

Written by the CEO of NEC Corporation, this was originally published first in Japan. It contains material on the history of Nippon Electric Company from 1899 onward and also his views on technology at large.

4319   Levine, G.B. "Computers in Japan," Datamation 13, No. 12 (December 1967): 22-24.

This is a history of the DP industry in Japan from 1958 to 1967.

4320   Magaziner, Ira L. and Hout, Thomas M. Japanese Industrial Policy. London: Policy Studies Institute, 1980.

Focus is on the role of the Japanese government on R&D, particularly on computers in the 1960s and 1970s.

4321   Matuyama, T. "History of Computer Development in the Fujitsu Company" (in Japanese) Bulletin Information Processing Society of Japan 18, No. 7 (July 1977): 664-674.

Begins in 1935 with a counter and goes down through electronic computers (1957-77); bibliography included.

4322   National Research Council, Computer Technology Resources Panel. The Computer Industry in Japan and Its Meaning for the United States. Washington, D.C.: National Research Council, 1973.

This was an early look at the Japanese DP industry as a threat to the U.S.

4323   National Science Foundation. The Five-Year Outlook for Science and Technology 1981. 2 vols. Washington, D.C.: National Science Foundation, 1981.

It predicted extensive competition from Japan on data processing; has a great deal of useful data on the 1970s.

4324   Suekane, Ryota. "Early History of Computing in Japan," in N. Metropolis et al. (eds), A History of Computing in the Twentieth Century (New York: Academic Press, 1980): 575-578.

A very short account with emphasis on the 1930s and 1950s.

4325   Tahara, Soichiro. "IBM is a Tiger Turned Loose in a Field," Bungei Shanju 60 (September 1982): 94-105 (in Japanese).

This is an interview with Fujitsu's chairman, Taiya Kobayashi, in 1982, in which he describes how his firm competes against IBM around the world with Amdahl.

4326   Takahashi, Sigeru. "Early Transistor Computers in
        Japan," Annals of the History of Computing 8, No. 2
        (April 1986): 144-154.

        Describes machines developed primarily in the second
        half of the 1950s, most of which were Mark class.

4327   Takahasi, Hidetosi. The Birth of Electronic Computers
        in Japan. (in Japanese). Tokyo: Chuokoronsha Publi-
        sher, 1972.

        Covers the period 1944 to 1964 with an illustrated,
        detailed account of the technology, companies and
        ends with an analysis of the situation as of 1971.

4328   Takahasi, Hidetosi. "Some Important Computers of
        Japanese Design," Annals of the History of Computing
        2, No. 4 (October 1980): 330-337.

        Surveys the subject from 1950 to the mid-1960s.

4329   Tarui, Yasuo. "Japan Seeks Its Own Route to Improved
        IC Techniques," Electronics (December 13, 1965): 90-
        93.

        Describes early efforts with ICs in Japan during the
        mid-1960s, in large part as a response to the
        announcement of the IBM S/360.

4330   The Future Group. The Impact of Foreign Industrial
        Practices on the U.S. Computer Industry. Glastonbury,
        Conn.: The Futures Group, 1985.

        This has comments on European and Japanese practises
        of the 1980s regarding the U.S.

4331   U.S. Congress, Committee on Science and Technology.
        Background Readings on Science, Technology, and
        Energy R&D in Japan and China. Committee Print,
        Committee on Science and Technology, 97th Cong. 1
        sess. Washington, D.C.: U.S. Government Printing
        Office, 1981.

        This was one of many publications from the U.S.
        Government to come in the 1970s and 1980s studying
        the impact of Japanese Government support of its
        DP industry and impact on U.S. computer business.

4332   U.S. Congress, Joint Economic Committee. International
        Competition in Advanced Industrial Sectors: Trade
        and Development in the Semiconductor Industry.
        Washington, D.C.: U.S. Government Printing Office,
        February 18, 1982.

        This contains a great deal of information on the DP
        industry in Japan.

4333   U.S. Congress, Office of Technology Assessment. U.S.
        Industrial Competitiveness. Washington, D.C.: U.S.
        Government Printing Office, July 1981.

This is an analysis of the Japanese DP industry and its influence within the U.S. industry.

4334   U.S. International Trade Commission. Foreign Industrial Targeting and Its Effects on U.S. Industries, Phase I: Japan. Publication 1437 (October 1983). Washington, D.C.: U.S. Government Printing Office, 1983.

It contains a great deal of material on the activities of specific Japanese computer companies with respect to their activities in the U.S. during the late 1970s and early 1980s.

4335   Yamamoto, Takuma and Inoue, Naotoshi. "History of the Development of FACOM," in The Collection of Ikeda Memorial Articles: Centered on the Development of FACOMS.(in Japanese) Tokyo: Fujitsu, 1978.

This describes Fujitsu's early interest in computers dating to the 1950s, and initial developments with that technology.

4336   Yasaki, Edward K. and Pantages, Angeline. "Japan's Computer Industry," Datamation 22 (September 1976): 97-102.

This is a brief overview of its size and function and includes a description of its major organizations as of the early to mid-1970s.

National Bureau of Standards (NBS)

4337   Archibald, R.C. "The New York Mathematical Tables Project," Science 96 (1942): 294-296.

Describes projects at NBS directed toward World War II needs using calculating and punched card equipment.

4338   Aspray, William and Gunderloy, Michael. "Early Computing and Numerical Analysis at the National Bureau of Standards," Annals of the History of Computing 11, No. 1 (1989): 3-12.

Surveys the important role played by NBS in early U.S. computing (1938-50s).

4339   Blanch, G. and Rhodes, I. "Table-Making at the National Bureau of Standards," in B.K.P. Scaife (ed), Studies in Numerical Analysis: Papers in Honor of Cornelius Lanczos (London: Academic Press, 1974): 1-6.

The project involved preparing basic tables of exponential and circular functions using desk calculators and punch card equipment (1938-40s).

4340   Cochrane, R.C. Measures for Progress: A History of the National Bureau of Standards. Washington, D.C.: U.S. Department of Commerce, 1966.

Deals with all aspects of NBS, not just computers.

4341   Curtiss, John H.   "Federal Program in Applied Mathema-
        tics," Science 107 (March 12, 1948): 257-262.

        The U.S. Government sponsored the bulk of all Ameri-
        can R&D in computers in the late 1940s; that effort
        is described by one active in the process.

4342   Curtiss, John H.   "The Institute for Numerical Analysis
        of the National Bureau of Standards," Monthly Research
        Report of the Office of Naval Research (May 1951): 8-
        17.

        He describes some of the very early projects and
        mission of the INA.

4343   Curtiss, John H. (With foreward by E.U. Condon). "The
        National Applied Mathematics Laboratories—A Pros-
        pectus," Annals of the History of Computing 11, No.
        1 (1989): 13-30.

        This documented was originally drafted in 1947 to
        suggest thinking about how to get more involved in
        computing projects. It is an internal NBS report and
        describes the mission of the INA.

4344   Curtiss, John H.   "The Program of a Large Computation
        Center," Annals of the History of Computing 11, No.
        1 (1989): 31-41.

        Delivered as a specch on September 9, 1950. He dis-
        cusses projects at the NBS at a time when he was the
        Chief of the National Applied Mathematical Laborator-
        ies.

4345   Curtiss, John H.   "Some Recent Trends in Applied Mathe-
        matics," American Scientist 37 (1949): 587-624.

        Describes the use of computers and the creation of
        the INA.

4346   Householder, A.S.   "The Gatlinburgs," SIAM Review 16
        (1974): 340-343.

        Details early professional meetings on the use of
        computers in scientific work hosted by NBS in the
        1940s and 1950s.

4347   Kevles, D.J.   The Physicists. New York: Knopf, 1978.

        This includes a description of computational work
        done by the NBS during World War II with MIT.

4348   Lowan, A.N.   "The Computation Laboratory of the Nation-
        al Bureau of Standards," Scripta Mathematica 15
        (1949): 33-63.

        Contains a description of computation with calcula-
        tors and punch card equipment at NBS in the 1940s
        and prior work of the 1930s. It is a good snapshot
        of contemporary scientific/numerical projects.

4349   MTAC Editors. "News," Mathematical Tables and Other
        Aids to Computation 5 (1951): 65-68.

        Describes an early professional meeting in computing
        hosted by NBS.

4350   Salzer, H.E. "New York Mathematical Tables Project,"
        Annals of the History of Computing 11, No. 1 (1989):
        52-53.

        He describes the NBS project that ran from early
        1938 to mid-1939 involving the use of computational
        equipment to produce numerous tables.

4351   Todd, J. "Numerical Analysis at the National Bureau
        of Standards," SIAM Review 17 (1975): 365.

        Provides some details on early projects at NBS of
        the late 1940s and 1950s, along with an explanation
        of the origins of the INA.

4352   Weber, G.A. The Bureau of Standards: Its History,
        Activities and Organization. Baltimore: The Johns
        Hopkins Press, 1925.

        Contains a description of some computational projects
        dating back to World War I, using office calculating
        equipment. The survey covers 1917 to 1924.

                    National Cash Register (NCR)

4353   Allyn, Stanley C. My Half Century With NCR. New York:
        McGraw-Hill, 1967.

        This senior executive at NCR describes the company
        during the middle decades of the 20th century.

4354   Bernstein, Mark. "A Self-Starter Who Gave Us the Self-
        Starter," Smithsonian 19, No. 4 (July 1988): 125-135.

        While this illustrated biography of Charles Ketter-
        ing focuses on his automotive achievements, it does
        discuss his work for NCR.

4355   Boyd, Thomas A. Professional Amateur: The Biography of
        Charles Franklin Kettering. New York: E.P. Dutton,
        1957.

        Kettering was actively involved with NCR in the early
        years of the 20th century; these activities receive
        treatment in this biography.

4356   Boyd, Thomas A. (ed). Prophet of Progress: Selections
        from the Speeches of Charles F. Kettering. New York:
        E.P. Dutton, 1961.

        Primary focus is on his automotive achievements and
        concerns.

4357   Bridge, James (ed). The Trust: Its Book.New York:
        Arno, 1973.

NCR constantly participated in trust activities and
had monopolistic problems with the U.S. Department
of Justice. This book provides useful background on
the general problem.

4358   Crane, Frank. Business and Kingdom Come. Chicago:
        Forbes & Co., 1912.

        Reviews NCR and business ethics in general at the
        height of that company's legal problems with the
        U.S. Department of Justice.

4359   Crowther, Samuel. John H. Patterson, Pioneer in Indus-
        trial Welfare. Garden City, N.Y.: Doubleday, Page,
        1923.

        This is a biography of NCR's founder and a major
        influence on Thomas J. Watson's business practices
        at IBM. It covers activities of the late 1800s.

4360   The Federal Antitrust Laws with Summary of Cases Insti-
        tuted by the United States, 1890-1951. New York:
        Commerce Clearing House, 1952.

        Commonly known as the Blue Book, it discusses NCR
        just before World War I and its legal problems.

4361   Flint, Charles R. Industrial Combinations. New York:
        Crawford, Printer, 1892.

        This describes his views on the subject.

4362   Flint, Charles R. Memories of an Active Life: Men,
        and Ships, and Sealing Wax. New York: Putnam, 1923.

        Describes in part his role at NCR in its early years.

4363   Fugitt, C.T. "Work of the National Cash Register
        Company," Cassier's Magazine 28 (September 1905):
        339-359.

        Describes NCR in 1905 in considerable detail.

4364   Fuller, Frederick L. My Half Century As An Inventor.
        N.C.: Privately printed, 1938.

        Reviews his work from 1880s through the 1930s. He
        worked first for NCR and later for IBM on cash regis-
        ters and other office equipment.

4365   Henry, Thomas Conner. Tricks of the Cash Register
        Trust. Winchester, Ken.: Winchester Sun, Printer,
        1913.

        Contains a great deal on NCR's marketing efforts
        before World War I.

4366   Johnson, Roy W. and Lynch, Russell W. The Sales
        Strategy of John H. Patterson, Founder of the

National Cash Register Company. Chicago: The Dart-
neli Corp., 1932.

This is a very detailed study of NCR prior to the
1920s.

4367   Kneiss, H.E. "First Electronics Research Lab. Redis-
       covered," NCR Dayton 6, No. 3 (April 11, 1973): 1-3.

       This is a short, illustrated review of the Electronics
       Research Laboratory where work was done on the NCR
       Electronic Calculator Project.

4368   Larson, Henrietta M. Guide to Business History.
       Cambridge, Mass.: Harvard University Press, 1948.

       Contains references to both NCR and IBM.

4369   Leslie, Stuart W. Boss Kettering: Wizard of General
       Motors. New York: Columbia University Press, 1983.

       This is the best available biography of Kettering
       with some comments on his role at NCR.

4370   Marcosson, Isaac F. Colonel Deeds: Industrial Builder.
       New York: Dodd, Mead, 1947.

       He was the senior executive at NCR in the 1930s and
       had been involved with the firm in one fashion or
       another since the start of the century; a biography.

4371   Marcosson, Isaac F. Wherever Men Trade. New York:
       Dodd, Mead, 1948.

       This is an early history of NCR.

4372   National Cash Register Company. NCR: Celebrating the
       Future, 1884-1984. Dayton, Ohio: NCR, 1984.

       This a collection of four well written, highly
       illustrated pamphlets on NCR. This represents the
       most complete history of the company available.

4373   Stevens, W.S. "Group of Trusts and Combinations,"
       Quarterly Journal of Economics 26 (August 1912):
       625-630.

       The focus is on NCR and its activities prior to
       World War II.

4374   "Three N.C.R. Pioneers Cited by Smithsonian for Elec-
       tronics Work," NCR Dayton 6, No. 3 (1973): 1, 3.

       Describes the careers of Joseph Desch and Robert
       Mumma who worked on NCR electronics, 1938-42, and
       on Don E. Eckdahl, head of MADDIDA project on an
       analyzer, complete in 1949.

4375   Whitney, Simon N. Antitrust Policies. New York: The

Twentieth Century Fund, 1958. Volume 2.

Includes material on NCR in the second volume.

4376   Work, E.W. "Trouble in the Cash Register Works,"
        Independent 53 (June 13, 1910): 1371-1373.

        This is a very early article on the cash register
        business in the U.S. in which NCR was already a
        major vendor.

                                RCA

4377   Rajchman, Jan. "Early Research on Computers at RCA,"
        in N. Metropolis et al (eds), A History of Computing
        in the Twentieth Century (New York: Academic Press,
        1980): 465-469.

        Describes his own work between 1939 and 1950 briefly.

4378   Rajchman, Jan. R.C.A. Computer Research: Some History,
        and a Review of Current Work. Princeton, N.J.:
        David Sarnoff Research Center, R.C.A. Laboratories,
        1963.

        This is an 8-page on the origins of computer-related
        research at RCA in 1939. It was done primarily for
        military projects.

4379   Rajchman, Jan. "Recollections of Memories from RCA in
        the Fifties," Computer Museum Report 13 (Summer 1985):
        11-13.

        Describes research on computer memories from the
        late 1940s and early 1950s conducted by him.

4380   Sobel, Robert. RCA. New York: Stein and Day, 1986.

        This is a useful history of RCA written by a business
        historian who has also written about IBM.

                        Semiconductor Industry

4381   Bank of America. The Japanese Semiconductor Industry:
        An Overview. San Francisco: Bank of America, 1979.

        In addition to surveying the industry of the 1970s,
        this contains data on Japanese hand held calculator
        sales during the same period.

4382   Borrus, M. et al. U.S.-Japanese Competition in the
        Semiconductor Industry. Berkeley: Institute of Inter-
        national Studies, University of California, 1982.

        Focuses on Japanese threats to the U.S. industry with
        data from the 1970s.

4383   Braun, E. and MacDonald. Revolution in Miniature.
        Cambridge: Cambridge University Press, 1982.

This is the best single-volume history of semiconductors available. Well-researched, it describes the evolution of the technology and its economics and includes a detailed bibliography.

4384   Chang, Y.S. "The Transfer of Technology: Economics of Offshore Assembly: The Case of the Semiconductor Industry" (Unpublished thesis, College of Business Administration, Boston University, UNITAR, 1971).

This was an early study of the international nature of the industry.

4385   Charles River Associates. International Technological Competitiveness: Television Receivers and Semiconductors. Boston: CRA, 1979.

Contains data on production and sales volumes for both for the 1970s and analysis of market conditions in the U.S., Europe and Japan.

4386   Dosi, Giovanni. "Technological Change, Industrial Transformation and Public Policies: The Case of the Semiconductor Industry". Sussex: Sussex European Research Centre, University of Sussex, 1981.

Describes a technological paradigm for the solution of technical problems in this industry evident in the late 1960s and early 1970s.

4387   Finan, W. International Transfer of Semiconductor Technology Through U.S.-Based Firms. New York: National Bureau of Economic Research, 1975.

This is a detailed look at direct foreign investments in the semiconductor industry in the 1960s and 1970s.

4388   Finan, W. "The Semiconductor Industry's Record on Productivity," in American Prosperity and Productivity: Three Essays on the Semiconductor Industry. Cupertino, Cal.: Semiconductor Industry Association, 1981.

Finan is a serious student of the industry's economy and this article, like his book, is an important source for the period beginning in the 1950s.

4389   Finan, W. and LaMond, Annette M. "Sustaining U.S. Competitiveness in Microelectronics: The Challenge to U.S. Policy," in Bruce R. Scott and George C. Lodge (eds), U.S. Competitiveness in the World Economy (Cambridge, Mass.: Harvard Business School Press, 1985): 144-175.

4390   Flaherty, M.T. "Field Research on the Link Between Technological Innovation and Growth: Evidence from the International Semiconductor Industry" Graduate School of Business Administration, Harvard University

43 (1984) in <u>American Economic Review, Papers and Proceedings</u> 74 (May 1984): 67-72.

This helps expand our understanding of the role played by users of semiconductor components of such technology in the 1960s and 1970s.

4391   Forester, R. (ed). <u>The Microelectronics Revolution</u>. Oxford: Blackwell, 1980.

Covers all aspects of the issue, reflecting technical, economic and social analysis, circa 1970s.

4392   Fox, M.B.   "The Role of Finance in Industrial Organization: A General Theory and the Case of the Semiconductor Industry" (Unpublished Ph.D. dissertation, Yale University, 1980).

Argues that financial strategies were crucial for a nation's development of a high technology item. His dissertation contains a great deal of information on semiconductor economics from the 1950s through 1970s.

4393   Freund, R.E.   "Competition and Innovation in the Transistor Industry" (Unpublished Ph.D. dissertation, Duke University, 1971).

The author actually discusses all types of semiconductors from the 1950s to 1970.

4394   Fusfeld, H. and Tooker, J. <u>Status of French and German Electronic Industry</u>. New York: Center for Science and Technology Policy, 1980.

This is a useful survey in English with considerable amounts of data on volumes and structure of semiconductor business in these two nations.

4395   Golding, A.M.   "The Semiconductor Industry in Britain and United States: A Case Study in Innovation, Growth and the Diffusion of Technology" (Unpublished Ph.D. dissertation, University of Sussex, 1971).

This is particularly useful for early developments dating back to the 1930s and 1940s at, for example, GE and at Bell Laboratories.

4396   Hazewindus, N. <u>The U.S. Microelectronics Industry</u>. New York: Pergamon Press, 1982.

This review documents technical innovations affecting development of semiconductor components in the 1950s to the 1980s.

4397   Kleiman, H.   "The Integrated Circuit: A Case Study of Product Innovation" (Unpublished Ph.D. dissertation, George Washington University, 1966).

More than a technical study, this is an early analysis of semiconductor economics.

4398   Kraus, J. "An Economic Study of the U.S. Semiconductor
        Industry" (Unpublished Ph.D. dissertation, New School
        for Social Research, 1973).

        Focus is on the period from the 1950s through the
        1960s with observations on historical issues while
        defining current patterns of economic behavior.

4399   Lake, A. "Transnational Activity and Market Entry in
        the Semiconductor Industry" National Bureau of Econ-
        omic Research Working Paper No. 126. New York: Nat-
        ional Bureau of Economic Research, March 1976.

        This reflects early concern over Japanese activities
        that threatened the U.S. position in semiconductors.

4400   Lamborghini, B. and Antonelli, C. "The Impact of
        Electronics on Industrial Structure and Firms' Stra-
        tegies," in Microelectronics, Productivity and
        Employment (Paris: OECD, 1981): 77-121.

        Focus is on LSI activities in Europe with material
        particularly useful on Germany and Italy in the
        1970s.

4401   Linvill, J.G. et al. The Competitive Status of the
        U.S. Electronics Industry. Washington, D.C.: Nation-
        al Academy Press, 1984.

        Questions U.S. effectiveness in the 1980s by survey-
        ing trends of the 1960s and 1970s.

4402   Malerba, Franco. Technological Change, Market Struc-
        ture, and Government Policy: The Evolution of the
        European Semi-Conductor Industry. Madison: Univer-
        sity Press, 1985.

        He describes the growing irrelevance of Europe's
        semiconductor efforts in the 1970s and 1980s.

4403   NEDO. The Microelectronics Industry. London: NEDO, 1980.

        Focuses on European and U.S. features of the 1970s.

4404   Nomura, Research Department. Microchip Revolution in
        Japan. Tokyo: Nomura, 1980.

        This Japanese survey has data on local semiconductor
        activities of the 1960s and 1970s.

4405   OECD. Gaps in Technology-Electronic Components. Paris:
        OECD, 1968.

        Discusses the status of the semiconductor industry
        in Europe during the 1960s.

4406   Pavitt, K. Technical Innovation and British Economic
        Performance. London: Macmillan, 1980.

        This is a particularly useful study for understanding

the semiconductor industry's weak performance in
Great Britain from the 1940s to the 1980s.

4407   Pavitt, K. and Walker, W. "Government Policies Towards
        Industrial Innovation: A Review," Research Policy 5,
        No. 1 (1976): 11-97.

        They concentrate on scientific and technological
        factors that influenced the European semiconductor
        industry in the 1960s and 1970s.

4408   Sciberras, E. Multinational Electronics Companies and
        National Economic Policies. Greenwich, Conn.: JAI,
        1977.

        Contains data on British and European semiconductor
        activities of the 1960s and 1970s.

4409   Semiconductor Industry Association. The International
        Microelectronic Challenge. Cupertino, Cal.: Semi-
        conductor Industry Association, May 1981.

        This sounds the alarm that Japan would come to
        dominate the world's semiconductor industry if steps
        were not taken to protect the U.S. manufacturers.

4410   Tilton, John E. International Diffusion of Technology:
        The Case of Semiconductors. Washington, D.C.: Brook-
        ings Institution, 1971.

        This details many of the financial programs of the
        U.S. Government in support of the DP industry during
        the 1950s and 1960s.

4411   Truel, J.L. "L'industrie Mondiale des Semi-Conducteurs"
        (Unpublished Ph.D. dissertation, Université de Paris-
        Dauphiné, 1980).

        The author provides material and reasons for how the
        industry developed in different countries with empha-
        sis on Europe and the U.S.

4412   United Kingdom Department of Trade and Industry. A
        Programme for Advanced Information Technology: The
        Report of the Advey Committee. London: H.M. Stationery
        Office, 1983.

        Describes a British government program to support
        basic research on VLSI and CAD technologies in the
        1980s.

4413   United Kingdom Electronic Components Economic Develop-
        ment Committee. The Electronic Component Industry.
        London: U.K. Electronic Components Economic Develop-
        ment Committee, March 1983.

        Contains data on the poor working relations between
        various British government agencies fostering LSI
        business in Great Britain during the 1970s and early
        1980s.

4414   United Nations, Centre on Transnational Corporations.
       Transnational Corporations in the International
       Semiconductor Industry. New York: United Nations,
       1983.

       Surveys how they develop and argues that automation
       and software also affects, e.g., pricing and not
       just the evolution of solid state physics, 1960s-70s.

4415   U.S. Department of Commerce. Report on the Semicon-
       ductor Industry. Washington, D.C.: U.S. Government
       Printing Office, 1979.

       Documents product and process innovations of the
       1970s.

4416   U.S. Department of Commerce, Business and Defense
       Services Administration. Electronic Components:
       Production and Related Data, 1952-1959. Washington,
       D.C.: U.S. Government Printing Office, 1960.

       This is a useful source for statistics on volumes,
       particularly for the U.S. for the 1950s.

4417   U.S., Trade Commission. Competitive Factors Influenc-
       ing World Trade in Integrated Circuits. Washington,
       D.C.: U.S. Government Printing Office, 1979.

       This was one of many U.S. studies on the industry
       documenting the threat to it from Europe and
       especially from Japan.

4418   Von Hippel, E. "The Dominant Role of Users in Semi-
       conductors and Electronic Subassembly Process
       Innovation," IEEE Transactions on Engineering Manage-
       ment EM 24 (May 1977): 60-71.

       He argues that innovations which were not apprecia-
       ted by users were not used. He also defines the role
       they played in the 1960s and 1970s.

4419   Webbink, D.A. The Semiconductor Industry: A Survey of
       Structure, Conduct and Performance. Staff Report to
       the Federal Trade Commission. Washington, D.C.: U.S.
       Federal Trade Commission, 1977.

       This offers statistics on volumes of components
       shipped in the 1960s and 1970s.

4420   Wilson, R. et al. Innovation, Competition and Govern-
       ment Policy in the Semiconductor Industry. Cambridge,
       Mass.: Lexington Books, 1980.

       This is one of the better descriptions available of
       the industry of the 1960s and 1970s.

4421   Yoshino, Michael Y. and Fong, Glenn R. "The Very High
       Speed Integrated Circuit Program: Lessons for Indus-
       trial Policy," in Bruce R. Scott and George C. Lodge

(eds), U.S. Competitiveness in the World Economy
(Cambridge, Mass.: Harvard Business School Press,
1985): 176-184.

While dealing with collaborative government-industrial
programs in high technology fields, they also discuss
the U.S. industry of the 1970s and 1980s.

Society and Computers

4422   Anshen, Melvin and Leland, George (eds). Management
        and Corporations, 1985. New York: McGraw-Hill Book
        Co., 1960.

        This is a collection of 15 papers read at a symposium
        at Carnegie Institute of Technology by leaders from
        business, law, education, social sciences and religion
        on future trends as viewed from the late 1950s and
        early 1960s.

4423   Aspray, William and Beaver, Donald deB. "Marketing
        the Monster: Advertising Computer Technology," Annals
        of the History of Computing 8, No. 2 (April 1986):
        127-143.

        Their analysis is of 10,000 advertisements from 1950
        to 1980, examining this technology within a social
        context.

4424   Auerbach, Isaac L. "Impact of Information Processing on
        Mankind; An Address, August 27, 1962," Vital Speeches
        28 (September 15, 1962): 729-732.

        A leading figure in the industry projects enthusiasm
        of the early 1960s into a projection of things to
        come.

4425   Bannon, Liam et al. (eds), Information Technology:
        Impact on the Way of Life. Dublin: Tycooly, 1982.

        This is an example of a growing body of literature
        on the impact of computers on society at large. This
        one is useful for Europe of the 1970s and 1980s.

4426   Barron, Iann and Curnow, Ray. The Future with Micro-
        electronics. London: Pinter, 1979.

        This report was prepared for the British Government.
        It surveyed the penetration of computers and argues
        that chips would replace workers in massive numbers;
        a controversial report at the time of publication.

4427   Bell, Daniel. The Coming of Post-Industrial Society:
        A Venture in Social Forecasting. New York: Basic
        Books, 1973.

        This is a highly influential book in which Bell
        argues that industrial society is ·evolving into a
        new, post-industrial phase characterized in part by
        the use of computers.

4428   Bell, Daniel. "Introduction," in Simon Nora and
        Alain Minc, The Computerization of Society: A Report
        to the President of France (Cambridge, Mass.: MIT
        Press, 1980): vii-xvi.

        The book was a significant piece, the introduction
        an important statement from Bell. The father of the
        concept of post-industrial society raises the ques-
        tion of the role of computers in an electronically
        based society and called for social policies that
        took that reality into account.

4429   Bell, Daniel. "The Social Framework of the Informa-
        tion Society," in Michael L. Dertouzos and Joel
        Moses (eds), The Computer Age: A Twenty-Year View
        (Cambridge, Mass.: MIT Press, 1979): 163-211.

        He continues to define society as one with a heavy
        reliance on electronics and computers.

4430   Bibby, Dause L. "Computers and World Leadership;
        Address, December 12, 1961," Vital Speeches 28
        (February 15, 1962): 285-288.

        Bibby was the president of the Remington Rand Divi-
        sion of Sperry Rand Corporation and this was his
        address to the Eastern Joint Computer Conference in
        Washington, D.C., December 12, 1961. He argues that
        computers can make the U.S. more productive.

4431   Bjorn-Anderson, Nils et al.(eds). Information Society:
        For Richer, For Poorer. Amsterdam: Elsevier, 1982.

        This is a collection of essays which, like so many
        other books on the subject, survey the impact of
        computers on industrialized society since the 1960s.

4432   Bolter, J. David. Turing's Man: Western Culture in
        the Computer Age. Chapel Hill: University of North
        Carolina Press, 1984.

        Focuses on the intellectual consequences of comput-
        ers and compares its impact to that of other tech-
        nologies, such as mechanical, clocks and earlier
        developments.

4433   Booth, A.D. Automation and Computing. New York: Mac-
        millan, 1959.

        Often pithy, he comments on computers and society
        and includes a section on the history of computers.

4434   Burck, Gilbert. "Knowledge: The Biggest Growth Indus-
        try of Them All," Fortune (November 1964): 128-131ff.

        By the early 1960s economists were defining knowledge
        and information as a new economic sector.

4435   Brzezinski, Zbigniew. Between Two Ages: America's Role

in the Technetronic Era. New York: Viking Press,
1970.

Argues that we are evolving into a technocratic society in which the computer will play a dominant role as
society moves away from an industrial-based economy.

4436   Clark, Jon et al. The Process of Technological Change:
        New Technology and Social Choice in the Workplace.
        Cambridge Studies in Management. Cambridge: Cambridge
        University Press, 1988.

        This is the latest of many such studies defining the
        influence of technology economically; this one also
        addresses the issue of electronics.

4437   "Computer Age," Business Week (April 7, 1956): 52-56ff.

        This may be the first use of the phrase "Computer
        Age" in print.

4438   "Computer Society," Time 111 (February 20, 1978): 44-
        59.

        This is a detailed look at the influence of computers
        on American society/economy, circa 1970s.

4439   Daglish, Robert (ed). The Scientific and Technological
        Revolution: Social Effects and Prospects. Moscow:
        Progress Publishers, 1972.

        This is a rare Soviet view of computing in which is
        presented a forecast of a world order in which scien-
        ce and technology lead to a new era.

4440   Diebold, John. Automation: Its Impact on Business and
        Labor. Planning Document No. 106, A Special Committee
        Report. Washington, D.C.: National Planning Associa-
        tion, 1959.

        This 64-page report is Diebold's view of future trends
        in business organization and function due to computers.

4441   Einzig, Paul. The Economic Consequences of Automation.
        London: Secker & Warburg, 1956.

        His focus is on the technological and commercial
        consequences of automation on society.

4442   Forester, T. (ed). The Microelectronics Revolution.
        Cambridge, Mass.: MIT Press, 1981.

        This is a collection of 41 articles on the impact of
        computers on all aspects of society, a major work.

4443   Galbraith, John Kenneth. The New Industrial State.
        Boston: Houghton Mifflin, 3rd rev. ed., 1978; origi-
        nal edition, 1968.

        This well known U.S. economist argues that American

society is headed toward greater consolidation of
power under larger corporations made in part possible
by developments in electronics and computers.

4444   Gerola, Humberto and Gomory, Ralph E. "Computers in
Science and Technology: Early Indications," Science
225, No. 6 (July 1984): 11-17.

Argues that they are becoming more obvious in
science.

4445   Gill, Colin. Work, Unemployment and the New Technology.
Oxford: Polity Press, 1985.

Gill looks at the impact of computers in Great Britain, circa 1970s and 1980s.

4446   Havelock, Eric A. The Literate Revolution in Greece
and Its Cultural Consequences. Princeton, N.J.:
Princeton University Press, 1982.

The lessons of the Greek experience with one knowledge revolution is instructive on the effects of
DP-based information societies.

4447   Hawkes, Nigel. The Computer Revolution. New York:
Dutton, 1971.

The author characterizes the introduction of the
computer as a major watershed in western civilization which he then describes.

4448   Hofstadter, Douglas R. Gödel, Escher, Bach: An External Golden Braid. New York: Basic Books, 1979.

This is a philosophical mirror of Turing's man,
reflecting commonly held views about data processing in the 1970s.

4449   Hunt, Earl. "What Kind of a Computer Is Man?," Cogni-
tive Psychology 2 (1971): 57-98.

This argues the case that man is similar to an
electronic computer.

4450   Inose, Hiroshi. Information Technology and Civilization. New York: W.H. Freeman and Co., 1984.

Includes a short history of data processing. The
study was commissioned by the Club of Rome on opportunities and problems arising from changes in DP
technology.

4451   Jacobson, Howard Boone and Roucek, Joseph S. (eds).
Automation and Society. New York: Philosophical
Library, 1959.

Nearly three dozen contributors from government,
education, and industry review automation's past and

future. Includes 37 case studies of applications in
the U.S. and in Canada.

4452   Johnson, John E. "Effects of Automation in Industry
        in the United States," Proceedings, Second Annual
        Conference on Automation and Personnel Administration,
        Society for Personnel Administration Pamphlet No. 19.
        Washington, D.C.: Society for Personnel Administra-
        tion, June 1963.

        The real concern was whether such technology would
        place large numbers of workers out of jobs.

4453   Johnson, Walter H. Man and Automation. New Haven: Yale
        University Press, 1956.

        This is an early, pioneering work on the impact of
        automation.

4454   Jones, Barcy. Sleepers, Wake! Technology and the
        Future of Work. Melbourne, Australia: Oxford Univer-
        sity Press, 1982.

        Covers all manner of automation on work in the 1970s
        with futuristic statements included.

4455   Kendrick, John W. Productivity Trends in the United
        States. Princeton, N.J.: Princeton University Press,
        1961.

        This is a major attempt to identify the economic
        basis for the output by industry in the U.S. in the
        twentieth century.

4456   Lawson, Harold W., Jr. (ed). Symposium Proceedings:
        Man and Society—Automated Information Processing.
        Royal Swedish Academy of Engineering Science Confer-
        ence, Stockholm, August 13-17, 1979. Atlantic High-
        lands, N.J.: Humanities Press, 1979.

        All the discussions were set in an historical pers-
        pective: machines, people, and society.

4457   Lipstreu, Otis and Reed, Kenneth A. Transition to
        Automation. Series in Business No. 1, University of
        Colorado Studies. Boulder, Col.: University of
        Colorado Press, January 1964.

        This is an analysis of the process at work in the
        U.S., part of which involved the use of computers.

4458   Macey, Samuel L. Clocks and the Cosmos: Time in West-
        ern Life and Thought. Hamden, Conn.: Archon Books,
        1980.

        The impact of clocks on Europe was significant; the
        lessons learned from the effects of that technology
        are useful to those looking at computers and society.

4459   Machlup, Fritz. Knowledge: Its Creation, Distribution,

and Economic Siginificance. 2 vols. Princeton, N.J.:
Princeton University Press, 1980-1982.

This is a major study that identifies the tasks and
industries involved in information transfer in U.S.
society. These are quantified and measured in economic terms.

4460 Machlup, Fritz. The Production and Distribution of
Knowledge in the United States. Princeton, N.J.:
Princeton University Press, 1962.

This was the initial version of his study cited in
the previous entry.

4461 Martin, James. The Wired Society. Englewood Cliffs,
N.J.: Prentice-Hall, Inc., 1978.

Martin describes the expanded use of computers and
telecommunications in the Western world right into
the home, and the effects on society in general.
Martin has published over 30 books on data processing technology.

4462 Mathews, Walter M. (ed). Monster or Messiah? The
Computer's Impact on Society. Jackson, Miss.: University Press of Mississippi, 1980.

Has material on the history of computers, impact on
society in the U.S., current uses and effect on
Western values.

4463 McCorduck, Pamela. The Universal Machine: Confessions
of a Technological Optimist. New York: McGraw Hill,
1985.

She argues that computers are humane and civilized,
amplifying human qualities. This is heavily historical and philosophical.

4464 Michael, Donald N. Cybernation: The Silent Conquest.
A Report to the Center for the Study of Democratic
Institutions. Santa Clara, Cal.: The Fund for the
Republic, Inc., January 1962.

Defines cybernation as both automation and computers.
He reviews early 1960s' thinking about advantages,
problems and control of cybernation and impact on
society in a 48-page booklet.

4465 Mills, C. Wright. White Collar: The American Middle
Classes. New York: Oxford University Press, 1951.

This great American classic in sociology also has
comments on the effect of office automation on white
collar workers.

4466 Morison, Elting E. Men, Machines and Modern Times.
Cambridge, Mass.: MIT Press, 1966.

The dynamics of one to the other are under study,
teaching us lessons applicable to computers.

4467   Mowshowitz, Abbe. The Conquest of Will: Information
        Processing in Human Affairs. Reading, Mass.: Addison-
        Wesley, 1976.

        One of several publications by this author on the
        social and cultural implications of computers, circa
        1970s.

4468   Mumford, Lewis. Myth of the Machine. 1: Techniques and
        Human Development, 2: The Pentagon of Power. New
        York: Harcourt, Brace & World, 1967-1970; originally
        published beginning in 1934, Technics and Civiliza-
        tion (New York: Harcourt Brace, 1934).

        One of the greatest American social critics of the
        20th century takes a critical and negative view of
        society's future relationship with technology in
        general. In the earlier work he links technological
        development to the patterns of Western Civilization
        since the Middle Ages.

4469   Murphy, Brian M. Computers in Your Life. London: Hutch-
        inson, 1971.

        His focus is on the economic impact of computers on
        society, especially in Europe and in North America
        during the 1960s and 1970s.

4470   Nass, Clifford I. "Society as Computer: The Structure
        and Skill of Information Work in the United States,
        1900-1980" (Unpublished Ph.D. dissertation, Prince-
        ton University, 1986).

        This continues the line of research begun by Fritz
        Machlup (nos. 4459 and 4460).

4471   "New Computerized Age; Potentiality of Automation
        Revolution and Its Implications for Our Society,"
        Saturday Review 49 (July 23, 1966): 15-25.

        Reports on a symposium held on the topic in 1966.

4472   Nikolaiff, George A. (ed). Computers and Society. New
        York: H.W. Wilson, 1970.

        The author, a political scientist, focuses on the
        impact of computers on American society and upon its
        institutions with various effects noticed.

4473   Nora, Simon and Minc, Alain. The Computerization of
        Society: A Report to the President of France. Cambri-
        dge, Mass.: MIT Press, 1980.

        This is the English translation of an important
        report that documented the expansion of electronics
        and computers throughout French society in coming
        years.

4474   Pacey, A. _The Culture of Technology_. Cambridge, Mass.:
        MIT Press, 1983.

        Argues that technical people, such as those in data
        processing, accumulate and concentrate power and
        thus weaken society's ability to control a technology
        making it a danger.

4475   Parkhill, Douglas F. _The Challenge of the Computer
        Utility_. Reading Mass.: Addison-Wesley, 1966.

        This short book is a response to the growing availa-
        bility of computing on society and affect on its
        activities.

4476   Pask, Gordon and Curran, Susan. _Micro Man: How Comput-
        ers are Revolutionizing Our Lives_. London: Century,
        1982.

        They argue that the influence is profound and coming
        quickly. In the process they survey events of the
        1970s.

4477   Peitchinis, Stephen G. _Computer Technology and Employ-
        ment_. New York: St. Martin's Press, 1983.

        This reflects a continuing concern about how compu-
        ters might displace workers; focus is on U.S. condi-
        tions in the 1970s and early 1980s.

4478   Philipson, Morris H. (ed). _Automation: Implications
        for the Future_. New York: Vintage Books, 1962.

        This anthology reflects concerns in the U.S. during
        the late 1950s in education, science, government and
        business.

4479   Pylyshyn, Zenon W. (ed). _Perspectives on the Computer
        Revolution_. Englewood Cliffs, N.J.: Prentice-Hall,
        Inc., 1970.

        Contains material on Babbage, Aiken, von Neumann,
        Bush, Shannon, Turing, and George Forsythe—papers
        written by each.

4480   Pratt, Fletcher. "The Human Relations of Computers
        and Automation," _Computers and Automation_ (December
        1954): 6-7.

        Considers labor's views and hostility toward this
        new technology.

4481   Rennekamp, Eugene E. "A Study of the Individual's
        Attitude Toward a Computerized Informational Sys-
        tem" (Unpublished M.A. thesis, University of Iowa,
        1967).

        This was an early study on a crucial aspect of appli-
        cation development and installation.

4482   Rose, Michael. Computers, Managers and Society.
        Baltimore: Penguin Books, 1969.

        This is an early recognition of the interrelationship
        among all three, the subject of this management book.

4483   Rosenbrook, Howard et al. "A New Industrial Revolution,"
        in Bruce R. Scott and George C. Lodge (eds), U.S.
        Competitiveness in the World Economy (Cambridge,
        Mass.: Harvard Business School Press, 1985): 635-647.

        They review the English Industrial Revolution of
        1780-1830 and conclude that we are not undergoing a
        special revolution of equal importance because the
        new information age is not causing a new way of
        living to come about.

4484   Rothman, Stanley and Mosman, Charles. Computers and
        Society; The Technology and Its Social Implications.
        Chicago: Science Research Associates, 1972.

        This is sociology at the macro level: computers and
        civilization, circa 1960s and 1970s.

4485   Rubin, Michael and Huber, Mary Taylor. The Knowledge
        Industry in the United States, 1960-1980. Princeton,
        N.J.: Princeton University Press, 1986.

        This updates statistical data on the same theme
        which concerned other authors cited in this section
        of the Bibliographic Guide.

4486   Sackman, Harold (ed). Computers and the Problems of
        Society. Montvale, N.J.: AFIPS Press, 1972.

        Shows that computers can have a positive effect.

4487   Sackman, Harold. Computers, System Science, and Evolv-
        ing Society; The Challenge of Man-Machine Digital
        Systems. New York: John Wiley & Sons, 1967.

        This nearly 650-page book describes computers of the
        mid-1960s with emphasis on the social impact of
        automation.

4488   Sackman, Harold. Mass Information Utilities and Social
        Excellence. New York: Auerbach Publishers, 1971.

        Offers considerable amounts of DP history, circa
        1950s-1970s, and describes the roles of communica-
        tions and automation in society at large.

4489   Sackman, Harold and Nie, Norman (eds), The Information
        Utility and Social Choice. Montvale, N.J.: AFIPS
        Press, 1970.

        This is a collection of papers presented at an AFIPS
        conference held at the University of Chicago dealing
        with social aspects of communications, including data
        processing.

4490   Sanders, Donald H. Computers in Society. New York:
        McGraw-Hill, 1973.

        A prolific writer on DP management issues of the
        1970s and 1980s comments on what computers are in
        general and how they were being used in society.

4491   Shaiken, Harley. Work Transformed: Automation and
        Labor in the Computer Age. New York: Holt, Rinehart
        and Winston, 1985.

        He provides a useful survey of the concern and goes
        farther than most writers to illustrate how labor
        has used computers, rather than just fear them.

4492   Smith, Gordon. "Computers: Man's New Freedom; Address,
        November 8, 1960," Vital Speeches 27 (January 1,
        (January 1, 1961): 186-189.

        Smith was Director of Marketing, Univac and this
        his presentation at Emory University on the use of
        computers and how useful they had become.

4493   Star, J. "Computer Data Bank: Will It Kill Your Free-
        dom," Look 32 (June 25, 1968): 27-29.

        This was an early article, but only one of hundreds
        in the decade, on the issue of loss of privacy due
        to computer data banks in the U.S.

4494   Stock, Brian. The Implications of Literacy. Princeton,
        N.J.: Princeton University Press, 1983.

        Contains observations relevant to the social impact
        of new forms of information transfer using data
        processing technology.

4495   Svedberg, T. Man and Machine: A Public Lecture Deli-
        vered at the Rice Institute, May 21, 1946. Rice
        Institute Pamphlet 33, No. 2. Houston" Rice Insti-
        tute, 1946.

        This is a very early lecture on the general theme,
        one that would draw a great deal of attention by
        1950.

4496   Taviss, I. (ed). The Computer Impact. Englewood
        Cliffs, N.J.: Prentice-Hall, Inc., 1970.

        More than an application brief, it describes how
        computers were already part of society's activities.

4497   Toffler, Alvin. Future Shock. New York: Random House,
        1970.

        This was a widely-read book when it first appeared.
        It was his view of society's future, one filled with
        computers and telecommunications.

4498   Toffler, Alvin. The Third Wave. New York: Morrow, 1980.

Although as not widely-read a volume as his earlier
one, this continues the theme of social change. He
pays particular attention to the role of information
and the role of data processing in society.

4499   U.S. Congress, Subcommittee on Economic Stabilization
        of the Joint Economic Committee, 84th Cong., 1st sess.
        Automation and Technological Change, Hearings . . . .
        Washington, D.C.: U.S. Government Printing Office,
        October 1955.

        This is a very early collection of American comments
        on automation, containing testimony by officials
        from unions, government, universities and corpora-
        tions.

4500   Vallee, Jacques. The Network Revolution: Confessions
        of a Computer Scientist. Berkeley, Cal.: AND/OR
        Press, Inc., 1982.

        Describes information networks and impact on humanity
        as of the start of the 1980s.

4501   Weizenbaum, J. "On the Impact of the Computer on Soc-
        iety," Science 176 (May 12, 1972): 609-614.

        A leading artificial intelligence expert comments on
        broader social issues and computing.

4502   Whittington, Dale (ed). High Hopes for High Tech.
        Raleigh: University of North Carolina Press, 1986.

        While a survey of contemporary trends by various
        experts, it also reflects economic and social develop-
        ments of the 1980s.

4503   Wooldridge, Susan and London, Keith. The Computer
        Survival Handbook. Boston: GAMBIT, 1973.

        Reflects hostility toward computing's pervasive
        influence on society, a lash back, of limited sorts.

4504   Zuboff, Shoshana. In the Age of the Smart Machine:
        The Future of Work and Power. New York: Basic Books,
        1988.

        This is a sociological study of the computer age in
        the U.S. with comments on its economic, social and
        emotional influences.

Sperry

4505   Brown, S.H. "Univac Isn't A Business to Jump In and
        Out of," Fortune 71 (April 1965): 120-123.

        This analyzes the role of Univac in the late 1950s
        and early 1960s as a business.

4506   Hughes, Thomas Parke. Elmer Sperry: Inventor and

Engineer. Baltimore: Johns Hopkins University Press, 1971.

This is an excellent biography of the inventor of the gyrocompass and founder of the Sperry Gyroscope Company, predecessor to Sperry-Rand Corporation.

4507   McLean, J. "Univac Disbanding Future Systems Plan," *Electronic* News 12 (December 1977): 1-28.

This is a detailed look at the firm and its actions during the 1970s, a decade about which little is available on the firm.

4508   Sperry Corporation. *Engineering Research Associates: The Wellspring of Minnesota's Computer Industry*. St. Paul, Mn.: Sperry Corporation, 1986.

This is an illustrated booklet on ERA on its fortieth anniversary. ERA became part of what eventually became Sperry Rand.

4509   Sperry Rand Corporation. *A History of Sperry Rand Corporation*. N.c.: Sperry Rand Corporation, 1964.

This is a 32-page history that includes discussion of the Eckert-Mauchly Company (acquired in 1949) and Powers Accounting Machine Co. (acquired in 1927).

4510   "Strong Combination," *Newsweek* 45 (March 28, 1955): 76ff.

This is a contemporary account of the merger of Remington Rand with Sperry to form Sperry Rand.

4511   Van Deusen, E.L.   "Two-Plus-Two of Sperry Rand," *Fortune* 52 (August 1955): 88-91ff.

This is a detailed analysis of the merger of Remington Rand and Sperry.

Telecommunications Industry

4512   Aldrich, Michael.   *Videotex: Key to the Wired City*. London: Quiller Press, 1982.

Describes the technology and its uses as of the early 1980s.

4513   Byron, Christopher M.   *The Fanciest Dive*. New York: W.W. Norton, 1986.

Describes the development of early commercial video (cable) enterprises in the U.S. during the early 1980s.

4514   Hollis, Timothy.   *Beyond Broadcasting: Into the Cable Age*. London: British Film Institute, 1984.

Suveys cable TV technology and connection to TP.

4515   Howeth, L.S. History of Communications—Electronics
       in the United States Navy. Washington, D.C.: U.S.
       Government Printing Office, 1963.

       Telecommunications technology and its use are des-
       cribed.

4516   Kahaner, Larry. On the Line. New York: Warner Books,
       1986.

       This is a history of MCI, a major rival of AT&T
       during the 1980s.

4517   Lizzeri, C. and Brabant, F. De. L'industria delle
       telecomunicazioni in Italia. Milan: F. Angeli, 1979.

       They describe telecommunications in Europe at large,
       not just in Italy of the 1970s.

4518   Martin, James. Viewdata and the Information Society.
       Englewood Cliffs, N.J.: Prentice-Hall, Inc., 1982.

       Describes videotext and TP technologies as they
       developed in the 1970s and speculates where they
       might go in the 1980s and beyond.

4519   Neustadt, Richard M. The Birth of Electronic Publish-
       ing: Legal and Economic Issues in Telephone, Cable
       and Over-the-Air Teletext and Videotext. White
       Plains, N.Y.: Knowledge Industry Publications, 1982.

       During the 1970s, DP, TP and TV began to merge to-
       gether; this book describes some of the non-technical
       issues that emerged as a consequence.

4520   OECD. Telecommunication Equipment Industry Study.
       Paris: OECD, 1981.

       This is a useful survey of telecommunications in
       Europe with data on the 1960s and 1970s.

4521   Shooshan, Harry M. III (ed). Disconnecting Bell: The
       Impact of the AT&T Divestiture. Elmsford, U.K.:
       Pergamon, 1984.

       This surveys the U.S. TP and DP industries as they
       involve telephonic technologies and then focuses on
       why the breakup of AT&T came about.

4522   Tolchin, Susan J. and Tolchin, Martin. Dismantling
       America: The Rush to Deregulate. New York: Houghton
       Mifflin, 1984.

       Comments on telecommunications within the broader
       context of deregulation of many industries in the
       U.S. during the 1970s and early 1980s. Discusses
       divestiture of AT&T.

4523   Wenham, Brian (ed). The Third Age of Broadcasting.
       London: Faber, 1982.

His focus is on telecommunication trends of the late 1970s involving voice, data and software applications.

U.S. Government Agencies.

4524   Albers, Donald J. and Alexanderson, G.L. (eds). Mathematical People: Profiles and Interviews. Boston: Birkhauser, 1985.

Includes an interview with Mina Rees, discussing her work during and just after World War II in fostering R&D with computers.

4525   Chu, J.C.   "Computer Development at Argonne National Laboratory," in N. Metropolis et al. (eds), A History of Computating in the Twentieth Century (New York: Academic Press, 1980): 345-346.

These are his recollections of the period 1949-53 working with the AVIDAC computer at Argonne.

4526   Curtiss, John H.   "The National Applied Mathematics Laboratories of the National Bureau of Standards," Annals of the History of Computing 11, No. 2 (1989): 69-98.

Originally written in 1953, but never published, this reports on the work of the NAML in its first five years.

4527   Curtiss, John H.   "A Review of Government Requirements and Activities in the Field of Automatic Digital Computing Machinery," in C.C. Chambers (ed), Theory and Techniques for Design of Electronic Digital Computers. Lectures Delivered 8 July 1946-31 August 1946. (Philadelphia: Moore School of Electrical Engineering, University of Pennsylvania, 1948): 29.1-29.32.

Curtiss described the computing needs of the period and then current projects underway around the U.S.

4528   England, James Merton.   A Patron for Pure Science: The National Science Foundation's Formative Years, 1945-1957.   Washington, D.C.: National Science Foundation, 1982.

Describes its legislative history (1945-50), early administrative structure and policies, then NSF's expanding role in the Cold War following Sputnik.

4529   Finch, James K.   History of the School of Engineering, Columbia University.   New York: Columbia University Press, 1954.

This school long used data processing equipment, was funded by various U.S. agencies and maintained ties to important vendors, such as to IBM.

4530   Leslie, Stuart W.   "Playing the Education Game to Win

The Military and Interdisciplinary Research at Stanford," Historical Studies in the Physical and Biological Sciences 18 (1987): 55-88.

Reviews the relationship between the U.S. military,
industry, and Stanford University in the development
of R&D projects, 1930s-1960s.

4531   Rees, Mina. "The Computing Program of ONR, 1946-1953,"
        Annals of the History of Computing 4, No. 2 (April
        1982): 102-120.

        Describes events at the U.S. Office of Naval Research
        and its relations with the National Bureau of Stan-
        dards.

4532   Rees, Mina. "The Computing Program of the Office of
        Naval Research," Communications, ACM 30 (1987): 832-
        848.

        This is a history of its extensive programs of the
        1940s.

4533   Rees, Mina. "Federal Computing Machine Program," Science
        112 (December 22, 1950): 731-736.

        She surveys major computer projects supported by the
        U.S. Government in the late 1940s.

4534   Rees, Mina. "The Federal Computing Machine Program,"
        Annals of the History of Computing 7, No. 2 (April
        1985): 156-163.

        This is an illustrated reprint of the previous cita-
        tion.

4535   U.S., Bureau of the Budget, Executive Office of the
        President. Inventory of Automatic Data Processing
        (ADP) Equipment in the Federal Government Including
        Costs, Categories of Use, and Personnel Utilization.
        Washington, D.C: U.S. Government Printing Office,
        May 1961.

        This is a comprehensive survey conducted by William
        A. Gill of 531 large processors in 1960; 755 were
        planned for 1961.

4536   U.S., Bureau of the Budget. Multi-Use of Automatic Data
        Processing Systems, Task Force Report to the Inter-
        agency Committee on Automatic Data Processing. Wash-
        ington, D.C: U.S. Bureau of the Budget, July 1958.

        This reports on "part-time and intermittent use of
        someone else's ADP facilities and services" in the
        U.S. Government, in the 1950s.

4537   U.S. Congress, Office of Technology Assessment. Infor-
        ming the Nation: Federal Information Dissemination in
        an Electronic Age. Washington, D.C.: U.S. Government
        Printing Office, 1988.

Describes how it was done in the 1980s and sheds
light on the specific uses of DP technology. It also
offers comments on the use of electronic publishing
in the 1980s.

4538   U.S. Congress, Subcommittee on Census and Government
        Statistics of the Committee on Post Office and Civil
        Service, House of Representatives. 86th Cong., 1st
        sess. Use of Electronic Data Processing Equipment.
        Hearings Before . . . . Washington, D.C.: U.S.
        Government Printing Office, June 5, 1959.

        Reproduces two important surveys on DP in the U.S.
        Government made by the General Accounting Office and
        Harry Fite of Lester B. Knight & Associates for the
        Bureau of the Budget.

                            U.S.S.R.

4539   Hoch, Paul. "(Russian Transistor Development) Held in
        Check by Years of Tyranny," The Times Higher Educa-
        tion Supplement, January 20, 1984, pp. 14-15.

        Describes some developments in the 1950s through the
        1970s, despite enormous bias against the U.S.S.R.

4540   Klass, P.J. "Soviets Improve Computer Technology,"
        Aviation Week 71 (November 16, 1959): 30-31.

        This is a status report on developments in the late
        1950s that recently became possible to discuss in
        the West.

4541   McHenry, William Keith. "The Absorption of Computer-
        ized Management Information Systems in Soviet Enter-
        prises" (Unpublished Ph.D. dissertation, University
        of Arizona, 1985).

        This is an historical study on the extent of DP use
        in the Soviet Union. It is a major source on the
        subject.

4542   Parry, A. "Are Soviets Ahead in Data Race?," Science
        Digest 52 (December 1962): 64-73.

        There was real concern about Soviet scientific
        achievements in the very late 1950s/early 1960s.
        This is reflected in the article on data processing.

4543   Wellman, David S. A Chip in the Curtain: Computer
        Technology in the Soviet Union. Washington, D.C.:
        National Defense University Press, 1989.

        This is a 185-page study of the computer industry in
        the Soviet Union.

4544   Wolcott, Peter and Goodman, Seymour E. "High-Speed
        Computers of the Soviet Union," Computer 21 (Septem-
        ber 1988): 32-41.

The survey covers activities from the mid-1960s to
the late 1980s; includes tables of machine features.

Xerox

4545   Dessauer, John H. My Years with Xerox. New York:

These are the memoirs of the director of research
who, in the 1940s, was instrumental in getting
xerographic products designed at Haloid Company,
predecessor to Xerox.

4546   Jacobson, Gary and Hillkirk, John. Xerox: American
Samurai. New York: Macmillan, 1986.

This is a lauditory history of the firm by two
journalists focusing primarily on the 1980s and
on Xerox's efforts to be successful in the copier
market.

4547   Pake, George E. "Research at Xerox PARC: A Founder's
Assessment" and Perry, Tekla S. and Wallich, Paul.
"Inside the PARC: The 'Information Architecture',"
IEEE Spectrum 22, No. 10 (October 1985): 54-75.

These accounts of Xerox's laboratory at Palo Alto,
California, include memoirs by Pake, its first
research director; articles cover the period 1950s-
1960s.

4548   Smith, Douglas K. and Alexander, Robert C. Fumbling
the Future: How Xerox Invented, Then Ignored, the
First Personal Computer. New York: William Morrow
and Co., Inc., 1988.

The authors argue that Xerox developed a micro called
the Alto in 1973, and that it elected not to market
the machine. It chose instead to invest in an office
computer system that did poorly in the market.

4549   Xerox Corporation. 1985 Fact Book. Stamford, Conn.:
Xerox Corporation, 1985.

This pamphlet contains a chronology of Xerox's
history and list of all its products.

4550   Xerox Corporation. The Story of Xerography. Stamford,
Conn.: Xerox Corporation, 1978.

This is a brief, well-illustrated history of Xerox.

4551   "Xerox: The McColough Era; Clashes With IBM," Forbes
104 (July 1, 1969): 24-26.

At the time competition between the two was heating
up; the article is a contemporary analysis of the
issues in the U.S. market.

Author Index

Subject Index

About the Author

JAMES W. CORTADA is a marketing manager at IBM Corporation. He is the author of several books on the history and management of information processing. His most recent books include the three volume *Historical Dictionary of Data Processing* (Greenwood Press, 1987) and *Archives of Data Processing History* (Greenwood Press, 1990). Dr. Cortada has also published numerous articles in a variety of journals. He is currently writing a major history of the U.S. information management industry, 1860s to 1956.